APPLIED
SOCIAL
PSYCHOLOGY

APPLIED
SOCIAL
PSYCHOLOGY

**Edited by Gün R. Semin
& Klaus Fiedler**

SAGE Publications
London • Thousand Oaks • New Delhi

SAGE Publications Ltd
6 Bonhill Street
London EC2A 4PU

SAGE Publications Inc
2455 Teller Road
Thousand Oaks, California 91320

SAGE Publications India Pvt Ltd
32, M-Block Market
Greater Kailash – I
New Delhi 110 048

British Library Cataloguing in Publication data

A catalogue record for this book is
available from the British Library

ISBN 0 8039 7925 8
ISBN 0 8039 7926 6 (pbk)

Library of Congress catalog record available

Typeset by Mayhew Typesetting, Rhayader, Powys
Printed in Great Britain by The Cromwell Press Ltd,
Broughton Gifford, Melksham, Wiltshire

Contents

Preface

This volume was conceived in a moment of folly in Santa Barbara. One of us proposed the idea which met the considerable enthusiasm of the other. The fact was that we had both encountered a comparable problem in the overall teaching responsibilities of our respective departments. There was really no volume in applied social psychology based on the expertise of social psychologists who not only did basic experimental research in social psychology, but also engaged in serious applications of this basic work. Since clearly we could not undertake such a task on our own we had to rely on the collective expertise of a number of our friends and colleagues who combined these two qualities. What's more, we had to rely on the expertise and good will of a number of other friends and colleagues who were prepared to give their time and attention to comment on these contributions. Having drafted a blueprint of the volume's structure, we were able to secure the good services of Sage, and in particular Ziyad Marar.

This book, in its conception, diverse drafts and final versions emerged between February 1994 and August 1995. It only emerged because of the good will and dedication of our contributors and this is an appropriate occasion to thank them for all the stresses that they suffered in the process. This is also the right moment to thank the reviewers who were kind enough to show such an interest in the work and to comment in so much detail. Their comments improved the contributions to this volume. They were: Stephan Hormuth, Klaus Jonas, William J. McGuire, J.A. Rothengatter, Stephan Schutz-Hardt, Carlo Michael Sommer, Eleanor Singer, Seymour Sudman, Ulrich Wagner, Hans-Werner Wahl, and Michaela Wanke.

The idea of this volume was to cover a range of themes in applied social psychology. It was obvious that it would be impossible to cover all the issues addressed by applied social psychology so we have missed out on certain topics or fields that could fruitfully be contained within a volume like this, such as the applications of social psychology to interpersonal relationships and families, in the clinical field, in the field of gender and sex differences. We could have expanded on central fields such as health. But then again, in a book such as this one, where each chapter could comprise an entire volume or more in its own right, specific types of decision regarding balance had to be made.

The volume is divided into four parts. The first contains *general frameworks* that are relevant to the application of social psychology. This part comprises four chapters on topics that have a broad range of relevance to applied social psychological issues. The first is the relationship between attitudes and behaviour. Questions about this relationship recur in one form or another in most of the topics covered in applied social psychology. Similarly, decision making and risk taking is a field of considerable relevance in the diverse applications of social psychology. This field spans a whole host of applied themes, ranging from consumer behaviour to environmental issues, to legal decision-making. The subject of the next chapter, survey research, is also central to nearly all the chapters in this volume. In doing applied research in any field that has some social relevance one must be able to address a number of questions: what is the sample that is the target of your problem?; how do you select it?; and, most importantly, how do you ask the right questions in the right order by creating the right context? For the final chapter in this part, we decided to offer an overview of the significant role that language and its strategic use plays in a variety of applied contexts. Although it is self-evident that linguistic behaviour is at the root of most types of social behaviour in everyday life, there is, to our knowledge, no contribution that brings together the investigation of linguistic behaviour across diverse applied contexts.

In Part 2, we decided to turn our attention to certain *focal behaviour domains*, and we have selected a number of these. One of the principal themes here is that of health-related behaviours. In recent years there has been a growing realization that the types of behaviour we engage in, and the types of habit we form, have dramatic consequences for our health. This has led to a rapid development of the applications of social psychology to health (Chapter 5). Similarly, the social psychology of economic and consumer behaviour as well as the social significance of our buying behaviour are central aspects of life in our current society. The implications of what we buy and why we do so are central behavioural themes within applied social psychology. These issues are addressed in Chapter 6. Another behavioural domain concerns the impact of human behaviour on the environment. The effects of air pollution, noise, natural and technological disasters, as well as the manner in which human behaviour impacts on the environment form the subject of the next chapter (Chapter 7). The final chapter in this part addresses the social psychological aspects of driver behaviour (Chapter 8). One of the most serious problems worldwide is that of road traffic accidents. A relatively recent development in this respect concerns the role played by social psychological factors that contribute to the understanding of driver behaviour. The focus of Chapter 8 is the contribution of social psychology of driver behaviour to the reduction of road accidents.

The third part covers the application of social psychological theories and methods to what one may broadly refer to as *social institutions*. The first chapter (Chapter 9) provides a new synthesis by presenting a systematic application of social psychological theories and perspectives to organizational phenomena. It does so by addressing organizational phenomena at the levels of individuals, groups and the organization as a whole, and by bringing relevant social psychological theories to bear upon each level of analysis.

Chapter 10 addresses a broad range of issues that give an idea of the applications of social psychology in legal contexts. This field, which has a long tradition, has revived in recent years and the current contribution focuses in particular upon the social and psychological aspects of issues that have to do with criminal law. The chapter on political behaviour (Chapter 11) focuses amongst other things on political knowledge and decision making as well as political attitudes and beliefs as they are structured around ideological principles, and considers how these attitudes and beliefs are influenced by the societal contexts within which people find themselves. Part 3 closes with the social psychology of the media (Chapter 12). This chapter focuses on what the contents of the media are, their impact, as well as their influence upon communication processes in general. It also addresses the different uses of the media as research tools in social psychology.

The closing part addresses issues at *a societal and cultural level*. These are also issues that touch our consciousness in our daily lives, for example the topic of violence and aggression (Chapter 13). We encounter it in the immediate context of soccer fields, the emergence of right-wing movements, the local but international scenes that occupy our daily concerns, such as events in the former Yugoslavian Republic. Other very modern phenomena, which have become increasingly important over the last thirty years, are ageing (Chapter 14) and migration and the emerging composition of multicultural societies in the West (Chapter 15).

Although it is impossible to cover all the possible applications of social psychology in a volume such as this, we have made what will hopefully be regarded as an interesting, useful and representative selection that will appeal to our readers' palate.

Gün R. Semin and Klaus Fiedler

Contributors

Günter Bierbrauer is scientific coordinator of a state-wide programme on peace and conflict research and Professor of Psychology at the Universität Osnabrück, Germany. His research interests cover social, legal and cross-cultural psychology. His most recent book is *Sozialpsychologie* (Kohlhammer, 1996).

Patrizia Catellani is a research scientist in the Department of Psychology at the Catholic University of Milan, Italy. Her research interests include political and legal psychology, with a stress on language and on reasoning processes.

Helga Dittmar works as a Lecturer in Psychology in the School of Social Sciences at the University of Sussex, England. Her most recent book is *The Social Psychology of Material Possessions* (Harvester Wheatsheaf/St Martin's Press, 1992) and her research interests include the links between self and material possessions, economic socialization, impulsive and compulsive shopping and adolescent body image.

Klaus Fiedler is a Professor of Social Psychology at the University of Heidelberg. His major research interests include language and social cognition, affect and cognition, lie detection, inductive information processing and stereotyping. Among his recent books is *Language, Interaction and Social Cognition*, edited with Gün R. Semin.

Jutta Heckhausen is a Senior Research Scientist at the Max Planck Institute for Human Development and Education in Berlin. Her primary research interests are the psychology of control and developmental regulation across the life span, with an emphasis on adaptive and successful development.

Günter Köhnken is a Professor in the Department of Psychology, University of Kiel. His research interests are in psychology and law, particularly credibility assessment and detection of deception, interviewing and eyewitness identification. His recent publications include *Psychological Issues in Eyewitness Identification* (co-edited with S.L. Sporer and R.M. Malpass, Lawrence Erlbaum, 1996).

Barbara Krahé is Professor of Social Psychology at the University of Potsdam, Germany. Her research interests include sexual violence with a current focus on date rape among adolescents, the attitude–behaviour relationship, and the measurement of prejudice. Her book *Personality and Social Psychology* was published by Sage in 1992.

Frieder R. Lang is a Research Scientist at the Department of Geronto-psychiatry of the Free University of Berlin. His research interests are the life-span development of social relationships, social and everyday competence and social support, with a focus on late life adaptivity and on processes of successful ageing.

Antony S.R. Manstead is Professor of Social Psychology at the University of Amsterdam. He has also held academic positions at the University of Sussex and the University of Manchester. He is an Associate Editor of *Personality and Social Psychology Bulletin* and of *Cognition and Emotion*. He is co-editor of the *Blackwell Encyclopedia of Social Psychology*. His publications focus on the psychology of emotion and the psychology of attitudes and attitude change.

John L. Michela is an Associate Professor in the Department of Psychology at the University of Waterloo, Ontario, Canada. His research interests include social and organizational psychological issues in quality management and continuous improvement in industry.

Dianne Parker is a Lecturer in the Department of Psychology at the University of Manchester. In addition to driver behaviour, her research interests include attitudes and attitude change and the impact of proceduralization on rule-related behaviour.

Paul Pedersen is Chairman of the Counseling and Guidance Program and Professor of Education at Syracuse University. He is the author and co-author of many books and articles, mostly on counselling and conflict management across cultures. His most recent book is *The Five Stages of Culture Shock* (Greenwood Press, 1995).

Joop van der Pligt is Professor of Social Psychology at the University of Amsterdam. His research focuses on human judgement and decision making and includes both basic research on these issues as well as applied research in areas such as health and environmental behaviour.

Norbert Schwarz is Professor of Psychology at the University of Michigan, Ann Arbor, USA and Research Scientist in the Survey Research Center and the Research Center for Group Dynamics of Michigan's Institute for Social Research. His research interests focus on human cognition and judgement, including their implications for data collection in the social sciences. His recent publications include *Thinking About Answers* (with S. Sudman and N. Bradburn, Jossey-Bass, 1996).

Gün R. Semin is Professor os Social Psychology at the Free University, Amsterdam and the Scientific Director of the Kurt Lewin Graduate School in Social Psychology and its Applications. He has also held academic positions at the University of London (LSE), University of Essex, University of Sussex and the University of Mannheim. His research interests focus on language and social cognition, cultural psychology and emotions.

Wolfgang Stroebe is Professor of Social, Organizational and Health Psychology at the University of Utrecht (Netherlands) and Director of the inter-university research institute Psychology and Health. A past president of the European Association of Experimental Social Psychology and a fellow of the Society of Personality and Social Psychology, he is the author of numerous scholarly books, chapters and articles on topics of social and health psychology, including *Social Psychology and Health* (with M.S. Stroebe, Open University Press, 1995).

Harald G. Wallbott is Professor of Social and Organizational Psychology at the University of Salzburg, Austria. His main research interests include psychology of the media, nonverbal communication, prejudice, person perception and the psychology of emotion.

John de Wit is an Assistant Professor in the Department of Social and Organizational Psychology at the University of Utrecht (Netherlands). His research interests involve the study of behaviour change and behavioural determinants with respect to HIV prevention. Currently he is involved in a study assessing the differential impact of interventions to promote safer sex.

PART 1

GENERAL FRAMEWORKS IN APPLIED SOCIAL PSYCHOLOGY

1

Attitudes and Behaviour

Antony S.R. Manstead

Contents

Why should we expect attitudes and behaviours to be correlated?

The study of the relationship between attitudes and behaviour has a long history in social psychology and is of particular relevance to applied social psychology. Some idea of the centrality of the attitude concept to social psychology can be gained from Gordon Allport's much-cited view that attitude 'is the most distinctive and indispensable concept in contemporary social psychology' (Allport, 1935, p. 798). The fact that Allport advanced this view as early as 1935 reflects the long history of attitude theory and research in social psychology, given that the discipline only really found a mature voice after World War II. What, then, do social psychologists mean by the term 'attitude'? Although there is no single, universally accepted definition, most present-day social psychologists would accept that the term 'attitude' should be used to refer to a relatively enduring tendency to respond to someone or something in a way that reflects a positive or a negative evaluation of that person or thing. Thus Eagly and Chaiken (1993) define attitudes as 'tendencies to evaluate an entity with some degree of favor or disfavor, ordinarily expressed in cognitive, affective, and behavioral responses' (p. 155). 'Entity' here means the object of an attitude, and can include individuals, inanimate objects, concepts, social groups, nations, social policies, behaviours, and so on; in fact anything to which one can respond favourably or unfavourably.

Table 1.1 *Different types of evaluative response*

Response mode	Response category		
	Affect	Cognition	Behaviour
Verbal	Expressions of feelings towards attitude object	Expressions of beliefs about attitude object	Expressions of behavioural intentions towards attitude object
Nonverbal	Physiological responses to attitude object	Perceptual responses (e.g. reaction time) to attitude object	Overt behavioural responses to attitude object

Source: after Ajzen (1988)

For the sake of clarity, the term 'attitude object' will be used in the rest of this chapter to refer to this large class of people and things towards which we can hold attitudes.

Eagly and Chaiken's definition of attitudes immediately raises the issue of the relationship between attitudes and behaviours, since 'behavioural responses' are listed as one of the ways in which an individual can express his or her evaluation of the attitude object. How, you might wonder, can we speak about an 'attitude–behaviour relationship' if behaviour is a component of attitude? In order to clarify this issue we need to examine the concept of attitude a little more closely. An attitude is, of course, a hypothetical construct, in the sense that we cannot directly sense or measure it. Its existence is inferred from certain classes of evaluative responses to the attitude object. If someone persistently expressed the view that members of a particular race are unintelligent, we would probably infer that this person has a prejudiced attitude towards members of that race. Likewise, if someone attended a football match every single weekend during the football season, we might infer that he has a positive attitude to football. Another way in which we might infer somebody's attitude is on the basis of their emotional responses. Thus if someone were to look angry and mutter expletives whenever she hears or sees the Prime Minister, it would seem reasonable to infer that she has a negative attitude to the Prime Minister.

Ajzen (1988) presented a useful way of summarizing the different possible types of evaluative response to an attitude object. He suggests that these evaluative responses can be organized in terms of two dimensions, one distinguishing between verbal and nonverbal responses, and the other distinguishing between cognitive, affective and behavioural responses. As shown in Table 1.1, this scheme enables us to make conceptual distinctions between the different responses that were given as examples in the previous paragraph. Thus making negative remarks about the intelligence of members of another race is a *verbal* expression of negative *beliefs* about that race. Regularly attending football matches is a positive *nonverbal* expression of *behaviour* in relation to football. Finally, looking angry at every mention of the Prime

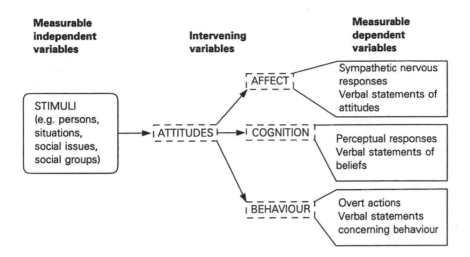

Figure 1.1   *Three-component structure of attitudes (Rosenberg & Hovland, 1960)*

Minister is a *nonverbal* expression of negative *affect* towards this particular object.

Now that we have a better sense of the different classes of evaluative response from which attitudes can be inferred, let us return to the issue of the relationship between attitudes and behaviour. As reflected in Ajzen's scheme, many attitude theorists assume that attitudes consist of three components: a set of cognitions about the object, typically referred to as *beliefs*; a set of affective responses to the object, typically referred to as *emotions* or *feelings*; and a set of *behaviours* or *behavioural tendencies* toward the object. This three-component view of attitudes was first articulated by Rosenberg and Hovland (1960). Figure 1.1 shows how the hypothetical construct of attitude to an object is inferred from observable responses to the actual or imagined presence of the object. The point is that if cognitive, affective and behavioural measures of evaluative responses to an object are all indices of the same underlying construct, attitude, then there should be some consistency between them. If measures of cognitive and affective responses to an attitude object fail to correlate with measures of behavioural responses to that object, then the assumption that attitudes consist of these three components would be called into question.

The three-component view of attitudes is one theoretical basis for expecting attitudes to be correlated with behaviour, but it is not the only one. Another important basis for such a prediction is Festinger's (1957) theory of cognitive dissonance. Festinger argued that humans are characterized by a need to maintain consistency between their cognitions. In Festinger's terms a cognition refers to any piece of knowledge one has about oneself or one's environment. Thus cognitions can include cognitions about one's own behaviour ('I told somebody else that I really enjoyed the new Tarantino movie') and cognitions about one's own attitudes ('At the time I saw the movie I did not like it very much'). If an individual becomes aware of inconsistencies between her cognitions, she is said to experience cognitive dissonance, an unpleasant state which she will be motivated to reduce or eliminate. It should be clear why cognitive dissonance theory leads one to predict that attitudes and behaviour will tend to be consistent with each other: to the extent that an individual becomes aware of inconsistencies between his attitudes and his behaviour, he will be motivated to reduce these inconsistencies and thereby reduce his dissonance. According to cognitive dissonance theory, dissonance reduction often takes the form of attitude change, bringing attitudes into line with behaviour. This line of reasoning therefore leads one to anticipate that where an individual has had some behavioural experience with the attitude object (even if this is limited to an expression of behavioural intentions, such as a declaration to others of how she intends to vote at the next election), there should be a positive correlation between attitudes and behaviour.

As noted at the beginning of this chapter, the attitude–behaviour relationship is one that is especially relevant to applied social psychologists. The ultimate goal of many applied social psychologists is to bring about a change in people's behaviour. The behaviour in question may be health behaviour (Chapter 5), consumer behaviour (Chapter 6), driver behaviour (Chapter 8), organizational behaviour (Chapter 9), criminal behaviour (Chapter 10), political behaviour (Chapter 11), aggressive or violent behaviour (Chapter 13), or environmental behaviour (Chapter 7). Those who study these behaviours from a social psychological perspective often do so with the implicit or even explicit goal of bringing about changes in behaviour, in order either to improve the quality of life for the individual or for society as a whole, or to increase the power or profits of political or commercial clients. These applied social psychologists often assume, either implicitly or explicitly, that the most effective means of bringing about a change in behaviour is to modify someone's attitudes. Effective advertising, for example, might help to create a positive attitude towards a product or a service, thereby (or so it is assumed) increasing the likelihood that the consumer will buy that product or service. The same line of reasoning underpins political campaigning, and all types of public education campaigns, ranging from advertisements encouraging people to practise safe sex to leaflets designed to encourage householders to take steps to protect their property against the threat of burglary. All of these different kinds of campaign are founded on the assumption that changing the way that people *think* or *feel* about an object will help to bring about a change in the way they *behave* towards the object.

There are different reasons for expecting attitudes and behaviour to be correlated. One set of reasons is grounded in theoretical assumptions that enjoy some currency in social psychology, such as the three-component view of attitudes, and Festinger's theory of cognitive dissonance. Another set of reasons is grounded in more practical issues, and concerns the motives of administrators, politicians, commercial organizations, educators and pressure groups to bring about changes in our behaviour. Especially in societies in which the media play such a well developed role in distributing information (see Chapter 12), it is attractive to such persons and organizations to try to achieve such behaviour change by changing our attitudes via campaigns conducted in and through the mass media. Now let us turn to the empirical evidence concerning the attitude–behaviour relationship, to see to what extent the theoretical and practical assumptions that these two constructs are positively correlated is borne out by the evidence.

Early research on the attitude–behaviour relationship

The first systematic study of the attitude–behaviour relationship was reported by Richard LaPiere (1934). LaPiere was interested in knowing whether people's behaviour towards members of an ethnic minority could be predicted by their self-reported attitudes towards that ethnic minority. To examine this issue he travelled around the United States in the company of a young Chinese couple. They stopped at a total of 251 establishments (e.g. hotels, restaurants); in all but one of these, according to LaPiere, the Chinese couple were treated courteously, despite the fact that in that era many Americans held negative attitudes towards Chinese people. On returning home, LaPiere wrote to each of the establishments they had visited, asking whether they would accept members of the Chinese race as guests. Of the 128 replies received, 92 per cent said that they would *not* serve Chinese guests. Taken at face value, these results suggest a sharp discrepancy between a measure of 'attitude' (the expressed policy of the establishment) and actual behaviour (how the Chinese couple were actually received). However, if one stops to think about the study more closely, one can see that the results are not all that damaging to the notion that attitudes and behaviour should be positively correlated. Perhaps the most basic flaw in LaPiere's procedure is that we have no way of knowing whether the person who was responsible for accepting the Chinese couple as guests was the same person as the one who replied to LaPiere's subsequent letter. If these two measures were *not* taken from the same individual, it is clearly inappropriate to conclude that the results indicate an inconsistency between attitudes and behaviour.

However, LaPiere's study was simply the first of many that reported a lack of correlation between measures of attitudes to some entity and measures of behaviours towards that entity. In many of these other studies the two types of measures *were* taken from the same individual, so the findings cannot be dismissed as readily as those of LaPiere's research on this issue. An example of such a study is the one reported by Corey (1937). He assessed his students' attitudes towards cheating and then measured the students' cheating behaviour on a test. To measure cheating he surreptitiously graded the students' performance on the test, whereas the students thought that they were going to grade the tests themselves on the basis of the feedback Corey gave them about right and wrong answers. The difference between the students' self-awarded grades and those awarded by Corey served as an index of cheating behaviour. The correlation between expressed attitudes to cheating and cheating behaviour was found to be near-zero, showing that students who had negative attitudes to cheating were just as likely to cheat as were those with positive attitudes.

DeFleur and Westie (1958) attempted to maximize the chances of finding a positive relationship between attitudes and behaviour by selecting for participation in their study only those with strong attitudes to the entity in question, namely black persons. They administered a questionnaire measuring attitudes to black persons to a group of 250 white college students in the United States. They then selected the 23 highest scorers (i.e. least prejudiced) and the 23 lowest scorers (i.e. most prejudiced) on this measure for participation in a study that would involve a measure of behaviour towards black persons. Subjects were shown slides of young people; in each slide there appeared one black person and one white person. The people in the slides were attractive and well dressed. It was explained that more slides of this type were needed, and subjects were asked whether they would be willing to be photographed with a black person of the opposite sex. If they agreed, they were asked to sign a 'photographic release form', authorizing the uses to which the resulting photograph could be put. These uses were graded, ranging from the most restrictive (use for laboratory research only) to the most permissive (use in a nationwide publicity campaign advocating racial integration). The correlation between the attitudinal measure and the behavioural measure was 0.40, which is significant and in the expected direction, but small in absolute terms in view of the fact that only subjects with strongly pro or anti attitudes participated.

Matters came to a head in 1969, when Wicker published an influential review of 45 studies on the attitude–behaviour relationship. He found that the correlation between measures of attitude and measures of behaviour rarely exceeded 0.30 and were often close to zero. The mean correlation was 0.15. Wicker concluded that 'Taken as a whole, these studies suggest that it is considerably more likely that attitudes will be unrelated or only slightly related to overt behaviours than that attitudes will be strongly related to actions' (Wicker, 1969, p. 65). In a later paper, Wicker (1971) went even further, suggesting that 'it may be desirable to abandon the attitude concept' (p. 29). While it is undoubtedly the case that there was a crisis in confidence in the attitude concept in general and in the attitude–behaviour relationship in particular in the early to mid-1970s, social psychologists have not abandoned the attitude concept and research on the attitude–behaviour relationship has flourished. The reasons why social psychologists were led to reconsider the implications of the early research on the attitude–behaviour relationship are considered in the following section.

The principles of aggregation and compatibility

The field of attitude–behaviour relations was transformed by the publication of an article by Ajzen and Fishbein (1977). In the course of this article, Ajzen and Fishbein developed two important principles, here referred to as the 'principle of aggregation' and the 'principle of compatibility'.

The *principle of aggregation* is a straightforward application to the attitude–behaviour issue of ideas well known to psychometricians. A standard notion in psychological measurement is that one should not try to measure anything but the simplest of constructs using a single item. Measures of personality or intelligence, for example, consist of multiple items, because the test developers recognize that these constructs are too complex to be reliably or validly measured by a single item. How one responds to a particular item on a measure of personality or intelligence may be influenced by a host of factors (such as a temporary mood state or a momentary loss of concentration) that have little or nothing to do with personality or intelligence. To overcome this problem, test constructors use multiple measures of personality or intelligence, the rationale being that individual differences in personality and intelligence will emerge more clearly from *consistencies* in the way that people answer a range of questions. One way to think about this problem is the following. Imagine that one is interested in assessing personality differences in extroversion. A typical item used to assess this construct is 'I enjoy going to parties', but nobody would seriously argue that everyone who agrees with this item is an extrovert, and that everyone who disagrees with it is an introvert. An extrovert might disagree with this statement because he or she does not enjoy dancing, for example, and interprets 'parties' as meaning parties at which one is expected to dance. The same logic applies to any other single-item measure of extroversion. To overcome this problem, the test constructor includes several items assessing extroversion; because the factors that lead an extrovert to disagree with items that measure how he or she seeks the company of others are random, the influence of these factors will be overwhelmed by any overall tendency for extroverts to be more likely to endorse items that measure the tendency to seek out the company of others.

Precisely the same argument can be applied to the measurement of attitudes and the measurement of behaviour. In attitude measurement the logic of this argument is generally recognized, and present-day researchers would not attempt to assess attitudes (as LaPiere did) using a single item ('Will you accept members of the Chinese race as guests in your establishment?'). However, researchers have not always been as careful to apply these elementary principles of psychological measurement to the assessment of behaviour. Take the DeFleur and Westie (1958) study, referred to above. These researchers used a multiple-item measure of attitudes to black persons, but a single-item measure of behaviour towards black persons, namely whether or not the subject was willing to be photographed with a black person of the opposite sex. How validly does this measure reflect a dispositional tendency to behave favourably or unfavourably towards black persons? Someone with non-racist attitudes may well refuse to have her photograph taken, not because she does not like black people but rather because she does not like being photographed, in which case the photographic release form measure is a poor way to assess the behavioural expression of an underlying evaluative tendency. The logical solution to this problem is to use more than one item to assess the disposition to behave positively or negatively towards black persons. If a subject refuses not only to be photographed with a black person, but also to work alongside a black person, live next door to a black person, allow his or her children to invite black friends home, and so on, a consistent pattern of discriminatory behaviour accumulates. This is the principle of aggregation at work: by aggregating across different measures of behaviour towards the entity in question, one arrives at a more valid and reliable index of an evaluative tendency expressed in behaviour.

The inference to be drawn from this analysis of aggregation is that it should be easier to find strong attitude–behaviour correlations where both attitudes and behaviour are measured using multiple items. A study reported by Weigel and Newman (1976) provides empirical support for this proposition. These researchers used a multiple-item measure to assess attitudes to environmental protection in a random sample of New England residents. Three months later, an interviewer visited each respondent to ask whether he or she was willing to sign one or more of three petitions that related to environmental protection (e.g. proposing more stringent regulation and punishment of people who removed anti-pollution devices from their cars' exhaust system). Each petition signed by the respondent was counted as one 'point' on a 'petitioning behaviour scale', and if the respondent agreed to keep a petition and circulate it to get new signatures, they gained an additional point (provided that the petition was returned with at least one new signature). Six weeks later, respondents were contacted by a different person and invited to participate in a roadside litter clean-up, and to bring a friend as well. They were given one point for turning up at one of the agreed times, and another if they brought a friend along. Two months later, the respondents were contacted by a third person who informed them about a local campaign to recycle newspaper, glass and cans that would be run for an eight-week period. Subjects were allocated one point for each week that they prepared materials for a weekly collection. Table 1.2 shows how well the single behaviours and the aggregated behaviours correlated with the previously measured environmental attitudes. It is clear that while the correlations between attitudes and any individual behavioural measure tended to be quite weak and variable, those between attitudes and aggregated behaviours were generally stronger and more consistent. The correlation between attitudes and the overall aggregate of all three aspects of environmental behaviour (i.e. petitioning, litter pick-up and recycling) was 0.62 – considerably larger than the values reported in the studies reviewed by Wicker (1969). The lesson to be drawn from this and other research is clear: if you are trying to measure general evaluative responses to some entity, do not depend on single items, whether you are trying to measure attitudes or behaviour.

The principle of aggregation leads to the conclusion that general measures of attitude should be better predictors of general measures of behaviour than of specific measures of behaviour. The *principle of compatibility* is a logical extension of this argument, being more precise about what is meant by 'general' and 'specific' in this context. Ajzen and Fishbein (1977) noted that a

Table 1.2 *The relationship between a general measure of attitude to the environment and (a) single behaviours, (b) categories of behaviour, and (c) a general index of behaviour*

Single behaviours	r	Categories of behaviour	r	General index of behaviour	r
Petitioning behaviours					
Offshore oil	0.41				
Nuclear power	0.36	Petitioning	0.50		
Car exhaust	0.39	behaviour scale			
Circulate petitions	0.27				
Litter pick-up behaviours					
Own participation	0.34		0.36		
		Litter pick-up			
Recruit friend	0.22	scale		General	0.62
Recycling behaviours				behavioural index	
Week 1	0.34				
Week 2	0.57				
Week 3	0.34				
Week 4	0.33	Recycling	0.39		
Week 5	0.12	behaviour scale			
Week 6	0.20				
Week 7	0.20				
Week 8	0.34				

Source: adapted from Weigel & Newman (1976)

behaviour (such as environmental behaviour) varies not only with respect to the *action* performed (e.g. signing petitions, engaging in litter pick-ups); other elements of behaviour that can vary are the *object* at which the action is directed (e.g. recycling newspaper versus recycling glass), the *context* in which the action takes place (e.g. at home, at work), and the *time* at which it takes place (weekdays versus weekends, summer versus winter, and so on). Thus a full account of a behaviour would specify not only what action is performed, but also the object, context and time of that action (e.g. recycling newspaper, at home, during the winter). The principle of compatibility states that measures of attitudes and behaviour are more likely to be correlated with each other if they are compatible with respect to action, object, context and time. Thus if your attitudinal measure is a *general* one (as was the one used by Weigel and Newman), and therefore not tied to any specific action, object, context or time, it should not be surprising to find that behavioural measures that *are* tied to specific actions, objects, contexts and times turn out to be poorly correlated with the attitudinal measure. Equally, it should not surprise us to discover that when the behavioural measure is aggregated across the specifics of actions, objects, contexts and times, it correlates better with the general attitudinal measure.

A logical corollary of this argument is that if the behaviour you are seeking to predict is *specific* with respect to action, object, context and time, then the attitudinal measure you employ should be compatible with the behavioural

Table 1.3   *Correlations between a specific measure of behaviour (use of oral contraceptives over a two-year period) and measures of attitude varying in specificity*

Attitudinal measure	Correlation
Attitude to contraception	0.08
Attitude to oral contraceptives	0.32
Attitude to using oral contraceptives	0.53
Attitude to using oral contraceptives during next two years	0.57

Source: adapted from Davidson & Jaccard (1979)

measure in these respects. Empirical evidence consistent with this argument comes from a study of family planning behaviours reported by Davidson and Jaccard (1979). One of the issues addressed in this study was whether use of oral contraceptives over a two-year period could be predicted from attitudinal measures. Note that the behavioural measure is quite specific: action (use of contraceptives), object (oral contraceptives), and time (during a two-year period) are all specified. Table 1.3 shows how well different kinds of attitude measure predicted the self-reported use of oral contraceptives during the two-year study period. Note that attitude to contraception was a poor predictor of the behavioural measure; attitude to oral contraceptives (object) was a better predictor; attitude to using oral contraceptives (action plus object) was still better; and finally, attitude to using oral contraceptives during the next two years (action and object plus time) was the best predictor.

Armed with the two principles articulated by Ajzen and Fishbein (1977), we are in a position to account for the early failures to find substantial correlations between attitudes and behaviour. LaPiere (1934), Corey (1937), DeFleur and Westie (1958), along with many others, used *general* measures of attitude (typically without specification of action, object, context and time) to predict very *specific* measures of behaviour, involving a specific action towards designated objects in a certain context and at a particular time. Indeed, Ajzen and Fishbein (1977) reviewed previous studies of the attitude–behaviour relationship in terms of whether or not the attitudinal and behavioural measures had been compatible. They found that where the measures were not compatible, the correlation was typically nonsignificant; but in *all* 26 studies in which the measures were compatible, the researchers found a significant correlation.

The principle of compatibility leads to the conclusion that attitudinal and behavioural measures have to be compatible in order to achieve substantial correlations. In order to predict whether someone will engage in action A toward object B in context C at time D, one should ideally measure the person's attitude toward performing that action toward that object in that context and at that time. As others (e.g. Dawes & Smith, 1985) have pointed out, there is something slightly dissatisfying about taking this line of argument to its logical conclusion. The heuristic value of attitudes, for many applied social psychologists, resides precisely in the fact that they are general dispositions to behave in a favourable or unfavourable way towards an entity, regardless of the particulars or action, time or place. If each behaviour we are interested in has to be predicted by its own, specially configured measure of attitude, much of this heuristic value would seem to be lost. Fortunately, researchers are not quite as restricted as the foregoing analysis might seem to imply. Probably the most important practical implication of Ajzen and Fishbein's analysis is that researchers interested in predicting and understanding behaviour should switch from measuring *attitudes to general entities* to measuring *attitudes to specified behaviours*. For example, if one wants to predict whether or not adolescents will use condoms when having sexual intercourse, it is far better to assess their attitudes to using condoms when having sexual intercourse than to measure attitudes to condoms: clearly, one can have positive attitudes to condoms in general, while at the same time having negative attitudes to using them oneself. Unless one really wants to be able to predict each and every occasion on which a respondent uses a condom, there is no need to measure attitudes to condom use in highly specific contexts and at precisely designated times. Thus observing the principle of compatibility does not necessarily entail losing the heuristic value of the attitude concept. Instead, it means that one needs to be rather more thoughtful in determining the appropriate level of specificity or generality when designing measures of attitudes and behaviour.

The conceptual analyses of the attitude–behaviour relationship reviewed in the present section were not the only responses to the 'crisis' stimulated by Wicker's (1969) pessimistic conclusions. In addition to addressing the question of what types of attitudinal and behavioural measures we should reasonably expect to be correlated with each other, social psychologists began developing theoretical frameworks in which the attitude–behaviour relationship was nested in a larger set of interrelated theoretical constructs. The central point of all these models is that thinking of behaviours as being determined exclusively or even principally by attitudes is a tremendous oversimplification. Moreover, this oversimplification sits rather strangely in a discipline, social psychology, whose primary focus of concern can be regarded as the impact of social factors on behaviour. Although attitudes are implicitly regarded as 'social products' by most attitude researchers, in the sense that attitudes are seen as being acquired in the course of experience, much of which takes place in a sociocultural context, in essence they are conceptualized as attributes of the individual. Thus much of the research effort on the attitude–behaviour relationship can be seen as rather narrow, concentrating on the way in which an individual's behaviour is shaped by personal attributes. Yet many of the classic studies in social psychology (e.g. Asch, 1951; Milgram, 1963; Sherif, 1936) testify to the powerful effects that the implicit and explicit expectations of others can have on the way that we behave. Thus it seems somewhat perverse to ignore the impact of social influence on individual behaviour. The best known of the theoretical frameworks in which the attitude–behaviour relationship was placed in the context of a larger network of causal relationships, including the impact of social factors, is one that came to be known as the theory of reasoned action.

The theory of reasoned action

As we have seen, the study of the relationship between attitudes and behaviour was for many years a problematic issue for researchers. In the mid-1970s, Martin Fishbein and Icek Ajzen (Fishbein & Ajzen, 1975) began developing a theoretical framework which went a long way towards resolving this problem. This framework, now known as the theory of reasoned action, has two key attributes. First, consistent with the literature on compatibility of measurement, reviewed above, it is argued that strong relationships between attitudes and behaviour will only be found where attitudinal measures and behavioural measures are compatible with respect to the action, object, context, and time elements of behaviour. The second key attribute of the theory of reasoned action is that attitude is construed as just *one* determinant of behaviour. The model is represented diagrammatically in Figure 1.2.

The immediate determinant of behaviour in this model is *behavioural intention*, in other words how the individual intends to act. This reflects an important assumption of the theory of reasoned action, namely that most of the behaviours that social psychologists are interested in studying are 'volitional' in nature. In other words, these behaviours can be performed if the individual chooses to perform them, or not performed if the individual chooses not to perform them.

Intention, in turn, is determined by the individual's attitude to the behaviour in question, and by his or her subjective norm. Attitude to behaviour is of course the individual's evaluation of the behaviour in question – broadly speaking, the extent to which the person sees performing the behaviour as good or bad. An example of how to measure such a construct is provided by Beale and Manstead (1991), who investigated mothers' attitudes to restricting the amount of sugar consumed by their infants. They measured attitudes with the item 'My not letting my baby eat or drink anything which contains sugar between meals', which had to be rated on each of four seven-point scales, anchored by the adjective pairs *good–bad, foolish–wise, beneficial–harmful* and *kind–cruel*. The overall measure of attitude to behaviour was derived by averaging the ratings on these four scales. This form of measure of attitude to behaviour is known as 'direct', in contrast to an 'indirect' measure that will be described below.

Subjective norm refers to the individual's belief that important others expect him or her to perform (or not to perform) the behaviour in question. In other words, subjective norm reflects the degree of perceived social pressure on the individual to perform or not to perform the behaviour. In the Beale and Manstead (1991) study, subjective norm was measured with the item 'Most people who are important to me think *I should–I should not* let my baby eat or drink anything which contains sugar between meals' on a seven-point scale. This is an example of a 'direct' measure of subjective norm. The relative contributions of attitude to behaviour and subjective norm in determining behavioural intentions is left open in the theory of reasoned action; which of these factors is more important in shaping intentions is thought to depend on

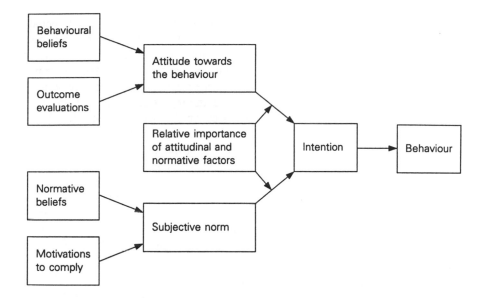

Figure 1.2   *The theory of reasoned action (after Fishbein & Ajzen, 1975)*

the behaviour in question and the individual in question. Clearly, some behaviours have more impact on our partners, families, friends and colleagues than do other behaviours; it seems reasonable to assume that those behaviours that have a greater impact on others will on average be ones where subjective norm (i.e. the perceived expectations of important others) will play a more prominent role. Similarly, some individuals are more inclined than others to take into account the perceived wishes and expectations of other people in their social environment (Snyder, 1974, calls these people high self-monitors); for these people it is likely that the role played by subjective norm in shaping intentions will be more important, as compared with individuals who are more concerned with achieving their own goals, regardless of others' expectations.

The model unfolds still further by specifying the determinants of attitudes to behaviour and of subjective norms. In the case of attitudes, the determinants are said to be *behavioural beliefs*, i.e. beliefs about the consequences of performing the behaviour; and *outcome evaluations*, or the individual's evaluation of each of those consequences. The behavioural beliefs assessed in Beale and Manstead's (1991) study were the beliefs that performing the behaviour in question would (1) help the baby to avoid tooth decay; (2) deprive him or her of treats; (3) help him or her not to get fat; (4) mean that he or she would not have a proper diet; and (5) help him or her to have a good appetite for meals. A sample item is 'My not letting my baby eat or drink anything which contains sugar between meals will help him/her to get less tooth decay.' Each of these beliefs was rated on a seven-point *likely–unlikely* scale. The corresponding outcome evaluations were measured on seven-point *good–bad* scales, an example being 'My baby getting less tooth decay is . . . .' In the theory of reasoned action, behavioural beliefs and outcome evaluations are regarded as joint determinants of attitudes to behaviour. More specifically, each behavioural belief is multiplied by the rating on the corresponding outcome evaluation, and an index of attitude to behaviour is provided by the summed products of behavioural beliefs and outcome evaluations. This summed products measure provides an 'indirect' measure of attitude to behaviour. Thus attitude to behaviour is treated in the theory of reasoned action as an evaluation of performing the behaviour, based on the perceived likelihood that carrying out the behaviour results in outcomes of which one approves or disapproves, or avoids outcomes of which one approves or disapproves.

In the case of subjective norms, the determinants are said to be *normative beliefs*, or the individual's beliefs that each of a number of significant others expects him or her to act in a certain way; and *motivations to comply*, or the individual's inclination to conform to these other people's expectations. Beale and Manstead (1991) assessed normative beliefs by asking each mother how each of six other people ('referents') expected her to behave with respect to the object behaviour. The six referent others used were (1) parents, (2) husband or partner, (3) sister, (4) dentist, (5) husband or partner's parents, and (6) doctor. Normative beliefs for each of these six referents were assessed using seven-point scales, an example being 'My parents think that *I should–I should not* let my baby eat or drink anything which contains sugar between meals.' Motivation to comply with each referent was measured on a four-point unipolar scale, anchored by *not at all* and *very much*. A sample question is: 'Generally speaking, how much do you want to do what your parents think you should do?' In the theory of reasoned action, normative beliefs combine with motivations to comply to determine subjective norms. Just as with attitude to behaviour, the manner of combination is seen as multiplicative: each normative belief is multiplied by its corresponding motivation to comply, and the sum of these products provides an 'indirect' measure of subjective norm. Thus subjective norm is conceptualized in the theory of reasoned action as based on the perceived expectations of others, weighted by the extent to which one is inclined to fulfil those others' expectations.

The theory of reasoned action has in many respects been a highly successful theory. It has been widely used by social psychologists, especially those working in applied domains, and it has generally performed quite well in terms of the ability of the constructs in the model to predict behaviour and behavioural intentions. For example, Smetana and Adler (1980) conducted a study of the intentions of women who were having pregnancy tests to have an abortion if the test proved to be positive. One hundred and thirty-six women awaiting the results of the pregnancy test completed questionnaires assessing their intention to have or not have an abortion, their attitude towards abortion, their beliefs about the consequences of having an abortion and their beliefs about the consequences of continuing with the pregnancy and having a child. The questionnaire included measures of all the components of the theory of reasoned action. Subsequently, the actual behaviour of the 59 women who tested positive was assessed. The correlation between behavioural intention and behaviour was 0.96 ($p<0.001$), providing support for Fishbein and Ajzen's contention that when behaviour is under volitional control, behavioural intention is the most efficient predictor of actual behaviour. Intention, in turn, was reasonably well predicted by attitude to behaviour and subjective norm, the multiple correlation being 0.76. In this case, subjective norm proved to be a more important predictor of intentions than did attitude to behaviour, the standardized regression coefficients being 0.46 and 0.21, respectively. Here, then, is an example of a study in which subjective norm outweighed attitude to behaviour in accounting for variation in behavioural intentions.

The performance of the basic theory of reasoned action (TRA) model has been assessed in two meta-analytic studies. In a widely cited meta-analysis of 87 separate studies, each of which used the theory of reasoned action model, Sheppard, Hartwick and Warshaw (1988) found a weighted average multiple correlation of 0.66 for the relationship between attitude and subjective norm, on the one hand, and behavioural intention, on the other. The average correlation between behavioural intention and behaviour was 0.53. Van den Putte's (1993) meta-analysis considered the results of 150 independent samples, reported in TRA studies published between 1969 and 1988. The weighted average correlation between attitude and subjective norm, on the one hand, and behavioural intention, on the other, was 0.68, while that between behavioural intention and behaviour was 0.62. It is clear, then, that behavioural prediction can be achieved with tolerable accuracy if one assesses behavioural intentions, rather than attitudes; and that behavioural intentions, in turn, can be predicted with tolerable accuracy if one assesses attitude to behaviour and subjective norm.

The theory of reasoned action is, however, concerned with more than simply the *prediction* of intentions and behaviours. It also attempts to provide an *explanation* for the way people behave, by specifying the determinants of intentions (i.e. attitude to behaviour and subjective norm) and also the factors that underlie these determinants (i.e. behavioural beliefs, outcome evaluations, normative beliefs and motivations to comply). How does this help to explain behaviour? Fishbein and Ajzen assume that the basic building blocks of volitional behaviour are beliefs, values and motives. Attitudes to behaviour are built up through experience (direct and indirect) of the behaviour in question, in the course of which individuals form and change beliefs about the consequences of the behaviour. They may also form or change their valuations of these consequences; for example, a mother having her first child might not evaluate the outcome 'deprive my child of treats' (meaning sugar-containing sweets or snacks) especially negatively, whereas a mother who already has one or more children may value this outcome more negatively, as a result of her experience with previous children of what happens when one does try to restrict such treats. If behavioural beliefs and outcome evaluations together determine attitude to behaviour, and attitude to behaviour in turn shapes behavioural intentions, then identifying which behavioural beliefs and outcome evaluations distinguish those with positive intentions from those with negative intentions helps us to understand and explain behaviour.

Exactly the same reasoning applies to the role of normative beliefs and motivations to comply in shaping subjective norm. To the extent that those who engage in a behaviour (or intend to engage in that behaviour) differ significantly on these variables from those who do not, it can be argued that key determinants of the behaviour in question have been identified. From an applied perspective, the importance of this process of identifying at the level of behavioural beliefs, outcome evaluations, normative beliefs, and motivations to comply which factors discriminate 'intenders' from 'non-intenders', or those who do perform the behaviour from those who do not, resides in the enhanced potential for designing effective interventions. In devising such interventions (e.g. to quit smoking, engage in regular exercise, drive within the speed limit, use condoms), it clearly makes sense to focus the communication on the factors that determine the behaviour you are trying to change. Imagine, for example, that you wish (on health grounds) to increase the incidence of breast-feeding of infants, and you discover (as did Manstead, Proffitt, & Smart, 1983) in the course of research using the theory of reasoned action that mothers who do intend to breast-feed do not differ from mothers who intend to bottle-feed with respect to the behavioural belief that breast-feeding helps to create a bond between mother and child. The implication is that an intervention arguing that breast-feeding is good because it strengthens the bond between mother and child would not be effective in changing the intentions of mothers who plan to bottle-feed, because the research shows that mothers who intend to bottle-feed hold this belief just as strongly as mothers who intend to breast-feed. Instead, it would be sensible to direct the intervention at those beliefs, values and motives on which the two groups of mothers *do* differ significantly from each other (for example the belief that breast-feeding helps to protect a baby against infection; Manstead et al., 1983). Herein lies the importance of the theory of reasoned action from an applied perspective: careful application of the model to a specific behavioural domain will (provided the indirect measures of attitude to behaviour and subjective norm are used, as well as or instead of the direct measures) help the researcher to pinpoint the determinants of that behaviour. Knowing what determines a behaviour can then be used to design persuasive communications that try to influence those determinants, rather than influencing irrelevant factors. An example of how an intervention was designed on the basis of prior research guided by the theory of reasoned action is provided in Chapter 8 of this volume, where a study by Parker, Manstead and Stradling (1996) is described.

It is worth noting that the above reasoning concerning the identification of the determinants of behaviour rests on the assumption that attitudes to behaviour and subjective norms exert a *causal influence* on behaviour. However, much of the evidence that is cited in support of the theory of reasoned action is correlational in nature; moreover, many of these correlational studies are cross-sectional in design, meaning that attitudes to behaviour, subjective norms, intentions and behaviours are all measured at a single point in time. This makes it difficult to infer whether the supposedly causal relationships specified in the model are in fact causal. One way to address this problem is to focus on those studies which measure behaviour at a different (future) time from the time at which attitudes and other constructs are assessed. Kraus (1995) has conducted a meta-analysis of 88 studies of the relationship between attitudes and future measures of behaviour. This analysis makes clear that the relationship between attitudes and future behaviour is substantial enough for it to be meaningful to say that measuring attitudes at time 1 helps to predict behaviour at time 2. The average correlation reported by Kraus is 0.38, and 52 per cent of the correlations in the studies he reviewed were above 0.30, while 25 per cent were 0.50 or greater. This pattern of relationships is clearly consistent with the notion that attitudes cause behaviour. However, conclusive evidence of a causal relationship demands experimental research designs in which the attitude construct is manipulated and the effects of this manipulation on behaviour are then assessed. There are relatively few such studies conducted within the framework of the theory of reasoned action or its successor, the theory of planned behaviour, which will be described and discussed below; however, those that have been conducted (e.g. Beale & Manstead, 1991; Parker et al., 1996) report results that are also generally supportive of the assumption that attitudes exercise a causal influence on behaviour.

Successful though the theory of reasoned action has undoubtedly been in terms of generating research and gathering supportive evidence, it has certain limitations. One common objection to the model is that the multiplicative formulae that are involved in the 'belief-based' measures of attitude to behaviour and subjective norm imply that routine behavioural decisions are based on complex cognitive calculations of likelihoods, costs and benefits, and so on. To a large extent this objection is based on a misunderstanding of the model. The theory of reasoned action was never intended by Fishbein and Ajzen to serve as a model of the cognitive processes involved in everyday behavioural decisions. Rather, the theory holds that such decisions are based on our evaluations of the behaviour in question (attitude to behaviour), and our perceptions of how key others expect us to behave (subjective norm). Attitude to behaviour and subjective norm can of course be stored in long-term memory in the form of summary evaluations of behaviour ('I like doing x', 'I hate doing y', and so on) and summary perceptions of others' expectations ('My friends don't want me to do x', 'My parents would really like me to do y', and so on). There is no need to build these evaluations and perceptions from scratch with each new behavioural decision, so the apparently effortful computation of summed products is not assumed to accompany every decision about action. Nor, indeed, is the summing of products itself supposed literally to simulate a cognitive process; rather, the factors which supposedly determine attitudes to behaviour and subjective norm are ones which in Fishbein and Ajzen's view are taken into consideration by the individual. How these different factors are weighted and integrated is another matter, and the theory of reasoned action can be seen as providing a logical account of these processes, rather than an account that reflects the actual processes involved.

This objection relates to a second kind of problem that is frequently raised in connection with the theory of reasoned action, namely that it is better suited to the prediction and understanding of challenging behavioural decisions that require the individual to deliberate the pros and cons of alternative courses of action than to the prediction and understanding of everyday, routine behaviours, or behaviours that have a strong habitual component.

Much of our everyday behaviour, according to this line of argument, is engaged in rather spontaneously and unthinkingly: it is more a matter of habit than of careful consideration. Consistent with this, various investigators have reported a significant direct link between previous behaviour and current behaviour, unmediated by the constructs of the theory of reasoned action. A widely cited study of this type is the one reported by Bentler and Speckart (1979), who studied alcohol, marijuana and hard drug use among college students. Among other things, they found that the statistical relationship between previous behaviour and present behaviour was not fully mediated by intentions, or by the other TRA constructs. This is certainly inconsistent with the theory of reasoned action, which leads one to expect that the influence of past behaviour on present behaviour will be mediated by constructs within the model. There is, of course, a conceptual problem with the past behaviour–present behaviour relationship. Past behaviour cannot in any real sense be said to 'cause' present behaviour, any more than the fact that you got out of bed at 7.30 this morning was 'caused' by the fact that you got out of bed at 7.30 yesterday morning. The fact that the two behaviours are statistically related suggests that they are governed by the same set of factors. The fact that the past behaviour–present behaviour relationship is (at least in some studies) independent of current attitudes to behaviours, subjective norms and intentions is more problematic for the theory of reasoned action. One explanation for this sort of finding is that both past and present behaviours are influenced by essentially non-cognitive factors, such as conditioning or addiction. Thus the fact that you continue to drive to an out-of-town shopping mall, while at the same time *intending* to shop locally and believing that unnecessary car journeys are bad for the environment and disapproved of by your friends, might be explained in terms of the automatized and non-thoughtful way in which you climb into the car and drive to the mall every Saturday morning: in this case, driving to the mall might be called a 'conditioned' response. Similarly, the fact that you continue to smoke, while at the same time intending to quit and believing that smoking is damaging your health and disapproved of by your friends, might be explained in terms of the cravings you have to light up a cigarette whenever you finish a meal: here, smoking can be seen as an addictive behaviour. The finding that past behaviour is sometimes related to present behaviour independently of the model constructs represents a challenge not only to the theory of reasoned action, but also to those researchers who are interested in explaining such associations in terms of the concept of 'habit'. The processes involved in the development of habitual behaviours need to be identified, and the concept of habit needs to be conceptualized and measured in a more sophisticated manner than simply correlations between past and present behaviours. Recent theorizing and research (e.g. Ronis, Yates, & Kirscht, 1989; Verplanken, Aarts, van Knippenberg, & van Knippenberg, 1994) holds out some promise with respect to better conceptualization and measurement of habit.

One way in which Fishbein and Ajzen could respond to the challenge presented by the notions of habit, conditioning and addiction would be to point out that the theory of reasoned action was developed in order to predict and understand behaviours that are engaged in *voluntarily* by the individual. Habitual behaviours, conditioned behaviours and addictive behaviours are not engaged in voluntarily, and therefore lie outside the model's explanatory scope. While this may seem to be a reasonable defence, this limitation of the model to the explanation of voluntary behaviours is more restrictive than one might at first imagine. Take a behaviour, namely having an abortion, which might be of some research interest. Here is a behaviour that may seem to be 'voluntary', in the sense that in the Western world very few if any pregnant women are compelled to have abortions against their will. However, the notion of voluntariness extends well beyond the issue of compulsion. A further issue is whether a woman can have an abortion if she wants one. Thus the model is well suited to the prediction and understanding of a behaviour such as 'having an abortion' – provided that the pregnant woman lives in a country where abortion is readily available, or at least has the resources available to travel to another country where abortion is readily available. However, in a country in which abortion is forbidden it is easy to see that a situation could arise in which a woman has a *positive attitude* to having an abortion, and she may perceive others who are close and important to her as *wanting her* to have an abortion, and yet she does not form the intention to seek an abortion because she knows full well that this is something that is simply not possible. In this context the object behaviour is said to be low in 'volitional control': it cannot be performed at will.

In other words, the restriction of the model to volitional behaviours excludes not only habitual behaviours, but also any behaviours that require special skills, resources or the cooperation of others. This point has been made most forcefully by Liska (1984), who argued that the successful performance of many social behaviours depends on some level of skill or ability on the part of the individual, on having the opportunity to carry out the behaviour, and/or on some degree of cooperation on the part of others. So only the simplest and most trivial of behaviours are entirely under volitional control, in the sense that performance of such behaviours is dependent only on the individual's motivation to perform the behaviour. Arriving at work on time might seem to be a simple behaviour, high in volitional control; if one intends to execute this behaviour, one surely can do so. Yet it is clear that success in performing this behaviour can depend on such factors as possession of money to buy a ticket, the reliability and punctuality of transport services, the traffic flow between home and work, the prevailing weather conditions, and so on. In short, there are many factors that can influence one's success in performing this behaviour, but which fall outside one's personal control. This issue of the role played by control over behaviour was the major reason for the development of a successor to the theory of reasoned action – the theory of planned behaviour.

The theory of planned behaviour

Ajzen (1985, 1988, 1991) proposed and developed the theory of planned behaviour (TPB) with the explicit goal of extending the scope of the theory of reasoned action. As we have seen, an important limitation of the earlier model was its restriction to behaviours that are under the volitional control of the individual. Recognizing that at least some of the behaviours that social psychologists are concerned to explain and understand are not under volitional control, Ajzen expanded the theory of reasoned action by adding a new construct, which he called *perceived behavioural control*. This construct represents the individual's perception of how easy or difficult it is to perform the behaviour in question. Clearly, a behaviour that is seen as easy to perform is one that is high in perceived behavioural control; a behaviour that is seen as difficult to perform is one that is low in perceived behavioural control.

The concept of perceived behavioural control overlaps to a large extent with Bandura's (1977, 1982) concept of self-efficacy, which in his view is central to the concept of human agency. According to Bandura (1982), 'Judgments of self-efficacy . . . determine how much effort people will expend and how long they will persist in the face of obstacles or aversive experiences' (p. 123). It is therefore a belief in one's own abilities and capacities that has motivational implications: if one believes that one can succeed in a task, one is more likely to attempt the task, and more likely to persist in one's attempts despite early setbacks. Similarly, the theory of planned behaviour argues that if an individual has high perceived behavioural control with respect to a particular behaviour, she is more likely to form the intention to perform that behaviour, and is more likely to act on that intention in the face of obstacles and setbacks, than if she is low in perceived behavioural control.

Just as there are both 'direct' and 'indirect' measures of attitude to behaviour and subjective norm, so too there are direct and indirect measures of perceived behavioural control. A typical item from a direct measure of perceived behavioural control would be the following: 'My not letting my baby eat or drink anything which contains sugar between meals is . . .', followed by a rating scale with endpoints labelled *easy* and *difficult* (cf. Beale & Manstead, 1991). Just as attitudes to behaviour and subjective norms are seen within the TRA as founded on the beliefs held by an individual, so perceived control is regarded within the TPB as being founded on another set of beliefs, namely control beliefs, and the indirect measurement of perceived behavioural control involves an assessment of these beliefs. Operationally this indirect measure has been defined as the sum of the perceived likelihood of these control beliefs (cf. Ajzen & Madden, 1986; Schifter & Ajzen, 1985). The beliefs are expected to reflect direct, observed and related experiences of the behaviour and 'other factors that may increase or reduce the perceived difficulty of performing the behavior in question' (Ajzen, 1988, p. 135). Examples of control beliefs concerning the limiting of infants' sugar consumption between meals, as assessed in the Beale and Manstead (1991) study, are the availability of sugar-free snacks (a facilitator of the object behaviour); the giving of sweets as a reward, bribe or gift (an inhibitor); and clear food labelling (a facilitator). It should be noted that methods for assessing perceived behavioural control, especially via indirect measures, are still being actively debated in the literature (see Manstead & Parker, 1995). Ajzen (1991) has recommended that such indirect measures should include assessments of

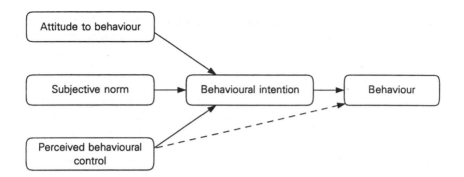

Figure 1.3   *The theory of planned behaviour (after Ajzen, 1988)*

how much a factor could inhibit or facilitate performance of the behaviour, weighted by the frequency with which such factors are encountered. This approach takes account both of the extent to which a caregiver thinks that a factor such as the availability of sugar-free snacks facilitates the restriction of a child's sugar intake between meals, and of the frequency with which she feels she is able to offer the child sugar-free snacks.

Ajzen's theory of planned behaviour is shown in Figure 1.3. The new construct, perceived behavioural control, is represented as jointly determining intentions (together with attitudes to behaviour and subjective norms) and also as jointly determining behaviour (together with intentions). Let us consider each of these relationships in turn. The joint determination of intentions is quite straightforward: the basic idea is that when individuals form intentions, they take into account how much control they have over the behaviour in question. Put concretely, we do not normally form *intentions* to do things (for example conduct a symphony orchestra, walk on the moon, score the winning goal in the cup final) unless we think there is some chance of converting our hopes and dreams into actions, irrespective of how positively we evaluate the behaviour and how much our friends and family would like us to perform the behaviour; hence the influence of perceived behavioural control on intentions.

Turning now to the role played by perceived behavioural control in co-determining behaviour (together with intention), we can understand this relationship in two ways. The first rationale is a motivational one that has not been emphasized by Ajzen himself, but it is consistent with the view that perceived behavioural control overlaps substantially with the concept of self-efficacy. Just as someone who is high in self-efficacy is predicted to persist in the face of obstacles, an individual who is high in perceived behavioural control and who has formed the intention to do something will simply try harder to carry out that action than another person who has an equally strong intention but who is lower in perceived behavioural control. As we saw earlier, even the execution of quite simple behaviours can depend on or be influenced by factors beyond the individual's control. Thus quitting smoking is something that an individual may sincerely intend to do, but as soon as he starts to quit he experiences withdrawal symptoms. If he has high perceived behavioural control with respect to quitting he is more likely to battle through these symptoms and become an ex-smoker than if he is low in perceived behavioural control.

The second explanation for the role played by perceived behavioural control in jointly determining behaviour is less psychological in nature, but is the rationale originally offered by Ajzen. The key point here is that when someone has the intention to perform a behaviour and then fails to act on that intention, that failure is often attributable to his or her lack of control over the behaviour. Imagine a busy lawyer who would like to play tennis every week during the coming year. She may express the intention to play tennis this regularly; however, she may also recognize, on the basis of past experience, that her work schedule sometimes does not permit her to take the necessary two hours away from work on the particular day of the week that the court is available. So her *intention* to perform the behaviour may be high, but her *perceived control* over the behaviour may be lower. If we assess how often she actually plays tennis during the year, we may find that she only played an average of once every two weeks, in which case her low perceived behavioural control would help to predict her behaviour, independently of her intentions. The role of perceived behavioural control here is 'non-psychological' in the sense that it is not the *perception* of control that is causing the failure to act in accordance with intentions; rather, it is the woman's lack of *actual* control over the behaviour. To the extent that her perception of control is accurate, and reflects her lack of actual control, a measure of perceived behavioural control will help to predict the frequency of her tennis playing; but note that if her perception of control was inaccurate, and she in fact had either more control or even less control than she thought she had, then a measure of perceived behavioural control is unlikely to improve the prediction of behaviour beyond what is explained by intentions alone. This is why the direct link between perceived behavioural control and behaviour is depicted in Figure 1.3 as a broken line, rather than a solid one: only when (a) the behaviour is not under volitional control, and (b) the individual has sufficient direct or indirect experience of the behaviour to be able to make a reasonably accurate estimate of his or her control over the behaviour will perceived behavioural control help to predict behaviour.

Ajzen's (1985, 1988, 1991) claim is that the theory of planned behaviour will provide a better description and explanation of behaviour than the theory of reasoned action when the behaviour in question is low in actual control. When the behaviour is high in actual control, he argues, the theory of planned behaviour will not add significantly to what can be predicted and explained on the basis of the theory of reasoned action. Consistent with this reasoning, Madden, Ellen and Ajzen (1992) found that the extent of the improvement in prediction resulting from the addition of perceived behavioural control as a predictor of behavioural intention and behaviour depended on how easy it is to control the behaviour. They included ten different behaviours in their study, ranging from those over which the subject could reasonably expect to exert a high degree of control, such as taking vitamin supplements, to those over which less volitional control may be exercised, such as getting a good night's sleep. The results indicated that the prediction of both behavioural intention and behaviour was enhanced by the inclusion of a measure of perceived behavioural control, but the extent of this enhancement was greatest for those behaviours that were classified as low in volitional control.

The number of studies using the theory of planned behaviour has grown rapidly in recent years. Ajzen (1991) reviewed the findings of more than a dozen empirical tests of the theory. In nearly all of these studies it was found that the addition of perceived behavioural control to the basic theory of reasoned action model resulted in a significant improvement in the prediction of intentions and/or behaviour. More recently, Godin and Kok (in press) reviewed the results of 54 empirical tests of the theory of planned behaviour simply within the domain of health behaviour, and came to broadly similar conclusions: adding perceived behavioural control enhanced the explained variance in intentions by an average of 13 per cent and the explained variance in behaviour by an average of 11 per cent. It seems safe to conclude that for most behaviours that are likely to be of interest to social psychologists, it is worth making the relatively small additional effort that is needed in order to use the theory of planned behaviour rather than the theory of reasoned action.

The importance of direct behavioural experience

As we saw in connection with Ajzen's notion of perceived behavioural control, direct experience with the attitude object can have an impact on the extent to which dispositional constructs such as perceived behavioural control are predictive of behaviour. Fazio (e.g. 1986, 1990) has developed a theoretical model in which the role played by direct experience is of central importance. Here, however, it is the influence of direct experience on *attitudes* to an object that is studied. Fazio's basic argument is that attitudes that are formed on the basis of direct behavioural experience with an object are more predictive of future behaviour towards that object than are attitudes that are based on indirect experience. The rationale for this argument is that attitudes based on direct experience with the attitude object are *stronger* (in the sense that they have greater clarity and they are held with greater certainty and confidence) and, relatedly, they are more *accessible*.

The strength of an attitude, in Fazio's approach, is treated as the strength of the association between an attitude object and the perceiver's evaluation of that object. The idea is that the more experience one has with the attitude object, the stronger will be this associative link between the object and the way in which it is evaluated. Thus the strength with which one positively evaluates another person is regarded as being determined by the amount of experience one has of interacting with that person. This makes good sense: one may have a positive first impression of someone, but the clarity, certainty and confidence of that positive evaluation will grow as a function of further interaction with him or her – assuming that this additional direct behavioural experience confirms the positive first impression.

A related consequence of having direct experience with the attitude object is that one's attitude towards it will be more accessible, in the sense that it will be more easily and quickly retrieved from memory. This is the reason why attitudes based on direct behavioural experience are more predictive of future behaviour, according to Fazio. Attitudes that are easily and quickly retrieved from memory are more likely than less accessible attitudes to be activated whenever the attitude object or cues relevant to the object are presented. Thus if you have frequent interaction with another person whom you like, and you therefore have a highly accessible positive attitude to this person, any sight or sound that is relevant to this person should automatically elicit this positive attitude. The result is that whenever one is responding to the actual or symbolic presence of that person, whether this is in the context of a questionnaire assessing attitudes or in the context of an assessment of behaviour towards that person, the same positive attitude should be rapidly and automatically elicited, and this attitude should guide both the questionnaire responses and the interpersonal behaviour. Attitudes and behaviour should be strongly correlated when the attitude in question is highly accessible.

To measure the accessibility of an attitude, Fazio has used the time taken to respond to a question about that attitude. If an attitude is highly accessible, he argues, it should take less time for subjects to retrieve their evaluation of the object in question from memory, and they should therefore be quicker to answer questions about attitudes to that object. Thus one should expect to find that, as compared with attitudes formed on the basis of indirect experience, attitudes based on direct behavioural experience with an object are (1) more accessible, in the sense that reaction times to questions about these attitudes should be faster (a prediction for which there is empirical support; e.g. Fazio, Chen, McDonel, & Sherman, 1982); and (2) that such attitudes are more predictive of behaviour towards that object (a prediction for which there is also empirical support; see Fazio & Zanna, 1981, for a review).

The significance of Fazio's theorizing and research in the context of the present chapter is that it shows that there are conditions under which reasonably strong attitude–behaviour relationships can be found even when one measures attitudes to the targets of behaviour, rather than attitudes to behaviour towards those targets. Thus the principle of compatibility as specified by Ajzen and Fishbein (1977) can, in certain circumstances, be violated without fatally weakening the relationship between attitudinal and behavioural measures. The condition that has to be fulfilled in order for this to apply is that the respondent has a highly accessible attitude towards the target of the behaviour. In terms of the principle of compatibility, accessible attitudes seem to have the capacity to close the psychological 'gap' that we saw earlier, in connection with Davidson and Jaccard's (1979) research on the contraception behaviours of women, between responses to being asked to evaluate 'oral contraceptives' and being asked to evaluate 'my using oral contraceptives over the next two years'. Following the logic of Fazio's reasoning, if all the women in Davidson and Jaccard's study had had highly accessible attitudes to oral contraceptives, their answers to the first question should have been predictive of their future behaviour, and perhaps as predictive as their answers to the second question.

Summary and conclusions

Social psychologists' understanding of the attitude–behaviour relationship has developed considerably since the publication of LaPiere's (1934) study. This study and its successors were seen as evidence of a worrying inconsistency between what people say (attitudes) and what people do. These studies were reviewed by Wicker (1969), who concluded that there was little evidence to support the idea of an underlying disposition to respond to a object favourably or unfavourably that influences both verbal expressions (attitude statements, responses to attitude scales) and overt actions. The crisis that ensued has to a large extent been resolved, partly by a careful conceptual and methodological analysis of the problem, and partly by locating the 'attitude–behaviour relationship' in a more general theoretical framework. The conceptual and methodological analysis focused on two principles: the *principle of aggregation*, which is founded on the psychometric fact that single items on any test are unreliable; and the *principle of compatibility*, which holds that substantial correlations between attitudinal and behavioural measures will only be found if these constructs are assessed at the same level of generality (or specificity).

The location of the attitude–behaviour relationship within a more general framework has been most successfully achieved by the theory of reasoned action and the theory of planned behaviour. As well as considering the role of attitudes in determining intentions, and thereby behaviour, these models give recognition to the role played by the perceived expectations of others (i.e. subjective norms). While Fishbein and Ajzen's (1975; Ajzen & Fishbein, 1980) theory of reasoned action has proved to be a successful model for predicting and understanding a variety of social behaviours, its restriction to behaviours that are largely under the individual's volitional control led Ajzen (1985, 1988) to develop an extended model, known as the theory of planned behaviour. The extended model includes a new explanatory construct, perceived behavioural control, and research to date suggests that the addition of this construct generally does improve the prediction of intentions and behaviour, especially where the behaviour involved is one over which the individual has less than perfect control.

Fazio's theorizing and research on the role played by direct behavioural experience with the attitude object, emphasizing the role played by the strength and accessibility of attitudes, demonstrates that there are conditions under which attitudes to targets can be predictive of behaviour towards those targets, without necessarily fulfilling the requirements of the principle of compatibility. It seems that direct experience with the attitude object serves to strengthen the attitude towards it, and to enhance the accessibility of this attitude. When the respondent subsequently encounters the attitude object, his or her evaluation of the object will quickly and automatically be activated, and will exert a directive influence on behaviour towards that object.

Future research in this field is likely to focus on three key issues. First, although the theory of planned behaviour has increased the predictive range and capacity of the basic TRA model, it is no better placed than its predecessor to shed light on the role played by *habit* in determining behaviour. As noted earlier, the field is in need of fresh ways of conceptualizing and measuring the notion of habit. Secondly, the theory of planned behaviour is in essence a subjective expected utility model (see Chapter 2), based on the assumption that individuals make rational decisions that are founded on beliefs about outcomes, weighted by evaluations of those outcomes. Both intuition and empirical evidence suggest that *affect* can play an important role in behavioural decisions: the emotions we expect to feel after we have engaged in a behaviour (Richard, van der Plight, & de Vries, 1995a) and/or the emotions we expect to feel while performing a behaviour (Manstead & Parker, 1995) may be as important as the more instrumental costs and benefits we expect to accrue as a result of our behaviour. Thirdly, there is a pressing need to integrate the theoretical models proposed by Ajzen and by Fazio. As Eagly and Chaiken (1993) have argued, these models should be regarded as compatible rather than mutually exclusive; one implication of Fazio's model is that attitudes to objects – when they are highly accessible – have a powerful and, perhaps automatic effect on attitudes to behaviour in relation to these objects, which would in turn have a major bearing on behavioural intentions. What remains to be researched is the extent to which the processes that follow from attitude accessibility, which are regarded by Fazio as automatic and unconscious in nature, can be married to the more deliberative and conscious processes which seem to be involved in the relationships between attitudes and intentions, and between intentions and behaviours.

This chapter has introduced the reader to theory and research on the attitude–behaviour relationship. The chapter began by considering why we should expect attitudes and behaviour to be related, and reviewed some of the early empirical research on this issue. Much of this early research found disappointingly weak correlations between these two constructs, which led some commentators to advise that the attitude concept should be abandoned. The chapter then discussed conceptual and methodological analysis of this problem which resulted in the articulation of two principles: the principle of aggregation and the principle of compatibility. Together these go some way towards resolving this problem of weak attitude–behaviour correlations. The contribution made by theoretical models, such as the Fishbein–Ajzen theory of reasoned action, which locate the attitude–behaviour relationship within a broader system of theoretical constructs, was discussed, along with the limitations which resulted in Ajzen's theory of planned behaviour. The penultimate section considered an alternative approach to the understanding of the attitude–behaviour relationship, which emphasizes the importance of direct experience with the attitude object. The chapter finished with some pointers to key issues that require further research.

Further reading

Ajzen, I. (1988). *Attitudes, personality and behavior*. Milton Keynes, UK: Open University Press. A very clear and readable introduction to the attitude–behaviour 'problem', as seen through the eyes of the developer of the theory of planned behaviour.

Ajzen, I. & Fishbein, M. (1980). *Understanding attitudes and predicting social behavior*. Englewood Cliffs, NJ: Prentice-Hall. The best introduction to the theory of reasoned action, complete with guidelines for developing a questionnaire to measure the key constructs.

Eagly, A.H. & Chaiken, S. (1993). *The psychology of attitudes*. Fort Worth, TX: Harcourt Brace Jovanovich. The most complete and authoritative overview of the literature on attitudes available. Chapter 4 discusses the attitude–behaviour issue.

Fazio, R.H. (1986). How do attitudes guide behavior? In R.M. Sorrentino & E.T. Higgins (Eds), *Handbook of motivation and cognition: Foundations of social behavior* (pp. 204–243). New York: Guilford. A good introduction to Fazio's approach to the attitude–behaviour relationship.

Manstead, A.S.R. & Parker, D. (1995). Evaluating and extending the theory of planned behaviour. In W. Stroebe and M. Hewstone (Eds), *European review of social psychology*, Vol. 6, (pp. 69–95). Chichester: Wiley. An analysis of the strengths and shortcomings of the theory of planned behaviour, with some suggestions for ways in which this model could be extended.

Ronis, D.L, Yates, J.F., & Kirscht, J.P. (1989). Attitudes, decisions, and habits as determinants of repeated behavior. In A.R. Pratkanis, S.J. Breckler, & A.G. Greenwald (Eds), *Attitude structure and function* (pp. 213–239). Hillsdale, NJ: Lawrence Erlbaum. An in-depth treatment of the habit construct and how to measure it.

2

Judgement and Decision Making

Joop van der Pligt

Contents

Human decision making has been studied by a variety of disciplines including philosophy, economics and psychology. Behavioural decision making, as the field is generally known in psychology, is being studied in all branches of psychology including social psychology. As will be made clear in this chapter, research on judgement and decision making has had a marked influence on both basic and applied research in social psychology. The first part of this chapter briefly describes *normative* approaches to the study of human judgement and decision making. Next the focus will be on *descriptive* approaches, followed by a brief overview of the *heuristics* people use in information processing. The emphasis will be on biases and errors, their effects on the quality of judgement and decision making, and possible ways to reduce their impact. The final section briefly summarizes research on group decision making and social dilemmas.

Normative theories of decision making

Imagine that you face the following decision problem. You are looking for a new apartment and have to choose between two options. The first apartment has three rooms, is relatively cheap but needs a bit of work. Moreover it is quite far from your work; the journey would take about 20 minutes by train. The apartment is close to a railway station, but rumour has it that this railway line will be discontinued. In that case your travel time would be increased by approximately 50 minutes. The other apartment is smaller, located in the centre of town and your work is within walking distance. Unfortunately, it is more expensive than the other apartment and there could be a major rent increase in about a year. What would you do? This is not an easy decision. You have to decide how much value you place upon space and travel time and compare the alternatives with respect to these two attributes. Moreover, you also have to deal with uncertainty; in both cases the attractiveness of the apartment could be affected by possible future developments (a rent increase for the second apartment and discontinuation of the railway line close to the first apartment).

The above decision problem is an example of a typical judgement or decision-making task used in this research area. Generally, tasks in this field of research have a *probability* component and/or a *value* component. Edwards (1954) provided the first major review of research on human judgement and decision making. He argued that normative and prescriptive models based on economic and statistical theory should also be relevant to psychologists interested in human judgement and decision making. Edwards introduced *subjectively expected utility* theory (SEU), which decomposes decisions or choices in probabilities and values or preferences, and provides a set of rules for combining beliefs (*probabilities*) and preferences (*values* or *utilities*). The SEU principle can be expressed as

$$\sum_i p_i.u(x_i),$$

in which p_i is the probability of outcome i and $u(x_i)$ the utility of outcome i. The weight p_i refers to a subjective or personal probability. SEU theory assumes that in choice situations people prefer the option with the highest subjectively expected utility. The theory is normative or prescriptive because it specifies how decisions *should* be made. If one accepts the axioms upon which it is based, then the most rational choice or decision is the one specified by the theory as having the highest subjectively expected utility. The theory thus provides rules to reach rational and consistent decisions on the basis of subjective, personal assessments of probabilities and values or utilities. Assume you have to make a choice between two job offers and that you make your choice on the basis of a comparison of the two jobs in terms of three possible outcomes or consequences that receive equal weight in terms of their importance: (initial) salary, career opportunities and work atmosphere. Initial salary is higher at firm A than at firm B. The salary offered by firm A is good, while the offer by firm B is more than adequate but not as good as that of firm A. Let us now replace these verbal descriptions of the two salaries by some (subjective) numbers which we call utilities. This would result in ratings of 8 and 7 respectively on a scale ranging from 1 to 10. Career opportunities seem better at firm B but this element cannot be assessed with certainty. Let us assume that career opportunities get ratings of respectively 8 and 9 but that these are less certain at firm A (subjective probability of 0.7) than at firm B (subjective probability of 0.9). Finally, the atmosphere at firm A seems to be

Table 2.1   *Choosing between two job offers*

	salary		career opportunities		work atmosphere		
	utility	(probability)	utility	(probability)	utility	(probability)	overall SEU
Job A	8	(1.0)	8	(0.7)	8	(0.8)	20.0
Job B	7	(1.0)	9	(0.9)	7	(1.0)	22.1

Utility scores range from 0 to 10.

better than at firm B, but you are certain about your judgement of the atmosphere at firm B and slightly less certain about firm A (probabilities of 1.0 (B) vs. 0.8 (A)). This leads to the following scores: Firm A ($1.0 \times 8 + 0.7 \times 8 + 0.8 \times 8 = 20.0$), Firm B ($1.0 \times 7 + 0.9 \times 9 + 1.0 \times 7$) = 22.1. Thus, according to this analysis, the job offer of firm B is more attractive than that of firm A (see also Table 2.1).

The axioms of SEU theory are all based on the work of von Neumann and Morgenstern (1944). Their work was purely mathematical and showed that if a person's choices follow certain rules or axioms, it is possible to derive utilities in such a way that a preference for a specific alternative implies that its expected utility is greater than that of the other alternative(s). Their approach assumes that it is possible to associate a real number with each possible consequence of the relevant alternatives. This number (e.g. a number between 1 and 10), as in the above example of the choice between two job offers, represents the utility of that consequence for the individual. The *expected utility* of a specific alternative is then the sum of the numbers associated with each possible consequence weighted by the probability that each consequence will occur. Thus a positive or negative outcome will be weighted by the probability of its occurrence: for example a certain outcome will be multiplied by 1.0, an outcome with a probability of 0.5 will be multiplied by 0.5, etc. The dictionary definition of utility focuses on 'immediate usefulness'. As argued by Dawes (1988), that is not what decision theorists have in mind when they employ the term 'utility'. Dawes prefers the term 'personal value', i.e. the personal evaluation of an outcome, taking into account both short-term and long-term usefulness as well as personal values.

SEU models have some constraints which make it difficult to represent real life decision making. A broader approach is to adopt a multidimensional definition of utility. Multi-Attribute Utility (MAU) theory has increased the scope of application of formal decision theory (see e.g. Von Winterfeldt & Edwards, 1986). It puts more emphasis on the clarification of the preference structure of the individual decision-maker. For instance, with MAU theory one could decompose a complex decision problem such as choosing between two or more personal computers by deciding how these alternatives score on the attributes one finds important (price, speed, memory, quality of the monitor, etc.), attach weights to these attributes, and combine the scores (weight × attribute score) to derive an overall evaluation of each computer.

Let us briefly return to our previous example concerning the two job offers.

Table 2.2 *Choosing between two job offers: weighted versus unweighted attributes*

	Attribute			overall utility (unweighted)	overall utility
	salary (weighted)	career opportunities	work atmosphere		
Job A	8 (0.2)	8 (0.6)	8 (0.2)	8.0	8.0
Job B	7 (0.2)	9 (0.6)	7 (0.2)	8.0	8.2

Utility scores range from 0 to 10, weights for the three attributes are given in parenthesis and should sum to 1.0.

A representation of the decision problem in terms of Multi-Attribute Utility is given in Table 2.2. The two offers have the same scores on the attributes as in the previous example (see Table 2.1). Generally, MAU models for preference among multi-attribute objects disregard uncertainty about the state of the world, so all attributes are seen as certain and differences in the likelihood of each of the attributes or consequences are ignored. Calculating the mean score on the basis of the scores on each of the attributes shows that the two offers are equally attractive. If we allow for differences in the importance of each of the attributes this could change. For instance, if the individual finds career opportunities by far the most important (a weight of 0.6) and assigns less weight to the remaining two attributes the overall score for job B would be 8.2 as compared to 8.0 for job offer A.

Both SEU theory and MAU theory have had a major impact on attitude theory and research. Several approaches in this area essentially employ a model based on SEU theory and MAU theory. The basic assumption of these approaches is that attitudes are based on the assessment of a variety of positive and negative attributes associated with a specific behavioural alternative or choice. Both Fishbein and Ajzen's *theory of reasoned action* (1975) and Ajzen's *theory of planned behaviour* (Ajzen, 1991) are based on the principles described earlier in this chapter. Decomposing complex issues into simpler elements is the crucial principle underlying these theories (see also Chapter 1 of the present book). Thus, individual attitudes are decomposed into a set of beliefs about possible outcomes or attributes. The attitude (A) towards an object, action or event is assumed to be a function of the beliefs (b) about the object's attributes or about the act's consequences or outcomes and the evaluations (e) of these attributes or consequences. According to Fishbein and Ajzen's model an individual's attitude can be estimated by multiplying the evaluation of each attribute or consequences associated with the object or action by the subjective probability that the object or action has that attribute or will lead to that consequence. Summing these products for the total set of beliefs results in an estimate for the attitude of the individual:

$$A \text{ thus equals } \sum_{i=1}^{n} b_i e_i.$$

For instance, a person's attitude towards a job offer would be a function of beliefs about attributes such as salary, career opportunities and work atmosphere and the evaluation of these attributes.

Not surprisingly, the validity of prescriptive, normative theories such as SEU theory as adequate *descriptions* of human choice and decision making has been a dominant theme in this research area for the past decades. This is partly based on the idea that the study of human decision making should focus on the perceptual and cognitive factors that cause human judgement and decision making to *deviate* from the predictions of normative models. Normative models such as SEU theory assume extensive information-processing capabilities and adopt a rational *homo economicus* model of human decision making. Simon (1957) argued that the limited computational capabilities of decision makers are likely to result in 'bounded' rationality, especially in the context of highly complex task environments.

People do not always behave as normative theories such as SEU theory claim they should. Research findings in cognitive psychology cast serious doubts on the *descriptive validity* of SEU theory. When there are many consequences and/or probabilities or unusual relationships between these elements, people tend to violate decision rules such as those proposed by SEU theory. Moreover, people find it difficult to learn and use the so-called weighted sum decision rule of SEU theory. An added difficulty is that people find it difficult to think probabilistically. These shortcomings also apply to applications of SEU theory such as the theory of reasoned action. Fishbein and Ajzen (1975) acknowledge that a person is capable of attending to or processing about five to nine beliefs about the attitude object. These beliefs are termed salient. Since it is impossible to obtain a precise measure of all possible beliefs underlying the attitudes of various individuals, they suggest that the so-called modal salient beliefs in a given population should be obtained. The most frequently elicited beliefs in a representative sample of the population are considered to modal salient beliefs for the population. Applied research in this field tends to use a considerable number of beliefs concerning possible consequences of a specific behavioural action or possible attributes of an object. Van der Pligt and Eiser (1984) argued that the inclusion of many beliefs seems the rule rather than the exception in this research area. Ajzen and Fishbein (1980), in their overview of steps in the construction of a standard questionnaire within the framework of their theory, recommend the inclusion of 20 beliefs. Other studies mentioned by van der Pligt and Eiser (1984) presented respondents with as many as 55 beliefs. All these examples resulted in relatively predictive attitudes. But what does this show? It could well be that the set of beliefs is predictive of the final attitude, but this does not necessarily reflect the actual decision-making process. Even if people want to, they would find it impossible to combine many beliefs with their evaluation and sum these products to form an overall attitude. Although scores on the various beliefs and their probabilities can be quite predictive of the individual's attitude they do not tell us much about the structure of the individual's attitude and thus *why* he or she holds that attitude.

All these findings suggest that the conscious thought preceding a decision may be of a relatively simple nature, given the difficulty of processing complex information. Quite often, people seem to rely on simple heuristics, and seem to use different decision-making strategies for different situations. As a consequence psychologists became more interested in understanding *how* people actually make decisions in the real world and attempted to develop *descriptive* models of judgement and decision making.

Descriptive approaches to decision making

Recent years have seen an increase of approaches attempting to provide adequate descriptions of human judgement and decision making. These range from comprehensive frameworks to approaches emphasizing specific factors that tend to be neglected in the mainstream literature on judgement and decision making. Prospect theory aims to provide a general theory of decision making under uncertainty and is probably the most comprehensive attempt to meet the various shortcomings of normative theories such as SEU theory. Other descriptive approaches will also be briefly discussed, followed by a summary overview of simplified rules that are often used in everyday judgement and decision making.

Prospect theory

Kahneman and Tversky (1979) developed prospect theory to remedy the descriptive failures of subjectively expected utility (SEU) theories of decision making. Prospect theory attempts to *describe* and explain decisions under uncertainty. Applications tend to focus on phenomena such as persuasion, negotiation and bargaining. Most of these applications concern the effects of 'framing' (the way decision alternatives are presented) on preference and choice (see for example Tversky & Kahneman, 1981). Like SEU theories, prospect theory assumes that the value v of an option or alternative is calculated as the summed products over specified outcomes x. Each product consists of a utility or value $v(x)$ and a weight $p(p)$ attached to the objective probability p of obtaining x. Thus the value v of an option is

$$\sum_i \pi p_i v(x_i)$$

Both the value function v and the probability weighting function p are non-linear. The two functions are not given in closed mathematical form but have several important features. The decision weight $p(p)$ is a monotonic function of p but is not a probability. Generally, small probabilities are overweighted, and large probabilities are underweighted. To give an example: An objective probability of 0.50 receives less weight than 0.50 (see Figure 2.1). Unfortunately, although $p(0) = 0$ and $p(1) = 1$, the probability weighting function is generally not well behaved near the endpoints. Extremely low probability outcomes are sometimes exaggerated, and sometimes ignored entirely.

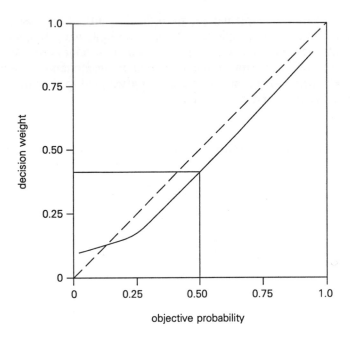

Figure 2.1   *Prospect theory: hypothetical probability weighting function*

Similarly, small differences between high probability and certainty are sometimes neglected, sometimes accentuated. According to Kahneman and Tversky this is so because people find it difficult to comprehend and evaluate extreme probabilities.

The value v is defined in terms of gains and losses relative to a psychologically neutral reference point. The value function $v(x)$ is S-shaped; concave in the region of gains above the reference point, convex in the region of losses (see Figure 2.2). Thus, each unit increase in gain has decreasing value as gain increases. In other words, the subjective difference between gaining nothing and gaining $100 is greater than the difference between gaining $100 and gaining $200. Finally, the value function is steeper for losses than for gains. This implies that losing $100 is more unpleasant than gaining $100 is pleasant. In other words, a given change in the status quo hurts more as a loss than it pleases as a gain (see also Figure 2.1). A later, extended version of prospect theory employs cumulative rather than separable decision weights (Tversky & Kahneman, 1992). A major change from the original version concerns the role of rank- and sign-dependency. This weakening of the view that the disentanglement of belief and value is essential to rational decision-making entails that probabilities can also be weighted by the rank order of the attractiveness of the outcomes. Overall, the theory retains the major features of the original version.

Two phenomena played an important role in the formulation of prospect theory: the *certainty effect* and the *reflection effect*. The first refers to the

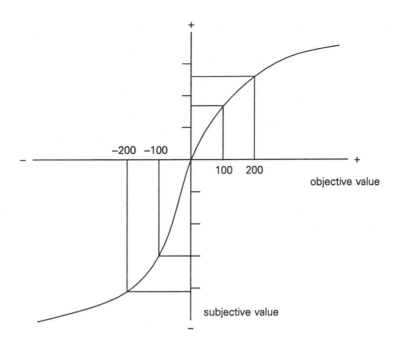

Figure 2.2   *Prospect theory: hypothetical value function*

tendency to give excessive weight to outcomes that are considered certain, as compared to outcomes that are 'merely' probable. Thus, most people would prefer a certain win of $300 as compared to an 80 per cent chance to win $400, although the latter has a higher expected utility. The second (the reflection effect) refers to the tendency to reverse the preference order between two alternatives depending on their sign (losses or gains). For instance, if presented with a choice between (a) a sure loss of $100, or (b) a 50 per cent chance of a loss of $200 and a 50 per cent chance of no loss at all, most people will prefer the uncertain, risky alternative (b). This risk-seeking preference is in sharp contrast with preferences when the choice is between a sure gain of (a) $100, or a 50 per cent chance of a gain of $200 *and* a 50 per cent choice of no gain at all (b). In this case most people will prefer the certain, risk-avoiding alternative. Inspection of Figures 2.1 and 2.2 will confirm the higher attractiveness of the risky option (in case of losses) and the risk-avoiding option (in case of gains). According to SEU theory the two options in each problem are equally (un)attractive. Both the reflection effect and the certainty effect violate expected utility theory.

The so-called 'editing phase' preceding the evaluation of options and the final choice plays an important role in prospect theory. The function of this stage is to organize and reformulate or 'frame' the available options in order to simplify the subsequent stages in the decision-making process (evaluation and choice). The frame that a person adopts is partly determined by external factors (the formulation of the problem) and partly by other factors such as experience, habits and norms. The most frequently studied framing effect concerns the reflection effect discussed earlier. Inducing people to adopt a gain frame when choosing between a gamble and a sure thing tends to result in a risk-avoiding preference (the certain alternative). Inducing people to adopt a loss frame, on the other hand, tends to result in a risk-seeking preference (the risky alternative). In a classic example of this effect ('The Asian disease problem') respondents were asked to imagine that the US is threatened with an unusual disease, expected to kill 600 people (Tversky & Kahneman, 1981). A choice had to be made between two alternative interventions with different consequences:

- If Programme A is adopted, 200 people will be saved.
- If Programme B is adopted, there is a one in three probability that 600 people will be saved, and a two in three probability that nobody will be saved.

Most subjects (72 per cent) opted for 'Programme A' in the gain frame. Another group was presented with the same problem in a loss frame:

- If Programme C is adopted, 400 people will die.
- If Programme D is adopted, there is a one in three probability that nobody will die, and a two in three probability that 600 people will die.

In this group, the majority (78 per cent) preferred the uncertain option (Programme D). This effect is most pronounced when subjects are presented with a gamble and a sure thing. In such cases both the value function and the probability weighting function would predict the described changes in preference. The reflection effect has been most clearly demonstrated in problems involving human lives (Tversky & Kahneman, 1981; Fischhoff, 1983; van der Pligt & van Schie, 1990; Miller & Fagley, 1991). Mixed effects are found in problems dealing with money (e.g. Hershey & Schoemaker, 1980; van der Pligt & van Schie, 1990) while the effect has rarely been found in more 'everyday' decision problems (e.g. Fagley & Miller, 1990; van der Pligt & van Schie, 1990). In the latter case it seems more difficult to induce people to adopt the frame suggested in the problem presentation.

The tendency to seek risk when confronted with possible losses is one of the important predictions of prospect theory. The relative attractiveness of risky options would explain the sometimes observed tendency to continue gambling after losses (not only in the casino but also in banking, as in the Barings Bank fiasco in 1995). Prospect theory can also be applied to processes of persuasion. For instance, one could describe a decision to reorganize a firm in terms of jobs lost but also in terms of jobs saved. A firm with 800 employees that needs to fire 400 of them could describe this option as a loss of 400 jobs. On the other hand one could use the maximum number of jobs lost (800) as a reference point (e.g. in case of bankruptcy) and present the alternative as a decision that saves 400 jobs. Comparing 400 job losses with a risky option that could result in the loss of 800 jobs or none would result in a different preference than comparing a gain of 400 jobs with a gain of 800 jobs or none.

In the latter case one would expect people to opt for certainty relative to the case when the alternative options are presented in terms of losses.

A further test of the reflection effect is to investigate whether subjects actually *adopt* the frame that corresponds with their preference (i.e. a gain frame when preferring the certain option, a loss frame when preferring the uncertain option). Research on this issue has obtained mixed findings, leading Slovic, Lichtenstein and Fischhoff (1988) to conclude that people seem to have considerable difficulties in introspecting the judgmental processes involved in framing, and that some natural frames (usually those concerning more familiar decision problems) may be so robust that it is difficult to persuade people to adopt a different frame.

Social psychological research in this area tends to focus on the effects of framing on individual attitudes and choice. Applications include medical decisions, preventive health behaviour and consumer behaviour (see e.g. Plous, 1993). Meyerowitz and Chaiken (1987) and Huber, Neale and Northcraft (1987) have investigated framing in the context of preventive health behaviour (breast self-examination) and selecting job candidates. Both studies confirm that emphasizing the positive outcome (gain) leads to risk avoidance, while emphasizing the negative outcome (loss) results in risk seeking. In Huber et al.'s study, interviewing more job applicants was considered as risk-taking behaviour and Meyerowitz and Chaiken viewed performing breast self-examination as risky behaviour (due to the possibility that one would find irregularities that could be related to a tumour, which would not be the case if one refrained from breast self-examination). One shortcoming of these two studies concerns the rather arbitrary selections of one of the alternatives as being risky. In both cases the presumably 'risky' alternative could also be seen as less risky than the remaining option (i.e. interviewing more job applicants and not performing breast self-examination), especially if one incorporates longer-term risks.

In other research inspired by prospect theory framing of the problem presentation involved selectively emphasizing the probability of success (gain or positive frame) versus emphasizing the probability of failure (loss or negative frame) (e.g. Levin, Johnson, & Davis, 1987; Wilson, Kaplan, & Schneiderman, 1987; Levin, Snyder, & Chapman, 1988; Marteau, 1989). Van Schie and van der Pligt (1995) refer to this manipulation as 'outcome salience'. This can be illustrated with a problem describing risky surgery used by Wilson et al. (1987). In the 'positive' frame, the problem presentation referred to a 40 per cent chance of surviving, and the 'negative' frame referred to a 60 per cent chance of dying. Respondents were requested to indicate whether they opted for the treatment or not. In the positive frame focusing on 'surviving' more subjects opted for the surgery than in the negative frame stressing the likelihood of losing one's life.

The effects of 'outcome salience' have been studied in a number of problem domains; e.g. medical decision-making (Marteau, 1989), consumer decision-making (Levin et al., 1987), and gambling (Levin et al., 1988). The effects of outcome salience obtained in these studies were similar to the findings of Wilson et al. (1987), described above, and show that the majority of respondents opt for the risky alternative if it is described in terms of chances of success. Presenting the complementary chances of failure tends to increase preference for the status quo, and leads to risk avoidance.

Other applications of prospect theory can be found in the literature on bargaining and negotiation. For instance, De Dreu, Lualhati and McCusker (1994) applied prospect theory to predict and understand individuals' satisfaction with social decision-making outcomes. Their findings showed that the satisfaction with own versus others' outcomes is partly determined by predictions based on prospect theory. Individuals with a loss frame were more own-outcome oriented than individuals with a gain frame. Thus loss frames led individuals to maximize their outcomes more than gain frames. Their findings implied that equity theory seems to apply more to gain frame situations than to loss frame situations, and show the potential relevance of prospect theory for our understanding of interdependence processes such as conflict management, negotiation and social dilemmas.

All in all, prospect theory may help our understanding of decision making under uncertainty. Insights derived from this field of research have considerable scope for applied research and include many issues that are of relevance to applied social psychology. Up to now applications of the theory focus on the effects of problem presentation, or framing, on decision making. Preferences for alternatives and satisfaction with these alternatives were the main dependent variables. Other possible applications concern the analysis of decisional conflicts. These conflicts could be the result of different frames employed by different individuals and/or groups. One possible shortcoming of prospect theory is the limited attention paid to the role of time in decision making. Quite often immediate and distant outcomes are given equal weight while people tend to discount events that will or could happen in the future. These discounting processes have been studied in research on intertemporal choice and only recently have there been attempts to relate the outcomes of this field of research to prospect theory (Mowen & Mowen, 1991) and expected utility theory (Quiggin & Horowitz, 1995). From an applied perspective these developments are important. One reason is that they could improve our understanding of the failure of many health education campaigns providing information about long-term risks associated with specific behavioural practices.

The next section presents a selection of other descriptive approaches to judgement and decision making. Most of these put more emphasis on everyday decision making and rely to a lesser extent on standard decision tasks such as the gambles discussed in this and previous sections. These approaches also recognize that ambiguity is an important feature of real-world decision problems.

Other descriptive approaches

Most of these approaches assume that people have available a variety of strategies for solving decision problems. Experience will affect the availability of these strategies, and strategy choice will also be affected by the expected advantages (benefits) and disadvantages (costs) of the chosen strategy. For many decisions an exhaustive analysis such as prescribed by SEU theory simply is not worth the trouble. Thus, for many problems people aim for an acceptable solution and not necessarily the optimal solution due to the costs (time, effort) of 'calculating' the best possible option. These approaches are direct extensions of the bounded-rationality concept we discussed earlier (see also Payne, Bettman, & Johnson, 1992).

Beach and Mitchell (1987) proposed *image theory*, which stresses the intuitive and automatic aspects of decision making. In this theory the decision maker's goals or values (images) play a crucial role and much attention is paid to simplified strategies. The theory emphasizes that individuals make judgements about the compatibility of an alternative with one's image. This assessment is assumed to be rapid and intuitive. More analytical and elaborate decision-making processes such as those assumed by SEU theory are expected to be evoked only in specific circumstances (e.g. decisions with possible severe consequences).

Image theory assumes that decision makers use three different schematic knowledge structures (images) in order to organize their thinking about decisions (cf. Beach, 1993, pp. 151–152). The first is the *value image*; this image is based on the decision maker's principles that serve as criteria for the rightness or wrongness of any particular decision about a goal or plan. The second image concerns the *trajectory image* (based on previously adopted goals). This image represents the hopes about achieving particular goals. The third image is the *strategic image* consisting of the various plans for achieving the goals on the trajectory image. Empirical research testing image theory is relatively scarce and focused on two more specific elements of the theory: the compatibility test and the profitability test. The *compatibility* test helps decisions to be made on the basis of the compatibility between images and the forecasted future if implementation of a given plan is adopted or continued. This assessment focuses on the lack of compatibility, with a decision rule based on a rejection threshold consisting of the weighted sum of a plan's violations of the images, where the weights reflect the importance of the violation. The *profitability* test refers to the repertory of choice strategies that the individual decision maker possesses for adopting the potentially most profitable plan. Beach (1993, p. 153) describes the profitability test as a 'tie breaker' when more than one plan passes the compatibility test screening. Thus, the compatibility test removes the wholly unacceptable candidate plans and the profitability test helps to select the best from among the remaining plans.

One study focused on the role of violations in executives' assessments of the compatibility of various plans for achieving a specified goal for their respective firms. Findings confirmed the presumed role of the sum of weighted violations of the particular firm's principles (value image) in assessing the compatibility of the plans (see Beach, 1993). Research on the profitability test confirms the contention that people possess a variety of choice strategies and that their selection of which strategy to use in a particular decision is contingent upon specific characteristics of the problem at hand, the decision environment, and the decision maker him- or herself. Image theory thus emphasizes the role of three decision-related images that constrain the decisions one can make:

(a)   how things *ought* to be in terms of one's belief and values (value image);
(b)   goals towards which one is striving (trajectory image);
(c)   plans to achieve these goals (strategic image).

These three images play a crucial role in all stages of decision making (including adoption, implementation and the monitoring of progress) via compatibility and profitability assessments.

Montgomery (1993), who developed a framework to describe the various stages of decision making, argues that people pass through several phases to redefine goals and options until one alternative becomes 'dominant' over the others. *Dominance testing* resembles what Beach called profitability testing. At this stage the decision maker tests whether any promising alternative dominates the alternatives. Montgomery argues that these tests can vary in how systematic and exhaustive they are. The next stage is called *dominance structuring*. In this stage the decision maker aims to restructure or reinterpret given information in such a way that a promising alternative becomes dominant. Methods used in this stage include *de-emphasizing* the likelihood or value of disadvantages and/or *bolstering* or enhancing the advantages of the promising alternative. The opposite is likely to happen with less promising alternatives. Svenson (1993) followed a similar approach and argues that human decision making should be seen as an active process in which one alternative is gradually differentiated from others. His *differentiation and consolidation theory* applies to the stages after the initial phase in the decision-making process in which one alternative is tentatively selected and gradually differentiated from the remaining alternatives. The differentiation stage resembles the profitability test of image theory and dominance testing mentioned earlier in this section. Consolidation processes in Svenson's approach are related to what Montgomery called de-emphasizing and bolstering processes, but can also be related to dissonance theory. Festinger's work on conflict, decision and dissonance (Festinger, 1964) also focuses on pre- and post-decision processes including the tendency to restructure a problem, and selectivity in information selection and processing after a decision has been made in order to reduce one's dissonance over the decision. Image theory, the dominance search model and differentiation and consolidation theory all try to incorporate elements of everyday decision making in a complex environment. This emphasis resulted in more general frameworks than the·earlier approaches, incorporating both pre- and post-decisional processes. Empirical tests of these approaches are relatively limited and tend to focus on specific aspects. One common element of these approaches is that people often rely on simplified decision rules when choosing a course of action.

Process tracing is one of the methods that can provide insight into the use of decision rules that serve a simplifying function, and helps to avoid complicated elaborate trade-offs between good and bad features of decision options. Process-tracing methods are used to investigate what information people seek before making a choice or decision, how this information is structured to form a cognitive representation of the decision problem, and how the information is used or processed in order to reach a decision or make a choice. This research confirms the view that people can use a variety of decision rules when confronted with a choice between alternatives that can be described in terms of several attributes. Most of these require less cognitive effort than a complete cost-benefit analysis of the available alternatives. Five simplifying decision rules are briefly discussed below, all of which apply to decision problems with certain outcomes.

The dominance rule states that alternative A should be chosen over B if A is better on at least one attribute and not worse than B on all remaining attributes (e.g. two more or less identical PCs but one has a better monitor).

The conjunctive decision rule requires the decision maker to specify a criterion value for each attribute. Any alternative that does not meet this minimally required value on one or more attributes is dropped from the list of remaining possible alternatives (e.g. a PC should have at least a 250 Mb hard disk, a colour monitor, etc.).

The disjunctive decision rule is the mirror image of the conjunctive rule, and also requires a set of criterion values of the attributes. In this case, a chosen alternative must have at least one attribute that meets the criterion while all remaining alternatives do not meet any of the criterion values (e.g. speed of the PC, followed by memory space, etc.).

The lexicographic decision rule prescribes a choice of the alternative which is most attractive on the most important attribute. If two alternatives are equally attractive in terms of the most important attribute the decision will be based on the next most important attribute, and so on.

The elimination by aspects rule is often interpreted as a combination of the lexicographic rule and the conjunctive rule. First, the most important attribute is selected. All alternatives that fail to meet the criterion on this attribute are eliminated. This procedure is repeated for each of the remaining attributes.

The last four decision rules in particular require considerably less cognitive effort than the decision rule required by SEU models. The latter require a compensatory decision rule (negative scores on one attribute can be compensated by positive scores on another attribute). The simplifying rules discussed in this section are used quite often in everyday decision making and can provide adequate short-cuts in complex decision environments. Research on consumer behaviour is one of the applied areas attempting to assess the prevalence of these different strategies and their consequences for marketing specific products and influencing consumer behaviour (e.g. Johnson, 1984). Knowing what decision rule is used helps to understand individual behaviour and also provides ways to help change this behaviour. Some of the rules could lead to faulty decisions if people are not aware of the kind of decision rule they employ.

Hammond and his colleagues (Hammond, Stewart, Brehmer, & Steinmann, 1975) also stress the comparison between analytical and intuitive decision making. They argue that the strategies available to a decision maker can be placed on a continuum ranging from intuition (with rapid and limited data processing, low cognitive control and limited awareness of processing) to analysis (slow data processing, high levels of control and high awareness of processing). Payne et al. (1992) also stress the constructive nature of human decision making. Both personal experience and characteristics of the problem at hand will determine the decision strategy. Payne et al. (1992) use the term contingent decision making in which the cognitive costs and benefits of the various strategies people might use determine their choice of strategy. Basic questions in this choice concern the balance between cognitive effort and accuracy, but factors such as decisional avoidance and accountability also influence strategy selection.

Affect and decision making

Other approaches have introduced added elements that play a role in judgement and decision making. One of these approaches is *regret theory* (Bell, 1982; Loomes & Sugden, 1982). The basic idea underlying this approach is that the value placed on the outcome of a specific choice or gamble also depends on the outcome that would have been achieved if one had chosen an alternative choice or gamble. Thus winning $100 is likely to be affected by the knowledge that one could have won $500 (versus e.g. $10) if one had selected another alternative. The major contribution of regret theory is that it has provided a framework to study affective factors as determinants of decision making and choice.

Research on the influence of affect on decision making tends to focus on the relationship between affective state and a variety of decision tasks such as risk estimation (Johnson & Tversky, 1983), and strategy selection in multi-attribute choice (Isen & Means, 1983). The growing recognition of the important role of affect in decision making and attitudinal processes has also led to research on the role of *anticipated* affective states. Janis and Mann (1977) already suggested that post-behavioural feelings can influence people's behaviour to the extent that these feelings are anticipated. Initially, research on the role of post-behavioural feelings focused on anticipated *regret*. Regret theory (Bell, 1982; Loomes & Sugden, 1982) has been applied to various behavioural domains including risk taking in gambles (DiCagno & Hey, 1988) and consumer behaviour (Simonson, 1992). After the initial focus on regret, later research addressed the effects of a variety of anticipated feelings on human judgements and decision making. These include guilt, sadness and anger (Baron, 1992), disappointment (Loomes & Sugden, 1986), embarrassment and pride (Simonson, 1989), and worry and tension (Richard, van der Pligt, & de Vries, 1995b). The possible role of anticipated affect in predicting behaviour is also studied in research on attitudes (see Chapter 1 of the present book). Recently, Wilson and Hodges (1992) argued that people often have contradictory beliefs about an issue or a behavioural option and that the corresponding attitude depends on the subset of beliefs to which they attend at a specific moment in time. Wilson and Hodges (1992) noted that the beliefs people attend to are influenced by both contextual factors and thought processes, and showed that attitudes are easily changed if people are led to attend to a particular subset of beliefs. Richard, van der Pligt and de Vries (1995b, 1996) argued that when people think about their feelings about a behavioural action, different beliefs could be salient than when they think about the feelings they would experience *after* carrying out the action. They argued that the behavioural activity itself is relatively salient when people indicate their feelings about the behaviour. In such cases the affective state associated with the behaviour itself will largely determine attitude. On the other hand, the (possible) consequences of the behaviour are likely to be salient when people think about the feelings they would experience *after* carrying out the behaviour. In this case, the affect associated with the consequences of a behavioural choice will also determine the attitude. Richard et al. propose that the distinction between people's feelings *about*, and their anticipated feelings *after* an action is likely to be most relevant for domains in which there is an affective discrepancy between the behavioural activity itself and the (possible) post-behavioural outcomes. For instance, in order to realize a positively valued outcome we sometimes have to carry out an unpleasant behaviour or refrain from a pleasant behaviour. If people focused on the feelings they would experience after such an action, a different (opposing) action tendency might emerge than if they focused on their feelings about the action itself.

Their research applied these insights to preventive sexual behaviour (see van der Pligt & Richard, 1994) and introduced a simple technique to increase the awareness that unsafe sex is likely to result in unpleasant feelings. Respondents were presented with scenarios describing a realistic situation in which they met an attractive other with whom they would like to have sex. In these studies respondents were asked to imagine either how they would feel about such an event or how they would feel *after* the event. With this simple procedure it was attempted to influence the time perspective of respondents and to make their feelings after the event more salient.

In a first study respondents were asked to answer a brief questionnaire. The first page introduced the issues of 'sexual intercourse' and 'condom use' and stressed anonymity. On the next page, respondents were asked to imagine the following hypothetical situation: 'Suppose, you are on a holiday and you meet a very attractive boy (girl) and after spending some time with him (her) the two of you have sexual intercourse.' Respondents in the first condition were asked to describe the feelings they would have about sexual intercourse (in the situation described earlier), using not a condom but another contraceptive. On the next page they were asked to describe their feelings about sexual intercourse (in that situation) when using a condom. Respondents in the other condition were asked to describe the feelings they would have *after* having had sexual intercourse. Thus in this condition respondents were encouraged to imagine how they would feel after having had (un)protected sex. It was expected that negative feelings about unsafe sex such as worries and regret would be more salient in this condition.

Results of this study can be summarized as follows: (a) Respondents listed significantly more negative feelings, such as regret, worries and anxiety, when asked to think about unsafe as opposed to safe sex. (b) This difference was more pronounced when respondents were asked to describe the feelings they would feel *after* the sexual act. (c) After answering questions about how they would feel after having had sex, respondents indicated a greater likelihood of using condoms. Thus a simple manipulation of time perspective when thinking about affective reactions resulted in the expectation to be more cautious in the future.

A later study confirmed these findings. In this study, time perspective also affected respondents' expectations to use condoms in the future. Those who were asked to imagine and describe their feelings *after* having had sex with a new partner had higher expectations that they would engage in safe sex, i.e. use condoms. Moreover, these respondents also reported more condom use in the five-months period following the experiment. These findings suggest that a simple straightforward intervention which consists of asking adolescents to think about how they would feel *after* unprotected sex can be effective in persuading them to take preventive action. Other research suggests that anticipated affective reactions can also influence such diverse behaviours as driving violations (Parker, Manstead, Stradling, Reason, & Baxter, 1992a, 1992b) and consumer behaviour (Simonson, 1992).

Research on affective determinants of preference and choice has a relatively short history but provides a wider perspective than the theories stressing the rational and reasoned aspects of judgement and decision making. This renewed interest in the role of affective factors can be seen in both the literature on judgement and decision making and in research on attitudinal processes (see also Chapter 1).

The next section discusses research on heuristics and biases. This research field focuses on discrepancies between normative theories and actual judgement and decision making, and has identified a number of heuristics that could lead to systematic errors in judgement.

Heuristics and biases

The study of heuristics and biases focuses on systematic errors and inferential biases in human judgement and decision making. The assumption is that investigating errors and biases can improve our insight into the psychological processes that govern judgement and decision making and hint at ways of improving the quality of our thinking.

Three heuristics that deal with probabilistic thinking have received considerable attention: (a) availability, (2) representativeness, and (3) anchoring and adjustment. The *availability* heuristic refers to the tendency to assess the probability of an event based on the ease with which instances of that event come to mind. This heuristic has been investigated in a variety of domains and relates probability estimates to memory access. Generally, people overestimate the probability of an event if concrete instances of that event are easily accessible in memory. Tversky and Kahneman (1973) argued that people learn throughout life that likely occurrences are easier to remember and imagine than unlikely ones, and subsequently use this knowledge in their probability judgements. Generally, ease of recall and frequency of occurrence are correlated. A number of factors that affect memory are, however, unrelated to probability. For example, vivid images are easier to recall than pallid ones. Heath, Tindale, Edwards, Posavac, Bryant, Henderson-King, Suarez-Balcazar and Myers (1994) provide many examples of the availability heuristic in more applied settings. The availability heuristic has been used to explain various effects in the perception of individuals and social groups (e.g. Taylor, 1982). The tendency to observe a relationship between minority groups and infrequent behaviours such as found in research on the illusory correlation effect can also be related to the availability heuristic. Infrequent behaviour stands out, and the same applies to minority groups; their combination is likely to be distinctive and hence more available. This could lead to the erroneous perception of a relation between group membership and specific behavioural practices. Some argue that these processes could underlie the formation of stereotypes (Hamilton & Gifford, 1976). Other examples include the work of Shiloh (1994) showing that genetic counsellors because of their repeated exposure to vivid and concrete abnormalities can easily be influenced by the availability heuristic. Dawes (1994) argues that the salience of negative and relatively extreme exemplars of drug addicts can bias policy makers' perceptions of the entire group and result in negative attitudes towards programmes such as the provision of clean needles to prevent further spread of the AIDS virus. The use of sterile needles for injecting drugs cannot result in HIV infection and would help to reduce the spread of HIV. Providing these needles could reduce the barriers to changing risky behavioural practices and this could be more effective than attempts to change the attitudes of intravenous (IV) drug users. Needle exchange programmes have been successful in a number of countries but attempts to get similar programmes off the ground in the USA have met with considerable opposition. According to Dawes this opposition is mainly caused by stereotypic or representative thinking and availability biases in the way people form social judgements. Dawes mentions a variety of examples in which the two biases seem to reinforce each other, leading to extreme views on IV drug users. First, extreme cases one has encountered or seen portrayed in the media are likely to be more available and receive excessive weight in perceptions of the group as a whole. In his view there is also an availability bias of focusing on personality characteristics (in accordance with attribution theory), a tendency to categorize people, and a tendency to infer other personality characteristics associated with a specific category as a result of representative thinking. These processes lead to a view of out-group members (in this case IV drug users) as extreme and alike and the view that their behaviour should be understood in terms of broad personality characteristics. Dawes provides many examples of the results of these processes, including a quote from *Time* magazine: 'To assume that anyone who is so irresponsible as to get on heroin then becomes sensible enough to use clean needles or sterilize them is as contradictory as a cat with wings' (Ellis, 1988, p. 10A).

Schwartz (1994) argued that availability can influence both patients' and doctors' judgements and decisions: the former are primarily influenced by concrete and vivid cases presented in the media; the latter are influenced by their own overexposure to illnesses. For instance, patients will overestimate the prevalence of specific diseases due to the excessive weight given to concrete cases in the media. Doctors, on the other hand, will overestimate the prevalence of specific diseases that are more common in their practice. In both cases, exposure to concrete cases will have more impact on prevalence estimates than statistics about the prevalence of each disease. This is also illustrated by differences between doctors. As a result of their experience, a heart surgeon will give higher estimates of heart-related diseases than a specialist in ophthalmology, who is likely to overestimate the prevalence of eye diseases. As we will see later in this chapter, the availability heuristic is also of relevance to issues of risk perception and the acceptability of risk. The *representativeness* heuristic refers to the tendency to assess the probability that a stimulus belongs to a particular class by judging the degree to which that event corresponds to an appropriate mental model. This heuristic can be associated with a number of cognitive errors such as insensitivity to prior probabilities.

A well-known example of how ignoring prior probabilities can affect judgement was reported by Kahneman and Tversky (1973). In their study, subjects were provided with brief personality sketches, supposedly of engineers and lawyers. Subjects were asked to assess the probability that each sketch described a member of one profession or the other. Half the respondents were told that the population from which the sketches were drawn consisted of 30 engineers and 70 lawyers; the remaining respondents were told that there were 70 engineers and 30 lawyers. The findings showed that the prior probabilities were essentially ignored, and that subjects estimated the probability of class membership by judging how similar each personality sketch was to their mental model of an engineer or a lawyer. Representativeness can also be related to a more general finding concerning the tendency to overuse categories in judgement, particularly in judgements about people or groups. Dawes (1994) argues that biases due to the use of categorical processing (e.g. stereotypes, schemas) can be regarded as instances of representative thinking. Some of the examples mentioned earlier (e.g. stereotyped views of drug addicts and patient groups) fall into this category. Other examples can be found in the literature on sentencing decisions showing that criminals are sometimes judged on the basis of their similarity to prototypical criminals (e.g. Lurigio, Carroll, & Stalans, 1994). Generally, representative thinking is a useful and functional strategy. Sometimes, however, it can lead to systematic biases and errors in judgement and decision making. The similarity between this heuristic and the availability heuristic is that concrete and vivid experiences do have a disproportionate influence on probability judgements.

Anchoring and adjustment refers to a general judgement process in which an initially given or generated response serves as an anchor, and other information is insufficiently used to adjust that response. The anchoring and adjustment heuristic is based on the assumption that people often start their judgmental process by focusing on some initial value that serves as an anchor.

The biases related to this heuristic stem from two distinct aspects. First, one could use irrelevant anchors. Secondly, one could insufficiently adjust up or down from an original starting value or anchor. Tversky and Kahneman (1974) showed that irrelevant information such as a randomly determined number influenced subjects' assessment of probabilities and frequencies. For instance, providing respondents with a randomly allocated number (by a turn on a wheel of fortune) affected their estimate of the percentage of African countries in the United Nations (Tversky & Kahneman, 1974). Respondents provided with an anchor value of 65 gave an estimate of 45 per cent while the remaining respondents provided with an anchor value of 10 responded with an estimate of 25 per cent. Van Schie and van der Pligt (1994) asked people to estimate the contribution of various factors to a specific problem (e.g. the contribution of various pollutants to environmental degradation). They argued that the number of categories provided implicitly determines anchor values for each of the categories. For instance, providing five categories or factors seems to lead to an (implicit) anchor value for each category of approximately 20 per cent. Categories received higher scores if fewer alternative categories were provided. Van der Pligt, Eiser and Spears (1987) applied this to public attitudes towards nuclear energy and renewable energy sources. Their findings show that providing people with fewer alternatives increased their estimates of the contribution of nuclear power to the generation of electricity in the UK. Moreover, providing fewer alternatives also resulted in greater preference for nuclear energy and even affected respondents' attitude towards nuclear energy and the building of nuclear power stations. This example can be related to both the anchoring heuristic and the availability heuristic and shows that both heuristics can also lead to systematic effects on preferences and attitudes.

Some other heuristics are also frequently mentioned in the literature. When Tversky and Kahneman (1974) introduced the availability heuristic they described two mental processes that can 'bring these to mind': retrieval of instances or exemplars, and the construction of scenarios or examples. The latter form of availability was originally referred to as the *simulation heuristic* (Kahneman & Tversky, 1982). Later research used the term *counterfactual thinking*, and focused on simulations that lead to other outcomes (counterfactuals), the ease with which these counterfactuals can be generated, and the consequences this has. Kahneman and Tversky (1982) showed that positive events that almost happened were rated as more upsetting than events that did not almost happen. The reason was that it was easier to generate alternative scenarios for undoing events that almost happened (e.g. missing a train by two minutes) than events that did not almost happen (e.g. missing a train by 30 minutes). Counterfactual thinking also has implications for judgements of responsibility for outcomes, with more responsibility and blame allocated to people if it is easier to generate scenarios to undo the particular outcome. Counterfactual thinking has been related to feelings of regret, with more intense regret being experienced if the negative outcome could have been prevented by easily imaginable alternative courses of action. The role of counterfactuals has been investigated in applied areas such as legal issues. Wiener and Pritchard (1994) argue that counterfactual thinking affects negligence judgements and propose that the outcome of the negligence judgement and the amount of damages awarded to the plaintiff is a function of the relative number and type of counterfactual created. If a large number of alternative courses of action were available to the defendant relative to the plaintiff then the overall judgement would favour the plaintiff, and vice versa. Similarly, Macrae, Milne and Griffith (1993) found that the amount of damages awarded to victims of a crime is affected by the ease with which counterfactuals to the negative outcome can be generated. When counter-factual alternatives to an outcome were readily available participants punished the perpetrators more severely, considered the incident to be more serious, and felt greater sympathy for the victim. Thus a scenario describing a victim who was mugged when walking his regular route home resulted in different judgements of the event than a mugging that occurred when the victim was taking a new route home. These effects generalized across different types of crime, and Macrae et al. argue that counterfactual (i.e. if-only) thinking affects the way in which an event is interpreted. The latter is likely to affect whether the event is reported to the police, how it is processed by the judiciary, how the victim is treated, and how the jury responds to evidence presented in court (Macrae et al., 1993, p. 125). Finally, two related biases need a brief mention: the hindsight bias and overconfidence. The *hindsight bias* (Fischhoff & Beyth, 1975) refers to the tendency to see events as not surprising and expected *after* they have occurred, even when they were seen as unlikely prior to their taking place. The effect of this bias is that it increases feelings of confidence in judgement after the fact and can lead to continued use of nonoptimal or faulty decision strategies. *Overconfidence* is a more general bias and applies to both lay people and experts. It refers to a tendency to assign higher than warranted probabilities to one's predictions. Oskamp (1965) was the first to provide empirical evidence for the apparent paradox that confidence increases while accuracy does not. He presented clinical psychologists with increasing amounts of case material and found that they became more convinced of the accuracy of their outcome predictions as the amount of information available to them increased. Unfortunately, their predictions were no more accurate than those based on less information. Heller, Saltzstein and Caspe (1992) showed that doctors' confidence in their diagnoses increases as they receive more information, even if this information is irrelevant and nondiagnostic.

All the heuristics discussed in this section can lead to the neglect of potentially relevant information. It needs to be added that the adaptive use of heuristics, even though leading to a neglect of some information, can save considerable cognitive effort and still result in adequate or even good solutions to decision problems. Most of the heuristics seem to operate across a wide range of stimulus materials. Some, however, appear to depend on a combi-nation of cognitive vulnerability and clever experimental tasks highlighting this vulnerability (see also Gigerenzer, 1991b). Although people may seem to use informal decision rules and simplifying heuristics rather than normative principles, it is certainly not the case that it is always maladaptive to do so. As argued before, cognitive heuristics may not only be functional, they may even be a valid basis for decision making in real-life contexts. An important shortcoming of the existing literature is that many studies of heuristics involve discrete judgmental tasks at a single point in time. In more natural and dynamic contexts, however, judgements and actions evolve and influence each other continuously over time (cf. Hogarth, 1990). Judgements and decisions in everyday life are typically made on a data base that is redundant and can be updated constantly. Moreover, correction through feedback may give rise to contingent decision making, resulting in adequate decisions. This is less likely in the typical tasks in this field of research, which generally require once-and-for-all judgements.

As argued by Payne, Bettman and Johnson (1992) the question is no longer *whether* biases exist, but *under what conditions* relevant information will or will not be used to arrive at a probability judgement. In their review of research on the use of prior probabilities or base-rate information Payne et al. (1992) conclude that research should not focus on the question of whether people are good or bad statisticians but on understanding the cognitive factors that determine the type of inference rule or decision strategy being employed. They argue that people seem to use a variety of approaches in their attempts to solve probabilistic reasoning tasks. How individuals use these methods contingent on the type of tasks and context variables has hardly been investigated.

The next section focuses on a research area that also deals with the judgement of probable outcomes. Perceived risk and related issues such as the acceptability of risk and the relation between risk and behaviour have been studied extensively in behavioural decision making, social psychology and health psychology.

Perceived risk, acceptability and behaviour

Risk perception and the acceptability of risks have been studied extensively in psychology. A formal definition of risk is the likelihood or probability p of the negative event or consequence i multiplied by the negative value or utility of that event or consequence u_i. If a negative event is characterized by multiple negative consequences, risk could be defined as

$$\sum_i p_i u_i.$$

This definition more or less coincides with dictionary definitions of risk; 'the possibility or chance of loss' is one frequently given definition. Other examples are: 'hazard or danger' and 'exposure to mischance or peril'. Although there is some disagreement about the precise definition of risk among researchers, most risk definitions are clearly related to the above general meaning of risk. Yates (1992) argues that there is considerable (often implicit) agreement on a fundamental conception of risk. He mentions three essential elements: (a) negative consequences or losses, (b) the value or significance of these losses, and (c) uncertainty associated with these losses or consequences. In medicine and epidemiology, risk is the chance of a specific adverse outcome such as death or the contraction of a particular disease. The risks of technological developments such as the use of nuclear power for generating electricity are often defined in terms of the chance of excess deaths per year.

Potential negative outcomes are sometimes quantified (e.g. financial loss, number of possible victims). Unfortunately, quantification of outcomes is often difficult and uncertain. There are different ways in which uncertainty can affect risk (see Yates, 1992). First, risk is said to exist whenever the (negative) outcomes of an action are not certain. Secondly, quite often decision makers are unable to foresee every significant consequence or outcome of their decision. This uncertainty concerns the relevant attributes or consequences that should be taken into account. Thirdly, even if one accepts that specific negative consequences can occur, there is still uncertainty about whether these consequences will occur. Fourth, it is necessary to distinguish different 'levels of uncertainty': i.e. the firmness of the basis on which the probability of a negative consequence is estimated. Levels of uncertainty range from complete ignorance (no basis whatsoever for estimating probabilities) via frequentistic probabilities (previous experience as the basis for estimating probabilities) to objective probabilities (e.g. if one decides that out of a group of five, one person will be selected by lot to be the spokesperson, the chance that anyone of the group members being selected is one in five). The quality of the database for frequentistic probabilities can vary substantially (a handful of experiences versus epidemiological findings based on large samples).

Two themes have dominated social psychological research on risk. First, perceived risk and the acceptability of risk have been studied extensively in the context of large-scale hazards such as nuclear power, toxic waste and a variety of technological developments with possible adverse consequences for the environment and public health. A second theme concerns individual risk-taking behaviour. Research on these more personal risks often concerns risks to one's health. These two themes will be central to the present section.

Perceived risk and acceptability

As we saw earlier, people have difficulties in estimating probabilities and understanding probabilistic processes. Sometimes uncertainty is simply denied, sometimes it is misjudged and often one is overconfident about one's judgement. Interestingly, experts appear to be prone to many of the same biases as lay people, especially when they cannot rely upon solid data. Initial research on risk perception aimed to develop a taxonomy of hazards in order to understand public responses to risks and why some hazards led to extreme risk aversion and others to indifference. One of the major conclusions of this research is that the public is much more likely to accept risks from *voluntary* activities as compared to *involuntary* activities. Voluntary risks which are up to a thousand times greater than involuntary risks with the same level of benefits, tend to be seen as equally acceptable (Starr, 1969). Thus, the risks associated with a skiing holiday are readily accepted while similar risks due to a governmental decision to cut the maintenance costs of bicycle tracks would be less acceptable. Similarly, people readily accept the risks of road traffic but are often opposed to risks associated with, for instance, the expansion of an airport. A frequently used paradigm in this line of research is to ask respondents to give their subjective estimates of the frequency of death from a variety of sources or activities (e.g. nuclear power, hang-gliding, different illnesses and accidents) for which objective estimates are available.

Results show that people are approximately accurate, but that their judgements are systematically distorted (see Fischhoff, Lichtenstein, Slovic, Derby, & Keeney, 1981). Overall, data suggest that people have a relatively consistent, subjective scale of frequency and that their judgements correlate fairly well with objective estimates. Thus, at ordinal level these estimates seem adequate. Results of this research also indicate a number of shortcomings in estimating risks. First, differences between the (subjective) estimated frequencies of the most and least frequent sources or events are considerably smaller than the corresponding differences in the objective, statistical estimates. In other words, larger risks are underestimated and smaller risks are overestimated. A second bias concerns the availability heuristic discussed earlier in this chapter. This heuristic results in large differences in the estimated frequency of events with similar statistical frequencies. People who use this heuristic tend to judge an event as likely or common if instances of it are relatively easy to imagine or recall. Unfortunately, availability can be affected by factors unrelated to frequency of occurrence. For example, a recent air crash or train disaster can have distorting effects on subjective risk estimates. A series of studies shows that overestimated frequencies or risks tend to be dramatic and sensational whereas underestimated risks are often related to less spectacular events that claim one or a few victims at a time and are also common in nonfatal form (see Fischhoff et al., 1981). Not surprisingly, overestimated hazards also tend to be disproportionately mentioned in the media, and media attention to specific risks and hazards shows a positive relationship with subjective estimates of these risks (Combs & Slovic, 1979). To summarize, lay people can assess annual fatalities if they are asked to, and generally produce estimates with the same general rank ordering as the existing statistical estimates. It seems, however, that their judgements are also related to other characteristics, such as dramatic impact and newsworthiness.

Generally, experts' judgements of risk differ systematically from those of non-experts. Experts' risk perceptions correlate quite highly with technical estimates of annual number of fatalities; their perceptions also reflect the complete range, from high to low risk. Lay people's perceptions of risk, however, are compressed into a smaller range and do not correlate as highly with annual mortality statistics.

A further line of research attempted to relate the acceptability of risk to characteristics such as familiarity, perceived control, catastrophic potential, equity and level of knowledge (see Fischhoff et al., 1981). In these studies, subjects were asked to judge a large number of technologies and risk-bearing activities on dimensions such as 'voluntary–involuntary', 'chronic–catastrophic', 'common–dread', 'not fatal–fatal', 'known to exposed–not known to exposed', 'immediate–delayed', 'known to science–not known to science', 'uncontrollable–controllable', and 'new–old'. The 'risk profiles' derived from this research showed that hazards such as nuclear power scored at or near the extreme high-risk end for most of the characteristics. Its risks were seen as involuntary, unknown to those exposed or to science, uncontrollable, unfamiliar, potentially catastrophic, severe and dreaded (see also Chapter 12 of this volume). These characteristics can largely be explained by two higher-order factors. The first is primarily determined by the characteristics 'unknown to exposed' and 'unknown to science', and to a lesser extent by 'newness', 'involuntariness' and 'delay of effect', while the second factor is defined by 'severity of consequences', 'dread', and 'catastrophic potential'. Perceived controllability of the risk contributes to both factors.

This research has helped to clarify structural aspects of the perception and acceptability of technological risks and has assisted the understanding of public reactions to specific technologies. An obvious case in point is nuclear power, including both the building and operation of nuclear power stations and nuclear waste repositories. The public's view of nuclear power risks is that these are *unknown, dreaded, uncontrollable, inequitable, catastrophic*, and *likely to affect future generations*. People's strong fears about nuclear power seem logical consequences of their concerns about these considerations. Furthermore, it seems likely that accidents occurring with unknown and potentially catastrophic technologies will be seen as indicative of the loss of control over this technology (see also van der Pligt, 1992). In Chapter 7 these issues will be discussed in more detail in the context of applications of social psychology to environmental issues. The next section focuses on research on personal risk, as opposed to the large-scale societal risks discussed above.

Perceived risk and risk-taking behaviour

Risk-taking behaviour has been studied in a variety of research traditions, some of which rely on insights derived from both the decision-making literature and social psychology. One research area that incorporates elements from both the social psychological and the decision-making literature concerns people's reactions to health risks. These have been studied extensively and will receive attention in this section (see also Chapter 6 of this book).

Increased epidemiological knowledge of the possible health consequences of behavioural practices has led to a situation in which a wide range of behaviours have been labelled as risky. Morbidity and mortality have increasingly come to be related to chronic conditions which are tied to lifestyle and behavioural practices. As a consequence there has been a significant increase in research attempting to understand these behaviours and to help design behavioural intervention programmes. Several models have been proposed to help understand and predict health-related behaviours. These theories are generally based on more general theories of decision making and risk taking and all incorporate the concept of perceived risk. For instance, the Health Belief Model (Janz & Becker, 1984) states that an individual will be prepared to undertake preventive behaviour(s) as a function of the perceived severity of the threat, the perceived benefits of the recommended health action, and the perceived barriers to taking the action. Protection motivation theory (Rogers, 1975) focuses on cognitive appraisal processes in response to messages about health risks that induce fear. This theory includes factors such as the perceived severity of the health threat and perceived vulnerability or susceptibility. Perceived risk is thus assumed to be an important determinant of behaviour. A more detailed discussion of these theories can be found in Chapters 1 and 6.

Unfortunately, individuals are not always accurate judges of their risk. One pervasive bias in people's judgements regarding their own risk is called *unrealistic optimism* (Weinstein, 1988). Weinstein argued that people tend to think they are relatively invulnerable: others are assumed to be more likely to experience negative health consequences. Each individual could be right in assuming that his or her risks are smaller than those of comparable others. However, if most people in a specific group rate their risk below average, a substantial part of them must be wrong or 'unrealistic'. Optimism has been found for a wide variety of life events. These include driving behaviour (Svenson, 1981), managerial decisions (Larwood & Whittaker, 1977) and entrepreneurship (Cooper, Woo, & Dunkelberg, 1988). Most research in this tradition focused on negative life events including negative health states. Initially, research tended to rely on college students; later research showed that even high-risk groups show an optimistic bias about their risks. Figure 2.3 summarizes the result of a study by van der Velde, van der Pligt and Hooykaas (1994) and shows that both low- and high-risk groups tend to be optimistic about their risk (in this instance the risk of contracting HIV).

Six possible causes have been mentioned in the literature on unrealistic optimism (see van der Pligt, Otten, Richard, & van der Velde, 1993, for an overview). The first is *perceived control*: when rating one's own risk status as compared to others, optimism tends to be greater for those risks judged to be under personal control. Findings also indicate that for any specific risk those who rate its controllability higher are more optimistic. This relation between perceived controllability and optimism is confirmed by research on perceived risk in a wide variety of domains including health. McKenna (1993) argued that unrealistic optimism could be equated with the illusion of control, and provided some evidence concerning people's perception of accident likelihood as a driver or a passenger. He found that uncontrollable events did not result in optimism. More recently, Harris and Middleton (1994) argued that this is not necessarily the case and found optimism to be unrelated to rating of the capacity to control outcomes.

A second factor that could be related to optimism is the so-called *egocentric bias*. When people are asked to assess their risks and those of others, they are bound to have more knowledge of their own protective actions than those of others. It seems that people tend to focus on their own risk-reducing practices

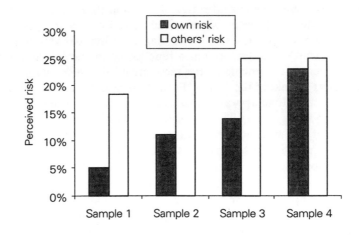

Figure 2.3   *Perceived risk for self and others as a function of own risk status (adapted from van der Velde et al., 1994, p. 27)*

Note: sample 1 (*n* = 437) low risk general sample; sample 2 (*n* = 241) low to moderate risk heterosexual sample with multiple partners; sample 3 (*n* = 147) high risk homosexual sample; sample 4 (*n* = 493) high risk heterosexual sample (visitors to an STD clinic engaging in prostitution contacts)

while they tend to forget personal actions or circumstances that increase their risks. Moreover, one's own actions are more available than those of others; people do not always realize that most other people also take protective action. This bias is also related to the availability heuristic discussed earlier in this chapter.

Thirdly, lack of previous *personal experience* tends to increase unrealistic optimism. Personal experience tends to be relatively vivid as compared to statistical information about risks, which enhances both availability and recall. Possible negative consequences for health and well-being that have been experienced more directly tend to result in less optimistic risk appraisals.

A fourth factor that could produce unrealistic optimism is related to *stereotypical* or *prototypical judgement*. People might have a relatively extreme image of those suffering from specific diseases. This extreme prototype is unlikely to fit one's self-image, hence it is concluded that the risk does not apply to oneself but primarily to others.

A fifth factor is *self-esteem maintenance* or enhancement. Generally, people seem to think that their own actions, lifestyle and personality are more advantaged than those of their peers. This mechanism would explain the fact that people are generally not optimistic about hereditary and environmental health risks, for the latter do not constitute a threat to their self-esteem. In contrast, a high-risk lifestyle could be seen to imply that we are ignorant of what we ought to do or are unable to exercise self-control. Both these factors concern a person's ability to cope effectively with life demands and have clear links to self-esteem.

The sixth and final factor is related to *coping strategies*. Under conditions of high stress or threat, denial is a response often used to protect against anxiety or worry. Denial can reduce emotional distress but can also reduce the likelihood of direct behavioural actions, which may be necessary to reduce one's risks. Unrealistic optimism is an illusion that can help the individual to adapt to threatening events.

Most research in this area relies on correlational analyses, and further research is needed to assess the precise causal role of the antecedents of unrealistic optimism. Moreover the effects of optimistic bias on preventive health behaviour need to be assessed more carefully. One of the basic rationales for this research is that optimism could undermine the effectiveness of health education campaigns. The assumption is that both perceived risk and optimism are important determinants of preventive behaviour. Gerrard, Gibbons, Warner and Smith (1993) provide an overview of research investigating the relationship between perceived risk and behaviour and conclude that perceived risk does affect behaviour. Otten and van der Pligt (1992), on the other hand, found no support for the mediating role of perceived risk after controlling for previous behaviour. Unfortunately, the impact of optimism and comparative risk appraisal on behavioural practices has hardly been investigated.

All in all, this research area provides interesting insights into possible biases of risk perception and their effects on behaviour. It seems essential however to expand the scope of this research and include both cognitive and motivational factors to explain these biases, preferably in experimental designs. Finally, more attention should be paid to the impact of perceived risk (both absolute and comparative) on behavioural choice.

An issue that received less attention in the decision-making literature – group decision making – will be discussed in the final section of this chapter. The popularity of this research field is increasing and it provides many opportunities to combine insights from both behavioural decision theory and social psychology.

Group decision making and social dilemmas

The literature on judgement and decision making tends to focus on the individual. Many problems are, however, solved by groups. The literature on group decision making is rapidly expanding, and the study of group decision making should provide many opportunities for social psychologists. This section briefly summarizes a number of issues in the literature on group decision making and interdependent decision making.

Group decision making

The stages of group decision making are similar to the stages of individual decision making. First the group has to identify the problem and develop a shared representation of the problem. This is followed by problem analysis (decomposing the problem into the relevant probabilities and values), and an evaluation of the various alternatives followed by the selection of the preferred alternative. Apart from these aspects, specific characteristics of the group will also play a role. Groups have characteristics such as mutual trust, cohesion and specific communication patterns that go beyond simple extrapolations of values and beliefs of the individuals participating in the group. Kleindorfer, Kunreuther and Schoemaker (1993) argue that the performance and quality of a decision-making group depend on many interacting factors. These include procedural aspects of the decision-making process, structural aspects of the group (size, homogeneity, knowledge), and intra-group processes (communication, cooperation, trust, responsibility) but also factors such as leadership style, time pressure, incentive structure and the resources available to the group.

Group processes were extensively studied in the 1950s and 1960s when group dynamics was a popular field of research. In these years research focused on structural aspects of groups and addressed issues such as power and influence, leadership styles and pressures to uniformity in groups (see e.g. Cartwright & Zander, 1968). This research emphasized processes in and between (sub)groups and paid relatively modest attention to the quality of group decision making. The popularity of this field declined due to the (expensive and time-consuming) reliance on observational techniques to assess the behaviour of groups and/or group members. This changed when research shifted its emphasis from process to outcome. In line with research on individual decision making, researchers also paid attention to discrepancies between normative models and the outcomes of group decision making. To a certain extent, the factors that influence group decision making are the same as those that influence individual decision making. A group is, after all, a collection of individuals, and the biases and shortcomings of individuals are likely to be found at group level too. It is possible of course that groups can overcome some of the biases shown by individuals because a group generally will have a mix of viewpoints and more expertise than a single individual. Most early attempts, however, stress the shortcomings of group decision making and reach the conclusion that groups amplify the shortcomings of individual decision making. For instance, groups tend to be more confident and often reach more polarized decisions than individuals. Janis (1982) studied the rationality of group decision making and the possible biases that can distort group decisions, and used the term 'groupthink' (borrowed from George Orwell) to refer to poor group thinking. Groupthink can be defined as an extreme concurrence-seeking tendency. Janis identified three major symptoms of groupthink:

(a) *Overestimation of the group*. Two phenomena fall under this heading. First, the *illusion of invulnerability*. This can lead to a serious under-estimation of the risks involved in a decision. Secondly, *belief in the inherent morality of the group*. This refers to a bias towards the morality of the ends of a decision which prevents group members asking whether the means are in fact justified in the case at hand.

(b) *Closed-mindedness.* Group members can convince themselves that there is no need to consider additional (outside) information or alternatives. This incomplete information search is one consequence of what Janis termed *collective rationalization.* Collective rationalization helps to alleviate incipient fears of failure and prevent unnerving feelings of personal inadequacy. Groups can also be overconfident in their own powers and morality and at the same time believe that their opponents are weak, foolish and immoral. This underestimation of opponents is termed *stereotypes of outgroups.*

(c) *Pressures towards uniformity.* Janis describes four related phenomena under this heading. First *self-censorship*, when group members hold back from mentioning their doubts about the chosen alternative. Self-censorship and other devices also create an *illusion of unanimity.* Sometimes group members exert *direct pressure on dissenters*, a task which is often carried out by *self-appointed mindguards.* Mindguards take it upon themselves to keep others in line with the supposed consensus.

Janis (1982, p. 244) mentions a number of antecedent conditions that may foster groupthink. These include the cohesiveness of the decision-making group, structural faults of the organization (e.g. insulation of the group, lack of norms requiring methodical procedures) and a provocative situational context (e.g. high stress from external threats, low self-esteem). Janis illustrated these processes with a variety of US foreign policy fiascos of recent decades such as the Korean War stalemate, the escalation of the Vietnam War, the Bay of Pigs blunder and the Watergate cover-up. Janis also argues that when good thinking occurs in groups there will be a commitment to an interchange of pro- and con-arguments, not to a decision already made. Thus, loyalty will be to the *process* of making the decision. Janis suggests that one way to prevent groupthink is to assign one member of the group to be the devil's advocate. More recent research on groupthink deals with the nature of conformity in groupthink and its causes (e.g. Tetlock, Peterson, McGuire, Chang, & Feld, 1992).

The term *groupthink* was chosen because of its Orwellian connotation (e.g. 'doublethink' and 'crimethink'), and the general acceptance of the model suggests that it has considerable heuristic value in the study of group decision-making processes. The model has stimulated research on group dysfunctions and also showed how the decision-making literature can be applied to a wide range of situations. It needs to be added, however, that the model has a relatively narrow focus and primarily addresses decision fiascos. Aldag and Riggs Fuller (1993) argued that the groupthink phenomenon has been accepted more because of its (considerable) intuitive appeal than because of its solid evidence. They argue that the reliance on anecdote in many studies of groupthink might have played an important role. More recent research attempts to integrate groupthink with other relevant literature. For instance, new approaches, such as the general group problem-solving model proposed by Aldag and Riggs Fuller (1993), aim to provide a framework for studying both the positive *and* negative aspects of group decision making.

Hastie (1986) reviewed many of the factors which can affect group judgement and decision making. He concluded that groups are usually slightly more accurate than individuals in their judgement of quantities and magnitudes. Hastie also found that groups outperformed individuals in reasoning tasks and general knowledge questions but that the best individual in a group often outperformed the group as a whole.

As argued, research on group decision making tends to focus on social and psychological processes between group members. Research on judgmental biases and heuristics has focused almost exclusively on the individual. The findings of this research, however, may also be of importance for understanding group decision making. For group decisions it is important how individuals in a group acquire, retain and retrieve information when performing a collective task. Individual heuristics and biases may affect the group in different ways.

A study by Tindale (1989) shows that groups tend to exacerbate the errors dominant at the individual level while attenuating those that are less dominant. A study on the use of base rate information or statistical summaries by individuals and by groups shows that groups appear to amplify the tendency of individuals to judge by representativeness when assessing category membership. Groups tend to rely more on concrete, individuating information about a person, and less on base rate information than individuals (Argote, Seabright, & Dyer, 1986). Results of an experiment on memory performance by decision-making groups and individuals showed that groups recalled information better than individuals in terms of accuracy, verbatim reproduction, volume of information revealed, and even reproduction of the serial order of presentation (Vollrath, Sheppard, Hinsz, & Davis, 1989). On the other hand, when the task is complex and many individual judgements are incorrect, exaggeration of common errors could reduce the quality of group performance (Timmermans, 1991).

There are a number of ways to help improve the quality of group decision making. The first concerns procedural aspects of the group decision-making process attempting to reduce the likelihood of intra-group processes with adverse consequences for the quality of the decision. These include the appointment of a devil's advocate as well as techniques such as the Nominal Group Technique and the Delphi method. The latter aim to reduce or prevent social interaction between the group members. In the Delphi technique (Linstone & Turoff, 1975) solutions and preferences dealing with a specific decision problem are elicited from individual group members and (anonymously) distributed to all group members. After this information exchange opinions and preferences are elicited again. This iterative process goes on until there is a majority favouring a specific solution or alternative.

Other ways to help improve the quality of group decision making are decision aids that help to structure the problem and provide computational help in comparing alternative options. For instance Multi-Attribute Utility (MAU) decision aids have been used to support group decision making. Group decision support systems help to decompose the problem into its constituents and can improve the information exchange between group members and the dynamics of group interaction. Timmermans (1991) concluded that these systems tend to be more effective for relatively simple problems and too elaborate for complex problems which require a comparison of many alternatives on many attributes. It seems essential to develop more transparent systems that are more in accordance with the decision strategies employed by real groups. Incorporating less complex decision rules (such as these discussed earlier in this chapter) might improve the user-friendliness of these systems.

Other decision support systems focus on aiding decisions for multiple interest groups. Value Oriented Social Decision Analysis (VOSDA) is such a system (Chen, Mathes, Jarboe, & Wolfe, 1979). This system helps to decompose the alternative actions in terms of the various possible effects *and* to uncover the various values of the groups or stakeholders involved. The method has been developed to improve the effectiveness of decision making on (controversial) public policy issues by enhancing the communication processes involved.

Because the quality of group decision making depends on so many different factors, it is difficult to draw general conclusions and reconcile mixed or contradictory results from group decision making. Plous (1993, p. 214) argues that notwithstanding these difficulties some tentative conclusions can be drawn from the literature:

(a) Most heuristics and biases operate both at individual and group level.
(b) Group discussion often amplifies existing tendencies.
(c) Groups usually perform somewhat better than their average member, provided all or most group members participate in the group decision-making process; on the other hand, the best member often outperforms the group.

Social dilemmas

Interpersonal decision making and choice can take the form of a social dilemma. Social dilemmas concern issues in which individual choices may have disastrous results for the group as a whole. For instance, let us assume that car drivers are asked to drive slowly and/or use cars with a smaller engine to reduce problems of pollution and the greenhouse effect. The individual complying with this request has a negligible impact on the general level of pollution and the greenhouse effect. On the other hand, the costs for the individual car driver could be quite noticeable (longer travel times, uncomfortable small cars, etc.). Clearly, on the individual level it seems more attractive to keep driving at the normal speed in a comfortable car. But we would all like pollution levels to be reduced and the probability of the greenhouse effect to be as small as possible. If enough car drivers comply, the problem will go away. Whether they do or don't, the fact that you drive a big car and like to drive fast will not make that much difference anyway.

Generally social dilemmas consist of two main elements: a 'social trap' (individual gains versus losses for the group) and a 'time trap' (immediate gains versus distant losses). An important feature of these situations is that individual group members engage in behaviour which has benefits for the individual but that would have negative consequences for all if everyone engaged in that behaviour. These social dilemmas can be either 'collective traps' or 'collective fences'. In traps, behaviours that are beneficial to individuals yield negative outcomes for all when exhibited by enough people. In fences, behaviours that are costly to individuals yield negative consequences for all when avoided by enough people. The example we discussed in the first paragraph of this section falls into the latter category. An example of a collective trap would be the tendency to keep increasing the size of the catch of fishing boats in the North Sea. For the individual boat and its crew this is attractive. However, the more boats adopt this behaviour the higher the chances that there will be few fish left in a number of years' time. This example points to the possible role of temporal delay between positive and negative outcomes which is an important characteristic of many social dilemmas. Dilemmas such as the one just described have been studied in research on N-person social dilemmas with the help of a number of specially developed games or paradigms. Messick and Brewer (1983) mention a number of important paradigms such as N-person prisoner's dilemma games, and delay fences. These paradigms seem especially relevant to public good issues such as environmental quality (see also Chapter 7).

The term prisoner's dilemma is derived from an anecdote about confessions to a bank robbery. According to the story, two men rob a bank. Both are apprehended but in order to make a case the district attorney needs confessions. The attorney succeeds by the following strategy. Each robber receives the proposal that if he confesses and the accomplice does not, he will go free and the accomplice will get a sentence of ten years. If both confess, both will get a jail sentence of five years, and if neither confesses both will be sent to jail for a year on the charge of carrying a concealed weapon. Each accomplice is told that the other will receive the same deal.

Research in this area focuses on *why* people choose to cooperate or defect. Research has shown that social values and motives influence behaviour in social dilemmas. Communication among group members can enhance co-operation. Others point to factors such as the desire to accumulate self-interest and subjective responsibility for the resource. Generally, social dilemma research focuses on the relative importance of self-interest versus group interest. One shortcoming of this tradition is the nearly exclusive reliance on rather pallid (temporary) experimental groups of subjects who do not know each other (cf. Levine & Moreland, 1990). On the other hand a social dilemma framework can be applied to many of the world's problems, such as pollution, overpopulation and depletion of natural resources.

Conclusions

Some four decades after the seminal work of Edwards (1954), decision-making research is becoming more prominent in psychology textbooks and a clear and separate research area has emerged, generally referred to as behavioural decision research. An important characteristic of this field of inquiry is that it adopts an interdisciplinary approach, relying on concepts and methods from economics, statistics and social and cognitive psychology. A second characteristic of this field of inquiry is that it often proceeds by testing the descriptive quality of normative theories of judgement and decision making. Unlike research on many social psychological issues such as aggression, helping behaviour, conformity and personal relationships, research on decision making pays considerable attention to the discrepancies between normative models and actual behaviour. Most of this research has focused on the information-processing strategies, or heuristics, that people use when making judgements or decisions. The final characteristic of this field of research is that many concepts and methods are being widely adopted in applied areas, including applied social psychology. Payne et al. (1992) mention areas such as environmental research, accounting, marketing, consumer behaviour, finance, law, medicine, and policy decision making.

Another research area incorporating insights and methods from cognitive, social and health psychology concerns the perception of risk. This research has shown that people are reasonably adequate judges of many risks. Their perception is biased, however. The availability heuristic is one of the distorting factors: sensational hazards and/or risks of which one has personal experience tend to be overestimated. Acceptability of large-scale technological risks seems to be primarily determined by qualitative characteristics of these risks such as the severity of the consequences, catastrophic potential, the novelty of the risks and low perceived controllability. People's perception of the possible risks of their own behavioural practices follows a different pattern. Generally, people seem rather optimistic about personal risks, an illusion that could reduce the need to take preventive action.

Finally, group and interpersonal decision making is an area on the crossline of social psychology and behavioural decision research. Many decisions are made by groups, and a better understanding of the relevant social and individual factors that determine the quality of group decision making requires a mixed approach incorporating insights from a variety of research traditions.

All areas discussed in this chapter could benefit from insights derived from social psychology; on the other hand, applied social psychology could benefit from the findings obtained in behavioural decision research. Combining these should increase the likelihood of providing adequate solutions to a variety of problems in present-day society. The complexity of these problems often requires a multidisciplinary approach in which both the social psychological literature and the literature on decision making can play an important role.

This chapter has presented an overview of the literature on judgement and decision making. First, normative theories of decision making were discussed. These basically decompose complex decisions into their constituents and provide rules for how to combine the possible positive and negative consequences of decision alternatives. Next, discrepancies between how people ought to make decisions according to these models and actual decision making were briefly considered. A number of approaches that attempt to provide more adequate descriptions of human judgement and decision making were briefly summarized, followed by a discussion of the impact of affective factors on judgement and decision making. Simplifying strategies or heuristics people use in decision making, as well as their impact on the quality of judgement and decision making, were also summarized.

The perception of risk and the acceptability of risk is the next issue. First the emphasis was on large-scale societal risks, their perception by lay people and experts, and factors underlying the limited public acceptability of technological risks such as nuclear energy. The perception of personal risk was discussed, and attention paid to the accuracy of people's perception of risk and the relation between perceived risk and behaviour. The final section described a selected number of issues in the area of group decision making. Some possible drawbacks and shortcomings were discussed, as well as ways to prevent these. Finally, the social dilemma literature was briefly considered, and its potential usefulness for applied research on many of today's societal issues such as environmental pollution and the depletion of natural resources.

Further reading

Dawes, R.M. (1988). *Rational choice in an uncertain world*. San Diego: Harcourt Brace Jovanovich. Introductory textbook on behavioural decision making comparing basic principles of rationality with actual behaviour in reaching decisions. This acclaimed textbook gives clear explanations of the basic principles and many illustrations of shortcomings of human decision making.

Janis, I.L. (1982). *Groupthink: Psychological studies of policy decisions and fiascoes*. Boston: Houghton-Mifflin. This second expanded edition of Janis's classic work on group decision making focuses on things that can go wrong, and ways to prevent this.

Klein, G.A., Orasanu, J., Calderwood, R., & Zsambok, C.E. (Eds), *Decision making in action: Models and methods*. Norwood, NJ: Ablex. This book focuses on naturalistic decision making and provides many applications of decision theory. Emphasis is on how people actually make decisions in complex real-world settings and on ways to support these processes.

Payne, J.W., Bettman, J.R., & Johnson, E.J. (1993). *The adaptive decision maker*. Cambridge: Cambridge University Press. This advanced textbook provides an alternative framework to study decision making, the basic argument is that people use many different strategies for making judgements and choices and that strategy choice is determined by effort and accuracy considerations.

Plous, C. (1993). *The psychology of judgment and decision making*. New York: McGraw-Hill. An introductory textbook linking cognitive and social psychology with behavioural decision making. Clear and well written, it covers both individual and group decision making.

3

Survey Research: Collecting Data by Asking Questions

Norbert Schwarz

Contents

Much of what we know about human behaviour is based on self-reports. This is particularly true for research in applied social psychology, as a perusal of the chapters in this book will easily confirm. When we want to learn about individuals' medical histories, employment histories, consumer habits, driving behaviour, family problems, media consumption or political beliefs, we ask appropriate questions. The answers provided to these questions not only serve as input into scientific analyses, but are also the basis of statistical indicators used to describe the state of a society and to monitor social change. Obviously, these data are only as meaningful as the questions we ask and the answers we receive. Moreover, whom we ask is of crucial importance to our ability to draw conclusions that extend beyond the particular people who answered our questions. Hence, both the processes underlying answers to questions about behaviours and beliefs and the appropriate selection of respondents are of considerable importance to many areas of social research.

The present chapter provides an introduction to these issues. The first section introduces the concept of a survey and reviews key issues of survey sampling. This section concludes with a discussion of the differences between surveys, experiments and quasi-experiments, comparing what we can learn from these different research designs. The second, and larger, section focuses on how to ask and reviews the cognitive and communicative processes involved in answering questions about one's attitudes or behaviours. The material covered in this section applies to surveys as well as to any other form of self-report, whether collected in the field or in the psychological laboratory.

Elements of survey design

What is a survey?

In its most general meaning, the term *survey* refers to systematic data collection about a sample drawn from a specified larger population. If data are obtained from every member of the population, the study is called a *census*. The best-known form of a survey is the opinion poll, in which information is gathered from a sample of individuals by asking questions. However, surveys may also be conducted of organizations or events (e.g. court sentences) and they do not necessarily imply question asking. The present chapter, however, deals exclusively with surveys of individuals.

Like any other research study, a survey must begin with a statement of its objectives. What does one want to study? The objectives determine the population of interest, from which the sample is to be drawn; the design of the survey (e.g. are respondents to be interviewed repeatedly or only once?); and the questions to be asked. The questions may be asked in face-to-face or telephone interviews, or by means of a self-administered questionnaire, which may be mailed to respondents. Following data collection, the answers must be coded for data analysis. Data analysis, interpretation of the results, and dissemination of the findings complete the research process. Next, we consider some of the key elements. More detailed discussions of many of these issues are provided by Bradburn and Sudman (1988), Schuman and Kalton (1985), and Weisberg, Krosnick and Bowen (1989).

Who to ask: populations and samples

The research objectives determine the population from whom data are to be collected. This may be the adult population of a country (as in national opinion polls), the members of an organization or patients suffering from a particular illness, but also the population of hospitals or car dealers in a country or in some specified region, and so on. As noted above, if data are gathered from all members of the population, the study is called a census. In most cases, however, this is not feasible and a sample will be drawn instead.

Drawing inferences from the sample to the larger population of interest requires that the sample be representative of that population. A biased sample, i.e. a sample that does not represent all parts of the sampling frame, will be devastating to the validity of the obtained survey results. Reflecting its crucial importance, survey sampling is a highly specialized field in its own right (see Kalton, 1983, for a mathematically oriented introduction and Sudman, 1976, for a nonmathematical discussion of applied sampling issues). Anyone who plans a survey is well advised to secure the services of a professional sampling statistician.

At a basic level, we can distinguish *probability* and *nonprobability* samples. A probability sample requires that each member of the population have a specifiable likelihood of being included in the sample. The most basic form of probability sampling is known as *simple random sampling*. In simple random sampling, each member of the population has an equal likelihood of being selected for the sample. For example, we may use a table of random numbers to draw a sample from the population of citizens living in a city, based on the city's register. Although this will result in a sample that represents the city's population at large, the chances are that small subgroups, for example the very old, will be represented by very few members. If we wanted to draw conclusions about the special situation of this subpopulation, simple random sampling would leave us with too small a number of respondents for reasonable analyses.

This problem is avoided by *stratified random sampling*, which is often combined with *oversampling*. Stratification has the advantage of increasing the power of a sample by reducing sampling error (to be discussed below). For example, if one is interested in comparing two or more subgroups in a population, the sampling error of the difference between groups is minimized when equal samples are taken from each group. To accomplish this, the sample is stratified into the subgroups of interest. If the groups are not of equal size, as is typical, the smaller group will be *oversampled*, i.e. represented by a number of respondents that is larger than its proportion in the population. In drawing inferences about the population at large, this oversampling will then be corrected for at the analysis stage.

Simple as well as stratified random sampling render survey research expensive, in particular if face-to-face interviews are used. This reflects the fact that the interviewer needs to track down and interview the specified respondents, who may live far apart. Moreover, contacting these respondents may involve numerous unsuccessful attempts, resulting in high travel costs. This is less of a concern if telephone interviews are used. For example, Traugott (1987) observed in a telephone interview survey that 39 per cent of the sample could be successfully interviewed on the first or second call and that this proportion increased to 57 per cent after three calls, 68 per cent after four calls, 92 per cent after ten calls and 96 per cent after fifteen calls. Survey researchers insist on interviewing as many members of the sample as possible because low *response rates* compromise the representativeness of the survey. In Traugott's study, for example, individuals aged 30 years or younger were underrepresented after the first call, since they were more difficult to reach at home. Hence, the proportion of young respondents increased from 23 per cent after the first call to 30 per cent after 15 calls. In most countries, response rates have been continuously declining over the last few decades (Steeh, 1981) and the response rates obtained in most high-quality surveys hover around 75 per cent. Investigating the determinants of respondents' decision to (not) participate in a survey provides a challenging agenda for psychological research (see Groves, Cialdini, & Couper, 1992).

To control the costs of data collection under face-to-face interview conditions, survey researchers often employ *clustering* strategies, which reduce the costs necessary to locate sample respondents. In this case, one draws a random sample of relevant locations at which respondents may be contacted and then randomly samples respondents at these locations. Some examples of widely used clusters include samples of schools and classrooms when students are the population, samples of shopping malls when shoppers are wanted, samples of airports and boarding areas when air passengers are sampled, and samples of cities and blocks within cities for household studies. It should be noted, however, that the reduction in costs comes with the disadvantage of increased sampling error. In general, clustering increases sampling error over simple random samples because the observations within a cluster are not independent. It is possible, however, to find optimal clustering procedures that provide the most information (i.e. smallest sampling error) for a given cost. Sudman (1976) provides a detailed discussion of relevant strategies.

The high cost of probability sampling and the problem of low response rates are avoided by *nonprobability sampling*, which for this reason is attractive to many market research companies – with negative implications for the quality of the data obtained. The main type of nonprobability sampling procedure employed in surveys is *quota sampling*. In this case, a sample is selected based on a set of characteristics in the population. For example, if the population of interest contains 40 per cent married people, 18 per cent black, and 35 per cent over the age of 45, we can select a sample that will conform to these characteristics. To accomplish this, interviewers are not given a specified list of respondents or addresses but are provided with the quota criteria and are free to select any respondent who fits these criteria. Although this method may seem similar to stratified random sampling, this similarity is misleading because each member in the quota specification group does *not* have an equal likelihood of being selected. Rather, the selection of respondents within those groups is left to the interviewer's discretion. Although this procedure reduces the cost of the study, it does not allow strong conclusions about the population, which requires the calculation of sampling error. Sampling error, however, can only be calculated for probability samples.

Sampling error reflects the discrepancy between the results one obtains from a particular sample and the results one would have obtained from the entire population. It is often referred to as the *margin of error* when survey results are reported. Suppose that a survey based on simple random sampling indicates that 70 per cent of the sample would vote for candidate A. With a sample size of N = 500 and a desired confidence interval of 95 per cent, sampling error would be around 4 per cent. Hence, one may conclude that between 66 per cent and 74 per cent of the population would vote for candidate A. Sampling error decreases with increasing sample size, but the decrease is nonlinear. For the above example, sampling error declines from 9 per cent for a sample of 100 to 4 per cent for a sample of 500. But doubling the sample size from 500 to 1,000 further decreases sampling error only modestly to 3 per cent, and to reduce sampling error to 1 per cent we would need a sample of approximately 10,500. For most national surveys, researchers aim for a sampling error of 3 per cent, requiring a sample of approximately 1,000 respondents. Because sampling error depends on sample size, the sampling error for any subgroup, e.g. 18–20-year-olds, is much larger than the sampling error for the sample as a whole. If it is important to obtain accurate estimates for specified subgroups we need to increase their representation through oversampling, as discussed above.

Note, however, that this relationship between sampling error and sample size holds only for probability samples. Sampling error cannot be estimated with the use of nonprobability sampling techniques, because the likelihood of being selected is unknown for nonprobability samples. Simply having a large number of respondents does not, by itself, allow us to draw any inferences about the population. This is particularly obvious for studies based on *convenience samples*, that is, samples which are readily available or comprised solely of volunteers. Such samples, be they college students who voluntarily sign up for a study or readers who respond to a questionnaire printed in a magazine, do not allow inferences to any population because their representativeness is unknown. Hence, such studies are useless if we are interested in learning about some specified population. Counterintuitive as it may seem, we can learn more about the population from a probability sample of 500 than from a convenience sample of 50,000 volunteers who respond to a magazine questionnaire. Convenience samples are very useful, however, in experimental research designed to explore the impact of some experimental treatment, as we shall see below.

Modes of data collection

Questions can be asked in face-to-face interviews, on the telephone, or in self-administered questionnaires, which may be mailed to respondents or administered in a group setting. Because face-to-face interviews require trained field staff at all interviewing locations, involving considerable administrative effort and travel costs, they are more expensive to conduct than telephone interviews. The latter may be completed by a smaller number of interviewers at a centralized telephone facility, which also facilitates interviewer supervision and quality control (see Frey, 1983, for an introduction to telephone surveys; Groves & Kahn, 1979, for a comparison of personal and telephone surveys; and Fowler, 1991, for a discussion of interviewer training). In developed countries, telephone coverage is likely to exceed 90 per cent, making telephone interviews feasible, although coverage may differ for some subgroups. Nowadays, telephone interviewing is usually conducted with the help of a computer system (called CATI – computer assisted telephone interviewing) that displays the question to the interviewer, who types in the respondent's answer, a procedure that reduces coding efforts and transcription errors. In addition, computer-assisted interviewing has the advantage that it facilitates the administration of complicated questionnaires. Such questionnaires may include elaborate branching sequences, where respondents are asked different follow-up questions depending on their previous answers, or the randomization of question order to control for order effects. To take advantage of these possibilities, face-to-face interviews may also be conducted with the help of laptop computers (called CAPI – computer assisted personal interviewing).

Mail surveys are the least expensive to conduct, and with proper procedures their response rates can approach those of face-to-face surveys. These procedures are described in detail in Dillman's *Telepone and Mail Surveys: The*

Total Design Method (1978), the standard reference on how to conduct a mail survey. Mail surveys require a particularly user-friendly questionnaire design to guide respondents through the question sequence (see Jenkins & Dillman, in press, for recommendations). Complicated skip patterns (which require respondents to proceed with different questions depending on the answer they have given) easily result in confusion, and open-ended questions that require more than a few words of writing may remain unanswered. Moreover, individuals who are particularly interested in the topic are more likely to return the questionnaire, introducing some risk of topic-related self-selection. This risk is less pronounced for face-to-face or telephone surveys, where respondents are unaware of the specific questions to be asked at the time they agree to be interviewed. On the other hand, the responses obtained in face-to-face or telephone surveys are susceptible to interviewer influences, which are largely absent in mail surveys (see van der Zouwen, Dijkstra, & Smit, 1991, and Hox, de Leeuw, and Kreft, 1991, for reviews).

Not surprisingly, the different modes of data collection also differ in the tasks that they pose to respondents. Most important, telephone interviews preclude the use of visual aids and put respondents under more time pressure, because periods of silence during which respondents think about their answers are experienced as more unpleasant on the phone. As a result, some of the influences of questionnaire design, to be reviewed below, vary as a function of the data collection procedure used (see Schwarz, Strack, Hippler, & Bishop, 1991 for a review). Accordingly, the intended mode of data collection must be kept in mind at the questionnaire construction stage.

Number of contacts

If a given sample is interviewed only once, the survey is often called a *cross-sectional survey*; if the sample is followed over time and interviewed repeatedly, the resulting longitudinal study is called a *panel survey*. Cross-sectional surveys provide a snapshot of the population's opinion or behaviour at a given point in time; their results can be compared with other snapshots and can be used to describe differences between subpopulations. However, cross-sectional surveys are limited in their ability to trace changes in opinion or behaviour over time. For example, if some people change their party preference from Liberal to Conservative, whereas others change from Conservative to Liberal, we can only see the net effect of both changes when we compare the results of two cross-sectional surveys. In contrast, panel surveys allow us to trace these changes in more detail, providing insight into who changes in which direction.

Occasionally, survey researchers employ experimental elements in a survey, for example by using different question wordings or different question orders for parts of the sample. The resulting between-subjects design, in which different respondents are asked different questions, is often called a split-ballot design in survey research.

Surveys and experiments: what can we learn from each?

The major strength of a representative survey is that it allows us to draw conclusions from a sample to a specified population. For example, we may infer, within the margins of sampling error, which percentage of the population is likely to vote for a given candidate. Accordingly, surveys provide an excellent source of descriptive data. Their major weakness, on the other hand, is that the resulting data are purely correlational, thus limiting our ability to draw causal inferences. We may observe, for example, that individuals who are concerned about inflation are less likely to vote for the candidate – but we can't tell if this reflects a causal impact of their concern about inflation or a causal impact of some other variable that covaries with this concern. One may control for the possible influence of such third variables with appropriate statistical techniques (see Weisberg et al., 1989, for an introduction to survey analysis), but this requires that we know which variables may be relevant and that we have assessed these variables in our study.

In contrast, the major strength of experiments is that they allow causal inferences (see Aronson, Brewer, & Carlsmith, 1985, for an introduction). By randomly assigning subjects to different conditions of an experiment, the experimenter can ensure that variables other than the ones manipulated in the experiment cannot exert a systematic influence. If we wanted to know, for example, if concern about inflation influences voting intentions, we could assign subjects to conditions that do or do not raise this concern and could subsequently assess their voting intentions. The major weakness of most experiments, however, is that they do not allow us to draw inferences to any specified population. This is because experiments are usually conducted with a small number of volunteers, comprising a convenience sample of unknown representativeness.

In most cases, this limitation is of little concern to the experimenter, who wants to test *if* a variable has a theoretically predicted causal influence. In the above example, observing an impact of increased inflation concerns on voting intentions would answer the experimenter's theoretical question – and whether this results in one or the other candidate being elected is of secondary interest. In contrast, survey researchers would typically want to predict the actual election outcome, which requires a representative sample. As this example illustrates, one may fruitfully combine both approaches by including experimental elements in representative surveys. For example, we may randomly assign half of a representative sample to a condition in which questions designed to raise concerns about inflation precede questions about voting intention. Such a research design would allow us to test the causal hypothesis and to estimate how the actual election outcome would be affected if inflation concerns increased in the population. At present, such experimental surveys are rare, although they provide a promising avenue for future research.

Asking and answering questions: cognitive and communicative processes

As noted above, survey data are only as meaningful as the answers that respondents provide. Although this fact has been recognized since the early days of survey research (see Payne, 1951, for a review), survey methodology has long been characterized by rigorous theories of sampling on the one hand, and the so-called 'art of asking questions' on the other. Only recently have the cognitive and communicative processes underlying question answering in surveys received theoretical attention. Drawing on psychological theories of language comprehension, memory and judgement, psychologists and survey methodologists have begun to formulate explicit models of the question-answering process and have tested these models in tightly controlled laboratory experiments and split-ballot surveys. Several edited volumes reflect the rapid progress made in this interdisciplinary area (Jabine, Straf, Tanur, & Tourangeau, 1984; Jobe & Loftus, 1991; Hippler, Schwarz, & Sudman, 1987; Schwarz & Sudman, 1992, 1994, 1996; Tanur, 1992) and a recent monograph (Sudman, Bradburn, & Schwarz's *Thinking about Answers*, 1996) reviews the current state of knowledge. Interested readers are referred to this book for a more detailed treatment of the material discussed below.

Respondents' tasks

From a cognitive perspective, answering a survey question requires that respondents perform several tasks, as shown in Figure 3.1 (see Strack & Martin, 1987; Sudman et al., 1996, Chapter 3; Tourangeau, 1984; Tourangeau & Rasinski, 1988, for more detail). Not surprisingly, respondents' first task consists in interpreting the question, to understand what is asked for. Next, respondents have to recall relevant information from memory. If it is an opinion question, respondents may sometimes be able to retrieve a previously formed opinion. In most cases, however, a previously formed opinion may not be accessible or may not match the specific aspects addressed in the question. Hence, respondents' third task is to 'compute' a judgement. To do so, they need to form a mental representation of the target and of some standard against which the target is evaluated. We will address these processes in more detail in the section on attitude questions.

If the question is a behavioural question, respondents need to recall or reconstruct relevant instances of this behaviour from memory. If the question specifies a reference period (such as 'last week' or 'last month'), they must also determine if these instances occurred during this reference period or not. Similarly, if the question refers to their 'usual' behaviour, respondents have to determine if the recalled or reconstructed instances are reasonably representative or if they reflect a deviation from their usual behaviour. If they cannot recall or reconstruct specific instances of the behaviour, or are not sufficiently motivated to engage in this effort, respondents may rely on their general knowledge or other information that may bear on their task to compute an

---

1. Interpret question to understand what is asked
2. Recall relevant information
3. Form a judgement
4. Format the judgement to fit the response alternatives
5. Report the judgement to the interviewer, editing it if necessary

---

Figure 3.1   *Respondents' tasks*

estimate. We will address these processes in the section on behavioural questions.

Once a 'private' judgement is formed in respondents' minds, respondents have to communicate it to the researcher. To do so, they may need to format their judgement to fit the response alternatives provided as part of the question. Moreover, respondents may wish to edit their response before they communicate it, due to influences of social desirability and situational adequacy.

Accordingly, (1) interpreting the question, (2) retrieving relevant information, (3) forming a judgement, (4) formatting the judgement to fit the response alternatives, and (5) editing the answer are the main psychological components of a process that starts with respondents' exposure to a survey question and ends with their overt report. Although it is useful to present these tasks in a sequential order, respondents may not always follow this sequence, as we shall see. Next, we consider each of these steps in more detail.

Question comprehension

The key issue at the question comprehension stage is whether the respondent's understanding of the question does or does not match what the researcher had in mind: is the attitude object, or the behaviour, that the respondent identifies as the target of the question the one that the researcher intended? Does the respondent's understanding tap the same facet of the issue and the same evaluative dimension? From a psychological point of view, question comprehension reflects the operation of two intertwined processes (see Clark & Schober, 1992; Strack, 1994; Strack & Schwarz, 1992).

The first refers to the semantic understanding of the utterance. Comprehending the *literal meaning* of a sentence involves the identification of words, the recall of lexical information from semantic memory, and the construction of a meaning of the utterance, which is constrained by its context. Not surprisingly, survey textbooks urge researchers to write simple questions and to avoid unfamiliar or ambiguous terms. Sudman and Bradburn's (1983) *Asking Questions* provides much useful advice in this regard and is highly recommended.

However, understanding the words is not sufficient to answer a question. For example, if respondents are asked, 'What have you done today?', they are likely to understand the meaning of the words. Yet they still need to determine what kind of activities the researcher is interested in. Should they report, for example, that they took a shower, or not? Hence, understanding a question in a way that allows an appropriate answer not only requires an understanding of the *literal meaning* of the question, but involves inferences about the questioner's intention to determine the *pragmatic meaning* of the question.

To understand how respondents infer the intended meaning of a question, we need to consider the assumptions that govern the conduct of conversation in everyday life. These tacit assumptions were systematically described by Paul Grice (1975), a philosopher of language (see Clark & Schober, 1992; Schwarz, 1994; Strack, 1994; Strack & Schwarz, 1992, for applications to survey research). According to Grice's analysis, conversations proceed according to a cooperativeness principle. This principle can be expressed in the form of four maxims. There is a *maxim of quality* that enjoins speakers not to say anything they believe to be false or lack adequate evidence for, and a *maxim of relation* that enjoins speakers to make their contribution relevant to the aims of the ongoing conversation. In addition, a *maxim of quantity* requires speakers to make their contribution as informative as is required, but not more informative than is required, while a *maxim of manner* holds that the contribution should be clear rather than obscure, ambiguous or wordy. In other words, speakers should try to be informative, truthful, relevant and clear. As a result, 'communicated information comes with a guarantee of relevance' (Sperber & Wilson, 1986, p. vi) and listeners interpret the speakers' utterances 'on the assumption that they are trying to live up to these ideals' (Clark & Clark, 1977, p. 122). These tacit assumptions have important implications for survey research.

Response alternatives

Suppose, for example, that respondents are asked in an open response format, 'What have you done today?' To give a meaningful answer, they have to determine which activities may be of interest to the researcher. In an attempt to be informative, respondents are likely to omit activities that the researcher is obviously aware of (e.g. 'I gave a survey interview') or may take for granted anyway (e.g. 'I took a shower'). If respondents were given a list of activities that included giving an interview and taking a shower, most respondents would endorse them. At the same time, however, such a list would reduce the likelihood that respondents will report activities that are not represented on the list (see Schuman & Presser, 1981; Schwarz & Hippler, 1991, for a review of relevant studies). Both of these effects reflect that response alternatives can clarify the intended meaning of a question, in the present example by specifying the activities the researcher is interested in. Whereas this example may seem rather obvious, more subtle influences are frequently overlooked.

Suppose that respondents are asked how frequently they felt 'really irritated' recently. To answer this question, they again have to determine what the researcher means by 'really irritated'. Does this term refer to major or to minor annoyances? To identify the intended meaning of the question, they may consult the response alternatives provided by the researcher. If the response alternatives present low-frequency categories, perhaps ranging from 'less than once a year' to 'more than once a month', they may conclude that the researcher has relatively rare events in mind and that the question cannot refer to minor irritations, which are likely to occur more often. In line with this assumption, Schwarz, Strack, Müller and Chassein (1988) observed that respondents who had to report the frequency of irritating experiences on a low-frequency scale assumed that the question referred to major annoyances, whereas respondents who had to give their report on a high-frequency scale assumed that the question referred to minor annoyances. Thus, respondents identified different experiences as the target of the question, depending on the frequency range of the response alternatives provided to them.

Similarly, Schwarz, Knäuper, Hippler, Noelle-Neumann and Clark (1991) observed that respondents may use the specific numeric values provided as part of a rating scale to interpret the meaning of the scale's labels. In their study, a representative sample of German adults was asked, 'How successful would you say you have been in life?' This question was accompanied by an 11-point rating scale, ranging from 'not at all successful' to 'extremely successful'. However, in one condition the numeric values of the rating scale ranged from 0 ('not at all successful') to 10 ('extremely successful'), whereas in the other condition they ranged from −5 ('not at all successful') to +5 ('extremely successful'). The results showed a dramatic impact of the numeric values presented to respondents. Whereas 34 per cent of the respondents endorsed a value between 0 and 5 on the 0 to 10 scale, only 13 per cent endorsed one of the formally equivalent values between −5 and 0 on the −5 to +5 scale. Subsequent experiments indicated that this difference reflects differential interpretations of the term 'not at all successful'. When this label was combined with the numeric value '0', respondents interpreted it to reflect the absence of success. However, when the same label was combined with the numeric value '−5', and the scale offered '0' as the mid-point, they interpreted it to reflect the presence of failure.

In combination, these findings demonstrate that respondents use the response alternatives in interpreting the meaning of a question. In doing so, they proceed on the tacit assumption that every contribution is relevant to the aims of the ongoing conversation. In the survey interview, these contributions include apparently formal features of questionnaire design, such as the numeric values given on a rating scale. Hence, identically worded questions may acquire different meanings, depending on the response alternatives by which they are accompanied (see Schwarz & Hippler, 1991, for a more extended discussion).

Question context

Respondents' interpretation of a question's intended meaning is further influenced by the context in which the question is presented. Not surprisingly, this influence is the more pronounced, the more ambiguous the wording of the question. As an extreme case, consider research in which respondents are asked to report their opinion about a highly obscure – or even completely fictitious – issue, such as the 'Agricultural Trade Act of 1978' (e.g. Bishop, Oldendick, & Tuchfarber, 1986; Schuman & Presser, 1981). Questions of this type reflect public opinion researchers' concern that the 'fear of appearing uninformed' may induce 'many respondents to conjure up opinions even when they had not given the particular issue any thought prior to the interview' (Erikson, Luttberg, & Tedin, 1988, p. 44). To explore how meaningful respondents' answers are, survey researchers introduced questions about issues that don't exist. Presumably, respondents' willingness to report an opinion on a fictitious issue casts some doubt on the reports provided in survey interviews in general. In fact, about 30 per cent of the respondents *do* typically provide an answer to issues that are invented by the researcher. This has been interpreted as evidence for the operation of social pressure that induces respondents to give meaningless answers in the absence of any knowledge.

From a conversational point of view, however, the sheer fact that a question about some issue is asked presupposes that this issue exists – or else asking a question about it would violate every norm of conversational conduct. But respondents have no reason to assume that the researcher will ask meaningless questions and will hence try to make sense of it. If the interviewer does not provide additional clarification, they are likely to turn to the context of the ambiguous question to determine its meaning, much as they would be expected to do in any other conversation. Once respondents have assigned a particular meaning to the issue, thus transforming the fictitious issue into a better defined issue that makes sense in the context of the interview, they may have no difficulty reporting a subjectively meaningful opinion. Even if they have not given the particular issue much thought, they may easily identify the broader set of issues to which this particular one apparently belongs. They may then use their general attitude to the broader set of issues to determine their attitude toward this particular one.

Supporting this assumption, Strack, Schwarz and Wänke (1991, Experiment 1) observed that German university students reported different attitudes towards the introduction of a fictitious 'educational contribution', depending on the nature of a preceding question. Specifically, some students were asked to estimate the average tuition fees that students have to pay at US universities (in contrast to Germany, where university education is free), whereas others had to estimate the amount of money that the Swedish government pays every student as financial support. As expected, many of the respondents interpreted the subsequent question about the fictitious 'educational contribution' to refer to students having to pay money in the former case, but to students receiving money in the latter case. Reflecting this differential interpretation, respondents reported a more favourable attitude to the introduction of an 'educational contribution' in Germany when the preceding question pertained to stipends students receive in Sweden than when it referred to tuition fees students have to pay in the United States.

As the preceding examples illustrate, question comprehension is not primarily an issue of understanding the literal meaning of an utterance. Rather, question comprehension involves extensive inferences about the speaker's intentions to determine the pragmatic meaning of the question. To make these inferences, respondents draw on the nature of preceding questions as well as the response alternatives. Accordingly, survey methodologists' traditional focus on using the 'right words' in questionnaire writing needs to be complemented by a consideration of the conversational processes involved in the question-answering process (see Bless, Strack, & Schwarz, 1993; Schwarz, 1994, for a related discussion of psychological experiments).

Recalling or computing a judgement

Once respondents determine what the researcher is interested in, they need to recall relevant information from memory. In some cases, respondents may have direct access to a previously formed relevant judgement that they can offer as an answer. In most cases, however, they will not find an appropriate answer readily stored in memory and will need to compute a judgement on the spot. The processes involved in doing so are somewhat different for behavioural questions and attitude questions, and will be discussed in the respective sections below.

Formatting the response

Once respondents have formed a judgement, they cannot typically report it in their own words. Rather, they are supposed to report it by endorsing one of the response alternatives provided by the researcher. This requires that they format their response in line with the options given. Accordingly, the researcher's choice of response alternatives may strongly affect survey results (see Schwarz & Hippler, 1991, for a review).

From a theoretical point of view, however, it is important to note that the influence of response alternatives is not limited to the formatting stage and that response alternatives are likely to influence other steps of the question-answering sequence as well, as we saw in the section on question comprehension. The only effects that seem to occur unequivocally at the formatting stage pertain to the anchoring of rating scales (e.g. Ostrom & Upshaw, 1968; Parducci, 1983).

As numerous studies demonstrate, respondents use the most extreme stimuli to anchor the endpoints of a rating scale. As a result, a given stimulus will be rated as less extreme if presented in the context of a more extreme one, than if presented in the context of a less extreme one. In Parducci's model, this impact of the range of stimuli is referred to as the 'range effect'. In addition, if the number of stimuli to be rated is sufficiently large, respondents attempt to use all categories of the rating scale about equally often. Accordingly, the specific ratings given also depend on the frequency distribution of the presented stimuli, an effect that is referred to as the 'frequency effect'. Daamen and de Bie (1992) provide an introduction to the logic of these processes and report several studies that illustrate their impact on survey results.

Editing the response

Finally, respondents may want to edit their response before they communicate it, reflecting considerations of social desirability and self-presentation. DeMaio (1984) reviews the survey literature on this topic. Not surprisingly, the impact of these considerations is more pronounced in face-to-face interviews than in self-administered questionnaires and interviewer effects are usually assumed to occur at the editing stage. For example, 'black respondents are less likely to express explicit distrust of whites when the interviewer is white, and white respondents mute negative sentiments about blacks when the interviewer is black' (Turner & Martin, 1984, p. 136; see Hox et al., 1991, for a review of interviewer effects).

However, it is important to emphasize that influences of social desirability are limited to potentially threatening questions and are typically modest in size. Moreover, *what* constitutes a socially desirable response depends on the specifics of the situation. For example, several researchers (see Smith, 1979, for a review) observed that respondents report higher levels of happiness and satisfaction in face-to-face interviews than in self-administered questionnaires. In contrast, Strack, Schwarz, Chassein, Kern and Wagner (1990) obtained a reversal of this effect under specific conditions. In their study, respondents reported deflated levels of happiness when they were interviewed by a handicapped interviewer, presumably because it seemed inappropriate to tell an unfortunate other how wonderful one's own life is. In contrast, the sheer presence of a handicapped confederate while respondents filled out a self-administered questionnaire resulted in increased reports of happiness, indicating that the handicapped person served as a salient standard of comparison, thus inflating respondents' private judgements. As this example illustrates, understanding issues of social desirability requires close attention to the actual social situation, which determines what is desirable and what is not.

Survey researchers have developed a number of different technical procedures designed to ensure the confidentiality of respondents' reports and/or to reduce respondents' concerns about their self-presentation. These procedures range from appropriate question wordings and sealed envelopes to complicated 'randomized response' procedures, which allow the researcher to estimate the frequency of an undesirable behaviour in the population without linking a given response to a given individual. Sudman and Bradburn (1983) review the various procedures in their chapter on threatening questions and provide detailed advice on how to use them.

Summary

This section has reviewed what respondents must do to answer a question. For ease of exposition, respondents' tasks were presented in a sequential order. Although this order is plausible, respondents may obviously go back and forth between different steps, revising, for example, their initial question interpretation once the response alternatives suggest a different meaning. In any case, however, they have to determine the intended meaning of the question, recall relevant information from memory, form a judgement, and format the judgement to fit the response alternatives provided to them. Moreover, they may want to edit their private judgement before they communicate it. Next, we turn to specific considerations that pertain to behavioural reports and attitude questions.

Asking questions about behaviours

Most survey questions about respondents' behaviour are frequency questions, pertaining, for example, to how often the respondent has bought something, has seen a doctor, or has missed a day at work during some specified period of time. Researchers who ask these questions would ideally like the respondent to identify the behaviour of interest; to scan the reference period; to retrieve all instances that match the target behaviour; and to count these instances to determine the overall frequency of the behaviour. This, however, is the route that respondents are least likely to take.

In fact, except for rare and very important behaviours, respondents are unlikely to have detailed representations of numerous individual instances of a behaviour stored in memory. The details of various instances of closely related behaviours blend into one global representation (Linton, 1982; Neisser, 1986): many individual episodes become indistinguishable or irretrievable, due to interference from other similar instances (Wagenaar, 1986; Baddeley & Hitch, 1977), fostering the generation of knowledge-like representations that 'lack specific time or location indicators' (Strube, 1987, p. 89). The finding that a single spell of unemployment is more accurately recalled than multiple spells (Mathiowetz, 1986), for example, suggests that this phenomenon not only applies to mundane and unimportant behaviours, but also to repeated experiences that profoundly affect an individual's life. Accordingly, a 'recall and count' model does not capture how people answer questions about frequent behaviours or experiences. Rather, their answers are likely to be based on some fragmented recall and the application of inference rules to compute a frequency estimate (see Bradburn, Rips, & Shevell, 1987; Schwarz, 1990; Sudman et al., 1996, for extensive reviews and the contributions in Schwarz & Sudman, 1994, for research examples).

Below, I address strategies that facilitate recall and subsequently turn to the estimation strategies that respondents are most likely to use.

Facilitating recall: recall cues

If researchers are interested in obtaining reports that are based on recalled episodes, they may simplify respondents' task by providing appropriate recall cues and by restricting the recall task to a short and recent reference period. There are, however, important drawbacks to both of these strategies. Although the quality of recall will generally improve as the retrieval cues become more specific, respondents are likely to restrict their memory search to the particular cues presented to them, indicating that the cues constrain the meaning of the question. As a result, respondents are likely to omit instances that do not match the specific cues, resulting in under-reports if the list is not exhaustive. Moreover, using a short reference period may result in many 'zero' answers from respondents who rarely engage in the behaviour, thus limiting later analyses to respondents with a high behavioural frequency.

If one decides to provide specific recall cues, one has to be aware that different cues are differentially effective. The date of an event is the poorest cue, whereas cues pertaining to what happened, where it happened, and who was involved have been found to be very effective (Wagenaar, 1986, 1988). In addition, recall will improve when respondents are given sufficient time to search memory. Recalling specific events may take up to several seconds (Reiser, Black, & Abelson, 1985), and repeated attempts to recall may result in the retrieval of additional material, even after a considerable number of previous trials (e.g. Williams & Hollan, 1981). Unfortunately, respondents are unlikely to have sufficient time to engage in repeated retrieval attempts in most research situations (and may often not be motivated to do so even if they had the time). This is particularly crucial in the context of survey research, where the available time per question is usually less than one minute (Groves & Kahn, 1979).

Moreover, the direction in which respondents search memory has been found to influence the quality of recall. Specifically, better recall is achieved when respondents begin with the most recent occurrence of a behaviour and work backward in time than when they begin at the beginning of the reference period (e.g. Loftus & Fathi, 1985; Whitten & Leonard, 1981). This presumably occurs because memory of recent occurrences is richer and the recalled instances may serve as cues for recalling previous ones. Given free choice, however, respondents tend to prefer the less efficient strategy of forward recall.

Even under optimal conditions, however, respondents will frequently be unable to recall an event or some of its critical details, even if they believed they would 'certainly' remember it at the time it occurred (e.g. Linton, 1975; Thompson, 1982; Wagenaar, 1986). In general, the available evidence suggests that respondents are likely to under-report behaviours and events, which has led many researchers to assume that higher reports of mundane behaviours are likely to be more valid. Accordingly, a 'the more the better' rule is frequently substituted for external validity checks.

Dating recalled instances

After recalling or reconstructing a specific instance of the behaviour under study, respondents have to determine if this instance occurred during the reference period. This requires that they understand the extension of the reference period and that they can accurately date the instance with regard to that period.

Reference periods that are defined in terms of several weeks or months are highly susceptible to misinterpretations. For example, the term 'during the last twelve months' has been found to be construed as a reference to the last calendar year, as including or excluding the current month, and so on. Similarly, anchoring the reference period with a specific date, for example 'Since 1 March, how often . . .?', is not very helpful because respondents will usually not be able to relate an abstract date to meaningful memories.

Not surprisingly, the most efficient way to anchor a reference period is the use of salient personal or public events, often referred to as 'landmarks' (Loftus & Marburger, 1983). In addition to improving respondents' understanding of the reference period, the use of landmarks facilitates the dating of recalled instances. Given that the calendar date of an event will usually not be among its encoded features, respondents were found to relate recalled events to other, more outstanding events in order to reconstruct the exact time and day (e.g. Baddeley, Lewis, & Nimmo-Smith, 1978). Accordingly, using public events, important personal memories or outstanding dates (such as New Year's Eve) as landmarks was found to reduce dating biases (e.g. Loftus & Marburger, 1983).

Without a chance to relate a recalled event to a well-dated landmark, time dating is likely to reflect both 'forward' and 'backward telescoping'. That is, distant events are assumed to have happened more recently than they did, whereas recent events are assumed to be more distant than they are (see Bradburn, Huttenlocher, & Hedges, 1994, for a review and theoretical model).

Respondents' estimation strategies

Given the inappropriateness of the 'recall and count' model, it is not surprising that respondents rely on different inference strategies to arrive at an estimate. Sudman et al. (1996) review these strategies and discuss how researchers can use them to their advantage. The most important strategies involve the decomposition of the recall problem into subparts, reliance on subjective theories of stability and change, and the use of information provided by the response alternatives.

Decomposition strategies

Many recall problems become easier when the recall task is decomposed into several subtasks (e.g. Blair & Burton, 1987). To estimate how often she has been eating out during the last three months, for example, a respondent may determine that she eats out about every weekend and had dinner at a restaurant this Wednesday, but apparently not the week before. Thus, she may infer that this makes four times a month for the weekends, and let's say twice for other occasions, resulting in about 'eighteen times during the last three months'. Estimates of this type are likely to be accurate if the respondent's inference rule is adequate, and if exceptions to the usual behaviour are rare.

In the absence of these fortunate conditions, however, decomposition strategies are likely to result in overestimates, reflecting the fact that people usually overestimate the occurrence of low-frequency events and underestimate the occurrence of high-frequency events (see Fiedler & Armbruster, 1994). As a result, asking for estimates of a global, and hence frequent, category (e.g. 'eating out') is likely to elicit an underestimate, whereas asking for estimates of a narrow, and hence rare, category (e.g. 'eating at a Mexican restaurant') is likely to elicit an overestimate. So the observation that decomposition usually results in higher estimates does not necessarily reflect better recall.

Subjective theories

A particularly important inference strategy is based on subjective theories of stability and change (see Ross, 1989, for a review). In answering retrospective questions, respondents often use their current behaviour or opinion as a benchmark and invoke an implicit theory of self to assess whether their past behaviour or opinion was similar to, or different from, their present behaviour or opinion. Assuming, for example, that one's political beliefs become more conservative over the life-span, adults may infer that they held more liberal political attitudes as teenagers than they do now (Markus, 1986). The resulting reports of previous opinions and behaviours are correct to the extent that the implicit theory is accurate.

In many domains, individuals assume a rather high degree of stability, resulting in underestimates of the degree of change that has occurred over time. Accordingly, retrospective estimates of income (Withey, 1954), or of tobacco, marijuana and alcohol consumption (Collins, Graham, Hansen, & Johnson, 1985) were found to be heavily influenced by respondents' income or consumption habits at the time of interview. On the other hand, when respondents have reason to believe in change, they will detect change, even though none has occurred (see Ross, 1989).

Response alternatives

A particularly important source of information that respondents use in arriving at an estimate is provided by the questionnaire itself. In many studies, respondents are asked to report their behaviour by choosing the appropriate alternative from a list of response alternatives of the type shown in Table 3.1. While the selected alternative is assumed to inform the researcher about the respondent's behaviour, it is frequently overlooked that a given set of response alternatives may be far more than a simple 'measurement device'. It may also constitute a source of information for the respondent (see Schwarz, 1994; Schwarz & Hippler, 1991, for reviews), as we saw in the section on question comprehension. Specifically, respondents assume that the range of the response alternatives provided to them reflects the researcher's knowledge of, or expectations about, the distribution of the behaviour in the 'real world'. Accordingly, they assume that the values in the middle range of the scale reflect the 'average' or 'usual' behavioural frequency, whereas the extremes of the scale correspond to the extremes of the distribution. Given this

Table 3.1 *Reported daily TV consumption as a function of response alternatives*

Low-frequency alternatives	%	High-frequency alternatives	%
Up to 0.5 hrs	7.4	Up to 2.5 hrs	62.5
0.5–1 hr	17.7	2.5–3 hrs	23.4
1–1.5 hrs	26.5	3–3.5 hrs	7.8
1.5–2 hrs	14.7	3.5–4 hrs	4.7
2–2.5 hrs	17.7	4–4.5 hrs	1.6
More than 2.5 hrs	16.2	More than 4.5 hrs	0.0

N = 132.

Source: adapted from Schwarz, Hippler, Deutsch, & Strack (1985). Reprinted by permission.

assumption, respondents can use the range of the response alternatives as a frame of reference in estimating their own behavioural frequency.

This strategy results in higher estimates along scales that present high- rather than low-frequency response alternatives, as shown in Table 3.1. In this study (Schwarz, Hippler, Deutsch, & Strack, 1985), only 16.2 per cent of a sample of German respondents reported watching TV for more than 2.5 hours a day when the scale presented low-frequency response alternatives, whereas 37.5 per cent reported doing so when the scale presented high-frequency response alternatives. Similar results have been obtained for a wide range of different behaviours (see Schwarz, 1990, for a review).

In addition to affecting respondents' behavioural reports, response alternatives may also affect subsequent comparative judgements. For example, a frequency of '2.5 hrs a day' constitutes a high response on the low-frequency scale, but a low response on the high-frequency scale shown in Table 3.1. A respondent who chooses this alternative may therefore infer that her own TV consumption is above average in the former case, but below average in the latter. As a result, Schwarz et al. (1985) observed that respondents were less satisfied with the variety of things they do in their leisure time when the low-frequency scale suggested that they watch more TV than most other people (see Schwarz, 1990, for a review).

To avoid these systematic influences of response alternatives, it is advisable to ask frequency questions in an open response format, such as, 'How many hours a day do you watch TV? ___ hours per day.' Note that such an open format needs to specify the relevant units of measurement, e.g. 'hours per day' to avoid answers like 'a few'.

As another alternative, researchers are often tempted to use vague quantifiers, such as 'sometimes', 'frequently', and so on. This, however, is the worst possible choice (see Pepper, 1981, for a review). Most importantly, the same expression denotes different frequencies in different content domains. Thus, 'frequently' suffering from headaches reflects higher absolute frequencies than 'frequently' suffering from heart attacks. Moreover, different respondents use the same term to denote different objective frequencies of the same behaviour. For example, suffering from headaches 'occasionally' denotes a higher frequency for respondents with a medical history of megrim than for respondents without that megrim history. Accordingly, the use of vague quantifiers reflects the objective frequency relative to respondents' subjective standard, rendering vague quantifiers inadequate for the assessment of objective frequencies, despite the popularity of their use.

Summary

The findings reviewed in this section emphasize that retrospective behavioural reports are rarely based on adequate recall of relevant episodes. Rather, the obtained reports are to a large degree theory driven: respondents are likely to begin with some fragmented recall of the behaviour under study and to apply various inference rules to arrive at a reasonable estimate. Moreover, if quantitative response alternatives are provided, they are likely to use them as a frame of reference, resulting in systematic biases. Although researchers have developed a number of strategies to facilitate recall (which are described in Sudman et al.'s *Thinking about Answers*, 1996, and the contributions in Schwarz & Sudman, 1994), it is important to keep in mind that the best we can hope for is a reasonable estimate, unless the behaviour is rare and of considerable importance to respondents.

Next, we turn to questions about respondents' attitudes and opinions.

Asking questions about attitudes: the emergence of context effects

The goal of many surveys is to learn about the distribution of opinions in a population by collecting reports from a representative sample. The extent to which the collected data do indeed inform us about the opinions held in the population depends crucially on the research instrument used. As we saw in the discussion of respondents' tasks, respondents' interpretation of a question, or the information they draw on in forming a judgement, may be strongly influenced by the specific wording of the question or by the content of preceding questions. As a result, the research instrument may draw respondents' attention to aspects they might otherwise not consider, or may bring information to mind that would otherwise go unnoticed. If so, the answers obtained from the sample do not reflect the opinions held in the population, because the answers are influenced by specific features of the research instrument that the population is not exposed to. Survey researchers refer to such influences of the research instrument as *response effects* or *context effects* (see Bradburn, 1983; Schuman & Presser, 1981, for reviews). Response effects are usually considered to be a component of measurement error, and hence were termed 'response errors' in the older literature. However, this is a somewhat misleading term in the case of attitude measurement. Whereas reports about behaviours or events can – at least in principle – be verified, attitude reports always reflect subjective evaluative judgements. Human judgement, however, is *always* context dependent. In essence, 'context free' judgements do not exist and the context effects that emerge in survey research reflect essential aspects of the nature of human judgement. Accordingly, if we want to talk of 'errors' in attitude measurement at all, we can only do so relative to what we were trying to do in the questionnaire, not relative to any objective standard that reflects respondents' 'true' attitudes.

A major source of context effects in survey measurement is the content of preceding questions, as numerous studies have demonstrated (see Schuman & Presser, 1981; Schwarz & Sudman, 1992; Tourangeau & Rasinski, 1988, for research examples and reviews). Sudman et al.'s (1996) *Thinking about Answers* provides a detailed discussion of different sources of context effects in the light of psychological theorizing. Unfortunately, a full discussion of this material is beyond the scope of the present chapter. Instead, I draw on one selected example to introduce basic theoretical principles and to illustrate the impact of question context on the results obtained in surveys as well as the psychological laboratory.

Information accessibility and use

As many psychological experiments have documented, individuals are unlikely to retrieve all information that may potentially bear on a judgement; instead they truncate the search process as soon as enough information has come to mind to form a judgement with sufficient subjective certainty (see Bodenhausen & Wyer, 1987; Schwarz, 1995, for reviews). Accordingly, their judgements strongly reflect the impact of the information that is most accessible in memory at the time of judgement. This is usually the information that has been used most recently, for example for the purpose of answering a preceding question.

The specific impact of the information that comes to mind depends on how it is used. In general, evaluative judgements require a mental representation of the target (i.e. the object of judgement) as well as a mental representation of some standard, against which the target is evaluated. If the information that comes to mind is included in the representation formed of the target, it results in an *assimilation effect*. That is, including a piece of information that has positive (negative) implications results in a more positive (negative) judgement. If the accessible information is excluded from the representation of the target, it may be used in constructing a representation of the standard. In this case, it results in a *contrast effect*. This reflects the fact that the inclusion of some very positive (or negative) information in the representation of the standard results in a more positive (or negative) standard, relative to which the target is evaluated more negatively (or more positively, respectively). Schwarz and Bless's (1992; see also Sudman et al., 1996, Chapter 5) inclusion/exclusion model of evaluative judgement provides a detailed conceptualization of these processes.

Marital satisfaction and the quality of one's life

Suppose that respondents are asked to evaluate how satisfied they are with their life as a whole. In social science research, questions about life satisfaction are used to gauge the well-being of a population and to monitor the subjective impact of social change (see Campbell, 1981; Strack, Argyle, & Schwarz, 1991, for reviews). To answer a life-satisfaction question, respondents may draw on a variety of different aspects of their lives and may evaluate them against a variety of different standards. Which aspects they actually draw on, however, may be influenced by which aspects were brought to mind by preceding questions.

In a test of this possibility, Schwarz, Strack and Mai (1991; see also Strack, Martin, & Schwarz, 1988) asked respondents to report their marital satisfaction and their general life satisfaction and varied the order in which these questions were asked. The results are shown in Table 3.2. When the general satisfaction question preceded the marital satisfaction question, both questions were correlated $r = 0.32$, suggesting that marital satisfaction contributes moderately to one's overall well-being. When the question order was reversed, however, this correlation increased to $r = 0.67$, suggesting that marital satisfaction is a major determinant of overall well-being. This increase in correlation illustrates that answering the marital satisfaction question brought information about one's marriage to mind, which respondents included in the representation that they formed of their lives in general.

If so, the increase in correlation should be less pronounced when the preceding questions bring a more varied set of information to mind, as may be the case when respondents are asked to report on their work and leisure time in addition to their marriage. Consistent with this assumption, the observed increase in the correlation of marital satisfaction and general life satisfaction was less pronounced, $r = 0.46$, and not significant, when questions about *several* specific life domains preceded the general one. This reflects that the impact of a given piece of information, e.g. pertaining to one's marriage, decreases as the amount of accessible competing information increases (see Schwarz & Bless, 1992).

However, highly accessible information is not always included in the representation formed of the target (in the present case, the target 'my life'). One of the many variables that discourages inclusion (see Schwarz & Bless, 1992, for a discussion of other variables) is the conversational norm of nonredundancy. Specifically, one of the principles that govern the conduct of conversation in everyday life (Grice, 1975) requests speakers to make their contribution as informative as is required for the purpose of the conversation, but not more informative than is required. In particular, speakers are not supposed to be redundant or to provide information that the respondent already has (e.g. Clark & Schober, 1992). Hence, respondents may hesitate to reiterate information that they have already provided in response to a preceding question. Accordingly, respondents who have just reported their marital happiness may consider the subsequent question about their happiness with life as a whole to be a request for *new* information. They may therefore

Table 3.2 *Correlation of general life satisfaction and marital satisfaction*

Condition	
Life–marriage	0.32
Marriage–life	0.67
Work, leisure, marriage – life	0.46
Marriage–life, with joint lead-in	0.18
Marriage–life, 'aside . . .'	0.20

Shown are Pearson correlations. N = 50 per cell.

Source: adapted from Schwarz, Strack, & Mai (1991). Reprinted by permission.

interpret the general question to refer to *other* aspects of their life, much as if it were worded, 'Aside from your marriage, how happy do you feel about the other aspects of your life?'

To test this possibility, Schwarz et al. (1991; see also Strack et al., 1988) explicitly assigned both questions to the same conversational context, by introducing them with a joint lead-in that read, 'Now, we would like to learn about two areas of life that may be important for people's overall well-being: (a) happiness with marriage; and (b) happiness with life in general.' Subsequently, both happiness questions were asked in the specific–general order, which had resulted in a correlation of $r = 0.67$ without this introduction. When both questions were introduced by a joint lead-in, however, this correlation dropped to a nonsignificant $r = 0.18$. This shows that respondents deliberately ignored information that they had already provided in response to a specific question when making a subsequent general judgement when the joint lead-in evoked the conversational norm of nonredundancy. In this case, respondents apparently interpreted the general question as if it referred to aspects of their life that they had not yet reported on. In line with this interpretation, a condition in which respondents were explicitly asked how satisfied they are with 'other aspects' of their life, 'aside from their relationship', yielded a nearly identical correlation of $r = 0.20$.

As the range of obtained correlations between identical questions, from $r = 0.18$ to $r = 0.67$, illustrates, we would draw very different conclusions from the answers given to two identically worded questions, depending on the order in which they were asked and whether or not they were introduced by a joint lead-in. Moreover, this impact of question order is not limited to the obtained correlations but is also reflected in respondents' mean reported life satisfaction, as we shall see below.

Mean differences: the conditionality of context effects

In examining the impact of question order on the obtained means, it is important to keep in mind that the preceding question *per se* does not do

Table 3.3 *Mean reported general life satisfaction*

	Respondents		
	Unhappily married	Happily married	All
Condition			
Life–marriage	6.8	8.5	8.3
Marriage–life	5.8	9.5	8.7
Work, leisure, marriage			
– life	7.1	9.1	8.6
Marriage–life, with joint lead-in	8.0	8.5	8.3

Ratings were on an 11-point scale, with 11 = 'very satisfied'.
Source: as Table 3.2. Reprinted by permission.

anything. Rather, it is the information that is brought to mind by the preceding question that has an impact. Thus, asking a question about marital satisfaction brings information about one's marriage to mind and the implications of this information may be positive or negative, depending upon the specifics of one's marriage.

As an example, let us consider the unhappily married respondents, i.e. the third of the sample that reported the lowest marital satisfaction. As shown in the first column of Table 3.3, these respondents reported lower general life satisfaction when the preceding question brought their marriage to mind ($M = 5.8$ on an 11-point scale) than when the life-satisfaction question was asked first ($M = 6.8$). Moreover, this decrease was not obtained ($M = 7.1$) when several specific questions were asked, reflecting that these questions brought (relatively) more enjoyable domains of life to mind. Finally, they reported higher life satisfaction when the joint lead-in ($M = 8.0$) induced them to disregard their marriage. The reports of happily married respondents (i.e. the third of the sample reporting the highest marital satisfaction), shown in the second column of Table 3.3, provided a mirror image of these findings.

However, none of these differences could be observed in the sample as a whole, as shown in the third column. This reflects that the opposite effects observed for unhappily and happily married respondents cancelled one another, with the third of the sample that reported moderate marital satisfaction adding additional noise. Had we only considered the sample as a whole, we would have concluded that question order had no impact. In this case, we could only have seen any differences if the unhappily married respondents outnumbered the happily married ones in our sample, or vice versa. It is therefore important that our analyses take respondents' substantive answers to preceding questions into account. This may be achieved by inspecting measures of association (such as the correlation coefficients reported above) or by conducting conditional analyses, as shown in Table 3.3. Unfortunately, context effects are often overlooked in survey research because their conditional nature is ignored in routine analyses (see Smith, 1992, for a more extended discussion).

On first glance, the finding that context effects may cancel one another in heterogeneous samples may suggest that they pose less of a problem to survey research than one might assume. This conclusion, however, is misleading. Although the mutual cancellation of context effects may result in a reasonably accurate estimate of the average opinion in the sample as a whole, it undermines comparisons of subgroups as well as the analysis of the relationship among different variables, which is at the heart of most scientific uses of survey data.

Summary

As the selected example illustrates, the order in which related questions are asked, either in the psychological laboratory or in opinion surveys, may greatly influence the obtained results. In fact, these influences may be so pronounced that researchers may draw opposite conclusions about the same substantive relationship, depending on the order in which they ask the relevant questions (see Schwarz & Bless, 1992; Schwarz & Sudman, 1992, for numerous examples). These effects reflect the impact of question order on question comprehension, information accessibility and information use. While much remains to be learned about these processes and their implications for survey research, there has been considerable progress in this field in recent years. The current state of knowledge is reviewed in Sudman et al.'s *Thinking about Answers* (1996), which provides a detailed introduction to the cognitive and communicative processes involved in survey measurement.

The present chapter has reviewed key elements of survey research, focusing on whom to ask and how to ask. The most important advice on whom to ask is to secure the help of a professional sampling statistician in drawing a representative sample. Accordingly, how to ask was covered in considerably more detail than whom to ask. Answering a survey question requires that respondents understand the question, retrieve relevant information from memory, form a judgement, format the judgement according to the response alternatives provided to them and report it to the researcher. Performance at each of these tasks is highly context dependent. Understanding the underlying cognitive and communicative processes, however, allows us to anticipate sources of systematic bias and to facilitate respondents' performance. In the case of behavioural reports, the research instrument may influence respondents' choice of recall and estimation strategies. In the case of attitude reports, the research instrument may influence the accessibility and use of information that respondents draw on in forming a judgement. It is therefore important to keep in mind that the obtained responses — in surveys as well as experiments — are always to some extent a function of the specific research instrument used.

Further reading

Numerous textbooks on survey research are available. As a general introduction, written for consumers of survey data with no prior knowledge of social science research methods, I recommend Bradburn and Sudman's *Polls and surveys: Understanding what they tell us* (1988).

A more technical, but very readable, introduction at the level of an advanced undergraduate textbook is provided by Weisberg, Krosnick and Bowen's *An introduction to survey research and data analysis* (1989).

More detailed treatments of numerous special topics can be found in Rossi, Wright and Anderson's *Handbook of survey research* (1983).

Bradburn and Sudman's *Asking questions. A practical guide to questionnaire design* (1983) offers hands-on advice on questionnaire construction and is the most useful compilation of survey researchers' accumulated wisdom on the topic.

Our current knowledge about the cognitive and communicative processes underlying responses to attitude questions and behavioural questions is reviewed in Sudman, Bradburn and Schwarz's *Thinking about answers: The application of cognitive processes to survey methodology* (1996), which provides detailed discussions of relevant psychological theorizing.

Conway's *Autobiographical memory: An introduction* (1990) offers an excellent introduction to this topic. Implications of autobiographical memory for survey research and the validity of behavioural reports are explored in the contributions to Schwarz and Sudman's *Autobiographical memory and the validity of retrospective reports* (1994).

Research on context effects in attitude measurement is reviewed in Schuman and Presser's classic volume *Questions and answers in attitude surveys* (1981) and the contributions to Schwarz and Sudman's *Context effects in social and psychological research* (1992).

4

Language in Applied Contexts

Klaus Fiedler and Gün R. Semin

Contents

One of the uncharted territories in applied social psychology is the systematic examination of the role that language plays in applied contexts. This is surprising if one considers the centrality of language in communication, which is at the heart of most of the issues in applied social psychology. This can be exemplified in abundance. Take, for instance, the patient–doctor communication in health-related contexts (cf. Chapter 5); the courtroom which constitutes the battleground for the skilful use of words in the pursuit of innocence or guilt (cf. Chapter 10); the mass media in which words are used to convey messages with an impact (cf. Chapter 12); political contexts of persuasion or conflict, negotiation or bargaining (cf. Chapter 11); close personal relationships where the expression of tenderness or distance is mediated by words; the use of language in expressing our attitudes (cf. Chapter 1); in therapy, in diagnoses, and so on. The list is endless. Language and language use is central to most if not all subjects that one can think of in an applied context and the surprising fact is that language receives so little systematic treatment within any of the multiple areas in which applied social psychology can be visualized.

Essentially, language can be treated as a tool (Semin, 1995), much like a chisel or a hammer, that is used to give shape to an intention, goal or desire. Such intentions, goals or desires have to be expressed in a communicative context such as an interview, a courtroom, an argument, a negotiation, or in order to convey an ailment or passion. The goal of this chapter is to provide an overview of how we deploy verbal tools strategically in the pursuit of such goals, intentions and desires, in a variety of contexts that are highly relevant to our daily lives.

One reason for the elusive nature of language research in applied contexts is that the diverse linguistic strategies that we employ are often too subtle and escape our conscious attention. Language use is a habitualized activity. For instance, men are generally not aware of the fact that they employ a sexist language style (for an overview, see Todd & Fisher, 1988). Defence attorneys would be hard pressed if they were asked to identify the differences between their style of language use and that of prosecutors, despite the fact that both are talking about the same defendant's behaviour in the same court case (Catellani, Pajardi, Galardi, & Semin, 1995; Schmid & Fiedler, 1996). And the same typically holds of politicians, therapists, and even advertising experts who may employ specific strategies consistently and often successfully without any meta-knowledge about the rules underlying their linguistic skills.

These observations become all the more important if one considers that the plasticity of language enables the same intention to be communicated in a variety of different ways. It therefore becomes interesting to consider why particular performers resort to one strategic expression or communication style in specific situations rather than another – consciously or unconsciously. Furthermore, it seems that, in order for a particular strategic use of language to be effective, it is critical that the linguistic strategy remain undetected or unconscious. The explicit and conscious availability of knowledge of such verbal strategies may in fact hinder their skilful performance. One reason is that the availability of such knowledge may hamper its spontaneous production, since the conscious monitoring of verbal performance may interfere with the production process. The other reason is that the conscious discovery of a linguistic strategy undermines its effectiveness by immunizing the receiver to its impact.

For instance, imagine that linguists or psychologists discover a highly effective verbal strategy for persuasion, ingratiation or deception. The strategy loses its effectiveness as soon as it is explicitly formulated. Once such knowledge is available explicitly and publicly, then people become immunized to it and the strategy loses its power. Consequently, language users would have to develop and learn new strategies that preserve their power until such time as they are unmasked again. As this example shows, there is always something creative and inventive in adaptive verbal communication. However paradoxical it sounds, while strategic language use is only possible as a convention, it nevertheless has to remain unconscious and implicit in order to preserve its power. One should not be surprised that even people who are highly skilled in rhetoric may not be fully aware of the verbal strategies they use regularly.

This chapter is devoted to a body of research that illustrates, explains and measures a number of subtle language tools that are often used unconsciously. We shall present the strategic use of these linguistic tools with reference to their characteristic fields of application or use. The chapter will cover a range of applied areas, each of which serves to illustrate specific principles of language use. Although the pertinent research has often developed in the psychological laboratory, a number of recent studies have extrapolated the empirical evidence to investigate the uses of linguistic tools in real settings.

Table 4.1 *Summary of topics and concepts covered in this chapter*

Field of application	Specific issues	Theories and methods
Interpersonal behaviour and personal health	Partner satisfaction	Attribution theory
	Identity management	Action identification theory
	Medical decisions	Framing illusions
Intergroup relations	Outgroup discrimination	Linguistic intergroup bias
	Group identity	Discourse analysis
	Dialects	Linguistic category model
	Sexist language	Speech accommodation theory
		Hedging and lexical choice
Social influence	Advertising	Elaboration likelihood model
	Camouflaging	Nominalization
	Deception	Lens model analysis
Juridical decision	Eyewitness testimony	Presuppositions
	Courtroom discourse	Leading questions
	Interrogation	Implicit verb causality
	Lie detection	Cognitive interview

Table 4.1 provides an overview of the topics that are covered in this chapter. The four broader fields of application in the left column are split into finer topics in the middle column. Column 3 indicates some of the associated theoretical and methodological concepts. As is evident from the table, this chapter has been organized along pragmatical lines. That is, it is structured in terms of the different fields of application rather than by theoretical principles or levels of analysis, such as the lexical, propositional or discourse levels.

Language and well-being

One of the interesting indications that language plays an important role in health-related issues comes from the field of traumatic experiences and health. Numerous investigations have demonstrated that the linguistic representation of a traumatic, strong or novel emotional experience leads to improved health. Thus if people who have experienced a powerful emotional experience are asked to write an essay about it, they exhibit superior health as a consequence when compared to persons who write essays about nonemotional events. The measures that have been utilized to assess health improvement include reduction in subsequent visits to physicians (e.g. Pennebaker, Kiecolt-Glaser, & Glaser, 1988) and response to latent Epstein-Barr virus reactivation (Esterling, Antoni, Fletcher, Marguiles, & Schneiderman, 1994).

One of the explanatory models was that not talking about the emotional experience, or not confronting it, was in itself stressful. This inhibition model (Pennebaker, 1989) has not been supported by empirical evidence. More recent research has focused on the role that representing an emotional experience in language plays in inducing cognitive changes (e.g. Murray, Lamnin, & Carver, 1989). It is undoubtedly the case that there is a link between representing a new and powerful emotional event in language and its health consequences. What future research in this field has yet to clarify is the precise nature of the relationship between the linguistic representation of such events in writing or talking and its health consequences.

Attribution and partner satisfaction

No other topic has attracted so much interest in social psychology as attribution research, and it is no wonder that attribution is also of central importance to applied psychology. However, as several authors have acknowledged (Antaki, 1981; Fiedler & Semin, 1992; Hilton, 1990), attribution is to a large extent conveyed through language, even though language users are rarely aware of their implicit attributions. In Fritz Heider's (1958) seminal writings, it was clearly recognized that ability or effort attributions have to do with the subtle implications of linguistic terms, such as 'can' and 'try'. When Heider introduced the concept of attribution as everyday thinking about the origins and causes of behaviour, he was well aware of the central role of language.

Although this part of Heider's message was almost forgotten for two decades, it is now being rediscovered and the fact that attributional styles and strategies are built into language is being recognized. For example, consider the vast body of evidence on the factors that discriminate between distressed and non-distressed couples (Fincham, 1985; Weary, Stanley, & Harvey, 1989). A reliable predictor of dissatisfaction, and even divorce, is a global attributional style that highlights stable, internal, uncontrollable causes within the persons themselves, as opposed to external circumstances or stressors. Quite analogous to the role of attribution in the genesis of depression and learned helplessness (Abramson, Seligman, & Teasdale, 1978), marital distress and partnership conflicts are fostered by the attribution of stress and failure to global and stable causes within the partner's personality. A particularly distress-prone attribution pattern involves global, dispositional attributions of negative partner behaviours and positive own behaviours, as compared with local, external attributions of positive partner behaviours and negative behaviours of oneself. For instance, the typically dissatisfied spouse would not simply blame the partner for the cold emotional climate, constant arguments and lack of delightful leisure activities. He or she would attribute these negative experiences to stable personality factors that promise little change over time. Moreover, the asymmetric tendency to attribute more stable negative characteristics to one's partner rather than one's self affords a permanent source of conflict that serves to perpetuate problems that already exist.

Translated into language behaviour, this unfortunate attribution syndrome amounts to a tendency to use abstract, dispositional trait terms in describing one's partner's negative and one's own positive behaviours, and to use much more specific terms and many adverbial qualifications and references to the situation in descriptions of one's own negative and one's partner's positive behaviours. Thus, using words like arrogant or selfish to blame one's partner (while interpreting the same behaviour in oneself as simply laughing and continuing talking) will inhibit conflict resolution, because trait adjectives do not clearly specify a behavioural prescription that could help to overcome the undesirable situation. Imperatives like 'Don't be so selfish!' or 'Stop being so arrogant!' are difficult to comply with, even when the partner is willing to comply, simply because the behavioural references are too diffuse. A study by Fiedler, Semin and Koppetsch (1991) suggests that, regardless of valence, there is a general tendency to describe one's partner in more abstract terms than oneself. This tendency can account for the joint occurrence of two opposing attribution biases, the so-called actor observer bias (i.e. more internal, dispositional attributions to others than to the self; Jones & Davis, 1965; Watson, 1982) at the level of abstract adjectives, and an egocentric bias (i.e. more internal attributions of responsibility to the self than others; Ross & Sicoly, 1979) at the level of concrete behaviour descriptions. Thus, regardless of valence, there is a tendency to attribute dispositions like arrogant or helpful to the partner, while at the same time claiming to contribute more than one's partner to various activities, like organizing leisure time, or starting discussion. The latter, egocentric bias has been shown to correlate with dissatisfaction in personal relationships (Fiedler et al., 1991; Thompson & Kelley, 1981).

One might wonder if the differential language styles that characterize distressed and non-distressed couples are merely a reflection of different attributions, rather than linguistic phenomena in their own right. However, self–other differences in language use have been shown to generalize far beyond the specific attribution effects. Thus, even when subjects are simply asked to describe others, with no explanation or attribution involved, they exhibit the same differential language use. Moreover, as will be seen in the next section, virtually equivalent language differences can be found in descriptions of ingroup versus outgroup behaviours, suggesting a basic perspective bias in verbal behaviour that is not merely a symptom but may be an essential determinant of pathogenic attribution. Granting the central role of attributions, and that attributions are mainly manifested in language, it seems worth basing therapeutic efforts on a modification of language style.

Action identification theory (Vallacher, Wegner, & Frederick, 1987) provides an interesting theoretical framework for the 'healthy' attributional biases that govern satisfied social relationships. In free verbalizations, people normally describe success at a higher level of behaviour identification (e.g. 'saving the drowning person', 'creating art') than failure (e.g. 'jumping into the water', 'drawing on paper'). High action identification of successful behaviours fosters the inference of positive internal personality attributes (courage, creativity). Departure from this self-serving tendency in attributional language affords a diagnostic symptom of pathogenic development.

Medical decisions

Effective communication and subtle linguistic factors play an influential part in medical decisions, too. A number of investigators have pointed out the importance of clear, empathic and patient-oriented language in medical treatment (Hinckley, Craig, & Anderson, 1990; Roter, 1984) and its impact on the patient's satisfaction and cooperation in the therapeutic process. In a typical investigation by Stiles (1979), medical interviews were analysed in terms of eight discourse categories: disclosure, question, edification, acknowledgement, advisement, interpretation, confirmation and reflection. Patient satisfaction was correlated, for example, with an exposition exchange pattern in which patients can start with their own stories while physicians encourage them with empathic responses (i.e. patient edifications and disclosures followed by physician acknowledgements).

While the method advanced by Stiles is based on the interpretation of discourse units or speech acts, other researchers have relied on simpler observation techniques requiring less subjective interpretation. For instance, Roter (1984) has modified the well-known Bales (1968) interaction analysis to meet the special requirements of the physician–patient interaction. In essence, the patient's as well as the physician's behaviour is observed and coded for categories of affectively positive communication (e.g. shows approval, agreement, personal remarks), negative communication (e.g. shows disagreement), and neutral items (e.g. gives information or opinion, gives instruction, requests medication, asks direct questions). Using this method, active patient participation is shown to be positively related to satisfaction. This general finding suggests that verbal communication provides an important component of medical success. Even when a somewhat extended medical interview increases the momentary treatment costs, it may actually help to reduce the costs of health care in the long run.

The necessity to communicate effectively about the patient's health situation and the causes and consequences of his or her disease is highlighted in a study by McNeil, Pauker and Tversky (1988), who were concerned with the impact of verbal framing on existential decisions. In one study, they confronted American medical students in a radiology course and students of medical and natural sciences in Israel with (fictitious) decisions about how to treat lung cancer. After they were informed about the two therapeutic alternatives – radiation and operation – the participants received statistical information on the lethal risk associated with these alternatives. The crucial manipulation pertained to the verbal framing of the risk information.

In the survival condition, the statistical information was framed in terms of positive survival outcomes. Participants learned that of 100 patients whose lung cancer is treated by surgery, 90 survive the operation, 68 are still alive after one year, and 34 have overcome the disease after five years. For comparison, if treated by radiation, all 100 people survive the treatment, 77 are still living after one year, and 22 survive the katamnestic test after five years. Given such a verbal focus on positive outcomes, the vast majority of respondents (88 per cent) favour surgery over radiation.

In contrast, when the same risk data are reframed in terms of mortality, or the complementary negative outcomes, the preferences change dramatically. Thus, when participants learn that mortality rates (out of 100) after surgery are 10 (immediately), 32 (after one year), and 66 (after five years), whereas mortality after radiation amounts to 0 (immediately), 23 (one year), and 78 (five years), only 53 per cent of the respondents favour surgery, while the preference for conservative therapy raises from 18 per cent to 47 per cent, even though the statistical data are exactly the same. These findings, like many related phenomena that highlight the importance of verbal framing in decision and choice, can be explained by the assumption of an S-shaped subjective value function as specified in prospect theory (cf. Kahneman & Tversky, 1984; see also Chapter 2). Such a function implies that with increasing gains or losses, the increments in positive or negative value become smaller and smaller; that is, the function is negatively accelerated. Therefore, the difference in the five-year survival rate after surgery and radiation appears much more significant in the survival condition (34 per cent vs. 22 per cent) than the complementary difference in the mortality condition (66 per cent vs. 78 per cent), simply because the same 12 per cent gains or losses are worth less in the range above 60 per cent than in the lower range around 30 per cent.

Although the explanations derived from prospect theory refer to a subjective value function in the first place, it is important to note that the psychologically significant implications of such modern decision theories draw heavily on the role of language and symbolic representations of decision alternatives. Many violations of rational norms in decision making, like the above preference reversal, would hardly occur if we had an unambiguous communication code for risks and probabilities, and if the translation of statistical data into ordinary language had not become an essential part of politics, decisions and public discussions.

For an even more striking illustration (taken from Gigerenzer & Hoffrage, 1995), consider the following two modes of conversing about the risk of breast cancer. In terms of the common probability format, you may be told that the base rate that a woman aged about 40 has breast cancer is 1 per cent, the hit rate of the common diagnostic instrument (i.e. the probability of a positive mammography if a woman really has breast cancer) is 80 per cent and the false-alarm rate (i.e. the probability of a positive mammography if the woman has no breast cancer) is 9.6 per cent. What is the probability that a woman whose mammography in a (non-selective) screening test happens to be positive actually has breast cancer?

A large majority of people who converse about this statistical problem dramatically overestimate the conditional probability of breast cancer. The normatively appropriate answer, according to Bayesian statistics, is 7.8 per cent. While this may be surprising, it is no less surprising that many people reach a much better understanding of the underlying statistics and arrive at accurate estimates if the same problem is phrased in a frequency format rather than the impairing probability format. For example, imagine you are told that there are 1,000 women altogether, of whom 10 (1 per cent) have breast cancer. Moreover, 8 of these 10 women get a positive mammography (80 per cent hit rate), but 95 of the 990 women who have no breast cancer will also get a positive mammography (9.6 per cent false-alarm rate). Given this framing, you will easily acknowledge that you only have to estimate the ratio of the eight people who have breast cancer and a positive mammography to all 8+95 people with a positive mammography.

Under realistic conditions, the conditional probability after positive diagnostic tests may be much higher if the patient sample is selective (e.g. because the patients already feel symptoms or pain). Moreover, the difference between hit and false-alarm rates can be sharply enhanced by conducting several parallel tests of the same patient. Remarkably, however, the fact remains that talking about frequencies regularly activates different routines of thinking (cf. Gigerenzer, 1991b) than talking about probabilities which are rarely given a frequentist interpretation in ordinary language. The term 'probability' refers to degrees of subjective confidence and beliefs in singular events as opposed to relative frequencies of repeated events. In contrast, the term 'frequency' primes people into extensional thinking about statistical samples and distributions of events.

Language and intergroup relations

Just as interpersonal conflicts may be due to conflict-prone language styles, as illustrated with reference to distressed couples, conflicts on the intergroup level are also manifested in, and supported by, characteristic language styles and language repertoires. After all, many ethnic prejudices or group stereotypes are often communicated by and socialized through language, without direct contact with the target group. Moreover, many language games (jokes about Jews, women, handicapped people; linguistic repertoires for discriminating against gypsies or immigrants, or for insulting members of political parties or soccer clubs) serve the purpose of keeping discrimination and hostility alive, often in an ironic, playful manner.

Group stereotypes and discrimination

There is a long tradition of studies showing that language styles and dialects can influence impressions of, and prejudice against, social groups (Bradac, 1990). In Giles's speech accommodation theory a tendency is postulated that members of ingroups react favourably to outgroup members who linguistically converge with them (Giles, 1973; Giles, Mulac, Bradac, & Johnson, 1987). However, people's natural reaction to like those who talk like themselves is moderated by other factors. For instance, the ultimate reaction to speech convergence may depend on the intention attributed to the speaker (e.g. ingratiation or authentic sympathy). Language divergence or a distinctive language style may also be maintained to assert a positive ingroup identity (Tajfel & Turner, 1979).

Empirical research on the role of language in diagnosing, creating and maintaining group distinctions relies heavily on the development of appropriate methods and research instruments. One particularly ambitious instrument is discourse analysis, as proposed by Edwards and Potter (1992). The aim of this approach is to analyse language in its natural, discursive context, in order to capture the interests and intentions that underlie all everyday communication, with special attention given to the speech acts of blame, denial, excuse and mitigation (Edwards & Potter, 1993). Since there is no simple algorithm to extract speaker intentions and motives, this approach relies strongly on the researcher's intuition and participation.

In contrast to discourse analysis, which attempts to assess illocutions and perlocutions rather than only words or linguistic forms, a different approach is advanced by the Linguistic Category Model (LCM) that was developed by Semin and Fiedler (1988, 1991). This approach leads to a simpler and more reliable coding procedure at the lexical level that is much less dependent the researchers' subjective judgements and intuitive insights. The LCM is a linguistically based classification of the four major word classes in text or discourse about interpersonal events and persons. The main objective of this model is the identification of the diverse inferences that these four classes of interpersonal terms can channel when used in a variety of discursive contexts. The four categories in this model are: descriptive action verbs (DAV), interpretative action verbs (IAV), state verbs (SV) and adjectives (ADJ). Examples of these four categories, their defining features, and their most important cognitive implications are given in Table 4.2.

The same behaviour can be often described at different linguistic levels, and this freedom of choice provides the potential for linguistic strategies, manipulations and self-deceptions. For instance, the same aggressive episode may be downplayed and localized as 'pushing' or 'shouting' (DAV) when oneself or one's group is the actor, but raised to the IAV level ('hurting', 'insulting') or ADJ level ('brutal', 'mean') when the behaviour refers to others or to an outgroup. Note that this tactical (self-serving or group-serving) choice of linguistic abstractness corresponds closely to the conflict-prone attribution styles in distressed couples already mentioned.

In several applications of LCM analyses to intergroup language, Maass and her colleagues (Maass & Arcuri, 1992; Maass, Arcuri, Salvi, & Semin, 1989; Maass, Milesi, Zabbini and Stahlberg, 1995) have demonstrated the so-called linguistic intergroup bias. This bias originates in the systematic utilization of the aforementioned strategy, namely, to use abstract language (ADJ, SV) for negative outgroup behaviours and positive ingroup behaviours, but to use more concrete terms (DAV, IAV) for positive outgroup and negative ingroup behaviours. Abstract terms imply temporal stability and trait-like dispositions within the sentence subject, whereas concrete terms imply less stability but emphasize the external, situational causes of behaviour. Therefore, the linguistic intergroup bias often serves to internalize ingroup assets and outgroup deficits, and to externalize ingroup deficits and outgroup assets.

In a series of studies, Maass et al. (1989) investigated the manner in which North Italian *palio* teams (*palio* is a competitive horse-riding game) described desirable and undesirable behaviours of members of their own team or of an opponent team. As expected, positive ingroup and negative outgroup statements were expressed at a higher level of linguistic abstractness than negative ingroup and positive outgroup statements. More recently, however, Maass et al. (1995) refined this linguistic-intergroup bias, demonstrating that the crucial factors underlying this bias are differential expectancies rather than

Table 4.2 *The classification of linguistic terms in the interpersonal domain and their classification criteria: the Linguistic Category Model*

Category	Examples	Characteristic features
Descriptive action verbs (DAV)	to call to meet to kick to kiss	Reference to single behavioural event; reference to specific object and situation; context essential for sentence comprehension; objective description of observable events

Classification criteria: refer to one particular activity and to a physically invariant feature of the action; action has clear beginning and end; in general do not have positive or negative semantic valence.

Category	Examples	Characteristic features
Interpretive action verbs (IAV)	to cheat to imitate to help to inhibit	Reference to single behavioural event; reference to specific object and situation; autonomous sentence comprehension; interpretation beyond description

Classification criteria: refer to general class of behaviours; have defined action with a clear beginning and end; have positive or negative semantic valence.

Category	Examples	Characteristic features
State verbs (SV)	to admire to hate to abhor to like	Enduring states, abstracted from single events; reference to a social object, but not situation; no context reference preserved; interpretation beyond mere description

Classification criteria: refer to mental and emotional states; no clear definition of beginning and end; do not take the progressive form; not freely used in imperatives.

Category	Examples	Characteristic features
Adjectives (ADJ)	honest impulsive reliable helpful	Highly abstract person disposition; no object or situation reference; no context reference; highly interpretive; detached from specific behaviours.

Sources: Semin & Fiedler (1988, 1991)

ingroup protection. Thus, positive ingroup behaviour is only raised to an abstract language level if it conforms to group-related expectancies. When expectancies suggest more negative ingroup than outgroup attributes, the linguistic intergroup bias will favour the outgroup.

In the context of political attitudes and social influence, a similar bias was demonstrated in the manner in which newspapers with a certain political affiliation report positive or negative events associated with their own group or preferred party, or an outgroup or opponent party (Maass, Corvino, & Arcuri, 1995). For instance, both Jewish and non-Jewish newspapers reported on anti-Semitic aggression in Italy in negative terms, but the non-Jewish newspapers formulated their negative statements in more concrete, less abstract language than their Jewish counterparts.

In general, then, the strategic use of linguistic categories provides a universal means of editing and optimizing one's utterances and public statements, in order to meet group interests and other motivational goals. While it would appear blatant and obtrusive to present one group in obviously more positive terms than the other, the subtle change of linguistic abstractness serves a similar purpose, but much more unobtrusively and presumably more efficiently.

Sexist language

One particularly prominent distinction in the social world is the ubiquitous grouping of people according to sex, or gender. While the term 'sex' refers to biological categories, 'gender' pertains to the different social roles associated with female and male people. Sex and gender differences have to be taken into account in socialization and education, marketing, television and politics. Two decades after the rise of the feminist movement, people have been sensitized to the disadvantaged and underprivileged status of women that still prevails in many modern societies. This has led to several changes in legislation, education, and has affected the job market, as well as giving rise to rules of non-sexist language, reflecting the insight that discrimination of women is partly due to crystallized language habits. As an illustration, the English language includes 220 terms for a sexually promiscuous female but only 20 for a sexually promiscuous male, although there are more words in the lexicon that refer to males than females (Ng, 1990). Gender differences are also prominent in conversation styles, with males interrupting females at a higher rate than vice versa, or females reacting more emotionally than men to conversation at the personal level.

In spite of, or because of, the enhanced cultural sensitivity to the gender groups issue, the instrument of language is multiplex and creative enough to offer various tools of subtle discrimination between gender groups. Not surprisingly, Fiedler, Semin and Finkenauer (1993) reported evidence of a similar type of linguistic intergroup bias that characterizes hostile or opposing groups. Analyses of free verbalizations provided by male and female speakers about males and females not only revealed a pattern of relative outgroup derogation and ingroup favouritism, but also the familiar tendency to raise stereotype-consistent statements on to a higher level of abstractness.

Closer inspection of verbalizations in different conversational categories (e.g. education of children, equality on the job, contraception, housework, car driving) has shown that the degree of discrimination is not higher in conflict-prone categories (e.g. equality on the job) than conflict-free categories (e.g. contraception). In fact, discrimination was most pronounced in certain unimportant topics (e.g. women as car drivers), which are only of symbolic value for the identification with one's gender group. It is often in these topics that people have acquired highly sophisticated language skills (words, jokes, material for conversation and small talk), providing efficient vehicles of gender discrimination.

Social influence through language

Modern approaches to persuasion and attitude change distinguish between two routes of communication (cf. Chapter 1): a central and a peripheral route (Petty & Cacioppo, 1986). While the central route is governed by the rules of consistency and argument quality, the peripheral route affords a channel for suggestive, irrational and emotional forces in social influence. Research has shown that receivers of a verbal message who are not distracted, highly involved and high in a personality trait called need for cognition give more attention to the central route. In contrast, when receivers are distracted, uninvolved or in euphoric mood, they are more amenable to cues conveyed via the peripheral route, such as the attractiveness of the communicator, conditioned associations (fear, erotic appeals), or sympathetic jargon or dialect.

Attempts to use verbal influence in advertising, medical consulting or political campaigns have to take these differences into account. In general, higher weight should be placed on peripheral cues (associated affect, erotic stimuli, mere visibility) when advertising is directed at ill-informed consumers, whereas more weight should be given to the central route (i.e. to arguments about product quality) when the message addresses highly informed expert consumers.

Again, the more subtle, less conscious influences of the peripheral route may appear to be more interesting, from a psychological point of view, than the overt arguments coming along the central route, which is obviously constrained by the actual quality of the arguments available. The peripheral route allows for creativity in suggestion, manipulation and deception, even when the arguments themselves are weak and unconvincing. Let us consider three instances of such linguistically mediated illegitimate or tricky influences via the peripheral route of persuasion: nominalizations, innuendo effects and verbal deception.

Nominalizations

One of the most common linguistic strategies for clouding the real nature of arguments or propositions is the use of nominalizations (Bolinger, 1973). The connotations of nominal phrases often evade the careful assessment that critical communication partners apply to propositions that are directly stated in the predicate of a sentence. For example, the nominal term 'insurance' mimics security and lack of threatening events, although hardly anybody would believe the direct assertion that an insurance company will actually increase the safety of one's home or health. It merely affords partial compensation for the insecurity and threat of terrifying, fatal events. Likewise, the term 'Ministry of Defence' may be used even when the ministry is more concerned with war and offensive action. Or the notion of 'innocence' may be used to evade a critical test of whether female virgin status is of positive valence.

The prominence and effectiveness of nominalizations in marketing strategies or political ideologies is due to the fact that appraisals and evaluations are not conveyed explicitly but hidden in presuppositions. In linguistics, the term presupposition refers to that part of communicated information that is taken for granted, as a given (Clark & Haviland, 1977), before the comprehension process can begin. Thus, the sentence 'You always find an agent of your insurance company in the neighbourhood' not only conveys the focused proposition in the predicate (i.e. that an agency is in the neighbourhood). An implicit statement is hidden in the depth of the nominal term 'insurance' (that insurance gives security) but this part of the message is presupposed as a premise and thereby protected from critical tests and objections. Other examples of presuppositions will be given below, in the section on eyewitness testimony.

Innuendo effects

Wegner, Wenzlaff, Kerker and Beattie (1981) have studied the phenomenon of incrimination through innuendo. Their studies show that incriminating statements (e.g. in newspaper headlines) may serve to devalue a target person regardless of whether the statement is affirmed, questioned or even denied. Thus, even when the headline reads 'No evidence for Politician X's red-light district affair', subsequent memory-based judgements reveal a negative impact on the impression of Politician X. The theoretical explanation of this phenomenon is related to the notion of constructive memory that will be dealt with in the later context of eyewitness memory. Apparently, the mere comprehension of incriminating statements involves the formation of transitory images, or representations, that may result in memory intrusions and distortions.

Verbal deception

Verbal deception is tantamount to lying. Protocol studies of everyday communication elucidate that not telling the plain truth is by no means an exceptional sin or criminal symptom, but quite common, and often serves a prosocial purpose (Turner, Edgley, & Olmstead, 1975). Most attempts to conceal the truth or to suggest invalid information use the peripheral route. Verbal deception strategies involve the avoidance of immediate references (e.g. Mehrabian, 1971), selective reporting, and switching from facts to subjective opinions and emotions.

Brunswik's (1956) lens model framework provides a useful and powerful research instrument for the empirical study of lying and deception (see Figure 4.1). This research tool is briefly outlined here because it can easily be used to analyse communication processes in many applied contexts. For example, to investigate the credibility of statements delivered by politicians in television during an election campaign, the researcher has to make a basic theoretical decision about a set of relevant cues that are supposed to mediate the credibility of the politician's statements. Depending on the researcher's background or hypothesis, these may be verbal, nonverbal or physiological cues, but let us assume the researcher is interested in the following five verbal-behaviour cues: richness of details reported, immediacy of response, emotional involvement, balanced arguments, and social desirability of utterances. (If the purpose is to derive practical recommendations, it is important that the cues

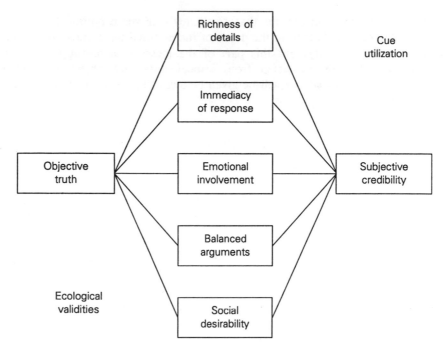

Cues mediating credibility judgement

Figure 4.1   *Brunswik's lens model (Brunswik, 1956)*

should refer to well-defined, deliberate behaviours that can be controlled voluntarily.)

The entire communication is then segmented into a sequence of singular statements that are scaled on the five cue dimensions, based on the judgements of experts or the television audience. In this way each statement is assigned a numerical value regarding immediacy, emotional involvement, etc. The next step is to obtain truth or credibility judgements from a sample of spectators who serve as lie detectors. Based on the correlations (across all statements) between the communication cues and the truth or credibility judgements, it is then quite easy to correlate the cue values with the judgements and to calculate multiple regression coefficients that reflect the weight each cue receives in the formation of credibility impressions. These empirically obtained weights can be directly transformed into concrete recommendations for communication styles.

If the truth of the statements is known, the same statistical procedure can be applied to figure out the actual diagnosticities of the cues, that is, the degree to which cues are related to the objective truth criterion. Note that the two sets of regression coefficients (the objective diagnosticities of the cues, and the weights they receive in subjective truth judgements) will usually diverge markedly (cf. Fiedler, 1989; Zuckerman, DePaulo, & Rosenthal, 1981), again reflecting the language users' lack of insight and the unconscious nature of the communication process. The same twofold multiple regression can be used in many applied settings to analyse the function of communication cues in mediating credibility, comprehensibility, advertising effects, television impact, or outcomes of interviews, and diagnostic conversations.

Language use in the legal context

Forensic lie detection

One prominent application of lie detection research is the courtroom and the forensic issue of judging the credibility of a defendant's or witness's reports. Although a good deal of this research has involved the measurement of physiological (rather than verbal) cues that can be displayed on the polygraph, this method is by no means free of language. While the measurement of blood pressure, skin conductance or respiration (supposed to assess excitation and guilt during lying) is based on purely physiological principles, the polygraph test depends crucially on the selection of questions used for interrogation. Typically, the test involves three types of item: (a) irrelevant questions for accommodation and warming up (e.g. 'What is your date of birth?'); (b) questions that directly pertain to the crucial issue (e.g. 'Did you rape the woman?'); and (c) control questions that also raise emotionally arousing issues but are not crucial to the judicial issue (e.g. 'Do you enjoy violent pornography?'). The decisive question is whether the respondents' autonomic reactions to crucial items exceed those to control items. It goes without saying that the success and accuracy of this method relies heavily on the selection of appropriate control questions. In any case, the polygraph test is of limited validity (Lykken, 1979; Szucko & Kleinmuntz, 1981) and not permissible in many countries.

Eyewitness testimony

Valid judicial testimony is not only contingent on informants' willingness to deceive or tell the truth but also on their ability to memorize relevant information. There are many reasons for expecting the less than perfect memory that may result in systematically biased reports, due to extreme fear and arousal, self-presentation concerns, and emotional involvement of witnesses or victims in the courtroom (see Chapter 10). However, aside from emotional and motivational distractions, the research by E. Loftus (1979) and colleagues has repeatedly shown that biased reports are partly due to linguistic suggestion and manipulation.

The notion of a presupposition provides a key concept for understanding the linguistic impact of particular question formulation strategies on eyewitness testimony (see Loftus, 1975). The open question 'Did the skinhead start the fight?' places the attentional focus on whether the proposition is true or false. In contrast, the question 'Why did the skinhead start the fight?' presupposes, or takes it as a given (Clark & Haviland, 1977), that the skinhead was the instigator, and focuses on the causal explanation of a granted fact. To repeat,

Table 4.3   *Variants of presuppositions*

Variant	Example
Nominalization	'Health insurance' suggests guarantee of health.
Attribute to nominal phrase	'Did the three Japanese tourists pose for a photograph?' The numerical attribute three will be hardly tested.
Implicit verb causality	'hurt', 'help' imply subject causation; 'admire', 'abhor' imply object causation.
Definite/indefinite article	'Did you notice the flash of lightning?' suggests that there was one.
Subordinate clause	'What did the skinhead say when he provoked the gentleman, before the fight started?' The suggested provocation is accepted uncritically.
Semantic connotations	'How fast were the cars going when they collided?' versus 'How fast were the cars going when they smashed into each other?'
Linguistic abstraction	'Politician took the present' versus 'Politician is corrupt'.
Syntagmatic order	'Brian continued to insult Mark before Mark started to fight' versus 'Mark started to fight after Brian continued to insult him'.

presuppositions afford a suitable means of suggesting the truth of the question content because they distract the conversation partner from critically assessing the truth of the proposition. Moreover, thinking about causal explanations (elicited by the 'why' question) can further increase the subjective truth of a statement (Wells & Gavanski, 1989). Numerous studies of the eyewitness paradigm have demonstrated that presuppositions can lead to memory intrusions and biased judgements. For instance, the use of the definite article in the question 'Did you see the stop sign?' in an interrogation about a traffic accident leads to considerably more positive responses than the same question with an indefinite article: 'Did you see a stop sign?' (Loftus, 1975). Using the definite article is but one of many different linguistic devices that may be used for presuppositions; a sample of such devices is given in Table 4.3.

Because eyewitness memory is susceptible to so many errors and suggestive influences, there is a strong need for methods to improve it. One such method is the cognitive interview developed by Geiselman, Fisher, MacKinnon and Holland (1986; see also Chapter 10). The cognitive interview is based on specific instructions to reinstate the context of the witnessed scenario, to report everything, to attempt recall in different orders, and to mentally change the perspective of reporting. This technique has been shown to elicit significantly more correct information, without increasing incorrect recall illusions and confabulations.

The strategic use of linguistic tools in interrogative settings

The background to some of the emerging work on the strategic use of language in legal settings finds its origins in some of the properties of interpersonal predicates that were discussed earlier. The stable finding that interpersonal verbs systematically mediate inferences about who initiates an event (Semin & Marsman, 1994) opens an interesting question. How does verb choice in question formulation influence the causal agency conveyed in the answers to these questions?

This question was investigated by Semin, Rubini and Fiedler (1995) and by Semin and de Poot (1995). The idea driving this research is simple. If one formulates questions with verbs referring to actions (e.g. 'Why did you join the Liberal party?' 'Why do you read the *New York Tribune*?') the choice of such verbs focuses the answer on the subject of the question. The respondents have to explain the event with reference to some properties of themselves. In contrast, if the same question is formulated with a verb of state, such as 'Why do you like the *New York Tribune*?' then the verb in the question focuses the answer on the sentence object, namely the newspaper. Thus, such answers have to explain the preference by reference to the qualities or properties of the newspaper. De Poot and Semin (1995) have shown this finding to hold systematically over a great variety of action verbs and state verbs and under conditions where the equivalence of the meaning between questions formulated by either verb class is ascertained. They have also demonstrated that subjects are not aware of the fact that different questions about the same event elicit different responses which have relatively dramatic implications (Semin and de Poot, 1995).

Finally, these authors have been able to show in a simulated rape interview that subjects whose expectations about the trustworthiness of the rape victim have been manipulated between trustworthy, not trustworthy and no expectations, display a systematic tendency to choose questions which systematically attribute inferred agency to the victim. Subjects who are led to believe that the victim is not trustworthy are more likely to pose a question formulated in the form of 'Did you dance with him?' In contrast, subjects who expect the victim to be trustworthy are more likely to choose a formulation that emphasizes the agency of the perpetrator: 'Did he dance with you?' Given the fact that they have danced prior to the incident, the answer is yes to both formulations. Furthermore, in a follow-up study it was shown that impressions that third parties form on the basis of listening to the chosen questions are biased accordingly. Cattelani et al. (1995) have shown that defence attorneys and prosecutors utilize precisely the same linguistic strategies when questioning witnesses, victims and defendants.

Subtle suggestive communications and manipulations in the courtroom are not confined to the manner in which witnesses are interrogated. Linguistic tools also play an important role in the manner in which the two opposing parties, prosecution and defence, describe the defendant's behaviour. This issue was addressed by Schmid and Fiedler (1996) in a language analysis of the protocols of the historical Nuremberg trials in which German Nazi generals had been accused of various crimes, with German defence attorneys and prosecutors from the USA, England, France and Russia. A number of distinct language strategies could be identified that enable attorneys to fulfil their roles without appearing too biased or dishonest. Note that any obvious tendency of defence attorneys to describe the defendant in less negative, more positive terms than prosecutors would appear to be obtrusive and partial, and would presumably be discounted by judges or jury members. However, lawyers may resort to more sophisticated and subtle strategies that are much less conspicuous.

It is indeed not surprising that defence attorneys use more positive predicates than prosecutors when talking about the defendant but, more subtly and more efficiently, their positive statements are conveyed at a high level of linguistic abstractness (e.g. the adjective level, according to the LCM model in Table 4.2 above). That is, they use the opportunities of positive statements to suggest stable, dispositional characteristics in the defendant's personality. Moreover, when defence attorneys talk about the defendant in positive terms, the sentence subject often has a clear-cut reference to the individual defendant, whereas (unavoidable) negative statements tend to refer to a larger group or collective, thus suggesting diffusion of responsibility. Moreover, defence attorneys tend to exploit the principle of implicit verb causality (Brown & Fish, 1983) in that they use many emotional state verbs (e.g. fear, like, respect) that express lack of voluntary control and external causation of behaviour. They talk about the defendant's inner feelings and emotional reactions to external provocations and restrictions. In contrast, prosecutors are not simply much more negative but they seek clear person references to the individual defendant (rather than a group or collective) and they express these negative statements on the concrete as well as the abstract level.

In general, then, research on language in the legal context corroborates the contention we have repeatedly made that the most interesting and impactful use of language tools is via the peripheral route, which is not subject to conscious awareness or control. In the central route, linguistic impact is limited by the actual validity and veridicality of the message. In the peripheral route there is always more latitude for suggestive, deceptive and distorting influences that can be used, and misused, to create an erroneous impression of a witnessed event or a defendant's personality. Since peripheral processes are less controllable and less conscious than the impact of arguments in the central route, one prominent aim of applied psychology is to sensitize language users to the subtle dangers and strategies of the peripheral route.

Our aim in this chapter has been to provide an overview of a number of linguistic tools that have been investigated in diverse applied settings. There is no coherent body of knowledge in this field that interfaces broadly with applied social contexts. The foremost reason for this is the implicit properties of language and linguistic tools. Nevertheless, it is possible to pull together a range of domains within which the subtle, often unconscious influence of different linguistic devices can be unambiguously demonstrated, including health-related issues, medical decisions, legal contexts, partner relationships and intergroup relationships. The effectiveness of different strategic uses of language in these contexts was reviewed.

Further reading

Giles, H. & Robinson, W.P. (1990). *Handbook of language and social psychology*. Chichester: Wiley. This is an outstanding sourcebook organized into six sections and covering a number of issues that are of relevance to the use of language in applied social contexts: the use of language in social relations, language and the law, amongst others.

Ng, S.H. & Bradac, J.J. (1993). *Power in language*. Newbury Park, CA: Sage. A most comprehensive volume on the relationship between verbal communication and social influence.

Semin, G.R. & Fiedler, K. (1992). *Language, interaction and social cognition*. Newbury Park, CA: Sage. An edited volume which brings together the recent developments in mainstream social psychology and language.

PART 2

FOCAL BEHAVIOUR DOMAINS

5

Health-impairing Behaviours

Wolfgang Stroebe and John de Wit

Contents

This century has witnessed a substantial increase in life expectancy in industrialized countries, due mainly to the virtual elimination of those infectious diseases as causes of death that were common at the turn of the century, such as pneumonia and influenza, tuberculosis and diphtheria. Thus, whereas approximately 40 per cent of all deaths were accounted for by 11 major infections in 1900, only 6 per cent of all deaths were due to these infectious diseases in 1973 (McKinlay & McKinlay, 1981). Today, the major killers are cardiovascular diseases (i.e. heart disease and stroke) and cancers. Among infectious diseases, the acquired immune deficiency syndrome (AIDS) is fast becoming a major cause of death.

These diseases are in some respects diseases caused by health-impairing behaviours such as smoking, drinking too much alcohol, overeating, leading a sedentary lifestyle or engaging in sexual risk behaviour (for a review, see Stroebe & Stroebe, 1995). The growing recognition that lifestyle factors contribute substantially to morbidity and mortality from the leading causes of death in industrialized countries was one of the reasons which led in the late 1970s to the development of health psychology as a field, integrating psychological knowledge relevant to the maintenance of health, the prevention of, and adjustment to illness. Because lifestyles are likely to be influenced by health beliefs and health attitudes, health psychology offers challenging opportunities to social psychologists, for whom the study of attitudes and attitude change has been a major research area for decades. Social psychologists can help to design effective mass media campaigns to inform people of the health hazards involved in smoking, drinking too much alcohol, failing to exercise, or engaging in sexual risk behaviour, and to persuade them to change their lifestyles.

The first part of this chapter examines the psychological processes which mediate the impact of persuasion or incentives on attitudes and behaviour: the first section discusses determinants of health behaviour, and the second section focuses on the modification of health-impairing behaviour through persuasive communications, as well as through changes in incentive structure aimed at increasing the cost of a particular behaviour (e.g. increases in cigarette price, seat-belt laws). The second part of the chapter will then discuss the application of these principles to two areas of health-impairing behaviour: smoking and sexual risk behaviour.

Determinants of health behaviour

The first step in attempting behaviour modification is the identification of the determinants of the target behaviour. Unless one knows *why* people behave in certain ways, it is difficult to persuade them to change. Models of behaviour not only identify general classes of determinants of behaviour patterns (e.g. attitudes, norms); they usually specify how these determinants interact to influence behaviour. Since general social psychological models of behaviour have already been discussed in Chapter 1, this section will focus on two models which have been developed specifically to predict health behaviour: the health belief model and protection motivation theory. We will also discuss implications of these models for the planning of interventions.

The health belief model

The health belief model was developed in the 1950s by social psychologists at the US Public Health Service in an attempt to understand why people fail to make use of disease prevention or screening tests for the early detection of diseases not associated with clear-cut symptoms (Janz & Becker, 1984). The model belongs to the family of expectancy-value models (cf. Chapter 2; Jonas, 1993). These models make the assumption that decisions between different courses of action are based on two types of cognition: (1) the individual's estimate of the likelihood that a given action will achieve a particular goal; and (2) the value placed on that goal by the individual. These models assume that individuals will choose from among various alternative courses of action that alternative which will most likely lead to the most positive consequences or avoid the most negative consequences. Like the theory of reasoned action (Fishbein & Ajzen, 1975), the health belief model attempts to explain behaviour that is under voluntary control of the individual. But unlike this theory it assumes a direct relationship between beliefs and behaviour, rather than a relationship which is mediated by intentions.

The model

Basic to the health belief model (Figure 5.1) is the assumption that health behaviour is determined by the following four health beliefs: (1) *perceived*

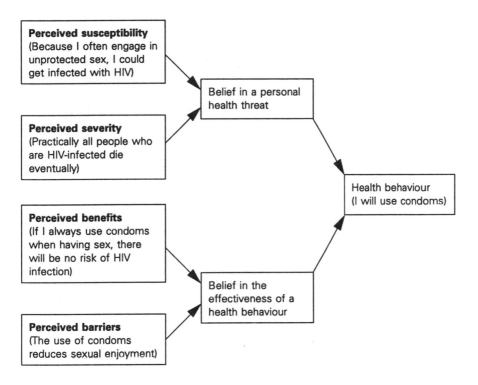

Figure 5.1   *The health belief model applied to the reduction of sexual risk behaviour*

susceptibility: the subjective risk of acquiring an illness, if no countermeasures are taken; (2) *perceived severity*: the severity of the physical (e.g. death, pain) or social (e.g. infecting others, inability to work) consequences of getting the disease; (3) *perceived benefits*: the degree to which a certain preventive behaviour will be seen as reducing the perceived susceptibility or severity of a particular health risk; (4) *perceived barriers*: the perceived negative aspects of a particular health behaviour: financial costs, effort, or side-effects of a medication may reduce the individual's willingness to engage in the behaviour. In addition, some cue is assumed to be necessary to trigger the behaviour (Rosenstock, 1974). This '*cue to action*' could be internal (e.g. a symptom) or external (e.g. a mass media campaign).

The factors 'perceived susceptibility' and 'perceived severity' determine the belief in a personal health threat, and produce the general, not yet goal-directed energy for action. Individuals who feel threatened will look for ways to reduce the threat. The cost-benefit analysis involving 'perceived benefits' and 'perceived barriers' determines the belief in the effectiveness of a particular health measure to reduce risk and guides the choice of a particular behaviour. For example, a sexually active student who engages in unprotected sex with a variety of partners might feel that he or she runs the risk of contracting a sexually transmitted disease. Obviously, getting herpes or even AIDS would have severe consequences. The student might therefore consider various alternative actions in order to reduce the risk, such as having sex only within a stable relationship, always using condoms, or giving up sex altogether. Each of these actions will reduce the risk but will also have some costs. For example, the use of condoms reduces not only the risk of infection, but also the enjoyment of sex. The student might continue to ponder over these alternatives without taking action, until there is some cue to action, for example a report in the papers that the spread of AIDS is accelerating or that other sexually transmitted diseases are on the increase.

The relation between the variables of the health belief model has never been formalized or explicitly spelled out. However, in most studies an additive combination is assumed. In the case of a health threat, an additive combination would imply that the threat of a disease is the function of the sum of 'perceived susceptibility' and 'perceived severity'. Thus, individuals should perceive a moderate threat if one of the two variables is perceived as high, even if the other approaches zero. In contrast, intuition would tell us that the perceived threat of an illness would be low if either of the two factors had a value of zero. For example, there may be many deadly diseases in the world (high severity) which do not worry us, because there is not the slightest chance that we could contract them (low susceptibility). This type of relationship would be better represented by a multiplicative combination, in which the perceived severity of a disease was multiplied by the subjective probability of contracting the disease.

Further weaknesses of the health belief model are its failure to consider potentially positive aspects of health-impairing behaviour patterns (e.g. smokers may disregard the health risk because they enjoy smoking) as well as the fact that many health behaviours are popular for reasons totally unrelated to health (e.g. much of weight control behaviour is driven by the wish to look good rather than be healthy). These aspects would be reflected by the beliefs underlying attitudes towards smoking or dieting in the models of reasoned action or planned behaviour (Chapter 1). The model also fails to include self-efficacy or perceived control as factors influencing behaviour. There is evidence from research on cognitive learning theory (e.g. Bandura, 1986) or the model of planned behaviour (e.g. Ajzen, 1991) to suggest that these variables improve predictions of behaviour. Finally, the model does not consider social influence variables like the subjective norm component included in the model of reasoned action and planned behaviour (Ajzen, 1988; Chapter 1).

Empirical evaluation of the model

A number of articles review the empirical research undertaken to test the health belief model (e.g. Harrison, Mullen, & Green, 1992; Janz & Becker, 1984). The review of Janz and Becker (1984) is based on 46 studies of which 18 used prospective and 28 retrospective designs. In order to assess support for the model, they calculated the number of positive, statistically significant findings for a given dimension of the model as a percentage of the total number of studies reporting significance levels for this dimension. The results were as follows: barriers (89 per cent), susceptibility (81 per cent), benefits (78 per cent), and severity (65 per cent). The authors interpret these results as providing substantial support for the model.

However, the fact that the association between two variables is statistically significant is not very informative concerning the strength of a relationship. To evaluate the strength of an association one would need information about 'effect sizes', which would allow us to estimate the variance of health behaviour that is accounted for by the various components of the model either separately or jointly. Such a meta-analytic review has been conducted by Harrison and colleagues (1992). Unfortunately, these authors were unusually restrictive in their selection of studies and based their analysis on only 16 studies (of which six had been included in the review of Janz and Becker, 1984). Harrison and colleagues found overall that all four dimensions of the health belief model were significantly and positively related to health behaviours, but that at best less than 10 per cent of the variance in health behaviour could be accounted for by any one dimension. This would indicate a very weak relationship. However, these results cannot easily be compared to those reported for the models of reasoned action or planned behaviour in Chapter 1, because Harrison and colleagues did not analyse the joint effect of the four dimensions of the model. The joint effect of all predictors taken together could be substantially greater than the independent effects.

Protection motivation theory

Protection motivation theory was originally developed in an attempt to specify the algebraic relationship between the components of the health belief model. According to the original model (Rogers, 1975), the intention to engage in some kind of health-protective behaviour depends on three factors: (1) the perceived severity of the noxious event; (2) the perceived probability of the event's occurrence, or perceived susceptibility; and (3) the efficacy of the recommended response in averting the noxious event. This version of the model assumed that the three factors combine multiplicatively to determine the intensity of protection motivation.

Since most of the empirical tests of the model (e.g. Rogers & Mewborn, 1976; see also Jonas, 1993) did not support the multiplicative combination of *all three* determinants of protection motivation, Rogers (1983) abandoned this assumption in a reformulation of the model. He also extended the model by including a number of additional factors. Probably the most important variable to be added was *self-efficacy*. The concept of self-efficacy refers to a person's belief that he or she is able to perform a particular action (Bandura, 1986) and is similar to the concept of perceived control of the model of planned behaviour (Ajzen, 1988; Chapter 1). Because people, despite their negative attitudes, might not be motivated to stop smoking or abandon unsafe sexual practices because they feel unable to do so, the inclusion of self-efficacy in a model of health-protective behaviour should improve predictions. The revision also incorporated the concept of perceived barriers of the health belief model

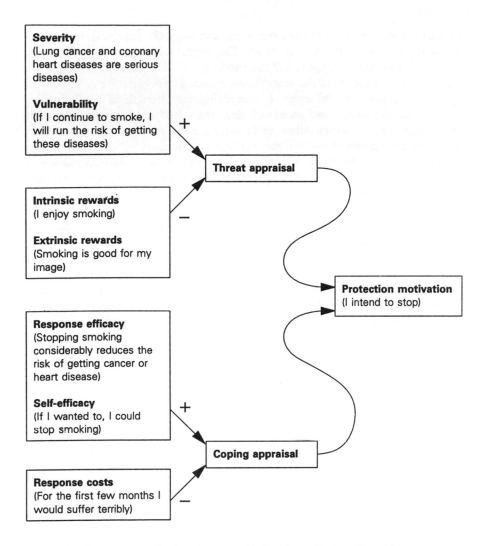

Figure 5.2 *Protection motivation theory applied to the reduction of smoking*

(labelled 'response costs'). As a related concept it also added the rewards associated with 'maladaptive responses', such as the enjoyment of continuing to drink, or the time or energy saved by not having health check-ups.

The revised model assumes that the motivation to protect oneself from danger is a positive linear function of four beliefs: (1) the threat is severe (severity); (2) one is personally vulnerable (vulnerability); (3) one has the ability to perform the coping response (self-efficacy); and (4) the coping response is effective in reducing the threat (response efficacy). Two further factors are assumed to have a negative influence on the motivation to perform the adaptive response: (5) the costs of that response; and (6) the potential intrinsic or extrinsic rewards associated with maladaptive responses (e.g. the enjoyment involved in continuing to smoke; peer approval). Rogers divided the six factors into two classes which he named threat appraisal and coping appraisal. Threat appraisal is based on the factors severity, susceptibility, and the intrinsic or extrinsic rewards of the maladaptive response. The factors assumed to influence coping appraisal are the effectivity of the coping response, perceived self-efficacy, and costs of the recommended behaviour. Rogers postulated an additive combination of factors within a given class but a multiplicative influence between classes. For example, given a positive coping appraisal, intention to engage in protective behaviour should increase with increasing threat appraisal. However, when coping appraisal is low, due, for example, to low self-efficacy, then increased threat appraisal should not result in an increased intention but might even lead to a 'boomerang effect' (i.e. negative change).

Empirical evaluation of the model

Protection motivation theory has been applied to a variety of health-related behaviours such as alcohol consumption (Kleinot & Rogers, 1982), smoking (Maddux & Rogers, 1983), breast self-examination (Rippetoe & Rogers, 1987), and exercise (Wurtele & Maddux, 1987). Results support protection motivation in so far as behavioural intentions were often found to be positively related to dimensions of the model such as severity, susceptibility, effectivity of the recommended action, and perceived self-efficacy. These results, which are also supportive of the health belief model, have typically been found in experimental studies (e.g. Maddux & Rogers, 1983; Rippetoe & Rogers, 1987; Wurtele & Maddux, 1987).

Empirical comparisons of protection motivation theory with the health belief model typically favour the former model. For example, Seydel, Taal and Wiegman (1990) found a superiority of protection motivation theory due to the inclusion of self-efficacy. Wurtele and Maddux (1987) observed in a study on exercise behaviour that the predictors of the health belief model affected behaviour through behavioural intentions rather than directly as assumed by the health belief model. Research was less successful, however, in clarifying the way in which the different components of the model combine to influence protective intentions. Like the multiplicative assumption of the original model, the assumption of the revised model that variables within a given class are combined additively, but that variables belonging to different classes should combine multiplicatively, could only be partially supported. Although some findings were consistent with the assumption of an interaction of variables belonging to different classes (e.g. Kleinot & Rogers, 1982; Self & Rogers, 1990) others were not (e.g. Maddux & Rogers, 1983; Mulilis & Lippa, 1990; Rippetoe & Rogers, 1987).

Implications for the planning of interventions

The implications of these models for interventions aimed at influencing some domains of health behaviour can be illustrated with the findings of a study which applied the health belief model to condom use among teenagers (Abraham, Sheeran, Spears, & Abrams, 1992). This study of more than 300 sexually active teenagers, which used behavioural intention as a proxy for behaviour and examined the relation between the four dimensions of the model to intention to carry and use condoms, found perceived severity of HIV infection, perceived vulnerability to HIV infection and perceived benefits of condom use to be only weakly related to intention. In contrast, perceived barriers to condom use (e.g. beliefs concerning pleasure reduction, awkwardness of use, and one's partner's likely response to suggested use) were found to be substantially related to intentions to carry and use condoms. These findings suggest that mass media campaigns which focus on social acceptability barriers to condom use might be more effective than the traditional strategy which emphasizes vulnerability to infection and the severity of the consequences of infections.

The inclusion of self-efficacy in the revised model of protection motivation also has important implications for intervention which have so far not been studied sufficiently. For example, if self-efficacy for a particular target behaviour (e.g. condom use, exercising) has been found to be high in the population for whom a campaign is being developed, the provision of information which increases susceptibility or severity should increase protection motivation. When self-efficacy is likely to be low, that is when most individuals feel unable to engage in a given action (e.g. dieting, stopping smoking), increasing vulnerability or susceptibility should not increase the recipient's intention to engage in protective actions. Under these conditions, information aimed at increasing recipients' feeling of self-efficacy might be more effective than a message which emphasizes susceptibility and vulnerability.

Summary and conclusion

Research guided by the health belief model and by the protection motivation model has substantially contributed to our understanding of the factors which determine health behaviour. However, with the emergence of general social psychological models of behaviour such as the model of reasoned action or planned behaviour discussed in Chapter 1, one must question the wisdom of investing further efforts in the scientific development of specific models of health behaviour. Such investments would be economical only if these models afforded a better prediction than the model of planned behaviour. This seems unlikely, however, because all of the components of the specific models can be integrated into the more general theory of planned behaviour.

The modification of health-impairing behaviour

How can we influence people to abandon health-impairing behaviour patterns and to adopt healthy lifestyles? There are basically two stages in the modification of health behaviour. The first involves the formation of an intention to change: individuals have to be informed of the health hazards of certain health behaviours and be persuaded to change. This can be effectively achieved with persuasive communications. However, persuasion may sometimes be insufficient to effect lasting changes in health behaviour patterns. Even if people accept a health recommendation and form a firm intention to change, they sometimes experience difficulty in acting on these intentions over any length of time. Thus, it is not only important to motivate people to change; they may also have to be taught how to change and how to maintain the change.

The next section will discuss strategies of behaviour modification based (1) on persuasion and (2) on planned changes in the incentive structure (e.g. increases in taxation). Although these strategies are often sufficient to induce people to change, clinical intervention may sometimes be necessary with behaviour such as substance abuse or excessive eating. However, the discussion of therapy programmes is beyond the scope of this chapter (see Stroebe & Stroebe, 1995).

Persuasion

Health promotion and education rely heavily on strategies of persuasion. During recent decades, research on persuasion has been dominated by cognitive theories of attitude change. These theories describe how attitudes change in response to complex verbal messages which typically consist of an overall position that is advocated (e.g. a health recommendation), and one or more arguments designed to support that position. Early cognitive theories of persuasion such as the cognitive response model emphasized the importance of the message recipient's *systematic processing* of argument content. They assume that if individuals are not able or not motivated to attend to the content of a communication, little attitude change will occur. In contrast, the more recent dual-process theories assume that, under certain conditions specified by these models, people will adopt attitudes on bases other than their systematic processing of the arguments contained in a message. These dual-process theories can thus be considered extensions of the cognitive response model. Although little research on these theories has been conducted in the context of health education, we will try to demonstrate their importance for the health area.

The cognitive response model: a theory of systematic processing

The cognitive response model of Greenwald and colleagues (e.g. Greenwald, 1968; Petty, Ostrom, & Brock, 1981) derives its name from the assumption central to this theory that it is not the arguments *per se*, but the recipient's thoughts or 'cognitive responses' produced while listening to a communication which *mediate* persuasion. Greenwald and colleagues suggested that when people receive a persuasive communication, they will relate the information contained in the arguments to their existing knowledge. They may even consider new material not contained in the communication. If these new, self-generated thoughts agree with the position taken in the communication, attitude change will result. If they refute the message or support a position other than the one advocated, the communication will not result in persuasion and may even lead to a 'boomerang effect' (an attitude change in the direction opposite to that advocated). Although a number of factors influence whether recipients of a message respond with predominantly favourable or predominantly unfavourable thoughts, the *quality* of the arguments contained in persuasive communications (e.g. well-reasoned, absence of logical errors, consistent with available knowledge) has proven to be a reliable determinant of the valence (i.e. positive or negative) of message-relevant thoughts elicited in the recipient.

The impact of a communication not only depends on the valence (i.e. favourable vs. unfavourable) of these responses but also on the extent to which recipients engage in message-relevant thinking. According to the cognitive response model, the *extent* to which individuals engage in message-relevant thinking depends on their *motivation* and *ability* to think about the arguments contained in a message. If people are highly motivated to think about a message and if they are able to process the argumentation, more message-relevant thoughts will be produced than if individuals are unmotivated or unable to do this. To give an example, suppose there is a programme on radio in which a dietician discusses the health risk people run by being overweight and suggests strategies for how to lose weight. Since listeners who have weight problems are likely to be more motivated to think about these arguments than those who keep slim whatever they eat, the former should respond with more message-relevant thoughts than the latter. Similarly, if recipients listen in the privacy of their home on a high-quality radio, they should be better able to process the message than if they listen in their car with the station fading or fellow passengers conducting a conversation.

According to the cognitive response model, variables that increase the extent of processing should enhance the impact of argument quality on attitude change, whereas variables which decrease the extent of processing should reduce the impact of argument quality. If the arguments contained in a message are of high quality and result predominantly in favourable thoughts, then the more recipients think about this message, the more favourable thoughts they should produce, and the more they should be persuaded. On the other hand, the more recipients think about a low-quality argumentation which results predominantly in negative thoughts, the more negative thoughts they should have, and the less they should be persuaded. Thus, the model predicts an interaction between determinants of thought-valence (i.e. argument quality) and factors which influence processing motivation or ability.

Dual-process models: the extension of the cognitive response approach

The dual-process models add a second process of persuasion which does not rely on the assessment of arguments contained in a message. Dual-process theories assume that as motivation and/or ability to process arguments is decreased, peripheral cues become relatively more important determinants of persuasion. We will discuss two dual-process models: the heuristic-systematic model of Chaiken and colleagues (e.g. Bohner, Moskowitz, & Chaiken, 1995; Chaiken, Liberman, & Eagly, 1989) and the elaboration likelihood model of Petty, Cacioppo and colleagues (e.g. Petty & Cacioppo, 1986a, b; Petty, Priester, & Wegener, 1994).

Both models assume that the persuasive impact of a communication can be mediated by two modes of information processing, which differ in the extent to which they are effortful. The heuristic-systematic model distinguishes between systematic and heuristic processing, the elaboration likelihood model between the central and the peripheral route to persuasion. Whereas the concepts of systematic processing and of the central route are identical, referring to message-relevant thinking that formed the basis of the cognitive response model, the concepts of heuristic processing and peripheral route differ in important aspects. Heuristic processing relies on simple decision rules or 'heuristics' to assess the validity of an argumentation. For example, as a consequence of invoking the simple rule that 'experts' statements can be trusted', message recipients may agree more with expert than inexpert communications, without carefully scrutinizing the content of a message. Thus, health warnings coming from a medical expert are more likely to be accepted without scrutiny than health warnings coming from a source considered non-expert. The concept of peripheral route is much broader than that of heuristic processing and includes, in addition, all forms of influence which do not rely on argument scrutiny, such as classic and instrumental conditioning. Both models assume that individuals will use the less effortful processing mode (i.e. heuristic processing or the peripheral route) if they are unable or unmotivated to engage in message-relevant thinking.

Empirical evaluation of the models

The ability to process and attitude change Much of the research on the impact of processing ability on systematic processing has focused on two variables: distraction and message repetition. By manipulating these variables jointly with argument quality, studies were able to assess the predicted interaction between the direction or favourability of the cognitive responses to the message (determined by argument quality) and the extent or quantity of cognitive responding (determined by distraction or repetition).

A good illustration of this strategy can be found in research on distraction. Distraction is an important variable in persuasion research, because in real life, unlike the laboratory, individuals are often disturbed while listening to persuasive communications. Thus, while a father who has had heart problems tries to listen to a TV programme recommending a low cholesterol diet, his son might begin a conversation with his mother or ask his father for a raise in pocket money. Early research on distraction had produced contradictory results, with some studies finding attitude change to increase with increasing distraction (e.g. Festinger & Maccoby, 1964), whereas others observed the opposite effect (e.g. Haaland & Vankatesan, 1968). Since, from a cognitive

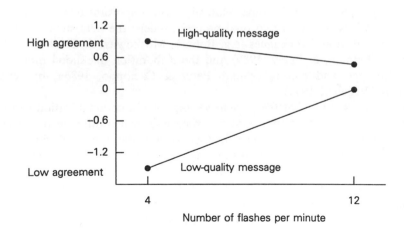

Figure 5.3 *Mean attitude score in relation to message and level of distraction (Petty, Wells, & Brock, 1976, experiment 2)*

response perspective, distraction should reduce recipients' ability to respond to a message, contradictory responses are to be expected, given variability of message quality between studies. Thus, with a high-quality message, likely to stimulate positive thoughts, distraction should reduce attitude change, whereas it should increase it in the case of a low-quality message likely to produce mainly unfavourable thoughts.

These predictions were tested in two experiments conducted by Petty, Wells and Brock (1976) which manipulated both argument quality and distraction. Consistent with predictions, increases in distraction reduced persuasion for the high-quality persuasive communication but enhanced persuasion for the low-quality argumentation (Figure 5.3). Additional support for the assumption that both the increase and the decrease in persuasion were due to thought disruption comes from the thought-listing task, which allows the experimenter to assess the extent and valence of the cognitive responses elicited by a communication. Distraction appears to have decreased recipients' negative thoughts in response to the low-quality argumentation and reduced the number of favourable thoughts in response to the high-quality version of the message.

Whereas the effect of distraction is to decrease processing ability, message repetition has the opposite effect. It allows the individual time to think about the message. Repetition should therefore result in increased attitude change for communications consisting of high-quality arguments, but decreased change for low-quality communications. Although there is empirical support for this hypothesis, there is also evidence that the positive impact of repetition of high-quality arguments is limited by a 'boredom effect'. Too frequent repetition results in rejection even of high-quality arguments (Cacioppo & Petty, 1979, 1985).

The motivation to process and attitude change The motivation to think about the arguments contained in a message has most frequently been studied by manipulating personal involvement (for a review see Eagly & Chaiken, 1993). In the context of health communication, personal involvement in an attitude issue would be influenced by factors such as personal vulnerability. We would thus expect frequent drivers to be more motivated to process car safety information than nondrivers, and individuals who know that they have high cholesterol to be more interested in information about diet and heart disease than those who have no reason to worry about their cholesterol level.

A classic study to assess the impact of personal involvement on message processing was conducted by Petty, Cacioppo and Goldman (1981). In this study, source credibility was manipulated in addition to argument quality in order to test the dual-process prediction that the impact of peripheral cues increases as the impact of argument quality decreases. Source credibility is a peripheral cue which allows individuals to form an opinion on the validity of the position recommended in the message without having to scrutinize the arguments. According to cognitive response and dual-process models, one would expect highly involved subjects to be more affected by argument quality than uninvolved individuals. In addition, dual-process models would suggest that uninvolved individuals should be more strongly affected by source credibility than would highly involved subjects. Results strongly supported both these predictions (Figure 5.4).

Although not typically discussed in this theoretical context, fear appeals also constitute attempts to manipulate processing motivation. Fear appeals which have frequently been used in the area of health education consist of information that establishes a personal health threat and is usually followed by some recommendation that, if accepted, would reduce or avoid the danger (for a review of classic research see Leventhal, 1970). In a typical study of the impact of fear appeals, smokers in a low-threat condition would be exposed simply to factual information about the dangerous health effects of smoking. In a high-threat condition, they would in addition be shown a film of a lung cancer operation. Under both conditions, a recommendation would be given that these negative consequences could be avoided if subjects gave up smoking. The majority of experiments on the impact of fear appeals have found that persuasion increases with level of threat imposed in the communication (see Boster & Mongeau, 1984; Sutton, 1982). This effect holds for behavioural intentions as well as actual behaviour, but tends to be stronger for intentions.

Most research on fear appeals was conducted before the development of dual-process theories, so these theories have been infrequently applied to this issue. From a dual-process perspective, one would predict that mild to moderate threats should increase the motivation of people who perceive themselves as vulnerable to scrutinize the message, and thus result in more systematic processing. This should increase the persuasive impact of communications consisting of high-quality arguments but decrease it for low-quality argumentations. With higher levels of fear, the emotional tension would probably disrupt people's capacity for systematic processing and they should become more reliant on peripheral cues. Moderate support for these predictions comes from studies by Jepson and Chaiken (1990) and Gleicher and Petty (1992).

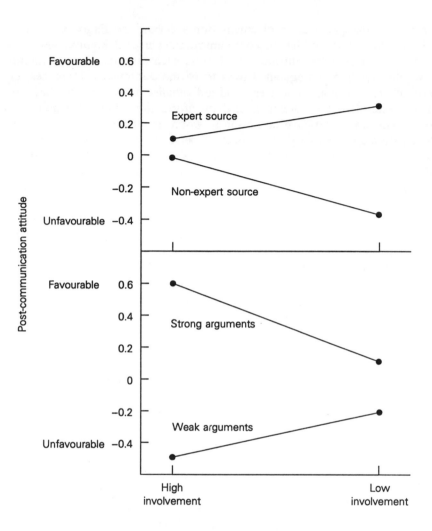

Figure 5.4 *Interactive effect of involvement, source expertise and argument quality on post-communication attitudes (Petty, Cacioppa, & Goldman, 1981)*

The persistence of attitude change Attitude change achieved through different modes of persuasion should differ in persistence. High levels of issue-relevant cognitive activity are likely to require frequent accessing of the attitude and the related knowledge structure (Petty et al., 1994). This activity should therefore increase the number of linkages between different beliefs forming the attitude, and make the attitude schema more internally consistent, and thus more enduring and more resistant to counterarguments. In support of this reasoning, a number of studies demonstrated that attitude change mediated by systematic processing (i.e. central route) is more persistent than changes that are accompanied by little issue-relevant thought (e.g. Haugtvedt & Petty, 1992; Petty & Cacioppo, 1986a, b).

Objective versus biased processing: an unresolved issue   So far we have described the information processing underlying attitude change as a relatively objective and unbiased activity. The elaboration likelihood model as well as the original version of the heuristic-systematic model postulate a single motive: people are motivated to hold correct attitudes. This *accuracy motivation* determines the processing goal, namely to assess the validity of persuasive messages. More recently, Chaiken and her colleagues (1989; Bohner et al., 1995) have extended the heuristic-systematic model to incorporate further goals for heuristic and systematic processing. Even though Petty, Cacioppo and colleagues (e.g. Petty and Cacioppo, 1986a, b; Petty et al., 1994) have also discussed the idea of biased processing in the context of the elaboration likelihood model, we will focus here on the work of Chaiken, because by incorporating the notion of multiple processing goals Chaiken and her colleagues (1989) have managed to systematically integrate the notion of biased processing into their revised dual-process model.

One class of motives likely to bias information processing has been labelled *defence motivation* by Chaiken and colleagues (1989). The processing goal of defence-motivated individuals is to confirm the validity of preferred attitudinal positions. The concept is important in the context of health communications, because defence motivation is likely to be aroused by health communications which are highly threatening, in particular when the recipient feels unable or unwilling to abandon highly pleasurable behaviour patterns. The defence-motivated perceiver is assumed to use the same heuristics as somebody who is accuracy motivated, but to use them selectively so as to support a preferred attitude position. Defence-motivated systematic processing is similarly selective, paying more attention to information that is attitude consistent. A third process not discussed by Chaiken and her colleagues (1989) is a reduction in the recipient's motivation to scrutinize the message. Thus, a smoker exposed to the outcome of recent research on the danger of smoking may be unwilling to think about this message, in particular if he or she has repeatedly failed in attempts to stop smoking.

Although biased processing has as yet received little attention in research on dual-process theories, the notion of defence-motivated processing is in line with one of the classic theories of social psychology, namely dissonance theory (Festinger, 1957, 1964). According to dissonance theory, individuals who have made a decision are in an aversive state of tension (called 'dissonance'), and are motivated to reduce this. Dissonance exists whenever a person has made a decision, because the negative aspects of the chosen alternative are incompatible with having chosen it (i.e. dissonant cognitions). The greater the number *and* the importance of cognitions which are dissonant, the greater the magnitude of the aversive state of dissonance and thus the pressure to reduce it. One way of reducing cognitive dissonance following a decision is to look selectively for decision-consonant information and to avoid contradictory information (for a review see Frey, 1987).

Thus, although a smoker should be more motivated than a non-smoker to process information about the health risks of smoking, according to early versions of dual-process theories, dissonance theory would predict that smokers tend to avoid such information, because it would increase their dissonance. If exposure to such information could not be avoided, dissonance theory would predict, smokers would engage in the type of defence-motivated processing suggested by the revised heuristic-systematic model.

Implications for the planning of interventions

According to the dual-process perspective, the major issue in designing persuasion campaigns is whether the target audience has the capacity to engage in detailed processing of the arguments employed in the communication and whether recipients of the persuasive communication either are, or can be, motivated to engage in systematic processing. Only if people can be assumed to have both the ability and the motivation to comprehend, scrutinize and evaluate the arguments contained in a communication, would it seem worth while to expend effort on developing a thoughtful, detailed argumentation. The development of such an argumentation should be based on careful analysis of the motives underlying a particular health behaviour.

If people are unable or unmotivated to engage in systematic processing, one could rely on mechanisms which do not depend on argumentation for their effectiveness. One could use classical conditioning, heuristic processing, or other peripheral mechanisms to influence the audience. It is no coincidence that most of the well-known advertisements for cigarettes, perfumes or sunglasses rely heavily on this peripheral route to persuasion. However, the disadvantage of this is that effects are less likely to last. For most health communications, long-term maintenance of attitude change is of great importance. It would therefore be worth developing strategies aimed at increasing processing motivation or ability. In the case of lack of motivation, one could use the health belief model or protection motivation theory to try to find out *why* individuals are not motivated to think about a health issue. This information could be used in the design of strategies to increase motivation. In the case of deficits of processing ability, for example due to very low educational levels or language problems in the case of foreign-language minorities, the message may have to be redesigned in a way that makes it understandable to these groups.

Beyond persuasion: changing the incentive structure

The major difficulty in persuading people to abandon unhealthy habits such as smoking or drinking too much alcohol is that they involve the renunciation of immediate gratification in order to achieve greater rewards or to avoid worse punishment in the remote future. One way to avoid this problem is to increase the immediate costs of a given behaviour through taxation or legal sanctions. By increasing taxes on tobacco and alcoholic beverages, governments have had some success in inhibiting unhealthy behaviours such as smoking and drinking excessive alcohol (see Stroebe & Stroebe, 1995). A review of econometric studies conducted in several countries concluded that, all else remaining equal, a rise in alcohol price generally led to a drop in the consumption of alcohol, whereas increases in the income of consumers generally led to a rise in alcohol consumption (Bruun et al., 1975). There is similar evidence for smoking, although less research seems to have been conducted on this issue (Walsh & Gordon, 1986). Finally, when persuasion campaigns failed to persuade drivers to use their seat belts, laws that made seat-belt use compulsory resulted in substantial behaviour change within a few months (Fhanér & Hane, 1979).

The usefulness of strategies which influence behaviour via changes in the incentive structure seems limited due to the tendency for changes in the 'price' of a given behaviour to influence mainly the attitude towards purchasing the product. Thus, although marked increases in the price of alcoholic beverages might induce people to buy less alcohol, they might drink at their old level whenever drinks are free. However, there are at least three conditions under which incentive-induced behaviour change could result in more general change: (1) when a habit is established which later continues even in the absence of incentives; (2) when expectations regarding the consequences of a given behaviour are unrealistic; and (3) when incentive-induced behaviour arouses dissonance.

For example, with seat belts it seems likely that once people get used to putting on their belts, it becomes a habit, and incentives are no longer necessary to maintain the behaviour. Furthermore, after having been induced through legal sanctions to use their seat belts, individuals might realize that this experience is much less unpleasant than they had anticipated. This might account for the findings of Fhanér and Hane (1979) showing that the introduction of the law on seat-belt use in Sweden brought about more positive opinions among those who complied. However, due to the arousal of dissonance, attitude change may even occur when individuals who have been induced through legal sanctions to engage in attitude-discrepant behaviour experience the negative consequences they had anticipated.

According to the theory of cognitive dissonance, engaging in attitude-discrepant behaviour can produce *cognitive dissonance*, an aversive state of arousal which motivates individuals to reduce it (Festinger, 1957). As we mentioned earlier (p. 127), whenever an individual chooses between alternative courses of action, there is always some information (dissonant cognitions) which would justify a different decision. The intensity of dissonance (and thus the motivation to reduce it) depends on the relative proportion of dissonant and consonant cognitions in the person's cognitive system. Since the reward anticipated for (or the sanction avoided through) the attitude-discrepant behaviour constitutes a consonant cognition, the theory predicts that dissonance should be greater when the reward anticipated for the attitude-discrepant behaviour is small rather than large. One way people can try to reduce their dissonance is by changing their attitude in the direction of greater consistency with their behaviour. The motivation to do this should be greater, the greater the dissonance.

Although the dissonance prediction of greater attitude change when small rather than large rewards are offered for attitude-discrepant behaviour is

counterintuitive and seems to contradict treasured principles of reinforcement theory, this negative relationship between the size of a reward and
the amount of attitude change was demonstrated in a classic study by
Festinger and Carlsmith (1959). In this experiment subjects who had performed a dull task were asked under some pretext to tell the next subject
the task was very interesting. They were offered either $20 or $1 for telling
the lie. The dependent measure taken after the lie was told consisted of a
rating of the interest value of the task. In line with predictions, subjects
who had been offered a small reward to tell the lie brought their attitude
more into line with their behaviour than did subjects who anticipated
receiving a large reward. Although this finding has frequently been replicated (see Eagly & Chaiken, 1993), subsequent research also revealed a
number of limiting conditions. Specifically, the negative relation between
magnitude of reward and amount of attitude change occurs only when
subjects feel free to refuse to engage in the attitude-discrepant behaviour
and when this behaviour has negative consequences either for themselves or
for other people.

An intriguing application of dissonance theory to the problem of AIDS
prevention among sexually active young adults has recently been reported by
Stone, Aronson, Crain, Winslow and Fried (1994). These authors made half
of the subjects, who had either been asked (or not been asked) to develop a
persuasive speech about AIDS and safer sex, to be presented in front of a
video camera, mindful of their own past failures to use condoms. Mindfulness
was achieved by asking subjects to describe the circumstances of their own
past failure to use condoms. At the end of the study all subjects were offered
the opportunity to buy condoms at a reduced rate from the student health
centre. The awareness that one has often failed in the past to use condoms is
inconsistent with the public speech in favour of condom use and should
produce dissonance. It was predicted that subjects who had prepared a public
statement and were made aware of their past failure to engage in safe sex
would reduce their dissonance by buying more condoms. In line with these
predictions, more than 80 per cent of the subjects in the high-dissonance
condition bought condoms as compared to 30 per cent to 40 per cent in the
other conditions.

The impact of incentives on attitudes investigated by Festinger and
Carlsmith (1959) occurs when individuals are offered incentives to behave in
ways that are discrepant from their attitude. Thus, if the offer of health
insurance at slightly reduced cost to regular joggers motivated some sedentary
people to overcome their aversion and begin to jog, the resulting dissonance
should lead them to develop a more positive attitude to jogging. However, this
positive effect might be counterbalanced by the unwanted negative effects such
an offer could have on the community of jogging enthusiasts. There is
evidence to suggest that the offer of incentives for the performance of a
positively valued behaviour can result in more negative attitudes towards that
activity (e.g. Lepper, Greene, & Nisbett, 1973). This so-called *overjustification
effect* occurs when people are rewarded for engaging in a behaviour that they
already find intrinsically interesting and pleasurable. The positive attitude

towards the behaviour is undermined by the positive incentives, perhaps in part because people attribute their behaviour to incentives rather than to their intrinsic interest in the activity (see Bem, 1972).

Summary and conclusion

Previous sections discussed the strengths and weaknesses of the use of persuasive messages as well as of changes in the incentive structure as intervention strategies in health behaviour change. Persuasion works best with individuals who are motivated and able to process persuasive communication, but some of the most promising target groups for health education are often unmotivated and sometimes also unable to process. Although the use of incentives to influence behaviour is particularly advantageous under these conditions, these strategies are subject to limitations. Thus, legal sanctions can only be used for behaviour which is publicly observable. While effective for publicly identifiable behaviour such as seat-belt use, or speeding, sanctions are difficult to impose if the behaviour one wishes to influence is difficult to monitor. However, monitoring is not necessary for behaviour modification relying on changes in price. Thus, although much drinking is done in private and so is not observable, the fact that alcoholic beverages have to be bought allows influence through increases in the price of liquor.

It should be emphasized that changing the incentive structure or using persuasive appeals should not be seen as competing strategies of attitude and behaviour change. After all, the effectiveness of legal sanctions is likely to depend on the acceptance of the law and the individual perception that violation of the law is associated with a high risk of sanction. For example, it is quite likely that the introduction of a law making seat-belt use compulsory would not have been as effective if people had not accepted that such a law was in their own best interest. In fact, without the persuasion campaign which made it widely known that the wearing of seat belts substantially reduced the risk of injuries in traffic accidents, it is unlikely that the introduction of such a law would have been politically feasible.

The identification and modification of health-impairing behaviour

This final section will discuss two areas of health-impairing behaviour, smoking and sexual risk behaviour, in which dramatic changes have been observed during the last decades. Despite great differences between them, what these two areas of behaviour have in common is that they had been considered of little consequence to health until they were suddenly discovered to be major risk factors for deadly diseases. Although in the beginning the information on the health risks of smoking or of unprotected sex was sufficient to achieve major behaviour change, substantial minorities are still engaging in these high-risk behaviours. The increasing loss of effectiveness of campaigns solely based on risk information has stimulated social psychological research into determinants of these behaviours.

The case of smoking

The health impact of smoking

Cigarette smoking has been identified as the single most important source of preventable mortality and morbidity in each of the reports of the US Surgeon-General produced since 1964. It has been estimated that an average of 5.5 minutes of life are lost for each cigarette smoked and that deaths from cigarette smoking in the United States exceed 320,000 annually (American Cancer Society, 1986). To claim an equivalent share of lives, the airline industry would have to experience three jumbo jet crashes every day of the year (Walsh & Gordon, 1986).

Thirty to 40 per cent of the deaths per year from coronary heart disease (the leading cause of death in most industrialized countries) can be attributed to cigarette smoking (Fielding, 1985). Overall, the mortality from heart disease in the USA is 70 per cent greater for smokers than for non-smokers (US Department of Health and Human Services, 1985). Similar excess rates have been reported for Canada, the United Kingdom, Scandinavia and Japan (Pooling Project Research Group, 1978).

The second leading cause of death in the United States and other affluent industrial nations is cancer. Lung cancer is responsible for more deaths than any other cancer. In the US it accounts for 25 per cent of cancer mortality and 5 per cent of all deaths (Fielding, 1985). Between 80 per cent and 85 per cent of deaths from lung cancer have been attributed to smoking (US Department of Health and Human Services, 1982). However, contrary to popular belief, coronary heart disease and not lung cancer is the major cause of smoking-related deaths, because many more people die of heart disease than of lung cancer.

Morbidity is also considerably higher among smokers than among non-smokers. Current smokers report more chronic bronchitis, emphysema, chronic sinusitis, peptic ulcers and arteriosclerotic heart disease than do persons who have never smoked (Schwartz, 1987). Data from the National Health Interview Survey conducted in the USA in 1974 suggest that there are more than 81 million excess work days lost and more than 145 million excess days of bed disability per year because of smoking (Schwartz, 1987).

The risk of morbidity and mortality for pipe and cigar smokers who do not inhale deeply is somewhat smaller than that for cigarette smokers but still considerably higher than that for non-smokers (Fielding, 1985). It is less clear whether smokers of filter cigarettes run a lower risk of morbidity and mortality than smokers of non-filter cigarettes. Although there is some evidence that changing from non-filter to filter cigarettes lowers the risk of lung cancer (e.g. Lubin, Blot, Berrino et al., 1984) it does not seem to reduce the risk of developing congestive heart disease (Fielding, 1985). Most surprisingly, a large-scale study conducted in Germany found that smokers of filter cigarettes died on average four years earlier than smokers of non-filter cigarettes (Krüger & Schmidt, 1989).

Smokers not only damage their own health, they also endanger the health of others. Epidemiological data suggest that cigarette use during pregnancy may be related to spontaneous abortion, premature birth, low birth-weight, and death of the infant during the first day of life (Kaplan, 1988; McGinnis et al., 1987). There is also evidence from studies assessing mortality from lung cancer among non-smoking persons exposed to smoking spouses that these 'involuntary' or 'passive' smokers have an elevated risk of lung cancer (see Stroebe & Stroebe, 1995). In the United States, such findings have led to the introduction of much more stringent restrictions on the places where tobacco can be smoked (US Department of Health and Human Services, 1986). Similar restrictions are now being considered in the UK after damages were awarded to an employee who claimed that sitting near seven chain-smokers for 14 months had permanently affected her health (*Independent on Sunday*, 31 January 1993).

Persuasive campaigns and behaviour modification

In 1964 the US Surgeon-General published the first report on the health risk of smoking and thus began the so-called 'war against smoking' which is still being waged today. The data on changes in per capita cigarette consumption in the USA during the latter half of this century certainly suggest that this anti-smoking campaign had a great impact (Figure 5.5). Yet, even with such apparently clear-cut data, it is difficult to decide how much of the decline in smoking behaviour should be attributed to the media campaign, and how much to other causes. To assess the impact of the media campaign, *experimental* studies are needed, in which one group of people is exposed to the campaign while an otherwise comparable group is not. If it can be shown that the experimental group has an advantage in cessation rates over the control group, this difference can be attributed to the communication.

Fortunately, such data are available from several major community studies which aimed at a reduction in smoking rates as part of their campaign to reduce the risk of coronary heart disease. The findings of these studies on smoking cessation have been summarized in one of the more recent reports of the US Surgeon-General (1984; see also Table 5.1). Probably the most successful community intervention was achieved in the North Karelia project conducted in northern Finland (Puska et al., 1985). As part of this project, an intensive educational campaign was implemented for the reduction of cigarette smoking. The neighbouring province of Kuopio was selected as a control group not exposed to the campaign. Self-reported numbers of cigarettes smoked per day fell by more than one-third among the men in North Karelia, compared to only a 10 per cent reduction among men in the control community. The campaign had no effect on the smoking rates of women. Although self-reports of smoking rates could be distorted by social desirability effects, it is encouraging that a 24 per cent decline in cardiovascular deaths

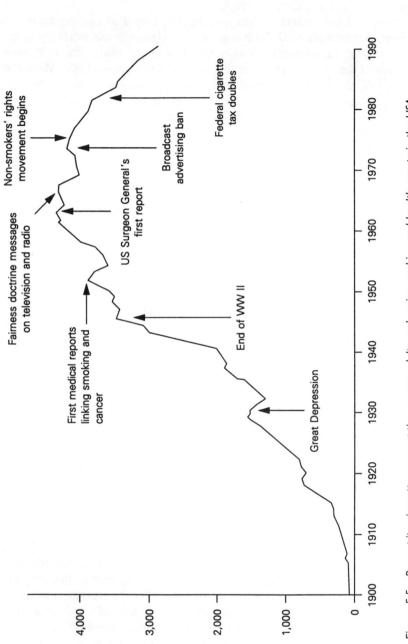

Figure 5.5 *Per capita cigarette consumption among adults and major smoking and health events in the USA, 1900–84 (Novotny, Romano, Davis, & Mills, 1992)*

Table 5.1 *Reduction in smoking observed in major community studies*

Study	Years of study	Net per cent reduction in smoking[a]
Stanford Three-Community-Study	3	15–20
Australian North Coast Study	3	15
Swiss National Research Program	3	8
North Karelia Project	10	25[b]
Other large-scale studies[c]	2–10	5–25

[a] Difference between per cent reduction in proportion of smokers in the maximum intervention versus control conditions.

[b] Difference between per cent reduction in the mean number of cigarettes smoked per day among men.

[c] Clinical and worksite trials, the London Civil Servants Smoking Trial, the Göteborg Study, the Oslo Study, the WHO Collaborative Trial and the Multiple Risk Factor Intervention Trial.

Source: adapted from US Surgeon-General (1984)

was observed in North Karelia as compared with a 12 per cent decline in other parts of the country (Puska et al., 1985).

In another well-known community study, the Stanford Three-Community-Study, only the experimental group which received face-to-face, intensive instruction in addition to media exposure achieved a significant reduction when compared to the control group (Farquhar et al., 1977). Two other community studies conducted in Australia (Egger, Fitzgerald, Frape, et al., 1983) and Switzerland (Autorengruppe Nationales Forschungsprogramm, 1984) achieved a net reduction of 8 per cent to 15 per cent. The US Surgeon-General (1984) concluded that a reduction of 12 per cent in smoking rate was usual in this type of community intervention.

Legal and economic measures and behaviour modification

The impact of persuasive campaigns can be supplemented by legal and economic measures such as further restrictions on the sale of cigarettes (e.g. stricter age limits) and increases in taxation. Increases in taxation should be particularly effective with teenagers, who, on average, have less disposable income than adults, so are more likely to be deterred from smoking by a marked rise in the price of cigarettes. It has been estimated that a 10 per cent increase in the price of cigarettes would result in a 14 per cent decrease in the demand for cigarettes in adolescents but only in a 4 per cent decrease in adults (Lewit & Coate, 1982).

On the basis of such estimates Harris (1982) predicted that the 1982 doubling of the excise tax on cigarettes by US Congress would produce a 3 per cent decline in the number of adult smokers but a 15 per cent reduction among teenagers. This would remove 1.5 million adults and 700,000 adolescents from the high-risk cohort of smokers (Walsh & Gordon, 1986). Because this doubling of the tax only involved a rise from 8 to 16 cents, more marked tax increases would seem a promising strategy to prevent young people from being recruited into smoking, particularly if these were combined with the various educational programmes described earlier.

Conclusions

Smoking has been identified as the single most important source of preventable morbidity and mortality and nowadays this fact is accepted by smokers and non-smokers alike. Most smokers admit that they would like to stop. Many smokers even seem to be able to stop without any help. Thus, surveys conducted by Schachter (1982) and Rzewnicki and Forgays (1987) suggested that approximately 60 per cent of the smokers who had attempted to stop had succeeded at the time of the interview. These latter results are consistent with epidemiological data which indicate that the significant reduction in smoking rates that could be observed during the last decades is largely due to people who stopped unaided. But since giving up a long-established habit like smoking is always difficult, the most promising strategy for smoking prevention would involve inducing people not to start smoking.

The case of AIDS

The epidemiology of AIDS

In many large cities of Australasia, North America and Western Europe, AIDS has become a major cause of death in young adults. By 1988, AIDS was the leading cause of death among young adults aged 25–34 in New York City. By 1989, HIV-related illness had become the second leading cause of death in men and the sixth leading cause of death in the United States among adults aged 25–44. According to the World Health Organization (WHO), almost one million AIDS cases had been reported by 1 July 1994, but allowing for under-diagnosis, under-reporting and delays in reporting, WHO estimates that there have been approximately 4 million AIDS cases worldwide (Global Programme on AIDS, 1994). Of these it is estimated that over three-quarters of a million are paediatric AIDS cases resulting from mother-to-child transmission, almost all of these having occurred in sub-Saharan Africa. The projected cumulative total of AIDS cases for the year 2000 is nearly 10 million.

Despite notable progress in treatment of infected persons, using pharmaceutical products that can slow down disease progression or prevent opportunistic infections, no effective cure or vaccine has been developed to date. Behaviour modification is the only available method to prevent HIV infection. Risk reduction guidelines have therefore been formulated to diminish further transmission. These instructions encourage the avoidance of exchange of body fluids during sex, refraining from unprotected sex, and either not sharing needles for intravenous drug use or adequately cleansing these needles.

The cause of AIDS

The cause of AIDS is a virus called the Human Immunodeficiency Virus (HIV), which directly attacks the human immune system. The immune system reacts normally by forming antibodies to counter the intruder. Unfortunately, however, these antibodies do not play a protective role as they do in more familiar virus infections, and the immune system does not succeed in eliminating the virus. Despite their limited role in fighting the virus, antibodies against HIV are used as indicators of the presence of the virus. These antibodies in the blood serum can be detected by simple tests. It can, however, take several months after infection with HIV before antibodies can be detected. During this latency period the individual can transmit the virus to others, for instance through sexual intercourse.

The period between infection with HIV and developing the symptoms of AIDS is unusually long compared with other communicable diseases, and is highly variable. Some individuals develop symptoms quite rapidly, whereas others remain free of symptoms for long periods of time, even more than 10 years (Rutherford, Lifson, Hessol, et al., 1990). The average incubation interval is now thought to be 7–10 years (Osborn, 1989). Between 50 and 75 per cent of homosexual men develop AIDS 8–10 years after infection with HIV. Due to this long incubation interval it is still not fully known what proportion of HIV-infected individuals will eventually progress to AIDS. However, the prognosis is not very favourable. Studies of long-term cohorts of seropositive individuals suggest that most, if not all, infected persons will develop AIDS (Curran, Jaffe, Hardy, Morgan, Selik, & Dondero, 1988). Once symptoms are present some patients deteriorate rapidly while others live for years. Mean survival time of patients with AIDS is one to three years.

HIV exerts its devastating effects on health by entering and killing important cells in the immune system, most importantly T-helper cells, a type of white blood cell. T-helper cells serve an important function in regulating the immune system. They stimulate other cells in the immune system to attack invading germs. By infecting and destroying T-helper cells, HIV stops the process of fighting invading germs at its root. The declining number of T-helper cells gradually reduces a person's ability to fight other diseases until the immune system finally breaks down altogether. Without a functioning immune system to defend the body against other germs, the individual is vulnerable to infection by germs (bacteria, protozoa, fungi, other viruses) and malignancies, which would not ordinarily have been able to gain a foothold. HIV can also attack the central nervous system and cause damage to the brain. This can lead to symptoms similar to dementia, and loss of control over bodily functions.

Modes of transmission

Identification of HIV, the aetiological agent of AIDS, and the subsequent development of immunological tests, made it possible to screen individuals at risk and to study risk factors for transmission of HIV in large sero-epidemiological studies. It was found that HIV is transmitted by exchange of cell-containing bodily fluids, notably blood, semen and vaginal secretions. Four main routes of infection can be distinguished: receiving infected blood or blood products, transmission from mother to child, sexual intercourse, and sharing needles for intravenous drug use (Curran, Morgan, Hardy, Jaffe, Darrow, & Dowdle, 1985).

Among homosexual men anogenital intercourse was repeatedly found to be the primary risk factor for HIV infection (e.g. Winkelstein, Samuel, Padian, et al., 1987a). For homosexual men the risk of HIV infection is highest when they are the receptive partner (Curran et al., 1988; Kingsley, Detels, Kaslow, et al., 1987). Recently, a small but growing number of cases has been reported in which receptive oral sex is the most likely cause of HIV infection (e.g. Keet, Albrecht-van Lent, Sandfort, Coutinho, & van Griensven, 1992). HIV transmission during anogenital or orogenital intercourse might occur without ejaculation since HIV was found to be present in pre-ejaculatory fluid (e.g. Ilaria, Jacobs, Polsky, et al., 1992).

Use of condoms during anal sex is promoted as an important prophylaxis against HIV infection for homosexual men. It has been found that gay men who used condoms only some of the time were six times more likely to become infected with HIV than those who used condoms all of the time (Detels et al., 1989). However, studies of HIV infection in serologically discordant couples suggest that condoms and spermicides are not completely safe (Hulley & Hearst, 1989). A study of the failure rate of condoms among homosexual men participating in an AIDS cohort in Amsterdam found that condoms tore or slipped off during anogenital intercourse on nearly 4 per cent of the occasions when they were used (De Wit, van den Hoek, Sandfort, & van Griensven, 1993). Failure rates depended highly on the type of lubricants used. Condoms used with water-based lubricants failed less often than condoms used with oil-based lubricants.

Laboratory and epidemiological studies have shown that HIV is *not* transmitted by everyday contact, by hugging, kissing, through food or water, or by mosquitoes and other biting insects (Global Programme on AIDS, 1994). The virus does not enter the body across intact skin, and is therefore not transmitted by sneezing, touching, hand-shaking, sharing eating utensils or living in the same household (Curran et al., 1988). In studies of households where one member was HIV infected, none of over 400 family members was infected except for sex partners or children born to infected mothers (Curran et al., 1988). HIV has been isolated from saliva, but the concentration is low and there is no evidence that the virus can be transmitted by (deep) kissing.

Behaviour change among homosexual men

When it became known that the risk of HIV infection can be considerably reduced or even eliminated by changing those behaviours that help to transmit the virus, the homosexual communities at the centre of the epidemic reacted with a variety of community-level interventions. These have rarely been formally evaluated. Indirect evidence regarding the effectiveness of prevention efforts aimed at increasing awareness and protective behaviours among homosexual men comes from a number of longitudinal studies that were initiated in several cities with large gay communities throughout the industrialized world, such as San Francisco, New York City, Vancouver and Amsterdam. These studies suggest that informing homosexual men about behavioural risks of HIV infection resulted in substantial behaviour change (Coutinho, van Griensven, & Moss, 1989).

Reductions of more than 60 per cent were observed in risk behaviours over four examination cycles between 1984 and 1986 in a subset of more than 600 homo- and bisexual men in a probability sample of single men in San Francisco (Winkelstein, Samuel, Padian, et al., 1987b). The fact that the proportion of men who were HIV-infected at the beginning of the study hardly increased in the studied period indicates that the reduction in high-risk behaviours resulted in a stabilization of the prevalence of HIV infections in this cohort. Analysis of behaviour change over 13 cycles in this cohort (van Griensven, Samuel, & Winkelstein, 1993) showed a steady decrease in the percentage of men reporting anogenital intercourse with ejaculation; from 84 per cent in 1984, to 30 per cent in 1987. From then onwards this percentage remained more or less stable. In addition, increases in condom use were found, among both seropositive and seronegative men. A similar decline in risk behaviour was reported in a study of a sample of gay men in New York (Martin, 1987).

The impressive number of epidemiological, behavioural and psychological studies concerning HIV infection that have been completed makes it clear that substantial behaviour change has occurred among homosexual men and that this has contributed significantly to the prevention of HIV infection. However, the evidence from San Francisco and New York City, both epicentres of the epidemic, may lead one to overestimate the extent of the behaviour change that occurred in gay communities as a result of the AIDS epidemic. Studies conducted in less affected areas typically reported higher levels of high-risk behaviours among homosexual men, even though substantial reductions in risk behaviour had occurred (see Catania, Coates, Kegeles, Ekstrand, Guydish, & Bye, 1989). For example, in the Amsterdam Cohort Study, a longitudinal study of more than 600 men who were repeatedly questioned about their sexual behaviours between 1984 and 1988, 46 per cent reported giving up unprotected anogenital intercourse, but nearly 30 per cent still regularly practised this technique, and a further 19 per cent engaged in unprotected anal sex some of the time (De Wit, de Vroome, Sandfort, van Griensven, Coutinho, & Tielman, 1992).

Furthermore, in recent years several behavioural studies have reported that observed groups of homosexual men at first successfully modified their behaviours but did not maintain these changes over time. A study among homosexual men in a probability sample of single men in San Francisco assessed longitudinal behaviour patterns in four annual intervals between 1984 and 1988 (Ekstrand & Coates, 1990). Findings from this study showed that 16 per cent had relapsed to unprotected insertive and 12 per cent to unprotected receptive anal sex. In a similar study in San Francisco among a convenience sample of gay men, initially recruited by soliciting bathhouse and bar patrons, relapse was found to be the predominant kind of high-risk sex (Stall, Ekstrand, Pollack, McKusick, & Coates, 1990). In the Amsterdam Cohort the percentage of men who reported engaging in unprotected anal sex increased from a low of 29 per cent in the first six months of 1991 to 41 per cent in the second half of the same year. Most of this change was related to an increase in unprotected anal sex with casual partners, from 13 to 24 per cent (De Wit et al., 1993).

There are a number of methodological limitations to cohort studies using convenience samples of participants which may bias the findings. The use of convenience samples and the possibly large refusal rate raise troublesome questions regarding the representativeness of the samples and the generalizability of the findings. Not only were the majority of respondents in these studies white and well-educated (Becker & Joseph, 1988), but the motivation underlying the decision to participate is also unclear (Catania, Gibson, Chitwood, & Coates, 1990). If individuals refuse to participate because they practise high-risk sexual behaviour which they do not want to admit, these studies might actually underestimate high-risk behaviour. Another potentially biasing factor arises from the longitudinal methodology used in most of these studies. Repeated assessments over time may elicit greater self-monitoring of one's sexual behaviours. It seems plausible, therefore, that repeated interviews of the same person may produce behaviour change that would not have occurred otherwise. However, Catania and colleagues (1991) recently compared the reports of a cohort with those of three cross-sectional samples of gay men interviewed at the same time and found similar increases in condom use across samples.

Behavioural determinants and interventions

To design and implement adequate interventions to promote protective behaviours it is necessary to understand the determinants of risk behaviours. Studies assessing behavioural determinants among homosexual men found a large number of variables to be related to high-risk sexual acts. In general, these investigations assessed variables specified in social psychological and health psychological theories of behaviours. Empirical evidence was collected concerning the importance of the following variables in changing high-risk sexual behaviours: knowledge (e.g. Kelly et al., 1990), significance of anal intercourse (McKusick, Coates, Morin, Pollack, & Hoff, 1990), condom acceptability (Valdiserri, Lyter, Leviton, Callahan, Kingsley, & Rinaldo, 1988), social norms (Joseph, Montgomery, Emmons, et al., 1987), beliefs of friends and lovers (McCusker, Zapka, Stoddard, & Mayer, 1989), communication about safe sex with partners (Linn, Spiegel, Mathews, Leake, Lien, & Brooks, 1989), perceived difficulty in changing one's behaviour (Siegel, Mesagno, Chen, & Christ, 1989), and personal efficacy with respect to sexual behaviour change (McKusick et al., 1990). Several studies also found younger age to be related to sexual risk behaviours (Ekstrand & Coates 1990; Kelly et al., 1990; McKusick et al., 1990). Hospers and Kok (1995) conducted a review of studies regarding determinants of sexual risk behaviour among homosexual men. They concluded that, in general, risk-taking behaviour is related to individuals' attitudes, subjective norm and perceived behavioural control.

However, as Fisher and Fisher (1992) have shown in their extensive review of intervention studies, few interventions have been stringently derived from social psychological theories of attitude and behaviour change. Instead, most interventions have been based on an 'informal blend of logic and practical experience' (p. 463). Fisher and Fisher observed that interventions based on formal theoretical conceptions were more successful. They also argued that although providing subjects with information about risk behaviours and motivating them to avoid risky sexual behaviours are necessary conditions to promote behaviour change, this may not be sufficient for a reduction in risk of HIV infection. They showed that health education interventions that also addressed behavioural skills were superior in terms of post-treatment attitude and behaviour change. Certain behavioural skills, such as the ability to communicate with and be assertive with a sexual partner, are necessary for practising protective sexual behaviours. Individuals must be able to negotiate HIV-preventive behaviour with a partner and be capable of leaving situations in which safe sex cannot be negotiated (Fisher & Fisher, 1992).

Several effective programmes have been developed and tested. These interventions included training of relevant behavioural and social skills. Kelly, St Lawrence, Hood and Brasfield (1989) randomly assigned 104 healthy homosexual men to an intervention group or a waiting list control group. Participants in the intervention group were taught, through modelling, role playing and corrective feedback, how to exercise control in relationships and to resist coercion by a sex partner to engage in unsafe sexual activities. Evaluation at the end of the training programme indicated that members of the intervention group had significantly reduced the frequency with which they practised unprotected anal sex and had increased the frequency of condom use. These changes were maintained at an eight-month follow-up: frequency of anal intercourse had decreased to near zero and condoms were used in 77 per cent of the few instances in which anal intercourse took place. Valdiserri, Lyter, Leviton, Callahan, Kingsley and Rinaldo (1989) found an intervention that included behavioural skills training to be more effective than an information-only programme.

In general, it is difficult to change behaviour once it has become habitual. This is an important consideration that underlies the introduction of HIV education programmes in school curricula. These programmes are especially important because they can help in forming habits that are protective before much unsafe behaviour has occurred. In recent years a substantial number of programmes have been developed to promote safe sex among adolescents. Most of these are intended to promote condom use; only a minority of programmes explicitly promoted delay of sexual intercourse as a preventive strategy. In general, these programmes were found to increase knowledge levels but did not appear to influence protective behaviour. Vogels and Danz (1990) found that in the Netherlands 60 per cent of sexually experienced adolescents did not consistently use condoms. Most adolescents primarily consider condoms to be a contraception device and either do not use them, or stop using them, when the female partner uses oral contraceptives. A second reason for the limited effectiveness of prevention programmes for adolescents is that they are generally not grounded in theoretical notions and empirical findings, a problem also faced with respect to HIV education programmes for gay men. An additional problem in relation to HIV education among adolescents is that cooperation of and support from high school teachers and administrators is needed to implement these programmes. Adoption of classroom-based HIV education can vary widely between schools and teachers and can be related to teachers' beliefs regarding the available programmes, and their role with respect to sex education in general and HIV education in particular, as well as school policy on sex education.

Summary and conclusions

The first part of this chapter focused on social psychological theories of attitude and behaviour change. From this discussion a number of simple principles can be derived for the design of campaigns aimed at changing health-impairing behaviour patterns. Once a behaviour has been identified as health-impairing, the first step in planning a campaign is to study the factors which determine this behaviour in the target population. This research should be based on models of behaviour such as the theory of planned behaviour, the health belief model, or protection motivation theory. The second step in campaign planning is to decide on the type of strategy of attitude and behaviour change to be employed. For example, it has to be decided whether to rely solely on persuasion or to complement persuasive messages with changes in incentive structure. Factors relevant to this decision are the processing motivation and ability of potential recipients of a health communication and/or whether the behaviour is amenable to influence by positive or negative incentives. For example, behaviour which is not publicly observable (and thus not easily open to sanctions) and which does not rely on substances which have to be purchased (and is thus difficult to influence via price increases) is clearly hard to modify via changes in incentive structure. Obviously, changes in incentive structure can be used not only to increase but also to decrease the costs of a certain behaviour. For example, since needle sharing among drug users is one of the sources of the spread of AIDS, making free needles available in needle-sharing programmes can help to reduce this risk factor. Finally, it should be remembered that strategies which rely on persuasion and those that use incentives are complementary and should be used in combination.

It is evident from our discussion of smoking and sexual risk behaviour as case studies of the application of social psychological theories of attitude and behaviour change that the scientific principles outlined in this chapter are not always heeded in the planning of health campaigns. Thus, most of the early campaigns against smoking or sexual risk behaviour relied on the power of the argument that these behaviours were dangerous and that engaging in them increased the risk of developing a deadly disease. Whereas this type information was effective in motivating change at an early stage when people were uninformed about these risks, it is no longer effective in individuals who persist in engaging in these behaviours despite the knowledge that they are dangerous. Any present-day information campaign aimed at these risk behaviours would have little chance of success unless it were based on the social psychological principles of attitude and behaviour change.

The growing recognition that lifestyle factors contribute substantially to morbidity and mortality from the leading causes of death in industrialized countries was one of the reasons which led in the late 1970s to the development of health psychology as a field, integrating psychological knowledge relevant to the prevention of, and adjustment to, illness. Because lifestyles are likely to be influenced by health beliefs and health attitudes, health psychology offers challenging opportunities to social psychologists for whom the study of attitudes and attitude change has been a major area of research for decades. This chapter demonstrates how social psychological theories can be applied to influence health-impairing behaviour patterns. The following key questions were discussed: why do people engage in health-impairing behaviours even if they know about their negative effect? How can people be influenced to change? In order to answer these questions, the first part of the chapter examined the psychological processes which mediate the impact of persuasion or incentives on attitudes and behaviour. The first section discussed models of health behaviour which identify general classes of determinants of behaviour patterns and specify how these determinants interact to influence behaviour. The second section focused on the modification of health-impairing behaviour by persuasive communications, as well as through changes in incentive structure aimed at increasing the cost of a particular behaviour. The second part of the chapter discussed the application of these principles to two areas of health-impairing behaviour: smoking and sexual risk behaviour.

Further reading

Fisher, J.D. & Fisher, W.A. (1992). Changing AIDS-risk behavior. *Psychological Bulletin*, *111*, 455–474. A comprehensive and critical review of research on interventions aimed at reducing sexual risk behaviour.

Petty, R.E., Priester, J.R., & Wegener, D.T. (1994). Cognitive processes in attitude change. In R.S. Wyer, Jr & T.K. Srull (Eds), *Handbook of social cognition*, Vol. 2 (pp. 69–142). Hillsdale, NJ: Lawrence Erlbaum. A very readable and state-of-the-art presentation of dual-process models, reviewing much of the research stimulated by these theories.

Schachter, S. (1982). Recidivism and self-cure of smoking and obesity. *American Psychologist*, *37*, 436–444. An intriguing study which indicates that the significant reduction in smoking rates observed during the last decades has largely been due to people who stopped unaided.

Stone, J., Aronson, E., Crain, A.L., Winslow, M.P., & Fried, C.B. (1994). Inducing hypocrisy as a means of encouraging young adults to use condoms. *Personality and Social Psychology Bulletin*, *20*, 116–128. The study presented in this article applies a new twist on cognitive dissonance theory to the problem of AIDS prevention among sexually active young adults. Dissonance was created after a pro-attitudinal advocacy by inducing hypocrisy–having subjects publicly advocate the importance of safe sex and then making subjects mindful of their own past failures to use condoms. In line with prediction from dissonance theory, these individuals were most likely to buy condoms at the completion of the experiment.

Stroebe, W. & Stroebe, M.S. (1995). *Social psychology and health*. Buckingham, UK: Open University Press. This book discusses major topics of health psychology from a social psychological perspective. It addresses two major factors detrimental to health and well-being: health-impairing behaviour patterns and stressful life events. It not only provides a more extensive coverage of the topics discussed in the chapter but also covers additional areas.

6

The Social Psychology of Economic and Consumer Behaviour

Helga Dittmar

Contents

Developing a *social psychology* of us as economic actors and consumers is crucial. Our economic and consumer activities are interwoven with our attitudes, beliefs and shared understanding. We negotiate our sense of identity, well-being and relationships with others in part through money and material goods. Yet, concern with gaining such a perspective on what it means for ordinary people to live in a modern Western economy and mass consumer society is relatively new, and research uneven. Cross-fertilization of economics, consumer research and psychology has not always been easy, given the traditional underlying assumptions in the three disciplines about the nature of the 'individual'. These can be caricatured by the stereotypes – respectively – of the 'rational economic man', the 'dispassionate purchase decision maker', and the 'psychological subject' abstracted from any material context. Economists have tended to neglect people's values and emotions, seeing them instead as actors who behave according to purely rational cost-benefit considerations (cf. Etzioni, 1988). Consumer research has concentrated on individuals as more or less competent information-processors, for whom the influence of emotions, symbolic images of consumer goods and cultural beliefs was not considered important (cf. Tybout & Artz, 1994). And, finally, in mainstream Anglo-American psychology, we have been regarded as decontextualized entities characterized by a set of internal, enduring attributes, rather than as beings dynamically interwoven with society, culture and the economy (Sampson, 1993).

By necessity this chapter has to be highly selective. It gives an introductory overview of those everyday activities, lay beliefs and development of ideas which deal most closely with money and material goods. The guiding theme concerns the relative contributions made by individual and social factors, and how we can best attempt to understand the links between them. In brief, it addresses the following issues:

Aspects of economic and consumer life
- 'Saving, spending and personal debt' discusses the relative influences of financial and social factors
- 'Psychological and social meanings of money' outlines the many roles of money over and above its use as a 'medium of exchange'
- 'The social psychology of material possessions' reviews biological, individual and social symbolic perspectives on the link between material objects and people's sense of self

Social belief and value systems
- 'Perspectives on mass consumer society' argues that materialism and shopping can have both liberating and entrapping effects on consumers
- 'Lay beliefs about wealth, poverty and social inequality' considers individual, social group and societal influences on everyday accounts

Economic and consumer socialization
- This section examines how children acquire an understanding of, beliefs about, and the ability to act in the economy and consumer society

Aspects of economic and consumer life

Saving, spending and personal debt

In our everyday lives, we are continuously faced with decisions about money. Should I save up for a holiday abroad? Should I add a further Access card bill to my already overdrawn account? Saving and borrowing are economic events, but do we deal with them like a calculator, considering only which option offers the best cost-benefit ratio or 'utility', as economists would say? Or do we deal with them as social beings whose decisions are influenced by attitudes, relationships with others, and the broader sociocultural context we live in, as this interview excerpt suggests?

> 'I think there's more people [now] that would pay weekly, monthly or whatever, than would pay outright. . . . It's the common attitude of keep up with the Joneses, next door's got a new car, so we'd better have one, we can't really afford it. Because of the society we live in, the pressure is on, and it's so easy to get credit facilities, they think it's what's expected of them . . . whereas in the old days . . . you saved until you could afford it.' (excerpt from focus group discussion, Lunt & Livingstone, 1992, p. 51)

This section focuses on saving, credit and personal debt, asking whether people's everyday management of their personal finances is best explained through economic constraints or social psychological factors.

Developments in 'modern' consumer spending

The everyday practice of borrowing money has shown rapid growth, particularly over the past decade or two. Moreover, the ways in which people can

Table 6.1 *Changes in consumer credit and credit card use in Britain**

	1976	1982	1992
Approx. amount of outstanding consumer credit in real terms (actual amount in brackets)	£5.5 billion (£5.5 billion)	£7.5 billion (£15.9 billion)	£15.2 billion (£52.9 billion)
Approx. number of credit cards in use	6.1 million	14.7 million	27.0 million

* £1 ≈ $1.5

and do borrow money seems radically transformed through the availability of consumer credit and the proliferation of plastic cards (the obvious influence of such macroeconomic factors as lender or retailer policies is beyond the scope of this chapter). Borrowing 'proper' is now complemented by 'lubricating liquidity' through credit and money transfers. If we take a look at some British figures (see Table 6.1), we can see that the yearly amount of outstanding consumer credit almost trebled between 1976 and 1992 in real terms, i.e. excluding the effect of inflation (*Social Trends*, 1994). The total number of credit cards in use more than quadrupled over the same time span (Rowlingson & Kempson, 1994). Different European and Anglo-American countries are bound to differ in their consumer spending profiles, but it is probably fair to conclude that, by now, almost everybody in modern Western societies uses credit to some extent.

Moving on to saving money, there is a commonsense assumption that saving and borrowing are opposite financial practices, i.e. if we have a surplus of money we save, and if we have less than we need we borrow. Yet, the relationship between borrowing and saving is far from this simple. Savings figures in Britain at the national (aggregate) level do not necessarily show a decrease as consumer credit and debt rise (*Social Trends*, 1994) and, at an individual level, many people borrow money and save at the same time (e.g. Lunt & Livingstone, 1992).

Economic approaches

Early theories that income was a main determinant of saving found little empirical support (Lea, Tarpy, & Webley, 1987). More influential are current economic (rationality) approaches which start with the assumption that saving means deferred consumption. At its simplest, the rational person's problem is to make choices between consuming now or later (i.e. spending or saving) so that her or his behaviour has the greatest utility. Theories are more sophisticated, of course, and deal with 'optimal' patterns of saving, spending and borrowing over time. The best known of these is Modigliani and Brumberg's (1954) *life-cycle hypothesis*, which proposes that people try to work out an optimum consumption plan for the whole of their life-cycle, which produces a 'hump-shaped' savings profile. Simply put, people should borrow before they reach peak income, then repay those debts during their middle years and save for old age, and once in retirement they should spend. While debt does tend to be more common amongst young people, empirical evidence shows that age-related variations are different from those predicted by the life-cycle hypothesis (cf. Lewis, Webley, & Furnham, 1994). A recent reformulation, *the behavioural life-cycle hypothesis*, offers a more promising model by including 'mental accounts' and the explicitly psychological concepts of self-control and framing (Shefrin & Thaler, 1988). The notion of mental accounts allows people to value, spend and save money differently, depending on its source (e.g. current income or assets), and framing emphasizes that their perceptions of these money categories are important. Self-control is exercised when we resolve the tension between far-sighted planning and wanting immediate consumption through self-imposed rules and external commitments (such as buying the latest computer model on credit, while leaving our savings intact). A clear strength of this model is that it *can* make sense of people borrowing and saving at the same time. However, like most economic approaches, it remains firmly committed to a 'utility maximization' model, which attempts to develop a universally applicable explanation for individual consumer spending.

Psychological factors

In contrast, research concerned directly with psychological factors has con-centrated on isolating *individual differences* in how people manage their finances, including differences in motivation, personality traits, abilities or preferences. For example, a recently proposed saving hierarchy identifies types of saver according to their underlying motives – the 'cash manager' (e.g. organizing money for everyday bills), the 'buffer saver' (e.g. for emergencies), the 'goal saver' (e.g. for durables, house, holidays), and the 'wealth manager' (e.g. investment). This has found some support in a Danish study of household finance surveys (Wärneryd, 1989). The idea that saving requires people to forgo the pleasure of immediate consumption has been investigated for some years, either in economic terms of 'time preferences' or in psycho-logical terms of 'ability to delay gratification' (see Lea et al., 1987). Evidence that individuals differ consistently in how strongly they prefer, or are able to resist, consuming now compared to consuming later is robust, but it comes mainly from laboratory experiments, rather than from studies of people's actual saving behaviour. On the plus side, this research makes it clear that people's financial behaviours can fulfil a range of different psychological functions, and so any single model of explanation, however elegant, is unlikely to capture their many facets. However, it is hard to see how a personality approach could account for a marked change in consumer spending in a short span of time, such as the recent boom in consumer credit. Taking a different angle, it can be questioned whether personal attributes and motives are best conceptualized as fixed and stable dispositions, or whether such a traditional conception of personality neglects the socially constructed aspects of person-hood (e.g. Semin, 1990). Moreover, the fact that systematic links exist between 'delayed gratification', for instance, and social class or ethnic group (see Lea et al., 1987) suggests that our orientations towards consumption are also influenced by attitudes, shared beliefs and social group membership.

Social psychological perspectives

Everyday financial decisions are influenced by individuals' attitudes, but they are also embedded in a moral and cultural context. In Britain, the Protestant work ethic – although possibly on the wane slightly – implies that saving is the right thing to do morally (result of hard work, effort and diligence), while borrowing money is wrong (result of idleness and careless spending of money), even if it is widespread in practice. Culturally, people are likely to feel under some pressure to consume and spend, because consumer goods are linked with identities and lifestyles, we are told that consuming means leisure and pleasure, and that we need to consume more and more. Of course, how individuals understand and relate to socially shared representations surrounding consumer spending will be crucially influenced by social group membership and personal history. For instance, people at different stages in their life course (single, couple, family, empty nest, retired) were found to save and spend according to characteristic generational beliefs, as well as according to life stage requirements such as providing for children (Lunt & Livingstone, 1992).

Although research on borrowing and saving is still too sparse for us to claim with certainty that social psychological variables enhance our ability to predict and explain who will save and who will get into debt, some recent British questionnaire studies have attempted to assess the relative influence of economic (e.g. income), sociodemographic (e.g. age, education) and social psychological factors (e.g. attitudes, locus of control beliefs, consumption styles). Two such studies use advanced statistical analyses (hierarchical multiple regression) which have the great advantage that they identify whether sociopsychological measures actually *improve* our ability to predict personal debt, once we have already taken economic and sociodemographic factors into account. Lea, Webley & Levine (1993) used the database of one of Britain's privatized water companies to draw samples of customers who had either no debts, mild debts or serious debts, and collected a range of economic indicators, demographics, responses to a pro-debt attitude scale and perceived social support for being in debt. This research design enabled them to compare people's self-reports of their financial circumstances with the records of the water company, and their finding that the great majority reported their debts quite truthfully can give us some confidence in such self-report surveys. Their main results were that pro-debt attitudes, knowing others with debts and thinking that debts are not perceived negatively by others were linked to being in debt, independent of economic and demographic variables, but that economic factors were the strongest predictors overall of whether somebody had no, mild or severe debts. Through grouping economic indicators together, but treating social support for debt and attitudes towards debt as separate factors, they concluded that the added increase in predictive power through the social psychological variables was relatively small – an interpretation which is not quite in line with the (very oversimplified) analysis of the relative predictive strengths of the different types of factors shown in Figure 6.1. Taking all their findings together, Lea et al. (1993) close by arguing that debt seems primarily a problem of financial difficulties: their serious debtors had

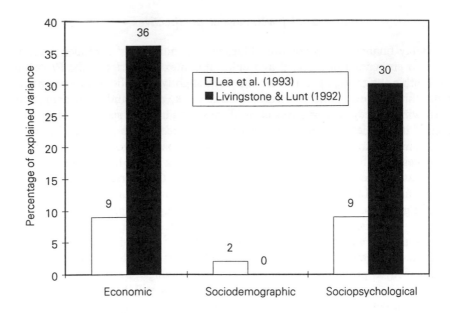

Figure 6.1 *Economic, sociodemographic and social psychological factors as predictors of personal debt in two British studies (Livingstone & Lunt, 1992; Lea et al., 1993). Percentages refer to amount of variance in amount of debt accounted for by the three factors*

lower incomes, lower occupational status, were less likely to own their homes, and had more children.

In contrast, Livingstone and Lunt (1992) found in a different British sample that disposable income and demographics were less powerful in predicting whether a person has debts or not than their social psychological measures. Livingstone and Lunt (1992) examined a more varied array of social psychological variables than Lea et al. (1993), and they conclude that,

> compared to those with no debts, those in debt . . . buy on impulse, feel less in control of their finances, feel less satisfied with their standard of living, have pro-credit . . . attitudes, blame their financial problems on convenience of credit facilities, high credit limits, enjoying shopping, careless budgeting and lack of self-discipline. (1992, p. 39)

However, economic factors – particularly income – became stronger when predicting the *amount* of debt, rather than determining whether or not somebody borrows in the first place, although sociopsychological variables were still important. Figure 6.1 provides a comparison between their findings and those of Lea et al. (1993).

How can we make sense of the apparently discrepant conclusions of these two studies? In addition to the fact that the two studies use somewhat different debt categories (no, mild, severe debt vs. no/some debt and amount of debt), one possibility are sample characteristics. The serious debtors in Lea et al. (1993) all faced legal proceedings for the recovery of their water bill, but also owed money for other basic household services (such as gas or electricity), which indicates poverty and extreme money problems. Lunt and Livingstone's (1992) sample was skewed towards average and higher-income brackets, and therefore less likely to contain people with problem debts. This interpretation may suggest that a severe lack of economic resources will almost guarantee debts, but that beyond a certain point of having sufficient financial resources for life's necessities, beliefs, attitudes and cultural factors become reasonably powerful determinants of credit and spending behaviour.

Whilst economic constraints and resources clearly play a powerful role in people's saving and borrowing, these nevertheless take place within a social context. Without diminishing their merits, the individualistic emphasis in dominant economic theories and static personality approaches will therefore always miss something. The contribution of social psychology lies in adding the dimensions of culture, communication and social groups to explanations of economic behaviour. Recent studies point to the importance of *within-household* dynamics, where gender and power relations between couples emerged as significant influences on spending decisions and the use of allegedly joint accounts (e.g. Burgoyne, 1990; see also Kirchler, 1995).

Psychological and social meanings of money

Apparently, money has been a fact of life for more than 2,500 years, yet we know surprisingly little about its everyday meanings and use. From a traditional economic perspective, money is nothing more than a generally accepted medium of exchange for goods and services. But we only need to consider that money is unacceptable as a present, that it can be 'dirty' or 'sacred', or that people seem to spend money more easily if they carry the same denomination as a coin rather than as a note (Lewis et al., 1994), to realize that money must have deeper psychological, social and symbolic meanings.

Money as non-social and social 'currency'

Economists view money as a non-social entity and argue that it is best understood in terms of the four main functions it fulfils. As a *medium of exchange*, it frees people from bartering only those goods which happen to be needed by each party at the time, and thus represents an all-purpose *store of value*. At the same time, it functions as a *standard unit of account* into which the value of any good can be translated, which also means that *payment for goods* can be deferred in time (Lea et al., 1987). However, while modern economies have such impersonal all-purpose money, many traditional societies have (or rather had) special-purpose money where use is regulated by social context. Thus, economic anthropologists have been more concerned with the role of money in the social relations between people, such as making visible and stable social roles and cultural categories. For instance, the use of two different forms of money on a Pacific island was described as highly gendered, where *ndap* (individual pieces of shell) was regarded as men's money, and *nko* (sets of ten shells) as women's money (Einzig, 1966). This suggests that money has important social and symbolic meanings.

Unconscious motivations and money personalities

Psychoanalytically informed approaches have in common that they view adults' relationships with money and possessions as the unconscious outcome of struggles between the infant's pleasure in dirt and excrement, and restrictions imposed on her or him by parents or society. Classic Freudian 'anal eroticism' suggests that money and possessions are 'symbolic faeces', which can compensate individuals for having to relinquish control over real faeces and the associated physical ('erotic') pleasure during restrictive toilet-training. Freudians claim that the anal theory of money is supported by many everyday expressions – 'filthy lucre', 'tight-arsed', 'stinking rich' – which are not confined to English or modern languages. Neo-psychoanalytic contributions shift their focus to infants' early experiences of social interactions during toilet-training through withholding, giving or struggling over faeces, so that money eventually comes to symbolize power, control and attachment (see Bloom, 1991).

The common emphasis in these approaches on unconscious motivations and pathologically exaggerated ways of dealing with money (e.g. the anal character 'hoards' and is 'miserly') is still evident in more recent typologies of money personalities, in which money is equated with power, love, security, freedom and self-expression. For example, Goldberg and Lewis (1978) identify four forms of 'money madness':

(a) *Security collectors* distrust others and use money to reduce their anxiety about being dependent on others.
(b) *Power grabbers* see money as strength, control and power; financial loss means helplessness and utter humiliation.
(c) *Love dealers* draw a parallel between love and money, where money symbolizes love, or money itself is loved, or love becomes a commodity that can be sold and bought.
(d) *Autonomy worshippers* use money to gain freedom and independence.

However intriguing, psychoanalytic concepts are notoriously difficult to pin down in empirical studies, and the research findings that do exist fail to provide convincing support for an anal personality (Kline, 1981). Moreover, these formulations have theoretical limitations, too. They tend to over-emphasize 'deviant' compared to everyday uses of money, and they cannot easily explain changes in an individual's money habits, or social group differences in the meanings of money. Their strength lies in highlighting money as a multiple symbol rather than a neutral 'medium of exchange'.

Everyday use and meanings of money

There is reasonable evidence that values and other social influences affect our perception of the physical attributes of money, making it social in nature. The most well-known paradigm examines whether values and needs influence judgements about the physical size of coins and banknotes (see Lewis et al., 1994, for a review). It was set in motion by Bruner and Goodman's (1947) classic experiment, which found that coins – as socially valued objects – were perceived as larger than cardboard disks of the same size, and that children from materially deprived families overestimated coin sizes more than those from affluent families.

Money may not be a unitary entity, given the disparate set of 'things' which function as money in modern economies. Some studies investigate the structure of people's concept of money by drawing on the notion of prototypical representations (e.g. Rosch, 1978), which would imply that we see some kinds of money as more typical than others of what we conventionally mean by 'money'. British and Dutch respondents agreed that cash – particularly the basic unit of a money system, such as the Dutch guilder – is a better example of money than plastic cards or cheques, while investment items (e.g. bonds) are least obviously included in our commonsense concept of money (e.g. Snelders, Hussein, Lea, & Webley, 1992). If plastic money is seen as somehow less 'real' than cash, this may explain in part why so many people get into credit card debt.

A number of studies examine money beliefs and attitudes. All confirm that the meanings of money are multidimensional. Wernimont and Fitzpatrick (1972) asked diverse groups of people to rate money on various attributes (e.g. good–bad, degrading–uplifting), and reported seven meaning dimensions of money, which differed on the basis of a person's sex, socioeconomic level and occupation. A more systematic scale was developed by Yamauchi and Templer (1982). This revealed five dimensions – power/prestige, retention, distrust, quality and anxiety – and systematic links with other (mostly psychopathological) personality measures (such as obsessionality). In an attempt to study links between money attitudes and social beliefs, as well as systematic group differences, Furnham (1984) found a six-dimensional structure of money attitudes in a British sample. Money attitudes were related to social beliefs (e.g. Protestant work ethic, conservatism) and showed differences on sex, age, education and income. For instance, people who were strongly concerned with obtaining money and believed that its accumulation is due to effort and ability, were more likely to be women and low-income earners, as well as those who endorse the Protestant work ethic. Tang's (e.g. 1992) recently developed Money Ethic Scale examines links between demographics, social values and orientations towards money.

Drawing on work concerned with material possessions, Prince (1993a, b) sees money as a self-extension and has demonstrated that certain self-concept dimensions are linked to materialistic values (e.g. success is equated with money), while 'money styles' were found to be highly gendered, with men emphasizing their competence in handling money and financial risk taking, whilst women felt more deprived of money as means of obtaining desired goods and enjoyable experiences. Lynn (1991) found cross-cultural differences, where people in affluent countries tended to attach less value to money than people in more deprived nations. More surprisingly perhaps, national money attitudes were found to be related to per capita incomes and economic growth, although the direction of cause and effect remains unclear.

Some of the symbolic qualities of money are perhaps most clearly revealed when we consider research on its unacceptability as a gift. On the surface, this seems odd because money should be more useful to the recipient than a present bought at the same price, which s/he may not like or have any use for. However, if a neighbour helps us out, we can give a small gift to show our gratitude, but not money – unless we are repaying a specific 'loan' of, say, milk (Webley & Lea, 1993). Money or a cheque is seen as an inappropriate present from a young adult to her or his mother by both parties (Webley, Lea, & Portalska, 1983). In this study, the time, thought and effort the giver invests in choosing a present was seen as the main reason why a present is valuable psychologically, and money does not involve such a process of choice. Burgoyne and Routh (1991) examined status and intimacy in *actual* gift-giving behaviour by asking British respondents to keep extensive diaries during the Christmas period. They found that only older, closely related family members (e.g. grandparents, aunts) can give an amount of money to a younger person without insult; other than that, money presents are acceptable only in the form of tokens which specify a particular kind of good (such as books or records). This suggests that money carries strong status-related messages, symbolizing both seniority and intimacy in certain gift-giving contexts. It may be inappropriate in most gift-giving situations because they often centre around symbolizing *particular* aspects of the giver (e.g. her or his thoughtfulness, perception of recipient) and the recipient (e.g. her or his taste, identity) – something money cannot provide.

This section has dealt with money generally. Reviews of specific types of money behaviour and decision making, such as tax evasion, ethical investment or the role of monetary incentives in work settings, can be found in recent economic (social) psychology textbooks (e.g. Lea et al., 1987; Lewis et al., 1994). Money clearly has important social and psychological meanings, which need further exploration. Thus, financial and debt counsellors may need to pay particular attention to their clients' beliefs and attitudes if they are to offer effective support and advice.

The social psychology of material possessions

We are surrounded by material possessions and consumer goods and, maybe because they are so commonplace, they may seem rather unremarkable at first sight. Self-evidently, many of the material objects we own are used as practical tools to make life easier, more comfortable and more efficient. Yet, rather than having mainly functional, pragmatic significance, there is accumulating evidence that they are intimately bound up with our psychological functioning. Possessions are perceived as parts of the self, can function as material symbols of identity, and their social psychological meanings change throughout our lives.

Material possessions as parts of the self

In a recent overview, Belk (1988) demonstrates that people perceive a whole range of material objects as a part of self, and concludes that possessions are 'self-extensions'. Tools, musical instruments, books, houses, cars, clothes and jewellery are just a few examples. A different and interesting illustration of the 'psychological nearness' of an object to its owner – which bridges self-perception and self-evaluation – is the 'mere ownership effect': the simple fact of owning an object makes it more attractive to us (Beggan, 1992). Moreover, respondents displayed a stronger mere ownership effect after an (experimentally induced) failure, which suggests that people may use possessions to re-establish a positive self-image: enhancing what they own serves indirectly to enhance themselves.

If we use possessions for defining and extending the self, it follows that their unintended loss should be experienced as a lessening of self. This seems true for people who lose their possessions through a natural disaster, as well as for victims of property crimes. Psychological reactions to burglary suggest that the ordeal people go through is related more to the perceived violation and shrinkage of self, security and privacy than to the financial value of property lost – which can be reclaimed for the most part – or to stress associated with police and insurance procedures (see Dittmar, 1992a). Victims, particularly women, often make an explicit analogy with rape, using expressions such as 'penetration', 'violation', and expressing revulsion at the idea of a 'dirty' stranger touching their private possessions (e.g. Maguire, 1980).

Biological, individual and social symbolic approaches to the self-possessions link

The notion of a genetic basis to an 'acquisitive instinct' was proposed initially at the turn of this century, but resurged in the more modern form of 'pop' human sociobiology, according to which the 'urge to possess' has evolved because it helps to maximize the likelihood that an organism (or rather its gene pool) will survive. Saunders (1990) suggests that the desire for home ownership may have some biological origins. However, evidence of cross-cultural variations in property-related behaviour, historical changes in children's collecting activities and – at best – only surface similarities between human and primate possessive behaviour suggests that any impact of biological factors is so diluted by social influences that it becomes uninformative as an explanation for the role that possessions play in our everyday lives (Dittmar, 1992a).

Psychological explanations which focus on the functions possessions fulfil for *individuals* have tended to conceptualize them as instruments of control. A prominent example is an interview study with children, adolescents and adults from America, Israeli kibbutzim and Israeli cities, asking them what possessions meant to them and their reasons for having them (e.g. Furby, 1978). The three cultures had different values with respect to possessions, with kibbutzim most collective and least materialistic, but Furby concluded that the main significance of possessions at all ages and in all three cultures resides in their instrumental use for exerting control over the physical environment and (indirectly) over other people, and that they are closely linked to self for precisely this reason. A recent experimental study partially confirmed that possessions satisfy a motivation for control, by showing that those individuals who generally believe they have control over their life (internal locus of control) compensate for a perceived loss of control by overemphasizing the control their possessions give them (Beggan, 1991). In contrast to this concern with an *intra-individual motivation* for *actual* control, psychoanalytically informed perspectives imply that material objects are important because they *symbolize* control and power (see p. 152).

Social symbolic perspectives claim that we draw on the socially shared meanings of material objects to communicate, maintain and transform aspects of our identity. Having a 'fashion' designer briefcase can only be an effective symbol of being 'up to date' if others share the belief that the briefcase is, indeed, fashionable. Identity includes both more private and personal aspects, such as beliefs, values and our personal history, as well as more public and social dimensions, such as social status, or the groups and subcultures we belong to. Goffman's classic analyses of 'self mortification' in prisons and mental hospitals (e.g. 1968) offer a vivid account of the identity-maintaining features of personal possessions by outlining how stripping inmates of all personal belongings takes away much of their previous basis of self-identification. That possessions help to maintain a sense of identity, integrity and personal history is also highlighted in empirical studies on the elderly, where people were found to adjust much better to nursing homes if they could take their cherished possessions with them (see review by Dittmar, 1992a). Wicklund and Gollwitzer (e.g. 1982) demonstrate that people make use of material symbols, amongst other strategies, to compensate for perceived inadequacies in certain dimensions of their self-concept.

Moving on to more social, group-related aspects of identity, possessions have been described as symbols of social status – particularly by sociologists – and a number of theories attempt to outline the processes through which social groups discard old status symbols and adopt new ones (see McCracken, 1990). Clothes are perhaps the most obvious example of goods through which we can signify social affiliations and standing, including sex-role identification, political orientation or socioeconomic status (e.g. Solomon, 1985). People can express the stereotypes they hold about different socioeconomic groups through material possession profiles (Dittmar, 1994). These examples also support the social symbolic notion that possessions are not only involved in the expression of our *own* identity; but that they are significant in our perceptions and judgements of *others'* identities, too.

Changing meanings and functions throughout life

The diverse meanings of possessions can be outlined in an integrative model (Figure 6.2), which proposes that they are self-extensions because they fulfil two major types of function: *instrumental use*, such as exerting control or making everyday activities easier; and *symbolic expression* of who we are.

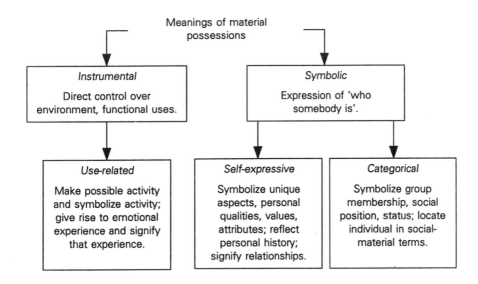

Figure 6.2 *The meanings and functions of material possessions (Dittmar, 1992a)*

Their symbolic functions can be further subdivided. First, as *categorical* symbols, they enable individuals to express their social standing, wealth and status, and they signify group membership, in terms both of broad social categories (such as gender) and of smaller groups or subcultures. Secondly, as *self-expressive* symbols, they can represent a person's unique qualities, values and attitudes, constitute a snapshot record of personal history, and signify interpersonal relationships. These distinctions are analytical rather than absolute. The use-related meanings of a car, for instance, can combine its utility as a means of transport with symbolizing the owner's freedom and independence. Despite some differences, there is reasonable overlap between private and public meanings of possessions (Richins, 1994).

There have been attempts to classify individuals into being either 'instrumental' possessors or 'symbolic' possessors (e.g. Prentice, 1987), but evidence suggests that the meanings and functions of possessions change dramatically throughout a person's life course. Kamptner's (e.g. 1991) life-span perspective proposes that individuals move through a series of different self-development stages, which are mirrored in their relationships with their favourite possessions. Having developed a sense of trust and security in early infancy, the central task of childhood is to build a sense of competence, whilst adolescents need to establish an autonomous self-identity. Adulthood is characterized first by finding intimate relationships, then by establishing social links with different generations and, finally, by a retrospective life review process. The meanings of possessions should therefore change from instrumental, control and activity-related concerns towards increasingly symbolic, social and contemplative functions.

In their first two years of life, infants often develop a special attachment to a cuddly toy (blanket, teddy), which gives emotional security and a first sense of separation from the nurturer. Both an ethnographic study in Chicago family homes (Csikszentmihalyi & Rochberg-Halton, 1981) and Kamptner's interviews with Californian respondents showed that children named toys and sports equipment because of the enjoyment and activities they make possible, while adolescents were more concerned with clothes, music and leisure objects, as expressions of an independent self. Whilst continuing to emphasize functional objects, adults increasingly preferred possessions which symbolized memories, social and familial networks and personal history, such as photographs or ornaments. Older people treasured personal possessions mainly as symbolic reminders of their past life and relationships. With death approaching, they even distribute their possessions as a symbolic means of preserving their identity beyond the grave (Unruh, 1983). So possessions seem to play a different role for people, depending on the stage they have reached in their life.

Yet the patterns of any self–possessions link are not universal, but are influenced by historical changes, socioeconomic status, gender and culture. A study on everyday consumer experience in Britain – which classified respondents into single, couple, family, empty nest and retired – found that the possessions people owned and whether they regarded them as necessities or luxuries depended on the specific requirements of each life stage (Livingstone & Lunt, 1992). Moreover, ownership of goods and attitudes towards them are affected by the sociohistorical climate individuals were socialized in, leading to generational differences. The most dramatic example of generation gaps in attitudes concerned a home computer, which less than 25 per cent of singles, couples and families saw as a luxury compared to almost 80 per cent of empty nests and retired (only people who actually possessed a computer gave a judgement). Compared to the sparsity of research on these social influences, consistent gender differences, permeating all age groups, have been documented in both American and British studies (see Dittmar, 1992a). It appears that women and men not only prefer different objects, but also relate to them in fairly distinctive ways. By comparison, women construe their personal possessions more in a relational and symbolic manner – focusing on connectedness with others and emotions – while men tend more towards an instrumental and self-oriented perspective – focusing on activities and usefulness. Of course, these differences are relative, not absolute, but they fit the descriptions of 'male' self-oriented functionality and 'female' symbolic, relationship-oriented concerns described in the gender identity literature. Finally, there is some indication that cultural differences in 'individualist' versus 'collectivist' construals of self (see Smith & Bond, 1993) are reflected in the meanings and functions of possessions. By comparison, 'individualist' conceptions tend to assume a *separate* self with stable attributes ('I'), while 'collectivist' conceptions involve a *relational* self embedded in social roles and networks ('we'). Differences in separate and relational self-construals exist at the level both of cultures and of individuals (Singelis, 1994). The great majority of American and North European infants seem to need a 'cuddly', but a first treasured possession is virtually unknown in such collectivist cultures as rural India, parts of Africa or Turkey (Gulerce, 1991). Wallendorf and Arnould (1988) compared urban Americans with African village inhabitants, and found an emphasis on possessions as reflections of a person's individual life history in individualist America compared to collectivist Niger, where possessions were important as signs of social status and conformity to shared community ideals.

Material possessions are perceived as functional and symbolic self-extensions. Their meanings and functions can change throughout the life course, partly as a reflection of different stages of self-development, but they are also subject to social influences, such as generational and cultural differences, socioeconomic constraints and socialization into major social roles, such as gender. Only a theoretical perspective which takes into account the interactions between individual and social determinants of people's relationship with their material possessions can hope to offer a comprehensive understanding of their role in Western mass consumer societies.

Social belief and value systems

Perspectives on mass consumer society: liberation or entrapment?

It seems that we have reached the point where consumption has penetrated and transformed not only our public existence, but also our private experiences. An article in the *Sunday Times Magazine* singles out five individuals for their curiosity value because they 'prefer ideas to objects', and because these 'consumer refuseniks stand out from the crowd . . . in an age where shopping is replacing sex as the most gratifying pastime, and designer tags say more about you than conversation' (Jaffé-Pearce, 1989, p. 8).

To talk about a social psychological perspective on mass consumption does not imply the existence of anything like a circumscribed field of research. We can only draw selectively – and somewhat tentatively – on a collection of ideas and studies around self-definition, materialistic values and shopping in order to illustrate the claim that mass consumption is intricately involved in our leisure activities, emotions, self-expression and social relations.

Mass consumption and self-definition

Theories of mass consumption are diverse (Bocock, 1993), but a central debate revolves around its contradictory nature, where arguments that it means greater choice and freedom for consumers to define their own lifestyle and identity clash with claims that it entraps us into a materialistic way of life, where endless chasing after material goods has become a poor substitute for fulfilment, self-development and meaningful relationships between people. This kind of debate can, of course, not be addressed directly by empirical research, but its existence should alert us to the possibility that consumer culture can have both positive and negative dimensions. Moreover, the tension

FIGURE

MOVEMENT OF MEANING

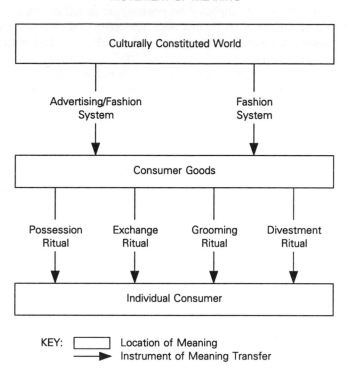

Figure 6.3 *McCracken's movement of meaning model (McCracken, 1990)*

between mass consumption as liberation and entrapment can often be found *within* a particular perspective. For example, McCracken (1990) claims that '[w]ithout consumer goods, certain acts of *self-definition* and *collective definition* in this culture would be *impossible*' (p. ix; emphases added), and proposes a model which sketches the transfer of meanings between consumer culture (fashion, advertising), consumer goods, and individual consumers (see Figure 6.3).

However, he also warns that 'displacing ideals', such as seeking happiness or fulfilling relationships through acquiring material goods and their associated images, can lead to discontent and dissatisfaction. Focus group interviews with British respondents revealed that commonsense or lay perspectives of ordinary people contain the same opposing themes of consumerism as empowerment and opportunity on the one hand, and as entrapment and persistent pressure on the other (Lunt & Livingstone, 1992).

Materialism as a value orientation

A preoccupation with material goods has links with commonsense notions of materialism, which have three distinctive themes: money and possessions are pursued for their own sake, are seen as the yardstick for judging success and well-being, and are used for status-seeking display (Fournier & Richins, 1991). Two main measures of materialism have been developed, both in the US. Belk's scale (e.g. 1985) concentrates on three supposed personal traits of materialists (possessiveness, envy of others, and non-generosity in sharing), placing emphasis on the last two themes of materialism, but not the first. The more recent scale by Richins and Dawson (1992) incorporates all three themes. It conceptualizes materialism as an individual value orientation, where the acquisition of material goods is a central life goal, key to happiness and well-being, and prime indicator of success. Their claim that materialistic values can influence individuals' thoughts and feelings is empirically supported. People who strongly endorse materialistic values hold more unrealistic expectations about the supposed psychological and social benefits they will derive from goods, experience more negative emotions after purchase, and attach different meanings to their possessions, with high materialists emphasizing their role as functional objects and status symbols compared to the greater concern of low materialists with material goods as symbols for interpersonal relationships and aids to enjoyment (Richins, 1994a). An impression formation study with British adolescents showed that strong materialists perceived a person as intelligent, successful and hard-working when s/he was portrayed as wealthy, while non-materialists did not see such a connection (Dittmar & Pepper, 1994).

Moreover, both Belk and Richins and Dawson report that materialists feel more unhappy and less satisfied with various aspects of their lives than other people. A more rigorous study of the 'dark side of the American dream' (Kasser & Ryan, 1993) found that young people's materialistic aspirations were associated with lower psychological well-being and adjustment. Materialism was defined as the relative centrality of obtaining wealth and money as a life goal, compared to self-acceptance, close relationships, or a sense of community. Using ratings from clinical interviews as well as self-reports, they showed that highly central materialistic aspirations were related to lower psychological adjustment and social functioning, and more depression and anxiety. Although these correlational studies cannot untangle questions of causality – whether materialism leads to poorer psychological adjustment, or whether those with psychological difficulties end up concentrating on material things – they nevertheless suggest deleterious consequences of an overly materialistic orientation. But, maybe, shopping as another important facet of mass consumption offers more positive psychological experiences.

Modern meanings and functions of shopping

Shopping has, of course, been studied extensively in consumer and marketing research. Traditionally, the emphasis has been on shopping as purchase behaviour, the individual consumer's decision making about what specific products to buy where and when, and making recommendations for marketing strategies (Tybout & Artz, 1994). An alternative *symbolic consumption* perspective has started to be recognized, but the still predominant traditional perspective – however valuable in its own right – tells us little about the emotional, social and symbolic dimensions of shopping beyond purchasing goods, which are the main concerns here. The focus is on 'high-status' shopping (consumer durables, shopping centres), rather than everyday groceries.

The nature of shopping seems to have shifted from provisioning physical needs towards becoming an important lifestyle, leisure and self-expression activity. British statistics suggest a change towards 'recreational' shopping, as the amounts of money for discretionary purchases increase relative to essential purchases. Americans spend more time in shopping malls than anywhere else outside home and work, and a survey of 600 mall visitors demonstrates that the 'shopping experience' entails a range of activities other than purchasing (Bloch, Ridgway, & Nelson, 1991). When asked what they did during their visit, 73 per cent had shopped to buy something, but 61 per cent had browsed in a shop without planning to buy something, 47 per cent had had a snack or drink, and 42 per cent had socialized with friends or others.

Diverse typologies of shopping motivations exist, which suggest that individuals differ in how involved they get in shopping, depending on the personal and social functions it fulfils for them, such as escape from daily routine, sensory stimulation, social encounters, or pleasure in bargaining (Gunter & Furnham, 1992). Stone (1954) suggested a more social psychological segmentation of shoppers. The 'economic shopper' is oriented to making efficient buying judgements, using price and quality, while the 'personalizing shopper' is most concerned with social interactions in shops. The 'ethical consumer' supports small, local shops, and the 'apathetic shopper', who hates shopping, cares most about convenience and minimum effort.

A recent study on a cross-section of British respondents examined everyday shopping experiences more holistically, focusing on dimensions of shopping often neglected in traditional market research, such as pleasure, impulse buying, or relationship with self and others (Lunt & Livingstone, 1992). It produced five shopper types:

- *Routine shoppers* (31 per cent of sample) rarely buy on impulse or for rewards, find little pleasure in shopping, and tend to use shopping centres when they need something.
- *Leisure shoppers* (24 per cent) buy rewards for self and others, buy on impulse, find pleasure in a range of different shopping experiences, and are close to the stereotype of modern consumerism: 'I shop therefore I am'.
- *Thrifty shoppers* (18 per cent) are economical, shop for the best deal and hardly ever buy on impulse.
- *Careful shoppers* (15 per cent) find shopping fairly pleasurable, are moderately economical in their shopping habits, and avoid impulse buys and rewards.
- *Alternative shoppers* (12 per cent) seem to stand outside modern consumerism, make use of second-hand markets, do not buy on impulse or for rewards, and do not see shopping as leisure.

These shopper types vary on a host of economic, psychological and socio-demographic factors. For instance, routine and careful shoppers are likely to be older and on better incomes, and there are more women and younger people amongst leisure shoppers, while thrifty shopping seems mostly a response to financial constraints. The idea that lifestyle, demographic and psychological factors need to be considered together is also taken up in 'consumer profiling' (Gunter & Furnham, 1992). And the argument that shopping has become increasingly self-oriented is also supported by recent research on self-gifts: goods we decide to buy for ourselves as special indulgences and rewards in order to repair self-esteem, mood, or tell ourselves that we are special (Mick & Demoss, 1990).

However, at the same time, shopping also seems to have an increasing potential to become excessive and dysfunctional for people. Very recent studies in the US, Canada, Germany and the UK estimate that shopping addiction or compulsive buying – involving considerable debts and distress – affects between 2 and 10 per cent of adults (Elliott, 1994). Sixty to 90 per cent of these self-identified samples were women, but it is unclear to what extent women are more prevalent or simply more likely to admit to their shopping problems. Two different theoretical perspectives address this 'urge to buy'. The first is a psychiatric or clinical model, where compulsive shopping is understood as a *disorder* of impulse control, mood or personality (e.g. Schlosser, Black, Repertinger, & Freet, 1994; see also O'Guinn & Faber, 1989). Accordingly, treatment may involve the administration of psycho-pharmaceuticals, such as antidepressants. The second perspective sees addictive buying more as a form of *compensatory consumption*, through which people try to deal with negative emotions, moods and aspects of self (Dittmar, Beattie, & Friese, 1995). In support, addictive shoppers have been found to have low self-esteem, want to spend money in a way that reflects status and power, buy to bolster their self-image and social image, and engage in mood repair (Elliott, 1994). With respect to treatment, this perspective implies that reducing the number of buying episodes through drug regimes is unhelpful, if underlying identity and emotional deficits are not addressed at the same time. However, addictive shoppers are probably not a homogeneous group, and differences in the biological, psychological and social functions shopping fulfils for them make a unidimensional explanation unlikely.

Consumption and consumer goods play an important role in reflecting and shaping individual and collective self-definition, but excessive involvement in material goods and shopping – where a 'having' mode predominates over a 'being' mode (Fromm, 1978) – may indicate consumption pathologies where people get trapped into filling an 'empty self' (Cushman, 1990) with transitory material gratifications.

Lay beliefs about wealth, poverty and social inequality

A greatly unequal distribution of personal wealth is pervasive in contemporary Western societies. In 1980, it was estimated that the most wealthy 50 per cent of the British population owned 94 per cent of its wealth, while the other half owned the remaining 6 per cent (Noble, 1981). Researching people's attitudes, explanations and perceptions with respect to poverty, wealth and inequality is interesting and important in its own right. But, furthermore, we need to know about their beliefs and values, because these are likely to influence how people interact with specific individuals, how they will vote, or what stance they take towards government policies concerning welfare or housing provisions. Put bluntly, 'as long as [we] attribute social problems to character defects, reform will be extraordinarily difficult' (Feagin, 1972, p. 103).

Lay explanations of poverty and wealth

Research on adults' beliefs about economic inequalities has mostly employed an attributional framework. Attribution theory is concerned with common-sense explanations of causes for social events, and has employed a central (though not unproblematic) distinction between causes internal and external to a person. Social psychologists have studied causal explanations for poverty longer and more extensively than those for wealth, sparked off by Feagin's (1972) study in which over 1,000 Americans rated the importance of 11 reasons why some people are poor. These were grouped into three main categories: *individualistic*, which place responsibility for poverty with the poor themselves; *structural*, which blame external social and economic factors; and *fatalistic*, which see poverty as a result of bad luck. Table 6.2 gives the percentage of his sample who rated each category as 'very important'.

Feagin found that poverty was overwhelmingly blamed on an individual's lack of effort, skills and motivation. However, beliefs differed according to sociodemographic variables, including age, income, education, religion and ethnicity. For instance, black, young, low-income groups did not explain poverty in mainly individualistic terms. A number of later studies built on this research, and – for example – Australians and, more recently, British people were found to be slightly less likely to attribute poverty to personal responsibility than Feagin's Americans, but individualistic accounts nevertheless predominated (Hewstone, 1989).

These and other studies also corroborated and extended findings on group differences in explanations by age, income and education. Political convictions and voting preferences are consistently linked to lay perspectives on poverty: right-wingers tend towards individualistic explanations and left-wingers towards societal explanations. Research evidence is more mixed concerning whether those with higher socioeconomic status, income and better jobs blame poverty more on individual responsibility than those less well placed. Whilst supported by a number of studies including Feagin, an analysis of over 1,000 responses to an American national election survey found only weak effects of socioeconomic position within an overwhelming bias towards individualistic explanations (Nilson, 1981). A 1990 survey by the CEC (Commission of the European Communities) found that education and income were the strongest influences on how people in 12 European countries saw and explained poverty. Poorly educated individuals were more likely to blame the poor themselves, and the better-educated unemployment. Interestingly, high-income

Table 6.2 *Perceived importance of causal explanations for poverty in America*

Type of explanation	%
Individualistic	53
lack of thrift and proper money management	
lack of effort by the poor themselves	
loose morals and drunkenness	
Structural	22
low wages in some businesses and industries	
failure of society to provide good schools	
prejudice and discrimination	
failure of private industry to provide enough jobs	
Fatalistic	18
sickness and physical handicaps	
lack of ability and talent	
just bad luck	

Source: Feagin (1972)

earners cited broken families, poor environment and unemployment more frequently as explanations than those on lower incomes (see Lewis et al., 1994).

Although this oversimplifies matters considerably, attempts to understand the factors which shape lay explanations for poverty can be placed at three different levels of analysis: individual, group and society. Research on self-serving biases in causal explanations suggests that individuals tend to blame failure on external factors, so that they do not have to take responsibility for it, and take personal credit for success (Hewstone, 1989). With respect to poverty (economic failure), such a simple self-interest hypothesis clearly does not hold. The European survey showed that high- rather than low-income earners referred to external causes for poverty, and Townsend's (1979) survey on poverty in Britain found that a larger percentage of the poor themselves blamed individuals for their poverty (30 per cent), rather than the system (25 per cent).

In addition to age, education, income and socioeconomic status, social and ideological beliefs such as religion or political orientation are also significant influences on poverty explanations. From a different angle, the importance of group differences is also highlighted by studies which ask respondents to explain poverty not only 'in general', but with respect to specific social groups. When people imagined four different poor individuals (black/white crossed with middle/working class), their explanations varied considerably (Furnham, 1982). Processes which explain how group differences come about in lay theories about poverty are far from understood, but Moscovici's (e.g. 1988) work on social representations suggests that people who are in regular contact with each other come to share and reiterate particular views of the world through everyday communication.

However, group differences tend to be relative and have to be understood in their broader cultural and economic context. Hewstone (1989) coined the term 'societal attribution' to express the view that explanations for social inequalities may reproduce 'collectively conditioned' beliefs. For instance, in India – a society with collectivist values and widespread poverty – system causes were seen as more important than personal ones by *all* political groups, just less so by right-wing activists (Pandy, Sinha, Prakash, & Tripathi, 1982). The CEC survey on poverty shows differences in explanatory patterns between the 12 European countries. Lewis et al. (1994) note that actual economic changes also influence how we explain events: the rise in unemployment across Europe seemed to be reflected in unemployment featuring as a common explanation in 1990, compared to poor luck and laziness in a similar survey in 1977.

Fewer studies examine lay explanations for wealth, but individualistic explanations seem less overwhelming than for poverty. A mixture between luck, help from others, and skilful use of opportunities emerged in British explanations, which were linked to politics, with Conservative voters believing more strongly than Labour supporters that wealthy people make more skilful use of opportunities or work harder (Lewis, 1981). Furnham (1983) makes the additional point that *evaluative* connotations of explanations need to be taken into account. Individual attributes were seen more positively by right-wingers (e.g. hard-working or thrifty) than left-wingers (e.g. ambitious or ruthless). A study in Australia, which collected explanations in an open-ended format rather than in the form of ratings, identified family background as an additional perceived route to wealth, and reported that wealth explanations differ, depending on the social group membership of the affluent individual whom respondents were asked to imagine (Forgas, Morris, & Furnham, 1982).

As for poverty explanations, cross-cultural differences emerge in wealth attributions, too. For example, whilst individual explanations were important in all three countries, wealth as an outcome of effort was most prominent in Australia (immigrant, multicultural), but tempered by family background and social explanations in the UK to some extent and more so in Germany (a traditional continental country, Germany is less individualist than the UK according to Hofstede's index, 1980). Forgas, Furnham and Frey (1988) concluded that 'explanatory strategies . . . by and large reflect the dominant functional ideologies and values of the surrounding society' (p. 654).

From the similar patterns of social group differences, we can conclude that some consistency seems to exist between people's tendency to use either individualistic or social causes to explain both wealth *and* poverty; that is, they have a relatively coherent view about social inequality.

Perception of individual attributes on the basis of relative wealth

The social representation of individualism links a person's material success, or lack of it, to individual attributes, such as effort, motivation and skills. A small set of studies has examined this link, not by asking people directly about their perceptions of social inequality, but by focusing on the inferences they make about a particular person's individual attributes, depending on whether s/he is portrayed as fairly poor or rich (see review in Dittmar, 1992a). For example, Belk (1978) used a 'lost property' paradigm, where American respondents were asked to reconstruct the owner's social and personal attribute profile from the contents of allegedly found hand luggage, which was varied to convey either a high or low level of wealth. The 'richer' traveller was judged higher on income and education, but also as more likeable, successful, interesting, generous, responsible, attractive and aggressive. However, the personal attributes of rich people are not seen in an unambiguously positive light. While favourable competence/dominance attributes (such as intelligence or assertiveness), are linked to wealth, affective qualities (such as warmth), are thought to be more characteristic of the less affluent. A study which used two types of video to depict the same person as either wealthy or fairly poor, found that British adolescents from a working-class and middle-class background shared a view of the wealthy person as able, skilled and in control, but lacking warmth (Dittmar, 1992b). This runs counter to expectations derived from social identity theory (e.g. Tajfel, 1981), which would suggest that the similarity in socioeconomic background between adolescents and video characters should influence perceptions, rather than both groups reproducing a shared wealth 'stereotype'.

These person perception studies cannot easily be accused of demand characteristics – 'if you ask for a stereotype you will get one' – because they usually ask people for their impressions after only one depiction (written description, photograph or video), so that respondents are unaware that relative wealth is being studied. Moreover, when asked directly in a small-scale survey, respondents denied that various individual attributes are in any way related to wealth (Dittmar, 1992a). These findings suggest that judgements about social-material standing systematically influence our perceptions of individual attributes, and possibly more strongly than we are aware of or comfortable with.

Explanations of social inequality show group differences and links with other social beliefs (such as politics or religion), but they are nevertheless influenced by societal factors: cultural values, ideology and economic climate. The sophistication of lay explanations might become more apparent if people were asked by researchers to consider causal chains (links between different types of factor), rather than to give ratings of single factors. The US, Australia and parts of Europe seem to have a particularly pervasive social representation of individualism, which is reflected in explanations, as well as person perception.

Economic and consumer socialization

Adult consumers and economic agents are not 'obstetric marvels' who 'leap fully developed from the womb', so to speak (Lewis et al., 1994). Children and adolescents have considerable spending power in their own right. For instance, in 1990, 14–16-year-olds in the UK each had about £10 (approx. $15) disposable cash per week. Early experiences and habits of spending, saving and shopping may lay important foundations for our beliefs and behaviour when we are adults. In other words, if we want to understand economic and consumer behaviour, we need to find out about their origins and development.

Consumer socialization

Consumer socialization has been defined primarily as the process through which 'young people acquire skills, knowledge, and attitudes relevant to their *functioning* in the marketplace' (Ward, 1980, p. 380; emphasis added). In research terms, this has meant a focus on children's actual consumer behaviour, and how it may be shaped by a range of socialization agents (McNeal, 1987). Parents and home environment, the consumer world itself (e.g. shops), peers, and the mass media are amongst the influences most studied, and can be illustrated by an example of each. A recent study of about 500 American mothers demonstrated that those who frequently go shopping with their children use this shared activity to model resistance to consumption pressures and socialize their children into making good (rational) consumer decisions (Grossbart, Carlson, & Walsh, 1991). In-store environments are laid out to capture children as a ready market for a variety of goods; for example sweets or toys are placed at children's eyelevel and near checkout counters, where adult shoppers are more likely to give in to their children's requests, in order to avoid embarrassment and frayed nerves (McNeal, 1987). With increasing age, peer influences become stronger, and adolescents start selecting and buying clothes, for instance, with friends rather than parents; girls even earlier than boys (Peters, 1989). A good deal of experimental research, mostly in the laboratory, has focused on the effects of television advertising on children. An example of a study in a real-life setting, involving actual consumer choices, is of children in a summer camp exposed to one of three different adverts (sweets, fruit, healthy nutrition) or no advert. Later in the day, when choosing foods to eat, most of the children who had watched the sweet advert chose sweets, while all others picked more fruit than sweets (Gorn & Goldberg, 1982).

Clearly, this type of research is valuable, but – similar to the traditional consumer and marketing perspective on adults – its focus on product-related behaviour has carried with it a relative neglect of how children develop beliefs about consumption, particularly with respect to symbolic meanings of products. There is suggestive evidence that children at the surprisingly early age of 5 to 6 years recognize what sorts of houses and cars function as symbols of affluence and status, and start making inferences about individual attributes of owners by the age of 10 or 11 (e.g. Belk, Mayer, & Driscoll, 1984). McNeal (1987) suggests that the symbolic meanings of a product can boost children's self-image, and notes that almost a third of American television adverts contain 'self-concept appeals'. Unfortunately, research on consumer socialization remains sparse, under-theorized, and consists of little more than a diverse collection of tantalizing findings.

The development of economic understanding and beliefs

Research on the development of concepts about economic reality has been dominated by a Piagetian perspective, guided by the assumption that similar stages will be found in children's economic thinking as in their understanding of the physical world (Lea et al., 1987). Essentially, this perspective holds that each individual child passes through a quasi-universal set of different stages of understanding, moving from simple-concrete to complex-abstract notions, towards an ideal end-state of full, adult understanding. The range of macro- and microeconomic institutions and processes investigated is broad, and includes buying and selling, profit and banking, ownership of the means of production and property (Berti & Bombi, 1988; Stacey, 1982). For instance, Furth (1980) outlines four main stages in children's conceptions of money and money transactions. Initially, they recognize that people have and spend money, but do not understand its role in transactions. Next, they understand that money is paid in exchange for goods bought, but not what happens with the money paid to shopkeepers. After realizing that shopkeepers buy goods on the basis of customer payments, they finally arrive at a basic understanding of profit and the societal use of money as a medium of exchange.

A prominent example of research on economic inequality in the Piagetian tradition is Leahy's (e.g. 1983) large-scale American interview study in the late 1970s. He interpreted his findings in terms of three main, consecutive stages of development: *peripheral-dependent* from 6 to 11 years of age, *psychological* between 11 and 14 years, and *sociocentric-systemic* from 14 to 17 years. Early conceptions (reflecting concrete-operational thinking) lack causal reasoning and focus instead on external, observable manifestations of wealth and poverty, such as differences in possessions or appearance. From the age of 11 onwards, explanations shift towards psychological conceptions (reflecting a transitional stage), when individuals at different levels of the socioeconomic hierarchy are described in terms of their inferred, underlying psychological qualities, such as individual differences in effort, intelligence or education. The sociocentric stage (reflecting proper formal operational thinking) is characterized by descriptions of inequalities as the outcome of different life chances, opportunities or other systemic factors.

Generally then, the contents of children's explanations is seen as a reflection of the qualitatively different stages of socioeconomic understanding each child passes through, although the precise number and contents of stages varies considerably for different socioeconomic concepts. However, the application of a cognitive-developmental approach to economic beliefs has begun to be challenged. Webley and Lea (1993) identify two important future directions for a 'more realistic psychology of economic socialization'. The first is the investigation of children's own economic behaviour, reflected in current work on children's playground economies in trading marbles, play economy experiments in which children can earn, spend and save tokens, or their use of pocket money (Lewis et al., 1994). The second concerns the need to relate the social, economic and cultural structure of society to children's and adolescents' economic ideas, which can be illustrated through research on wealth and poverty.

Social influences on children's representations of economic inequalities

Leahy's findings showed, inconsistent with a pure stage model, that individualistic, psychological explanations for inequality continued to predominate in late adolescence, which he later (1990) suggests indicates that 'inequalities become increasingly legitimated by reference to individual differences rather than social-structural . . . factors. . . . One might argue that the functionalist socialization to perceive inequality as legitimate is so strong as to *override formal operational thinking*' (pp. 115–116; emphasis added). This last comment makes reference to more sociologically oriented work, which sees economic socialization as children's progressive alignment with 'dominant ideology', leading to their positive acceptance of Western, capitalist economic systems, and the economic inequalities associated with them (e.g. Connell, 1983). A recent review concludes that late adolescence is characterized by a tendency to view a greatly unequal distribution of wealth as both necessary and good (Furnham & Stacey, 1991). This perspective provides a much-needed social framework for the development of beliefs about inequality, but tends to imply a deterministic and passive shaping of young people's ideas.

A study on differences between Scottish state and private school children in perceptions and explanations of income differentials (Emler & Dickinson, 1985) can serve as an example of a third perspective, which attempts to pin down some aspects of the dynamic interaction of individual development and social factors. Privately educated children perceived greater disparities in income between four occupations than did state-educated children, and gave more elaborated and diverse explanations for these disparities. These findings were explained through socially shared ideas about income differentials – maybe discussed during a family meal – being much more information rich in a middle-class than a working-class environment. These differences suggest tentatively that the contents of children's ideas about inequality may be shaped in part by the knowledge and representations prevalent in their social environment, but some age-related differences in income estimates and explanations point to the importance of cognitive and linguistic abilities in children's development of economic beliefs.

A recent extensive cross-cultural study in 12 diverse countries points to a possible avenue for integrating cognitive-developmental and social constructionist perspectives on economic socialization (Leiser, Roland-Lévy, & Sevón, 1990). To aid comparability – a problem with earlier studies carried out in different countries – researchers used exactly the same method and questions when interviewing children and adolescents of three age groups: 8, 11 and 14 years. They examined a broad range of core areas of economic reality, and found that children's developing understanding of *economic processes* and *institutions* – such as banking, taxation or profit – followed a general stage model and was hardly influenced by culture. Children's understanding of these particular aspects of the economy seem heavily constrained by their cognitive capabilities. In contrast, children's explanations for wealth and poverty – representing *economic beliefs* and *attitudes* – showed great cultural diversity and fairly stable proportions of individualist, society, family and luck explanations across age groups. For instance, in (non-kibbutz) Israel, a highly individualistic society, 76 per cent of all responses referred to individual ability as a cause of economic inequalities and a mere 3 per cent to systemic factors. In (the then) Yugoslavia with a socialist heritage, 37 per cent of explanations were individual-centred, whereas a full 49 per cent referred to social-structural causes. The prominence of individualistic explanations also showed some links – although by no means perfect – with countries' individualist-collectivist rankings. Economic beliefs appear to be more strongly shaped by prevalent cultural values.

We know less about children's socialization into mass consumer society than about their representations of economic reality. A reasonable extrapolation from findings might be that family environment, schooling, peers, mass media and predominant cultural values are important influences on the development of children's ideas and behaviour, possibly more so on their beliefs and attitudes, and less on their understanding of complex economic and consumer transactions and institutions.

This chapter dealt with aspects of our everyday involvement in the economy and mass consumer society. The first section reviewed perspectives and research on our activities with respect to money and material goods: saving and spending money, the social and psychological meanings of money, and the social psychology of material possessions. The second focused on broader social beliefs and values: the positive and negative dimensions of materialism and shopping in mass consumer society, and our perceptions and lay beliefs of economic inequalities. The third concerned the origins and development of our ideas about the economy and consumer issues. The theoretical developments and scope of empirical studies in each section are uneven, and specific conclusions are therefore drawn with respect to each. Overall, it can be concluded that, despite their merits, the individualistic emphasis in dominant economic theories, static personality approaches in psychology and information-processing models in market research neglect the *social* nature of economic and consumer behaviour. The special contribution of social psychology lies in adding the dimensions of culture, communication and social groups to our understanding.

Further reading

Dittmar, H. (1992). *The social psychology of material possessions: To have is to be*. Hemel Hempstead, UK: Harvester Wheatsheaf; New York: St Martin's Press. The first explicitly social psychological attempt to give a theoretical and empirical perspective on the link between possessions and identity.

Lewis, A., Webley, P., & Furnham, A. (1994). *The new economic mind: The social psychology of economic behaviour*. Hemel Hempstead, UK: Harvester Wheatsheaf. A lucid and thorough introduction to theory and research by both economists and psychologists concerned with economic social psychology.

Lunt, P.K. & Livingstone, S.M. (1992). *Mass consumption and personal identity*. Buckingham, UK: Open University Press. An eminently readable and relevant account of our ordinary experiences of mass consumer society.

McCracken, G. (1990). *Culture and consumption*. Indianapolis: Indiana University Press. An interdisciplinary and lively discussion of the role played by consumer goods for individuals and social groups in advanced Western societies.

Rudmin, F.W. (Ed.) (1991). *To have possessions: A handbook of property and ownership*. Special issue of the *Journal of Social Behavior and Personality, 6*. A useful compendium of articles which capture the diversity of people's behaviour with respect to possessions and their psychological significance.

Tybout, A.M. & Artz, N. (1994). Consumer psychology. *Annual Review of Psychology, 45*, 131–169. A condensed, but comprehensive 'state of the art' overview of the main theoretical and research developments in consumer psychology.

7

Social Psychology and Environmental Issues

Joop van der Pligt

Contents

Over the past decades social psychologists have become more involved in research on environmental issues. This research is often done in conjunction with researchers from other disciplines, most notably environmental psychology, health psychology, economics, medicine, political sciences and sociology. Major themes in this field of research concern both the impact of the environment on human behaviour and the impact of human behaviour on the environment. The study of these effects led to the growth of environmental psychology. Early research tended to focus on the impact of environmental factors such as crowding. Later, interest broadened to include effects of air pollution, noise and natural and technological disasters. Other research focused more on the (negative) effects of human behaviour on the environment and ways to promote positive changes in this behaviour. In the 1970s and 1980s much attention was paid to energy conservation. At present a wide variety of behaviours are being studied, including recycling behaviour and behaviours that are related to the greenhouse effect.

This chapter is divided into two sections. The first focuses on the impact of adverse environmental conditions on human behaviour. The emphasis will be on hazards related to technological developments such as nuclear energy. Public attitudes and the role of risk perception and more general values as determinants of these attitudes will be discussed. This will be followed by an overview of research on the effects of large-scale accidents and an analysis of public reactions to siting hazardous facilities such as nuclear power plants and toxic waste facilities. The first section ends with the issue of risk communication. It will be argued that social psychology could help to improve the quality and effectiveness of risk communication efforts, not only in the context of large-scale accidents but also in the context of increasing public awareness of the adverse consequences of a variety of behavioural practices. The second section addresses the impact of human behaviour on the environment and describes the possible role of social psychology to help stimulate environment-friendly behaviour.

Effects of the environment on human behaviour

Obviously the environment affects our behaviour; research tends to focus on factors that have a detrimental effect on human behaviour. Environmental stress refers to human reactions to noxious stimuli and/or perceived threats. One such factor is noise. Noise diminishes behavioural effectiveness not only in the laboratory but also in daily life. Children who are regularly exposed to noise of motorway traffic or of airports perform more poorly on problem-solving tasks and related achievement tests (Cohen, Evans, Stokols, & Krantz, 1986). Exposure to unpredictable noise in particular has negative effects on performance. Exposure to loud unpredictable noise in everyday life is also associated with reduced well-being, and with health risks. This is due to the fact that such stimulation is arousing and stressful. Noise is only one example of an environmental stressor. Generally it is regarded as an 'ambient stressor', a term introduced to describe the more continuous, stable and relatively intractable conditions of the physical environment. Like noise, most ambient stressors are background conditions (e.g. air pollution, poor climate control and bad lighting). Cataclysmic events constitute another type of environmental stressor. These are sudden catastrophes that demand major adaptive responses of those directly affected. Later in this chapter the effects of a number of major accidents or catastrophes will be discussed. Generally, environmental stressors result in more extreme reactions if the stressful event is unpredictable and uncontrollable. These two factors also play an important role in the context of a number of technological hazards such as nuclear energy and toxic waste, which will be discussed later.

Environmental hazards

There are clear differences between the general public and experts in how they perceive environmental hazards. Table 7.1 lists sources of hazards that people in the United States are concerned about and contrasts these with hazards that scientific experts are concerned about. The table shows that the general public tends to worry more about immediate, short-term hazards, while the scientific experts tend to be more concerned about hazards with long-term consequences for the environment and health. The table also indicates that experts are more

Table 7.1 *Concern about technological hazards*

Issues of concern to:	
General public	Experts
Contaminated drinking water	Global climate change
Storage of toxic chemicals	Species extinction, loss of biological diversity
Cancer-causing chemicals	Soil erosion and deforestation
Pesticide residue in food	Herbicides and pesticides
Air pollution	Pollution of surface water
Nuclear power accidents	Acid rain

Source: based on Baron & Byrne (1991, p. 564)

concerned about global environmental changes. Opinion polls among the Amsterdam population illustrate the priority of concrete environmental hazards over the more abstract, long-term hazards. In the late 1980s the most often mentioned environmental problem was the (then abundant) presence of dog excrement in the streets of Amsterdam.

Since the 1970s, policy makers have been confronted with vehement public opposition to various new technologies with possible adverse consequences for public health and the environment. Most prominent amongst these has been nuclear energy. Other developments concern toxic waste disposal, and large-scale projects such as the construction of major airports and motorways. In this section the focus will be on nuclear energy and (toxic) waste facilities. Frameworks developed in this area of research also apply to other large-scale hazards. Moreover, these issues are likely to remain prominent in the near future. The nuclear and toxic waste problem will be with us for some time, given the tendency to postpone adequate solutions to these problems.

Public opinion and nuclear energy

Generally, people tend to view current risk levels as unacceptably high for quite a few technological activities. All in all, there seems to be a substantial gap between perceived and desired risk levels. Slovic (1987) concluded that this difference clearly suggests that people are not satisfied with the way risks and benefits are balanced in present-day society. One example is nuclear energy. In the late 1970s the public became more involved in nuclear energy issues, and since then public acceptance has become a crucial issue in the nuclear debate. Rosa and Freudenburg (1993) show that nuclear attitudes tend to be consistently more negative than attitudes towards other energy sources (coal, natural gas and oil). The NIMBY (Not In My Back Yard) phenomenon is clearly reflected in public opinion data concerning nuclear issues. Generally, residents oppose local construction of nuclear and other hazardous facilities. This opposition is often a function of the (im)balance of health and safety hazards versus economic benefits. Nealey, Melber and Rankin (1983) show that the NIMBY effect is not restricted to ordinary citizens; they report the results of a study showing that 63 per cent of the interviewed politicians would be more likely to support waste disposal initiatives if these were not located in their state. Waste disposal issues also play an important role in public opinion. Recent polls conducted in the UK show that more than 60 per cent of the respondents worried about this issue (van der Pligt, 1992). As mentioned earlier, the perception of risk plays an important role in this context and seems a prime determinant of public opposition.

Risk assessment versus risk perception

The rapid development of nuclear and chemical technologies in the past decades has been accompanied by the potential to cause catastrophic and long-lasting damage to both the environment and public health. Quite often the most harmful consequences of these technologies are rare, delayed and difficult to assess by statistical analysis. Moreover, they are not well suited to management by trial-and-error learning (Slovic, 1987). Risk assessment techniques aim to help identify and quantify risk. Since the introduction of these techniques policy decision making has become increasingly dependent on quantitative risk assessments. Politicians, regulatory agencies and experts frequently refer to probabilistic criteria and rely on risk assessment to evaluate hazards. The public and its representatives have often been confused by the use of risk assessment in policy decision making.

Slovic, Fischhoff, Lichtenstein and colleagues showed that the way people perceive risk is both predictable and quantifiable. As argued by Fischhoff, Slovic, Lichtenstein, Read and Combs (1978), biases in perceived risk can be related to one of the most general judgmental heuristics: *cognitive availability* (see also Chapter 2). People who use this heuristic judge an event as likely or common if instances of it are relatively easy to imagine or recall. Slovic, Fischhoff and Lichtenstein (1979) argue that the most over- and under-estimated risks illustrate the availability bias; in their study overestimated risks (e.g. nuclear accidents, air crashes, botulism) tended to be dramatic and sensational whereas underestimated risks concerned less spectacular events that claim one or a few victims at a time and are also common in nonfatal form. Further support for this view is provided by Combs and Slovic (1979), who found that overestimated hazards also tend to be disproportionately mentioned in the news media.

Fischhoff et al. (1978) attempted to assess the causes of the low acceptability of some technological hazards, and asked respondents to rate nuclear power and 29 other hazardous activities on nine characteristics which were expected to influence risk perceptions and acceptability. The 'risk profiles' derived from these data showed that nuclear power scored at or close to the extreme high-risk end for most of these characteristics. Its risks were seen as involuntary, unknown to those exposed or to science, uncontrollable, unfamiliar, potentially catastrophic, severe and dreaded. Nuclear power was rated far higher on the characteristic 'dread' than any of the 29 other hazards studied by Fischhoff et al. (1978). Overall these ratings could be explained by two higher-order factors. The first factor is primarily determined by the characteristics 'unknown to exposed' and 'unknown to science', and to a lesser extent by 'newness', 'involuntariness' and 'delay of effect'. The second factor was defined most strongly by 'severity of consequences', 'dread', and 'catastrophic potential'. Controllability contributed to both factors. Nuclear power scored high on all these characteristics.

Lindell and Earle (1983) followed a similar approach and related judgements of the minimum safe distance from each of eight hazardous facilities to their ratings on 13 risk dimensions. The eight facilities were: natural gas power plant, oil power plant, coal power plant, oil refinery, liquefied natural gas (LNG) storage area, nuclear power plant, toxic chemical disposal facility and nuclear waste disposal facility. Their findings revealed a cluster of high-risk facilities (nuclear waste and toxic chemical waste facilities and nuclear power stations). At the low-risk end facilities included natural gas power plants, oil power plants and coal power plants.

Figure 7.1 shows the risk profiles for two high-risk facilities (nuclear power plant and toxic chemical disposal factory) and one low-risk facility (natural gas power plant) on the risk dimensions. Respondents were 396 people including environmentalists, urban residents, residents of hazardous facility communities, science writers, nuclear engineers, and chemical engineers. Overall, nearly 80 per cent were willing to live or work within a ten-mile radius of a natural gas power plant; percentages for a nuclear power plant and a toxic chemical disposal factory were 35 per cent and 29 per cent respectively. Interestingly, only 23 per cent of the nuclear engineers were willing to live within ten miles of a chemical waste facility as compared to 55 per cent of the chemical engineers. Percentages for a nuclear waste facility showed a reverse difference (60 per cent for nuclear engineers, 47 per cent for chemical engineers).

Overall, results of these studies help to clarify the structure of the perception of technological risks and could also help to understand public reactions and predict future acceptance and rejection of specific technologies. An obvious case in point is nuclear power. Findings presented in this section clearly reflect the public's view that nuclear power risks are unknown, dreaded, uncontrollable, inequitable, catastrophic, and likely to affect future generations. It has been argued that people's strong fears of nuclear power and their opposition to it are not irrational, but are logical consequences of their concerns (cf. Slovic, Lichtenstein, & Fischhoff, 1979).

It would be incorrect, however, to reduce the whole nuclear debate to differences in perceived risk between experts, policy makers and lay people. Attitudinal research provides more information about the reasons underlying public opposition to nuclear energy.

Attitudes to nuclear energy

Results from a series of studies by Eiser, van der Pligt and Spears (see van der Pligt, 1992; Eiser, van der Pligt, & Spears, 1995 for an overview) provide

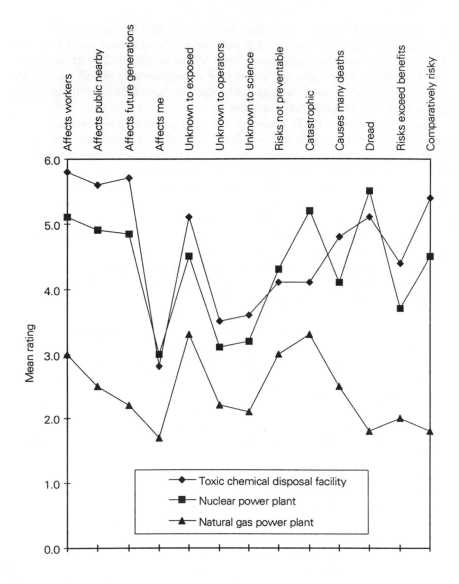

Figure 7.1   *Risk profiles for selected hazardous facilities (adapted from Lindell & Earle, 1983, p. 250)*

strong support for the view that individuals with opposing attitudes tend to see different aspects of the issue as salient, and hence will disagree not only on the likelihood of the various consequences but also about their importance. In other words, each group has its own reasons for holding a particular attitude; the 'pro' group saw the potential economic benefits as most important, while the 'anti' group attached greater value to environmental and public health aspects. Conflicts between opponents and proponents of nuclear energy quite often take the form of accusations about missing important key aspects. What constitute 'key aspects' is, of course, the central question in controversies of this kind. It seems that the pro- and anti-nuclear groups tend to see different aspects of the issue as *salient*, and tend to disagree not only over the validity and reliability of certain facts but also over their importance. The finding that separate dimensions of the issue appear differentially salient (in terms of their contributions to the prediction of overall attitude) for the different attitude groups has important practical implications for communication and mutual understanding between the different sides in the nuclear debate.

Later in this chapter the possible role of general values as a determinant of attitudes and environment-friendly behaviour will be discussed. To investigate whether attitudes about nuclear energy are also related to more general values Eiser and van der Pligt (1979) asked participants attending a one-day workshop on 'The Great Nuclear Debate' to select the five factors which they felt would contribute most to an improvement in the overall quality of life from a list of nine. Results show substantial differences between the two groups, with pro-nuclear respondents stressing the importance of advances in science and technology, industrial modernization, security of employment and conservation of the natural environment. The anti-nuclear respondents put even more emphasis on the last factor and stressed the importance of decreased emphasis on materialistic values, and improved social welfare. In a later study van der Pligt, van der Linden and Ester (1982) presented a sample of the Dutch population with a similar list of more general values. Results were in accordance with the above study and showed that pro-nuclear respondents emphasized the importance of economic development, whereas anti-nuclear respondents put more emphasis on conservation of the natural environment and the reduction of energy use. Finally, the anti-nuclear group thought the issue of increased public participation in decision making to be more important (see Table 7.2).

These results clearly indicate that attitudinal differences to nuclear energy are embedded in a wider context of attitudes to more general social issues. Public thinking on nuclear energy is not simply a matter of perceptions of risk but is also related to more generic issues such as the value of economic growth, high technology and centralization. It seems impossible to detach the issue of nuclear energy from questions of the kind of society in which one wants to live.

The fact that public attitudes to nuclear energy issues are relatively stable and embedded in a wider context of values suggests that large-scale attitude conversion may be quite difficult. People may, however, change their attitudes as a function of serious accidents that attract widespread attention, such as those at Three Mile Island (1979) and Chernobyl (1986). It seems much easier for nuclear attitudes to become suddenly more anti-nuclear because of a major accident or a series of smaller accidents than it would be for nuclear attitudes to become more pro-nuclear as a result of an extensive period of safe operations. Changes in a pro-nuclear direction are more likely to be gradual and to result from events related to energy supply, for example developments that would make non-nuclear energy much more expensive or more damaging to the environment (such as the greenhouse effect caused by fossil fuels).

Table 7.2 *Importance of various social issues as a function of attitude*

		Pro-subjects	Neutral subjects	Anti-subjects
(a)	Maintaining the present material standard of living	31[1]	33	28
(b)	Improvement in the strength of trade and industry	76	63	37
(c)	Conservation of the natural environment	28	31	58
(d)	Reduction in the level of unemployment	64	75	71
(e)	A stricter criminal law	35	42	24
(f)	Providing a less complex society	17	17	29
(g)	Greater public participation in decision making	3	1	12
(h)	Increase of defence spending	24	11	3
(i)	Reduction of energy use	16	18	26

[1] Scores represent the percentage of subjects selecting each issue among the three most important. The three columns do not add up to 300 because of the inclusion of subjects who chose fewer than three issues (total N = 600).

Source: adapted from van der Pligt, van der Linden, & Ester (1982, p. 226)

Environmental catastrophes

Since the early 1980s there has been a marked increase in research on disasters involving radiation or toxic waste. Residents' experiences at Love Canal in the USA (a leaking toxic chemical waste dump) appear to have been quite stressful and could have chronic consequences for some victims. The nuclear accident at Three Mile Island in 1979 generated extensive research on both immediate and longer-term effects on people living near the reactor site. This research supplemented self-report data with behavioural and biochemical measures for a number of years. This section presents a brief overview of research on the aftermath of the Chernobyl accident, as well as looking at Three Mile Island.

Three Mile Island

The accident at Three Mile Island (TMI) began at about 4 a.m. on Wednesday, 28 March 1979, when the TMI nuclear plant outside Harrisburg, Pennsylvania experienced a major accident. During the following days radio-active material was released from the plant in an uncontrolled and sporadic manner. Goldhaber, Houts and Disabella (1983) argued that psychologically and emotionally, the nearby population experienced a disaster. Because of the highly charged issue of nuclear safety, the TMI incident attracted an unprecedented number of investigations.

The amount of stress experienced by people around TMI was primarily determined by the perceived threat to physical safety and the perceived reliability of the information about the amount of threat. The perceived amount of threat varied considerably among individuals. Nearly 70 per cent of respondents thought the threat was very serious or serious (Flynn, 1981). Quite a few studies have found considerable psychological effects of the events at TMI, ranging from demoralization, threat perception and fear, to increased symptom reporting and negative emotional reactions (see, for example Davidson, Baum, & Collins, 1982; Dohrenwend, Dohrenwend, Kasl, & Warheit, 1979; Flynn, 1979).

A number of studies have examined the effects of living near TMI over longer periods of time. These indicated that problems decreased somewhat after the accident, but remained at higher levels as much as two years after the accident (see van der Pligt, 1992 for an overview). Davidson, Baum and Collins (1982) investigated control and stress-related responses of people living near TMI. They expected long-term effects of the accident, since a number of sources of stress remained at TMI. Their findings showed that residents reported less ability to control their surroundings than residents of communities further away. Loss of perceived control often leads to cognitive and motivational deficits, and this seemed to be the case for residents in the TMI area. TMI residents exhibited greater symptom distress, more behavioural difficulties on tasks, and increased physiological arousal than did residents in a comparison group. Feelings of control mediated the stress response; TMI area residents who reported lower expectations of being able to control their experience also reported greater symptom distress, showed poorer task performance and higher levels of physiological arousal than TMI residents who reported greater expectations of control. More recent research confirms the important role of the appraisal of control as a mediator between perceived threat and psychological symptoms for residents of TMI (Prince-Embury, 1992). All in all, research indicates a persistent stress response psychologically, behaviourally and biochemically *up to two years* after the accident. TMI residents expressed more concern about possible radiation leaks and about the threat to their personal health than residents of control areas.

Chernobyl

The reactor accident at Chernobyl in the Ukraine on 25–26 April 1986 is best described as a 'worst case' accident scenario in which a large reactor unit with a mature fuel inventory breached containment and released some of its radionuclide inventory. The accident at Chernobyl had a series of important consequences. Although the number of immediate fatalities was surprisingly low (31), over the next 50 years there may be up to 28,000 delayed fatalities worldwide, about half of them in the Ukraine and neighbouring states and half in Europe.

A number of issues played an important role in the aftermath of the accident. Most published research on the immediate impact of the accident was conducted in locations in Western Europe, and *not* in the area around Chernobyl. The psychological and behavioural reactions that have been extensively studied around TMI will be more or less absent in the next sections due to the unavailability of published research findings. This section will focus on public reactions and institutional reactions and will end with some implications of the accident for risk management and risk communication.

Opinion polls show that support for nuclear power declined in most West European countries while opposition increased. This immediate change was followed by some recovery but as long as a year after the accident overall figures imply that the recovery to pre-accident levels of support was not complete. It seems, therefore, that the Chernobyl accident had similar effects to the TMI accident: a dramatic initial increase in opposition followed by moderation but not a complete return to previous levels. Findings obtained in Sweden (Drottz & Sjöberg, 1990) indicated increased stress in the most affected areas in Sweden. Not surprisingly, the effects were less extreme than those at Three Mile Island but they give a clear indication of the effects in areas closer to the accident. Other reports suggest that the combination of health threats and negative consequences to one's livelihood (e.g. farmers in various countries) may have led to stress reactions (see e.g. Wynne, 1989).

Loss of trust and belief in the relevant agencies did play a major role in some countries. For instance, public opinion polls in Italy and France reported 70 per cent or more of respondents feeling distrust towards and lack of confidence in the government (Otway, Haastrup, Connell, Gianitsopoulos, & Paruccini, 1987). It needs to be added that trust in the government was not high in these two countries before Chernobyl, and their rather restrictive handling of information may have aggravated this feeling.

An analysis of newspaper reports by Otway et al. (1987) provides anecdotal evidence of stress-related reactions of the general public in a number of countries. In their study Otway et al. report a variety of reactions; quite often these constituted a higher risk than the one they tried to combat (see also Renn, 1990). Some examples:

- a significant increase in the number of abortions (reported in both Austria and Italy);
- panic buying of tinned, frozen and other long-life foods, reported in various countries, but reaching near-riot proportions in Greece;
- buying of radiation-measuring equipment for personal use (reported in Germany and Great Britain);
- uptake of potassium iodine (sometimes in substantial overdoses), reported in Denmark, Germany and Poland;
- an increase in suicides, partly attributed to the inability to cope with the threat, partly attributed to the financial consequences for small farms (reported in Italy and Greece).

Although these extreme reactions received quite extensive press coverage they were not typical of the majority of the population.

Hohenemser and Renn (1988) argue that since governments were simply not prepared for the transnational character of the accident, most protective actions involved a good deal of improvization, inconsistency, and at most a modest amount of prior planning. Many countries failed to take or recommend immediate protective action for the population at risk and also failed to convince the public that a clear and consistent risk management strategy was being implemented. The resulting confusion was further enhanced by inconsistent use of measurement units to indicate radiation levels (rem, rad, sievert, becquerel were all used, sometimes by the same agency). Overlapping responsibilities of the authorities also complicated things: quite often several ministries and health authorities provided information and advice.

Inadequate risk communication was the major shortcoming of the institutional reactions. Nearly all countries affected by the fallout had extremely limited experience of communicating these specific risks to the general public. The sensitivity of the issue (radiation) and the fear of the general public of this type of risk required an extremely careful approach. People confronted with information in terms of 'becquerel per kilogram or litre' in lettuce or milk had no reliable way of translating this information to possible health effects and/or comparing the risks with other health hazards. Too often the highly technical information was unintelligible to the average lay person (see e.g. Hohenemser & Renn, 1988; Wynne, 1989).

Siting hazardous facilities: attitudes, risk perception and equity

As we saw earlier in this chapter, local attitudes towards nuclear facilities tend to be negative. Harvey Brooks (1976, p.52), for instance, noted that 'almost from the first consideration of nuclear power as a realistic possibility, the public has viewed radioactive waste management as the primary obstacle to its ultimate technical success and social acceptability'. Numerous empirical studies underline this sombre appraisal. Initial attempts to explain these reactions focused on the 'irrational fear' of the public. References have been made to 'panic' and 'irrationality' with regard to radiation and chemicals.

The presence of fear in public reactions to nuclear and chemical waste is indisputable. It is disputable, however, that fear is the dominant factor. Studies of the fear hypothesis have not supported the proposed relationship (Cunningham, 1985; Freudenburg & Baxter, 1984). Brown, Henderson and Fielding (1983) found concern (a cognitive concept) to be far more pervasive than anxiety. Johnson (1987) notes that despite the lack of evidence for irrational fear as the primary factor in attitudes to nuclear waste, it should not be dismissed entirely. Fearful aspects of exposure to radiation or chemical risks are especially salient for local residents in the area where these facilities are sited. However, dismissing public concerns as entirely irrational is not likely to enhance the acceptability of waste facilities. Instead, more attention should be paid to risk–benefit equity and safety.

From a local perspective there is generally an imbalance between the risks and the benefits associated with hazardous facilities. The risk to the environment and health are for the locality while the benefits (e.g. solving a toxic waste problem) are for the country as a whole. To improve this inequity one could provide financial compensation at community and/or individual level. There is only limited experience of financial/economic compensation for local risks related to the siting of toxic waste facilities, and the assessment of the compensation to be awarded to the locality tends to be extremely complicated. As noted by Kasperson, Derr and Kates (1983) this would require an analysis of the distribution of benefits and harms to some specified population which would result from the siting decision. This entails (a) a specification of the economic, social, psychological and health-related aspects whose distribution is being investigated; (b) an explicit delineation of the population and relevant subpopulations to be included in the analysis; and (c) an estimate of the actual impact distribution as defined by (a) and (b) – which would result from siting a hazardous facility in a particular location. Next we would need a set of normative standards or principles by which the equity or 'fairness' of particular distributions may be judged and by which preference of one distribution over another may be determined (Kasperson et al., 1983, p. 332).

Unfortunately, the current understanding of the possible impact distributions from a hazardous waste facility at a particular site is quite limited. Reasons for this limited knowledge include (a) the relatively underdeveloped state of theory supporting approaches to social impact assessment; (b) the limited siting experience in recent years; and (c) the highly site-specific nature of social impacts (cf. Kasperson, 1985). In one of the few elaborate analyses of equity at a hazardous waste site, Kates and Braine (1983) painted a complex picture of gains and losses over more than a dozen locations stretching across the entire United States: benefits for some corporations, institutions or governments, and local residents; losses for others; and mixed balance sheets for still others. One of the major problems of this type of impact assessment concerns the limited knowledge about socioeconomic impacts and delayed health effects, and how to translate these possible futures into immediate compensatory (economic) benefits.

Communicating risks

The previous sections frequently referred to the importance of communication. For instance, experts and lay people seem to differ widely in their perception of environmental hazards. Similarly, pro- and anti-nuclear groups tend to adopt widely differing frames of reference to assess the acceptability of nuclear facilities. Risk communication is also important during siting procedures, after major accidents and in increasing the awareness of long-term risks to the environment that require behavioural change. Generally, three types of risk communication tasks are of relevance: (a) general information and education; (b) hazard awareness and emergency information; (c) policy decision making and conflict resolution. As noted by Covello, von Winterfeldt and Slovic (1986) these tasks frequently overlap, but can be conceptually differentiated. This section presents a brief overview of the major problems that hinder adequate risk communication and suggests a number of ways to improve risk communication efforts.

General information and education

General information and education is the aim of a wide variety of communication efforts. One recent example concerns information about radon risk. Radon is an important health risk and this gas is the second leading cause of lung cancer in the United States. Kerry Smith, Desvouges and Payne (1995) report the results of a study investigating the effects of different radon risk information booklets on households' decisions to undertake some mitigating action. Their results indicate that the amount and the format of risk information affects risk perceptions, behavioural intentions and mitigation. Concise information and clear instructions about when to act and take mitigating action seems most efficient. Risk communication aiming to increase *hazard awareness and provide emergency information* is becoming increasingly important. In Europe this is partly due to recent EC policy. The Seveso directive (named after a catastrophe in the chemical industry in northern Italy) focuses on the exchange of information between governments, industry and the general public. The directive requires the active provision of information by hazardous industries to residents nearby who could be affected by an accident. Generally it is expected that (local) government and industry should design the information programme together. In the Netherlands risk communication within the framework of the Seveso directive had three objectives: (1) to increase public knowledge about technology and risks related to technology; (2) to raise (or not damage) the public's confidence in policy concerning technological risks; and (3) to provide the public with behavioural guidance in disasters and emergencies. Some progress has been made in this area, and present practices have learned from previous failures, as in the aftermath of the Chernobyl accident. Finally, risk communication in the context of *policy decision making and conflict resolution* is probably the most difficult of the three. An example is the communication provided in the context of selecting sites for hazardous facilities. The major difficulties of risk communication can be summarized as follows:

(a) *Complexity.* Risk information is often highly technical and complex. Quantitative risk information is difficult to comprehend and relatively meaningless for the average lay person. Complexity is increased by the need, sometimes the habit, to present this information in scientific, legalistic and formal language. All these factors can lead to the view that risk communication efforts are evasive and not to the point. Suspicion and confusion are two of the most likely consequences.

(b) *Uncertainty*. Limited experience with nuclear accidents, insufficient data-bases and shortcomings of available methods and models lead to substantial uncertainty. This has also led to disagreement between experts about the validity of risk assessments. Improvement of both databases and assessment techniques generally result in more reliable risk assessment. Rapid changes, however, also create discontinuity and confusion in the public.

(c) *Frame of reference*. Lay people and experts often use different definitions of risks, and a different frame of reference when evaluating risks. Lay people tend to focus on factors such as catastrophic potential, fairness of the distribution of risks and benefits, effects on future generations, voluntariness and controllability. Experts, on the other hand, tend to define risks in terms of expected annual mortalities.

(d) *Trust and credibility*. Governmental agencies and industry sometimes lack public credibility and trust. Recent history has shown examples of the provision of limited information and/or deliberate withholding of information, usually because agencies, the industry and other relevant bodies feared emotional reactions and/or panic. This has severely damaged public trust in and the credibility of some governmental agencies and industry.

(e) *Involvement and concern*. Sometimes it is difficult to predict public involvement with and concern about specific risk issues. On the one hand people can be far *less* interested in risks than governmental agencies: in these cases it is difficult to get people to pay attention to risk information. On the other hand people can be far *more* interested in risks than governmental agencies. The latter is most often the case in highly charged areas such as industrial accidents and nuclear radiation leaks. Risk communication is then particularly hard and needs very different strategies from situations in which one tries to attract the attention of the public to less salient risk issues (e.g. seat belts, global warming).

These five problem areas give an indication of the difficulties of risk communication. The first two are related to the characteristics of the issue, the third and fifth to differences in conceptualization between lay people and experts. The fourth factor refers to lack of experience of the relevant agencies, underestimating the public, and consequently, a relatively poor history in the recent past. Some progress has been made and, as argued before, social psychology could help to make further progress by investigating the frame of reference of the various groups involved, but also by pointing to other important factors that determine the effectiveness of communication such as source characteristics (e.g. credibility and trust) and a variety of message characteristics (e.g. consistency, vividness and concreteness). Communication also plays a crucial role in the issues to be discussed in the next section of this chapter.

Understanding and changing environmental behaviour

Since the early 1970s, social psychologists have examined ways to encourage environmentally sound behaviours such as conserving energy, recycling, reducing detergent use, and not littering. This research has focused primarily on behaviour modification and has identified a number of principles that can help to foster environment-friendly behaviour. First, the role of environmental concern and attitudes and their relationship to environmental behaviour will be discussed. Next, the emphasis will be on changing environmental behaviour; strategies to promote environmental-friendly behaviour will be illustrated with research on recycling behaviour and energy conservation.

Environmental concern, attitudes and behaviour

Environmental concern has been investigated by sociologists, social psychologists and environmental psychologists. Their interest is based on the assumption that concern for the environment is a necessary condition for the development of successful environmental protection and behaviour modification programmes.

The presumed role of environmental concern can be related to a long-standing research tradition in social psychology: investigating *values* as guiding principles in the life of a person or group. Rokeach (1973) argued that the ordering of values according to their importance forms a relatively enduring system that serves as a standard when forming and expressing attitudes, and when selecting and rationalizing actions. Values share elements with concepts such as attitudes, but transcend specific situations and might be conceptualized as attitudes towards abstract end-states or goals of human activities. Values and differences in value priorities have been studied in the context of environmental behaviour and many other behaviours (e.g. friendship, health, consumer, delinquent, occupational). There is some evidence for the causal impact of values on behaviour (see Ball-Rokeach, Rokeach, & Grube, 1984). Rokeach and Ball-Rokeach (1988) provided experimental evidence for the role of values as a predictor of behaviour. Stressing the value of equality in an American television programme resulted in more positive attitudes to ethnic minorities and women and higher donations to the movements against racism and sexism. Generally, however, the impact of general values on specific behaviours is limited. Although incorporating general values can help our understanding of attitudes (see also the earlier discussion on the relation between values and nuclear attitudes), their predictive power over and above these attitudes is modest.

From the late 1970s onwards researchers have explored the role of broad attitudes towards the environment in predicting attitudes to specific conservation issues and conservation behaviours. One widely used measure of environmental concern is the so-called 'New Environmental Paradigm'

Balance of nature
  When humans interfere with nature it often produces disastrous effects
  Humans must live in harmony with nature in order to survive
  Humans have the right to modify the natural environment to suit their needs

Limits to growth
  The balance of nature is very delicate and easily upset
  There are limits to growth beyond which our industrialized society cannot expand
  We are approaching the limit of the number of people the earth can support
  The earth is like a spaceship with only limited room and resources
  Mankind is severely abusing the environment
  To maintain a healthy economy we will have to develop a 'steady state' economy
    where industrial growth is controlled

Humanity over nature
  Plants and animals exist primarily to be used by humans
  Mankind was created to rule over the rest of nature

Figure 7.2 *New Environmental Paradigm scales (Vining & Ebreo, 1992, p. 1591)*

(NEP) developed by Dunlap and van Liere (1978). The NEP incorporates a series of attitude statements representing a worldview of the relationship between humanity and the environment. It is often contrasted with the 'Dominant Social Paradigm' (DSP) with an emphasis on progress and economic growth (see Dunlap & van Liere, 1984). High scores on the NEP indicate pro-environmental attitudes. Milbrath (1984, 1986) also used the distinction NEP versus DSP and employed a two-dimensional structure to describe these two values. One dimension refers to social change (advocacy versus resistance); the other contrasts the value given to the environment and that given to material wealth and economic growth. In this two-dimensional structure those who adhere to values typical of industrial society resist social change and emphasize material wealth. Those with more radical, pro-environmental values emphasize the environment and the necessity for social change.

Initially the NEP was seen as a unidimensional concept, but later research indicated that the NEP is multidimensional. For instance Albrecht, Bultena, Hoiberg and Nowak (1982) found that the NEP scale can be decomposed into three distinct dimensions labelled 'Balance of Nature', 'Limits to Growth' and 'Humanity over Nature'. Figure 7.2 summarizes the items of the NEP in terms of these three dimensions. Hacket (1992) also developed a multivariate model of environmental concern.

A number of studies indicated that the NEP is reliable and valid. For instance the NEP was useful in differentiating members of environmental groups from the general public (Dunlap & van Liere, 1978; Steger, Pierce, Steel, & Lovrich, 1989) and higher scores on the NEP are also related to greater knowledge about environmental problems (Arcury, Johnson, &

Scollay, 1986). Other research shows that the NEP is predictive of more specific environmental attitudes. Shetzer, Stackman and Moore (1991) found that attitudes of business students to the position of business on environmental issues were positively related to the NEP. Similarly, Vining and Ebreo (1992) found that NEP scores were positively related to more specific attitudes, in their case recycling. It needs to be added that this relationship was modest (approximately 16 per cent of the variance in specific attitudes could be explained by general environmental concern).

Others argue that general environmental concern can help the understanding of more specific attitudes by placing these in a wider context. For instance, Kempton, Darley and Stern (1992) argue that a profound change in the 1990s concerns the role of more general moral values in the debate about energy use and conservation. Many of the more serious consequences of present-day environmental policy will occur far in the future, to other nations or to other species. This is especially the case for global climate change, caused by the so-called greenhouse gases that humans are releasing into the atmosphere. Although there is uncertainty about the effects, many climatologists expect warmer weather, disruption of agriculture, forced migration and the extinction of many species. The expected modest rise in sea level is likely to have a profound effect on countries that simply lack the resources to combat these changes. Most of the reported consequences will not be felt by us, but by future generations. Moreover most of the worst consequences will be experienced by nations and species less well able to adapt. In this context Kempton et al. (1992) point to the changes in more general values that provide some hope for the future. Since 1981 US opinion polls have included one question that asks respondents whether they agree or disagree with the statement: 'Protecting the environment is so important that requirements and standards cannot be too high, and continuing environmental improvements must be made regardless of cost.' The percentage of US adults in agreement with this statement increased from 45 per cent in 1981 to nearly 80 per cent in 1989. Kempton (1990) found that more than 80 per cent of respondents expressed concern about future generations. MacLean (1983) argued that a commitment to securing resources and opportunities for future generations expresses the belief that society and culture matter to us and should survive into the future. For this reason he is quite hopeful about the future because the actions intended to pass on an intact environment to descendants will make our own lives more meaningful and of a higher quality.

Vlek and Keren (1992) are less optimistic and argue that environmental risk management can be characterized in terms of four different types of dilemma: benefit-risk, temporal, spatial and social traps in which long-term risk receives less weight than immediate benefits, and risks for other groups and/or nations receive limited attention. Most conservation behaviours can also be interpreted as a social dilemma; i.e. the self-interests of each individual actor are often incompatible with those of society at large. Similarly the self-interests of nations are often incompatible with those of the planet as a whole. In many situations such as limiting pollution or increasing energy conservation the individual actor (person, group or nation) may have strong incentives to deny cooperation and become a 'free rider'. The costs of the needed changes will then be shifted to the collective.

The impact of general environmental concern on behaviour seems limited. For instance Vining and Ebreo (1992) found that general environmental concern as assessed by the NEP accounted for only 5.6 per cent of the variance in self-reported recycling behaviour. In their study specific recycling attitudes were much more predictive, accounting for approximately 35 per cent of the variance. Not surprisingly, some reviews of the conservation literature (e.g. Cook & Berrenberg, 1981; Stern & Oskamp, 1987) argue that less attention should be paid to factors such as general environmental concern, given their limited predictive power. Oskamp, Harrington, Edwards, Sherwood, Okuda and Swanson (1991) also argue that much of the existing literature focuses on general environmental concern rather than on more specific attitudes and beliefs. Given the modest relationship between this general factor and behaviour, a number of researchers have argued in favour of investigating more specific environmental issues such as energy conservation and resource recycling.

Notwithstanding the obvious problems related to inducing behavioural change on the basis of more general values such as environmental concern and moral considerations about fairness and equity, their relevance should not be underestimated. Kempton et al. (1992) acknowledge that given the gap between general attitudes and behaviour one should not have high expectations that appeals focusing on these general values will produce concrete behavioural change. They recommend distinguishing between concrete consumer behaviours and political actions and argue that more general values may have a greater effect on the environment through the results of political behaviour such as voting for 'green' candidates in elections. These behaviours may produce changes in policy making and eventually lead to changes in a pro-environmental direction. One could argue that this is exactly what happened with policy making concerning a number of environmental hazards.

The social psychological literature generally pays more attention to attitude as a primary determinant of behaviour. Although most findings indicate a modest relationship between specific attitudes and environmental behaviour, this relationship tends to be stronger than the relationship between general values such as environmental concern and environmental behaviour. Newhouse (1990) summarizes some factors that could explain the modest power of attitudes to predict environmental behaviour: temporal instability, direct versus indirect experience, normative influences, and attitude–behaviour measurement correspondence. Vining and Ebreo (1992) focus on the latter two factors. In accordance with Ajzen and Fishbein (1977) they propose a hydraulic relationship between the predictive power of social norms and attitudes. If social norms are absent the relationship between attitudes is expected to be quite strong. When strong social norms exist, they can prevent people from acting in accordance with their attitudes. For instance, a person may feel very strongly about energy conservation, but the prevailing social norms prevent him/her from taking action. The second factor concerns the general requirement that behavioural antecedents such as beliefs, attitudes and social norms should be measured at the same level of specificity as the behaviour itself (see Ajzen & Fishbein, 1977 and Chapter 2 of this volume). This lack of specificity could well be a major cause of the limited predictive power of general environmental concern. Vining and Ebreo (1992) showed that attitudes, if assessed on the same level of specificity, can be a reasonable predictor of behaviour (in their case recycling behaviour). It needs to be added, however, that the total amount of variance explained by attitudes remained modest (approximately 35 per cent). Other findings indicate even less impact of attitudes on environmental behaviour, especially in behavioural domains, in which habits play an important role. For instance, Aitken, McMahon, Wearing and Finlayson (1994) found attitudes to have no significant impact on residential water use. Similarly, Verplanken, Aarts, van Knippenberg and van Knippenberg (1994) found a weak attitude–behaviour relation in the domain of travel mode choice (travelling by car versus train) if travel mode choice was primarily determined by habit, i.e. without deliberate consideration.

Changing environment-related behaviour

Since the early 1970s psychologists have examined ways to promote environment-friendly or conservation behaviours. Early research focused on litter behaviour and energy conservation. More recent research also focused on behaviours such as recycling (e.g. Katzev, Blake, & Messer, 1993), car use (Verplanken et al., 1994), and water use (Aitken et al., 1994). Psychological research should help to determine how to encourage or discourage environment-related behaviours, and, in the past decades research has identified some basic principles that can help make behaviour modification programmes successful. The major lesson from these efforts concerns the need to adopt a *multitude of approaches* in order to increase the effectiveness of behaviour modification programmes.

First this section describes two specific cases of a behavioural change programme in more detail; this is followed by a discussion of strategies to reduce energy consumption. The section ends with a new challenge for social psychology: i.e. improving programmes that aim to help delay or reduce global environmental change such as the greenhouse effect.

Aitken et al. (1994) attempted to evaluate methods to encourage the reduction of residential water use. They built upon earlier studies relating social psychological concepts to resource conservation, and identified three concepts that were expected to be relevant for domestic water consumption: attitudes, habits and values. Their results showed that all three concepts were poor predictors of water consumption. A total of 60 per cent of the variance of water consumption was explained by three variables (number of residents in the household, clothes-washing machine loads, and property value). Katzev et al. (1993) provide further support for the important role of situational factors in changing environment-related behaviour. In their study the main determinants of recycling behaviour was the 'user-friendliness' of the recycling system, while psychological variables had a modest impact or no impact at all. These results indicate a limited impact of psychological variables and can be added to the body of research showing a poor relationship between values, attitudes and behaviour. A follow-up study by Aitken et al. (1994) was based on the assumption that freely performed behaviour that is inconsistent with an attitude results in dissonance, and one way to reduce this dissonance is to change one's behaviour. Two conditions were created, which were quite similar. In both, respondents received a postcard containing information about their water use, and the average consumption for a household of the same size. In the dissonance condition respondents were reminded of their agreement with the fact that they were also responsible for the conservation of water resources. Both interventions resulted in a reduction in residential water consumption, especially in high-consuming households. The households receiving both dissonance and feedback information exhibited the greatest reductions, followed by households receiving feedback only. As noted by Aitken et al., the results of their two studies suggest an interesting paradox. On the one hand attitudes were shown to be poor predictors of water consumption; on the other hand householders made significant behavioural changes in order to align their water consumption with their expressed attitude. The latter suggests that attitudes are important determinants of behaviour. The limited insight into the impact of one's own behavioural practices due to the prevailing limited feedback on water use could explain the lack of correspondence between attitudes and behaviour in this specific domain. Providing information about behaviour can highlight possible discrepancies between attitudes and behaviour one simply was not aware of, and result in behavioural change.

Another example concerns energy conservation and illustrates the need to provide clear, practical and vivid information. The programme was developed in the United States, a country that consumes far more energy, per capita, than any other nation in the world. Aronson and his colleagues (see Aronson, Wilson, & Akert, 1994 for an overview) argued that people's attention tends to be directed to those aspects of their environment which are most salient and vivid, and assumed that energy conservation in the home is not a particularly vivid problem. To test whether making the sources of home energy consumption more vivid would affect energy use, the researchers collaborated with several energy auditors. In California energy auditors provide (free) advice on request and give customers an assessment of what needs to be done to make their homes more efficient. The problem was that fewer than 20 per cent of the individuals requesting audits were actually following the auditors' recommendations. Aronson et al. (1994) give an example concerning home insulation. To increase compliance the auditors were trained to present their findings in a more vivid manner. For most people, a small crack under the door did not seem to cause a significant loss of energy, so generally the auditor's recommendation to put in some weather stripping had limited success. The resolution was to present this type of information more vividly:

> Look at all the cracks around that door! It may not seem like much to you, but if you were to add up all the cracks around and under each of these doors, you'd have the equivalent of a hole the size and circumference of a basketball. Suppose someone poked a hole the size of a basketball in your living room wall. Think for a moment about all the heat you'd be losing from a hole that size – that's money out the window. You'd want to patch that hole in your wall, wouldn't you? That's exactly what weather stripping does. And that's why I recommend you install weather stripping. (Aronson et al., 1994, p. 573)

Similar attempts were made to make other problems more concrete and vivid – for example, referring to an attic that lacks insulation as a 'naked attic' that is like 'facing winter not without an overcoat, but without any clothing at all'. Results showed an increase in the percentage of home owners who followed the vivid recommendations to 61 per cent. This study demonstrates that if old habits are involved, the communication should be vivid enough to break through those established habits.

Research in related domains shows that attitudes are often not sufficient to induce environment-friendly behaviours or reduce environment-destructive behaviours. Factors such as convenience, costs associated with the behavioural alternatives and trust in the authorities recommending specific behavioural practices also play an important role as behavioural determinants. The complex and often changing determinants of environmental behaviour make it necessary to use a combination of intervention techniques to address the most important barriers to the desired behaviour. As mentioned before, these barriers can be related to internal variables such as attitudes, values and perceived responsibility, but also to external factors such as convenience and costs related to the behaviour.

Kempton et al. (1992) describe five standard policy strategies that are generally used to change a specific environmental behaviour: energy consumption. These are (1) information or feedback, (2) persuasion, (3) altering incentives, (4) commands or mandates, and (5) developing new technologies. Each of these will be briefly discussed below.

Early research during the energy crises in the 1970s tended to focus on *providing information* to citizens about the necessity to save energy and providing *feedback* about their energy use. Providing information about the costs of energy use is most likely to be successful when energy prices are high and public awareness and involvement are considerable. Even if these conditions are met, the information should include practical tips on saving energy while the costs in terms of convenience have to be modest. One could also provide information about nonfinancial matters, and focus on more altruistic motives such as reducing national energy dependence on imported oil and preserving environmental quality for future generations. *Persuasive* approaches focusing on these nonfinancial motives can be effective; this seems especially true when one adopts a community-based approach as opposed to large-scale campaigns via the mass media. Successful examples are provided by Dietz and Vine (1982) and Vining and Ebreo (1992). Both the provision of information and persuasive attempts could benefit from insights derived from the social psychological literature. First, in accordance with the main findings obtained in the area of judgement and decision making one would expect concrete and vivid information to be more persuasive (see Chapter 2). Secondly, it is essential to take into account the involvement of respondents in environmental issues. If this is low more attention should be paid to so-called peripheral cues such as the credibility of the source that provides the information (see Chapter 1). If involvement is high the information could be more detailed and does not necessarily have to rely on heuristic information processing and more peripheral cues. Policy strategies often use *financial incentives* to help change behaviour. Examples are tax increases on fossil fuels. Positive incentives include tax rebates for installing insulation, and reduced prices for energy-efficient household appliances. National or local authorities can *mandate* energy conservation efforts by law. One example concerns fuel economy standards imposed on car manufacturers (see Kempton et al., 1992, p. 1217). Similar examples concern emission thresholds for industry and legal measures to control toxic waste dumping. Finally, *technological development* can also provide solutions to energy conservation and related environmental problems. Technology could help to design more energy-efficient appliances, production processes and cars.

Quite often a mix of these five strategies is essential to generate adequate levels of behavioural change. Thus successful programmes should provide concrete and practical information by reliable sources that are trusted and, if possible, also offer financial incentives (tax deductions or other measures). Simultaneously, attention should be paid to legal measures to stimulate individual and corporate behaviour. Finally, technological development can help to provide solutions and these should also be stimulated by a mix of the first four strategies.

Global environmental change

These five strategies also apply to global environmental change. Over the past decade both scientists and policy makers have become more concerned about global environmental change because of the unprecedented rate of this change. Human activities can have global effects in two ways: they can alter (eco)systems such as oceans or atmosphere, or the combined localized changes can become global cumulatively (see Stern, 1992). As argued by Stern and others, psychology is relevant to issues of global environmental change because of the role of human activities. Psychological expertise is essential in helping to bring about the changes in human behaviour necessary to forestall or slow down processes of global change. This provides a major challenge to the behavioural sciences, and has many sides. First it is essential to convince policy makers and the public that there is a problem. Particularly worrying in this context is the long time lag of many global environmental changes. Moreover, uncertainty about these changes is high, while the possible consequences are serious and may be difficult to control; by the time a catastrophe is foreseen, it may already be too late to prevent it. The uncertainty often results in contradictory statements from the scientific community. Adequate communication about the risks of global change and their uncertainties is the first task in which social psychology could play an important role. The second task concerns the framing of the problem. Global change is a prime example of a dilemma in which long-term consequences for other continents, countries or species tend to receive less weight than more immediate and concrete consequences. Convincing policy makers and the public to adopt a wider perspective is a difficult task, and will often be a prerequisite for behavioural change programmes.

The third task concerns behavioural change. This requires a multidiscip-. linary approach, since a first step must be to identify the human behaviours that have the greatest impact on global change. Without such an analysis behavioural change programmes could be targeted on the wrong behavioural practices. Stern (1992) illustrates this nicely, arguing that past research often focused on behaviours that intuitively were expected to have the greatest impact. For instance, much attention has been paid to daily practices of households concerning energy use and solid waste generation while investment decisions by households and corporations generally have a more profound impact on the environment. In the case of the greenhouse effect, fossil fuel burning is a major contributor and this can be subdivided by type of user (households, industries, etc.) and purpose (transportation, space heating). A wide variety of activities have energy consequences: these include the design of products, purchase behaviour of consumers, everyday use of products, and even the discarding of these products. For instance, fuel consumption for personal transportation is determined by the fuel efficiency of the available automobiles (design of the product), purchase behaviour of the consumers (the weight assigned to fuel efficiency), miles driven per automobile (user behaviour). The relative impact of each of these elements should be known before starting interventions to stimulate behavioural change. For instance, car design and purchase decisions in the United States would have a considerable impact on carbon dioxide emissions (one of the major contributors to the greenhouse effect) and hence the global climate. If the fuel efficiency of cars doubled, worldwide emissions would fall by 2.5 per cent (Stern, 1992).

Research on reduction of energy use is most relevant to global change. During the 1970s and 1980s a considerable number of studies focused on ways to promote energy conservation. Earlier in this section Kempton et al.'s (1992) proposal to distinguish five standard policy strategies was discussed. Stern's (1992) review confirms most of Kempton's conclusions. Providing information and feedback are most likely to be successful if one adopts techniques that rely on simple, concrete and clear language with concrete, practical recommendations and credible sources. More intensive, personalized community based interventions tend to be more successful but these also tend to be more expensive and more difficult to implement on a large scale. Most research, however, focuses on the use of equipment (household appliances, heating, cars, etc.) already 'in place'. It could be more efficient to influence purchase decisions. Research on this issue is less prominent but shows some promising results (energy-efficiency labelling of appliances, cars, etc.). Social psychologists could help to increase the weight of energy conservation in purchase decisions and should be more involved in informational programmes aiming to change purchase behaviour. Stern also refers to the potential contribution of financial incentives, regulation and technical developments. In accordance with Kempton et al. (1992) he concludes that combining the various techniques after careful analyses of the behaviour and its relevance to global change seems the best approach in developing effective and practical programmes to change behavioural practices. In this way it is possible to overcome a number of barriers that may hinder behavioural change.

Finally, some neglected issues in research on global change should be mentioned. First, social psychological research tends to focus on the individual consumer and pays limited attention to other actors (politicians, industry) who also play an important role in processes that have severe consequences for the global climate. In collaboration with political scientists and economists more effort should be made to study their decision-making processes and to develop ways to influence these. This research should also address issues such as public participation in policy decision making and communication between the various actors and the public.

Conclusions

This chapter has provided a number of applications of social psychological methods, concepts and theoretical frameworks to environmental issues. It was argued that insights derived from social psychology can help to increase our understanding of public reactions to technological hazards such as nuclear power stations and toxic waste facilities. The major contribution of social psychological research is that it helps to analyse the points of view of the various stakeholders in these controversial issues. These viewpoints vary with respect to the perceived costs and benefits of the developments and their relative importance. Other contributions concern the importance of equity in siting hazardous facilities. Social psychology could help to foster efficient communication and mutual understanding between experts, policy makers and the lay public. Recent history has shown that improved communication is essential in environmental policy decision making about siting hazardous facilities, waste disposal issues and risk management after major accidents.

Social psychology can also contribute to the efficiency of programmes to stimulate environment-friendly behaviour. Basically it seems essential to rely on different strategies to help change behaviour in a more environment-friendly direction and focus on both internal (e.g. values, attitudes, perceived responsibility) and external factors (e.g. convenience, costs). To enhance the role of social psychology in these processes it seems essential to collaborate with researchers from other disciplines. This applies to most environmental issues; their importance and urgency require a multidisciplinary approach within which social psychology can make a useful contribution.

This chapter focuses on the role of social psychology in understanding the impact of the environment on human behaviour and the effects of human behaviour on the environment. The first part briefly described the impact of adverse environmental conditions on human behaviour. The effects of ambient stressors (such as noise) and cataclysmic stressors (e.g. major catastrophes) are discussed. Much attention was paid to nuclear energy and toxic waste facilities: public attitudes, the role of equity in siting procedures and the importance of risk communication were briefly discussed. The second part focused on the effects of human behaviour on the environment. The role of habits, values and attitudes as determinants of environment-related behaviour was discussed. This was illustrated with research on a variety of environmental behaviours such as recycling, energy conservation and domestic water use. This was followed by an analysis of the effectiveness of interventions that aim to stimulate environment-friendly behaviour and the possible role that social psychology can play. The chapter ended with a consideration of the human dimensions of global environmental change.

Further reading

Cohen, S., Evans, G.W., Stokols, D., & Krantz, D. (1986). *Behavior, health, and environmental stress.* New York: Plenum Press. This book provides an overview of the stress paradigm and discusses research findings concerning a variety of environmental stressors. The consequences of these stressors and their explanations, as well as coping mechanisms people use to deal with environmental stressors, are discussed.

Stern, P.C. (1992). Psychological dimensions of global environmental change. *Annual Review of Psychology, 43,* 269–302. This review article provides an overview of the issue of global environmental change and discusses the possible contribution of psychology to changing behavioural practices with adverse effects for the global environment. Problems and opportunities for the behavioural sciences to help solve these issues are summarized.

Stokols, D. & Altman, I. (Eds) (1987). *Handbook of environmental psychology,* 2 vols. New York: Wiley. This two-volume handbook provides a comprehensive overview of environmental psychology with theoretical, methodological and empirical contributions. It attempts to identify linkages among various research traditions. Much attention is paid to the applicability of environmental psychology to the analysis and resolution of environmental problems.

Sundstrom, E., Bell, P.A., Busby, P.L., & Asmus, C. Environmental psychology 1989–1994. *Annual Review of Psychology, 47,* 485–512. This article reviews new contributions to theory and empirical research published in major journals of environmental psychology in the period 1989–1994.

Van der Pligt, J. (1992). *Nuclear energy and the public.* Oxford: Blackwell. This book provides an overview of public reactions to nuclear energy and related technological hazards. Public attitudes and differences between the frame of reference of experts, policy makers and the lay public are discussed. The book also covers issues such as risk communication and decision aids that could help improve the quality of policy decision making.

8

The Social Psychology of Driver Behaviour

Dianne Parker and Antony S.R. Manstead

Contents

Road traffic accidents constitute a serious social problem across the world. Governmental statistics show that in Great Britain during 1992 there were over 233,000 reported road traffic accidents, of which 3,855 were fatal, leading to a total of 4,229 deaths (Department of Transport, 1994). This represents a death rate of 7.5 per 100,000 population. The equivalent figures for other countries are as follows: Germany, 10,631 (13 per 100,000); France, 9,900 (17); Japan, 14,886 (12); and the USA, 39,235 (15). It is evident, then, that the problem is substantial worldwide, despite a downward trend in accident numbers during the last 20 years. Every accident is a traumatic – if not tragic – event for those involved, and the costs to society are enormous. For while the human suffering that occurs as a result of road traffic accidents cannot be quantified, efforts can be and have been made to calculate the economic costs. Taking factors such as police time, use of emergency services, and damage to vehicles and property into consideration, it has been estimated that each injury accident in Great Britain in 1993 cost over £38,000, while each fatal accident cost over £863,000 (Department of Transport, 1989). The corresponding figures would of course be even higher today. Moreover, the data show that the most vulnerable groups are the young. While 0.7 per cent of all deaths among the general population of Great Britain in 1992 were the result of a road traffic accident, the corresponding figure for 16–19-year-olds was 35 per cent, and for 20–29-year-olds 19 per cent (Department of Transport, 1994), although it should be noted that not all of these road deaths involve young people as drivers.

It is now commonly acknowledged that human factors play an important role in road traffic accident causation (Grayson & Maycock, 1988), and a great deal of research effort has been devoted to improving our understanding of those factors. Within human factors research broadly conceived, a distinction has been made between driver *performance*, which reflects what a driver *can* do, based on his or her physical and mental capabilities, and driver *behaviour*, which involves what a driver *does* do and which may to a great extent be culturally and socially determined (Evans, 1991). In a widely cited four-year study of accident causation in Great Britain, Sabey and Taylor (1980) reached the conclusion that in 95 per cent of the 2,041 accidents investigated, driver and/or pedestrian error and impairment were significant contributory factors. In attempting to devise ways to reduce error among drivers, human factors specialists have addressed a wide range of driving-related topics, including driving task analysis, driver selection, training and retraining, and human engineering as applied to highway and vehicle subsystems (OECD, 1970). The efforts of psychologists have in the main been directed towards the explanation of differential rates of accident liability in terms of individual differences (Grayson & Maycock, 1988; Noordzij, 1990). Concepts and methods borrowed from cognitive psychology have been employed in studies focusing on driver performance, attempting to identify individual differences in variables such as the management of attentional resources, reaction times and information processing capabilities, and in the analysis of driver errors (e.g. Groeger, 1989, 1991). Research on driver behaviour, on the other hand, has tended to adopt a psychometric perspective, aiming to develop scales consisting of items which are capable of differentiating between various driver groups in terms of accident liability (e.g. Elander, West, & French, 1993; Gulian, Matthews, Glendon, Davies, & Debney, 1989).

A recent review of individual differences in accident liability (Lester, 1991) identified and evaluated human factors research in seven main areas: psycho-motor skills, perceptual style, cognitive abilities, performance measures, personality, social and family context factors, and attitudes. Lester observed that research in the first four of these areas, which can be broadly categorized as measuring skills and abilities, has failed to demonstrate a relationship between driving performance and accident liability. However, several studies have suggested that there *is* a significant association between accident liability and social and attitudinal factors. Lester concludes that 'further work in these complex areas [of higher-order cognitive and risk perception skills together with attitudinal and social factors] would appear to provide the best prospects of understanding the determinants of driver behaviour in the longer term' (p. 18). In recent comments other researchers have also begun to acknowledge the potential of social psychological methods and theories to contribute to our understanding of driver behaviour, and thence to the reduction of road traffic accidents (e.g. Evans, 1991; Grayson, 1991; Quimby & Downing, 1991).

Methodological issues

The psychologist involved in researching the determinants of driver behaviour faces a daunting set of methodological problems. The three main methodological options available are direct observation, simulation of the driving task, and self-report, each of which has its limitations. Direct observation of driver behaviour may be conducted unobtrusively, from the roadside or from a separate vehicle, in order to avoid observer effects (Baxter, Manstead, Stradling, Campbell, Reason, & Parker, 1990). The collection of data of this type may require specialized equipment such as radar, or induction loops. This method is most useful for the collection of data on the prevalence of observable driver behaviours such as the use of seat belts, headway (gaps) between vehicles, and speed choice which, whilst uncontaminated, is necessarily of a fairly crude nature. Another approach involves in-car observation, a situation in which the researcher travels as a passenger in the observed driver's own vehicle, or in a test vehicle supplied by the researcher (Rolls, Hall, Ingham, & McDonald, 1991). There are two main problems with this approach. The first involves the possibility of experimenter effects, and the second involves either the difficulty of comparing drivers' performance when each has used a different vehicle, or the problems arising from unfamiliarity with the vehicle if a 'standard' test car is used. Moreover, establishing a link between behaviour and accidents using any of these observational methods would require an enormous amount of time and effort, given that accidents are both infrequent and difficult to predict, for which reason traffic conflicts are often used as a surrogate measure for accidents.

More detailed information on driver behaviour can be collected when normal driving is simulated. Some researchers have used instrumented vehicles for this purpose (Casey & Lund, 1987; Mourant & Rockwell, 1972). The use of a standard test car removes the possibility that observed differences in driver behaviour are due, at least in part, to differences in the characteristics of the vehicles driven. Moreover, standard test vehicles can be adapted so that multiple measures of cognitive and physiological reactions to the driving situation can be assessed. However, such a vehicle will inevitably be unfamiliar to the observed driver, so there are problems with the validity of the resulting measures. The performance of a driver in a standard test car is unlikely to reflect his or her normal driving performance. The same problems arise when using a specific test route in order to maintain standardization. Whilst this allows the researcher to ensure that each observed driver encounters the same physical hazards on the test route, the route chosen may be familiar to some, but not all, of the drivers observed. The driver under study is unlikely to behave in a 'natural' way while being observed by an experimenter, or monitored by equipment. Driving simulators developed for use in a laboratory, which usually involve seating the subject in front of a screen showing a range of driving situations, allow for the introduction of tighter control into the experimental situation. However, they are comparatively expensive and lacking in ecological validity. The social and motivational context in which normal driving occurs is completely removed, as are the real consequences of risky driving. Nevertheless, the use of a standard test car is eminently suitable for studying within-subject variations in driver behaviour which may result from experimental manipulations of driver state (e.g. through fatigue, stress or alcohol use), task difficulty, instruction or feedback on performance.

The collection of self-report data remains the simplest and least expensive way to gain information about driver behaviour, and is the method most often employed in the studies reported in this chapter. However this method of data collection, dependent as it is on the ability and willingness of respondents to produce truthful and meaningful responses, is open to criticism as lacking in validity, given its obvious susceptibility to social desirability effects. Some support for the validity of self-reported measures of driver behaviour has been provided by several studies, using a variety of methods for cross-validation (see Ingham, 1991; West, French, Kemp, & Elander, 1993). In an unusual study in which both self-reported and actual behaviour were measured, Vogel and Rothengatter (1984) reported a correlation of 0.56 between reported speed and registered speed. Furthermore, it can be argued that the effect sizes reported in the studies reviewed below would have been suppressed rather than inflated if social desirability biases had been operating. For example, Parker, Reason, Manstead and Stradling (1995) found a significant link between reported tendency to commit driving violations and accident involvement. It seems reasonable to argue that this relationship would be weakened rather than enhanced by the operation of social desirability biases, since those who regard their driving violations as a mark of their superior driving ability (and may therefore be inclined to overestimate the number of violations they commit) would presumably also be inclined to under-report the number of accidents in which they are involved.

There is also some evidence concerning the reliability of self-reported measures of driver behaviour. The test-retest reliability of the Driver Behaviour Questionnaire (DBQ; a self-report measure of driver behaviour discussed below) was assessed by having 54 drivers complete the instrument twice, with an interval of seven months between the two measurements. The correlations between the two sets of scores for the three subscales ranged from 0.69 to 0.81. This demonstrates that it is possible to develop reliable self-report measures of driver behaviour.

A valid and reliable measure of driver behaviour designed to investigate the behavioural predictors of road traffic accidents also has to take account of the effects of *exposure* and *experience* on accident liability. Measures of exposure, which may be indexed by annual mileage, or by number of trips taken, reflect the amount of time an individual spends driving and therefore exposed to the possibility of accident involvement. Patterns of exposure vary considerably among individuals. Experience, on the other hand, increases inevitably from the time the driving test is passed, although there is variation in the rate at which experience is gained. While accident likelihood decreases with experience (and with age), it increases with exposure.

In summary, although each of the methodological strategies open to researchers in driver behaviour has drawbacks, each is nonetheless suitable for investigating some research questions. Significant improvement in our understanding of the social psychology of driver behaviour will require the judicious use of each of the strategies outlined above, as and when appropriate.

The link between violations and road traffic accidents

Reason, Manstead, Stradling, Baxter and Campbell (1990) conducted a survey of the types of aberrant driving behaviour which are associated with accident involvement.

A 50-item driver behaviour questionnaire (DBQ) was developed, in which respondents were asked to report on a six-point scale (ranging from 'never' to 'nearly all the time') how often they committed each of 50 types of behaviour while driving.

Factor analysis of the results suggested that a distinction should be made between errors, violations and lapses. Errors, defined as 'the failure of planned actions to achieve their intended consequences' (p. 1315), included behaviours such as misjudging the speed of an oncoming vehicle when overtaking. Violations, which were defined as 'deliberate . . . deviations from those practices believed necessary to maintain the safe operation of a potentially hazardous system' (p. 1316), included behaviours such as driving especially close to the car in front in order to signal its driver to move over, and disregarding the speed limit. Lapses, which only cause embarrassment and inconvenience to the perpetrator, included items such as switching on the headlights when intending to switch on the windscreen wipers.

Young drivers, male drivers, those who drive a high annual mileage, and those who reported that their driving was affected by their mood had higher scores on the *violation* factor. Moreover, high violators reported themselves to be less law-abiding, but also better than average drivers. Those who reported that their driving was susceptible to mood, that they used motorways (freeways) infrequently, and that they considered themselves to be relatively unsafe and error-prone drivers scored relatively high on the *error* factor. Those who reported that their driving was affected by their mood and that their driving was error-prone also scored higher on the *lapse* factor. Women scored higher on this lapse factor than men did.

This study demonstrated a clear distinction between driving errors and driving violations. In further research a reduced, 24-item version of the DBQ, containing eight error items, eight violation items and eight lapse items, was completed by 1,656 drivers. Again, there were significant age and sex differences in self-reported commission of violations, as illustrated in Figure 8.1.

Data on these drivers' accident records had previously been collected as part of a separate investigation. When the data on self-reported behaviour and accident data were analysed together, the error–violation distinction was replicated, and it was shown that while violations were associated with

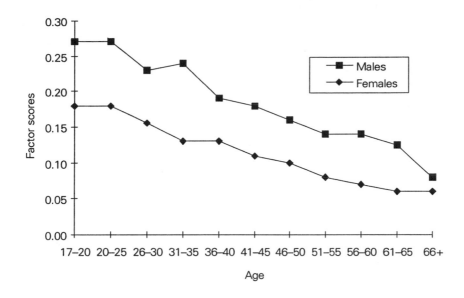

Figure 8.1 *Violation factor scores, by age and sex*

accident involvement, errors were not (Parker, Reason et al., 1995), a finding illustrated in Table 8.1. This finding calls into question the conventional wisdom that road traffic accidents arise as a result of lack of skill on the part of drivers, and that the most effective way to reduce the number of accidents is therefore to provide better training (or retraining) of driver skills. While the need for training in perceptual and decision-making skill is certainly necessary, Parker, Reason et al.'s results suggest that a successful approach to road safety might include a focus on reducing the commission of violations, by persuading or compelling drivers not to deviate deliberately from safe practices when driving. This implies that any effective strategy for promoting road safety needs to identify the reasons why some drivers elect to drive in a dangerous manner.

For the purposes of this chapter, the importance of the error–violation distinction is that violations, being at least partly intentional in nature, are rooted in motivational factors, and thus fall squarely within the social psychologist's domain of interest. Much of the remainder of this chapter is devoted to reviewing the ways in which social psychological methods and theories have been recruited in order to improve understanding of driver behaviour and to devise ways of persuading drivers to behave more sensibly behind the wheel. It begins with a review of research that considers deviant driving behaviour in the context of social deviance in general, and suggests a significant association between the two. The following section contains a review of studies that focus more specifically on driver behaviour, using the conceptual framework offered by widely used attitude–behaviour models to investigate the beliefs, values and attitudes which are associated with

Table 8.1 *Predictors of accident rate*

Step	Predictor	R^2	Increment	Beta	Significance
1	Mileage	0.04	0.04	−0.09	0.001
2	Age			0.25	<0.001
	Sex	0.15	0.11	0.12	<0.001
3	DBQ violation			−0.12	<0.001
	DBQ error			−0.04	ns
	DBQ lapse	0.16	0.01	0.02	ns

The accident rate variable was inversed in the course of transformations designed to reduce skewness and kurtosis in its distribution. Thus, the negative beta weight for DBQ violation factor score, for example, reflects the fact that respondents with violation factor scores tended to have higher accident rates.

Source: Parker, Reason, Manstead & Stradling (1995, p. 1043)

unsafe driving. The behavioural domains considered include a range of specific driving violations and the use or non-use of seat-belts. Then research which investigates the role of a range of cognitive biases and misperceptions in determining driver behaviour is reviewed. In the final section three approaches to the modification of driver behaviour are described. The first involves the provision of feedback designed to counter the type of cognitive biases that are known to occur. The second approach focuses on changing drivers' behaviour directly, operating on the assumption that once behaviour is changed, drivers' attitudes will be brought into line with behaviour. The third approach involves attempting to bring about changes in the beliefs which underpin attitudes, on the assumption that lasting behavioural change will only be achieved following attitude change.

General social deviance and driver behaviour

Some researchers with an interest in driver behaviour have tried to assess the extent to which deviant behaviour on the road is related to more generalized social deviance. A great deal of early driver behaviour research focused on the role of deviance in general (for a review see Elander, West, & French, 1993), although many of the studies were methodologically flawed, particularly in failing to take account of variables such as age, sex and annual mileage of drivers. The results consistently suggested that there was a positive association between accident liability and 'deviance', however the latter construct was measured. There is also some evidence from the criminological literature that crime is positively associated with accident-involvement (Junger, 1994; Sivak, 1983). Attempting to clarify the nature of such a link, West and his colleagues (West, Elander, & French, 1993) devised a self-report scale of mild social deviance containing 11 items, each of which carried a risk that it would cause harm to others, directly or indirectly. West et al. were keen to establish whether the demonstrated association between accident risk and social deviance holds good only for a minority of drivers who are extremely socially deviant, or whether it applies equally to those drivers who fall within the 'normal' range of social deviance.

It was hypothesized that mild social deviance would be associated with increased accident risk independent of other personality measures and demographic factors. It was further hypothesized that this association would be mediated in part by speed or commission of driving deviations. A total of 108 subjects provided data from three time points. The main dependent variable in subsequent analyses was accident involvement, obtained by summing the data from the surveys at times 1 and 3.

Social deviance was found to be negatively associated with age, and males' scores were higher than those of females. There were significant positive associations between social deviance, high preferred driving speed and relatively frequent commission of driving deviations. Number of accidents was significantly associated with higher annual mileage, faster reported driving, higher levels of deviations, lower age, and higher social deviance. Number of accidents was shown to be independently associated with faster driving speed and with higher levels of mild social deviance, but not with the measure of driving deviations. This absence of an independent relationship between driving deviations (i.e. violations) and driving accidents is puzzling, given the results of Parker, Reason et al.'s (1995) study, referred to above. This apparent inconsistency seems to be attributable to the fact that West, Elander et al.'s measure of violations consisted of just two items, whereas the DBQ measure used by Parker, Reason et al. included eight violation items and eight error items. In a more recent study, Lawton, Parker, Stradling and Manstead (1994) used the DBQ to measure aberrant driving, and also administered West, Elander et al.'s mild social deviance scale and a measure of accident involvement. They found a stronger independent association between DBQ violation score and accident involvement than between mild social deviance score and accident involvement. A path analysis revealed that tendency to commit violations was independently and positively associated with annual mileage and social deviance, and independently associated with age and gender, reflecting the fact that older drivers and females reported committing fewer violations. At the same time accident involvement was independently associated with age and violation score. This pattern of relationships suggests that the effects of social deviance, mileage and gender on accident involvement are mediated by tendency to commit violations. Thus it seems that one of the ways in which mild social deviance manifests itself is in the commission of driving violations. On the other hand, the association between age and accident involvement works both indirectly, via the tendency to violate, and directly. This suggests that there is something about being young which increases the likelihood of accident involvement, above and beyond the tendency of the young to commit relatively high levels of driving violations. It is of course possible that the direct relationship between age and accident involvement reflects the greater inexperience of younger drivers.

A different approach to examining the relationship between social deviance and driving deviance, with special reference to the behaviour of adolescents, has been taken by Jessor (1987), using the theoretical framework of problem-behaviour theory (Jessor and Jessor, 1977). Problem-behaviour theory was developed to account for a wide range of potentially problematic and health-compromising behaviours among young people, including drinking alcohol, smoking, delinquency, drug use and sexual promiscuity. In a study of almost 1,800 American adolescents, almost two-thirds of males and one-third of females reported having taken risks while driving during the previous six months. The correlation between risk taking while driving and other forms of risk taking was 0.51 for males, and 0.42 for females. Variation in risky driving behaviour was associated with variation in psychosocial proneness to engage in problem behaviour in general, as measured within this theoretical approach. Jessor concluded that in order to reduce risky driving (among adolescents, at least) it is necessary to address interventions at the level of lifestyle, rather than at the problematic behaviour alone. This, of course, makes the development of feasible interventions extremely difficult. The rather general and inclusive nature of problem-behaviour theory helps to explain why few attempts have been made to test it, with the result that its value cannot properly be assessed (but see Beirness & Simpson, 1988).

Social cognition models and driver behaviour

Although theories linking general deviance and driving deviance provide food for thought, they are not particularly useful for those interested in applying the results of research to social problems such as road traffic accidents. Although distal social structural variables such as social class and level of education may well be important in the aetiology of dangerous driving, these factors cannot easily be tackled in interventions designed to promote road safety. More readily addressed are the proximal psychological variables through which social structural variables presumably influence behaviour. What is required, then, is a means of identifying these psychological variables. Fishbein and Ajzen's (1975; Ajzen & Fishbein, 1980) theory of reasoned action, renamed in its extended form the theory of planned behaviour (Ajzen, 1988, 1991), provides just such a means (for an introduction to these models, see Chapter 1). The theory of planned behaviour specifies the ways in which three theoretical constructs – attitudes to behaviour, subjective norms, and perceived behavioural control – jointly determine intention to behave, and thereby the behaviour itself. Intention is seen as the product of attitude to the behaviour, subjective norm and perceived behavioural control. Attitude to the behaviour is based on a relatively small set of salient beliefs about the consequences of a given behaviour (behavioural beliefs). Subjective norm derives from the individual's beliefs concerning the expectations of a relatively small set of 'significant others' with respect to his or her performance of the behaviour (normative beliefs). Perceived behavioural control reflects beliefs about the degree to which performance of the behaviour is under one's volitional control (control beliefs). The model lends itself to application, positing a simple and clearly defined set of pathways between beliefs and behaviour, together with explicit instructions concerning the ways in which the model's constructs should be operationalized. Readers are referred to Chapter 1 of the present volume for further description and discussion of this model.

Attitudes to driving violations

In a series of three studies, Parker and colleagues have investigated intentions to commit a total of nine driving violations (Parker, Manstead, Stradling, Reason, & Baxter, 1992a; Parker, Manstead, & Stradling, 1996; Parker, Manstead, Stradling, & Lawton, 1995). In terms of theory development, the studies were used to research ways in which the perceived behavioural control construct can best be operationalized, and to assess the predictive utility of variables that are not included in the model. With respect to application the main aim was to use the model as a means of identifying beliefs, values and motives that differentiate high-violating drivers from their low-violating counterparts, the idea being that these beliefs, values and motives can then be targeted in campaigns designed to reduce the commission of violations on the road.

The performance of the model in predicting intentions was generally satisfactory. In every case, all three of the model's main predictors (attitude to the behaviour, subjective norm and perceived behavioural control) were significantly and independently associated with behavioural intentions. The amount of variance in intentions accounted for by the basic model components varied between 23 per cent (close following) and 47 per cent (speeding). Interestingly, for seven of the nine violations the association between subjective norm and intention was stronger than that between attitude and intention. This is a highly unusual finding in the context of research using the theory of reasoned action/planned behaviour, and appears to reflect the relative importance of the perceived expectations of others in shaping intentions to commit driving violations. In all three studies perceived behavioural control proved to be a statistically significant addition to the basic theory of reasoned action model.

In the second and third studies two extra constructs were added to the model, in order to assess whether the prediction of intentions to commit violations could be enhanced. One item assessed *moral norm*, asking respondents to what extent they agreed that 'It would be quite wrong for me to [commit the violation in question]'. Two other items provided a measure of *anticipated regret*, asking respondents how positive or negative they thought they would feel if they had committed the violations (cf. Richard, van der Pligt, & de Vries, 1995). These items were intended to measure respondents' personal norms concerning driver behaviour, in contrast to the more usual measure of subjective norm, which assesses respondents' perceptions of how others expect him or her to behave. Moral norm and anticipated regret both proved to be statistically significant additions to the model, together making a further contribution of between 6 per cent (driving through traffic lights just after they have turned red) and 15 per cent (overtaking on the inside – an illegal manoeuvre in the UK) to explained variance in intentions. Thus it seems that internalized notions of 'right' and 'wrong' driver behaviour play a significant role in determining behavioural intentions, over and above considerations of consequences, social norms and the perceived controllability of the behaviour.

The scores of groups of drivers (young vs. old, male vs. female) who are known to vary with respect to the frequency with which they commit violations and/or are involved in traffic accidents (Harrington & McBride, 1970; Storie, 1977) were compared. Taking speeding as an example, it was found that older respondents felt it was more likely that speeding in the specified context would result in their being stopped and fined, and that it would endanger the lives of pedestrians. They also saw their same-sex friends and their partners as more likely to disapprove of their speeding than did younger respondents. There were no differences in other beliefs about the consequences of speeding, or in relation to other reference groups (Parker, Manstead, Stradling, Reason, & Baxter, 1992b). The results of this type of analysis of individual items have important implications for the targeting of road safety education campaigns.

Vogel and Rothengatter (1984) used the theory of reasoned action to study speed choice. Their results showed that the multiple correlation between the model's predictors (attitude and subjective norm) and behavioural intention was 0.67, and that the correlation between behavioural intention and behaviour was 0.81. On the basis of the behavioural belief items salient in relation to speed choice, four motivational factors were identified. These were labelled *pleasure in driving, traffic risks, driving time* and *expense*. Of the four, pleasure in driving contributed most to drivers' attitudes to speeding. There were significant differences between speeders and nonspeeders on all four factors. In relation to pleasure and risk the observed differences pertained to the strength of drivers' beliefs about the likelihood that pleasure and/or risk would be a consequence of speeding. However, in relation to travel time and expense the observed differences were in drivers' evaluations of those consequences. The authors concluded that those who drive fast are not unconcerned about risk, but believe less strongly that they increase their own risk by increasing their speed. All drivers in the sample believed equally strongly that driving fast increases the expense of driving and decreases journey times. However the faster drivers in the sample evaluated increased expense less negatively, and decreased journey time more positively than did the slower drivers.

Considered together, these studies suggest that the theory of reasoned action and the theory of planned behaviour can help researchers to predict the commission of driving violations and to understand why these violations are committed. Inspection of the mean scores on specific belief, value and motive items enables the identification of those items which discriminate groups known to be over-represented in road traffic accident statistics (e.g. young drivers, especially males, or fast drivers) from other drivers.

Attitudes to the use of seat belts

Attitudes to the use of seat belts has attracted a lot of research attention, mainly because usage remained fairly low despite the overwhelming evidence that the wearing of seat belts substantially reduces the severity of injuries in the event of a collision. Wittenbraker, Gibbs and Kahle (1983) used the theory of reasoned action in conducting a longitudinal study of seat-belt use among psychology undergraduates. Cross-lagged panel correlation analysis showed that the correlation between attitudes at time 1 and behaviour at time 2 was significantly greater than that between behaviour at time 1 and attitude at time 2. Wittenbraker et al. concluded that it is legitimate to infer a non-spurious relationship between attitudes and subsequent behaviour. However, habit ($\beta = 0.49$) was found to be a stronger predictor of time 2 behaviour than was intention at time 1 ($\beta = 0.30$). It is important to note that this study operationalized the reasoned action model, rather than the planned behaviour model. The study therefore did not include a measure of perceived behavioural control, which was added to the model specifically with a view to accounting for behaviours that are not entirely under volitional control. The important role played by habit in Wittenbraker et al.'s study shows that seat-belt use can be just such a nonvolitional behaviour, and it seems likely that the observed association between habit and behaviour would have been mediated by perceived behavioural control. Assuming that the wearing of a seat belt is generally regarded as desirable, drivers low in perceived behavioural control with respect to this behaviour would presumably be those who had a strong 'non-use' habit.

The studies reported above, all of which employed the reasoned action/ planned behaviour models, are vulnerable to the criticism that they pay too little attention to the role played by affective factors in determining intentions and behaviours. There is an assumption in the reasoned action/planned behaviour model that the decision to behave in a given way is based on a rational assessment of salient information. The costs and benefits of performing the behaviour are evaluated, but little or no explicit cognizance is taken of the positive and/or negative feelings one might have concerning that behaviour. In relation to driver behaviour it seems intuitively plausible to suggest that these rational considerations are not the only factors determining behaviour. For example, the kinds of affect that one might expect to feel while engaging in driving violations could include the excitement of driving fast or the fear engendered by risk taking.

However, the way in which behavioural beliefs are selected for assessment in reasoned action/planned behaviour research militates against the inclusion of affectively loaded evaluations of the behaviour, and encourages a relatively dispassionate and thoughtful consideration of the consequences of the behaviour. Parker, Manstead, Stradling and Lawton (1995) asked respondents what they *liked or enjoyed*, and what they *disliked or hated* about engaging in a number of driving violations, including speeding in different physical contexts. The findings suggested that behavioural beliefs about and affective evaluations of driving violations can be distinguished, in that the responses to the affective evaluation items did not overlap at all with the behavioural beliefs derived from the questions typically employed in such research. When asked what they liked or disliked about speeding, respondents tended to say that speeding made them feel exhilarated, or nervous, or powerful, or frightened. When asked the 'standard questions' about the advantages and disadvantages of speeding, respondents tended to say that speeding reduces journey times, can cause an accident, might result in being stopped by the police, and so on. Thus it seems that there may be real potential in differentiating behavioural beliefs and affective evaluations, in order to extend the scope of the model.

Social and cognitive biases and driver behaviour

A different approach to understanding drivers' motivations takes as a starting point the notion that drivers who take risks are prone to biases, for example in risk perception, and draws on the social cognition literature to explain how such biases operate. An impressive amount of work has been done on risk perception, and a review of this literature is beyond the scope of the present chapter (but see Chapter 2 of the present volume).

Reviewing the evidence, Jonah (1986) concluded that young people are at increased risk of traffic accident involvement, and that this elevated risk is mainly a function of their increased willingness to take risks. A study by Finn and Bragg (1986; replicated by Matthews & Moran, 1986) reported age differences in perceptions of accident risk. Young drivers perceived themselves as less likely to be involved in an accident than did older drivers. This perception is clearly at odds with the published statistics, which show that young drivers, especially males, are over-represented in accidents. Finn and Bragg (1986) also found that young drivers believe themselves to be less likely than their peers to be involved in an accident.

Attributional bias

Attribution refers to the process by which social perceivers arrive at causal explanations for their own and others' behaviours (see Hewstone, 1989 for a review). 'Bias' in this context refers to the fact that social perceivers arrive at causal explanations which deviate systematically either from a normative standard that is supposed to represent 'rational' information processing or from the explanations made by other perceivers. A classic example of the latter type of bias is the so-called 'actor–observer' effect, whereby those who perform a behaviour (actors) tend to arrive at different explanations for that behaviour than do those who witness the behaviour (observers). The typical finding is that actors see situational causes as more important than do observers, who tend to explain the actor's behaviour in dispositional terms.

Baxter, Macrae, Manstead, Stradling and Parker (1990) investigated the actor–observer attributional bias in the context of driving violations. Two descriptive vignettes were developed, each of which portrayed the commission of a driving violation. The violations used were running traffic lights (i.e. accelerating through traffic lights while they are amber) and close following (i.e. tailgating). There were two versions of each vignette. They differed only in that for the 'actor' version the vignette was written in the second person singular, whereas for the 'observer' version the vignette was written in the third person singular. Thus subjects read either about a violation as if they themselves had committed it, or about the same violation committed by another driver. Subjects were then required to rank in terms of likelihood four possible explanations for the behaviour portrayed in the vignette. The explanations had previously been rated by a different sample of subjects, two of the explanations being judged to be dispositional, and the other two as situational. Analysis of the results showed that there was a marked tendency for drivers to attribute their own driving violations to situational factors, while attributing the same behaviours in another driver to dispositional factors. These findings suggest that at least some of the hostility that is evident on the roads may have its roots in attributional bias: when I commit a driving violation it is due to situational circumstances; when you commit the same violation, it is because you are a stupid or aggressive person. Making drivers more aware of the operation of this bias may help to reduce its operation and thereby to reduce hostility towards other drivers.

False consensus

Perceptions of consensus have been studied by psychologists for many years (see Marks & Miller, 1987; Spears & Manstead, 1990). One aspect of this research is the work on 'false consensus' that was triggered by the publication of Ross, Greene and House's (1977) paper. There the authors described a series of studies in which they showed that attributes and behaviours are seen as relatively more common by persons who have those attributes or engage in those behaviours than by people who do not. Subsequent research has shown that this tendency to engage in false consensus is very reliable and of moderate effect size (Mullen et al., 1985; Mullen & Hu, 1988). If false consensus operates in perceptions of driver behaviour, drivers should see those errors and violations in which they personally engage as being committed by a higher percentage of other drivers than should drivers who do not commit these errors and violations. This possibility was examined by Manstead, Parker, Stradling, Reason and Baxter (1992). As part of a larger investigation, more than 1,500 drivers were asked how often they committed each of eight violations and eight errors. At a later point in the survey booklet, respondents were asked to estimate the approximate percentage of other road users who commit each of the same 16 behaviours 'on a fairly regular basis'. For 14 of the 16 behaviours considered, those who reported regularly committing the behaviour themselves (the 'regulars') made higher percentage estimates than did those who reported committing the behaviour hardly ever, if at all (the 'irregulars'). Thus the false consensus effect was demonstrated for both errors and violations. It was also found that 'regulars' significantly overestimated the degree of consensus on their behaviour, while 'irregulars' significantly under-estimated consensus on their position. The degree of false consensus was found to be greater for violations than for errors. These findings suggest that violators may derive some psychological support from thinking that their behaviours are routinely performed by others, and that attempts to persuade them to change their own behaviour would benefit from removing this comforting perception. Indeed, as is shown below, there is evidence that information about the behaviour of other drivers can be effective in changing driver behaviour.

Illusion of control

The effects of other cognitive biases on perceptions of personal safety on the road have also been studied. McKenna (1993) sought to disentangle the effects of unrealistic optimism and of the illusion of control on people's perceptions of their own relative invulnerability. Unrealistic optimism is said to exist when 'as a group, the vast majority perceive their chances of a negative event as being less than average' (McKenna, 1993, p. 39). Unrealistic optimism has been demonstrated across a range of domains, and manifests itself both as a decreased perceived probability of negative events and as an increased perceived probability of positive events. McKenna argues that the operation of unrealistic optimism might increase the likelihood of drivers taking risks, and/or reduce the probability that they will take steps to protect themselves from harm, for example by using seat belts. Such a bias might also undermine the impact of media safety campaigns, since individuals may be inclined to regard safety messages as relevant to other drivers but not to themselves; they do not see themselves being at risk. Indeed, Tyler and Cook (1984) provided some support for this suggestion, showing that media campaigns on the risk of crime serve to increase people's perceptions of societal risk, but have little effect on perceptions of personal risk.

A second theoretical construct, illusion of control, can also be used to explain underestimations of own risk. The illusory perception of control refers to the tendency for individuals to see themselves as having more control over their own behaviour and their environments than is actually the case (Langer, 1975). In the realm of driving, one source of such illusory perceptions is having an inflated estimate of one's own ability. There is ample evidence that most drivers do see themselves as 'above average' with respect to driving ability (Svenson, 1981). For example, Reason et al. (1990) found that only 2 per cent of more than 1,500 drivers considered themselves to be below average, while 48 per cent considered that they were above or well above average, compared to other drivers of their age and sex.

McKenna (1993) pointed out that although unrealistic optimism and the illusion of control can both contribute to an overall 'rosy picture' of the world, it is important to distinguish between these two explanations. Optimism refers to the expectation of positive outcomes, irrespective of the source of those outcomes. By contrast, illusory perceptions of control will only result in positive expectations where the outcome could conceivably be influenced by the skills or abilities of the perceiver. In situations where no skill is involved personal control should not play a role. So, for example, whereas the illusion

Table 8.2 *Mean judgements (and standard errors) of likelihood of own involvement in a road traffic accident in high- and low-control scenarios*

	High-control	Low-control
Driver	−1.92	−0.53
	(0.20)	(0.17)
Passenger	−0.31	−0.20
	(0.20)	(0.13)

−5 = much less likely compared to the average driver; +5 = much more likely compared to the average driver.

Source: based on data reported by McKenna (1993)

of control should not influence estimates of the likelihood of an earthquake occurring, it could well play a role in estimates of the likelihood of being involved in a road traffic accident. McKenna distinguished between these two sources of bias by asking subjects to make judgements about the likelihood of their being involved in an accident under one of two conditions. In the first (high-control) condition, subjects made judgements on the likelihood that they would be involved in an accident when they were driving, compared to other drivers. In the second (low-control) condition, the same subjects made judgements about the likelihood that they would be involved in an accident when they were a passenger, compared to other drivers. The results showed that subjects judged themselves to be considerably less likely than other drivers to be involved in an accident when they themselves were driving. However, subjects rated their accident likelihood as a passenger to be no better or worse than that of other drivers. These findings are consistent with the view that the source of perceived invulnerability in the realm of driving behaviour is illusory perception of control, rather than a generalized optimism about future outcomes.

Support for this interpretation was obtained in a further experiment which specified various negative occurrences that might happen on the road. Level of control was manipulated by using six scenarios depicting events high in controllability (e.g. driving your car into the back of another) and six scenarios depicting events low in controllability (e.g. skidding on black ice). As in the earlier experiment, subjects rated their risk as a passenger to be higher then their risk as a driver. Although accident likelihood was rated higher for low-controllability events than for high-controllability events, there was also an interaction between controllability and role, such that in the 'driver' role accident likelihood was judged to be lower in the high-control scenarios than in the low-control scenarios, whereas there was no such difference in the 'passenger' role, as shown in Table 8.2.

McKenna interpreted these results as indicating that level of control is the critical factor producing perceptions of relative invulnerability. Drivers believe that they are in control and that they can use their skill to avoid potentially aversive events. When their feelings of control are removed, judgements of invulnerability relative to other people disappear. As McKenna points out, the operation of this particular cognitive bias may serve as a disincentive for the adoption of safety-related behaviours, and may thus mitigate the effectiveness of media road safety campaigns.

Cognitive misperceptions

Jaccard and Turrisi (1987; Turrisi & Jaccard, 1991) have employed psychological theories of judgement and decision making to research cognitive judgement processes in relation to drink-driving. In an experimental study, Jaccard and Turrisi (1987) used hypothetical scenarios to assess subjects' judgements of whether the actor in the scenarios had exceeded the permitted blood alcohol level for driving. Three types of cue were manipulated in order to study their effects on judgements. The cues related to type of drink (wine, beer, or both), number of drinks taken (two, three, four or five) and time taken to consume the drinks (one, two or three hours). Factorial manipulation of the cues produced 36 scenarios, each of which was considered by every subject. For each scenario subjects were required to rate the extent to which they judged the actor to be over or under the legal blood alcohol limit. Measures were also taken of subjects' locus of control in relation to driving, sensation-seeking tendencies, risk-taking tendencies and drinking experience.

Analysis showed that several misperceptions were operating in subjects' estimations of blood alcohol levels: the impact of drink taken over longer time periods was underestimated; the effects of a single type of drink (beer or wine) were underestimated relative to the effects of mixed drinks; and the relative consequences of a moderate number of drinks were also underestimated. Moreover, measures of some psychological constructs were found to influence the accuracy of such cue-based judgements. Risk-taking and sensation-seeking measures proved to be highly correlated and were therefore averaged. Subjects high on this combined measure were more likely than other subjects to judge actors who were in fact over the limit to be under the limit. This was interpreted as supporting the hypothesis that high risk takers rely less on external cues and more on internal impulse than do low risk takers. Those with an external locus of control made fewer judgmental errors than did those with an internal locus of control. Jaccard and Turrisi argue that one possible explanation for this is that those with an external locus of control are more cautious about drinking and driving, and pay more attention to external cues.

Turrisi and Jaccard (1991) extended the range of judgements made by subjects to include judgements of the likelihood of being stopped and arrested, and of being involved in an accident while drink-driving. In this study subjects consisted of persistent drink-driving offenders, those with one drink-driving conviction, drink-drivers who had never been convicted, and drivers who claimed never to drink and drive. Systematic cognitive biases were again found, and this was true of those with a history of drink-driving, including convictions, as well as those who claimed never to have driven after drinking. Judgements of the likelihood of accident involvement and of being stopped and arrested were also related to the experimental manipulations. Finally, the data suggested that perceptions of drunkenness were less important than were perceptions of the likelihood of having an accident in influencing the decision to drive.

Jaccard and Turrisi conclude that the misperceptions that they have shown to be consistent across these two studies should be addressed in educational programmes. They suggest that their data could be used to guide the development of campaigns which would focus on debiasing drivers' judgements by addressing the most commonly made errors. For example, the provision of information concerning the cumulative effects of alcohol over time could serve to correct some of the misperceptions shown to be important. Drivers would also benefit from clear information about the potentially dangerous effects of low levels of alcohol. Jaccard and Turrisi point out that stable personality traits such as locus of control and risk-taking tendency cannot easily be changed, and that it is in any case notoriously difficult to teach people how to assess their own level of intoxication with any accuracy. They therefore advocate the development of heuristics, involving external cues such as number of drinks and time taken to consume them, which could alert drivers to the dangers of making such perceptual errors and facilitate accurate judgements.

MacDonald, Zanna and Fong (1995) show that alcohol itself can result in cognitive biases that play an important role in the decision to drive while intoxicated. They compared the intentions, behavioural beliefs, attitudes, subjective norms, and perceptions of moral obligation concerning drink-driving of subjects who were either sober or intoxicated. While it is known that the vast majority of individuals have highly negative attitudes towards drink-driving, drink-driving remains a social problem of some importance. MacDonald et al. investigated the possibility that the physiological state of intoxication serves to change attitudes and intentions, with the result that some people engage in drink-driving in spite of the negative attitudes they espouse when sober. The researchers employed Steele and Josephs's (1990) notion of 'alcohol myopia' to explain this discrepancy between attitude and behaviour in relation to drink-driving. Specifically, they suggest that in deciding whether or not to drink-drive the individual is influenced both by negative inhibiting cues (e.g. the likelihood of an accident, the likelihood of getting fined) and by positive impelling cues (e.g. the saving of time and money, avoiding the hassle of leaving your own car behind). In making the decision whether or not to drink-drive the conflict between these two sets of cues has to be resolved. MacDonald et al. suggest that a sober person is capable of attending to and weighing up both sets of cues, and will typically find the inhibiting cues to be more influential than the impelling ones. However, the state of intoxication induces a state of 'alcohol myopia', meaning that the intoxicated person is more likely to focus on and respond to whichever cues are most salient at the time of decision making. In the drink-drive situation, the cues impelling the intoxicated individual to drive are typically more salient than are the cues restraining him or her from driving. In other words, the hassle and expense of having to arrange alternative transport tend to be more salient than the possibility that one might have an accident or be stopped and breathalysed.

In the course of a laboratory experiment and two field studies, MacDonald et al. showed that when general, non-context-specific questions about drinking and driving were posed, subjects reported negative attitudes and intentions, whether they were sober or intoxicated. However, when the same questions were embedded in 'contingent items', which included an impelling reason to drink-drive, intoxicated subjects were significantly less negative than their sober counterparts, in both attitudes and intentions. This pattern of findings is consistent with the notion of 'alcohol myopia', in that intoxicated subjects tended to respond to the most salient cues in their environment. MacDonald et al. conclude that making inhibiting cues more salient than impelling cues should lead to the development of more negative attitudes, intentions and behaviours relating to drink-driving. In practical terms inhibiting cues could be made salient by the placing of reminders of the possible costs of drink-driving in drinking venues such as bars. The authors also suggest that drivers could be trained to anticipate the effects of 'alcohol myopia' and warned that their attitudes and intentions may well change as a consequence of drinking.

Modifying driver behaviour

Cognitive debiasing techniques

Having examined the bases of drivers' perceptions of relative invulnerability, McKenna and Lewis (1991) went on to investigate various techniques for changing their biased perceptions. Laboratory experiments were conducted in which memory search strategy, accountability and mood were each manipulated in order to assess their role in the operation of illusory positive perceptions of skill and safety. McKenna speculated that one of the mechanisms underlying illusory positive perceptions might be the selection from memory of information which accords with the individual's prevailing positive view of his or her own ability. Experimental manipulations were devised with the aim of increasing the availability to subjects of information incompatible with unrealistic assessments of skill and safety. In one condition subjects were sensitized to their own skill deficiencies by being asked about times when they might have had problems manoeuvring their vehicles. In another condition, subjects were prompted to recall personal experiences with road accidents. Control group subjects were not exposed to either of these debiasing techniques. The results revealed no significant differences between experimental and control subjects. Assessments of skill and safety did not differ between the three groups of subjects.

In a second study subjects in the experimental group were required to judge their own skill and safety immediately before performing a driving simulation task which, they were told, would provide a relatively objective measure of their performance. Any overoptimistic self-ratings would conflict with this objective assessment. Consistent with the social psychological literature on accountability (e.g. Tetlock & Kim, 1987), it was reasoned that making subjects accountable for the accuracy of their self-assessments in this way should reduce the operation of bias. A control group made the same self-assessments but did not take part in the driving simulation test. Although the group means for ratings of own skill and safety differed in the expected direction, the difference between the experimental and control groups was not significant.

A third study investigated the phenomenon of depressive realism, i.e. the notion that while a 'normal' individual is prey to a range of self-enhancing cognitive misperceptions, the depressed individual is much less susceptible to such illusions (see Taylor & Brown, 1988 for a review). McKenna examined the effect of mood on judgements of driving skill and safety, in an attempt to determine whether being in a depressed mood would reduce or eliminate illusions of skilfulness and safety. The Velten mood induction procedure was used to induce a depressed mood in experimental group subjects. Again, there were no significant differences in the judgements of skill and safety made by subjects in the depression condition, as compared to control subjects whose mood was not manipulated.

McKenna and Lewis (1991) concluded that although the operation of illusory enhancement of judgements of own driving skill and safety seem to be resilient and resistant to all three of the debiasing techniques they attempted, further research into the causes and consequences of such biases could play an important part in road safety research. More recently, McKenna has developed a debiasing strategy which seems more promising. It was noticed that drivers who had actually been involved in road traffic accidents made lower estimates of their own safety, and reported lower intended speeds, than did non-accident-involved drivers. An attempt was made to reproduce this effect among the non-accident-involved by having them generate an imaginary scenario in which they personally were involved in a road traffic accident. Preliminary results suggest that this technique can be successful in lowering drivers' estimates of their own safety (McKenna, 1992).

Providing feedback

Studies of the practical effectiveness of interventions intended to change driver behaviour are few, and the results are mixed. In a series of five studies van Houten and Nau (1983) assessed the efficacy of feedback in producing reductions in driving speed. They tested the effects of feedback based on two definitions of 'speeding' (either 20km per hour above the speed limit or 10 km per hour above the speed limit), showing that the more lenient criterion, which allowed for feedback to show a greater percentage of drivers not speeding, was the more successful. They also demonstrated that feedback in combination with other speed control methods, such as the deterrence provided by a parked police vehicle (unmanned) nearby, or a police air surveillance programme, served to reduce the incidence of speeding. Finally, van Houten and Nau reported on a police programme which involved issuing speeding motorists with warning tickets plus feedback on the number and types of accident occurring on the road on which they had been stopped. This approach proved more effective than a traditional speeding enforcement programme using a radar trap. Van Houten and Nau (1983) recommend that the use of a feedback sign would be an effective first step in a multi-step approach to the widespread problem of speeding.

However, Nau, van Houten, Rolider and Jonah (1993) examined the effectiveness of feedback in reducing the level of drink-driving and obtained less encouraging results. In order to establish baseline levels of drink-driving behaviour in the two bars chosen for this research, patrons were asked to complete a questionnaire in which they were asked about their drinking behaviour on that occasion and how they planned to get home. A randomly chosen one-third of those who completed the questionnaires were also asked to provide a breath sample so that their blood alcohol levels could be measured. In order to assess the reliability of their self-reported behaviour a randomly selected one-fifth of those who provided this breath sample were also covertly observed. After baseline drink-driving levels had been established, the intervention began. A guide to safe drinking was handed to each person entering the bar. The guide indicated how a driver can maintain a blood alcohol level below the legal limit, separately for each of six body weight categories. Customers who were interviewed on leaving the bar were given private feedback on their blood alcohol level, and those who were over the limit were advised either to ask to get someone else to drive or else to take a taxi. In addition, public feedback on the percentage of drinkers who had driven home while impaired during the previous weekend was posted in the bars. Increased enforcement was introduced at a later stage, when a well-publicized police campaign, involving increased rates of breath-testing, was introduced.

The results showed that the provision of information on how to remain within the legal limit, accompanied by both private and public feedback on levels of impaired driving, had no measurable effect on behaviour. However, following the introduction of increased law enforcement there was a 66 per cent drop in the mean blood alcohol level of drivers, a decrease that persisted for a month after the enforcement campaign ended. Nau et al. point out that it is not possible to determine whether the observed change was solely the result of the enforcement campaign, or whether the combined effects of information and enforcement was effective, since there was no condition in which increased enforcement was attempted without the information campaign. They also suggest that feedback might be more effective if it is provided before the drivers have become impaired. Although this may be sensible in terms of feedback on general levels of impairment, individual feedback is only useful after some drinking has occurred. Finally, Nau et al. suggest that an alternative information feedback strategy would involve providing feedback on the percentage of drivers choosing low-alcohol drinks during the last week, since this would highlight a positive course of action which drivers could take in order to remain within legal blood alcohol limits.

Changing behaviour

Interventions have also taken the form of initially trying to change drivers' behaviour, on the assumption that attitudinal change will then follow and thereby serve to sustain the behavioural change (see Festinger, 1957). In relation to driving behaviour, individuals have been persuaded in a variety of ways to commit themselves to behavioural strategies which they would not have adopted spontaneously, including carrying pledge cards, making a public verbal commitment and displaying a car sticker. The act of committing oneself to a course of behaviour is thought to lead one to develop a *post hoc* justification for that behaviour, and thereby to bring about a change in one's beliefs and attitudes towards the behaviour (see Eagly & Chaiken, 1993, Chapter 11). In relation to the use of seat belts, commitment to the behaviour has been manipulated in several studies, with or without the accompaniment of an incentive for behavioural change, with mixed results. Ludwig and Geller's (1991) study indicated that a personal commitment to seat-belt use by employees of the target company served to increase actual belt use, particularly among younger drivers. On the other hand, Cope and Grossnickle (1986) concluded that neither pledge cards nor incentives led to an increase in seat-belt use over and above the improvement achieved by holding awareness sessions, during which employees of the target company took part in discussions or heard lectures about seat-belt safety. However, in another study which included both incentives and commitment, Geller, Kalsher, Rudd and Lehman (1989) demonstrated a 'substantial' increase in seat-belt use. Moreover, when drivers made a commitment to fix a sticker to the dashboard of their car encouraging use of seat belts among their passengers, use of seat belts among the drivers themselves increased (Thyer & Geller, 1987).

Changing attitudes

The research on behavioural commitment starts from the assumption that an enforced change in behaviour will lead to a change in attitudes. Other researchers have taken the view that a change in behaviour is likely to follow a change in the attitudinal factors which underpin it. Rothengatter, de Bruin and Rooijers (1989) tested various types of publicity and enforcement measures designed to bring about changes in drivers' speed choice on 80 km per hour roads in the Netherlands. Questionnaire measures of attitudes and behaviour were supplemented by speed measurement via radar detectors and continuous-loop speed registration pads. These self-report and behavioural measures were taken while different levels and methods of interventions involving publicity and enforcement were introduced.

Interventions were divided into five categories. First, surveillance by patrolling police vehicles was designed to increase subjective risk of apprehension, although objective apprehension probability remained low. Secondly, the introduction of obtrusive surveillance and radar detection was intended to increase both subjective and objective risk of apprehension. Thirdly, general behavioural feedback was provided by posting each day the percentage level of speed limit compliance. Fourthly, information campaigns involving leaflets, posters and press announcements were used to provide information about the negative consequences of speeding. Finally, a combination of intensified publicity and increased surveillance (the second and fourth of the previously mentioned interventions) provided increased information together with increased risk of apprehension.

The results of these interventions showed that increasing surveillance without increasing objective risk of apprehension, as in the first strategy, has no effect on speed choice. However a marked reduction in the percentage of drivers speeding was achieved by increasing the objective level of risk of apprehension (as in the second strategy), by using radar. Survey results indicated that while drivers had noticed the increased level of surveillance, their attitudes towards speeding were unchanged, compared to those of a matched control group. Feedback (strategy 3) had a noticeable effect on speed choice, consistent with Manstead et al.'s (1992) argument that perceptions of consensus on one's own behaviour can influence one's subsequent behaviour, although alternative explanations such as implied threat have also been suggested. Examination of the survey results showed that drivers were adapting their own speed choice on the basis of the information provided about average speed choice. They regulated their behaviour in relation to other drivers' speeds, rather than in relation to the speed limit. The publicity campaign (strategy 4) was as effective as obtrusive radar surveillance in reducing speeds. Moreover, when publicity and increased obtrusive surveillance were combined (strategy 5), a still greater reduction in speeding behaviour was achieved. Although publicity was not found to change drivers' attitudes towards speeding or their expressed intentions to speed, increased enforcement was evaluated less negatively when it was preceded by a publicity campaign. This suggests that the publicity may have had a beneficial effect, preparing drivers to accept the introduction of increased enforcement. Such a role for the otherwise undetectable effects of health education campaigns aimed at changing beliefs, values and attitudes has also been suggested by others (e.g. Eiser, 1986).

As argued earlier, one benefit of using theory-guided approaches to the issue of predicting and understanding how intentions to commit driving violations are influenced by variables such as attitudes is that the models typically used for this purpose (i.e. the theory of reasoned action or the theory of planned behaviour) help to identify the beliefs, values and motives that distinguish likely from unlikely violators. A logical next step is to design persuasive communications which target these key belief, value and motive items. Parker, Manstead and Stradling (1996) developed four short videotapes designed to change beliefs or values relating to speeding in an urban

Table 8.3   *Mean attitude to speeding by type of video seen*

Type of video seen

	Normative belief	Behavioural belief	Perceived behavioural control	Anticipated regret	Control
Mean	21.58[a]	20.88[a]	21.47[a]	23.49[b]	19.73[a]
(SD)	(6.02)	(4.95)	(6.13)	(6.49)	(5.95)

Means not sharing a common superscript differ significantly ($p<0.05$).

Source: Parker, Manstead, & Stradling (1996)

residential area. Three of these videos addressed one of the key theoretical constructs of the theory of planned behaviour: attitudes, subjective norms, or perceived behavioural control. The fourth video addressed personal norms concerning speeding in residential areas, since this had been shown to be a useful predictor of intention to commit lane-change violations (Parker, Reason, Manstead, & Stradling, 1995). More specifically, this video attempted to increase the viewer's level of anticipated regret if he or she were to commit the violation. A control video of similar length, and which featured the same principal actor, was also used. Between 45 and 50 drivers, with approximately equal numbers of males and females, were randomly assigned to view one of the five videos. A standard thought-listing task (Greenwald, 1968) was used, in which subjects recorded the thoughts they had while viewing the video. Their thoughts were subsequently coded as favourable, unfavourable or neutral with respect to the anti-speeding message of the video. For each of the four experimental videos the number of favourable (anti-speeding) thoughts greatly exceeded the number of unfavourable (pro-speeding) thoughts, demonstrating that the videos had the potential to change attitudes in the desired direction. In addition, subjects' general attitude to speeding was assessed, together with measures of behavioural beliefs, normative beliefs, control beliefs and anticipated regret with respect to speeding in residential areas. The results showed that two of the videos produced significant changes in the desired direction on key variables. Those who had seen the normative beliefs video differed significantly from other groups on items measuring normative beliefs, while those who had seen the anticipated regret video differed from other groups on one of the two items measuring anticipated regret. Those who had seen the anticipated regret video also expressed more negative attitudes to speeding than did subjects in the control group (see Table 8.3).

Thus two of the four videos resulted in significant effects on key dependent variables, despite the entrenched nature of the target behaviour, the brevity of the videos (average length 2.25 minutes), and the fact that the videos were only seen twice by subjects. A logical and potentially effective way to proceed in devising interventions in the realm of driver behaviour is to use existing social psychological models of attitude–behaviour relations to identify the key determinants of the behaviour in question, and then to target those determinants in persuasive communications.

Summary and conclusion

Despite some improvement in accident statistics in different countries during the past five years, large numbers of people die or are injured each year as a result of road traffic accidents. Quite apart from the sheer misery caused by these deaths and injuries, road traffic accidents are very expensive. Analysis of accident causation shows that driver behaviour plays a major role in bringing about road traffic accidents, which suggests that psychologists should be in a position to identify the factors that increase the likelihood of accident involvement. In this chapter the social psychological research on this issue has been selectively reviewed. Despite the substantial methodological problems confronting the researcher who studies driver behaviour, considerable progress has been achieved.

Research points to the conclusion that a self-reported tendency to commit violations while driving is associated with greater involvement in accidents. Our review focused on three approaches to studying this tendency to commit violations and other unsafe driving behaviours. Research using the concept of deviance treats deviant driver behaviour as part of a larger tendency to engage in 'deviant' or 'problem' behaviours. Research using theoretical models such as the theory of reasoned action or the theory of planned behaviour treats driving violations as a product of beliefs, values and motives. Finally, research focusing on cognitive biases treats dysfunctional driver behaviour as arising from or sustained by one or more misperceptions. These misperceptions range from the role played by perceptions of control in underpinning undue optimism about one's chances of avoiding involvement in an accident to underestimating the impairing effects of different types and amounts of alcoholic beverages on driving ability. These different approaches should not be regarded as mutually exclusive. People whose deviant lifestyle is reflected in their behaviour as drivers may also have different beliefs, values and motives than people with a less deviant lifestyle. Equally, drivers who (for example) believe that their speeding behaviour is unlikely to cause an accident may also be inclined to underestimate their likelihood of being involved in an accident because of their control over the driving situation. In other words, although different researchers have elected to adopt different approaches to studying this issue, it is most unlikely that the various risk factors they have identified operate in isolation from each other.

In the final section of this chapter research in which investigators tried to modify driver behaviour was reviewed. Although there has been less research on this issue than on the determinants of unsafe driver behaviour, it is evident from the work that has been conducted that changing driver behaviour is a challenging task. It seems safe to conclude that deeply entrenched behaviours such as driving with excessive speed will not be changed simply by means of a public education campaign. The effectiveness of such a campaign can be enhanced by tailoring it on the basis of prior research examining the determinants of the target behaviour. However, while this sort of approach undoubtedly has an important role to play in changing driver behaviour in the direction of greater safety, it is clear that the chances of success will be greatest if the intervention combines educational efforts with more salient and more stringent enforcement. The fact that attitudes, social norms and behaviours relating to drinking and driving have changed so dramatically in the last 30 years shows that intervention efforts of this sort *can* be effective. Although such interventions are expensive to implement and may take a long time to achieve measurable effects, the statistics cited at the start of this chapter concerning the human and material losses resulting from road traffic accidents show that doing nothing to address this problem is also a costly course of action.

This chapter has provided a selective review of the literature in which social psychological concepts and theories have been applied to the study of driver behaviour. The potential of social psychology to make a contribution to our understanding of driver behaviour has only recently been widely recognized, and some of the research leading to that recognition is described. The usefulness of attitude–behaviour models, especially of Ajzen's (1985) theory of planned behaviour, was discussed, and examples of the application of such models to various aspects of road user behaviour were described. Some ideas for improvements and extensions to the model were briefly introduced. Investigations of the operation of cognitive biases, including attribution bias, false consensus bias, unrealistic optimism and the illusion of control were reviewed. Finally attention turned to the use of social psychological concepts and theories in the development of interventions. Several approaches to the design of interventions grounded in theory were discussed.

Further reading

Elander, J., West, R., & French, D. (1993). Behavioral correlates of individual differences in road-traffic crash risk: An examination of methods and findings. *Psychological Bulletin, 113*, 279–294. This review chapter provides a useful summary of the methodological issues connected to the study of differential road traffic accident involvement.

Evans, L. (1991). *Traffic safety and the driver.* New York: Van Nostrand Reinhold. A book which admirably summarizes a wide range of traffic safety topics, primarily from a North American perspective.

Parker, D., Manstead, A.S.R., Stradling, S.G., Reason, J.T., & Baxter, J.S. (1992). Intentions to commit driving violations: An application of the theory of planned behaviour. *Journal of Applied Psychology, 77*, 94–101. This paper reports in detail the application of the theory of planned behaviour to four driving violations.

Parker, D., Reason, J.T., Manstead, A.S.R., & Stradling, S.G. (1995). Driving errors, driving violations and accident involvement. *Ergonomics*, *38*, 1036–1048. An exposition of the link between driving violations and accident involvement.

Rothengatter, J.A. & de Bruin, R.A. (Eds) (1988). *Road user behaviour: Theory and research*. Assen/Maastricht, the Netherlands: Van Gorcum. A compendium of approaches to road user behaviour, illustrating the breadth and multidisciplinary nature of this field of research.

PART 3

THE SOCIAL PSYCHOLOGY OF SOCIAL INSTITUTIONS

9

Social Psychology and Organizations

John L. Michela

Contents

In modern societies, most of the necessities of life, and many of its pleasures, derive from the actions of production and service organizations such as manufacturing plants, agribusinesses, retail stores, entertainment conglomerates, and so forth. From a global perspective, today's world is one in which various societies' organizations are engaged in competition for market share, capital, and ultimately wealth (Fukuyama, 1995). Consequently, the effectiveness of organizations is a matter of societal as well as individual concern. Applied social psychology has the potential to contribute to organizational effectiveness by providing insights into how people's contributions in organizations can be maximized, and some of the topics in this chapter emphasize this potential contribution. Research questions in this category include how to motivate employees to high levels of effort and how to promote creativity or innovation.

There is another, more immediate reason why organizations are important in modern life: many people live their lives, for many of their waking hours, as members of organizations. In these hours, fundamental social psychological phenomena such as social acceptance, rejection and dominance occur regularly. Social psychological processes in organizations are also important because of their consequences on impactful experiences such as success or failure, stress, injustice, security, and satisfaction.

These two concerns – organizational effectiveness and personal experiences in organizations – arise throughout the research literature that applies social psychological perspectives to organizational phenomena. This chapter will

Sabbatical support from the Universities of Amsterdam and Waterloo made it possible to undertake this project. Kim Baron provided helpful comments on a draft of this chapter.

review some of this literature. Coverage has been selected partly to reflect these two concerns, but also to reflect a longstanding distinction in social psychology. This is the distinction between problem-centred and theory-centred research (e.g. Deutsch & Hornstein, 1975). The problem-centred researcher brings to bear whichever theories or concepts from social psychology or other disciplines as may help to solve the problem. For example, in order to promote innovation, it might be discovered that social-cognitive, group, and organizational-level phenomena all play a role and must be understood in order to identify specific managerial actions to address this problem. In contrast, the theory-centred researcher is a researcher first and a problem solver second. This researcher asks, for example, 'How do causal attribution processes unfold in the organization? When and where might we look to see these processes? What consequences do these processes have for matters of significance to the organization and its members?' Accordingly, this chapter is organized most broadly along these lines of problem-centred and theory-centred approaches.

The first part of the chapter is theory-centred. It reviews research pertaining to the beliefs and thought processes that are encompassed by theories of attribution and social cognition. In order to illustrate how far a single domain's set of ideas may reach, and still remain within the bounds of a single textbook chapter, it was necessary to exclude other equally appropriate domains of social psychology, such as attitudes (which could include topics of job satisfaction: Oskamp, 1984; organizational commitment: Mathieu & Zajac, 1990; Meyer & Allen, 1991; and organizational justice: Cropanzano, 1993; Greenberg, 1990), group and intergroup processes (Goodman, Ravlin, & Schminke, 1987; Kramer, 1991; Levine & Moreland, 1990), power and leadership (Bass & Avolio, 1990; Srivastva & Associates, 1986), and culture and socialization (Kilmann, Saxton, Serpa, & Associates, 1985; Schein, 1992). The selection of attribution and social cognition is at least partly a function of the author's interest in, and dissatisfaction with most textbook (organizational behaviour) treatments of this topic – though there is also a possibility of some influence from the predominant focus of North American social psychology upon the individual level of analysis (Steiner, 1986).

In any case, this individualistic (and North American) focus is less evident in the second, problem-centred part of the chapter, in which three current concerns of organizations are addressed: organizational change, technological change, and innovation. Here again the coverage is selective, both in terms of the problems addressed and the perspectives discussed for each problem.

Theories of attribution and social cognition as applied to organizations

Social psychologists have devoted a great deal of attention in recent years to understanding people's perceptions and beliefs about the social world. Questions of how these cognitions are acquired and organized, and how they affect motivation, behaviour and emotional experience have been studied. The products of this research have accumulated as theories of social cognition and attribution. In this section we will discuss some of the applications of these theories in organizational research.

Perceiving causes of individual performance

Causal attributions are explanations that people hold for events. They have special significance in organizations because people's emotional and behavioural reactions to an event at work can depend on attributions for its cause. For example, a manufacturing engineer's attempts to design a new process for microchip production may prove to be a failure when the manufactured microchips are found to be defective at a high rate. Research indicates that in response to this outcome, the engineer is likely to seek a causal explanation.

Weiner, Frieze, Kukla, Reed, Rest and Rosenbaum (1971) proposed a model for categorizing the kinds of causal explanation that people give for success and failure outcomes. These researchers were able to locate specific causes, such as lack of ability or unfortunate luck, in a two-dimensional scheme. The first dimension distinguishes between factors pertaining to the person whose performance led to the outcome (e.g. ability, which is a characteristic of the individual) and those pertaining to the environment in which the performance occurred (e.g. luck). This is the internal–external dimension. The second dimension focuses on the permanence of the cause, and is called the stable–unstable dimension. Luck is an unstable causal factor by definition – it can change rapidly – and ability is stable, because once acquired, it tends to remain characteristic of a person and available for use.

The importance of the dimensions is that these underlying attributes of perceived causes are, in theory, the determinants of various reactions to success and failure. For example, laboratory research has shown that affective or emotional reactions such as pride in success or shame because of failure are heightened when attributions are made to internal factors rather than external ones (Weiner, 1982). Concretely, an engineer's failure because of lack of effort, an internal, unstable cause, is more shameful than failure due to difficulty of the task (external, stable).

Perceiving one's own performance

Research on these points has been conducted primarily with students in laboratory settings (for reviews see Weiner, 1982, 1979). Some especially intriguing studies have involved attribution 'retraining' in relation to real-life experiences. Wilson and Linville (1982) investigated the impact of attributionally relevant information on students in the first year of university studies. Students were randomly assigned either to a no-information control group or to an experimental group in which (a) statistical data were supplied to show that the majority of students' grades improve over time; and (b) students in their later years of studies described on videotape how their grade point averages increased substantially from the first to later years. Noting that their procedure entailed little cost to its administrators or participants, Wilson and Linville commented that their results were 'nothing less than dramatic' (p. 374). Most striking were the significantly greater grade point averages in the experimental group, one year after the informational presentation. In addition, a higher dropout rate was seen in the control condition.

The investigators interpreted their results as evidence of the importance of the underlying dimension of stability of attribution, which is to say, of perceived changeability of the causal conditions leading to performance. By design, specific causes of performance were not manipulated; instead, expectations for higher performance in the future, or, at least, a perceived potential for higher performance in the future, was the belief targeted in the information supplied. Weiner's (1979) theory holds that these beliefs provide a link between attributions to specific causes and motivation to strive in future performances.

A study by Curtis (1992) demonstrated successful use of attribution retraining with a specific occupational group, physiotherapists. The problem addressed was slightly unusual: it appears that physical therapists experience considerable frustration at the dominant position of power held by physicians, and this frustration may be partly responsible for a high rate of attrition in this occupational group. The attribution retraining (received by a randomly assigned group) required attendance at three two-hour sessions in which emphasis was placed on the strategy or approach taken by the physical therapist to influence the physician. The retrained group showed increased attributions to strategy, increased expectations of success in influence attempts, and increased rates of promotion in the next six months (39 per cent vs. 10 per cent for the control group).

Implications for employee development It seems likely that greater attention to attributional factors in performance at work could be helpful in a wide variety of positions, particularly for people who are new to their positions (just as participants in Wilson and Linville's study were new to being undergraduate students). Research on newcomers to organizations has been concerned more with instilling the organization's values and norms (e.g. van Maanen, 1978), a process called organizational socialization. The socialization process can be valuable to organizational effectiveness, but it does not deal with what happens when someone's efforts fall short when trying to meet the goals instilled by the organization. The techniques of attribution retraining might be especially useful with positions in which there are many things to know and it is important to learn how to learn (i.e. positions with similarities to being an undergraduate student). An example might be the position of customer service representative in a service organization (such as a bank) in which the employee provides a variety of services; requires skills in diverse areas such as use of computers and communicating with customers; must keep up with changing products, procedures or other conditions; has substantial decision latitude; and receives periodic and specific feedback about performance (such as rate of failed loans).

A related area of theorizing, which has seen some application to organizations (e.g. Bernardin & Beatty, 1984; see also Kanfer, 1992), concerns self-efficacy belief. This is the belief that one has the ability to perform effectively in a particular manner. These beliefs are important in individual motivation because, lacking this belief, a person has no reason to exert effort toward a goal. Schunk and Carbonari (1984) have discussed links between attribution theory and social learning theory, which is the framework within which the concept of self-efficacy has been developed. According to social learning theorists (Wood & Bandura, 1989), self-efficacy is instilled not only by the kind of vicarious experience illustrated in the Wilson and Linville (1982) study, but also by direct experience (among other means). For example, a bank trainee could make simulated loan decisions using files of past applicants, and then receive feedback concerning which of the applicants defaulted on the loans. Self-efficacy would be instilled as the trainee experienced success in making correct decisions.

Finally, a body of research has developed on the effect of preferential hiring practices on self-evaluations of ability and performance, motivation, task interest, and related outcomes. Preferential hiring in the United States is practised in support of 'affirmative action' to redress past discrimination on the basis of race, sex or other demographic factors. Attribution theory predicts that when individuals are aware that these factors have contributed to their hiring they may question whether their abilities are equal to those of others not hired preferentially. (A theoretical rationale for this prediction derives from the discounting principle in attribution theory, which will be described in a later section concerning perceptions of causes of behaviour by groups or role incumbents.) Studies reviewed by Turner and Pratkanis (1994) provide qualified support for this prediction. For example, Heilman, Simon and Repper (1987) found that women's (though not men's) evaluations of their leadership ability suffered when told in an experiment they had been given the leader role on the basis of sex, relative to women told that a test had indicated that they were qualified to serve as leaders. Turner and Pratkanis go on to discuss the implications of the research and theory for effective management of affirmative action programmes.

Supervisors' responses to employee performance

Up to this point we have been focusing on the point of view and responses of the employee or other individual who succeeds or fails at a task. However, the dimensional model applies as well to how others' successes or failures are viewed. A programme of research by Mitchell and his colleagues (Mitchell, Green, & Wood, 1981) sought to apply some of these ideas to attributions made by supervisors for their subordinates' performance. Because *poor* performances especially may require a response by the supervisor or the organization, performance failures have been the focus in this programme.

Figure 9.1 presents a simplified version of the theory underlying the research, derived from Mitchell and Wood (1980). The figure describes a sequence that begins with a subordinate's behaviour and ensuing outcome.

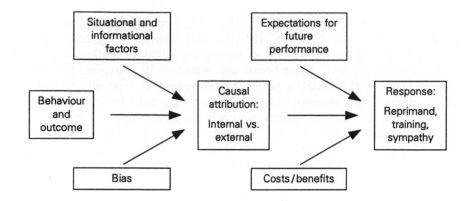

Figure 9.1   *A simplified attributional model of a supervisor's response to a subordinate's performance failure (Mitchell & Wood, 1980, reprinted by permission of Academic Press, Orlando, FL)*

Here the term 'outcome' connotes both the failure itself and its consequences. After seeing or learning of the poor performance, the next step for the supervisor in this sequence is to form a causal attribution. Influencing this judgement are various situational and informational factors, the behaviour, the outcome, and biases that the supervisor may hold.

Using an example from materials used in these studies, imagine that a nursing supervisor has learned that a nurse neglected to put up the side railing on a patient's bed. Informational factors include those identified by Kelley (1967) in his model of how people are able to process information systematically to reach causal judgements. For example, the supervisor may consider whether other employees also neglect to put up the side railing; Kelley calls this 'consensus' information. Further, the supervisor may consider 'consistency' information – in this case, whether the side railing was left down on other occasions or a single occasion – and 'distinctiveness' information, which is situation specific and here might refer to whether the employee neglects other tasks. Kelley's theory describes the attributional implications of specific patterns of consensus, consistency and distinctiveness information. As one such pattern, the behaviour is most likely to be attributed to the employee if it shows low consensus, high consistency and low distinctiveness (i.e. if few other nurses are neglectful in this way and this nurse is neglectful consistently in this way and has been neglectful in other ways).

In one study of supervisors' attributions (Mitchell & Wood, 1980, Study 1), 23 nursing supervisors read brief descriptions of six incidents said to have occurred on hospital wards, and they made judgements about causes of these events and appropriate supervisory responses to them. Informational factors were varied in the descriptions in a general manner by describing the work history of the nurse involved in the incident (good, poor, or none supplied). Outcome severity (severe, not severe) was also varied (e.g. the patient in the bed with the lowered railing was described as having been injured severely or not).

One set of results indicated that work history information influenced the exent to which the nurse's behaviour was seen as due to 'personal characteristics (such as ability, attitudes, mood, and so on)' as opposed to 'characteristics of the situation (e.g. busy ward)' (p. 127). These factors correspond to the internal vs. external distinction in Figure 9.1. Poor work history led to higher ratings for personal characteristics and lower ratings for the situation. This finding was to be expected from the authors' predictions, from Kelley's model (though its application is not so straightforward to this general presentation of information), and, perhaps, from conventional wisdom.

Among the remaining influences on attributions made, it was of special interest that attributions to personal characteristics were higher when the outcome was more severe. Other studies, not confined to work or organizational settings, have not been consistent in showing this effect of severity (see Kelley & Michela, 1980, for references). Although this effect does not violate conventional wisdom in the sense that it is not surprising to learn of it, there is no logical reason (certainly not from the perspective of Kelley's information-processing model) why severity should have this effect. In any case, the effect of severity on internal attributions was not large compared with the effect of work history, so in this sense the results are in line with the overall thrust of the research on severity.

Mitchell and Wood also looked for evidence of bias in causal attributions. Biased observers are prone to see things in a particular way, and thus violate the systematic and rational information processing described in Kelley's model. Attribution research indicates that we are all biased in various ways (Nisbett & Ross, 1980), in and out of the work setting. One bias is so prevalent it has been called the 'fundamental attribution error' (Ross, 1977). This is the tendency to attribute behaviour to internal factors – something about the person enacting the behaviour – as opposed to external or situational factors. Because it is impossible to say what the true causes are of any given behaviour, 'proof' of the fundamental attribution error comes from many different kinds of observation. Though not definitive, Mitchell and Wood's evidence on this matter is consistent with these observations: the mean rating of whether the behaviour was due to personal characteristics exceeded the mean rating for characteristics of the situation.

Results for ratings of supervisors' responses to the poor performance also showed effects of both work history and severity. For example, 'punitive responses' such as verbal reprimand, written reprimand and termination were rated as more appropriate under conditions of poor work history and high severity. More directly apropos to the model in Figure 9.1, responses of this kind were found to be correlated significantly with attributions made. For example, a correlation of 0.55 was obtained between the summary question of whether the behaviour was due to personal characteristics and a summary question of whether the supervisor's response should be directed towards the nurse.

Other studies by Mitchell and his colleagues have addressed some of the limitations of this study. For example, the correlational findings, presented immediately above, do not establish a causal direction between attributions and responses. Consequently Mitchell and Wood (1980, Study 2) conducted a follow-up study in which they varied attributions directly to see whether responses would correspond to predictions from attribution theory. The following is an example of an internal-cause induction:

> From your discussion with Nurse Connally and some other nurses on the ward, you believe that the failure to tape down the catheter was due to a lack of effort on Nurse Connally's part. She had not spent sufficient time or thought on her duties at the time of the incident. This lack of attention to detail had caused an error on a somewhat simple task at a time when the ward was not very busy.

Results of this study were consistent with those of the earlier one. Supervisors' ratings of specific 'punitive' or negative responses (e.g. written reprimand) again were affected by both severity and the supplied attribution, with the more negative responses occurring for high severity and internal attribution. Also, in analysis of summary questions about directing a response at the nurse or the situation, the supplied attribution had the predicted effect on both measures, and the severity information affected the person measure (response directed at the nurse) significantly. In discussing their results, Mitchell and Wood noted that supervisors' *ratings* of how they would respond under the various conditions may not be completely accurate. In particular, the element of costs (see Figure 9.1) associated with actually carrying out a punitive or other response may operate more in real situations than in the imagined situations of this study. We may also speculate that the benefits or need – for the reputation of the hospital – to 'do something' after an event such as a patient being harmed, could increase the likelihood of a 'punitive' response even if the supervisor's attribution would not recommend its use. (This is an example of a 'political' force operating to produce a punitive response.) Thus, attributions are one of many influences on responses to the behaviour of others in organizations.

Other researchers have probed further questions connected with various parts of the scheme in Figure 9.1. Pence, Pendleton, Dobbins and Sgro (1982) questioned whether the internal–external distinction between attributions is most fundamental to generating responses to others' behaviour. For example, in the preceding description of the internal-cause induction concerning Nurse Connally, the specific cause, lack of effort, was not only internal to the person but also unstable and controllable in terms of Weiner's (1979) theory. Drawing on Weiner's and others' research, Pence et al. predicted that failure due to lack of effort would lead to particularly unfavourable responses by supervisors. Pence et al. tested this prediction by asking undergraduate students to review portions of files (which were actually fictitious) of private-sector employees who had performed poorly in the past year. Included in the file were comments and ratings by the supervisor which signalled the supervisor's attribution for the performance. For example, the supervisor commented: 'Carl/Carla was simply at the wrong place at the wrong time' for the employee assigned an attribution to luck.

Findings from a set of responses termed 'coercive' actions, which included reprimands, punishments and termination, are most comparable logically to the findings for the 'punitive' responses in Mitchell and Wood (1980). Most striking in these findings were the especially high ratings for coercive actions, given lack of effort as the attribution for poor performance. The significant difference between these ratings given lack of effort versus lack of ability suggests that something else besides internality of the cause is the basis of the response. Controllability, which is a property of some internal and unstable causes, varies between these causes (Michela, Peplau, & Weeks, 1982) and so controllability may be this 'something else'. However, a further complication is that there appear to be a great many dimensions on which attributions may be distinguished, and the specific language used in giving a causal explanation may be important in responses (Wimer & Kelley, 1982). In Pence et al., the supervisor's comment in the lack of effort condition was: 'Michael/Michelle is one of the laziest people I've ever met.' It seems likely that this wording injects extra negativity into the explanation. Attributions serve functions for individuals who make attributions about themselves and for observers who communicate attributions about others. The Pence et al. study seems to illustrate in part how a supervisor's strategically chosen comments may denigrate an employee and influence others to support punishment of the employee.

A final set of issues arises from a study by Heneman, Greenberger and Anonyuo (1989), which examined whether supervisors' attributions varied as a function of the nature of the relationship between the supervisor and the subordinate. Supervisors from 37 organizations (N = 188) described an instance of effective and ineffective behaviour by two of their subordinates. These two were selected under instructions to identify the worker with whom the supervisor had his or her best and worst working relationship (e.g. 'Who would you most likely depend upon to get things done?') Supervisors rated each behaviour and each subordinate separately for the extent of causality from the subordinate's ability, effort, luck, and difficulty of the task. For the two internal causal factors, ability and effort, 'best' working relationship subordinates as compared with 'worst' relationship subordinates received higher ratings for effective behaviours and lower ratings for ineffective behaviours. From the point of view of the model in Figure 9.1, we could consider these results to point to bias in attributions. The exact nature of the bias is not established by these results, however. Often it is important to know whether the source of attributional bias is motivational or cognitive (see Tetlock & Levi, 1982). An example of a motivated bias in this instance might be the desire to maintain a favourable view of the other person when a positive relationship exists (e.g. a wish not to think badly of a liked and trusted person, because this way of thinking would be uncomfortable for the perceiver). Cognitive biases stem from properties of the way people process information. Heneman et al. posited this kind of explanation for their results. They suggested that supervisors have mental categories for good and poor performers, and once someone is in a category it is a relatively mindless process to assign attributions for performance – because presumed attributions are part of the category.

Organizational implications Accurate evaluations of workers' performances are important to organizational effectiveness in several respects. Not only should remedial action be taken for poor performers, but also, in general, the best performers should be promoted. From the point of view of how individuals experience the workplace, accurate evaluations are important for achieving fairness in the allocation of rewards.

However, this discussion of attributions for workers' performance suggests that there are many sources of inaccuracy or bias in employee evaluations. From the findings of an influence of severity of consequences on attributions and responses to poor performance, we may wonder whether there are millions of supervisors out there who have unwisely given less attention than they should to events that could have had bad consequences but didn't. In Mitchell and Wood's words, this tendency 'can lead to serious negative consequences at some later time and is clearly not an effective means of feedback' (1980, p. 258). Conversely some supervisors may unfairly give more attention than is warranted to events that have generated bad consequences but for which the employee is not responsible.

Evidence has also been presented of biases to attribute too much causality to the worker and too little to his or her circumstances, and to make more favourable attributions for performance of employees with whom one has a favourable relationship. The literature on attribution theory in social psychology suggests that the sources of these biases are deep-seated and resistant to change. Nevertheless, it may be worthwhile to implement suggestions by Mitchell, Green and Wood (1981) to provide training to supervisors specifically geared towards minimizing attributional errors and biases. Recent research by Crant and Bateman (1993) suggests that as part of this training, supervisors should be made aware of how attributions of blame are affected by employees' impression-management behaviours such as claiming to have been handicapped by circumstances or otherwise providing excuses or justifications of behaviours or outcomes.

Perceiving causes of behaviour by groups or role incumbents

As noted earlier, the research on supervisors' attributions and responses to subordinate performance has been guided by a model in which organization members actively process social information (albeit in a more or less biased way). Some applications of attribution theory to work life have drawn upon the notion that, at times, perceivers process relatively little information and respond on the basis of assumptions, untested expectations, and other prior beliefs (see Kelley & Michela, 1980, for references on the operation of beliefs in attributions). These uses of attribution theory have suggested that attributions, responses and further consequences of these responses may form a dynamic system that feeds back on itself, thus maintaining the original attribution and response.

Figure 9.2, adapted from Pinder (1984), illustrates a circular process of this kind. The starting point lies at the left of the figure, in management's beliefs in theory X. McGregor (1960) described theory X as one of two sets of beliefs

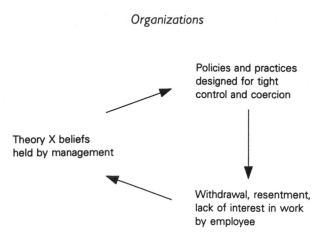

Figure 9.2   *The self-fulfilling prophecy of managers' theory X beliefs (adapted from Pinder, 1984)*

commonly seen among managers concerning employees under their supervision. Under theory X, a manager assumes that employees prefer to avoid work and responsibility when they can, among other unflattering characterizations. Consistent with these beliefs about human nature, managers holding theory X then tend to institutionalize policies and practices promoting tight control over employees. For example, assembly-line workers may be given little discretion in their work activities, may be closely observed, and may even be required to obtain a pass from their supervisors when they want to leave the line to use the toilet. Encountering these demeaning practices, employees respond with withdrawal from work – which is perceived by management as evidence of the initial beliefs.

Strickland (1958) conducted research which provides a laboratory analogue to some aspects of this cycle (see also Deci, Benware, & Landy, 1974). In Strickland's study, participants took the role of a supervisor over identical, boring work performed by two other participants. The experimenter randomly selected one worker for the supervisor to monitor and possibly punish (as a means of inducing higher levels of performance) on nine of ten trials of the task; the second worker was monitored and potentially punished on two trials. After all trials, the supervisor was told that the two workers' performance was identical. Then the supervisor was allowed to decide the extent of monitoring of the two workers in ten subsequent trials. Supervisors chose to do more monitoring of the previously more-monitored worker. This finding is understandable if we posit that social perceivers use a cognitive heuristic called the discounting principle (Kelley, 1971). According to this heuristic, when external causes of behaviour are made more salient, internal causes are presumed to be less operative. Thus the worker seen to have been exposed to more external inducements (monitoring and punishments) is assumed to be less internally motivated to perform the behaviour. This lower attribution to internal motivation implies to the perceiver that external inducements need to be maintained – thus maintaining the kind of cycle described by McGregor.

Correlational observations by Kipnis, Castell, Gergen and Mauch (1976), concerning a real-life supervisory relationship, are quite consistent with the laboratory research reported by Strickland. In Kipnis et al., 25 women who employed housemaids provided ratings of (a) how frequently they tried to influence their employee's work; (b) attributions of the causes of good work by the maid; and (c) evaluations of performance of the maid in terms of initiative, quality of work and three other dimensions. Frequency of influence was correlated 0.56 with the attribution that the supervisor's instructions caused the maid's good work; −0.69 with the attribution that the maid's own motivations caused her good work; and −0.73 with a sum of the five evaluation dimensions.

According to McGregor (1960), in order to break the self-fulfilling and dysfunctional cycle that derives from theory X beliefs, managers need to act in accordance with theory Y beliefs. Under theory Y, managers hold that people do, in general, have the capacity and desire to develop, take responsibility, and promote the well-being of the organization (not just their own well-being). In the decades since McGregor's analysis, corresponding policies and practices have been implemented in many (though certainly not all) organizations in connection with a variety of initiatives: empowerment, total quality management, continuous improvement, and so forth. Common to these initiatives are increases in worker participation in goal setting, decision making, or other activities that are the exclusive province of management under theory X. Although the relatively few evaluations that have been made of the effect of enhanced participation generally have weak designs (owing to small sample sizes, unreliable measures, inappropriate comparison groups, etc.) reviewers of these evaluations have concluded that worker satisfaction, productivity and organizational effectiveness have been enhanced by participative supervisory practices (Guzzo, 1988) – although the strength of this effect has been questioned (Wagner, 1994).

The mechanisms of enhanced productivity and organizational effectiveness in these initiatives are not yet clear. Two categories of mechanism are structural and motivational. In this context the term 'structural' includes improved information flow that occurs when employees are involved (e.g. Locke & Schweiger, 1979). Another example of the structural aspect of some of these initiatives involves changing the range and nature of tasks assigned to specific jobs (e.g. assembler, clerical worker), which may yield gains in flexibility and efficiency (as when workers are more able to help or substitute for one another). One aspect of the motivational effect of participation may be its enhancement of the relationship between the subordinate and supervisor (Kanfer, 1992). From an attributional perspective, the favourable motivational effect of a shift from management under theory X to theory Y may stem from the sense of ownership over one's work that is fostered under participative conditions. That is, instead of perceiving one's work as being performed in order to remain employed, get paid, and other extrinsic inducements, the employee experiences intrinsic satisfaction from his or her more autonomous actions to solve problems and produce output. The psychology of intrinsic motivation is discussed further in the next section.

Intrinsic motivation

What happens when an employee receives a reward, such as money, for doing something that he or she would have done regardless of the reward? Does the activity become more valued, because of its association with the reward? Research on intrinsic motivation shows that the activity may become *less* valued under these conditions. A study by Deci (1971) illustrates this phenomenon. University students were given the task of solving a type of puzzle generally found to be interesting in this population. Thus some amount of intrinsic motivation to perform the task could be assumed. The key experimental manipulation was whether students were paid or not for solving puzzles. After a period in which puzzle-solving activity varied between experimental groups in this way, all students were given an opportunity to solve additional puzzles without pay. Students *not* paid earlier were found to spend more time solving puzzles in the later period. Deci interpreted this behaviour as a reflection of the greater intrinsic motivation in the group not paid. Evidently the paid group experienced a reduction in intrinsic motivation. Calder and Staw (1975) supplemented behavioural data from this and other studies with self-reports of lower enjoyment of an activity in a group given extrinsic rewards for an intrinsically interesting activity.

Extrinsic rewards' undermining of intrinsic motivation appears to stem at least in part (cf. Deci & Ryan, 1980) from the discounting principle, as defined in the preceding section. When an extrinsic reward is made salient as a possible cause of the behaviour, the employee may infer that intrinsic causes, such as enjoyment of the task itself or of the achievement it represents, are less influential as causes. In other words, the employee believes 'I do this work for the money' (or award, praise, etc.). As belief in the intrinsic value of the activity diminishes, the employee is less likely to expend effort on the work unless the extrinsic reward is available. As one research team put it, play has been turned into work (Lepper & Greene, 1978).

Naturally things are not so simple in organizations as in the psychology laboratories that have made us aware of the potential effects of extrinsic rewards. It is not possible to stop paying employees and expect them to continue to come to work. It is probably not wise, either, to stop giving praise and awards or other recognition, because any gains for improvement in intrinsic motivation could be offset by losses in the quality of the relationships between employees, their supervisors and their organizations. What's a supervisor to do?

A partial answer comes from cognitive evaluation theory (Deci, 1975). This theory distinguishes between the two aspects of rewards identified in Table 9.1. The controlling aspect has the potential to undermine intrinsic motivation, as when an employee infers having less intrinsic motivation in light of extrinsic motivators received. The informational aspect can promote intrinsic motivation, as when a reward signals that one's goals for achievement, mastery and similar accomplishments have been met. Thus the challenge to the supervisor is to accentuate the informational aspect and minimize the controlling aspect of rewards. Research by Smith (1974), which seems to contradict the implications

Table 9.1   *Two aspects of rewards identified in cognitive evaluation theory*

Aspect	Example
Informational	By receiving a raise, an employee learns that she has been accomplishing her own goal of providing high levels of customer satisfaction.
Controlling	Having received an extrinsic reward (money) for providing high customer satisfaction, the employee may perceive her behaviours as partially under the control of this reward and therefore less intrinsically motivated.

of the controlling–informational distinction, suggests that meeting this challenge requires skill and subtlety. Smith's experiment with university students varied praise for performance, which would seem to capture the informational aspect of rewards and thus to yield greater intrinsic motivation with praise. Instead, the opposite occurred. Deci and Ryan (1980) argue that the way the praise was delivered had the effect of making its controlling aspect dominant over the informational aspect, and, for this reason, they consider this study to support cognitive evaluation theory. Specifically, praise was given in a context that made it salient that the recipient was being evaluated.

Drawing on an analysis of the literature by McGraw (1978), Deci and Ryan (1980) note further that there may be situations in which an extrinsic reward facilitates performance instead of undermining it. With unattractive tasks, rewards can promote performance, 'presumably by adding some hedonically positive elements to the aversive situation' (Deci & Ryan, 1980, p. 46). With attractive tasks, a critical factor seems to be whether a task requires 'resourcefulness', as in the case of the puzzle-solving activity. In this case, rewards undermine, yet if the task is one that is completed more mechanically, rewards tend to facilitate performance.

The general implication for individual supervisors and designers of reward systems is that the *meanings* of rewards should be considered when deciding whether to supply them. It seems likely that these meanings can be managed to some extent by managing the cultural context of messages to employees surrounding recognition programmes, pay administration, and the implicit or psychological contract (Rousseau & Parks, 1993) between the employer and employee. For example, if an organization signals a cultural value that employees have worth and rights as human beings (e.g. by providing opportunities for personal or professional development and by ensuring respectful treatment and fair procedures of various kinds), employees may be more likely to view pay for performance as the organization upholding its side of a mutually beneficial relationship (instead of as applying leverage in a manner suggesting theory X predominance).

Perceiving the environment in terms of a causal map

So far we have considered causal thinking about oneself and about others in the organization. Organizational effectiveness is also influenced by causal

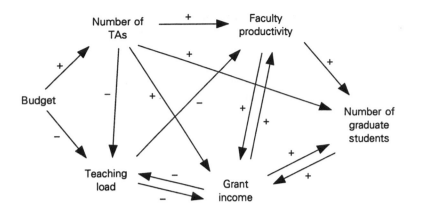

Figure 9.3 *Hypothetical perceived causal structure for an academic department (Salancik & Porac, 1986, reprinted by permission of Jossey-Bass)*

thinking about the organization itself, about the organization's environment, and about the relation of the organization to the environment. An organization populated by people with invalid 'cognitive maps' about these matters is doomed to take wasteful, ineffective or counterproductive actions, such as producing goods with no buyers.

Figure 9.3 presents a cognitive map of this kind. Salancik and Porac (1986) constructed this map as a hypothetical illustration of the causal thinking that academics may have about the interrelations of the variables named in the map. The map indicates, for example, existence of beliefs that as an academic department's budget is increased, its number of teaching assistants (TAs) will increase and the teaching load of faculty members will decrease. This decrease is partly a result of the increased number of TAs (as indicated by the negatively signed arrow leading from 'Number of TAs' to 'Teaching Load') and partly a result of other, unspecified factors (the arrow from 'Budget' to 'Teaching Load'; e.g. more faculty might be hired). Maps of this kind have been developed for strategic decision makers (e.g. when deciding which products to produce), employees involved in quality improvement activities (when analysing factors and processes involved in production), and for other groups and individuals. There are several social psychological aspects of maps of this kind. First, if the map includes agents – such as students, employees or customers – then beliefs about the psychology of these agents may be the basis of the perceived causal relations represented in the map. For example, in the map in Figure 9.3, the basis of the positive arrow linking 'Faculty Productivity' with 'Number of Graduate Students' may be the belief, held by the person or group whose beliefs have been mapped, that prospective graduate students will be attracted to enrol in a department in which they expect the prestige of faculty with higher productivity to be beneficial to their careers.

Another social psychological aspect to these maps arises with work groups, when there are important points of disagreement across group members in their maps. Different maps usually imply somewhat different responses to situations and different priorities among alternative emphases. Given sufficiently deep disagreements about these matters, the group will not be able to function as a group.

Eden, Jones, Sims and Smithin (1981) describe the construction of individual and group maps and ways of resolving disagreements among cognitive maps. On the basis of their experience as consultants in the development of maps for groups involved with policy and decision making (in housing policy, publishing and health care), they recommend that a group map be constructed from the set of individual maps, as a starting point for group discussion about the common understanding of the problem. Eden et al. make a point of not assigning strengths or importances to specific links or beliefs, so that group members will be more likely to consider all aspects of the map open to revision during discussion. When appropriate, they follow the development of a group map with computer simulation exercises, and they encourage group members to test the map against whatever data they may have.

These follow-up activities and the development of the maps themselves can be quite time consuming, and the final group map can be quite complex, even daunting. Nevertheless, Eden et al. suggest that the expenditure of effort may be worthwhile not only for the improvement in work effectiveness gained from having a more valid map, but also for the improvement that group members may experience in their ability to understand other group members' priorities, rationales for favouring particular courses of action in the past, and so forth. Quite possibly this greater perspective could lead to improved interpersonal relations in the group and greater clarity of communication in the future.

Actions, justifications and organizing

This discussion of causal structures in organization members' thinking would not be complete without mentioning the respected work of Karl Weick (1993). Weick describes a cycle in which cognitive, motivational and social processes at the individual level of analysis give rise to social and organizational structure, culture and norms. The cycle begins not with thought but with public, voluntary and irrevocable actions. Having taken such actions, organizational actors often must justify them to others (because organizations are self-examining by nature). These justifications invoke organizational goals, social obligations such as requirements of one's role, norms including those entailed in organizational culture, and other mutually held beliefs and values. Providing a justification has the effect of committing the actor to the course of action. Indeed, continued action, in line with the original justification and commitment, further justifies the action. Commitment here implies predictability and regularity of action, which is the stuff of structure. Commitments also constrain interpretations of future events for the actor and others, thus reinforcing and potentially diffusing to others the cognitive structure that generated the organizational structure in the first place. Weick's description underlines the cyclical nature of this process:

> Organizations begin to materialize when rationales for commitment become articulated. Since the decisions that stimulate justification originate in small-scale personal acts, organizational rationales often originate in the service of self-justification. Only later does justification become redefined as collective intention. Justifications can easily be transformed into organizational goals because these goals themselves are so general. But collective goals can best be understood as embellishments of earlier direct efforts to validate the soundness of individual commitments on a smaller scale. (1993, p. 13)

Two additional observations by Weick (1993) are noteworthy. First, cognitive maps are fundamentally unlike geographic maps because there is no objective reality. Instead there is only a socially constructed reality, which is always in flux. Secondly, Weick (p. 24) holds that macro phenomena (such as organizational culture) are best understood *not* as distinct and emergent (which is the conventional view) but as 'constructed and pursued within micro interaction' (interaction of the kind in the cycle described above). People find it useful to reify institutions such as the market or the corporate culture, in part because necessary justifications are supported in this way – but this does not make these institutions real. Weick is saying, in essence, that these institutions exist in people's heads, not in reality. Organizational reality is a dynamic process of social interaction and sense making by participants.

Schemas and information processing

So far, this discussion of social cognition and attribution in organizations has emphasized the effects of causal understanding of events. However, judgements and behaviour in organizations are influenced by other aspects of social perception and thought.

Schemas

The concept of cognitive schema is central to the social psychology of these other influences. A schema is a cognitive structure that promotes the integration of incoming information so as to render the information meaningful. Meaning in this instance is obtained by linking the incoming information to knowledge within one's total store of knowledge. Interconnections of beliefs and knowledge, and the elements of belief and knowledge so connected, constitute the schema. Schemas may concern anything we perceive. Social schemas concern matters among people.

Social schemas differ from one another in various respects (see Taylor & Crocker, 1980). For example, some schemas organize generic information about occupational and social roles such as firefighters and police officers, or supervisors and subordinates. Other schemas provide meanings in relation to prototypic conceptions such as social introvert and extrovert. Still others allow us to anticipate sequences of events, or to know what to do in sequence, in 'scripted' interactions such as going through the supermarket checkout line.

Variations in schemas such as their generality vs. specificity have been described. An example is the distinction between a generic script (event sequence schema) for what one does as a patron of a restaurant, as opposed to how to phone in a delivery order to your local pizzeria in a way that produces the greatest chance of ending up with what you wanted in the first place (taking account of what is meant by a 'medium' pizza, 'extra' cheese, and so forth).

These definitional statements suggest that schemas are important to judgements and behaviour in organizations in many ways. First, schemas are necessary because in order to respond appropriately to events, people must use schemas to derive the meaning of the event and thus be able to develop a response. Many of the difficulties encountered by people new to their jobs are a result of inadequate schemas to allow rapid, confident and effective responses (cf. Lord & Foti, 1986). These schemas must be built up through direct experience, training and other learning. Lord and Kernan (1987) suggest that training for some jobs benefits from being organized around scripts. At the same time there is the hazard that scripted behaviour, as in an employee–customer interaction, may become 'mindless' and lead to *reduced* customer satisfaction when the employee is not truly responsive to the customer.

Further, once acquired, schemas may bias our interpretations and responses. The Heneman et al. (1989) study of causal attribution may illustrate this point. As noted earlier, Heneman et al. suggested that instead of taking account of all the information available, supervisors may simply note the category membership, good or poor performer, of the subordinate, and then favour the attribution that already exists as part of the schema for the good or poor performer.

Information processing

The psychological term 'information processing' encompasses a wide range of cognitive processes, such as attention, categorization, recall and information integration. Feldman (1981) has illustrated the application of these concepts to organizations in an analysis of supervisors' appraisals of employee performance. The picture that emerges of performance appraisal (and, by implication, other social-perceptual activities in organizations) is even more complex than our discussions of attributions and schemas have indicated. For example, Feldman distinguishes low depth-of-processing uses of categories and schemas – as illustrated in the Heneman et al. (1989) study described earlier – and controlled or higher depth-of-processing uses. Controlled processing requires more conscious effort and tends to occur when events are more unexpected or of more significance to the perceiver; low depth of processing is essentially automatic and outside of awareness.

Feldman's information-processing account of performance appraisal has some interesting implications. One is that previous researchers' emphasis on trying to find just the right evaluation form or procedure for appraisals is unlikely to lead to more accurate appraisals. Instead, a better understanding is needed of how appraisers acquire and integrate information for appraisals. Another is that the strengths and weaknesses of various formats for recording evaluations (trait ratings, behavioural ratings, forced-choice formats, etc.) may be analysed and improved by focusing on the aspects and stages of information acquisition and processing at which they are especially prone to bias or error.

Assessing the applicability of attributional and social-cognitive theory

We have seen that the single (though broad) domain of attributional and social cognitive theory within social psychology has a good deal to say about a variety of everyday events and problems in organizations, such as motivating employees, coordinating their efforts, and assessing their performance. Nevertheless, even as broad a theoretical domain as this is inadequate to fully explain these phenomena. Reality is vexingly complex. Theories are deliberate oversimplifications of reality, constructed so as to provide an identifiable toehold on an otherwise slippery reality. All we can reasonably ask of any one theoretical perspective is for one solid toehold – perhaps one insight or, better yet, one recommendation for action in relation to a problem. Thus when the focus is on the problem instead of the theory, we tend to seek out multiple theoretical perspectives in order to derive as many insights and recommendations as possible. This problem-focused orientation is illustrated in the next major section of this chapter.

Social psychological perspectives on contemporary problems for organizations

'Change' is the watchword of the decade in which this chapter was written. Three problems related to change were selected to reflect the times and what social psychology may have to contribute. These are: aligning the goals and activities of various individuals and groups when their organization undergoes large-scale change; implementing new technology in ways responsive to human needs; and promoting innovation and creativity.

Organizational change

Organizations exist because collective efforts, properly organized, accomplish more than isolated, individual efforts. A key problem for any organization is to align members' efforts with one another (Katz & Kahn, 1978). A variety of processes in organizations promote this alignment. For example, employees may be selected for positive attitudes to customer satisfaction; new hires may be trained in the importance of customer satisfaction and how to achieve it; and continuing members of the organization may receive 'cultural' messages (Trice & Beyer, 1993) about customer satisfaction through symbols (e.g. photographs of customers on the walls of the workplace), stories (as about a department store employee who took initiative to deliver goods to a customer in urgent need), and structures (such as the ways rewards are allocated).

When properly managed, these processes support one another and tend to provide a degree of stability and consistency of purpose and practice in the organization. At this point the various groups within the organization are likely to have accommodated locally to these and other processes. For example, the managers of a manufacturing plant may have implemented particular authority structures and management practices with the belief that these are appropriate and effective under the circumstances.

Then comes the need for change. Many forces originating inside and outside the organization may exert pressures for change, including a declining competitive position in the marketplace, availability of new technologies or other opportunities, and societal trends such as changing demographics or values of the workforce. Whatever the origin, forces of these kinds may have far-reaching implications for various groups' activities and relationships to one another.

Bartunek (1993) has described how the concept of schemas can inform efforts at organizational development and change in response to forces like these. Drawing on others' writings, Bartunek distinguishes between organizational change initiatives that involve first-order change, which is quantitative in nature (e.g. seeking greater amounts of employee input) and second-order change, which is qualitative and transformational. As an example of the latter, management's understanding of 'participation' might shift from seeking employee input for decision making to initiating a stock ownership programme for all employees. In other words, in second-order change there is change in the meaning of some concept.

As described earlier in this chapter, schemas are crucial to meaning because they organize knowledge and beliefs that impart meaning. In Bartunek's use of this concept, schemas also connect with feelings and action orientations, in a manner similar to the connections described earlier for attitudes. (This point of similarity between schemas and attitudes is consistent with theoretical work by Pratkanis and Greenwald, 1989. In the present discussion, schemas imply greater cognitive elaboration.) Thus, Bartunek's schemas are quite encompassing, incorporating various evaluations along with beliefs about likely consequences of actions, and in this respect they are similar to the implicit theories X and Y described earlier.

A key barrier to change is the variety of schemas that different groups within an organization may hold. Bartunek offers the bold assertion: 'When multiple schemata are present, successful consultation can only result when consultants initiate second order change processes rather than facilitate participants' achievement of first order change' (1993, p. 345). Table 9.2 provides an illustration from Bartunek's efforts to foster quality of work life

Table 9.2   *Schemas of the different groups at FoodCom*

Group	Label for schema	Valued outcome(s)	Expressed concerns
Consultants	Cooperation	Productivity and QWL (QWL = mutual respect and communication)	None
Corporate management	Control	Productivity	Productivity might decrease
Local management	Paternalism	Productivity and QWL	Decreased productivity and decreased QWL
Line employees	Dependence	QWL (QWL = acquisition of amenities)	None
Machinists	Competition	Maintain influence and pay differential	Influence and pay differential might decrease

QWL = Quality of Work Life. LMC = Labour–Management Committee.

Source: Bartunek (1993) (Reprinted by permission of Prentice-Hall, Upper Saddle River, NJ)

(QWL) changes at a food-processing plant ('FoodCom'). The table lists various groups with a stake in QWL change and key elements of their beliefs. At a minimum we would expect from social cognitive theory that these differences in schemas would impede mutual understanding and communication about a possible organizational change. Bartunek noted that 'none of the groups really appreciated the different perspectives of the other groups' (p. 337) and this was an impediment to change in the direction of the greater productivity wanted by management and greater autonomy wanted by employees.

Bartunek comments that this lack of appreciation of others' views probably stems partly from a general tendency to overestimate similarities between one's own and others' views. This tendency crops up in other social domains and has been the focus of social cognitive research, originally under the rubric of 'false consensus bias' (e.g. Dunning, Griffin, Milojkovic, & Ross, 1990).

Bartunek has suggested further that different groups' schemas often involve conflicting interests connected with the prospect of change; consequently a conflict over the schema itself may emerge. For example, local management might insist that its paternalistic orientation is necessary for everyone's ultimate benefit; line employees are unlikely to agree with this orientation if it means that their wishes will receive little weight in the decision process.

Because conflicts of this kind are so prevalent, Bartunek has supplemented the schema-based analysis of organizational change with social psychological (and what we may call 'social technological') approaches to conflict and negotiation (e.g. van de Vliert & Mastenbroek, in press; Ury, Brett, & Goldberg, 1988). In consulting practice, Bartunek induces the various groups to address each other's perspectives (schemas) explicitly. One of the functions of this direct engagement of each other's perspectives is to avoid falling prey to a form of the attribution biases discussed earlier, namely experiencing differences between schemas as 'personality conflicts' (see also Mitchell et al., 1981, p. 215). When differences are experienced in this personalized way, they are seen as more intractable. However, by working to understand the other's view, it is likely that legitimate interests of the other will be discovered and a basis for negotiation may become visible. Subsequently the parties in the conflict can negotiate ways of satisfying each other's interests. Another function of direct engagement of perspectives is to stimulate a dialetical process in which the status quo thesis and an alternative antithesis may become seen as reconcilable in a synthesis. Bartunek describes such an outcome for a religious order which arrived at a synthesis of two seemingly incompatible roles for itself in its community. Finally, in direct engagement it may be discovered that notions about the legitimacy of conflict itself and acceptable ways of handling conflict are intrinsic to one or more groups' schemas, and that these notions must be addressed at the outset of these processes of analysis and negotiation.

Job design and technology

Given the direction of progress in the nineteenth and twentieth centuries, the future seems to hold ever-greater pervasiveness and complexity of technology in work life. Some researchers and consultants with a social psychological orientation have examined some of the resulting issues for the management of people in relation to technology.

Majchrzak (1988) opens her book on human aspects of factory automation by citing failure rates of 50 to 75 per cent when implementing advanced manufacturing technology (AMT). She attributes much of this failure to shortcomings in 'organizing, motivating, and directing the people involved in designing, implementing, and using the new technology' (p. xi). Although some of these shortcomings may reflect the sheer complexity of the human, technological and organizational systems involved (not to mention the myriad points of contact among these systems), many stem from what Majchrzak calls 'status quo' assumptions about people and technology. These include: technology is paramount in competitiveness, people are more flexible than machines, and little is known about human-oriented engineering. A more productive orientation is to see people and technology as elements or facets of a production system functioning in an organizational context. With this orientation Majchrzak describes how chances for success in factory automation may be enhanced by undertaking appropriate personnel practices, management of organization climate and culture, realignment of organizational structure, and other actions.

Among these other actions is the design of 'shop floor' work to meet human needs. Majchrzak lists nine options for job design in automated factories. One of these, Taylor's 'scientific management', continues in the tradition of re-organization of work into assembly lines or other low-skilled and constrained job design. It is scientific in the sense that it is based on observation of how some given technology may be used most efficiently, accurately and so forth, e.g. in terms of specific operator movements ('time and motion studies'). However, it is not social–scientific in that the technology is taken as given, and little or no account is taken of human preferences or needs. A review of case studies of firms implementing flexible automation found that 'in all companies where jobs were designed according to scientific management principles . . . operators experienced increased stress and the system was less cost effective' (Butera, 1984 as described by Majchrzak, 1988, p. 58). Among the other job design options are job enrichment as defined in Hackman and Oldham's (1980) job characteristics model (JCM), and sociotechnical systems (STS) inter-ventions (Pasmore, 1988).

To define 'job enrichment,' as opposed to 'job enlargement', we may contrast horizontal loading of tasks into a job (enlargement) with vertical loading (enrichment). In horizontal loading, a greater number of tasks is specified as part of the job, but the jobs are all at a similar level of complexity and responsibility. For example, horizontal loading of work for data entry personnel might be accomplished by requiring a given worker to do initial entry of some data and verification of other data. Vertical loading involves increased control or autonomy in ways such as giving workers authority to set schedules and priorities. In the case of data entry work, authority might also be given about when to verify one's own work (e.g. depending on the legibility of the material from which entry was done). Other aspects of determining work methods can also be an aspect of vertical loading, as when school-teachers are given more authority over choosing lesson plans and textbooks. Ultimately the goal of job enrichment, according to Hackman and Oldham (1980), is to enhance internal work motivation by enhancing three 'critical psychological states': experienced meaningfulness of the work, experienced responsibility for outcomes of the work, and knowledge of the actual results of the work activities. Other actions besides vertical loading for achieving these states, as described by Hackman and Oldham, include forming natural work units, establishing client relationships, and opening feedback channels. For example, a specified group of data entry workers could serve a particular part of an organization, communicate directly with people in that part of the organization about their needs for timeliness and accuracy of data entry, and receive feedback about timeliness and accuracy.

STS interventions are highly human- and process-oriented and are part of the collaborative organizational development tradition introduced in the previous section (in connection with Bartunek's writings). Application of STS typically involves formation of a design team with representatives from various levels, functions and jobs in the organization, including operators of the equipment to be redesigned. Analyses are undertaken of both the technical and social considerations before decisions are made about the design of technology and work. These decisions are likely to be consistent with STS principles of job design, which overlap those of JCM considerably but also include somewhat more specific features such as 'ability to control critical variances that impact on work outcomes' (Majchrzak, 1988, p. 63).

Wall, Corbett, Martin, Clegg and Jackson (1990) undertook research in a manufacturing plant to examine the effects of two arrangements for worker control over technologically sophisticated equipment. Wall et al. distinguish between specialist control and operator control. With specialist control, equipment problems requiring readjustment are handled by specialists who are called upon by operators as the need arises. In this case the operator's job is primarily to load, monitor and unload materials from the manufacturing machine. With operator control, readjustment problems are handled directly by the operator, who has been trained to deal with the most frequently occurring problems previously handled by specialists. Wall et al. collected data before and after changing operators' jobs from specialist- to operator-controlled design. A key finding was a 40 per cent reduction in downtime for the most complex machines used by these operators. The less complex machines, which had relatively little downtime initially, did *not* also show a statistically significant reduction in downtime. Reviewing these findings, Wall and Davids (1992) note that these more complex machines were, ironically, the ones that management was somewhat reluctant to include in the change to operator control, because of their complexity; management's underestimation of employees' ability and motivation nearly deprived all of an opportunity for work improvement. Wall and Davids also note from this study that operators were found to be 'appreciative of the change, and reported increased intrinsic job satisfaction, reduced job pressure, and no detrimental stress effects' (p. 381).

A further study described by Wall and Davids illustrates the interplay of job design and technology with human resource management policies and procedures. Specifically, equipment downtime was found to decrease gradually after introduction of a pay-for-results policy. At first this payment scheme seemed inappropriate because the automated robotics manufacturing line was under specialist control as defined previously. However, close examination of data on the operation of the machines and specialist call-outs suggested that operators wrested a degree of control nevertheless. Soon after the pay policy began, operators increased the number of short stoppages for preventive or rectifying actions. Because these stoppages were too short for specialist intervention, and the logs of specialist call-outs did not show an increase, the operators themselves must have been doing something with the machines. Wall and Davids note: 'The rise in short stoppages was more than compensated for by reduced downtime in excess of 15 minutes. . . . The opportunity for fault rectification not only brings direct benefit through enabling a quicker response to operating errors, but also provides the platform from which fault prevention skills develop' (p. 386).

Issues of people in relation to technology have been salient in offices as well as factories. Many of these issues were reviewed by Frese (1987). One issue concerns the design of work in terms of its effect on internal work motivation and job satisfaction. Based on his review, Frese comments:

There is overwhelming evidence that there is a *danger* of Taylorization of office work with the advent of computers. This could occur by bringing to the office the kind of division of labor that is boring and tedious with planning of work being placed outside of the working person's control. . . . There is also evidence, however, that it is possible to use alternative (often sociotechnical) job design methods and, additionally, that it pays to proceed with a more holistic and humane approach. . . . Thus it is not the technology that determines the human consequences of computer use, but how computer use is organized. (p. 126)

Other key issues include how to design the technology and how to train the worker so that optimal performance is attained. These issues are intertwined: 'The less complicated the commands, the rules, and the interface of a system . . . the less there is a need for training' (p. 134). Nevertheless, some empirical findings and general principles for these issues may be found in Frese (1987). They are not pursued further here because they would take us from social to cognitive psychology.

It is important to note that the theoretical perspectives used, such as JCM and STS, are as much subject to criticism and improvement as, say, attribution theory as presented in detail in earlier sections. For example, Hackman and Oldham (1980) comment that the appeal of the general notion in STS theory of the need to harmonize the social and technical factors of work is not matched by specific guidance on how to do this. The JCM has also been criticized on empirical and conceptual grounds – for example, subjectivity and, thus, variability in the perception of job characteristics (see, for example, Griffin, 1987). In the problem-oriented mode of this part of the chapter we are glossing over these important qualifications in order to see the practical possibilities of ever-incomplete theories.

Innovation

Orlikowski (1992) has observed that the very technology which has permitted the kind of progress seen in the nineteenth and twentieth centuries can also inhibit progress when people get into a rut of applying a particular technology in a particular way. Innovation with respect to developing and applying technology, managing employees, and satisfying customers is widely believed to be key to organizational success into the twenty-first century.

'Innovation' means a lot of things in the organizational literature at present. One aspect is sheer creativity – arriving at ways of doing things or at things to do (e.g. products to produce) previously unknown. Amabile (1988) has investigated a variety of individual and organizational factors that promote creativity. In one of her studies, Amabile asked research and development scientists about characteristics of the organizational environment that facilitate or inhibit creativity. The inhibitors most frequently mentioned by the scientists included social and organizational conditions such as an organizational climate marked by lack of cooperation across divisions and levels, and lack of value placed on creativity by the organizational culture. Inhibitory organizational structures and policies, such as inappropriate reward systems, also were mentioned frequently. The facilitators mentioned by the scientists were, largely, the flip sides of these same factors (e.g. creativity–promotive organizational culture). Noteworthy among the facilitors was a sense of freedom particularly in the day-to-day conduct of one's work. Amabile cites other research pointing to similar findings.

In discussing her results as a whole, Amabile emphasizes the delicate balancing acts required of managers who want to promote creativity. For example, the wrong amount or wrong kind of performance evaluation is detrimental. Too much or overly specified criteria for evaluation may inhibit risk taking which is, of course, absolutely necessary for creativity. Too little evaluation leads employees to feel forgotten and thus unmotivated. Amabile recommends 'a constant, constructive, less formal exchange of information about a project's progress on the part of all team members and management' (p. 149). Arriving at a recommendation about another balancing act, applying the right amount of pressure, is more difficult. On the one hand, some amount of time pressure and possibly competition appears to be facilitative; too much pressure appears to lead to unimaginative solutions.

Amabile has offered an encompassing model of creativity and innovation that incorporates factors ranging from those at the highest level of organization (e.g. the mission statement for the organization as a whole) to the individual level (e.g. skills). One further factor to highlight from this model is resources. This factor was mentioned frequently by the scientists on both the facilitating and the inhibiting side (lack of resources). Falling within this category are not only material resources but also knowledge about technology and customers, access to various databases, and appropriately trained employees.

West (1990) has also offered a social psychological analysis of factors that promote innovation. Not surprisingly, this analysis highlights some of the factors mentioned by scientists in Amabile's survey. Nevertheless, West's scheme seems to place greater emphasis on values and norms that favour innovation. The relevant values and norms include those holding that innovation is good and that it is safe to suggest new approaches ('participative safety' in West's terms). Such values and norms may be instilled explicitly via socialization or implicitly via cultural messages. In addition, although it does not directly influence innovation, a value on excellence may be helpful, because people striving for excellence will naturally seek innovation when appropriate. Similarly, a clear, attainable and consensually shared vision or mission is helpful because people become motivated to reach the goal by appropriate means.

Kanter's (1988) discussion of innovation touches on some of these same topics. However Kanter gives special emphasis to the implications for innovation stemming from organizational politics and the interdependence of organizational units. As Kanter flatly states:

> The innovation process is controversial. Innovations always involve competition with alternative courses of action. The pursuit of the air-cooled engine at Honda Motor, for example, drew time and resources away from improving the water-cooled

engine. Furthermore, sometimes the very existence of a potential innovation poses a threat to vested interests – whether the interest is that of a sales person receiving high commissions on current products, or of the advocates of a competing direction. (p. 171)

Kanter's inclusion of these observations is consistent with the list of four tasks she has identified for those who would innovate: idea generation, coalition building, idea realization, and transfer or diffusion into the market. The potential threat of innovation to vested interests has implications for all of these tasks but especially for coalition building. Kanter defines coalition building as 'acquiring power by selling the project to potential allies' (p. 184). This acquired power can derive from the power of specific individuals' positions in the organizational hierarchy or from the collective effect of many individuals in a coalition that supports the innovation. When one individual, such as a high-level executive, provides the power base for the innovation, this individual may take on the role of innovation 'orchestrator' (Galbraith, 1982). The orchestrator gives special attention to political issues for the innovation-in-progress. Intermediate between the originator of the innovation and the orchestrator there may be a manager acting as 'sponsor', who, after having 'discovered' the innovation (really someone else's innovation, typically a nonmanager), provides resources for development and testing of the innovation.

However, there are many possible patterns of support for innovation, so Kanter favours the broader notion of coalition building over that of sponsorship as an explanation for why some innovations advance to realization and diffusion. Kanter argues that individuals and groups tend to join coalitions favourable to the innovation when its consequences are directly favourable to those individuals and groups. Opposed coalitions form because of unfavourable direct consequences. For example, the finance department is responsible for acquiring and analysing financial information. Innovations that promote this task are likely to be supported; those that make accounting difficult are likely to be resisted. The interests of other stakeholders, such as suppliers and investors, also may come into play. Innovations that affect a greater number of interests need larger coalitions in order to survive.

Kanter has identified formal and informal mechanisms for building coalitions or otherwise aligning various interests with the innovation and overcoming resistance. Informally, a variety of tactics are available to deal with opponents: waiting them out, wearing them down, appealing to larger principles, inviting them in, sending emissaries to smooth the way and plead the case, displaying support from others, reducing the stakes for the opponents, and warning the opponents that they will be publicly challenged.

Formal structures become especially important in the later stages of development and implementation of innovation, so that required resources, information and support will be brought to bear in a way that reconciles various interests and otherwise solves problems. These structures tend to be 'overlays' upon the functionally or departmentally dominated organizational chart. That is, cross-functional groups such as task forces, joint planning groups and information-spreading councils get involved in the innovation.

This later formalization of organizational structure in relation to the innovation contrasts with what is believed to promote invention in the first place, namely, isolation of the group responsible for innovation. Kanter describes safe havens or 'reservations' that may be permanent or temporary, and internal or external to the organization. In this connection Kanter quotes Galbraith (1982): 'the odds [for innovation] are better if early efforts to perfect and test new "crazy" ideas are differentiated – that is, separated – from the function of the operating organization.'

Concluding comments

This chapter has, in effect, argued the case that social psychological processes and phenomena are as pervasive and fundamental to organizations as sand is to the Sahara. Social psychological processes studied in laboratories often turn out to be demonstrable and in some way applicable to work life.

Despite this definite applicability, social psychological research in organizations is challenging. Ideally, theory-oriented researchers should go beyond showing that laboratory phenomena play out in organizations, by showing their significance to organizational effectiveness or personal experience, as defined in the introduction. One way to do this is by implementing theory-based programmes and practices in organizations. However, few examples of such a strong theory base for action exist. Theory-based action tends to be multiple-theory-based, in the interest of having practical impact but at the likely expense of ability to make inferences about theory. The challenge for the problem-oriented researcher-practitioner is to integrate the insights of social psychology with the technical, political and organizational-cultural realities in the organization (cf. Tichy, 1983). This integration requires a set of skills and experiences not automatically acquired by studying, even understanding social psychology. Nevertheless, an understanding of social psychology and of psychology more generally can help the practitioner not only at the level of conceptualizing what is going on, but also at the level of doing something about it as a consultant, human resource professional or manager. For example, the social psychologist working as a consultant is particularly well prepared to avoid attributional biases such as over-attributing behaviour to the individual as opposed to the situation; acknowledge there are often multiple legitimate interests that must be reconciled through negotiation; and appreciate the visceral depth of distress employees may feel when cultural premises are challenged. Indeed, Brief and Dukerich (1991) have argued that the primary benefit of theory applied to organizations is its potential to raise consciousness in ways such as these. Hopefully this chapter has shown that organization members who are not social psychologists can acquire and use similar understandings and insights in order to improve organizational effectiveness and life at work.

Two approaches to social psychological research and analysis in organizations were described and illustrated. The first approach, theory-centred, examined whether particular theoretical concepts developed outside organizations (for example, in laboratories or in other applied domains) can help in understanding social phenomena in organizations. This approach was illustrated by reviewing the applicability of research on social cognition and attribution to a variety of organizational concerns, such as employee motivation, supervisory behaviour, and perception of people and the environment. The second approach, problem-centred, began with a focus on an organizational concern, such as the need to promote innovation, and drew upon various social psychological theories or concepts depending on their usefulness for addressing the concern. In illustrating this approach, theories of social climate and culture, motivation, attitudes, and cognition and attribution were all applied.

Further reading

Katz, D. & Kahn, R.L. (1978). *The social psychology of organizations* (2nd ed.). New York: Wiley. A major undertaking which spans many topics in the field. For several of these topics the authors develop original integrative frameworks for the purpose of organizing large literatures. In other instances, links with sociological or other writings in the social sciences are revealed. Use of a systems-theoretic perspective on various topics, introduced in these authors' earlier edition, is maintained.

Martinko, M. (Ed.) (1995). *Attribution theory: An organizational perspective*. Delray Beach, FL: St Lucie Press. Additional illustrations of the many applications of attribution theory to organizational life (e.g. leadership, absenteeism) are to be found here, along with discussions of measurement. (This book was released after completion of the present chapter, so this description is based only on an announcement of the contents of the book.)

Murnighan, J.K. (Ed.) (1993). *Social psychology in organizations: Advances in theory and research*. Englewood Cliffs, NJ: Prentice-Hall. The product of a series of conferences on social psychology and social phenomena in organizations. Conference participants review their programmes of research.

Oskamp, S. (Ed.) (1984). *Applied social psychology annual, vol. 5: Applications in organizational settings*. Beverly Hills, CA: Sage. Opens with trenchant comments on the gap between social and organizational psychology, and illustrates through specific examples some of the methodological issues that confront researchers in this area.

Schein, E.H. (1980). *Organizational psychology* (3rd ed.). Englewood Cliffs, NJ: Prentice-Hall. A brief textbook which provides an introduction to many of the topics covered in this chapter. Most longer textbooks concerning organizational behaviour – an applied field which draws on social psychology and other disciplines to explain behaviour in organizations – also address many of the topics in the present chapter.

Sims, H.P., Gioia, D.A. & Associates (Eds) (1986). *The thinking organization: Dynamics of organizational social cognition*. San Francisco, CA: Jossey-Bass. Leading researchers present their work concerning how organization members' beliefs are organized and how beliefs influence behaviour in organizations.

Wilpert, B. (1995). Organizational behaviour. In J.T. Spence, J.M. Darley, & D.J. Foss (Eds), *Annual review of Psychology*, vol. 46 (pp. 59–90). Palo Alto, CA: Annual Reviews, Inc. This chapter is the most recent among those on organizational behaviour in this annual book series, and is the first with special concern for including European contributions to the field (e.g. in action theory, new technology and participation).

In addition, there are other works that span a range of social psychological topics applied to organizations. These include:

Argyle, M. (1989). *The social psychology of work* (2nd ed.). Harmondsworth: Penguin.
Glen, F. (1975). *The social psychology of organizations*. London: Methuen.
Smith, P.B. (1973). *Groups within organizations: Applications of social psychology to organizational behaviour*. London: Harper & Row.

Various 'handbook' volumes contain authoritative reviews of many topics in organizational psychology, theory and behaviour. These include:

Dunnette, M.D., Hough, L.M., & Triandis, H. (Eds) (1990–94). *Handbook of industrial and organizational psychology* (2nd ed., Vols 1–4). Chicago: Rand-McNally.
Hofstede, G. & Kassem, M.S. (Eds) (1976). *European contributions to organization theory*. Assen: Van Gorcum.
Lorsch, J. (Ed.) (1987). *Handbook of organizational behavior*. Englewood Cliffs, NJ: Prentice-Hall.
March, J.G. (Ed.) (1987). *Handbook of organizations*. New York: Garland. (Reprint. Originally published 1965 by Rand-McNally.)
Thierry, H., Drenth, P.J.D., & de Wolff, C.J. (Eds) (in press). *A new handbook of work and organisational psychology*. Hove, UK: Lawrence Erlbaum.

Many 'readers' are also highly relevant. A good starter is:

Pugh, D.S. & Hickson, D.J. (Eds) (1993). *Great writers on organizations* (omnibus ed.). Brookfield, VT and Aldershot, UK: Dartmouth.

10

Social Psychology and the Law

Günter Köhnken

Contents

Psychological research in legal contexts has a long tradition with an initial flourishing period at the beginning of this century (see, for example, Binet, 1905; Lipmann, 1906; Marbe, 1913; Münsterberg, 1908; Stern, 1903; for historical reviews see Sporer, 1982; Undeutsch, 1992). Moreover, it was one of the first areas of experimental applied psychology (e.g. Stern, 1903; Wertheimer, 1906). Following a less active period, we are now witnessing a strong revival of psycholegal research. Evidence for this revival is found in the publication of more and more books on various aspects of psychology and law (e.g. Bull & Carson, 1995; Gudjonsson, 1992; Kaplan, 1986; Kerr & Bray, 1982; Konecni & Ebbesen, 1982; Lösel, Bender, & Bliesener, 1992; Ross, Read, & Toglia, 1994; Sporer, Malpass, & Köhnken, 1996; Stephenson, 1992; Wegener, Lösel, & Haisch, 1989), the establishment of journals (e.g. *Law and Human Behavior*; *Behavioral Sciences and the Law*; *Law and Psychology Review*; *Expert Evidence*; *Public Policy, Psychology, and Law*), the constitution of national and international professional organizations, the growing number of national and international conferences and symposia, and the strong increase in empirical publications during the past twenty years.

Lösel (1992) describes six trends that have emerged during recent research:

1. research activities have expanded from a primarily psychotechnical orientation towards a greater autonomy;
2. there is a strong increase in empirical, particularly experimental, research;

3. more emphasis is being laid on theory-guided research;
4. more research is being conducted on behaviour within the legal system, e.g. on jury decision making and sentencing;
5. research results have increasing impact on legal practice;
6. research activities are expanding from criminal law to civil law.

The results of psychological research are applied to legal practice in various ways and at a number of levels within the criminal and civil justice system. For example, in the investigation of crime the police may use techniques of offender profiling to draw conclusions about the lifestyle, criminal history and residential location of a person who had committed a number of crimes (e.g. Canter, 1994, 1995; Holmes, 1989). Witnesses are interviewed using interview techniques which are based on research on memory and communication (Fisher & Geiselman, 1992). Line-up identifications are constructed according to guidelines which are derived from psychological research (e.g. Sporer et al., 1996). At trial, attorneys may rely on advice and empirical analysis of social scientists when selecting juries (Hans & Vidmar, 1982). Courts employ psychologists as expert witnesses to assist in evaluating witness statements. Finally, if a defendant is convicted he or she may be subject to correctional treatment that is derived from research on behaviour modification and psychotherapy.

This brief (and incomplete) overview illustrates that the field of legal psychology entails more than the application of social psychology alone, although, for example, social cognition plays a prominent role in the psychology of eyewitness testimony. Likewise, research on jury selection and jury decision making draws heavily on theories of attribution, stereotypes and group decision making. However, in addition to the application of social psychology cognitive psychology and developmental psychology are important pillars of, for example, witness psychology. Theories of criminal behaviour would hardly be possible without research on personality and clinical psychology, and the police and prisons have been investigated from the perspective of organizational psychology.

It would be impossible to cover all areas of psycholegal research in this chapter. The discussion will therefore focus on psychological research in the area of criminal law. The vast majority of research has focused on various levels of the criminal justice system; civil proceedings have received considerably less attention. This chapter will address topics from four areas which have received particular attention in previous research: the explanation and prediction of criminal behaviour, the investigation of crime, the criminal trial, and offender treatment.

Criminal behaviour: explanation and prediction

How criminal behaviour is explained and predicted has enormous influence on all levels of the criminal justice system. Theoretical models of criminal behaviour will more or less determine how a society deals with the phenomenon of crime. Such models can, for example, be used to assist the investigation of crime; crime prevention programmes are influenced by theories of criminal behaviour and this is even more so with regard to the treatment of offenders. There appears to be some consistency about criminal behaviour which calls for psychological explanation. Cross-sectional as well as longitudinal epidemiological research on criminal behaviour has repeatedly shown that the prevalence of offending (officially recorded as well as self-reported) increases with age to reach a peak in the teenage years and from then on decreases through the twenties and thirties (e.g. Farrington, 1990; Gottfredson & Hirschi, 1988; Stephenson, 1992). There is also a remarkable continuity of offending over time. In other words, the best predictor of offending at one age is offending at a preceding age. In a prospective longitudinal study Farrington and West (1990) found that of those convicted as juveniles (age 10–16) almost 75 per cent were reconvicted between the ages of 17 and 24, and nearly half of the juvenile offenders were reconvicted between the ages of 25 and 32. Furthermore, those convicted early tend to become the most persistent offenders, committing large numbers of offences at high rates over long periods.

From a psychological point of view offending is a certain type of behaviour, similar in many respects to other types of anti-social or deviant behaviours. Offending has indeed been found to be part of a more general anti-social behaviour syndrome that arises in childhood and persists into adulthood (Robins, 1979). Farrington and West (1990) report that the most serious offenders at each age were deviant in a number of other aspects. Among other things, at the age of 18 offenders drank, smoked and gambled more, used more drugs, admitted to drinking and driving, and fought more than did the nonconvicted peers. Of 110 18-year-old males diagnosed as anti-social on noncriminal criteria, 70 per cent were convicted up to the age of 20, and this anti-social tendency persists into adulthood.

Offending and anti-social behaviour in general seems to be linked to a configuration of personality factors variously termed hyperactivity-impulsivity-attention deficit. For example, Farrington, Loeber and van Kammen (1990) found that diagnosis of this syndrome at age 8–10 predicted juvenile convictions independently of conduct disorders at that age. Delinquency has also been related to certain patterns of thinking. In particular, criminal activities are associated with a strong tendency to justify and excuse criminal behaviour. For example, Farrington, Biron and LeBlanc (1982) reported that offenders tend to blame the world for their problems and to believe that they had a lot of bad luck. Mitchell and Dodder (1983) found that delinquents attempt to neutralize their guilt feelings by finding excuses and justifications for their behaviour. They deny their responsibility as well as the injury of the victim. Over time, the justification employed to explain past delinquency may subsequently be used in an anticipatory way to justify future, intended deviation (Stephenson, 1992).

Does this pattern of results indicate that offending is a stable personality characteristic, a trait, or that the possession of certain normal personality characteristics facilitates criminality? Eysenck (1977) and Eysenck and Eysenck (1978) have put forward a theory that suggests just that. These authors hypothesize that extroverts are less well conditioned than introverts and therefore more difficult to socialize. They are said to be more sensation-seeking and less likely to feel anxious when contemplating or performing a criminal act. This theory links criminal behaviour to genetics in that extroversion–introversion is assumed to have a biological basis and that this is to a considerable degree rooted in genetics. Eysenck's theory on criminal behaviour has been strongly criticized (e.g. Sarbin, 1979). Moreover, the empirical data do not seem to support this position. For example, Hollin (1989) concluded from a literature review that studies on the relation of extroversion and offending have had inconsistent results. Some did find the predicted relationship, others found no difference while still others reported lower extroversion scores in offender groups. Furthermore, Raine and Venables (1981) failed to confirm the notion that poorly socialized people are less conditionable than better socialized individuals. West and Farrington (1973) reported that convicted juveniles did not differ in extroversion and neuroticism from their nonconvicted peers.

Based on their prospective longitudinal study and on literature reviews Farrington (1992; Farrington & West, 1990) has suggested that a combination of factors eventually leads to delinquency. West and Farrington (1973) and Loeber and Stouthamer-Loeber (1986) reported that poor parental supervision and monitoring, erratic or harsh parental discipline, cruel, passive or negligent parental attitude and parental conflicts and separation were all important predictors of offending. Criminal, anti-social and alcoholic parents tend to have criminal sons (Robins, 1979). These results suggest that offending occurs when the normal social learning process is disrupted by erratic discipline, poor supervision and unsuitable parental models. These children tend to have below-average intelligence (Wilson & Herrnstein, 1985; West & Farrington, 1973). Farrington (1992) hypothesizes that, because of their poor ability to manipulate abstract concepts, they have problems in foreseeing the consequences of their offending and in appreciating the feelings of victims. He further assumes that children with low intelligence are likely to fail in school and later to have erratic employment careers. As a consequence, they are less able to satisfy their desires for material goods, excitement and social status by legal or socially approved methods and so tend to choose illegal or socially disapproved methods (Farrington, 1986).

Apparently, no definitive answer can be given yet as for the ultimate causes of criminal behaviour. Empirical research in this area is extremely difficult due to the impossibility of experimental control. As a consequence, the available data are sometimes vague and inconclusive and subject to highly controversial debates. However, the recent longitudinal studies seem to be a promising approach and have already provided some new and promising insights into this complex phenomenon.

Investigation of crime: interviewing eyewitnesses

Whatever the causes of criminal behaviour, when a crime has been committed it is the task of the police to initiate an investigation and to identify the perpetrator. Apart from primarily criminalistic aspects this is the point where eyewitness psychology comes into play. Much of the relevant information is provided by witnesses and/or victims of the crime. Hence, one major part of the police investigation is to interview witnesses, victims, and perhaps suspects. If, in the process of a criminal investigation, a suspect has been arrested the police may require an eyewitness to identify this individual. Finally, the witness statements have to be evaluated in terms of their credibility or sincerity. These topics will be discussed in the following section.

For the police, interviewing is one of the major tools of investigation. Research in Germany has shown, for example, that police officers spend approximately 70–80 per cent of their total working time interviewing witnesses, victims and suspects (Herren, 1976). With regard to criminal investigations, collecting as many accurate facts as possible is of primary importance for the police. Fisher and Geiselman (1992) cite a comprehensive study of criminal investigation processes by the Rand Corporation where it was found that the principal determinant of whether or not a case is solved is the completeness and accuracy of the eyewitness's account. There are basically two psychological techniques available for enhancing memory retrieval: *hypnosis* and the *cognitive interview*. Gudjonsson (1992) lists a third: drug-aided interviews; however since the use of drug-aided interviews is highly controversial and since this technique is not admissible in many countries it will not be discussed here.

Forensic hypnosis – or, as Reiser (1980) terms it, *investigative hypnosis* – attempts to improve the interviewee's recall by means of hypnotic techniques. The empirical evidence for the memory-enhancing potential of hypnosis is equivocal. Whereas some anecdotal reports claim that hypnosis may enhance memory in criminal cases (cf. Reiser, 1980), controlled laboratory studies have produced mixed results (Smith, 1983; Wagstaff, 1984; Yuille & McEwan, 1985; see Gudjonsson, 1992; Geiselman & Machlowitz, 1987 and Orne, 1979, for reviews). Geiselman and Machlowitz (1987) report that of 38 experimental studies on hypnosis, 21 found significantly more correct information with the use of hypnosis, 13 reported no effect, and four reported significantly less correct information. With respect to incorrect information generated under hypnosis, eight experiments showed a significant increase in errors with hypnosis, whereas ten showed no effects.

In their review, Geiselman and Machlowitz (1987) could link the equivocal nature of the results, in part, to methodological differences between the experiments. They conclude that a combination of three methodological factors account for the variability of effects: type of interview (interactive vs. fixed, prearranged questions or free recall), length of the retention interval, and sample size. Hypnosis appears to be more effective if an interactive interview style is used after a long retention interval and if the sample size is large. Furthermore, it seems that hypnosis is more effective if more realistic stimulus material is used (i.e. films or live events).

Although these results suggest that hypnosis may indeed have, at least under certain conditions, some potential for enhancing memory retrieval it

1. Reinstatement of the environmental and personal (emotional) context of the witnessed event
2. Instruction to report everything, even partial and seemingly trivial information
3. Instruction to report the event in various temporal orders (e.g. beginning at the end and moving backwards)
4. Instruction to recall information from various perspectives (e.g. from the perspective of another person)

Figure 10.1   *The four mnemonic aids of the original form of the cognitive interview*

remains a controversial technique. It has been argued that hypnosis may contaminate memory (Haward, 1988, 1990). Gudjonsson (1992) lists three possible ways in which hypnosis may interfere with normal memory processes: first, subjects may be particularly prone to confabulate whilst under the influence of hypnosis. Secondly, witnesses may be more susceptible to (mis)leading questions; and thirdly, hypnosis may lead witnesses to feel overconfident in the accuracy of their recollections. In part as a consequence of these problems the admissibility of evidence obtained during hypnosis has been (and still is) an issue of controversial debate (see, for example, Haward, 1990; Orne, 1979; Morris, 1989).

A less controversial technique for improving memory retrieval is the cognitive interview. It is based on two main principles of memory: encoding specificity (Flexser & Tulving, 1978; Tulving & Thomson, 1973) and varied retrieval (Tulving, 1974; Anderson & Pichert, 1978). The cognitive interview was developed by Geiselman and Fisher (Geiselman, Fisher, Firstenberg, Hutton, Avetissian, & Prosk, 1984). In its original form the cognitive interview comprises of four basic retrieval aids or mnemonic strategies, together with some ways of helping witnesses to recall specific bits of information (see Figure 10.1). First, interviewees are instructed to mentally reconstruct the context of the witnessed event, to form an image or an impression of the environmental aspects of the scene, and to remember their emotional feelings and thoughts. The second strategy is to encourage witnesses to report everything they remember, even if they think the details are not important. The third component is to ask witnesses to recall the event in a variety of temporal orders or to make retrieval attempts from different starting points, for example from the most memorable element. Finally, witnesses are encouraged to recall the event from different physical locations, just as if they were viewing it with another person's eyes.

Fisher and Geiselman later refined the technique considerably, particularly by addressing the social dynamics and communication between the interviewer and the eyewitness (e.g. interview structure, rapport building, using nonverbal responses, witness-compatible questioning) and called this refined version the enhanced cognitive interview (Fisher, Geiselman, Raymond, Jurkevich, & Warhaftig, 1987; for recent overviews see Bekerian & Dennett, 1993; Fisher

& Geiselman, 1992; Fisher & McCauley, in press; Fisher, McCauley, & Geiselman, 1994; Memon & Köhnken, 1992).

During recent years more than 30 experiments that evaluate the effectiveness of the cognitive interview have been reported. In a series of experiments conducted by Geiselman and Fisher, the original version of the cognitive interview generated about 25–30 per cent more correct information without increasing the number of false details. The cognitive interview enhanced memory in written reports (Geiselman et al., 1984) as well as in oral interviews (Fisher, Geiselman, & Amador, 1989; Geiselman, Fisher, MacKinnon, & Holland, 1985). This effect has been demonstrated with a variety of interviewees including, for example, adults (Geiselman, Fisher, MacKinnon, & Holland, 1986), children (Geiselman & Padilla, 1988; Saywitz, Geiselman, & Bornstein, 1992; McCauley & Fisher, 1995) and people with learning disability (Brown & Geiselman, 1990). It has also been shown that the cognitive interview may decrease the effect of misleading post-event information (Geiselman, Fisher, Cohen, Holland, & Surtes, 1986). Whereas all of the initial research on the cognitive interview was conducted in the laboratories of Geiselman and Fisher and their colleagues, in recent years a growing number of studies have been reported in Germany and the United Kingdom (e.g. Aschermann, Mantwill, & Köhnken, 1991; George, 1991; Köhnken, Schimossek, Aschermann, & Höfer, 1995; Köhnken, Thürer, & Zoberbier, 1994; Mantwill, Köhnken, & Aschermann, 1995; Memon, Holley, Milne, Köhnken, & Bull, 1994).

A recent meta-analysis (Köhnken, Milne, Memon, & Bull, 1994) including 36 experiments with more than 1,400 participants obtained a significant overall effect size d = 0.83 for the difference in correct information between cognitive and conventional or standard interviews. The overall difference for the amount of incorrect information, although considerably smaller, was also significant (d = 0.33). However, the average accuracy rate (i.e. the proportion of correct details relative to the total number of recalled details) was similar in both types of interview (85 per cent for the cognitive interview compared to 83 per cent for the standard interview). Thus, the cognitive interview generates more information than a standard police interview and this larger amount of information is no less accurate. But the results indicate that the cognitive interview may not work with children younger than seven years.

These data suggest that the cognitive interview may, in certain circumstances, be a useful tool for criminal investigations. It can help to increase the amount of information extracted from a witness substantially without sacrificing accuracy. Whether or not the risk of an increase in the absolute number of incorrect details is acceptable depends on the purpose of the interview. For example, in the early stages of an investigation it may be important for the police to generate a large amount of information in order to establish as many leads as possible. Similarly, when interviewing a suspect who claims to have an alibi, it may be important to get as much information as possible in order to be able to investigate the correctness of this claim. This information is likely to be cross-checked in the later course of the investigation and errors have a good chance of being discovered.

Eyewitness identification

According to studies by Brandon and Davies (1973), Frank and Frank (1957), and Rattner (1988), mistaken identification is one of the most important sources of the miscarriage of justice. In a survey of 205 cases of wrongful convictions mistaken identification was found to be involved in 52 per cent (Rattner, 1988). Most of these convictions had severe consequences for the defendant, due to the seriousness of crimes with which he or she was charged.

Why do false identifications occur? On the one hand, witnesses may have had a poor view of the criminal; a long delay between the encounter and the recognition test may have weakened the memory representation of the culprit, or post-event information (e.g. a photo of an innocent suspect) may have contaminated the witnesses' memory. These and similar factors have in common that they are usually not under the control of the criminal justice system. Their likely effects on identification accuracy in a given case can only be post-dicted or estimated. Wells (1978) has labelled these variables *estimator variables*. On the other hand, the police may conduct the recognition test in a way that it is biased towards the suspect (e.g. because he is the only blond person among a group of dark haired foils) or the witness may have observed the suspect being escorted by police officers. These factors are called system variables because they are under the control of the criminal justice system. Empirically based knowledge on the potential effects of estimator and system variables may help attorneys, judges and juries to assess the accuracy of eyewitness identification and can be used by the police to apply state-of-the-art recognition procedures in order to avoid the destruction of vital evidence (Cutler & Penrod, 1995b; Köhnken, Malpass, & Wogalter, 1996; Wells, 1993).

Estimator variables

Shapiro and Penrod (1986; see also Cutler & Penrod, 1995a, b; Narby, Cutler, & Penrod, 1996) conducted a meta-analysis in order to assess the effects of various estimator variables on identification accuracy. This meta-analysis included 128 experiments with 960 experimental conditions, almost 17,000 subjects, and more than 700,000 separate recognition judgements. The authors discuss the results of this analysis with regard to seven classes of variables:

1. stable characteristics of eyewitnesses (e.g. personality factors);
2. malleable characteristics of eyewitnesses;
3. additional eyewitness testimony (e.g. expressed confidence in the accuracy of identification);
4. stable target characteristics (e.g. attractiveness);
5. malleable target characteristics (e.g. disguises);
6. environmental conditions (e.g. exposure duration, presence of a weapon);
7. post-event factors (e.g. the length of the delay between the crime and the recognition test).

The results of the meta-analysis suggest that stable characteristics of eyewitnesses such as intelligence, gender and personality traits (e.g. self-monitoring) are only weakly, if at all, related to identification accuracy. In particular, self-reported facial recognition skill is not reliably associated with actual performance. However, children and the elderly tend to perform more poorly than other adults. The most interesting result with regard to malleable characteristics of eyewitnesses is perhaps the finding that, contrary to widely held beliefs, neither training in face recognition nor the expectation of a later recognition test substantially influences identification accuracy. However, a deeper processing (Craik & Lockhart, 1972) of facial characteristics seems to enhance performance in a recognition test.

Police or jurors often refer to *additional information from eyewitnesses* when evaluating the likely accuracy of identifications. They assume, for example, that the eyewitnesses' confidence, the amount of information they recall, or the degree of consistency between multiple descriptions of the same event or person are valid indicators of recognition accuracy. In contrast to these beliefs, neither consistency nor confidence were found to be reliable predictors of actual accuracy. However, in most studies the confidence–accuracy relationship was examined based on all subjects, regardless of whether or not they attempted an identification. Sporer, Penrod, Read and Cutler (in press) have recently reported data which suggest that the confidence–accuracy relationship is consistently stronger for choosers (i.e. witnesses who have identified a person) than for non-choosers.

The most important variable of the *stable target characteristics* seems to be facial distinctiveness. Faces that are highly attractive or highly unattractive are substantially better recognized than nondistinct faces. Whereas neither the race of the perpetrator nor the race of the witness alone is strongly associated with recognition performance, these variables interact such that cross-race identifications are less accurate than own-race identifications (Bothwell, Brigham, & Malpass, 1989; Chance & Goldstein, 1996). However, almost all of this research used African-American and white subjects and relatively little is known about the identification accuracy with regard to Mediterranean or North African individuals. *Malleable target characteristics* are important predictors of identification accuracy. In particular, if the perpetrator wore a disguise or changed facial appearance between initial exposure and recognition test, identification accuracy is significantly reduced.

The majority of experiments on estimator variables have looked at the effects of *environmental conditions* at the time of the crime. In general, these situational factors were found to be important predictors of identification accuracy. For example, recognition performance is reduced for less salient targets if the exposure duration is short, if the crime is less serious, if a weapon was present during the crime (see the meta-analysis of studies on the weapon focus effect by Steblay, 1992), and if the witness was intoxicated. The effects of stress and arousal are less clear due to ethical restrictions in the manipulation of high levels of arousal. However, there appears to be a tendency for extreme stress to reduce identification accuracy.

With regard to *post-event factors* Shapiro and Penrod (1986) found that face recognition accuracy shows a linear decline with retention interval. Interestingly, time delay has a smaller impact on the number of false identifications than on the proportion of correct recognitions. Witnesses are often requested by the police to provide a description of the perpetrator, to help in generating a facial composite, or to search through mug shots. The available research results suggest that facial composite procedures are not particularly successful (Shepherd & Ellis, 1996), and that verbal descriptions are sometimes more helpful than facial composite productions (Sporer, 1996). Furthermore, misleading information can lead to inaccurate facial composites, which in turn leads to inaccurate identifications (Jenkins & Davies, 1985). Mug-shot searches may bias the witness towards (correctly or incorrectly) identifying a person from the line-up who appeared in the mug shots (e.g. Gorenstein & Ellsworth, 1980).

System variables

Factors that are under the control of the criminal justice system are called system variables (Wells, 1978). This term describes the characteristics of a recognition test. With regard to recognition tests (line-ups or photo arrays) false identifications can have two causes (see Figure 10.2). On the one hand, random error can occur. In this case, the witness chooses the suspect purely by chance. Any other member of the line-up is just as likely to be selected as the alleged offender. Secondly, a false identification may result from systematic error. A systematic error occurs when certain properties of the line-up procedure or the composition of the line-up lead the witness to choose the suspect even if he or she is not the criminal.

Random errors

Witnesses may want to present themselves as good and constructive persons who can help the police catch the offender and thereby solve the crime. Further, witnesses tend to see the whole line-up procedure as a technique to convict an already well-known criminal (e.g. Malpass & Devine, 1984). In the erroneous belief that the police are best served by a positive identification of one of the individuals in the line-up, they may choose the individual who most resembles the fuzzy picture of the offender in their memory. As long as no systematic errors are made that would direct the witnesses' choice to a specific individual, the selection is likely to be more or less random. In these circumstances the likelihood that an innocent suspect will be selected is inversely related to the number of foils in the line-up or the photo array (Köhnken et al., 1996; Wells & Turtle, 1986). Consequently, the larger the pool of foils from which the suspect is chosen the more informative is the identification (Cutler, Penrod, & Martens, 1987). A line-up without foils does not provide valid evidence (Wells & Turtle, 1986).

Systematic errors

A line-up is conducted in order to test the hypotheses that (a) the suspect is the guilty party, and (b) the suspect is not the criminal (null hypothesis). The

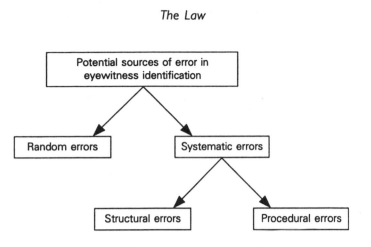

Figure 10.2   *Potential sources of error in eyewitness identification*

line-up recognition test thus resembles an experiment and the general methodological principles for experimental research and hypothesis testing apply (Wells & Luus, 1990). From this point of view two types of systematic error can be distinguished (Köhnken et al., 1996; Malpass & Devine, 1983): (1) the composition of the line-up or the arrangement of the photographs can lead to the suspect standing out from the other individuals. Malpass and Devine (1983) referred to this as a structural error; (2) errors can occur during the procedure of the recognition test that would lead the witness to select the suspect. This type of error is referred to as a procedural error.

Structural errors   Several experiments have demonstrated that unfair line-ups where the suspect stands out from the foils can dramatically increase the risk of false identification. For example, Lindsay and Wells (1980) found that an uninvolved person who was noticeably different from the other foils in a photo array was incorrectly identified by 70 per cent of the subjects. It is therefore essential to select foils who are sufficiently similar to the suspect. This can be achieved by using a combination of objective and subjective selection procedures (Köhnken et al., 1996). In the objective selection procedure, selection of alternatives is determined by the presence of a few objectively important personal characteristics (e.g. size, weight, age, facial hair, race). However, the selection of alternatives on the basis of objective physical characteristics does not always ensure the formation of a fair group for the line-up. Often, when comparing his or her memory of the culprit to the individuals in the line-up, the witness is guided by highly subjective impressions. These impressions noted by the witness should also be taken into account in selecting the foils (Luus & Wells, 1991).

Procedural errors   Procedural errors are present when peculiarities during the preparation and execution of a line-up cause the witnesses to draw their attention to the police suspect. Such errors may, for example, result from repeated recognition tests. Sometimes the police requests a witness to do a mug-shot search. If a person is recognized on one of the mug shots he or she is arrested and a line-up identification may be staged by the police. However, several experiments have shown that witnesses tend to repeat their first decision in later line-ups even if they are false (Gorenstein & Ellsworth, 1980; Brigham & Cairns, 1988). This perseverance of a false identification may be caused by a contamination of the witnesses' memory or by a tendency to cling to publicly made decisions (commitment effect; see Kiesler, 1971). As a consequence, the evidentiary value of repeated identifications can never be greater than the value of the first identification. False identifications can also result from clothing bias. Lindsay, Wallbridge and Drennan (1987) found that the rate of false identifications was highest when an innocent substitute was dressed like the perpetrator while the other foils wore different clothes.

Whereas these and some other potential sources of procedural errors are fairly obvious, false identifications may also result from more subtle, maybe even unintended manipulations like systematic changes in the nonverbal behaviour of a police officer (e.g. Fanselow, 1975; Smith, Pleban, & Shaffer, 1982). In order to avoid such biases it has been suggested that a recognition test be conducted by a police officer who was not involved in the investigation and who has no knowledge as to who the suspect is (Köhnken et al., 1996).

To summarize, during the past three decades numerous experiments have demonstrated that eyewitness identification accuracy can be affected by a number of factors. There can be no doubt that psycholegal research has raised the stakes for identification evidence. However, improving the procedure of recognition tests and avoiding structural and procedural errors helps to prevent innocent suspects from false identifications while the correct identification of a criminal is not substantially impaired.

Children as witnesses

The past fifteen years have seen a dramatic increase in the number of eyewitnesses and victims who are children, as well as in research on the accuracy and credibility of child witness statements (see, for example, recent books by Ceci, Leichtman, & Putnick, 1992; Ceci, Ross, & Toglia, 1989; Ceci, Toglia, & Ross, 1987; Dent & Flin, 1992; Doris, 1991; Spencer & Flin, 1993). A particular research interest has been the suggestibility of children. Ceci and Bruck (1993) point out that in the past ten years, more research has been conducted on the suggestibility of child witnesses than in all of the prior decades combined (p. 403). Since 1979, more than 100 studies on children's suggestibility have been reported. Two questions have dominated this research: are children more suggestible than adults? and under which conditions are child witness statements distorted by suggestions?

In their comprehensive review Ceci and Bruck (1993) conclude that there appear to be significant age differences in suggestibility, with pre-school children being more suggestible than school-aged children and adults. In approximately 83 per cent of the developmental studies that have compared pre-schoolers with older children or adults, pre-schoolers were the most suggestible group. Not only peripheral details are vulnerable to suggestions. Contrary to expectation, the available results indicate that suggestibility effects occur even when the act in question is a central action, when the child is a participant, or when the report is a free narrative (Ceci & Bruck, 1993). Both social and cognitive factors have been found to be capable of distorting children's statements or creating memories of nonexistent events. Lepore and Sesco (1994), Leichtman and Ceci (in press), and Tobey and Goodman (1992) found that inducing a negative stereotype of a person increases the danger that children will answer a leading question in the direction of that stereotype. If an interviewer is convinced that a certain event has happened, this belief may influence his or her emotional tone, linguistic behaviour, type of questions asked, etc., which in turn may promote a child's false report (e.g. Ceci, Leichtman, & White, in press; Clarke-Stewart, Thompson, & Lepore, 1989; Pettit, Fegan, & Howie, 1990). If children have to go to court they are often questioned several times about an event. Whereas repeated open-ended questions seem to have little effect (positive or negative) on children's responses (Poole & White, 1991) the repeating of specific questions may signal to a child that their first response was not acceptable. As a consequence they may change their answer even though the first response was correct (Moston, 1987; Poole & White, 1991). Some recent studies have demonstrated that suggestive questioning and the imagination of fictitious events may even create memories of highly involving personal experiences that never actually have happened (e.g. Ceci, Leichtman, & White, in press; Ceci, Loftus, Leichtman, & Bruck, 1994; Ceci, Crotteau, Smith, & Loftus, in press). Referring to a source-monitoring framework (Johnson & Raye, 1981; Lindsay, 1994), it is assumed that these imaginations create new memories and that young children have particular difficulties in distinguishing between imagined and actual actions (Lindsay, Gonzales, & Eso, 1994; Lindsay, Johnson, & Kwon, 1991).

However, this does not mean that children are in principle incompetent witnesses. There is considerable agreement in the literature that children – even pre-schoolers – are indeed capable of providing accurate testimony. Their statements may be less detailed than those of older children or adults but what they report in a free narrative can be highly accurate – provided that they are questioned in a neutral, non-suggestive manner (Bull, 1992; Ceci & Bruck, 1993; Davies, 1996; Goodman & Reed, 1986; Johnson & Foley, 1984; Marin, Holmes, Guth, & Kovac, 1979; Spencer & Flin, 1993). Guidelines for appropriate interviewing techniques have been described in the 'Memorandum of good practice for video recorded interviews with child witnesses for use in criminal proceedings' (see Bull, 1994a, b).

Evaluating witness statements: assessment and attribution of credibility

Witness statements, whether descriptions of events or person identifications, can rarely be taken at face value. Numerous factors have been found to be able to cause discrepancies between statements and the actual facts. These factors can be distinguished into two different classes: on the one hand, witnesses, although trying to give a correct and complete report of an event or an accurate description of a person, may be subject to unintended errors and distortions, caused for example by forgetting, suboptimal perception conditions or misleading post-event information. The term 'accuracy' describes the extent to which statements are free of this kind of unintended error. On the other hand, a statement may deviate from reality because the witness deliberately tries to deceive the police or the court. Intentional deceptions or lies affect the truthfulness or credibility of a statement. In forensic psychology the term 'credibility' describes the witnesses' motivation to give a truthful account of his or her experiences.

Deception is a communication phenomenon that involves at least two individuals: a communicator (or witness in the present context) and a recipient (e.g. a detective, a judge or a juror). Consequently, research can focus on each of the two participants of an interaction. With regard to the communicator (or witness) it can be examined whether or not there are any behaviours that are systematically associated with the deceptiveness of a statement. Such behaviours have been called *correlates of deception* (Zuckerman, DePaulo, & Rosenthal, 1981), *authentic cues of deception* (Fiedler & Walka, 1993) or *objective indicators of deception* (Vrij, 1991, 1994). From a different point of view, a set of content characteristics have been proposed as indicative of the truthfulness of a statement. These are called *reality criteria* (Steller & Köhnken, 1989).

Regarding the recipient or evaluator of a statement, research has predominantly been concerned with the investigation of people's efficiency when attempting to judge the credibility of statements. More recently, attention has shifted somewhat to the factors that cause people to ascribe credibility or dishonesty to a statement. Classifying statements as either truthful or deceptive based on the analysis of objective or authentic indicators of credibility is called *assessment of credibility*, whereas the judgement of credibility by the recipient has been called *attribution of credibility* (Köhnken, 1990).

Assessment of credibility

Objective indicators of truth and deception have been examined in four behavioural areas:

1. the content of the statement (e.g. amount and type of detail, logical consistency; see Steller & Köhnken, 1989);
2. the way the statement is verbally presented, i.e. speech behaviour (e.g. speech rate, speech disturbances) and stylostatistic characteristics (e.g. word frequency statistics; see Morton & Farringdon, 1992; Köhnken, 1985);
3. the accompanying nonverbal behaviour of the witness (e.g. arm movements, facial expression; see Zuckerman et al., 1981);
4. psychophysiological phenomena (e.g. electrodermal responses, heart rate, blood pressure; see Reid & Inbau, 1977; Raskin, 1989). The polygraph

technique – the analysis of psychophysiological responses for credibility assessment – will not be discussed here because it is not admissible as evidence in most European countries.

Research on nonverbal and speech behaviour suggests that some observable behaviours are indeed associated with deception. Several meta-analyses (Zuckerman et al., 1981; Zuckerman & Driver, 1985; DePaulo, Stone, & Lassiter, 1985) have shown that of 24 different verbal, nonverbal and speech behaviours, 14 are significantly related to deception. There appears to be a tendency for highly motivated compared to less motivated liars to decrease the frequency of a number of nonverbal behaviours. In the area of speech behaviour liars engage in more and/or longer speech hesitations, produce more speech errors (e.g. stutter, repetition) and grammatical errors, and show longer response latencies. However, the association of these behaviours with deception, although statistically significant, is rather weak. It is certainly not strong enough to serve as a way of assessing the credibility of a witness statement. A possible explanation for the generally weak relationships may be found in the meta-analytic technique itself, which averages group differences across various studies. However, some of these individual studies have led to contradicting results. The frequency of eyeblink, for example, was found to decrease in some studies and increase in other experiments. Averaging across these results will necessarily lead to overall weak correlations.

Another very interesting explanation has recently been offered by Burgoon and Buller (1994), who propose an interpersonal deception theory. They claim that most investigations on deception have used a unidirectional view, such that a liar actively transmits signals which a receiver passively absorbs. This paradigm lacks the interpersonal communication that involves feedback and mutual influence. In an ongoing conversation the character of deceit may change when deceivers continually monitor their own performance while adapting to the receivers' feedback. As a consequence, behavioural patterns evidenced at the outset of an exchange may differ radically from those manifested later (Buller & Aune, 1987). According to this position, averaging behaviour frequencies across a lengthy interaction may produce weak effects or even no effects at all although clues to deception may indeed exist.

A very different approach to the assessment of the credibility of a statement has been developed in literature research and in psycholinguistics. In order to assign pieces of literature of unknown authorship to a certain author the style of the disputed document was analysed according to various statistical parameters (hence the term 'stylostatistics') which are then compared with the respective data derived from an undisputed text. Such parameters are, for example, the number of words per sentence, the number of different words relative to the total number of words in a text body ('type-token-ratio'), the average word length, the proportion of verbs to adjectives and the proportion of grammar words (prepositions, articles, etc.) as an indicator of the grammatical complexity of a sentence (Yule, 1944; Herdan, 1964). Köhnken (1985) found that some of these stylostatistic parameters did reliably discriminate between truthful and fabricated statements.

General characteristics

1. Logical structure
2. Unstructured production
3. Quantity of details

Specific contents

4. Contextual embedding
5. Descriptions of interactions
6. Reproduction of conversation
7. Unexpected complications during the incident

Peculiarities of content

8. Unusual details
9. Superfluous details
10. Accurately reported details misunderstood
11. Related external associations
12. Accounts of subjective mental states
13. Attribution of perpetrator's mental state

Motivation-related contents

14. Spontaneous corrections
15. Admitting lack of memory
16. Raising doubts about one's own testimony
17. Self-deprecation
18. Pardoning the perpetrator

Offence-specific elements

19. Details characteristic of the offence

Figure 10.3   *CBCA criteria (Steller & Köhnken, 1989)*

An alternative way to assess the truthfulness of a statement was developed in German forensic psychology by Undeutsch (1967, 1984) and Arntzen (1983). Based on their work, Köhnken and Steller (1988) and Steller and Köhnken (1989) have compiled a list of criteria and described a procedure for evaluating the veracity of a statement which led to the development of Statement Validity Assessment (SVA) as a comprehensive method for evaluating witness statements (for detailed descriptions of SVA see Raskin & Esplin, 1991; Steller & Köhnken, 1989; Steller & Boychuk, 1992). In contrast to research on nonverbal detection of deception, this approach focuses on the content of a statement rather than on the witnesses' nonverbal and speech behaviour. Furthermore, SVA is not a verbal lie detector. Instead of searching for 'lie symptoms' it focuses on specific content characteristics which, if present in a statement, support the hypothesis that the account is based on genuine personal experience.

SVA consists of three major elements:

1. a structured interview;
2. a criteria-based content analysis (CBCA) (see Figure 10.3);
3. the integration of all obtained case information, including information on

the witnesses' cognitive, verbal and social abilities, into a final judgement as to whether or not the account is based on genuine personal experience.

CBCA is based on the hypothesis, originally stated by Undeutsch (1967), that truthful and fabricated statements differ in content and quality. This basic hypothesis comprises two components, one cognitive and the other motivational. The latter can be related to impression management theory (Tedeschi & Norman, 1985). The cognitive part of the hypothesis states that, given a certain level of cognitive and verbal abilities, only a person who has actually experienced an event will be able to produce a statement with the characteristics that are described in the CBCA criteria (see Figure 10.2). It is, for example, deemed unlikely that a child who fabricates an account will deliberately invent unexpected complications that allegedly happened during the incident. The impression management component relates to motivation and social behaviour. It is assumed that lying is a goal-directed behaviour and that a person who deliberately invents a story wants to be perceived as honest in order to achieve his or her goals. Therefore, the person is likely to avoid behaviours which, in his or her view, may be interpreted as clues to deception. For instance, if a liar believes that admitting lack of memory will undermine his or her perceived credibility, he or she will try to avoid such behaviour. This impression management approach assumes that people have a common stereotype of the typical behaviour accompanying a lie. Provided that a particular behaviour can be sufficiently controlled it is expected that a liar, to conceal his or her lie, will attempt to avoid such behaviour. If empirical research can show that such stereotypes exist it would be possible to formulate specific hypotheses concerning additional criteria to discriminate truthful from fabricated statements. Interestingly, four studies that have examined beliefs about deceptive behaviour in the USA, the Netherlands, Germany and Great Britain support the assumption that these stereotypes do indeed exist (Zuckerman, Koestner, & Driver, 1981; Akehurst, Köhnken, Vrij, & Bull, in press; Köhnken, 1990; Vrij & Semin, in press).

Several studies have demonstrated that SVA can be a useful tool in distinguishing truthful from fabricated accounts. Although early reports from German practitioners like Arntzen (1983), according to which SVA had proven its validity in more than 30,000 court cases, have been criticized for methodological reasons (Köhnken & Wegener, 1982, 1985), they give at least a hint at its potential. In addition, some recent controlled experiments and field studies support the Undeutsch hypothesis (for overviews see Horowitz, 1991; Lamb, Sternberg, & Esplin, in press).

Using children of various age groups or adolescents, Esplin, Boychuk and Raskin (1988), Joffe and Yuille (1992), Köhnken and Wegener (1982), Steller, Wellershaus and Wolf (1992) and Yuille (1988) found significant differences in at least some of the CBCA criteria or hit rates that were significantly better than chance level if the decisions had been based on CBCA. Three recent studies have also demonstrated that CBCA may reliably discriminate between truthful and fabricated adults' accounts (Landry & Brigham, 1992; Höfer, Köhnken, Hanewinkel, & Bruhn, 1993; Köhnken et al., 1995).

So the hypothesis that CBCA criteria can reliably distinguish truthful from fabricated or deliberately distorted accounts has received some, although not completely unequivocal, support. However, given the disappointing judgement accuracy that has been found in nonverbal detection of deception studies (see p. 271), the SVA approach is well worth further research. Recently, Alonso-Quecuty (1992), Sporer (1995) and Porter and Yuille (1995) have suggested supplementing the CBCA criteria with reality-monitoring criteria (Johnson & Raye, 1981).

Attribution of credibility

Research on the attribution of credibility has examined how successful people are in discriminating truthful and deceptive statements, which behavioural cues they utilize for their judgements, and how access to different communication channels influences their attributions. How accurate are people when they attempt to judge the credibility of a statement? The results of several meta-analyses of more than 50 experimental studies provide a rather disillusioning picture. In these experiments the hit rates (i.e. the proportion of correct judgements) generally falls into a range between 45 per cent and 60 per cent, where 50 per cent correct decisions can be expected by chance alone, i.e. simply by guessing. Hit rates above 60 per cent are reported very rarely. The mean detection accuracy across all studies is only slightly (although significantly) better than the 50 per cent chance level (DePaulo et al., 1985; Zuckerman, De Paulo, & Rosenthal, 1981; Zuckerman & Driver, 1985).

This poor judgement accuracy stands in sharp contrast to people's self-assessment of their judgement ability. A survey study on various aspects of credibility judgement found that people tend to overestimate their ability to detect deception considerably (Köhnken, 1990). The reason for this unrealistic self-confidence is simple. When we are asked to estimate our ability to detect deceptions, we remember only the gross and awkward lies which were easily detected. Most of the skilful, clever, successful lies, on the other hand, are rarely noticed. Hence, they will not influence our judgement of our own judgement accuracy. Not surprisingly, the correlation of the accuracy of credibility judgements and the self-assessed level of confidence in this accuracy tends to be rather low (Vrij, 1994).

Interestingly, people with experience in credibility judgements (e.g. police and customs officers) achieve no better results than inexperienced subjects (DePaulo & Pfeifer, 1986; Kraut & Poe, 1980; Vrij & Winkel, 1992, 1993, 1994). Experienced subjects are, however, more confident in the correctness of their judgements than are lay people. Apparently the mere frequency of credibility judgements does not help to improve judgement accuracy because subjects receive no detailed feedback (DePaulo & Pfeifer, 1986; Fiedler & Walka, 1993; Vrij, 1994). Nor does training help to improve judgement accuracy (Köhnken, 1987; Fiedler & Walka, 1993; Zuckerman, Koestner, & Alton, 1984; Zuckerman, Koestner, & Collela, 1985; Vrij, 1994).

The attribution of credibility appears to be an exceptionally difficult task.

Hit rates rarely exceed chance level and neither on-the-job experience nor training improves judgement accuracy substantially.

Psychology in the courtroom: jury decision making

Psychological research on courtroom proceedings differs from the other areas of research outlined in this chapter in one important aspect. Whereas, for example, psychological aspects of eyewitness testimony or correctional treatment are relevant regardless of the specifics of national law, courtroom proceedings differ in various countries. Within the adversarial system of justice, which is by and large characteristic of English-speaking countries, the proceedings are structured as a dispute between two sides (Damaska, 1973). The role of the judge is kept to a minimum and can best be described as that of a referee. The evidence is presented by the prosecution and the defence. Although the jury trial is not an essential element of adversarial procedure, it is found most regularly in Anglo-Saxon countries (McEwan, 1995). An adversary process is marked by a clear distinction between matters of fact and matters of law. Matters of fact are for the lay persons (the jury) whereas matters of law are for the judge (Sealy, 1989). In contrast, in inquisitorial systems, which are roughly descriptive of continental Europe, judges have a considerably more active role. They play a major part in the preparation of evidence before the trial and in the questioning of the defendant and the witnesses. Most important, the judge or the panel of judges decides on guilt or innocence of the defendant whereas in the adversarial system this decision is for the jury.

The vast majority of psychological research on decision processes in the courtroom has focused on jury decision making rather than decision processes of professional judges (although see van Koppen, 1995). The first substantial contribution by psychologists to an understanding of jury functioning was presented by Kalven and Zeisel (1966), a survey of trial judges' opinions concerning jury verdicts, the determinants of jury verdicts, and the judges' evaluations of the quality of those verdicts. Another major landmark was the research programme conducted by Thibaut and his associates (e.g. Thibaut & Walker, 1975) which had a significant impact on social psychology and its application to law. The jury has now become, besides the witness, the most popular research object in the entire area of psychology and law, especially in the criminal trial (Davis, 1989). Psychologists have, for example, examined the impact of jury size, decision rules, jury composition, instructions to the jury from the trial judge, and the evaluation of evidence by juries.

Jury size

Most countries applying the adversarial system have opted for 12-member juries, although proposals have been made in the USA to reduce the jury to six members. It has been argued that larger juries have a better chance of being representative of the various social groups in a community and that the margin of error would diminish, the larger the size of the jury. Different 12-member juries would therefore be more likely to reach the same decision than different six-member juries (Hans & Vidmar, 1986). Numerous experiments have been carried out to examine the effects of jury size on decisions (usually verdicts). As Vollrath and Davis (1980) conclude in their review, the surprising outcome from this now rather large body of data is that no significant size-attributable differences in verdicts have been found.

Jury composition

Since the seminal work of Kalven and Zeisel (1966) the possibility that jurors could be subject to judgement biases has received much attention in the literature. In search of factors that could cause such biases the impact of personality variables, gender, demographic factors and experimental influences on group performance in general has been examined in a number of studies. The basic idea underlying these efforts was that identification of variables that could cause bias would enable scientifically based procedures for the selection of jurors and thus reduce decision biases. However, the results of this line of research are mixed. For example, some studies found that men's verdicts differed in some cases from those of women (Efran, 1974); other studies did not find any differences related to gender (Griffitt & Jackson, 1973). In their review, Hans and Vidmar (1982) suggest that men are less likely to convict rapists than are women, and that younger people are generally less conviction prone. Research on the effects of race has been equally inconsistent and the same is true for various personality variables. Acre, Sobral and Farina (1992) suggest that personality variables require particular circumstances for their effects to be manifested. Thus, efforts at scientific jury selection (Kairys, Schulman, & Harring, 1975) seem to lack conclusive empirical support (Hans & Vidmar, 1982).

Evaluation of evidence and decision making

How individual jurors and juries as groups evaluate the evidence and finally reach a decision has been investigated from two different perspectives. On the one hand, psychologists have examined the cognitive processes in individual juror decision making. The other major research interest has concerned the social dynamics of group decision making.

With regard to individual jurors' decision processes, up until the early 1980s research was dominated by the application of algebraic or stochastic models, mostly derived from Bayesian probability models (reviewed by Pennington & Hastie, 1981). The typical research paradigm was a laboratory experiment using undergraduate psychology students as mock jurors who read brief 10- to 20-sentence summaries of imaginary evidence. Usually, little attempt was made to mimic the conditions, procedures and instructions of a typical jury trial (Pennington & Hastie, 1990). A shift in perspective was initiated by Pennington and Hastie (1986), who criticized the artificiality of laboratory research on juror decision making. In contrast to previous research methods, these authors attempted to create conditions and stimulus events that were comparable to those at an actual trial. The participants were sampled from courthouse jury pools rather than from undergraduate psychology students and the analyses of evaluation and decision processes were based on think-aloud protocols.

From this research Pennington and Hastie concluded that the traditional mathematical models were inadequate and proposed an alternative model to explain evidence evaluation and decisions that is embedded in cognitive psychology (e.g. Kintsch & van Dijk, 1978; Rumelhart, 1977; Schank & Abelson, 1977): the *story* or *explanation model*. This model is supposed to provide a framework for explaining how jurors comprehend, recall and use the evidence in criminal trials in terms of verdict categories. The idea is that jurors attempt to make sense of the entirety of evidence by imposing a summary structure on it that they feel captures what is true about the events referred to in the testimony. Furthermore, it is assumed that jurors engage in a deliberate effort to match the explanatory story that they had constructed with the verdict categories, seeking a best fit between one of the verdict categories and their story (Pennington & Hastie, 1990). In other words, it is hypothesized that the 'story' mediates between the evidence presented and the final judgement or decision.

The story approach introduces some clarification regarding the mixed results on the effects of psychosocial variables on verdicts by suggesting that these variables are not related to verdicts directly. Instead, they are linked to stories, which in turn are related to verdicts. For example, Pennington and Hastie (1990) report that in some of their studies social class of the juror was related to the harshness of verdicts. They found that jurors from poorer neighbourhoods did not find the possession of a weapon particularly surprising, whereas jurors from a wealthier suburb did find this fact remarkable. As a consequence, the latter jurors inferred that the defendant had a special purpose in mind for the knife – namely to injure or kill the victim. This example shows that social class is related to particular life experiences which influence the way the jury members construct a story for this particular case but perhaps not for different cases.

Jury deliberation and group decision making

Two of the central assumptions underlying the trial by jury are that (1) the deliberation will act as a countermeasure against individual biases; and (2) group decisions are superior to individual decisions. In particular, information seeking and processing is assumed to be more efficient in groups than individuals. However, in contrast to these assumptions, research by Janis

(1972, 1982) has shown that under certain conditions (especially homogeneity, isolation, structural faults, lack of decision procedures) groups may be affected by the phenomenon of 'groupthink'. In these circumstances groups tend to develop an illusion of invulnerability, a belief in a shared morality, closed-mindedness, and exhibit pressure on individual group members to conform with the majority opinion (e.g. Park, 1990; Tetlock, Peterson, McGuire, Chang, & Feld, 1992). One important consequence of these processes on the evaluation of evidence and the construction of a story is the tendency towards a biased search for and evaluation of information. This would then result in a strong confirmation bias (Snyder, 1984).

A series of studies by Frey and colleagues (Frey, Schulz-Hardt, Lüthgens, & Moscovici, 1995) has demonstrated that groups do indeed show a greater confirmation bias than individuals: they were both more confident about the correctness of their decision and more selective when seeking information. This was particularly the case in homogeneous groups (i.e. when group members share the same initial opinion). Furthermore, the more certain the group members are, and the more they deem themselves to be unanimous, the more they look for consistent information (Frey, 1995).

Acre, Sobral and Farina (1992) have examined the impact of group homogeneity on jury decision making by forming ideologically homogeneous juries (only conservatives or progressives) and attributionally homogeneous juries (subjects preferring either internal or external attribution). They found that in some criminal cases these juries differed in post- but not in pre-deliberation verdicts, indicating that the bias derived from the deliberation of homogeneous groups. Pennington and Hastie (1986) found that evidence that is incongruent with the verdict is not equally considered. Acre (1995) concludes from these data that the appreciation of evidence during the deliberation is selective, that homogeneous juries either avoid using certain information that is not congruent with their bias or that they interpret it according to their bias. Hence, contrary to the assumptions underlying the idea of trial by jury, individual bias is magnified rather than reduced in deliberation under homogeneous conditions.

Correctional treatment of offenders

The conviction of a criminal in a trial, and imprisonment is not the end of the story. Psychology, particularly clinical psychology, has long emphasized the importance of behaviour modification programmes in order to prevent criminal offenders from recidivism after they are released from prison. This discussion has been accompanied by various attempts to reduce recidivism. During the 1960s and 1970s an apparently ever-increasing number of research programmes were initiated to examine the effectiveness of a wide variety of behaviour modification techniques for correctional treatment. Particularly popular were individual and group counselling, family counselling, and behaviour therapy, to name just a few (Lipsey, 1992). By the end of these two decades several hundred studies on correctional treatment had accumulated, the vast majority (80 per cent) in the field of juvenile delinquency (Lösel, 1995). The major question that these studies tried to answer was: 'Does it work?' In other words, is correctional treatment capable of reducing the risk of recidivism, and, if so, what works?

A number of reviews of the existing body of research, published during the 1970s, gave a discouraging answer to this question: nothing works in criminal rehabilitation (e.g. Brody, 1976; Greenberg, 1977; Lipton, Martinson, & Wilks, 1975; Martinson, 1974; Sechrest, White, & Brown, 1979). Although there were a few exceptions to this pessimistic view (e.g. Gendreau & Ross, 1979; Palmer, 1975) the idea of rehabilitation declined and 'the spirit of the times moved on to other concepts, such as just-deserts punishment, retribution or deterrence' (Lösel, 1995, p. 78).

However, in recent years we are witnessing a strong revival of research on offender treatment which is largely due to the availability of meta-analytic techniques. Meta-analysis had already been used successfully to assess the effectiveness of psychotherapy in general and, just as in psychotherapy research, it had become almost impossible to evaluate hundreds of empirical studies with a large variety of procedures and settings using the traditional method of literature reviews. Hence, it was necessary to re-examine the full corpus of the delinquency treatment research literature using meta-analytic techniques. In a recent review Lösel (1995) lists a total of 13 meta-analyses of correctional treatment studies published since the mid-1980s (e.g. Garrett, 1985; Gottschalk, Davidson, Gensheimer, & Mayer, 1987; Lipsey, 1992; Lösel & Köferl, 1989; Whitehead & Lab, 1989). Lipsey's (1992) meta-analysis alone includes more than 400 studies of juvenile delinquency and examines a total of 157 variables describing details of the methods, treatment circumstances, and study context. Altogether, the available meta-analyses now cover more than 500 primary evaluation studies (Lösel, 1995).

In contrast to most previous literature reviews all meta-analyses reveal a modest but significant positive effect for offender treatment. Lösel (1995) estimates the mean effect size at around 0.10. This is indeed modest and certainly much smaller than the effect sizes found in meta-analyses of psychotherapy effectiveness studies. However, it clearly contradicts the once fashionable 'nothing works' statement. Furthermore, reductions in recidivism of 10 per cent (Lipsey, 1992) or 15 per cent (Prentky & Burgess, 1992), although not spectacular, are not negligible and may indeed lead to substantial cost savings.

The finding that something does work in correctional treatment leads to the question 'What works?' Not surprisingly, the effects of different treatment approaches differ substantially. Although, due to inconsistencies and methodological problems, it is often difficult to draw clear-cut conclusions, there is at least a tendency for skill-oriented, cognitive-behavioural and multimodal programmes (i.e. those which target specific skills such as professional or interpersonal skills) to be more effective than traditional counselling and casework approaches which have less specific goals. Lipsey (1992) found reductions of recidivism of 20 per cent or more for these more successful approaches. On the other hand, some treatments (e.g. measures of deterrence) may even have negative effects.

One would expect the setting as well as institutional characteristics to affect the outcome of correctional treatment. These were indeed found to be important moderator variables in many meta-analyses. In general, treatments in community settings have stronger effects than those in residential/institutional settings (Lösel, 1995). However, this pattern of results is not easy to interpret because variables are frequently confounded. Only very few individual studies directly compared imprisonment and community-based interventions using appropriate control procedures with regard to other variables (e.g. sample characteristics such as age, personality or staff characteristics). For example, incarcerated offenders are normally more persistently anti-social, disordered or dangerous than those who are treated in community settings (Lösel, 1995). It is likely that these offenders will be more resistant to treatment, and effect sizes can thus be expected to be smaller, regardless of the setting. If appropriate control procedures are applied, setting has only a weak effect on the outcome of correctional treatment (Lipsey, 1992).

To summarize, several recent meta-analyses covering more than 500 empirical studies have shown that correctional treatment does have a small though significant effect on recidivism. The relatively small effect of correctional treatment may reflect the fact that anti-social disorders are particularly difficult to treat. On the other hand, it may also be a consequence of the unfavourable conditions (e.g. motivational deficits, organization of prisons) which limit the effects of behaviour modification attempts (Lösel, 1995). Despite the large database, it is difficult to evaluate the differential effects of a number of important factors such as offender characteristics or settings. Although there appears to be a tendency for cognitive-behavioural techniques to be more effective than other methods, there are still too few controlled evaluation studies available to allow more detailed conclusions.

Conclusion

Psychology and law is an exceptionally broad field of applied psychology. It covers a wide variety of subdisciplines (e.g. social psychology, clinical psychology, cognitive psychology) and employs a number of rather diverse research approaches (laboratory experiments, field studies, surveys, longitudinal studies). This diversity has stimulated many fruitful exchanges between basic and applied research, perhaps more so than in many other areas of psychology. Furthermore, it seems that psycholegal research has often exercised more methodological rigour than some other fields of applied (social) psychology. This comes as no surprise, given the fact that its results are applied in highly controversial settings where they face very rigorous questions by the opposing parties. As a consequence, psychology and law is not simply a 'consumer' of the results of basic research. Instead, there is a growing number of examples where psycholegal research has discovered new phenomena which have subsequently become relevant to basic research.

With regard to research on the explanation and prediction of criminal behaviour, various research approaches and theories were discussed which attempt to explain why people commit crimes. The second section focused on psychological facets of the investigation of crime, i.e. eyewitness psychology. Four areas of research were presented: investigative interviewing, eyewitness identification, children as eyewitnesses, and the evaluation of the credibility of eyewitness statements. The third section discussed the extensive research on jury decision making, and the final section reviewed the research on correctional treatment of offenders, raising the question of the effectiveness of offender treatment.

Further reading

Bull, R. & Carson, D. (Eds) (1995). *Handbook of psychology in legal contexts.* Chichester: Wiley. This reader provides one of the most exhaustive overviews of a wide range of topics in psychology and law.

McGuire, J. (Ed.) (1995). *What works: Reducing reoffending: Guidelines from research and practice.* Chichester: Wiley. This comprehensive overview of research on offender treatment includes, among other topics, a review of various meta-analyses on the efficiency of treatment programmes.

Ross, D., Read, J.D., & Toglia, M. (Eds) (1994). *Adult eyewitness testimony: Current trends and developments.* London: Cambridge University Press. This is the most recent collection on adult eyewitness psychology. It includes chapters on various aspects of eyewitness identification, interviewing, and evaluating eyewitness evidence.

Sporer, S.L., Malpass, R.M., & Köhnken, G. (Eds) (1996). *Psychological issues in eyewitness identification.* Hillsdale, NJ: Lawrence Erlbaum. Readers who are interested in recent developments in eyewitness identification research are referred to this book. It includes chapters on voice identification, recognition performance of children and elderly witnesses, cross-race identification, and face construction systems.

11

Political Psychology

Patrizia Catellani

Contents

The scope of political psychology

Imagine a typical meeting between a nonmilitant and a militant during a period of great public ferment, like the 'events' of 1968. When the nonmilitant says 'I'm not interested in politics', the militant invariably replies, 'You can't say that. Every choice you make, all your behaviour, even the most private, is political because it reflects the current political and ideological system and, along with the choices and behaviour of everyone else, influences the form it takes.' This kind of answer already shows how difficult it is to define the scope of politics and, more specifically, say where the political sphere ends and the social sphere begins. The difficulty is illustrated by the fact that the limits of the political sphere change during different historical periods (and under different political regimes). In the Ancient World, for example, the scope of politics was extremely broad because it embraced everything to do with the *polis*, and so all social relationships within a given community. Politics is usually less all-embracing in the modern world, although regimes do differ appreciably. There are those in which politics governs all aspects of behaviour, including what seem extremely private matters like deciding to marry or have children. In others, perhaps ideal ones like the minimal state advocated by liberals, politics is confined to the administration of the state and the exercise of power in relation to just a few specific functions.

Irrespective of how the limits of the political sphere are determined, which is the proper concern of other disciplines, we could define political psychology in operational terms as the discipline that studies the mental functioning and actions of political 'actors', that is, of any subject seen as a (potential or actual) citizen, leader or member of a group or movement whose aims are public and collective. The scope of politics depends on how these roles are interpreted in different historical periods and under different political regimes.

Most political scientists are also extremely interested in analysing politics in terms of the 'actors' who participate in it. Until the end of the last century, politics was dominated by a European and continental perspective in which ideologies and institutions were the major focuses of study. Since then, the emphasis has shifted to the more empirical Anglo-Saxon concept that politics is a direct expression of the people or forces involved in it, whether leaders or public opinion. This shift of interest towards the 'actors' of politics has led some political scientists to borrow theories and methods from psychology in their studies; others have developed implicit political psychologies of their own.

However, few university syllabuses today are designed to train specialists in political psychology, with the notable exception of American universities which have produced a large proportion of our political psychology studies to date. Inevitably, then, American culture and politics have had an important influence on the content and methods of political psychology. As regards content, we might reflect on the appropriateness or otherwise of generalizing from data gathered in one specific political system to studies of other different systems; as regards methods, the longstanding emphasis on the intra-individual dimension is now being challenged and modified by a growing interest in the inter-individual and group dimensions.

Historical stages

Let us now survey briefly the major stages in the development of political psychology studies (see Amerio, 1991; McGuire, 1993).

Psychology and personality

In the 1940s and 1950s, most studies focused on the role of personality factors in the exercise of political power, with special emphasis on political leaders. Political behaviour was seen as the expression of stable personality traits and needs, whose origins were traced back to early childhood development and explained in predominantly psychoanalytical terms. One example is the work of Lasswell (1948), who located the origins of politicians' commitment to public affairs in their need for external reassurance to dispel unresolved ego anxieties and remedy low self-esteem. The method was both qualitative and quantitative (see McGuire, 1993). In qualitative terms, the key consideration is historical reconstruction, or psychohistory, based on detailed biographies of individual politicians starting from early childhood. This approach is still used by researchers. One example is Barber's study (1985) of American presidents, which concludes that presidents with low self-esteem were incapable of changing their policies during their terms of office, even when they were shown to be misguided, as with President Johnson's commitment to American intervention in Vietnam. Other more quantitative studies have surveyed the political views of ordinary people using scales and questionnaires administered to broad samples of subjects. One example, which we shall return to later, is Adorno's study of the authoritarian personality (Adorno, Frenkel-Brunswick, Levinson, & Sanford, 1950).

Attitudes and voting behaviour

The 1960s and 1970s saw an explosion in studies of public opinion and voting patterns. Large-scale surveys showed how little information subjects actually make use of when making political choices, and concluded that people behave in largely irrational ways. The prevalent explanation at the time (see Campbell, Converse, Miller, & Stokes, 1960) attributed this to family influence and, more generally, to the process of socialization. As well as explaining political attitudes in developmental terms, some studies also employed theories dominant at the time, like functionalism, which relates attitudes to motivation, and cognitive style, which assumes that a subject's fundamental need is to restore balance when faced with contradictory attitudes.

Political cognition and information processing

From the 1970s through to the late 1980s, researchers shifted their attention away from attitudes and behaviour as such to the information-processing mechanisms that underlie them, and from explanations based on motivation to explanations based on the cognitive capabilities of subjects. Using results obtained from social cognition studies, they developed a line of research based on political cognition (see Lau & Sears, 1986) in which the assumption was not, as before, that political behaviour is largely irrational, nor even (as economic theories would suggest) that it is completely rational, but that its rationality is conditioned by the limited information-processing capability of individual subjects.

Current trends

Although assessing the present is always a difficult task, we can now say with reasonable certainty what the latest research trends are, or at least which trends may hopefully carry political psychology beyond the impasses of current cognitivist approaches. One important trend is that political psychology is now more genuinely social than political cognition would strictly allow it to be. The reasons for this derive from four considerations that apply to social knowledge in general, and even more so to political knowledge (see Amerio, 1991; Catellani & Quadrio, 1991).

(a) Political knowledge is social in origin. It is created and reinforced through interaction and, more than in other knowledge domains, is acquired not directly but through intermediary sources strongly influenced by social and cultural context like newspapers, television, opinion leaders and politicians themselves.

(b) Studies of social and political cognition have treated the social and political dimensions as *objects of perception*, not as dimensions that influence the *person who perceives*, with the result that intrapersonal processes have attracted more attention than interpersonal and group processes. The relationships cognizers have with others, and the fact that they belong to one group rather than another, are factors that have an important influence on cognitive processes, and are themselves important topics for study in political psychology.

(c) The study of political psychology cannot be confined to the micro dimension; it must also be extended to the macro dimension that embraces relationships between individual mental functioning and social and political reality. Only in this way will it be possible to study issues that are crucial to the discipline, like migration (see Chapter 15 of this volume), social change, the distribution of power, relations between the public and private spheres, etc.

(d) The study of basic cognitive processes is certainly essential, but studying their articulation in a variety of social and political contexts could be useful too. Among other things, this will draw attention to the complex relationships between the contents and the processes of knowledge.

This brief summary of major issues in political psychology will first of all be concerned with the basic cognitive processes that govern the acquisition of political knowledge and decision making, although we shall also take full account, where studies have already raised the issue, of how these processes interact with the social dimension and specific features of political content.

We shall then consider attitudes and political beliefs and, more specifically, how they are structured around ideological principles and more inclusive values. Finally, we shall look at political participation, whose prerequisites include knowledge and attitudes, but whose actualization is influenced by the context the subject lives in.

Political knowledge

Political cognition research has dominated political psychology studies in recent years. This section will deal mainly with the results obtained using this approach. The basic assumptions are similar to those of social cognition: man is seen as a subject who actively processes information, has limited cognitive capacities and so necessarily adopts strategies of simplification that enable him to perform the cognitive task in hand, although this means that not all the available information can be processed. Taking for granted that the processing system itself is limited, the amount of information processed and the types of strategy used are influenced by factors like personality and motivation, the goals subjects set themselves and other factors generated by the context in which the cognitive process is activated. One of the most important of these is degree of accountability (Tetlock, 1983), that is, the perceived need (induced by social context) to account for reasoning and judgements based on it. Thus, a subject involved in a bar-room discussion of how to deal with drug pushers in public parks will probably use simpler strategies than someone who has to discuss the same issues in a neighbourhood committee meeting.

A growing number of studies in this specific context have drawn attention to aspects of political cognition that are different from those of cognition in other contexts, most notably the role of the media as information filters and the consequences of this in terms of information processing. Although we cannot look at them in detail here, we should note in passing that a substantial number of studies have been made, mainly in the United States, of the way information is presented (selected, manipulated, etc.) by television and the press, and how this affects human information processing. The order in which events are narrated, the presentation of political issues in an abstract rather than a concrete way and the source through which information is supplied are only some of the factors that make certain pieces of information seem more important than others, and guide the information acquisition process of subjects.

Which information is processed in a political context? Obviously, a large portion consists of everything that falls within the scope of politics in the strict sense, issues like economic reform, privatization, social welfare, armaments, defence and so on that concern the life of a community and determine the political stances of the parties involved. However, another significant portion consists of information about people. In a democratic system, political activity depends on delegation and so also on choosing people we think will represent us effectively.

In a given situation, the subject's attention may focus more on issues or on people, depending on the subject's aim. A programme of economic reform proposed by a politician may be perceived and processed in one way if the aim is to form an opinion on the matter, and in another if the aim is to decide whether to vote for that politician in the next election. In the former case, I might code the politician's arguments in terms of their theoretical economic plausibility; in the latter, I might code them as indications of the politician's greater or lesser competence and powers of persuasion. Although one might think that information about people is more important than information about issues in the run-up to elections (see Iyengar & Ottati, 1994), the question of whether voting is based on people or issues is still an open one (see pp. 305–307) and probably depends on the particular system and political situation.

Although increasing attention is now being paid to the special features of the political sphere, many of the results obtained so far from political cognition studies are essentially replications of results obtained from social cognition studies with different content. For this reason, a summary of what happens during information processing is given in Figure 11.1, while the text examines only a few specific points, mainly those concerning the way in which knowledge of politicians and of political issues is organized and represented in the subject's mind (for a fuller discussion of political cognition results see Iyengar & Ottati, 1994). Obviously there are close links between knowledge of politicians and of political issues: we think of people in terms of the ideas they advocate, and vice versa. Generally speaking, researchers have tended to deal with the two areas separately, so we shall do the same here.

1. *Coding*

    In this stage new information is collated with concepts which are already present in subject's mind. The degree of accessibility of these concepts is determined by a range of factors, such as:
    - perceiver's aim
    - frequency of previous use of concept
    - recency of previous use of concept

2. *Organization and representation*

    In this stage new and existing information is integrated. To describe how this happens, models based on semantic networks are frequently used. These networks consist of: (a) nodes, which correspond to concepts; (b) links, which correspond to the relationships between concepts.

3. *Retrieval*

    In this stage information is retrieved from memory. Which information is retrieved depends on:
    - the way information was coded
    - the way information was transformed into representation
    - the aim pursued at the moment of recall
    - retrieval cues

Figure 11.1 *Stages in human information processing: notions developed by social cognition studies and shared by political cognition studies*

Perception of politicians

The results of studies of political cognition can be summarized using the various stages in human information processing.

Coding

In the coding phase new information is collated with known concepts and given meaning. The same piece of information about a politician may be relevant to more than one concept, so different people will code it in different ways. For example, when a head of government says, 'I swear on the life of my children that I have never offered kick-backs to financiers', we may interpret this statement either as a passionate denial of any involvement in corruption, or as the (inappropriate) involvement of a politician's private life in public affairs.

One of the factors which determine the accessibility of one or the other of the concepts to the subject's mind is the aim being pursued: when interpreting the head of government's statement, most people's aim would be to form an accurate picture of the politician, although a minority might have other aims and code the message differently as a result. For example, a psycho-biographer (or psychoanalyst) might interpret the politician's statement as an expression of latent conflict between his role as a leader and his role as a father.

The other factors that influence accessibility – how frequently and recently the concept has been used – are related to the subject's existing knowledge base. Someone who has recently seen a TV programme about the misconduct of a politician who is a close friend of the head of government in our example will probably interpret the message differently to someone who has recently learned of judicial errors that have led to the public and private disgrace of unjustly accused politicians. The interpretation of the message may be influenced not only by a subject's existing knowledge of the matter in hand, but also by his or her knowledge of the person involved. This knowledge may be schematic – the person may be seen not as an individual but stereotypically with all the typical features of the category (whether a political party or a social class) he or she belongs to (see Lodge & Hamill, 1986) – or piecemeal – the person's individual physical features or character traits may remind the subject of another similar person (see Fiske and Pavelchak, 1986), even if the other person belongs to a different category. Which of the two perceptions will prevail in various circumstances is unclear, but in both cases, existing knowledge (schematic or piecemeal) will influence the accessibility of concepts when the message is being perceived, and therefore its encoding.

So far, we have seen that information is coded in relation to concepts that are accessible to the mind: basically, the process seems to involve integrating new information with existing information. However, when it proves difficult to assimilate new information to available concepts – indeed, when the opposite applies, and the new information *challenges* available concepts – a different process may be activated, based on contrast rather than assimilation. When this happens, existing knowledge is used not to assimilate new information but to highlight the difference between the two classes of knowledge (old and new). Thus, the liberal proposal that investment funds above a certain amount should be taxed may be coded as even more liberal if it comes from a conservative party.

When this contrast-based process is not activated, it seems likely that content which cannot be related to easily accessible concepts is simply not coded: as we have seen, information is processed selectively as an adaptive response to the limitations of human reasoning.

Organization and representation

We have said that information coding is profoundly influenced by existing knowledge. Now we must see how new information is integrated with existing knowledge both in the short-term memory and in the complex storage systems of the long-term memory. To describe the organization of knowledge and its representation in the long-term memory, most cognitivists use a semantic network model (see Collins & Loftus, 1975).

McGraw, Pinney and Neumann (1991) have tested three different semantic network models for the representation of political actors (Figure 11.2), each based on a different dimension (attribute type, partisanship, evaluation type). Using the results of a pre-test, McGraw et al. drew up a list of 16 statements about an imaginary political candidate, each characterized by one ideological and one evaluative trait that were both clearly evident, uncorrelated, and shared by the pre-test subjects. For example, a statement like 'restoring capital

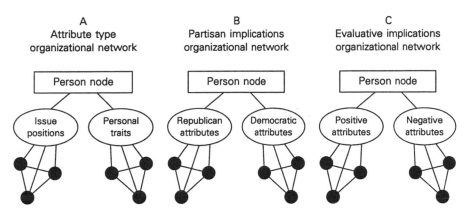

Figure 11.2 *Comparison of three alternative organizational strategies for the representation of political actors (McGraw, Pinney, & Neumann, 1991)*

punishment in New York State' was evaluated by pre-test subjects as a typical Republican attitude, and the subjects themselves judged it positively, irrespective of their own ideological stances (Republican, Democrat, nonpartisan). The list of 16 statements was completely balanced in terms of attribute type (eight issue attitudes, eight personal traits), partisan implications (eight Republican, eight Democrat) and evaluative implication (eight positive, eight negative).

Sample students were given the statements one after the other, having being told that the aim of the study was to see how people form impressions about political candidates. After a distracting task, the subjects were given without warning a recall task to which their responses had to be as accurate as possible. After analysing the results, McGraw et al. concluded that the first of their models best reflected how information about politicians is organized. Like the other models, this one has a hierarchical structure in which a super-ordered node representing the candidate is linked vertically to two information clusters, one containing information about the candidate's personality traits, the other information about his or her stances in relation to political issues. These clusters may in turn be organized hierarchically, in the sense that, for example, information about personality traits may be organized under a few more inclusive dimensions like leadership/competence on the one hand, and integrity/empathy on the other (Kinder, 1986).

Retrieval

Obviously, the fact that information is coded on the basis of existing knowledge and converted into representations determines how information is subsequently retrieved. In retrieval, as in coding, the aim of the person who is processing the information is important. If, as is usually the case in the political sphere, the aim is to form a judgement about a person (as voting day draws near, for example), subjects will first scan their short-term memory and then turn to long-term memory if they fail to find the information they need to form an opinion. Retrieval cues are also important: assuming that the network model we looked at earlier is valid, the presence of one or another cue will activate one mental chain rather than another and therefore determine which information is retrieved.

Perception of political issues

As with the perception of people, we can describe knowledge of political issues using the various stages in human information processing.

Coding

If the essential elements we need to define a person are his or her traits and/or belonging to a certain social group or class, the elements that help us to understand a political issue, event or proposal are its temporal and/or causal antecedents and consequents. Thus, coding a political event entails the construction of a mental scenario that includes not just the event itself, but also an assessment of what might have caused it and what might result from it. In the case of a political proposal, attention would focus mainly on its possible consequences.

The sheer complexity of reality means that any event will have many possible antecedents and consequents, even before we distinguish between those that operate in the short term and others that operate in the long term. Whether one rather than another antecedent or consequent is accessible to the subject's mind depends, as always, on the subject's existing knowledge of the issue, but here especially we have to remember that this knowledge is almost never acquired through direct experience, but through other intermediate sources like history books and newspapers which will already have selected some antecedents and consequents rather than others. Thus, if there is some prospect of a left-wing government coming to power, the scenario and its possible consequents will probably be based on the outcome of a similar situation in other countries, as presented in the sources of information at our disposal.

Organization and representation

We can make a useful distinction between intra-issue and inter-issue organization (Iyengar & Ottati, 1994). The former describes how the event is represented in the subject's mind, together with antecedents/consequents and corresponding evaluations; the second describes how different issues are organized in the subject's mind around a number of super-ordered unifying principles.

Once again, the network models used to describe politicians, which we looked at earlier, are employed here to describe inter-issue organization. One example is Judd and Krosnick's model (1989), in which nodes representing both individual political actors or parties and individual political issues are linked to other nodes representing abstract values or ideological principles.

Each node has a certain strength (level of accessibility or activation) and evaluative connotation (negative or positive) and the links between them (confirmation, inclusion, exclusion, etc.) also have varying degrees of strength.

Judd and Krosnick used this model in a study of the factors that influence the coherence of subjects' attitudes to political issues, and so the extent to which these issues are mentally organized around certain core values. A sample of adults was interviewed to measure their attitudes to political issues, candidates and parties, the importance they attributed to those political issues, and political competence. The results showed that both the importance they attributed to political issues, and their political competence, influenced the coherence of their attitudes, and so also the extent to which issues are mentally organized around core values. Political competence seems to generate more numerous relationships between the various nodes, and the importance attributed to an issue seems to increase the likelihood that the corresponding node will be activated once other linked nodes have already been activated.

The notion that specific policies are organized around a number of core values or abstract principles like freedom or equality is a feature not only of Judd and Krosnick's model, but also of other models that attempt to describe how attitudes to and beliefs about issues are structured. There is broad agreement on this point, but the same cannot be said of attempts to explain exactly what these organizing principles are (liberal/conservative ideological dimension, abstract values like liberty or equality, etc.), and if they operate in the same way for all issues. On the other hand, these attempts transcend the aims of political cognition studies in the strict sense, in that they imply not so much the processes of political cognition as their articulation in terms of culturally and socially mediated content. We shall return to this problem later when we look at attitudes and political beliefs.

Retrieval

As with the retrieval of any other kind of mental content, what is retrieved about political issues obviously depends on how information is organized in memory, and the subject's aim when retrieval takes place. Thus, if mental coding and organization are based on temporal/causal sequences of events, retrieval may include references to the possible antecedents and consequents of an event, as well as to the event itself. Similarly, a subject may retrieve some of the core values the issue relates to, rather than the detail of the issue itself.

Expertise

Political cognition studies have shown that the kind of information processing we have looked at so far varies according to the political expertise of subjects. The study of expertise in various domains of knowledge assumes that cognitive processes are linked to knowledge contents and the way they are organized. This means that we have to explore these various domains of knowledge if we want to understand how the minds of individuals actually work.

Like the other social sciences, politics is an 'ill-defined' domain; its contents cannot easily be reduced to rules and algorithms, and it straddles not one but several disciplines which it usually assimilates from a variety of sources. So political expertise is difficult to define, and further difficulties arise from the fact that studies have tended to concentrate on different aspects of expertise, which in turn have been operationalized in different ways. Despite this, we can still identify the most important factors in political expertise (see Fiske, Lau, & Smith, 1990).

Political knowledge

Up to now, many indicators have been used to measure political knowledge, usually general notions of civics, political events and figures and current affairs. However, many of these indicators are based on static concepts and statements; few are concerned with procedural knowledge or problem-solving ability. Essential political knowledge apart, another four factors have been identified that contribute to political expertise, in the sense that they operate simultaneously as both causes and consequences of it.

Media use

Political knowledge may be acquired through systematic study of disciplines like political science, but it can certainly also be got from nonsystematic sources embedded in the specific historical and cultural environment subjects live in, and from subjects' interests and choices. The media are one such source, and magazines and newspapers, which stimulate political interest more effectively than television, appear to be the most important.

Political self-concept

This term describes the importance of a subject's political interest and ideological stance in determining the concept of self. Few studies have dealt with the concept, although the factor does seem to play an important role.

Political interest

This factor is generally measured using self-report instruments, and studies agree on its importance in measuring political expertise.

Political activity

Although several studies have found a link between this factor and political expertise, opinion is divided over whether political activity is a factor in itself, that is once other factors have been excluded. For example, Hamill, Lodge and Blake (1985) and Fiske, Lau and Smith (1990) found no correlation between political activity and political knowledge.

The issue has been further explored in a study by Catellani (1995) of a sample of young subjects involved in political activity to varying degrees. A

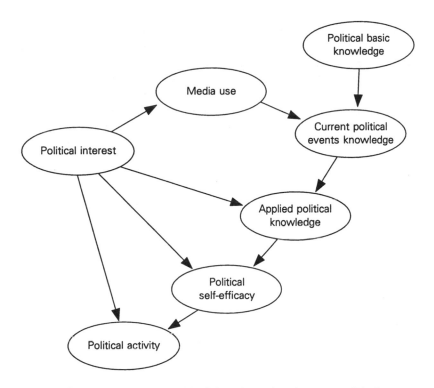

Figure 11.3   *Structural equation model of the relationships between political knowledge and political participation (Catellani, 1995)*

questionnaire provided data about three types of political knowledge – basic (e.g. functions of governmental institutions), current affairs (e.g. names of party leaders and government figures) and problem-related, or applied. In the case of the third type of knowledge, subjects were presented with a variety of political problems (e.g. welfare state, defence budget, privatization of public services) and were asked to say what they would do to solve these problems, and which people or government figures could bring influence to bear in solving the problem. Degree of applied knowledge was measured using an index that integrated the quantity and quality of the responses given.

The aim was to see how each of these knowledge types is linked not only to the others, but also to factors like political interest and political activity. Political interest was measured using three indicators: declared interest, political discussion and emotional involvement. Political activity was measured using a list of support activities (e.g. 'I distributed leaflets'), organizational activities (e.g. 'I helped organize some demonstrations') and official activities (e.g. 'I had an official position within the party').

Structural equation models applied to the various factors revealed that basic political knowledge and media use are linked through current-affairs knowledge to applied knowledge (Figure 11.3). The study also revealed a strong link between political interest and all the various knowledge types, whereas the link between political knowledge and activity was found to be weaker once the influence of political interest was excluded. Political activity seems to be linked only to applied political knowledge, and then only indirectly through the mediation of a further factor known as political self-efficacy, that is, the subjective perception that one's own action can achieve hoped-for outcomes (see pp. 309–310). On the whole, the results show that the discrepancy between the competence of people who act in this domain and people who merely have some interest in it is less marked than in other domains, probably because the shift from interest to action heavily depends on non-knowledge-related factors, such as the perception of one's power to influence people and events.

Another study of the relationship between political activity and knowledge has examined how the concepts of *politics* and *politician* differ in militants and nonmilitants (Catellani, 1990; Catellani & Quadrio, 1991). The hypothesis was that the different sociocultural backgrounds of subjects would result in different perceptions of the two concepts in both quantitative and qualitative terms. Quantitatively, the study shows that militants have a more complex perception of the abstract concept (of politics), in the sense that they see it as having more defining traits, whereas the opposite is true of the concrete concept (of politician). This is probably because greater familiarity with politicians produces the perception that politicians vary widely in type, and a corresponding reluctance to identify defining traits. In qualitative analysis, attention shifts from the processes to the contents of the representation so as to explore any differences between the perception of politics in the two groups, and how this perception relates to the perception of politicians. The results showed that the traits both groups perceived as most typical of politicians (ambition, interest in power, etc.) are fairly consistent with the militant concept of politics as gaining and exercising power, but not with the more moralistic nonmilitant concept of politics which sees power as a means to achieve personal ends rather than a functional aspect of practical politics.

Generally speaking, the relationship between political involvement and knowledge deserves to be studied more closely, and may benefit from a more explicitly social approach to the study of knowledge. To understand when and how knowledge is translated into action, we cannot take as our only object of study a cognizer who is isolated from the rest of reality. We must also take into account the social context the subject lives in, the notions he or she shares with other people, relationships with other people, the actions these relationships make possible, and so on.

Decision making

One of the subject's aims in processing political information is to be able to choose between political alternatives (e.g. when voting). Economic decision-making models (see Chapter 2 of this volume) assume that subjects behave rationally when deciding how to vote: their aim is to derive maximum personal utility from their decisions, so they use economic indicators (e.g. inflation, unemployment) to help them to decide. However, in real life subjects are often unfamiliar with these indicators; and even if they were not, the fact remains, as we have repeatedly observed, that the information available to them is usually not acquired first-hand but mediated through other sources, and has probably been manipulated or distorted along the way. If to this we add the fact that a country's economic and political situation is influenced by complex international trends and adjustments, it is easy to see that subjects are unable to predict with any accuracy what the consequences of their decisions are likely to be. And yet, economic theories still assume that people behave rationally – even in cases (as here) of decision making under uncertainty – and that statistics, and probability theory especially, are what influence decision makers most.

More recent psychological studies of decision making have abandoned this approach (cf. Chapter 2), embracing instead the cognitivist tenet that rationality is limited by human memory and information-processing capability, and is also influenced by many other psychological factors. Tversky and Kahneman's prospect theory (1981) adopts the newer approach, and has also been applied to the political sphere.

Economic theories usually conclude that people are basically risk averse. In voting, this means that they tend to vote for the known rather than the unknown, even if the unknown seems more attractive. By contrast, Tversky and Kahneman's prospect theory (1981) says that the attitude towards risk is influenced by how information is presented or framed. What matters is how individuals evaluate the outcomes of the choices posed by the decision-making problem, and how this evaluation explains their attitudes towards risk. On the whole, people tend to avoid risk if the future looks good, and accept it if the future looks bad.

Quattrone and Tversky (1988) have applied prospect theory to voting decisions. In a series of experiments, they gave subjects different information regarding the possible effects of choosing either one or the other of two economic or political policies, and then asked them to say how they would vote. In one experiment, subjects were told that, according to the predictions of economists, choosing party A would result in 12 per cent inflation, while choosing party B would result in a 0.5 probability of zero inflation *and* a 0.5 probability of 24 per cent inflation. When inflation figures showed that the future would probably be an improvement on the past, most subjects chose party A, but when they showed a worsening they chose party B, the riskier option.

Prospect theory has also been used to explain the political decision-making processes that come into operation when tackling serious international political issues. One example is McDermott's study (1992) of President Carter's behaviour during his mission to free American hostages in Iran in April 1980. The home and overseas political situation was crumbling, so after much diplomacy Carter decided to accept the risks of hard-line military action to avoid further setbacks in a home political context that was already extremely difficult. However, as prospect theory says, running great risks also implies accepting the possibility of great losses, and in fact, Carter's mission ended in a dramatic defeat.

Of the psychological dimensions that influence the decisions of both political leaders and ordinary voters, social factors linked to the presence of other people in the decision-making context are certainly among the most important. Leaving aside group decision-making, which has been widely studied in any case, it will be useful here to mention another two social factors which influence decision making in leaders and ordinary citizens respectively.

Decision making in leaders is a matter of consensus (Farnham, 1990). The aim of politicians is to act effectively in the context in which they find themselves, and to do this they must have an adequate consensus. In this respect, the political context differs from other contexts where the principal aim is usually to maximize utility. Politicians are mainly interested in the *acceptability* of their decisions, not simply because they need approval but because consensus is the prerequisite for every effective political action.

In the case of ordinary citizens, especially when they have to vote, it is obvious that an individual's decision will result in a hoped-for outcome only if many other people make the same decision. In a study of what determines the decision to vote rather than abstain, Quattrone and Tversky (1984) showed that deciding to vote for a certain party is usually supported by the subjective perception that other supporters of the same party will make the same decision, and the party will win. This process is known as 'voters' illusion', the fact that subjects mistakenly believe that their own choices have influenced the choices of others. One cognitive explanation for this is that subjects tend to extend to others the attitude–behaviour coherence they themselves show when they choose to vote for the party they support.

Attitudes and political beliefs

We have already seen that, in a political context, evaluation is a crucial component of knowledge itself. The reason for devoting a separate section to attitudes and political beliefs is not that they lie outside the cognitive domain, but that their study cannot be limited to the cognitive processes that underlie them, and must extend to a whole range of other personal and situational factors that interact with cognitive factors. The 'social cognition' approach has certainly given an important boost to attitude studies because it emphasizes the cognitive processes that determine attitudes, but it is equally true that a comprehensive study of attitudes both inside and (especially) outside the laboratory includes other factors like the role of affect in expressing attitudes, the motivations that underlie attitudes, the functions that attitudes perform, and the impact that contingent situational factors and more general cultural factors have on attitudes.

Evaluation of candidates and political issues

Cognitively, evaluation is the process by which subjects integrate the information available to them. One crucial issue here is the relative importance of the various types of information available, and when this information is actually integrated. Two explanations have been proposed, and both have been partially validated by research results. The first is that integration occurs after information relevant to the judgement has been retrieved; the second is that integration happens before this, on-line, simultaneously with the subject's exposure to the information.

Another critical issue in evaluation is a restatement of an issue we raised earlier in relation to the acquisition of knowledge: when subjects evaluate a politician, are their assessments based on their schematic perception of the category the politician belongs to, or on the piecemeal information they have about him (cf. Fiske & Pavelchak, 1986)? In the first case, evaluation is based on a group stereotype or the category the politician belongs to; in the second, it is based on the candidate's specific 'distinguishing' features. The second explanation has been advanced by, among others, Fishbein and Ajzen (1981), whose now classic study shows that evaluation of a candidate is a cumulative process in which all the pros and cons are added up and assessed. Subsequent studies have shown that, in evaluation, piecemeal knowledge takes priority over (more simplified) schematic knowledge when the judgement itself is complex and the interval between acquiring information and making the judgement is short.

Everything that has been said so far assumes that political knowledge influences attitudes, or rather, that available information is important in shaping evaluations. However, this does not exclude the opposite case: that political attitudes, once formed, can influence political knowledge. One example of this is the tendency to perceive as similar to one's own the political stance of a candidate we have already judged favourably for other reasons. A heuristic affective balance may be at work here which leads subjects to attribute ideas they like (ones that are similar to their own) to a person they like, and ideas they don't like to a person they don't like.

A study by Ottati, Fishbein and Middlestadt (1988) attempted to gauge to what extent a heuristic balance of this sort may be influential, irrespective of the objective information a subject has about a candidate. During the Reagan vs. Mondale presidential campaign, a sample of subjects was given a series of statements describing candidates' attitudes to a number of political issues. Some of the statements could be classified as true, in the sense that they reflected the real attitude of the candidate (e.g. 'Reagan is in favor of increased defense spending', 'Mondale is in favor of defense cuts'), while others could be classified as false (e.g. 'Reagan is in favor of defense cuts', 'Mondale is in favor of increased defense spending'). For each statement, subjects were asked to indicate the probability that it was true on a scale from −3 (improbable) to +3 (probable). Subjects' attitudes to the two candidates, and to the political issues contained in the statements, were also measured.

The results were used to divide the subjects into two groups. In group 1, true statements matched the subjects' own statements but false statements did not; in group 2, the opposite was the case. Obviously, if the heuristic balance had not had some influence, the truth value attributed to the true statements would have been the same in both groups. But, as Figure 11.4 shows,

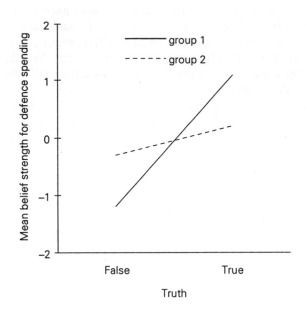

Figure 11.4   *Effect of an affective balance heuristic (Ottati, Fishbein, & Middlestadt, 1988). Mean belief strength for the defence spending issue as a function of truth of candidates' statements. In group 1 true statements match the subjects' own positions; in group 2 they do not match*

attributed truth value is greater in group 1, in which the statements themselves are coherent with those of the subjects expressing judgement.

From these results and those of other studies, we may conclude with Ottati and Wyer (1993) that knowledge of a candidate is both the determinant (reason) and consequence (rationalization) of a subject's attitudes to that candidate.

The problem of the relationship between attitudes and behaviour has featured widely in attitude studies (cf. Chapter 1). The problem is especially relevant to political attitudes because one of the most urgent demands that politicians make of both sociologists and psychologists is that they should find ways of describing attitudes that also provide the most accurate forecasts possible of how people will vote. Responding to this need, pre-election opinion polls of the relative popularity of political parties are now so commonplace that we might well ask whether knowledge of the results of these polls in itself constitutes information that may influence the attitudes of voters. Some governments believe that this is the case, and impose strict controls on the publication of opinion-poll results in the period immediately before an election. Research results to date have more or less repeated the findings of general attitude studies, and have usually adopted (though with some critical reservations) Ajzen and Fishbein's (1980) theory of reasoned action. A fuller discussion of this theory is given in Chapter 1.

Affect and cognition

Although cognitive factors play a important part in determining political attitudes, the fact remains that these attitudes are influenced by other factors, of which one, the affective dimension, has recently been the subject of several political cognition studies.

Abelson, Kinder, Peters and Fiske (1982) have examined the influence of cognitive and affective elements on evaluations of certain American politicians, including Kennedy, Carter and Bush. Cognitive elements were determined using a list of 16 traits (eight positive, like honest and smart; eight negative, like weak and power hungry) which subjects were asked to rate as more or less typical of each politician by responding to questions such as: 'Does the word *honest* describe Carter extremely well, very well, pretty well, or not very well at all?' Affective elements were determined using a list of positive (e.g. happy, proud) and negative (e.g. sad, angry) emotions. Subjects were asked to say (yes–no answers) which of these emotions the politicians elicited in them, by responding to questions like: 'Think about your feelings when I mention Carter. Now, has Carter – because of the kind of person he is or because of something he has done – ever made you feel: angry? happy?. . . etc.'. Finally, evaluations were obtained by asking subjects to express their preference for each politician on a scale ranging from 0 (extremely unfavourable) to 100 (extremely favourable). The results showed that emotions (especially positive ones) are good predictors of evaluative response, and that this effect is independent of and greater than the predictive value of politicians' personal traits.

In addition to the direct influence they have on evaluation, emotions probably have other more indirect, mediated effects. Some studies indicate that the emotions experienced when political information is acquired may be stored in the memory as part of the representation of the message referent, even if the emotions were caused by something other than the message itself. People who create election advertising deliberately try to achieve effects of this type. For example, a candidate's message may be accompanied or immediately preceded by situations or scenarios that involve viewers and elicit positive emotions.

Conservatives/liberals

In moving from the study of individual attitudes to how they are organized in more complex structures, we immediately encounter a factor that is crucially important in political psychology: the ideological dimension. Political cognition studies see the ideological dimension mainly as a way of organizing political knowledge, but it can also be seen, and has already long been studied, in relation to other factors that may be individual (personality, values, motivation, ultimate needs) as well as social (role, position of power, social and political context). So here we shall examine the ideological dimension as an organizing principle of attitudes in terms of function and content, rather than as a universal human process.

The ideological dimension is usually described in terms of liberal/conservative polarity. The political organization of many countries is based on this duality: even where there are more than two political parties, they tend to be located across a broad spectrum that unites the two poles. This said, people have been arguing for years over *which* dimensions political beliefs are organized around, and psychology has a long way to go before it can supply a satisfactory answer to this question. In the mean time, let us look at some of the major approaches to the problems ideology raises.

The fundamental text, now universally cited, is Adorno's collective study *The Authoritarian Personality* (1950) which presented the results of a wide-ranging quantitative survey of racial prejudice, and anti-Semitism in particular, in the United States. Its key assumption was that individual political beliefs are the expression of a system, and that this system in turn consistently reflects the profound dynamics of human personality, which Adorno and his colleagues interpreted psychoanalytically. A variety of structured and nonstructured instruments were used to explore a range of issues in the study, in the hope of finding some correlation between them. These issues were (a) anti-Semitism; (b) ethnocentricity; (c) political and economic conservatism; (d) anti-democratic tendencies and potential fascism. In their study of (d), Adorno and his colleagues used the so-called F Scale, which itemizes what were taken to be the three principal traits of the authoritarian personality: *conventionality*, strict adherence to conventional middle-class values; *authoritarian submission*, uncritical, unrealistic, emotion-based respect for idealized moral figures; and *authoritarian aggression*, hostility towards people who violate widely-held conventional values.

In keeping with their psychoanalytical approach, Adorno and his colleagues located the origin of these authoritarian traits in early childhood experience, and in relationships with parental authority figures especially. Since then, others have analysed their material in a rather different, functionalist way to demonstrate that specific attitudes and prejudices may be expressions of ego-defensive needs.

Adorno's pioneering work has been indispensable to many later studies of both the authoritarian personality and ideological orientation, although it has also received its share of criticism. Purely methodological criticisms have been made of Adorno's sampling procedures, which many now regard as unsatisfactory, and his formulation of F-Scale items, which some believe may have encouraged acquiescent answers in subjects. These criticisms have led to the development of new scales, like Altemeyer's RWA Scale (1981) (Figure 11.5).

What interest us most here, however, are criticisms of Adorno's account of the relationship between authoritarianism and the conservative/liberal (or right-wing/left-wing) ideological dimension. The suitability of the F Scale as a measure of potential fascism or right-wing authoritarianism can already be challenged on the basis of Adorno's own data, which did, admittedly, establish a correlation, though not a very significant one, between authoritarianism and the ideological dimension. Subsequent research has confirmed that

1. Laws have to be strictly enforced if we are going to preserve our way of life.
*2. People should pay less attention to the Bible and the other old traditional forms of religious guidance, and instead develop their own personal standards of what is moral and immoral.
3. Women should always remember the promise they make in the marriage ceremony to obey their husbands.
4. Our customs and national heritage are the things that have made us great, and certain people should be made to show greater respect for them.
*5. Capital punishment should be completely abolished.
*6. National anthems, flags and glorification of one's country should all be de-emphasized to promote the brotherhood of all men.
7. The facts on crime, sexual immorality and the recent public disorders all show we have to crack down harder on deviant groups and troublemakers if we are going to save our moral standards and preserve law and order.
*8. A lot of our society's rules regarding modesty and sexual behaviour are just customs which are not necessarily any better or holier than those which other peoples follow.
*9. Our prisons are a shocking disgrace. Criminals are unfortunate people who deserve much better care, instead of so much punishment.
10. Obedience and respect for authority are the most important virtues children should learn.
*11. Organizations like the army and the priesthood have a pretty unhealthy effect upon men because they require strict obedience of commands from supervisors.
12. One good way to teach certain people right from wrong is to give them a good stiff punishment when they get out of line.
*13. Youngsters should be taught to refuse to fight in a war unless they themselves agree the war is just and necessary.
14. It may be considered old-fashioned by some, but having a decent, respectable appearance is still the mark of a gentleman and, especially, a lady.
15. In these troubled times laws have to be enforced without mercy, especially when dealing with the agitators and revolutionaries who are stirring things.
*16. Atheists and others who have rebelled against the established religions are no doubt every bit as good and virtuous as those who attend church regularly.
17. Young people sometimes get rebellious ideas, but as they grow up they ought to get over them and settle down.
*18. Rules about being 'well-mannered' and respectable are chains from the past that we should question very thoroughly before accepting.
*19. The courts are right in being easy on drug offenders. Punishment would not do any good in cases like these.
20. If a child starts becoming a little too unconventional his parents should see to it he returns to the normal ways expected by society.
21. Being kind to loafers or criminals will only encourage them to take advantage of your weakness, so it's best to use a firm, tough hand when dealing with them.
*22. A 'woman's place' should be wherever she wants to be. The days when women are submissive to their husbands and social conventions belong strictly in the past.
*23. Homosexuals are just as good and virtuous as anybody else, and there is nothing wrong with being one.
24. It's one thing to question and doubt someone during an election campaign, but once a man becomes the leader of our country we owe him our greatest support and loyalty.

*Figure 11.5 Altemeyer's RWA (right-wing authoritarianism) scale (Altemeyer, 1981). Each item is valued on a six-point scale, ranging from 'disagree strongly' to 'agree strongly'. Items marked * are reversed items*

authoritarian attitudes are more common in right-wing subjects than in left-wing subjects, although in some cases authoritarianism is more often found in left-wing subjects than in moderate subjects. More generally, it seems likely that the sample material in both Adorno's and other later studies is biased in any case because it was gathered in countries like the United States and Great Britain where left-wing subjects are on the whole well educated and politically aware, and form a fairly homogeneous minority. By contrast, left-wing authoritarianism may well be a feature of Communist countries, where any sample would perforce be more heterogeneous.

Irrespective of whether a relationship between ideology and authoritarianism can be demonstrated, studies of the conservative/liberal dimension continue to run into problems, if only because there is some doubt as to whether this dimension is the only, or at least the most important, principle that shapes political attitudes.

In Tetlock's value pluralism model (1986), conservative and liberal stances differ in terms of reference values. Tetlock maintains that in all political ideologies we can identify a set of core or 'terminal' values (see Rokeach, 1973) that define the ultimate aims of any political act (e.g. social equality, economic efficiency, individual freedom). According to Tetlock, the two stances, conservative and liberal, differ in both 'terminal' reference values, and in their tolerance of conflict between these values. For example, the centre-left ideology of Western democracies is characterized by high levels of value conflict, and issues such as redistributive income policies have to be tackled by trying to reconcile values like social equality and economic freedom, which usually conflict with each other in some way. As we shall see in the next subsection, greater conflict produces greater cognitive complexity in subjects who share this centre-left ideology.

Perhaps a better understanding of how the ideological dimension influences attitudes to political issues may come from studies that go beyond differences of political opinion as such to address differences in the causal structures that underlie them. One example is a study by Heaven (1994) which explores the perception of poverty in subjects of different ideological orientations. Side-stepping the problem of scale-based measurement of ideological orientation, Heaven instead asked people who had voted respectively Conservative and Labour to say what they thought the probable causes of poverty were. Using structural equation models to reconstruct the hierarchical structure of immediate and remote causes, he found that ideological differences appear not so much in immediate causes (which in both groups were largely social, e.g. prejudice, exploitation of the weak by the strong) as in remote causes (mainly internal in Conservatives, e.g. moral or intellectual poverty, and both internal and social in Labour supporters).

Some studies have attempted to explore the relationship between conservative vs. liberal ideology and moral reasoning. According to Emler, Renwick and Malone (1983), individual differences in moral reasoning reflect differences in political ideology. Thus, the kind of moral reasoning we use when judging issues does not depend on our level of cognitive development, as Kohlberg claims (1976), but on the political ideologies we possess. Liberal ideology is typically opposed to the status quo, so the people who share it will be more inclined to use general moral principles when describing their political stances, rather than simple rules or conventions. Their reasoning will be post-conventional, the highest level of moral reasoning in Kohlberg's hierarchy. By contrast, those who share right-wing ideologies, and support tradition and the maintenance of the status quo, will argue that law and order in society should be upheld. As a result, they will use conventional reasoning, which comes lower down in Kohlberg's hierarchy of moral development.

Ideological orientation and cognitive style

Conservative-liberal ideological orientation has also been related to other dimensions of mental functioning. In a long line of studies (for a review see Tetlock, 1993), Philip Tetlock has explored one particular aspect of cognitive style called *integrative complexity* by analysing texts written by politicians on a given issue and coding two features of the text called differentiation and integration. Differentiation is measured by the number of distinct dimensions subjects take account of in an issue, and integration is measured by the number of links subjects make between the various dimensions. Initially, and very much in line with previous studies, Tetlock measured integrative complexity using sentence-completion tests, but later used archive material (speeches by politicians, American Supreme Court rulings) to enhance the external validity of his research.

The relationship between ideological stance and cognitive style has been explained in at least two ways. One explanation, which Tetlock defines as the 'rigidity of the right', derives substantially from Adorno, and says essentially that the reasoning of right-wing subjects is more dogmatic and rigid, less subtle – in a word, simpler – than that of left-wing subjects. Tetlock defines the other explanation as 'ideological', in the sense that it is extremists in general, of either the right or the left, rather than right-wing extremists only, who are more dogmatic, rigid, etc. than moderate subjects. The inconsistent results Tetlock obtained in his various studies prevent us from confirming either hypothesis. This has led to the formulation of more complex hypotheses that take into account the context in which integrative complexity is measured and, more specifically, the issue the subject is reading about and the role he played when the text was formulated. Let us look at these two features separately.

In keeping with the value pluralism model he proposes, Tetlock claims that some issues are related to only one core value, so that an individual's attitude to the issue reflects the force of that particular value. Other issues may relate to a set of conflicting values, which makes the subject integratively more complex.

In his study of the value pluralism model (1986), Tetlock recorded the preferences of a sample of subjects regarding six political issues that would presumably lead to conflict between a variety of terminal value pairs in the Rokeach Value Survey (Rokeach, 1973). Subjects were asked questions like:

'Would you be willing to pay higher taxes in order to provide more assistance to the poor?' (conflicting values: social equality vs. comfortable and prosperous life); or, 'Should the United States spend more on national defense even if such spending requires lowering the standard of living of most Americans?' (conflicting values: national security vs. comfortable and prosperous life). Tetlock then gave his subjects the Rokeach Value Survey to obtain their terminal value hierarchies. Finally, subjects were asked to write down their thoughts about each of the six political issues, and the integrative complexity of what they wrote was measured.

Regression analyses showed first that the best predictor of a subject's attitude is which of the two conflicting values the subject attributes most importance to. They also showed that the integrative complexity of what the subjects wrote increases proportionally to similarity in the degree of importance subjects attribute to the pair of values the issue itself raises, and so also proportionally to the value conflict the issue provokes in the subject. This would explain why the integrative complexity of subjects varies depending on the issue in question.

The subject's role – for example, being or not being in a position to exercise power – also influences integrative complexity. Tetlock and Boettger (1989) analysed speeches by Soviet politicians before and after they rose to power and found that integrative complexity was greater once they were in power. Their explanation is that people fighting for power win consensus by giving clear, simple messages that clarify how their political stances differ from those of other politicians. By contrast, politicians who have gained power have to reconcile and mediate a variety of stances, so level of integrative complexity tends to rise. This explanation contains echoes of studies of minority influence (see Moscovici, 1976), and research of this issue might progress even further if a more explicitly psychosocial approach were adopted.

Tetlock draws the following conclusions from his research: (a) centre and left-of-centre subjects show greater integrative complexity in response to certain issues because they have to reconcile conflicting values; (b) irrespective of ideological stance or issue, some situations (e.g. being in a position of power) call for greater integrative complexity than others.

Political participation

In this final section we shall shift our attention away from conceptual and evaluative politics to political activity itself. We have already looked several times at the question of political behaviour, and of voting behaviour especially, because political attitudes and knowledge are often regarded as precursors of behaviour. However, in this section devoted entirely to political behaviour, or rather, political *activity*, we shall look at more obviously social factors which are essential to understanding how an action takes place because they operate both alongside and in addition to individual ones. Focusing attention on action and, more specifically, political action, entails studying individuals not just as reasoning beings who take decisions and make judgements in variously rational and/or emotional ways, but also as subjects who perform all these functions in a social context which they influence with their actions, and are influenced by in turn. It is certainly both possible and appropriate to identify the fundamental processes that guide mental activity, but it is also true that how these processes work in real life is influenced by the social situations (couple, group, collective) an individual's life is composed of.

This is even more so when politics is the object of study. What is politics if not a system created to regulate the relationships between people and groups? In the end, politics is essentially a matter of social and power relationships. By studying these relationships, we can finally arrive at a social psychology of politics in the narrower sense of the term.

The political action we shall be concerned with here is not the action of politicians, which is the prerogative of a small number of people, even if what politicians do is of absorbing interest to everyone because of the effects it has on society. The actions of politicians have been the subject of many studies of decision making, conflict management and political negotiation in national and international contexts, so for reasons of space we shall concentrate, first, on political action that involves the greatest number of citizens, that is, voting; and secondly, on militant action, which is much more limited and yet highly relevant to the study of social change.

Choosing a political party

Descriptions of the cognitive processes that underlie political evaluation have now reached highly sophisticated levels, but despite this, the factors they employ have not proved especially reliable predictors of voting behaviour.

While political cognition studies have concentrated on psychological factors of exclusively individual origin, studies of voting behaviour have long had a sociological orientation that highlights the structural factors (e.g. sex, age, education, residence, occupation) one can use to predict voting behaviour. That said, the predictive reliability of sociostructural factors is not particularly impressive either. Only recently have we seen psychosocial studies that attempt to integrate structural and individual factors in an effort to explain more satisfactorily how people really behave when they vote. We shall look at these studies, after a brief survey of some of the more important models used to describe voting behaviour.

Any survey of these models must begin with the work of Campbell, Converse, Miller and Stokes (1960), which will henceforth be referred to as the 'Michigan model'. Campbell and his colleagues broke with the explicitly sociological orientation of previous studies because they wanted to explain voting behaviour using the psychological factor of identification with a political party. According to Campbell, voting choices are not based on political knowledge, which is usually minimal and inconsistent, but on party affiliation rooted in tradition and, especially, the family environment individuals grow up in. Campbell explains this psychoanalytically as identification with the party, which is remarkably stable because it is acquired at an early age.

Later studies have challenged the Michigan model. Himmelweit's 'consumer model' (Himmelweit, Humpreys, Jaeger, & Katz, 1985) developed from studies of British voting behaviour, and points to substantial congruence between individuals' and parties' positions on political issues, which suggests that, when historical and political situations change, it is more appropriate to speak of 'issue-voting' rather than identification with political parties. Again based on the British situation, Heath, Jowell and Curtice's 'ideological model' (1985) claims that voting is influenced not by issue-beliefs but by more general belief structures to which individual issues can be related. Heath et al. go even further when they claim that people support political parties whose attitudes are similar to their own in terms of the two specific ideological dimensions of equality and liberalism/conservatism (see pp. 299–303).

One criticism levelled at all the models we have looked at so far is that they fail to make any significant conceptual or explanatory distinction between dependent and independent variables (Evans, 1993). Campbell's model explains voting by identification with the party, but then uses voting to measure degree of identification, so models like Himmelweit's consumer model, which explains voting for a certain party in terms of sharing its position on general or specific political issues, are perhaps unconvincing in the last analysis. And there is still the problem of how to reconcile mutually contra-dictory models and establish exactly what determines whether voting is based on candidates/parties or on issues.

One solution may be to try to explain voting using models that integrate sociostructural factors with individual psychological factors. Several social psychologists have attempted to do this using social identity theory (e.g. Tajfel and Turner, 1986), in which 'social identity' means the awareness of indi-viduals that they belong to a certain social group, combined with the signifi-cance of this sense of belonging in evaluative and emotional terms. The basic assumption is that individuals actively seek a positive social identity because it boosts their positive self-esteem, and that they try to form this identity by comparing their own social group with other groups and displaying 'positive in-group distinctiveness'.

Social identity has been used in psychosocial interpretations of regional and local variations in voting patterns, an issue to which sociologists (e.g. Heath) have repeatedly drawn attention. Abrams and Emler's study (1991) of the political choices of young Scots and Britons has shown that identification with a political party for regional reasons may serve to uphold the portion of the subject's social identity that specifically derives from a sense of regional belonging. Thus, if being a Labour supporter is part of the Scottish identity, identification with the Labour party will serve to strengthen this identity, even when it conflicts with the subject's personal interests. Expressive values like identification with particular groups seem to take priority over instrumental values like choosing a party on the assumption that it will secure economic advantages for the voter.

The question of the stability of this identification with political parties, which Campbell describes but others have not always confirmed, has also been tackled in a new way by borrowing from general studies of social identity. For

Table 11.1 *Percentage of each political category giving different reasons for voting decisions*

Support party because ...	Non/ uncertain voters (n=408)	Labour/ Tory voters (n=1252)	Minority voters (n=347)	Chi square (non versus majority versus minority)	Chi square (majority versus minority)
Has best leaders	47.3	54.1	30.3	62.09**	60.79**
Agree with basic ideals	92.6	94.3	98.1	13.40*	7.82*
Best policies	90.0	87.0	77.1	28.43**	18.84**
Represents people like me	76.5	77.2	84.7	10.08*	130.88**
Family supports it	11.3	50.1	15.6	275.50**	130.88**

* p<0.01; ** p<0.0001

Source: Abrams (1994)

example, Abrams (1994) borrowed and applied to the issue of political party belonging an insight from studies of group belonging in other fields; namely, that medium-sized groups probably work better from the psychological point of view because they encourage identification. In the political sphere, this may mean that stable identification with a party is more likely in the case of minority parties because they are structured in ways that encourage identification.

Abrams's data source is the same as that in the previous study, i.e. a large-scale survey of young Britons. One question subjects were asked was which party they would vote for if there were an election; a later question asked them to say why they would have voted in that way. Table 11.1 lists the reasons given by subjects who were uncertain how to vote, subjects who supported majority parties, and subjects who supported minority parties. Supporters of minority parties tended to say that they agreed with the basic ideals of the party of their choice, and that this party represented people like them. By contrast, supporters of majority parties tended to say that the party of their choice had the best leader or the best political programme, or that they had chosen the party simply because their parents would have chosen it. Thus, Abrams's results show that support for majority parties is an outcome of rational and instrumental reasoning, while support for minority parties is more closely linked to identification.

Political activity

While voting (or deciding not to vote) is something that affects all adult citizens, the same cannot be said of other types of political activity that call for active involvement in public affairs. It may be true that periods of transition or institutional crisis tend to generate greater desire for political involvement on the part of citizens, but several recent studies, mainly of younger people in Western countries (e.g. Breakwell, 1992), seem to indicate widespread disenchantment with political involvement. This may be linked to a deeply rooted ideological crisis that is deterring young people from identifying with conventional political categories. Some confirmation of this comes from the activities of environmental and voluntary groups, which now seem magnets for political involvement. Clearly, the desire for involvement is not extinct, but is seeking other outlets. For this and other reasons, our definition of political activity here will be rather broad so as to include nonparty groups. In general, the focus will be on purposefully voluntary action whose principal aim is to influence political decisions.

One of the first questions we have to answer is: how can political activity be measured? Measuring instruments usually record the perceptions of subjects using indicators like frequency of party or group meetings, leafleting, etc. Obviously, people will not always have an entirely accurate perception of their own political involvement, but for the purposes of psychological research, subjective involvement is a useful, if not the most useful, indicator. Another question is whether political activity is a one-dimensional or multidimensional construct. Some studies have used factor analysis techniques to identify various dimensions of involvement, but the results have been challenged on methodological grounds. However, in trade union involvement at least, a one-dimensional model seems the most accurate and realistic. More specifically, it may be possible to measure level of involvement on a Guttmann scale, assuming that participation in high-level activities (e.g. being a member of a union commission) includes (or has included in the past) participation in lower-level activities (e.g. voting to elect union representatives) (Kelloway & Barling, 1993).

Another distinction frequently used in describing political activity is the one between 'conventional' and 'unconventional' activities. The kind of involvement and the personal characteristics called for by these two types of activity may be different, although we should not forget that an activity which starts off as unconventional may later acquire conventional forms of organization and expression. This shift from one type of activity to another may often coincide with a process widely studied in social psychology (see Moscovici, 1976) that enables an active minority to influence a majority. For example, an activity like throwing rotten eggs at women wearing fur coats to opera premières, which would be regarded as unconventional for an environmental group, may eventually prove so popular that it transforms itself into a conventional activity like signing petitions to have fur factories closed.

As with voting behaviour, studies of political activity have borrowed widely from sociology, especially in its use of sociostructural factors linked to political involvement, including sex and level of education, with greater political activity in highly educated males. Psychological studies of this initially placed the accent on personality factors like authoritarianism and dogmatism which encourage political activity, but more recent theoretical studies of personality have adopted a more interactive approach which sees personality not as a given entity, but as the outcome of interaction between individuals and the situations they have to act in (see Krampen, 1991). These and other more explicitly psychosocial studies have enabled us to identify a series of psychosociological factors associated with the desire for involvement in collective action (see Kelly & Kelly, 1994; Klandermans, 1995). We shall look here at the three that have been studied most widely.

Relative deprivation

One factor that seems to generate collective action is a subject's perception that he or she has suffered injustice and has been discriminated against. This factor includes not only the perception of breakdown in values that are held to be important (e.g. the right to work, education), but also the perception that others are responsible for this breakdown, and that a different states of affairs might be possible. This 'trigger' for political action has so far been the most widely studied factor in social psychology. Deprivation has been defined as *egoistic* when an individual believes that he or she has been discriminated against with respect to others, and *collective* when the individual believes that his or her group has been discriminated against with respect to others. Several studies have now shown that collective deprivation correlates with collective action.

Social identity

Our discussion of collective deprivation already implies the concept of ingroup and outgroup, 'us' and 'them'. We have seen that social identity is based on the sense of belonging to a group and, we should perhaps now add, on shared beliefs and aims. There has been speculation that strong social identity is one of the factors that generates collective action, but only when this identity is the outcome of belonging to particular types of group. Borrowing a distinction made by Hinkle and Brown (1990), Kelly and Kelly (1994) stress that social identity generates collective action if it is the outcome of belonging to a group that is oriented anyway towards collective action and human relationships (political groups, trade unions, environmental groups, etc.), and not to groups that encourage individualism and independent activity (hobby groups, sport, etc.). We now also know that there is a two-way relationship between social identity and collective action: involvement in collective action boosts a group's identity.

The emphasis on social identity has also raised the question of whether other factors that correlate with this construct, for example stereotyped perception of the outgroup, level of intergroup conflict, are also linked to collective action, but research results so far have been inconclusive.

Perceived self and group efficacy

Researchers have hypothesized that individuals are unlikely to undertake political action unless they believe they will obtain something by doing so. Psychologists have long regarded self-efficacy – an individual's expectation that he or she will help to produce a successful outcome – as a key factor in political involvement. However, predictions of the outcome of a political action can also be interpreted in a more social way by taking into account the fact that the success of a collective action depends precisely on the fact that it involves several people, and that predictions of the outcome of an action must be based on the contributions of all these other people, as well as on the individual's own contribution. Self-efficacy is only one of a subject's expectations: there are also two other expectations, or perceived probabilities, one concerned with the behaviour of others, the other concerned with the perceived likelihood of success if many others participate in a given political action.

These three factors, or rather, classes of factors, are probably interrelated, although to what extent and in what ways is still unclear. For example, Kelly and Kelly (1994) have found some (slight) confirmation of the hypothesis that relative deprivation plays an important role in generating political action when social identity is strong, whereas self-efficacy plays a more important role when social identity is weak. Another study by Catellani, Balzarini and Cardinali (1995), dealing with local, national and European political identity and action, has found a positive link between weak social identity and self-efficacy. Not surprisingly, it shows that self-efficacy decreases as the range of possible actions increases (e.g. from a local to a European context). And yet, despite this, the factor is a reliable indicator of European identity (weak in the study), but a poor one of national and local identity (strong in the study). The reason for this may be that an individual trait like self-efficacy starts to generate political involvement mainly (if not exclusively) when social identity fails to materialize, although only future research will be able to confirm this.

In this chapter we have regarded political psychology as a discipline that studies the cognitive, evaluative and behavioural dimensions of political 'actors', whether these be ordinary citizens or the politicians elected or delegated to represent them.

In examining the cognitive dimension, we looked at how information about political issues and politicians is processed, crucial factors in determining the formation of political competence and decision-making processes. In tackling these questions, researchers have sometimes limited themselves to extending to the political sphere models developed in other fields of inquiry, and to replicating with political content results already obtained with different content in other areas. However, further studies have revealed features that seem more specific to the political sphere, like the importance of the media as information filters, and the consequences this has on information processing and the acquisition of competence.

In examining the evaluative dimension, we looked at how people judge the people called upon to represent them, and discussed in some depth an issue of crucial importance to political studies, namely ideological stance, as revealed in studies based either on traditional left/right or conservative/liberal dichotomies, or on several dimensions, meaning that political attitudes are organized around certain core values.

In examining the behavioural dimension, a number of more strictly social variables were highlighted. In particular, we saw that social identity influences voting choice and political activity, and that these in turn tend to reinforce social identity. Social variables certainly merit much closer study on the part of political psychologists because, in the last analysis, politics is nothing other than a system created to regulate interpersonal and intergroup relationships.

Further reading

Granberg, D. & Holmberg, S. (1988). *The political system matters: Social psychology and voting behavior in Sweden and United States.* Cambridge: Cambridge University Press. This volume presents a detailed instance of collaboration between a social psychologist and a political scientist. It is also a good example of empirical research in the domain of voting behaviour.

Iyengar, S. & McGuire, W.J. (Eds) (1993). *Explorations in political psychology.* Durham, NC: Duke University Press. Provides an excellent overview of research in political psychology.

The journal *Political Psychology* is also an excellent source for further reading.

12

Social Psychology and the Media

Harald G. Wallbott

Contents

- Do you watch MTV a lot and what has that done to your musical taste?
- Is *Rambo* dangerous to your health?
- Why did CDs win the battle against the old vinyl disc that fast?
- Why are portable telephones such a big success?
- When James Dean or Kurt Cobain died, what was the role of media coverage?
- How do you feel, when you try to call somebody and unexpectedly encounter a telephone answering machine?
- Do people commit suicide after listening to 'Judas Priest' records?
- Do you use the Internet or e-mail, and if yes, do you communicate different there compared to face-to-face communication?

These are just a few questions related to psychology of the media. This chapter provides an attempt to shed some light on at least some of these questions, though not on all, and to introduce theories and findings from social psychology pertinent to them.

The media and social psychology

Usually, social psychology and psychology of the media are considered as being rather different areas of research. The former is a distinct field in psychology, while the latter has some problems in being viewed as a part of psychology at all. This is because media scientists, sociologists, teachers or philosophers are keen to comment on topics related to 'mass media'. Media is a topic which seems to be of acute interest to researchers from different fields and to the general public. This is probably because media consumption occupies a substantial amount of our lives. It comes as no surprise that, for instance, the writings of Neil Postman (e.g. 1985) reached the status of bestsellers. This, in itself should be an argument for why the media are of interest to social psychology. In fact, Oskamp (1986) considers mass media research to be one of the centrally important future areas for applied social psychology (among other topics like international affairs, environmental issues, legal issues and the like).

On the other hand, social psychology was concerned from the beginning with the media, and especially in its central areas of research. Many factors concerning sender, message and receiver of persuasive messages have been studied extensively to identify central aspects which foster attitude change, such as speaker credibility, quantity vs. quality of arguments, fear induction and so on (for overviews see McGuire, 1985; Eagly & Chaiken, 1993). Most of this research is indeed not concerned with face-to-face communication, but with communication mediated by technical means such as written messages, tape recordings or video clips used to convey persuasive messages.

The same is true for most research in person perception and attribution. Usually, subjects are not confronted with other persons face to face, but instead with information about persons, be it lists of personality traits characterizing a person in the tradition of Asch (1946), standardized photographs or video recordings, or written vignettes (see Cline, 1964). The point to be made in this chapter is that much of social psychological research is concerned with the media, partly because media are used to a large degree in social psychology and partly because they are an integral part of modern life worthy of study by social psychologists.

The following first of all attempts to distinguish between several types of media then to shed some light on three areas in which media and social psychology are related: (1) *media as research devices in social psychology* describes how the media help and foster research in social psychology. It is argued that, for instance, research in nonverbal communication in its present form would not be possible without the availability of video technology; (2) *mass media contents and impact as research topics* discusses how media affect our knowledge of the world, shape our beliefs, and our behaviour. Effects on behaviour will be described in a consideration of one of the most prominent research topics – aggression and the media; and finally (3) *the influence of mediated communication on communication processes* focuses on aspects of new communication media, like picture telephones and teleconferencing and their psychological implications. In the first part of the chapter these three issues will be addressed more theoretically, while in the second part several research examples of the issues are reported. Obviously, it will not be possible to cover all topics exhaustively. The intention is to demonstrate the importance of social psychological theories and ideas for media research, especially in media areas with strong impact on daily life, like television, which should not be the sole domain of culture-pessimistic philosophers or *feuilleton* authors.

The media and communication

We will distinguish here between face-to-face communication on the one hand and communication via media on the other. Such media can be very diverse, ranging from smoke signals to television. Winterhoff-Spurk (1989) distinguished media for individual communication from mass communication media, and introduced further subclassifications: whether these media are transport media (the information has to be consumed immediately) or fixation media (the information is fixed to paper, etc.), or whether they carry speech and speech-related information or other signal/symbol information. His overview is reproduced in Table 12.1.

A subdivision can be made between what is usually termed *mass media* and *mediated communication*. While Winterhoff-Spurk's classification focuses mainly on transmission codes, here the aspect of interaction will be stressed. 'Mass media' include, according to the definition of Harris (1989; see also Maletzke, 1978), all media where the communication process is public, diverse, indirect, via a technical medium, basically one-sided and usually addressed to a more or less large, and more or less anonymous audience. In contrast, 'mediated communication' refers to all types of communication processes where face-to-face communication is mediated by technical devices: for example telephone, electronic mail message, video conference, talking drum, or letter.

Both areas can be further subdivided with respect to the question of whether real interaction is possible or not. Most mass media by definition of course are *non-interactive* media, i.e. what is broadcast on television, for instance, cannot be influenced by the viewer at that moment. Nevertheless, recent technical developments may make real interactive television possible in the not too distant future. Furthermore, new forms of broadcasting both on radio and on television are becoming more and more interactive. Examples

Table 12.1   *A classification of communication media*

Individual communication	Speech media	Signal/symbol media
Transport media	Telephone, audio- and video-conferencing, etc.	Signal lights, flag signals, drum signals, etc.
Fixation media	Notes, tapes, films, videorecordings, e-mail etc.	Pictures, photographs etc.
Mass communication		
Transport media	Radio, television, etc.	Horn signals, light signals, etc.
Fixation media	Print media, tapes, films, etc.	Pictures, photographs, etc.

Source: after Winterhoff-Spurk (1989)

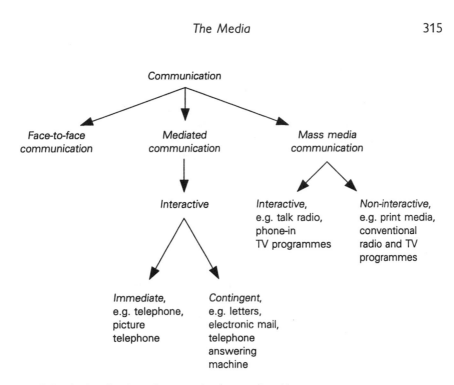

Figure 12.1 *A classification of communication media with respect to interactive aspects*

include recent developments like talk radio broadcasts, or special phone-in television shows.

Mediated communication usually entails interaction which may consist of immediate exchange, for example via the telephone, or delayed interactive communication or contingent exchange, as in the case of an exchange of letters or e-mail messages or leaving messages on a telephone answering machine, where no immediate feedback from the addressee is possible. This classification is depicted in Figure 12.1.

In recent years, mediated communication has increasingly become important with the development of more sophisticated technical devices. Such new forms of communication include electronic mail, the telephone answering machine, telephone conferencing (allowing more than two participants to share a telephone link), as well as teletext services, home banking, video-conferencing, and portable telephones, the picture telephone, and finally integrated multimedia communication as it has become available in the context of the information highway on the home computer.

Media as research devices in social psychology

Many recent developments in psychology would not have been possible without the employment of media. This is especially true of video technology, but more and more also for computers: no longer mere devices for statistical analysis, instead they are a stimulus presentation, measurement and storing device for subjects' reactions. It may for instance not be pure coincidence that the increase in research in nonverbal communication which started in the late 1960s (for overviews see Harper, Wiens, & Matarazzo, 1978; Scherer & Ekman, 1982; Feldstein & Rimé, 1991) happened at the same time as video recorders and video cameras became increasingly more available to the general public outside of large television production studios. The availability of video technology at a comparatively low price contributed substantially to the fostering of research in areas where storage of visual information in a cheap and efficient way is essential to facilitate repeated viewing, slow motion, still-frame viewing, etc. Before the advent of home video, researchers in the area of nonverbal communication had to work with tremendously expensive studio video equipment, which was outside the financial realm of most researchers, or they had to use film (8mm and 16mm), which was also quite costly, did not allow immediate viewing, and was limited by the short duration of films. Gigerenzer has described and analysed the 'tools-to-theories heuristic' within cognitive psychology. His central idea is that quite often theories and concepts in research emerge from methods and tools available (for cognitive psychology specifically statistical models like the analysis of variance or computers; for details see Gigerenzer, 1991a). A similar analysis concerning the impact of media on research in social psychology and communication remains to be written.

Video not only helped to store nonverbal behaviour, it also allowed the development of sophisticated observation and coding techniques. Most of these techniques in fact require storage of behaviour (i.e. video recordings) and cannot (or only with great difficulty) be used for on-the-spot, immediate observation of behaviour. Two illustrative examples will be mentioned.

Frey (1987) developed the Bernese System for Movement Notation, which attempts to code the position of all bodily parts exhaustively. Coders watch video recordings of the person whose behaviour is to be coded, frame by frame, and locate for each video frame (or for each nth frame, if a less than optimal temporal resolution is chosen) the position of each bodily part with respect to the spatial dimensions the respective part of the body is able to move in. Head movements – to give just one example – are coded with respect to the sagittal dimension (head lifted or lowered), to the rotational dimension (head turned right or left) and to the lateral dimension (head tilted right or left). This coding procedure results in time series of codes for the respective parts of the body. In fact, if all codes for head, arms, upper body, legs, etc. are employed, this procedure approximates a complete description of human movement in time. The categories to code head positions are depicted in Figure 12.2.

A second example is the Facial Action Coding System (FACS), developed by Ekman and Friesen (1978), and now widely shared as a coding device for the analyses of facial expression by numerous researchers. FACS is based on observation categories, the action units, which are the smallest visible and distinguishable units of facial expression. A coder's task is to analyse facial expressions with respect to these action units, or to decompose a complex expression into the constituting action units. Furthermore, FACS optionally

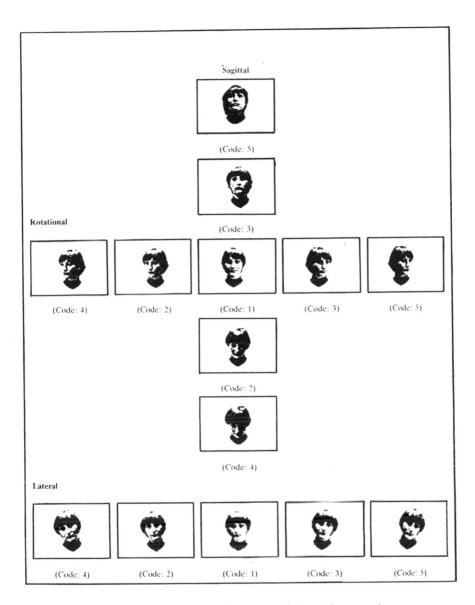

Figure 12.2 *An example of a coding technique employing video to code head positions with respect to the three spatial dimensions (after Frey, 1987)*

allows for the coding of action unit intensities, as well as for location in time and duration of events coding.

Given this short description it should be immediately evident that these coding systems can only be used when video recordings (or films, i.e. stored behaviour) are available. Only facilities like slow motion, shuttle search, or frame-by-frame viewing make these systems a meaningful research device.

Outside of social psychology, video is becoming a more and more important research device, in developmental psychology or in organizational

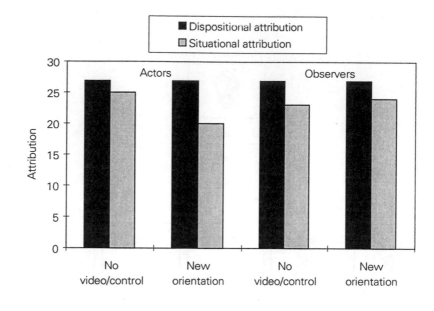

Figure 12.3 *Changes in actors' and observers' internal and external attributions after exposure to a new perspective via video (Storms, 1972)*

psychology, for example. Classical fields in social psychology have employed video to a growing degree, either as a means of stimulus presentation, or as a device to store behaviour. Person perception and attribution research was for a long time restricted to person or event descriptions as stimuli, or to trait lists characterizing persons in the tradition of Asch (1946). For obvious reasons this research was criticized as lacking validity (cf. Krauss, 1980). Nowadays, more and more video presentations are used in person perception research. The often cited paper by Storms (1972) represented something like the video advent in attribution research. Storms showed that by exposing actors and observers to information they usually do not receive (e.g. exposing an actor to a video recording of his/her own behaviour) a reversal of the usual actor–observer bias is possible. Actor–observer bias is a finding often replicated in attribution research. It implies that an actor tends to locate reasons for her or his behaviour in external causes (the situation, other people, etc.), while an observer of the same behaviour will locate reasons more often in internal causes (personality traits of the actor, intentions, etc.). Exposing the actor to video recordings of her or his own behaviour changes the actor's perspective to more internal attributions, while providing situation information (e.g. the actor's interaction partner) to the observer via video changes the observer's perspective to more external attributions (see Figure 12.3). The strong effect of changing information access and perspective via video demonstrated by Storms's study provided the rationale for video feedback. Since then video feedback has been a popular method in clinical psychology, training and applied areas (see Dowrick & Biggs, 1983).

Mass media contents and mass media impact as research topics

There is no doubt that the mass media shape and influence our cognition, attitudes and behaviour to some degree. The question to be addressed should be how influential mass media are. McGuire (1986) arrived at the conclusion that the effects of mass media are in general small, despite the fact that 'with all this watching [of TV], there must be some effect' (McGuire, 1986, p. 175). The discussion seems to oscillate between the view that media have no direct impact at all and if there is any influence it is mediated via personal communication with opinion leaders, and the opposite view that the mass media are our central source of knowledge, that they determine our view of the world, and, consequently, our behaviour. The latter position is advocated by culture-pessimistic philosophers and some media scientists, but also by the proponents of a strong version of the *cultivation of beliefs hypothesis*, i.e. the idea that very often we do not have direct access to events and information, but that the mass media deliver the information, thereby shaping and determining our view of the world (Gerbner & Gross, 1976; p. 331ff.).

It seems that the question of the (often negative) impact of mass media contents comes up regularly with the arrival and increasing popularity of new media. One example is the old and still unresolved question of media impact on aggression and violence. Mass media which address adolescents in particular seem to become the black sheep now and again. In the 1950s, for instance, comic books were blamed for influencing adolescents negatively, in the 1960s it was television, and in the 1980s the cinema (especially the growing popularity of horror and splatter movies and the like). This was replaced in the 1990s – among other media contents – by music videos (hard rock, rap and heavy metal), which are held to be responsible for aggression and violence (see Wallbott, 1992a).

Other popular research on media contents besides aggressive behaviour is concerned with prejudice as conveyed via media. Topics include *gender stereotypes* as communicated by such diverse media as television drama, advertisements and children's books. *Ethnic characterization*, *race*, etc. are other topics research has focused on (for overviews on these topics see McGuire, 1986; Harris, 1989). Questions here include the roles and function of African-American people in (US-American) advertisements or television drama, the importance of media during elections and political debates, imitative suicides after media coverage of prominent suicides, the influence of ethnic characterization on guilt attributions for criminals and cross-racial rape as presented via newspaper articles.

Mediated communication

When the telephone – nowadays certainly the most prominent medium of mediated communication – entered the stage about a century ago, social psychology was not there to study the massive impact of this medium on communication. Research on the impact of newly introduced media on communication and interaction processes should be a central question for social psychology. This is true both from a theoretical point of view (in which ways does mediated communication differ from face-to-face communication? Which advantages and disadvantages do different media have? Which social psychological theories may account for such differences?), as well as from a practical point of view. New media like the fax or e-mail today are sold and used in tremendous quantities, but social psychological research on user habits, attitudes, etc. is basically nonexistent. In 1982, about 10,500 fax machines were in use in Germany. Ten years later this number was nearer to a million!

The introduction of new media is indeed a chance for social psychology, because their introduction opens the possibility of examining the formation and change of user habits and attitudes. The recently introduced picture telephone and teleconferencing systems may provide just one example.

Picture telephones have a long tradition. In the 1920s Bell Laboratories introduced the 'Picturephone', without much success. During the world exhibition in 1964 a different picture telephone was launched on the market, with the prediction which we in hindsight know to be absolutely wrong: that such systems would replace conventional telephones by the beginning of the 1970s (see Egido, 1988). The vice-president of Bell Laboratories in 1969 stressed the advantages of this new communication device which were stated as: 'face-to-face mode of communication . . . enhanced feeling of proximity and intimacy with the other party . . . [it can] convey much important knowledge over and above that carried by the voice alone'. In a similar vein picture telephones and teleconferencing were considered 'the closest thing to being there', and research indicated that 41 per cent of all business meetings could be replaced by teleconferencing (Harkness, 1973).

As it turned out, these new media were less than a success; indeed, they were commercial failures. As a consequence, some researchers stressed that it was not just the efficiency of problem solving using teleconferencing or economic advantages that should be studied, but that 'one must consider the process of communication as well as the product' (Weeks & Chapanis, 1976). Or: 'To reach . . . understanding requires the answers to at least two questions: How do people naturally communicate with each other? And, how are natural human communications affected by devices through which people converse?' (Chapanis, Parrish, Ochsman, & Weeks, 1977).

Kiesler, Siegel and McGuire (1984) have taken these suggestions seriously and have reported a number of studies addressing the issue of communication changes via computer-mediated communication. They were able to demonstrate that computer-mediated communication affects participation, decisions and interactions among group members differently from face-to-face communication. They attribute this difference to lack of norms and informational feedback, absence of social influence cues, and depersonalization due to the lack of nonverbal involvement in computer-mediated communication. Similarly, Kiesler and Sproull (1992) found that computer-mediated group discussions compared to face-to-face discussions lead to more delays, more unconventional and risky decisions, but also to more explicit advocacy, and more equal participation of group members. Whether this 'equalization phenomenon' (Dubrowsky, Kiesler, & Sethna, 1991) can be considered positive or negative certainly depends on the context and the norms and aims of a group or an organization.

Certainly, picture telephones, teleconferencing or e-mail may have advantages compared to face-to-face communication: interactions are more problem-centred, and less concerned with relationship aspects and emotions (Stoll, Hoecker, Krueger, & Chapanis, 1976). Economically, they help to reduce travel and accommodation costs (Dickson & Bowers, 1973) and may allow decentralization of project teams, and installation of home workplaces. But the low acceptance rate (which is nowadays changing somewhat in industry) indicates that social psychological processes have to be taken into account. One aspect may be that 'being on camera' restricts behaviour and induces negative emotions (Weeks & Chapanis, 1976). This prediction of negative emotions is also made by the social-psychological concept of 'objective self-awareness': when confronted with oneself via a camera or a mirror this theory predicts that shortcomings and negative discrepancies between the ideal self and the real self will usually be detected and will result in negative moods and emotions (Duval & Wicklund, 1972). A 'social embarrassment' situation (Egido, 1988), with a 'sense of social presence and mutual knowledge' (Egido, 1988) is created with which users are not yet familiar.

Furthermore, in comparison to direct face-to-face interaction, information which is important in direct interaction is lost, like gaze and eye contact or spatial proximity, which implies reduced social feedback (Strickland, Guild, Barefoot, & Paterson, 1978). 'A group's culture sets the tone for its meetings, and the physical environment in which meetings take place is not only a direct reflection but a facilitator of this culture' (Egido, 1988, p. 17). This reduced nonverbal exchange between interaction partners results, for instance, in reduced consensus in discussion groups, and less stable group hierarchies and leader structures (Strickland et al., 1978). 'Less time is spent socializing,' according to Egido. Furthermore, subjects find it more easy to communicate assertive messages via letter or telephone than in face-to-face interaction (Furnham, 1986). It may well be that this lack of hierarchy is one reason why some media are not accepted widely, despite their advantages (Mintzberg, 1973). Even repeated exposure to teleconferencing does not seem to change these aspects to a large degree (Strickland et al., 1978).

Social skills we have acquired in early childhood when using conventional telephones are not developed when we are confronted with new media like the picture telephone. In fact, this medium – if it becomes a success (which seems doubtful when one considers the above-mentioned optimistic predictions and their failure, an interesting question for social psychology in itself) – may require the establishment of new norms and regulations of communicating. When using a conventional telephone one, for instance, does not have to bother about clothing or hair-do, or one may use a telephone while being in the bathroom. With a picture telephone this all changes drastically, especially in less private and more formal communications, as in business. A picture telephone, on the other hand, might also become a status and power symbol, an instrument to impress others, a status which portable telephones have reached today in certain populations.

Norms might also have to be established when one wants to switch off the camera of the picture telephone. Attribution theory informs us that such behaviour may lead to inferences that the person has something to hide and it may become difficult to explain to an interaction partner why one does not want to expose oneself to the camera. But would such media allow new (and commercial) applications? (Think what possibilities there might be for telephone sex!)

After these more general remarks on relationships between the media and social psychology, some research examples for different areas will now be presented. No attempt can or will be made to be exhaustive; instead the selection of studies has been guided by topics which are considered attractive and interesting and which may be of specific interest to researchers in social psychology.

Research examples

Research in impression formation via media

Research in impression formation has made considerable use of stimulus presentation via different media to answer questions such as, for example, to what degree impressions of other people are determined more by the visual channel of information transmission than by the vocal channel. Such studies are often referred to as 'multichannel' studies. The general aim is usually to determine the relative impact of different cues or channels on impressions and attributions. Similar attempts may be found in the area of studies on attitude change, where the aim is to compare the efficiency of different media in changing attitudes (e.g. television vs. radio vs. print media; Chaiken & Eagly, 1976; Andreoli & Worchel, 1978).

Mehrabian's well-known 'formula' stating that impressions are determined 55 per cent by visual information, 38 per cent by vocal cues and 7 per cent by verbal content (Mehrabian, 1972), is an extreme (and much discussed) example in this area of research. The superiority of the visual channel over the vocal channel in transmitting information and determining impressions claimed by Mehrabian was also found in studies by Burns and Beier (1973) and Archer and Ackert (1977). Studies showing that in general nonverbal behaviour is more important in determining impressions than verbal behaviour are reported by Argyle, Salter, Nicholson, Williams and Burgess (1970), and by Argyle, Alkema and Gilmour (1971). Studies that tried to distinguish information within the visual channel (for instance facial expression and bodily posture) were conducted by Dittmann, Parloff and Boomer (1965) and by Domangue (1978). Contrary to most studies, Domangue (1978) found that verbal information dominates the impact of nonverbal information cues. It seems that there is no general dominance of one or the other channel in determining attributions, but that, depending on the situation, one channel may become more salient than others (Domangue, 1978).

It is impossible here to mention or discuss the multitude of multichannel studies conducted so far, so only a few other examples will be given. Rosenthal and his collaborators found that the dominance of the visual channel claimed by Mehrabian seems to be true in general but that differential effects due to the type of information transmitted (here different emotions were studied) and the channel have to be taken into account (compare Zuckerman, Lipets, Hall, & Rosenthal, 1975; DePaulo, Rosenthal, Eisenstat, Rogers, & Finkelstein, 1978). This means that some emotions are detected more easily when one has access to visual information (e.g. the smile as a powerful indicator of joy), while other emotions are at least equally well detected via the vocal channel (e.g. anger). Similar effects were found by Scherer, Scherer, Hall and Rosenthal (1977), though this study was not concerned with emotion attributions but with personality attributions. Using the 'profile of nonverbal sensitivity' (PONS; a test intended to measure the ability to 'read' other persons; Rosenthal, Hall, DiMatteo, Rogers, & Archer, 1979), this research group again was able to show that although there seems to be a general dominance of the visual channel, especially in facial information, differential effects have to be taken into account. For instance, when facial and bodily posture cues are given simultaneously, the latter seem to distract attention from the facial information, thus leading to less reliable judgements of emotions.

Ekman, Friesen, O'Sullivan and Scherer (1980) stressed the importance of such effects by concluding for their study that 'no single channel (face, body, or speech) was consistently most highly correlated with the whole person judgments' (p. 272). Friedman (1979) arrived at the same conclusion, stating that his results 'support the notion that the whole scenario (that is not only one nonverbal channel, but the combination of all nonverbal channels given) is crucial' (p. 465).

Research predominantly concerned with discrepant cues between nonverbal channels (e.g. a positive verbal message spoken with an angry voice and an angry facial expression) was conducted by Bugental and collaborators. In a series of studies (Bugental, Kaswan, & Love, 1970; Bugental, Kaswan, Love, & Fox, 1970; Bugental, Love, Kaswan, & April, 1971; Bugental, 1974), they were able to show that given discrepant messages in different nonverbal channels the visual channel accounted for about twice the size of variance of judgements than both the verbal (content) and the vocal (tone of voice) channel. Bugental, Kaswan and Love (1970) conclude that 'any model (linear or nonlinear) of conflicting communication would thus have to include a strong weighting for the visual component of messages' (p. 652). This implies (like the results found by Rosenthal and others) that in terms of information integration simple additive or averaging models are not sufficient to describe the processes going on.

Another aspect relevant to person perception and to media is the *situational context* in which a specific behaviour is embedded. Movie director Alfred Hitchcock once argued that in a movie it is not the actor's task to produce affects and tension. Instead, the director creates contextual information, using cutting and editing techniques, which would guide a viewer to infer certain attitudes or emotions not immediately evident from the actor's expressive behaviour itself (Truffaut, 1975). Soviet movie director Lew Kulechov in the 1920s argued in a similar way and at one time produced three short movies showing in a first take either a dead woman, a dish of soup, or a girl playing, and in all three movies an identical second take presenting an actor with a neutral facial expression. It is said that viewers were very impressed by the thoughtfulness expressed by the actor when viewing the dish of soup, by the sadness expressed when watching the dead woman, and by the happy facial expression when confronted with the playing child (see Kristaponis, 1981), a phenomenon later referred to in cinematography literature as the 'Kulechov effect'. A neutral facial expression is interpreted as containing some emotional meaning, but this meaning is in fact conveyed by contextual information (for an overview of this area of research see Wallbott, 1990).

Such anecdotes point to the importance of a longstanding question which is discussed in research on emotion attributions: whether person information (especially facial expression) or contextual information (for instance, information on situation antecedents presented in movie takes) is more important in determining emotion attributions. Figure 12.4 presents an example of a stimulus combination, where the emotion of the woman depicted on the left had to be judged (from Wallbott, 1990). The reader when looking at this figure may realize that the context (here the second person depicted) may indeed influence impressions of the target person to some degree.

In a review concerning this question Ekman, Friesen and Ellsworth (1982) arrived at the conclusion that in general facial expression will dominate contextual information in determining emotion attributions, the only exception being that contextual information becomes more influential when facial expression is more ambiguous and less intense than context information. Unfortunately, this review does not distinguish between different modes of presentation of information within the person domain and the context domain. Person information (facial expression) may be presented using photographs or the dynamic presentation of film or video. Context information may be presented using verbal descriptions of emotion-arousing situations, photographic depiction, or dynamic presentation via film or video. It seems necessary to distinguish between different paradigms (see Wallbott, 1990).

One of the most influential paradigms within this realm was introduced by Goodenough and Tinker (1931) using a *person-scenario* approach, in which static person information (photographs of facial expression) is combined with verbal context information (verbal descriptions of emotion-arousing situations). This paradigm was used in more or less the same way in studies by Frijda (1958, 1969), Watson (1972), Knudsen and Mutzekari (1983), and

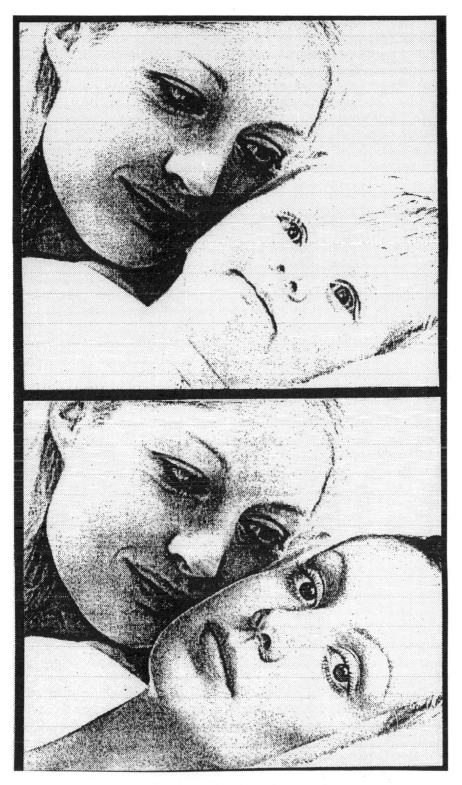

Figure 12.4   An example of context manipulation demonstrating context effects on the recognition of emotional facial expression (from studies in Wallbott, 1990)

Wallbott (1986, 1988). The general conclusion that can be drawn from these studies is that facial expression dominates context information in determining emotions attributed to the person.

The second paradigm relevant to this question uses *candid pictures* (Munn, 1940), i.e. photographs of situations that have actually occurred and which may be found in magazines and newspapers. The photographs depict persons experiencing an emotion within a context indicating what elicitors aroused this emotion. As with the person-scenario approach the experimental design is the following: one group of judges is confronted with the person information only (by masking parts of the photograph conveying situation information), a second group is confronted with context information only (by masking the person), and a third group of judges is confronted with the combined information (in the person-scenario paradigm, photograph plus verbal situation description; in the candid picture paradigm the complete photograph). Studies using the candid picture paradigm were conducted by Vinacke (1949), Cline (1956), Turhan (1960), Forgas and Brown (1977), Spignesi and Shor (1981), and Wallbott (1988). Interestingly enough, these studies found that in most cases contextual information was at least as influential as person information. This contrasts with the findings of studies using the person-scenario paradigm. The visual presentation of context information may lead to more 'vividness' or 'immediacy', resulting in a larger impact on emotion attributions.

Studies trying to replicate experimentally the ideas of Hitchcock or Kulechov by employing dynamic stimulus presentation are relatively rare. Goldberg (1951) studied the phenomenon within a *movie clip* paradigm by producing two short movies consisting of four takes each, the last take of which was identical in both movies (showing a woman screaming). Context information suggested a fear experience in the first movie, and a joyful experience in the second movie. Results supported the Kulechov effect: the fear context led to more fear judgements while the joy context resulted (though not as powerfully) in more joy judgements. Isenhour (1975) cites unpublished studies by Foley (1966) and Kuiper (1958). In both studies a neutral facial expression presented in the last take of several films – each time preceded by different context information – was judged according to the emotion suggested by the situation information provided in the preceding take.

Finally, research is available concerning certain *formal aspects of media presentation*, such as camera angle, and possible ways of recipient manipulation. To cite Zillmann, Harris and Schweitzer (1993): 'He or she [the photographer] may elect to take a shot of a person's face from above or below, from the front or the side, with light coming from the left or the right, from close range or afar. It is this selectivity, in fact, that has been suspected of giving photographers the power to wield undetectable influence' (p. 107).

A number of studies indicate that certain photographic aspects are indeed able to influence impressions. Tannenbaum and Fosdick (1960) have shown that the light angle used on photographs may influence sympathy ratings for the persons depicted. In this study persons lighted from a 45-degree angle were judged more positively than those lighted from other angles. Fosdick and

Tannenbaum (1964) demonstrated that camera angle (frontal, frog-like perspective, bird-like perspective) influences judgements of activity and potency. Other studies indicate that even very minute manipulations of camera angle may have similar effects (cf. Mandell & Shaw, 1973; McCain, Chilberg, & Wakshlag, 1977; Tiemens, 1970; Kepplinger, 1987). Often these studies found that a frog-like perspective enhances judgements of potency. Zillmann et al. (1993) manipulated perspective (close range, intermediate, and distant) as well as camera angle (frontal level, lateral level, lateral below, and lateral above) and found a number of significant effects on personality and competence judgements. Frontal-level portrayals, for instance, generally resulted in more negative evaluations of the persons depicted than other camera angles, while lateral non-level portrayals in particular lead to more positive evaluations.

Mass media contents

Here only two examples for research topics will be mentioned: *gender stereotypes* and prejudice as conveyed by the mass media; and *ethnic groups* and related prejudices. Research on gender stereotypes has a long tradition. It has been demonstrated that, for instance, evaluation of the quality of manuscripts depends on the ascribed gender of the author (Cline, Holmes, & Werner, 1977). If manuscripts are attributed to female authors, people tend to judge them more negatively. Males and females are portrayed rather differently – usually to the advantage of males – in TV shows, advertisements or children's TV programmes (cf. McArthur & Eisen, 1976; Goffman, 1979; for an overview see Harris, 1989). An experimental study by Walstedt, Geis and Brown (1980) demonstrated that such stereotypes as transmitted by the mass media are by no means without effect. The authors were able to show significant effects of TV advertisements with conventional gender roles in contrast to advertisements with reversed gender roles on female subjects' self-confidence and independence of judgement. Both, self-confidence and independence, were significantly reduced after exposure to gender stereotype-confirming advertisements. Some results of this study are depicted in Figure 12.5.

Another example of gender discrimination in the mass media is the 'face-ism' concept, introduced by Archer, Iritani, Kimes and Barrios (1983), and confirmed by a number of studies (see Sparks & Fellner, 1986; Schwarz & Kurz, 1989; Zuckerman, 1986). Face-ism starts from the idea that people can be depicted in photographs in different ways, i.e. a close-up or a full-body presentation. Archer et al. (1983) found that not only in newspapers and magazines but even in art portrayals females are usually depicted with a predominance of the body, males with a predominance of the head/face (i.e. males are more often shown in close-up). On the other hand, photographs of persons in close-up are judged more positively than full-body representations. Archer et al. argue that these findings taken together indicate discrimination against females in the (print/photo) media.

A number of studies have shown that cues like race or ethnically un-equivocal names may elicit prejudices against members of outgroups (see

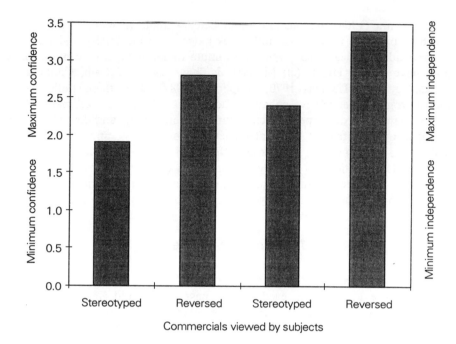

Figure 12.5 *Impact of TV commercials with traditional and reversed gender roles on women's self-confidence and conformity (data from Walstedt, Geis, & Brown, 1980)*

Wallbott & Schleyer, 1990). It is important to note that for some subjects 'everything we know about some kinds of people comes from television' (Harris, 1989, p. 37) or the mass media in general. This implies that the media may induce stereotypes or at least may strengthen them. Clark (1969) has identified four stages of portrayal of minority groups in television: (1) nonrecognition (total ignorance); (2) ridicule (members of a minority group are shown as dislikeable or incompetent); (3) regulation (few, but some members of the minority group appear in positive roles); and (4) respect (the group appears in the same full range of roles as the majority). A good example of a process (moving from stage (1) to stage (4)) is the function of African-American people in US-American television. While African-Americans were almost nonexistent in television during the 1960s, since than at least some blacks have appeared in advertisements, and some even in leading roles (the prime examples being Sidney Poitier and Bill Cosby). Studies from the 1970s indicate that at that time about 8 per cent of all prime-time television characters were African-American (Gerbner & Signorelli, 1979), which is still not 'respect', but certainly an improvement.

Although the picture is improving, it still seems that cues identifying a person as a member of a minority group may foster prejudice and stereotypes. A recent discussion in the German print media was concerned with the fact that quite often in newspaper reports on crimes the ethnicity of the wrongdoer is

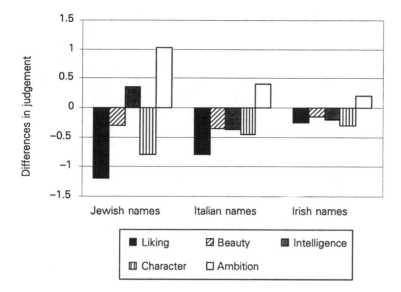

Figure 12.6 *Differences in judgements of portrait photographs with and without ethnically unambiguous names attached to photographs (data from Razran, 1950)*

explicitly mentioned (i.e. a Turk, a Bulgarian, or a member of another immigrant group). One may ask whether this explicit information may direct readers' impressions and attributions into a biased direction. In a recent study (Wallbott, 1994) it was tested whether such cues, as presented in newspaper reports on criminal delicts, would result in similar changes in recipients' perception of criminals. From daily newspapers 40 reports concerning criminals were selected. These reports were presented to judges, whose task was to determine the wrongdoer's responsibility for the crime, his or her intention, guilt, etc. on five-point-scales, as well as the number of days, months, etc. the person should spend in jail. A Latin square design was used to vary the ethnic characterization of wrongdoers (no characterization, 'West German', 'Turkish', 'East European immigrant', and 'Black African'). Results indicated significant interactions between ethnic characterization and judges' gender. Females in particular were somewhat prone to prejudice elicited by the ethnic characterization, especially when the wrongdoer was introduced as being of Turkish origin.

These results can be interpreted with respect to the possible effects of newspaper reports on recipients' perception of criminals. A number of studies arrived at similar conclusions. Razran (1950), in an old but ingenious study, showed that ethnically unambiguous names changed the impressions perceivers had of persons as depicted in photographs in the direction of the respective stereotypes, in this study especially for Jewish names (for a similar approach see Wallbott & Schleyer, 1990). Some of Razran's results are depicted in Figure 12.6. Ugwuegbu (1979) demonstrated that reports on cross-racial rape led to much stronger guilt attribution when the defendant was characterized as being of the other race (white vs. black), especially when the race of the victim was the same as the judges' race.

It is interesting to note (and this is also true for the present chapter) that most of the research and the discussions concerning mass media have almost exclusively focused attention on negative, 'bad' influences of the media. It is rarely mentioned what positive, 'good' influences the media (especially TV) may have, with the notable exception of the 'Children's Television Workshop' and its studies concerning the positive influences of *Sesame Street* and other children's programmes (see Bryant, Alexander, & Brown, 1983) on children's abilities, social competence, etc. It might also be worth studying positive impacts of the mass media in other areas outside specific children's programmes. Consider, for instance, *Star Trek* fans. It might be an interesting research question to examine whether such people are less prejudiced than other groups. Given that the *Enterprise* crew is, among others, composed of an African-American, an Asian, a Russian, and an alien, one might expect fewer stereotypes in the *Star Trek* fandom, since they are exposed to such positive role models and examples of outgroup members!

Mass media impact

Winterhoff-Spurk (1989) has described the history of media impact research as starting from the idea of a strong, direct and uniform media impact (the campaign research by Lasswell, 1927), which soon had to be revised because it was shown that 'opinion leaders' may mediate media's direct influence on the recipient (Lazarsfeld, Berelson, & Gaudet, 1944). Furthermore, the uses-and-gratification approach (see Roberts & Bachen, 1981) and different attempts at recipient typologies demonstrated that the impact of the mass media is far from uniform, resulting in a number of theories of 'weak' media impact, such as the knowledge gap hypothesis (Tichenor, Donohue, & Olien, 1970). This theory states that both well and less well educated persons benefit in terms of knowledge from mass media information, but the better-educated benefit more: i.e. the gap is enlarged by the mass media. The agenda-setting hypothesis (McCombs & Shaw, 1972) asked to what extent topics of discussion are 'made' by the media and to what extent just a reflection of society and daily life. Most important are different theories concerning the *cultivation of beliefs* (especially Gerbner, Gross, Morgan, & Signorelli, 1986).

The hypothesis concerning cultivation of beliefs exists in different shades of weak or strong relations postulated between media exposure and acquired beliefs (for an overview see Winterhoff-Spurk, 1989). It basically states that in contrast to pre-mass-media times our knowledge of the world, our beliefs and attitudes are not shaped by our everyday experiences, but instead by the mass media, and here the most predominant medium is television. Fiske and Hartley (1978) described television as being dramatic, episodic, mosaic-like and concrete, thus focusing attention on singular events, and hindering complex thinking and understanding of abstract relationships. An anecdote may help to explain the cultivation of beliefs hypothesis. Recently, German newspapers reported on a study with young Bavarian pupils whose task it was to name the predominant colour of cows. It was reported that the majority of the pupils believed that cows are lilac! It comes as no surprise that one of the most popular Swiss chocolate and sweets producers, which advertises heavily in German television and in the print media, uses a lilac cow as its brand symbol!

Most influential may have been Gerbner's studies and ideas (see Gerbner & Gross, 1976). He argued that if television does indeed cultivate our beliefs this should be even more so for those who watch more television than others. A famous study by Gerbner and Gross (1976) illustrates that idea. The authors found that heavy TV viewers were more prone to the belief that they were likely to become a victim of a crime themselves than were those who watched less TV. Others studies in the same vein indicated that TV users tended to overestimate the percentage of certain occupations in modern society (like policeman or detective, medical doctor – those occupations often seen in TV drama; see Winterhoff-Spurk, 1989).

A simple test may demonstrate the plausibility of the cultivation of beliefs hypothesis. The reader may try to guess the percentage of all crimes committed in Germany during 1993 which were murders. Well, the answer is much less than 1 per cent. The prediction would be that most people, and again especially heavy TV users, would overestimate this percentage to a large degree, because our knowledge concerning crime is for the most part second-hand knowledge we receive from the mass media. Murder is shown far more frequently in the media (whether on news programmes or crime drama) than crimes like fraud or theft, which in reality are far more frequent.

On the other hand, two arguments show that the cultivation of beliefs hypothesis may be too simple. Winterhoff-Spurk (1989) has conclusively demonstrated that people are well able to distinguish between what he termed personal-real knowledge (knowledge from our own immediate experiences), medial-fictional knowledge (knowledge gathered from fictitious TV programmes), and medial-real knowledge (knowledge gathered from non-fictitious media coverage such as news programmes). Thus, we usually do not confuse media information with own personal experiences. Secondly, some studies (cf. Doob & MacDonald, 1979) were able to demonstrate that the relation Gerbner and Gross (1976) found between TV consumption and fear of becoming the victim of a crime is a correlational one, but not in any case a cause–effect relationship. One simple mediating variable identified was the neighbourhood where people lived. Those living in areas with high crime rates also tended to watch more TV, or to put it in other words when crime rate was used as a covariate the relationship vanished (for a general, also methodological critique see Hirsch, 1980, 1981).

Another aspect of the influence of the media on beliefs and attitudes may be mentioned. Especially in the USA, the role of different media, specifically radio and television, on *political election processes* is a matter of debate. McLuhan (1964) claimed that during the Kennedy–Nixon debates in the early 1960s radio listeners got a rather positive impression of Nixon, while Kennedy

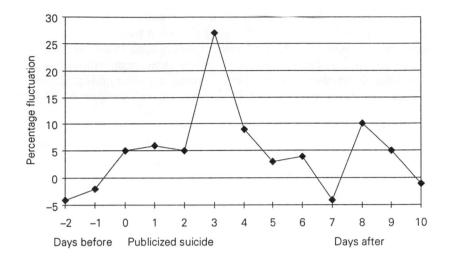

Figure 12.7   *Changes in motor vehicle accident fatalities before, during and after suicides covered in the mass media in California, 1966–73 (data from Phillips, 1986)*

gained much sympathy from TV viewers. Meyrowitz (1985) argued that the movie camera allowed US President Wilson to appear larger than he actually was, that on radio President Roosevelt could communicate powerfully without the fact that he was hampered in walking being revealed, and that television was the ideal medium for the young Kennedy and his style of delivering talks. Research in attitude change has demonstrated in a similar way that television compared to radio or to print media focuses recipients' attention more on the communicator than on the message (cf. Chaiken & Eagly, 1976). This implies that in television it may be less important what arguments a communicator is presenting, and more important how these are presented. A sympathetic and attractive person should profit from television, and President Kennedy was just that: young, good-looking, attractive. Less physically attractive communicators (Nixon, for example) on the other hand should not benefit from television appearances; their impact might be stronger via radio, and in fact probably strongest in the print media, where recipients' attention is almost totally focused on the message, and not on peripheral communicator characteristics.

Finally, there is ample evidence that the media shape not only our beliefs, but to some degree also our behaviour. The most dramatic examples of such an influence are studies on *suicide in reaction to media coverage* of the suicide of other people. The effect found in a number of studies is sometimes called the 'Werther' effect (Remember Goethe!) (Wasserman, 1984). Imitative suicide was found, i.e. a significant increase in suicides after soap opera suicide stories (Phillips, 1982), in general after publicized suicides (Phillips, 1979; for some results see Figure 12.7), and especially after celebrity suicides (Wasserman, 1984). Wasserman (1984) conducted a very elaborate analysis of suicide data from 1968 to 1977, controlling for economic shifts, seasonal effects and other potential influence factors, but still found a significant relation for celebrity suicides. An overview of studies in this area also covering statistical and methodological problems is provided by Phillips (1986). Another example of dramatic media influence is a study by Phillips (1983), which analysed the incidence of homicides during the period 1973–78 in the USA after heavy-weight boxing prize fights. He was able to show that immediately after prize fights homicides increased by about 12 per cent, with the greatest increases after heavily publicized fights. This impressive finding leads straight to the next aspect to be discussed: the relation between aggression, aggressive media content and media consumption.

Far from being resolved is the question of aggression and the media. It seems that the amount of aggressive portrayals, especially on television, is increasing over the years (see Gerbner's reports on the 'violence profile' in US-American television; cf. Gerbner, Gross, Signorelli, & Morgan, 1980). Different hypotheses have been proposed concerning the relationship of media consumption to aggression, ranging from the idea of catharsis, to general arousal theories, whereby heightened arousal may lead to aggression (cf. Zillmann, 1979), to habituation processes, i.e. that repeated exposure to aggression in the media may lower thresholds for one's own aggression, to postulated contrary inhibition effects, i.e. that exposure to aggression may even inhibit aggressive behaviour.

It is not possible here to review the multitude of studies and books published on the topic. Reviews concerning the relation between TV violence and viewer aggression tend to find some positive relationship, but usually a very weak one, and often the direction of causality is unclear (Andison, 1977). In a review concerning the effects of media violence on children, Heath, Bresolin and Rinaldi (1989) postulate a positive relationship, but identified as mediating variables among others the predisposition to aggression, a violent family environment, identification with aggressive media characters, belief in the reality of the media presentation, and the depicted consequences of media violence. In a meta-analysis of 32 samples where the relationships between television violence viewing and peer-nominated aggression were measured Rosenthal (1986) found a median correlation of $r = 0.19$ (with a maximum $r = 0.38$ and a minimum $r = -0.16$). His conclusion is that the effects are small indeed, but still do exist. A similar but far more extensive meta-analysis was presented by Hearold (1986). She analysed 230 studies (resulting in 1,043 statistical effects reported) for a ten-year period, which were published in about 40 leading psychology journals. This analysis resulted in an average effect size of 0.25 for anti-social behaviour. Some of Hearold's results concerning the effects of different portrayals of TV violence are illustrated in Table 12.2. The effect sizes reported there indicate, for instance, that human or real violence is more influential than cartoon violence, or that justified violence is more influential than unjustified violence, while rewarded vs. punished violence or motives of the TV aggressor do not seem to make much of a difference.

Though this finding is fairly typical, the discussion about whether there

Table 12.2 *Effect sizes for different types of media violence*

Comparison	Average effect size	Standard deviation	No. of effects	% negative
Human or real vs. cartoon violence	0.48	0.67	5	20
Real vs. fictional or stylistic violence	0.30	0.65	20	25
Without consequences vs. consequences shown	0.26	0.53	19	42
Justified vs. unjustified violence	0.39	0.46	12	17
Rewarded vs. punished violence	−0.01	0.70	10	30
Mixed vs. all bad motives or actions	0.15	0.29	5	40

Based on N = 71 studies or effects. The effect size is computed by subtracting the mean of the treatment type listed second (e.g. 'cartoon') from the mean of the treatment type listed first (e.g. 'Human or real'). A positive effect means that the treatment type listed first is, on the average, more powerful; standard deviation = standard deviation of effect sizes. No. of effects = number of studies in which the respective effect was found. % negative = percentage of studies in which the respective effect has not been verified.

Source: data from Hearold (1986, p. 103)

exists a positive relationship between media violence and aggression, and if so, whether this is a causal one, still is far from being resolved. Friedrich-Cofer and Huston (1986), for instance, argue that there is strong evidence supporting a positive relationship, while Freedman in the same issue of *Psychological Bulletin* (1986) maintains that data so far are too weak to make any causal statements. Some studies indicate that the causality may not go from TV viewing to aggression, but the other way around, i.e. from aggression to TV viewing (people tend to watch aggressive programmes when they feel angry or aggressive; cf. Gunter, 1983; Fenigstein, 1979). Huesmann and Malamuth (1986) nevertheless arrived at the conclusion that 'the majority of the researchers in the area are now convinced that excessive violence in the media increases the likelihood that at least some viewers will behave more violently' (p. 1). The authors state that some of the divergent results may be due to economic interests (the media industry), to selectivity in reviews and meta-analyses (some authors do not consider laboratory studies to be relevant), and finally to the theoretical orientation of the researchers. Their hunch is that psychologists with a developmental social-learning perspective take the problem of aggression and media somewhat more seriously than others. Still, even the conclusion by Huesmann and Malamuth is far from satisfying. 'Likelihood' and 'some viewers' indicate that many factors are involved in the relationship and any direct and monocausal relationship between media consumption and violence is an oversimplification. In an interesting study Bybee, Robinson and Turow (1985) asked experts in the field (486 mass media scholars) what their beliefs were concerning the effects of TV on children. Two results are of specific interest: first, TV's ability to increase aggression was given a relatively low emphasis in comparison to other topics like 'decrease in reading behaviour'; and secondly, highly published experts tended not to judge TV's effects as negatively as their lesser-published colleagues!

Some authors' mistrust in laboratory studies of the topic also demands critical acclaim. For such studies it is very often true that:

- Subjects are exposed only very briefly to media violence (only during the short laboratory session).
- Only immediate effects are tested (often employing Buss's 'aggression machine'; see Buss, 1961; a methodology criticized with respect to external validity).
- Only a certain form of aggression is studied (dependent on the operationalization: in the aggression machine paradigm this is usually the number, intensity or duration of electric shocks administered to a confederate of the experimenter).
- Cumulative and long-term effects of media violence are not studied.
- The subject usually is alone when confronted with the violence, while in reality TV or movies are quite often watched together with friends or peers, i.e. audience effects or emotional contagion cannot be taken into consideration, though these might be of crucial importance (Leyens, Herman, & Dunand, 1982; Dunand, Berkowitz, & Leyens, 1984).
- The target of subjects' potential aggression is usually fixed: either a second 'subject', as in the aggression machine paradigm, or the experimenter.
- For subjects it is often quite easy to detect that the media violence they are exposed to is fictitious (in many older studies Kirk Douglas in the movie *The Champion* was presented to many, many subjects; nowadays scenes from *Rambo* and similar movies are used again and again).
- It is often neglected that much of media violence (for example on TV) is not at all fictitious, but very real – reports about wars, assaults, etc. in news programmes, the popular 'reality TV' shows, aggression in sports. Whether exposure to 'real' as compared to 'fictitious' violence makes a difference has rarely been studied.
- In laboratory studies subjects are primed to concentrate on aggressive contents (stimuli are edited, for instance, so that only the aggressive incident from a movie is presented, and this stimulus is decontextualized from the non-aggressive parts).

Still the number of studies and experiments concerned with aggression and media influences is abundant. A literature search in *Psychological Abstracts* reveals more than 5,000 journal articles, not to mention book chapters, and publications outside of psychology. As noted above, some recent concern has focused on aggressive rock music videos. MTV made Beavis and Butthead dumb, subversive and aggressive because of their heavy exposure to rock videos. As one example, a small study will be described, concerned with a recent aspect of aggression in the media, namely aggression in rock music videos (especially rap and hard rock), whose discussion arose with the advent of MTV and other music video channels, and their success with young viewers in particular. Based on a study by Wallbott (1989), it asked whether different types of content of (rock) music videos affect recipients' judgements of emotions and general impression qualities conveyed by a piece of music (for details see Wallbott, 1992a). Forty judges were confronted with 30 music videos (10 each with neutral, sexual and aggressive content) or the respective pieces of music without pictures and were asked to judge the emotions conveyed, as well as the amount of interest etc. of the videos and pieces of music. Results indicate that a 'euphorizing' effect of music videos (more positive emotions and less negative emotions are ascribed to the videos than to the pieces of music; see also Wallbott, 1989) can be confirmed, but only for videos with neutral or sexual content. Aggressive videos on the other hand conveyed more negative emotions (especially anger, but also sadness). Furthermore, videos with sexual or aggressive content were not judged as more interesting or more dynamic than neutral videos or the respective pieces of music. With respect to the recent discussion of the potential dangers of sexual and aggressive videos, results indicate that the 'dangers' may not be too large.

This short discussion of media exposure and violence can be closed with a citation from Huesmann (1986):

> the conditions most conducive to the learning of aggression seem to be those in which the child has many opportunities to observe aggression, in which the child is reinforced in his or her own aggression, and in which the child is the object of aggression. Nevertheless, in such situations only some children become seriously aggressive . . . no single factor by itself seems capable of explaining more than a small portion of the individual variation in aggression. (p. 127)

This it not to deny possible media influences, but one should keep in mind that media violence (especially movies and TV) is only one of this multitude of factors.

Mediated communication influences

In olden days calling somebody on the telephone was a relatively straight-forward business. Either the person would be reached and would respond, or the person would be away from the telephone, and one had to try again later. Nowadays, things have changed. For some time now, *telephone answering machines* (TAMs) have been around, and they are supposed to make life with the telephone easier, both for the caller and the person called. The caller may leave a message and thus may hope for a return call, and the person called may leave home or work, still being sure that telephone calls will reach her/him, though some time after the event. Commercially, TAMs are a big success and are sold in ever increasing numbers. Besides portable telephones, the fax, and electronic mail, the TAM is certainly one of the most important and influential developments of modern telecommunication technology.

To my knowledge not much research has been conducted to date to test how this telecommunication facility affects communication via the telephone line. Social psychology enters the scene in several ways when encountering a TAM:

- Some money is lost because one has to pay for the (possibly futile) call. Before the age of TAMs one either reached the person one wanted to reach (and had to pay for the call) or one did not (and had to pay nothing). Now one has to pay even if one would hang up and try again later, with the chance of not reaching the other person again, but being confronted with the TAM a second time. On the other hand, it may be cheaper to leave a short message, thus delegating the expenses for the later call to the partner.

- One may experience a loss of subjective freedom. One wanted to talk to somebody, but instead one has to talk to a TAM (this aspect is certainly different in some areas of business. When calling a telephone shopping agency one might expect to be confronted with a TAM). Loss or restriction of subjective freedom is a key feature of the theory of psychological reactance (Brehm, 1966). This theory predicts that in such situations people tend to restore their freedom and will become increasingly angry when this turns out to be difficult.

- When complying with the TAM's request to leave a message one may be confronted with another problem: one is instructed to present a free, unrehearsed speech which will be recorded in front of an audience (even if it is an audience of one) without receiving any feedback. The theory of objective self-awareness (see p. 321) and its extensions to trait characteristics (Duval & Wicklund, 1972; Wicklund, 1975) incorporates predictions for these types of situations: specifically, enhanced negative emotions, arousal and 'stress'.

Recently Wallbott conducted two studies addressing some of these questions in relation to TAMs (Wallbott, 1995). A questionnaire approach to attitudes toward TAMs and feelings/emotions and strategies when confronted with TAMs revealed that in general subjects' attitudes were moderately positive. Their emotional reactions when confronted with a TAM are not very pronounced, with the possible exception of reported anger. That subjects on average report more anger than other feelings and emotions is in line with predictions derived from the theory of psychological reactance (see above). It seems indeed that TAMs evoke more anger than other negative (and also positive) feelings. Thus, the prediction that encountering a TAM implies a momentary loss of freedom can be confirmed.

In a second (experimental) study, type of task and type of TAM message were varied in order to study possible effects on subjects' feelings and evaluations and on their speech behaviour during the telephone conversations. The results confirm that the type of message used on a TAM had a rather profound effect on subjects' evaluations. In general a warm message was evaluated more positively than either a cold or a neutral one. Furthermore, subjects reported feeling more unpleasant and more angry when being confronted with a cold message rather than a warm one. Thus, the data indicate that the type of message on a TAM may influence emotions and evaluations in a negative way. As the TAM message may quite often be the first information about a possible interaction partner (if this number/person is unknown and called for the first time), one might expect strong 'primacy' effects on impression formation, especially rather negative impressions, if the message is a cold one. These negative first impressions may be accentuated by the emotion of anger when a cold message is encountered during the delivery of a rather difficult task. This result is in line with predictions made on the basis of the theory of psychological reactance. It seems indeed that reactance is fostered especially when a task is difficult and the caller is confronted with a cold message on a TAM.

So one might want to pay more attention to the characteristics of the TAM message one uses on one's own TAM in order to preclude such negative impressions and emotions. It should be mentioned that the evaluations and emotions subjects reported were in general more favourable when they were confronted with a human interaction partner instead of a TAM. This finding may indicate that at least the majority of the subjects might prefer to talk to a human being instead of a TAM. This aspect certainly demands further research.

Picture telephones and teleconferencing have been mentioned before. Besides problems of acceptance and efficiency it is important to know how picture quality (which is reduced in commercially available picture telephones compared to TV quality standards) affects person perception and impression formation. This question is of some importance to telecommunication, especially low-cost teleconferencing (projects are in progress on the feasibility of using ordinary personal computers as terminals in teleconferencing systems). The term 'low-cost teleconferencing' implies that the pictorial quality of such systems is somewhat limited, for instance with respect to spatial resolution, contrast resolution, picture size and frame rate.

Wallbott (1991, 1992b) conducted two studies testing the impact of pictorial distortion on emotion recognition. Results of one study (1991) using still photographs of facial emotional expression indicated that variation in three modes of deterioration (spatial resolution, contrast resolution and picture size) in general did not affect recognition rate or mean intensity of emotion judgements within a very large range. If at all, recognition rate dropped only when spatial resolution of stimuli was reduced to about 38×38 pixels and further when this highly reduced spatial resolution was combined with a highly reduced contrast resolution. In all other conditions, i.e. for manipulations of contrast resolution and picture size, recognition rate remained fairly high and stable.

In the second study (Wallbott, 1992b) video stimuli were distorted both with respect to spatial (pixel) resolution and with respect to temporal resolution (frame/refreshment rate). Furthermore, judges were confronted with a control condition, presenting the undistorted stimuli. Type of information provided (close-up of the face versus full body recording) was also manipulated. Results indicated (besides main effect for type of emotion encoded as well as for type of information provided) that emotion recognition was somewhat impaired by reduction of both spatial resolution and temporal resolution.

While for reduction of spatial resolution a linear decrease in recognition rate was found, indicating that the worse spatial resolution is, the worse emotion recognition is, for the manipulations of temporal resolution the decrease in recognition rates was already evident at the first step of distortion, and further reductions in temporal resolution did not lead to further decreases in recognition rate. Rather slight manipulations of frame rate reduced recognition rate, but then no further changes occurred, while slight manipulations of spatial resolution did not have such a strong effect. Restrictions in temporal resolution seem to impair decoding of emotion in general, to some degree independently of the type of emotion conveyed and also of the fact whether facial or bodily expression information is provided, while impairment of spatial resolution leads to differential effects on emotion recognition, depending on type of information provided (recognition from bodily expression in particular is impaired) as well as on type of emotion encoded.

Research concerned with teleconferencing and especially with the picture telephone is still rare, though if this medium is more widely distributed, this area might be a challenging and fascinating topic for social psychology. The same seems to be true for other newly introduced telecommunication media. The fascinating research by the Kiesler group on the effects of e-mail conferences on group structures and group decisions was described above. All these new media, their acceptance and usage, and especially their effects on interaction and communication, should be fruitful and highly important research topics for social psychologists in the future.

Final comments

No attempt has been made at an exhaustive coverage of media psychology in the present chapter. This would be virtually impossible, if one thinks, for instance, only of the numerous books written on just one topic in this area: aggression and the media. Instead an (admittedly heavily biased by the personal interests and research topics of the author) attempt was made to demonstrate the importance of social psychology for research in the media. If one defines media psychology more broadly than is usually done, classical social psychological topics like research and theorizing on attitude change or on impression formation are concerned with media. On the other hand, there seems to be some kind of reluctance of classical social psychology to address topics that are becoming evident with the advent and rise of new media. Changing communication habits and norms in association with picture telephones, and the problems of acceptance and reactance with respect to the telephone answering machine were just some of the topics mentioned.

Social psychology should take note of these changes in communication structures and opportunities. This seems important both from a theoretical perspective and from an applied point of view. From a theoretical perspective the introduction of new communication media, especially when these are as successful as the fax, e-mail, or answering machines, provides researchers with huge, but so far rarely used opportunities for all kinds of studies. Introduction of such new communication media provides giant field experiments in changing communication habits which ought to be studied. It may be that nowadays traditional research topics in media psychology and media sciences, which were mostly concerned with the 'mass media', will indeed become less important (that is not to say unimportant) in comparison to the vast changes and new possibilities new devices of mediated communication will bring to our daily lives, in private and in business. We are just one step away from the 'information highway' or we may already have entered it without realizing it, and it should be of vital interest to social psychology to learn more about the ways we use it and how this usage influences us. Taking the culture-pessimistic stance again and warning of possible dangers is no solution. Empirical research is needed and social psychology is the field of psychology to take care of that.

In this discussion of the relations between the media and social psychology, several types of media were distinguished, specifically mass media communication from mediated communication. An attempt has been made to shed some light on three areas in which media and social psychology are connected: (1) the use of media as a research tool in social psychology, which is important for instance in the area of non-verbal communication and impression formation research; (2) mass media content and impact, where among other topics the dissemination of stereotypes and prejudice via the mass media, aggression and the media, and the cultivation of beliefs hypothesis were discussed; and (3) influences of the media on communication processes, discussed here with respect to teleconferencing and telephone answering machines. Besides general considerations of the different topics, some selected research examples were presented for the different areas.

Further reading

Fowles, J. (1992). *Why viewers watch: A reappraisal of television's effects.* London: Sage.

Harris, R.J. (1989). *A cognitive psychology of mass communication.* Hillsdale, NJ: Lawrence Erlbaum.

Neuman, W.R. (1991). *The future of the mass audience.* Cambridge: Cambridge University Press.

Oskamp, S. (Ed.) (1988). *Television as a social issue.* Newbury Park, CA: Sage.

Sproull, L. & Kiesler, S. (1994). *Connections: New ways of working in the networked organization.* Cambridge, MA: MIT Press.

PART 4

THE SOCIAL PSYCHOLOGY OF SOCIETAL ISSUES

13

Aggression and Violence in Society

Barbara Krahé

Contents

There can be no doubt that aggression and violence are among the most pressing social problems facing the world today. While large-scale aggressive conflicts between nations, ethnic groups and rival political factions have always been a reality, recent years have witnessed a number of particularly acrimonious conflicts, such as the Gulf War, the civil war in the former Yugoslavia, the battle over political power in Rwanda, and, most recently, the war between Russia and Chechnya over Chechen independence. It is a depressing, but realistic expectation that new examples will have to be added to this list by the time the present volume is published. In each of these conflicts, incredible hardship is inflicted on the civilian population, claiming the lives of innocent people or destroying their livelihoods. Beyond the political level, aggression and violence are widely perceived to be on the increase in our everyday social life as well. Crime rates have reached alarming figures across the Western world, and virtually all areas of life are affected by specific forms of aggressive behaviour. Reckless driving, sexual and racial harassment, bullying at school, child and elder abuse in the family, robbery, hooliganism and vandalism are key words which illustrate the widespread nature of aggression and violence affecting people's lives.

Given the negative, often devastating impact of aggressive actions, two questions are of primary importance:

1. What are the origins and causes of aggressive behaviour?
2. What can be done to control aggression and reduce the incidence of aggressive acts?

Psychology in general, and social psychology in particular, have been centrally involved from the beginning in the attempt to answer these two questions. In the present chapter, theoretical work and empirical evidence are drawn from different areas of psychology to bring together the current state of knowledge about the causes, manifestations and consequences of aggressive behaviour as well as possibilities for its prevention. While this analysis must of necessity be highly selective, several recent volumes document the richness and diversity of psychological aggression research (e.g. Baenninger, 1991; Baron & Richardson, 1994; Berkowitz, 1993; Felson & Tedeschi, 1993; Goldstein, 1994a; Huesmann, 1994; Peters, McMahon, & Quinsey, 1992).

Starting from a brief discussion of how to define and measure aggression and violence, the present chapter offers a summary of the main theoretical approaches for explaining aggressive behaviour. This review will be followed by a look at attempts to identify determinants of aggression, distinguishing between determinants located at the level of the individual person (e.g. sex differences) and those located in the situation or social environment (e.g. media influences). In the remainder of the chapter, specific forms of aggression will be examined in more detail, organized into the broad categories of *interpersonal aggression* and *intergroup aggression*. The final section will be devoted to strategies and proposals for reducing aggression and violence, ranging from individual-centred psychological intervention to long-term measures implemented at the sociopolitical level.

Aggression and violence: definition and measurement

While 'aggression' is an established term not just among psychologists but also in the vocabulary of ordinary language, defining its exact meaning is by no means a straightforward task. As Krebs and Miller (1985) point out, definitions can focus on different aspects, varying in their implications for the identification and classification of behaviours as 'aggressive': they may concentrate on observable behaviours as opposed to intentions and motives, on verbal as opposed to physical aggression expressed in direct or indirect forms, on the psychological vs. physical effects of aggression, either immediate or long term. There appears to be general consensus nowadays that a purely behavioural definition of aggression, as 'a response that delivers noxious stimuli to another organism' (Buss, 1961, p. 1), falls short of capturing the psychological significance of the concept. Additional aspects have to be included in the definition to eliminate behaviours not commonly thought of as aggressive:

- the *intention* to cause harm to a person or damage an object (e.g. to exclude the driver killing a pedestrian who crosses the road without looking);
- the *expectancy* that the behaviour will result in harm to the target (e.g. to exclude the helper who aggravates the injuries of an accident victim by taking the wrong actions through lack of competence);

– the willingness on behalf of the target person *to avoid* the harmful treatment (e.g. to exclude the doctor who performs an operation on the patient's request).

The actual consequences of an aggressive action do not feature in the definition of aggression along these lines. The intention to cause harm is sufficient for labelling the action as aggressive irrespective of whether or not the intended effect is actually achieved: even a failed murder attempt represents an instance of aggression according to this rationale. The extent of the inflicted harm does, however, play an important role in deciding on sanctions to penalize the behaviour.

There has been some controversy about the aspect of norm violation as a further defining feature of aggression. Disciplinary measures taken by teachers or acts of physical self-defence are examples of behaviours which satisfy the criteria of intention, expectancy and desire of avoidance and should, accordingly, be classified as aggressive. Yet they are covered by social norms which turn them into accepted forms of social behaviour. However, as Berkowitz (1993) argues, limiting aggression to norm-violating or socially disapproved behaviour ignores the problem that the normative evaluation of a behaviour frequently differs depending on the perspectives of the people involved, rendering the identification of aggressive behaviours ambiguous. For example, some people regard corporal punishment as an effective and legitimate child-rearing practice, while others consider it to be a form of aggression.

A definition which takes these considerations into account was offered by Baron and Richardson (1994, p. 7) who define aggression as any form of behavior directed toward the goal of harming or injuring another living being who is motivated to avoid such treatment.

The broad definition adopted here covers diverse subcategories of aggressive behaviour, such as physical and verbal aggression, legitimate and illegitimate aggression, individual and group aggression. In contrast, the term 'violence' is more specific in meaning and usually refers to 'physically damaging assaults which are not socially legitimised in any way' (Archer & Browne, 1989, p. 11).

Concerning the psychological functions of aggressive behaviour, a fundamental distinction runs through the literature between affective (or hostile) aggression and instrumental aggression. This distinction reflects the awareness that the primary motive for the aggressive behaviour may be either the desire to harm another person as an expression of negative feelings or the aim to reach an intended goal by means of the aggressive act. The two types of motivation for aggressive behaviour may frequently coexist. Nevertheless, it makes sense to tease them apart because of the specific psychological processes involved.

Aggression has been *measured* in a variety of ways, depending on the type of question addressed by the specific research. Special measurement problems arise, however, from the socially unacceptable and harmful character of aggressive behaviour, often precluding the elicitation of overt aggression by the investigator. Available methods to study aggression can be assigned to two broad categories: *observation* and *asking* (cf. Baron & Richardson, 1994).

Observational methods can be used to record aggressive behaviour as it occurs in a natural context (e.g. Archer, 1989) or to examine the effects of specific experimental manipulations in a laboratory situation (e.g. Berkowitz, 1989a; Carlson, Marcus-Newhall, & Miller, 1989). Methods which ask for the occurrence of aggressive behaviour without actually observing it include the use of self and peer reports of aggressive behaviours (e.g. Pan, Neidig, & O'Leary, 1994), the analysis of archival records (e.g. Anderson, 1989) and the application of personality scales as well as projective techniques to assess dispositional tendencies towards aggression (e.g. Buss & Perry, 1992; Rosenzweig, 1981). Each of these different methodologies, as well as their respective advantages and shortcomings, will be illustrated by specific examples in the course of this chapter.

Theoretical explanations of aggression and violence

The variety of forms and contexts in which aggressive behaviour presents itself is matched by the diversity of theoretical explanations of the causes and origins of aggression. In trying to come to terms with this diversity, four main lines of theorizing can be distinguished, each focusing on different psychological mechanisms in explaining aggression: aggression as an innate instinct, aggression as a goal-directed drive, aggression as mediated by cognitive appraisal, and aggression as learned behaviour.

Aggression as an innate instinct

The first and earliest line of theoretical development regards aggressive behaviour as the expression of a genetically rooted *instinct* which is an innate part of human (and animal) nature. Freud (1920), in his dual instinct theory, proposes that individual behaviour is driven by two basic forces: the life instinct (*eros*) and the death instinct (*thanatos*). While *eros* drives the person towards pleasure-seeking and wish-fulfilment, *thanatos* is directed at self-destruction. Due to their antagonistic nature, the two instincts are a source of sustained intrapsychic conflict which can be resolved by diverting the destructive force away from the person on to others. Thus, acting aggressively towards another person is seen as a mechanism for releasing destructive energy in a way which protects the intrapsychic stability of the actor. In his notion of *catharsis*, Freud acknowledges the possibility of releasing destructive energy through expressive behaviour, but with only temporary effects. According to this view, aggression is an inevitable part of human nature beyond the control of the individual, and it is interesting to note that Freud revised his earlier model, centering on *eros* only, by adding a destructive force after witnessing the violence of World War I.

From an entirely different perspective, a very similar account of aggression was offered by Lorenz who, as an ethologist, developed his ideas about human aggression mainly from the study of animal behaviour. Arguing that aggressive behaviour serves an adaptive function in the evolutionary development of a species by favouring the survival of its strongest and genetically fittest members, he proposes a detailed model of how aggressive energy is set free (Lorenz, 1966). He assumes that the organism continuously builds up aggressive energy. Whether or not this energy will lead to the manifestation of aggressive behaviour depends on two factors: (a) the amount of aggressive energy accumulated inside the organism at any one time; and (b) the strength of external stimuli (e.g. the sight or smell of a predator) triggering an aggressive response. These two factors are inversely related: the lower the energy level, the stronger the stimulus required to elicit an aggressive response, and vice versa. If the energy level becomes too high without being released by an external stimulus, it will overflow, leading to spontaneous aggression. In applying this model, well supported by animal studies, to human aggression, several additional assumptions have to be made. Most notably, it has to be explained why the inhibition against killing members of their own species, widely observed among animals, obviously fails to generalize to humans. Here, Lorenz (1974) argues that strong inhibitions against intraspecies killing were superfluous in the early history of mankind when fists and teeth were the only, relatively innocuous, weapons with which to attack each other. With the development of ever more sophisticated and lethal weapons, the fact that there is no innate inhibition to counterbalance the potential for destroying one's own species has given rise to basically uncontrolled levels of aggression and violence. Like Freud, Lorenz regards aggression as an unavoidable feature of human nature. However, he assigns greater significance to the possibility of releasing aggressive energy in a socially acceptable way, e.g. through sports competitions and noninjurious aggressive actions, by which highly destructive forms of aggression may be avoided.

Aggression as a goal-directed drive

The reception of instinct-related explanations of aggression has been a critical one for several reasons, not least because of a shortage of empirical evidence to support them (cf. Baron & Richardson, 1994). However, the idea that there is a force within the organism which, in conjunction with external events, leads to aggressive behaviour has been retained by an influential line of research postulating an aggressive *drive* as motivating aggressive behaviour. Unlike an instinct, a drive is not an ever-present, continuously increasing source of energy but is activated only if the organism finds itself deprived of means to satisfy a vital need. A drive then serves as an energizing force directed at terminating the state of deprivation.

In the famous *frustration-aggression hypothesis* (Dollard, Doob, Miller, Mowrer, & Sears, 1939; Miller, 1941), aggression is explained as the result of a drive to end a state of frustration, whereby frustration is defined as external interference with the goal-directed behaviour of the person. Thus, the experience of frustration activates the desire to act aggressively against the source of the frustration, which in turn precipitates the performance of aggressive behaviour. Whether or not frustration will eventually lead to an aggressive response depends on the influence of mediating variables, such as fear of punishment for overt aggression or unavailability of the frustrator as inhibiting factors or the presence of aggression-related cues as promoting factors. These factors may also explain why aggression is frequently 'displaced' away from the frustrator on to a more easily accessible or less intimidating target.

As Berkowitz (1989b) points out in his reformulation of the frustration-aggression hypothesis, negative affect induced by the experience of frustration is another important mediating variable between frustration and aggression. In predicting when frustration will lead to aggression through the mediation of negative affect, the appraisal of the frustrating experience plays an important role. Aggressive responses are more likely to be triggered via negative affect if the frustration is perceived as deliberate and illegitimate by the target person than if it is seen as accidental or covered by social norms. Frustrations arising out of competitive interactions are also particularly prone to lead to aggressive responses via the elicitation of negative emotional arousal. It is important to note that according to this view, frustration is but one source for the generation of negative affect. Other types of aversive stimulation, such as fear, physical pain or psychological discomfort, through their capacity to produce negative affect, are also recognized as antecedents of aggression (cf. Berkowitz, 1993).

Aggression as mediated by cognitive appraisal

Whether or not an individual will react with an aggressive response to an aversive stimulation depends to an important degree on how the stimulation is interpreted by the recipient. As we saw above, frustrations are especially likely to cause aggression if they are interpreted as being deliberate and unjustified interferences with the actor's goal-directed activities (cf. also Geen, 1990 on the role of attributional mediators of aggression). Moreover, if emotional arousal is unspecific and its origins not readily apparent to the individual, he or she tries to make sense of the arousal by drawing on informational cues present in the situation. In his 'excitation transfer' model, Zillmann (1978) argues that aggression can be triggered by physiological arousal from a neutral or irrelevant source in conjunction with the attribution of this arousal to aversive stimulation within the situation. He found that individuals who carry residual arousal from a physical activity into an unrelated social situation in which they are exposed to a provocation are more likely to respond aggressively to the provocation than non-aroused individuals. The affectively neutral arousal serves to intensify the negative arousal caused by the provocation in that it is interpreted in the light of the salient situational cue, i.e. the provocation.

Another model stressing the impact of cognitive processes on aggressive behaviour was proposed by Huesmann and Eron (1984; Eron, 1994). In their social cognitive approach, they propose that social behaviour in general, and aggressive behaviour in particular, is controlled by behavioural repertoires acquired in the process of early socialization. Behaviour routines or 'scripts' are acquired by the child to regulate his or her behaviour in a wide range of situations. Incorporated in the scripts are guidelines as to the appropriate forms as well as contexts in which scripted behaviour may be performed. For example, failure to learn the limiting conditions for the expression of overt aggression and to develop alternative behavioural programmes for the settlement of conflicts will lead to the inappropriate enactment of aggressive scripts which may form the basis for long-term adjustment problems.

Aggression as learned behaviour

Unlike the view that aggressive behaviour is an inevitable expression of human nature, learning theorists have stressed that aggressive behaviour is produced to a large extent by 'nurture', i.e. acquired through learning processes like most other forms of social behaviour (e.g. Bandura, 1983). Both learning through reinforcement and punishment as well as observational learning have been shown to be powerful mechanisms for the acquisition and performance of aggressive behaviour. To the extent that individuals are rewarded for aggressive behaviour, e.g. a boy being praised for settling a disagreement with a peer by pushing him to the ground, the likelihood is increased that the same or a similar behaviour will be shown again in the future. Equally, if influential others are seen as acting in an aggressive way, this has been shown to instigate aggressive response in the observers as well. In the classic study by Bandura, Ross and Ross (1963), children were shown films of two adult models behaving either in an aggressive or a nonaggressive way towards a large inflatable doll. When the children were subsequently given the opportunity to play with the same doll, those who had watched the aggressive model showed more aggressive behaviours towards the doll than those who had watched the nonaggressive model. These findings suggest that observing an influential model (such as a person of high status or competence, a well-liked model, or a popular TV character) may lead to the acquisition of the observed behaviour even if the model has not been reinforced for his or her behaviour. In predicting whether or not the learned behaviour will actually be *performed*, the perceived consequences of the model's as well as the observer's behaviour do play an important role. These external stimuli, along with the person's internal standards and normative knowledge, regulate the performance of aggressive behaviour. The more positive the effects of the aggressive behaviour, the greater the likelihood that it will be imitated. The social learning perspective has been the major theoretical approach for understanding the effects of media violence on aggressive behaviour, which can be regarded as a paradigmatic case of observational learning.

Altogether, the approaches reviewed in this section have shown that there is a diversity of theoretical accounts of how and why aggressive behaviour occurs, each highlighting different aspects in answering this basic question. One important point of comparison refers to their implications concerning the controllability and reduction of aggressive behaviour. While the early instinct- and drive-related approaches entail a basically pessimistic view, theories stressing the mediating role of cognitions and learning processes imply possibilities of strengthening the inhibitory factors against the performance of overt aggression.

Determinants of aggression

The broad theoretical perspectives discussed in the previous section seek to provide general explanations of how aggressive behaviour is instigated and performed. In the present section we will look at variables which allow a differential diagnosis of aggression, i.e. serve as contributory or counteracting factors with respect to the performance of aggressive behaviour. Three groups of determinants will be examined: (1) variables at the personal level which may help to distinguish between more or less aggressive individuals and groups of individuals; (2) situational influences of a transient or continuous nature which have an effect on the performance of aggressive behaviour; and (3) factors in the physical or social environment which influence the likelihood of aggression and violence.

Personal variables

A variety of variables have been examined as potential candidates for identifying individual differences in aggression (Baron & Richardson, 1994; Berkowitz, 1993). In the present section, we will concentrate on two prominent examples: sex and genetic make-up.

The assumption that men are generally more aggressive than women is well established in everyday observation, crime records as well as lay conceptions about gender. Systematic empirical research lends qualified support to this position. Meta-analyses of studies looking for sex differences in aggression confirm the claim that men consistently show more aggressive behaviour than women (e.g. Hyde, 1984; Eagly & Steffen, 1986), even if the difference is less pronounced than commonly assumed. It is larger for physical than for verbal aggression, but even on measures of verbal aggression, men tend to score higher than women. This is not so say, however, that female aggression does not exist (Keeney & Heide, 1994). A recent volume by Björkvist and Niemelä (1992) provides a comprehensive coverage of the different aspects of female aggression, including both biological and cross-cultural analyses (cf. also Farabollini, 1994).

Two models have been contrasted to account for the stronger aggressive tendencies among males: a biological and a social role model. According to the biological model, sex differences in aggression may be attributed at least in part to higher levels of testosterone in males. While some studies have found higher testosterone levels in aggressive as compared to nonaggressive males, the overall evidence is inconsistent, prompting the search for moderating variables that may affect the link between hormones and aggressive behaviour (Benton, 1992). From a sociobiological perspective, it has been argued that aggressive behaviour has been favoured by natural selection in the evolutionary history of the human species. Aggression represents a highly adaptive behaviour pattern for males in that it facilitates access to attractive (i.e. young and healthy) females for the purpose of reproduction (e.g. Thornhill & Thornhill, 1991; Wilson & Daly, 1985). In contrast to both hormonal and evolutionary explanations, the social role model argues that stronger male tendencies towards aggressions and stronger female inhibitions against aggression are largely the result of gender-role socialization (Eagly, 1987). Findings which show that women more frequently report feelings of guilt and anxiety as accompanying responses of aggressive behaviour support this line of reasoning. Unlike the evidence on the existence of sex differences in aggression, which is fairly clear-cut in suggesting higher levels of aggression in males, the task of explaining why these differences occur is far from being resolved.

The second variable proffered to account for individual differences in aggression has to do with a specific genetic make-up characteristic of aggressive individuals. According to this view, aggression is linked to a particular genetic code resulting in an increased likelihood of the carrier becoming aggressive and criminal (cf. Baron & Richardson, 1994, for a more detailed discussion). Indeed, there is evidence to suggest that abnormal sex chromosome patterns (i.e. an extra Y chromosome) are related to higher levels of aggression. Some authors have argued, however, that the apparent relationship between chromosome abnormalities and aggression is due to the mediating influence of low intelligence frequently observed in these individuals. Twin studies provide another source of evidence for the impact of genetic factors on aggression, showing that monozygotic twins tend to be more similar in their aggressive dispositions than dizygotic twins. Demonstrating the impact of genetic make-up on aggression does not, however, imply a deterministic view of the manifestation of aggressive behaviour. Instead, situational and environmental factors are likely to interact with these person variables in producing aggressive behaviour (DiLalla & Gottesman, 1991; Widom, 1989). While certain situational factors exacerbate aggressive tendencies, others exert a mitigating influence. In the next section we will look at situational factors shown to increase the likelihood of aggressive behaviours. Situational forces leading to a reduction in overt aggression will be considered in the final section.

Situational variables

As part of the frustration-aggression hypothesis reviewed above, it has been claimed that aggression is a likely, but not an inevitable consequence of frustration. In predicting when exactly frustration will give rise to aggression, Berkowitz and LePage (1967) were the first to highlight the importance of *aggressive cues in the environment* in triggering aggressive responses. They showed that subjects who had previously been frustrated and were thus in a state of negative arousal were more likely to act aggressively towards the frustrator in the presence of a weapon than in the presence of a neutral object. A meta-analysis by Carlson, Marcus-Newhall and Miller (1990) confirms the impact of situational aggressive cues as mediators of aggression across a wide range of studies. They even found an effect, albeit weaker, of aggressive cues on subjects in a neutral mood state, supporting the view that aggressive cues within a situation activate ('prime') cognitive schemata related to aggression and thus increase the salience of aggressive response options. This line of research has immediate practical implications concerning the availability and accessibility of weapons and other aggression-related objects. It has been shown consistently that the very fact that a weapon is visually present within the situation increases the likelihood of aggressive responses.

Another variable to be discussed in this context is *alcohol consumption*. While this is not strictly speaking a situational influence, it still represents a situation-specific, transient state which may explain why individuals show aggression in one situation and not in others. The meta-analysis conducted by Bushman and Cooper (1990) clearly supports a causal link between alcohol intake and aggressive behaviour. Experiments on this issue typically administer controlled amounts of alcohol to the subjects and then compare their levels of aggressive behaviour to those who received a placebo (who thought they would receive alcohol but were given a nonalcoholic drink instead). Other studies have included a control group of subjects who were correctly informed that they would receive a nonalcoholic drink, still others had an additional 'anti-placebo' group of subjects who were led to believe that they would receive a nonalcoholic drink but were given an alcoholic drink instead (see Figure 13.1).

Comparisons between the two placebo groups and the control group speak to the impact of cognitive expectations concerning alcohol intake on the performance of aggressive behaviour. Across a range of 56 studies, Bushman and Cooper (1990) found that subjects who had been given alcohol scored higher on measures of aggression than subjects who received the placebo, suggesting that the pharmacological effects of alcohol are responsible to a large extent for the enhanced levels of aggression. This conclusion needs to be qualified, however, because of the failure to find a significant difference between the anti-placebo and control groups: both groups believed they had not received alcohol, but the anti-placebo group had in fact been given an alcoholic drink. If the effects of alcohol were purely pharmacological, there should have been an aggression-enhancing effect of the anti-placebo manipulation. As Bushman and Cooper (1990) point out, the pharmacological and psychological effects of alcohol consumption occur together in real life: people usually know whether or not they have drunk alcohol. Therefore, the alcohol vs. control group comparison is seen as the most realistic measure of alcohol effects on aggression. Here, evidence from a range of 32 studies shows that alcohol is, indeed, a significant contributory factor to the manifestation of aggressive behaviour. This conclusion is supported outside the laboratory by Wolfgang's (1958) comprehensive analysis of homicide statistics.

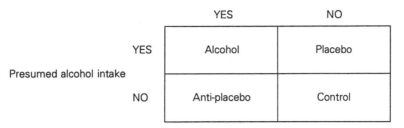

Figure 13.1 *Experimental comparisons for studying the effect of alcohol on aggression (based on Bushman & Cooper, 1990)*

Beyond the role of alcohol and specific aggression-related situational cues, a variety of environmental stressors have been identified as causes and/or mediators of aggressive responses (cf. Baron & Richardson, 1994; Geen, 1990). *Temperature* has been found consistently to be linked to aggression in naturalistic observations and archival analyses of criminal records: uncomfortably high temperatures are related to increased levels of aggression (Anderson, 1989). Rates for homicide and other violent crimes are highest during the hot summer months and in years with particularly high average temperatures. They were also found to be higher in hotter as opposed to more temperate geographical regions, even within the same country (Goldstein, 1994a; cf. however, Nisbett, 1993, for a disconfirming analysis of the temperature hypothesis and alternative interpretation of regional differences). Evidence from laboratory studies is less consistent, but a number of potential artefacts in laboratory experiments are discussed to account for this discrepancy (cf. also Geen, 1990).

Noise is another environmental stressor linked to aggressive behaviour. In its capacity as intensifier of ongoing behaviour, noise can reinforce aggressive behavioural tendencies already present in the actor. In a study by Geen and O'Neal (1969), subjects were shown either a violent or a nonviolent film and subsequently instructed to deliver electric shocks to another person as punishment for errors on a learning task. While they administered the shocks, half of the subjects were exposed to a loud noise. It was found that the noise manipulation only led to higher aggression in those subjects who had previously seen the violent film. Another effect of noise is to impair the person's tolerance for frustration, thereby increasing aggressive behavioural tendencies following a frustration. However, it does not seem to be the noise *per se* which facilitates aggression but the fact that noise is often an uncontrollable aversive event. If the noise is perceived as controllable by the person, its impact on aggressive behaviour appears to be greatly reduced.

Finally, *crowding* has also been found to intensify aggression. Unlike density, which is defined in terms of objective spatial constraints, crowding refers to the perception of those constraints as aversive. The same level of spatial density may give rise to feelings of crowding for some people but not others or in certain contexts only. While density as such cannot be linked to aggression in a conclusive fashion, crowding has been found to increase the likelihood of aggression in a variety of settings, such as crowded living conditions of families, prison environments and violation of personal space (Geen, 1990). It appears that the primary effect of crowding is to produce negative feelings which, in turn, lower the threshold for aggressive behaviour; and it seems that men are more negatively affected by crowded conditions than women.

Goldstein (1994a) has presented a comprehensive review of the effects of ecological factors on aggression, going beyond the impact of specific environmental stressors. He breaks down environmental influences into physical and social aspects, each considered at the micro level (e.g. the street), the meso level (e.g. the neighbourhood) and the macro level (e.g. the region). Conceptualizing aggression as the product of person–environment interaction, he also provides strategies of 'ecological intervention' designed to prevent or reduce the occurrence of aggression.

Media influences

In the public debate on aggression and violence, media influences are commonly quoted as *the* most powerful environmental factor responsible for the apparently increasing levels of aggression, especially among children and adolescents. Indeed, a cursory and occasional 'sampling' is sufficient to suggest to the everyday observer that television programmes are full of aggressive episodes, often of a highly violent nature, easily accessible even to young viewers. The same is true for home videos, cinema films, computer games, comics, etc. In conjunction with alarming figures on the average number of hours per week spent using these media by children from pre-school age, these observations foster the conviction that the portrayal of violence in the media has a causal effect on viewers' readiness for aggression. Some critics even claim that media consumption, irrespective of its aggressive contents, works as a contributory factor for aggression and anti-social behaviour.

Over the past twenty years or so, a large body of evidence has been accumulated to examine this view through systematic empirical research (see Berkowitz, 1993). Focusing on the adverse effects of depictions of physical violence, two main lines of inquiry can be identified in this research:

(a) studies on the immediate and short-term effects of violent media contents on aggressive behaviour;
(b) research on the long-term consequences of sustained and prolonged media exposure.

While the latter research has concentrated on children and adolescents as primary target groups, the former has also been concerned with media effects on adult viewers.

Among the short-term effects of media violence, two issues have received considerable attention: the direct imitation of specific violent acts observed in

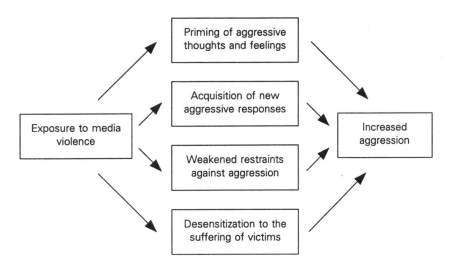

Figure 13.2 *Psychological effects of media violence (adapted from Baron & Byrne, 1991, p. 412)*

films, videos, or on TV, and the effects of exposure to pornographic material on sexual aggression. Direct imitation, or copycat violence, features with some regularity in crime reports. Deliberate as well as accidental killings were shown to have resulted from children's re-enactments of scenes they had observed in the media. In adults, copycat imitations of specific fictional actions or widely publicized real events, such as hijackings, are also well documented in the literature, including the impact of spectacular self-killings on subsequent suicide rates (the 'Werther' effect; see Jonas, 1992 and Chapter 12, this volume). Additional evidence by Miller, Heath, Molcan and Dugoni (1991) identified a significant link between heavyweight boxing fights and increases in homicide rates. Apart from the direct imitation of specific forms of violence publicized through the media, the aggression-enhancing effect of exposure to violent media contents has been demonstrated in laboratory as well as natural contexts (Wood, Wong, & Chachere, 1991; cf., however, Freedman, 1988, for a challenge of the view that there is a *causal* link between TV violence and aggression). In trying to explain *how* the observation of violent interactions works to increase aggressive tendencies in the observer, several mechanisms have been identified (Figure 13.2).

First of all, aggressive episodes serve as cues priming aggressive thoughts and feelings in the observer (Rule & Ferguson, 1986). There is evidence showing that subjects exposed to a violent videotape reported more aggressive thoughts and stronger feelings of hostility than those exposed to a nonviolent film (e.g. Bushman & Geen, 1990; Langley, O'Neal, Craig, & Yost, 1992). This priming mechanism is particularly obvious with regard to copycat crimes in which not just a general readiness for aggression but a highly specific course of action is triggered by the observed media violence. Secondly, the consequences of the aggressive act for the model play a decisive role: if the model's behaviour is rewarded by success or presented as acceptable (e.g. as a form of revenge), then it is more likely to be imitated. Finally, exposure to violent media contents may weaken the viewers' inhibitions against aggression by making aggression appear a common and pervasive feature of social interactions. Repeated exposure to media violence also leads to habituation, which in turn reduces the viewers' sensitivity to the victims' suffering. Evidence for the disinhibiting role of media influences comes from a wide range of studies into the effects of pornography on sexual aggression. These studies show that subjects exposed to violent pornography rated the impact of a subsequently presented rape scenario on the victim as significantly less severe and express more permissive attitudes about sexual violence than those without prior exposure to the pornographic material (Linz & Malamuth, 1993; Linz, Wilson, & Donnerstein, 1992).

Beyond the demonstration of short-term aggression-enhancing effects of media violence, several studies have examined the long-term implications of continuous exposure to violent media contents (see Huesmann & Miller, 1994, for a review). Longitudinal studies are also better equipped than cross-sectional analyses to address the crucial issue of a *causal* link between media violence and aggression. After all, in contrast to the hypothesis that viewing violence leads to aggression it may reasonably be argued that higher levels of aggression lead to a stronger preference for aggressive media contents. Eron and his colleagues conducted an extensive longitudinal study, starting with a sample of eight-year olds in 1960. At the first data point, measures of aggressiveness and preference for violent TV programmes were obtained for each child. These measures were taken again 10 years later. Cross-lagged panel analyses revealed that for boys preference for violent programmes at third grade was significantly related to aggressiveness 10 years on, while aggressiveness at age eight turned out to be unrelated to preference for TV violence a decade later. These findings suggest that television violence acted as a causal influence on aggressiveness rather than the other way round. (Lefkowitz, Eron, Walder, & Huesmann, 1977). Subsequent studies, including cross-national comparisons, show consistently that boys become more aggressive the more they are exposed to violence in the media (Huesmann & Eron, 1986; Singer & Singer, 1981). For girls, the evidence is less conclusive. Lefkowitz et al. (1977) failed to find a significant relationship between media violence and aggressiveness for their female sample, yet other studies found parallel patterns of results for boys and girls (e.g. Botha, 1990; Milavsky, Kessler, Sipp, & Rubens, 1982).

Thus, there is ample evidence to support the view that exposure to violence in the media leads to the development and performance of aggressive behaviour, by instigating aggressive thoughts and feelings, by conveying more or less explicit evaluations of aggression as rewarding and/or justified, and by demonstrating specific ways of acting aggressively that may be incorporated into the behavioural repertoire of the viewer. As we saw in the course of this section, other variables have been identified which also exert a significant influence on the manifestation of aggressive behaviour. While we are still a far cry from having the total picture of why and when aggressive behaviour occurs, at least some basic pieces of the jigsaw are now more fully understood.

Aggression and violence as social problems

Up to this point, we have been talking about aggression as an umbrella term covering a wide range of distinct forms of aggressive behaviour. It is now time to examine in more detail a number of specific manifestations of aggression in society, each of which carries its own unique characteristics. This analysis will begin with aggressive behaviours located within the context of *interpersonal encounters* in which participants interact as individuals rather than members of particular social groups. Next, different forms of aggression will be examined which involve *intergroup encounters* and arise out of confrontations between different groups or between individuals by virtue of their group membership.

Interpersonal aggression

Aggressive behaviours performed by one person against another can take many forms, varying in terms of the means employed (direct vs. indirect; verbal vs. physical) as well as the severity of the consequences for both actor and target. The present discussion will be limited to severe forms of aggressive behaviour which not only have dramatic effects on the targets and perpetrators of such acts but also pose a challenge to society at large.

Criminal homicide

Taking another person's life is clearly the most extreme form of aggressive behaviour. Most legal systems distinguish between different forms of criminal homicide, depending on the intentionality and foreseeability of the killing. While *murder* requires premeditation, intent and malice on the part of the killer, behaviour which leads to the death of another person is qualified as *manslaughter* if the lethal consequences were the result of prior provocation or caused by criminal negligence.

Berkowitz (1993) presents a detailed discussion of the psychological literature on criminal homicide. He points out that the killing of a stranger and the killing of a person known to the offender have very different dynamics and underlying motives. Killings between previously acquainted persons frequently arise from arguments which get out of hand under the influence of strong affective responses (often aggravated by alcohol). In these cases, the victim has typically played an active part in the cycle of violence culminating in his or her death (see Goldstein, 1994a, on victim-precipitated murder). In terms of a distinction introduced earlier, many cases of lethal violence against a victim known to the assailant are instances of *hostile aggression*. In contrast, killings of strangers are more likely to be acts of *instrumental aggression* in that they are committed in pursuance of some other goal (e.g. covering up a criminal offence, robbing a bank). Across a range of studies it has been found that homicides of both types are frequently committed by individuals with a previous record of criminal violence, suggesting that criminal homicide may be the extreme expression of a more general tendency towards physical violence rather than an isolated outburst of intense aggressive impulses. Leaving aside aggressive tendencies resulting from psychiatric disorders, such general inclination towards violence is likely to be the result of adverse socialization experiences (e.g. childhood abuse, association with delinquent peers) in combination with poorly developed skills for coping with these negative experiences (Blaske, Borduin, Henggeler, & Mann, 1989; Browne, 1994; Gresswell & Hollin, 1994). Socioeconomic stressors like low income, poor education and poor housing are additional, though not independent factors contributing to violent behaviour (Hsieh & Pugh, 1993). These factors may also serve to explain the disproportionately high rate of homicides committed by black offenders and the higher frequencies of homicide in large cities as opposed to smaller towns and rural settings.

Bullying

Lethal violence has always been at the forefront of public awareness of aggression as a social problem. In contrast, bullying is a relatively new addition to the list of anti-social behaviours recognized by the public and investigated by social as well as developmental psychologists. Even though it does not represent a criminal offence, bullying can have highly negative effects, clearly marking it as a form of aggressive behaviour.

The most extensive research programme into the causes, manifestations and consequences of bullying has been conducted in Norway by Olweus and his colleagues. According to Olweus (1994, p. 98), a person is bullied 'when he or she is exposed, repeatedly and over time, to negative actions on the part of one or more other persons'. In addition, bullying involves an imbalance of strength and power leaving the victim unable to defend him- or herself effectively against the negative behaviour. Unlike other aggressive acts which involve one-off or short-term attacks, bullying typically occurs continuously over extended periods of time, leaving the victim in a sustained state of anxiety and intimidation. Bullying can take both direct and indirect forms: direct bullying involves open, physical harassment of the victim, while indirect bullying consists of strategies leading to the exclusion and social isolation of the target. Bullying has been recognized as a social problem primarily among schoolchildren, and most of the research has been conducted with this group (e.g. Olweus, 1991; Rivers & Smith, 1994).

According to the findings reported by Olweus (1994) based on a sample of 130,000 Norwegian pupils aged between 8 and 16, bullying shows considerable prevalence rates. Nine per cent of his sample reported being bullied; 7 per cent admitted bullying others 'frequently' or at least 'now and then'. Studies from other Western countries suggest even higher figures (e.g. Bowers, Smith, & Binney, 1994; Branwhite, 1994). In the Norwegian study, boys featured more prominently as both targets and perpetrators of direct bullying than girls. Victimization for both sexes showed a steady decline with age, while active bullying rates remained relatively stable across age groups. Thus, it seems that the youngest and most vulnerable students are particularly affected by harassment from bullies.

Moreover, Olweus's data provide clear-cut evidence as to the typical characteristics of victims and bullies, which confirms commonsense notions about bullying. The typical victim is an anxious, socially withdrawn child or adolescent, isolated from his or her peer group and likely to be physically weaker than most peers. In contrast, bullies are typically strong, dominant and assertive, showing aggressive behaviour not just towards their victims, but also towards parents, teachers and other adults. These findings suggest that bullying is part of a more general pattern of anti-social behaviour which is associated with an increased likelihood of deviant behaviour in adolescence and adulthood. A detached parent–child relationship, parents' tolerance of aggressive behaviour by the child and the use of aggressive child-rearing practices were found to play a crucial role in producing this anti-social behaviour pattern (Olweus, 1991).

Abuse and neglect in the family

While the ideal image of family life is one of warmth, affection and mutual support, reality shows that a range of serious, often prolonged forms of aggression occur within the family setting: the physical, sexual and emotional abuse of children, sibling aggression, marital violence and the problem of elder abuse and neglect by relatives (Browne, 1989).

As relatively powerless members of the family system, children are particularly at risk of becoming targets of aggressive behaviour from parents and other adult relatives. Corporal punishment is still practised in the vast majority of families, at least occasionally, as an accepted means of discipline. According to incidence rates reported by Straus and Gelles (1990), nearly 100 per cent of parents of young children reported having hit their child at least once in the preceding year. Serious forms of physical violence, leading to injuries in the child, were found at a rate of 110 per 1,000 children. In the UK, about 200 children are estimated to die every year as a result of injuries or maltreatment inflicted on them by their parents (Browne, 1989). Reliable incidence rates are hard to establish because many acts of child abuse go unreported or undetected, and true figures are likely to be much higher than those reflected in official crime statistics. This is particularly true for the sexual abuse of children, where despite rising reporting rates experts still estimate the true scale of the problem to be much greater than the available figures suggest (cf. Browne, 1994; Finkelhor, 1986).

Violence between spouses is an equally widespread, but under-reported problem. Survey data analysed by Straus and Gelles (1990) suggest that male and female partners are equally involved in violent exchanges. Other authors point out, however, that women more frequently engage in retaliatory rather than initiating acts of physical aggression and suffer more serious injuries than their male counterparts (e.g. Frude, 1994). Community- or charity-run shelters for battered women, which have mushroomed in recent years, reflect the growing threat posed to women and children by violent partners.

The problem of elder abuse and neglect by their caregivers has been recognized as another significant manifestation of domestic violence. Apart from the physical abuse of elderly family members, emotional abuse and material abuse have been identified as additional forms of maltreatment of the elderly (Eastman, 1989; Hornick, McDonald, & Robertson, 1992). Incidence rates are even harder to establish for elder abuse than for the other forms of domestic violence because the victims are usually confined to the domestic setting and have limited contact with people in the outside world who might be alerted to their situation. Moreover, the very fact that they are dependent on the care provided by the abuser works against the disclosure of abuse experiences.

Researchers on domestic violence stress that despite the different forms of aggression in the family, the underlying causes and mechanisms are quite similar (Berkowitz, 1993; Browne, 1989). They identify several interlocking factors common to the different forms of abuse discussed in this section:

- the existence of a clear-cut power differential, substantiated by economic factors, enabling the dominant person to enforce his or her needs through the use of physical aggression;
- childhood experiences of family violence by the abusive adults;
- a normative structure which condones the use of violence as a strategy of conflict resolution, leading to the transmission of aggressive response modes from one generation to the next;
- adverse social and economic conditions, such as unemployment and poor housing conditions.

In addition, both short-term and enduring behaviour patterns of the target persons, such as antagonistic behaviour of the child or dependent elder, play an important role in precipitating violent behaviour by family members.

Sexual aggression

Rape and other forms of sexual aggression against women have received growing attention over the last two decades, both in public awareness and by psychologists of different disciplines (Koss, Goodman, Browne, Fitzgerald, Keita, & Russo, 1994). While clinical psychologists have been concerned primarily with the immediate and long-term effects of sexual violence on the victim and with the development of appropriate intervention strategies (Koss & Harvey, 1991), social psychologists have concentrated on the antecedents and consequences of sexual violence in the context of social norms and gender roles.

In trying to identify the *causal factors* that lead to sexual violence, the majority of research has focused on the *offender*. A variety of interlocking causes has been suggested that induce men to commit sexually violent acts against women, such as emotional deficits in early socialization, biological processes including the operation of evolutionary principles, exposure to pornography, and exposure to a social environment which accepts interpersonal violence (Hall & Hirschman, 1991). Moreover, aspects of the social climate, such as widely shared gender stereotypes and the portrayal of sexual violence in the media, have been shown to contribute to the problem of sexual violence (Linz et al., 1992).

In studying the *consequences* of sexual violence, the emphasis has been on the *victim* and on *others* who learn about and react to her fate. Two major issues have been explored as part of a social psychological perspective on rape. The first refers to the reactions to victims of rape by members of the police, the legal system and the medical profession. This concern arose out of widespread public dissatisfaction with the way these institutions responded to the needs of victims of sexual violence. Systematic investigations demonstrating biased perceptions and unfavourable evaluations of rape victims by police officers, judges and jurors have played a significant role in prompting institutional changes to achieve a more sympathetic treatment of victims. The second line of inquiry refers to the social perception of rape victims in society at large. This research has its roots in the conceptual framework of attribution theory where the question of when and why there is a tendency to attribute responsibility to victims of rape has generated a large body of evidence (Krahé, 1988, 1991). It was shown that certain victim characteristics, such as low social status, higher number of sexual partners, pre-rape behaviour that is at odds with female role requirements, are linked with higher attributions of responsibility to the victim (and often correspondingly lower responsibility attributed to the attacker). At the same time, individual differences between observers have been found in the sense that individuals with a more traditional sex-role orientation or with a greater readiness to accept 'rape myth' as true tend to assign more responsibility to victims of rape (Lonsway & Fitzgerald, 1994). Sex differences, with men attributing more responsibility to victims than women, were found regularly, but not pervasively in the literature. Both institutional and individual responses to victims of rape frequently amount to the experience of 'secondary victimization' which can seriously impair the process of coping with sexual assault.

Recent years have also seen a rapid increase in research on two types of sexual assault: date rape and child sex abuse (Browne, 1994; Parrot & Bechhofer, 1991). Prevalance studies revealing that date rape is a large-scale problem in adolescents' and young adults' sexual relationships have been complemented by evidence on predictors (e.g. peer pressure) as well as perceptions of responsibility for date rape (e.g. as a function of who paid for the dating expenses). A related issue refers to the problem of marital rape, to which most countries still do not assign the status of a criminal offence (Russell, 1990). Child sexual abuse is a form of sexual violence committed mostly by members of the child's family or circle of acquaintances. In contrast to rape and sexual assault of adult victims, the sexual abuse of children is rarely confined to a single incident. It typically extends over multiple occasions, often continuing for several years. Sexual abuse by people from the child's immediate social environment can lead to traumatizing effects, especially since the child does not usually have a chance to escape from the abusive environment (Hanson, 1990).

Finally, psychologists have begun to explore the problem of sexual harassment, placing special emphasis on sexual harassment in the workplace and over the telephone (Koss et al., 1994; Sheffield, 1993). Even though in the public understanding these forms of sexual aggression are still widely regarded as more or less innocuous, there is now ample evidence documenting the lasting negative effects of prolonged sexual harassment.

Aggression as an intergroup phenomenon

In the previous section, different types of aggressive behaviour were examined which arose out of a confrontation between persons as individuals, regardless of their identity as members of a particular social group (cf. Mummendey & Otten, 1993, for a discussion of the relationship between interpersonal and intergroup aggression). We will now turn to instances of aggressive behaviour which are driven primarily by group processes, both within the aggressive group and in relation to the target group.

Rioting, hooliganism and gang violence

Following LeBon's (1896) early work on crowd behaviour, social psychologists have explored the notion that membership of large, anonymous groups leads individuals to behave in a more aggressive and anti-social fashion than they would on their own (Goldstein, 1994a). This notion has received considerable support through laboratory studies showing that groups do indeed show more aggressive behaviour than individuals. To explain this effect, Zimbardo (1969) introduced his theory of *deindividuation*, claiming that by becoming submerged in an anonymous group, individuals lose their sense of personal identity and responsibility and are thus less inhibited about showing negative social behaviour normally suppressed by their internal standards. Subsequent research has qualified the claim that individual behaviour always becomes more negative as a result of deindividuation (Diener, 1976; Reicher, 1984). Instead, a number of laboratory experiments showed that behaviour changes in accordance with the norms prevailing in the group context: when, for example, people were deindividuated by being dressed in Ku Klux Klan outfits, their behaviour became more aggressive; when they were deindividuated by having to wear a nurse's uniform, they showed less aggression than people acting as individuals (Johnson & Downing, 1979). Thus, there is clear evidence that individual behaviour becomes more extreme as a function of group membership, but the direction of the change towards either increased or decreased aggression is determined by the norms and salient cues inherent in the situation.

Systematic analyses of riots also disconfirm the earlier view that crowd action is uncontrolled, disorganized and irrational. In a detailed case study of a riot in the St Paul's area of Bristol, UK in 1980, Reicher (1984) showed that the riot was confined to specific targets within a confined geographical area and that the rioters had developed a sense of shared identity *vis-à-vis* their common enemy, the police. In his sociological analysis of 341 urban riots in the United States during the 1960s, McPhail (1994) rejects the view that rioting is the result of structural strain particularly affecting young black males living in socially deprived ghettos. Instead, he proposes a model in which rioting is seen as a behavioural response adopted by a person to meet a particular aim (e.g. pursuing a political goal, acting out aggressive feelings against another group). In summarizing his 'purposive action model', McPhail concludes that 'violent actors are neither the hapless victims of structural strain nor of psychological deindividuation. Purposive actors adjust their behaviors to make their perceptions match their objectives. They bear responsibility for those violent objectives and for the violent actions in which they engage' (McPhail, 1994, p. 25).

Football hooliganism represents a special case of crowd violence featuring prominently in Western Europe. Beyond dramatic incidents like the Heysel Stadium disaster in Belgium in 1989, violence arising in the context of football matches has led to a tragic number of deaths and serious injuries as well as to large-scale violent exchanges between rival football fans and the police. To come to grips with the problem, a variety of restrictions and control mechanisms have been introduced in recent years, such as banning the sale of alcohol before matches, developing strategic seating arrangements for opposing groups of fans and segregating opposing fan clubs on their way to and from the stadium. While the success of these measures has been limited, the need for security measures surrounding matches has, in itself, proven to be a serious safety hazard by impeding escape in the case of emergencies.

In their explanation of football hooliganism, Murphy, Williams and Dunning (1990, p. 13) argue that football hooliganism is a form of aggression typically engaged in by young working-class males. They identify a subculture of aggressive masculinity, 'predominantly, but not solely lower class', which provides the normative framework for the performance of violent behaviour by football fans. The significance of violence-condoning social norms is also reflected in an Italian study in which violent fans cited 'solidarity with the fan club' as their primary motive for participating in disturbances around football matches (Zani & Kirchler, 1991). Moreover, the assertive nature of the game itself as well as the aggression displayed by the players in the course of the match provide additional cues which may reinforce aggressive tendencies in the spectator.

In contrast to rioters and hooligans who form relatively transient social groups restricted to particular events and/or settings, *delinquent gangs* usually exist over a longer period of time, at least as far as their core members are concerned. While group criminality is by no means confined to adolescence, research has focused primarily on juvenile gangs, not least because membership of a juvenile gang may well be the pathway into an adult criminal career. The scale of aggressive behaviour shown by delinquent youth gangs is illustrated in Figure 13.3.

It is hard to imagine that the participants in this assault would have shown the same behaviour if they had been on their own. Rather, deindividuation and substitution of their personal identity by the social identity of the group suggest themselves as crucial mechanisms to account for this type of aggressive behaviour (Turner, Hogg, Oakes, Reicher, & Wetherell, 1987). Like the other

A gang of 50 youngsters, including girls and children as young as seven, terrorised and assaulted passengers on a bus in Birmingham yesterday, before robbing them at gunpoint.

A 24-year-old man was dragged from his seat and had a hand gun held to his head while he was robbed of his bus pass and loose change. Gang members then dragged another man to the front of the bus, punched him in the face and robbed him. A woman was also assaulted and had her handbag stolen before the gang jumped off the bus and fled.

Figure 13.3   *A case of gang violence (The Independent, 28 February 1995)*

forms of group violence considered in the present section, the actions of delinquent gangs typically show a discernible pattern rather than being impulsive, uncontrolled outbursts of violent impulses in the individual: 'The contemporary American juvenile gang may have a structured organization, identifiable leadership, territorial identification, continuous association, specific purpose, and engage in illegal behavior' (Goldstein, 1994a, p. 256). The inter-group dynamics of gang behaviour is reflected in the observation that gang cohesiveness is reinforced by the arrest and incarceration of gang members.

Noting the difficulties in obtaining accurate statistical evidence of gang violence, Goldstein attempts to pinpoint the characteristic features of juvenile gangs and their members. According to his review, gang violence is primarily a male problem, with males outnumbering females at a rate of 20:1. The age range of group membership has gone up in recent years, not least because drug trafficking plays an increasing role in juvenile gangs. Poor socioeconomic background, preventing legitimate forms of access to material resources and status symbols, in combination with a sense of social identity provided by membership of successful gangs, are identified as factors explaining why young people are attracted to this type of group. This may also explain the high proportion of juvenile gang members from ethnic minorities who are affected by both adverse socioeconomic conditions and lack of acceptance by the dominant social group. Even though criminal aggression committed by gangs accounts for only a small proportion of total crimes, serious acts of violence, such as aggravated physical assault and homicide, are committed more frequently by gangs than by individual offenders (Goldstein, 1994a).

Ethnocentric and racial aggression

In the previous section we looked at aggressive behaviour arising out of the membership of the *actor* in a crowd or defined social group. We will now examine instances of aggression in which the group membership of the *target person* motivates or triggers aggressive acts towards that person. Hostility against members of particular ethnic and racial groups is a widespread phenomenon giving rise to a range of aggressive behaviour from verbal derogation to serious forms of violence (cf., however, O'Brien, 1987, on the intricacies of assessing interracial crime rates). Examining evidence from crime surveys on racial harassment and victimization in Britain, Bowling (1993) concludes that racial harassment of members of ethnic minorities presents a large-scale problem. Members of ethnic minorities were found to have generally higher victimization rates than the white majority, suffering a high proportion of racially motivated attacks, predominantly by groups of young white men. In Germany, dramatic incidents of ethnocentric violence, committed by perpetrators close to or part of extreme right-wing groups, have been witnessed in recent years, directed in particular against foreign refugees seeking political asylum, at the long-established Turkish community and against Jewish institutions and memorials.

Prejudicial attitudes against members of different racial and ethnic groups have been investigated as potential predictors of heightened aggression against members of those groups. However, as Baron and Richardson (1994) point out, there is no straightforward relationship between prejudice and aggression. Whether or not prejudiced people will respond more aggressively to members of the rejected groups depends on the influence of mediating factors, such as fear of retaliation and anonymity. If whites holding strong prejudicial attitudes towards blacks had to perform aggressive behaviour in public, they showed 'reverse discrimination', i.e. acted less aggressively towards a black than towards a white target person. If their behaviour was recorded anonymously, however, they did show more aggression towards the black person (e.g. Donnerstein & Donnerstein, 1978). Moreover, it has been demonstrated that rather than discriminating between the targets of aggression, prejudiced people show a higher general tendency towards aggressive behaviour.

According to Bar-Tal (1990), *delegitimization* is an important process mediating between the ethnocentric devaluation of an outgroup and the performance of harmful action against outgroup members. Delegitimization refers to the '*categorization of a group or groups into extremely negative social categories that are excluded from the realm of acceptable norms and/or values*' (Bar-Tal, 1990, p. 65, emphasis in original). If the perception of an outgroup as different and inferior is accompanied by feelings of fear, then delegitimization is likely to occur in order (a) to maximize the difference between one's own reference group and the outgroup; and (b) to provide a justification for the exploitation or other ill-treatment of the outgroup. The treatment of Jews in Nazi Germany or of black citizens under the South African apartheid regime provide extreme examples of how delegitimization provides the basis for justifying the oppression, persecution and killing of outgroup members (cf. also Staub, 1989). On an everyday level, delegitimization strategies are frequently employed to shift responsibility for aggressive behaviour from the actor on to the target persons who are said to elicit, or at least deserve, the negative actions directed at them.

Political violence: terrorism and war

Outgroup devaluation with the aim of justifying aggressive actions against members of the devalued group also plays an important role in aggressive conflicts at the political level. While terrorism refers to acts of violence aimed at making an impact on the power holders within a particular country, wars involve the use of force against other nations (unless they are civil wars in which different political, religious or ethnic groups fight each other within a nation). If the aggression is directed at the persecution and killing of entire groups for racial, political, religious or other reasons, then it takes the form of genocide (Staub, 1989).

In defining 'terrorism', Friedland (1988) points out that definitions should concentrate on acts rather than persons, because the labelling of people and groups as terrorist is ambiguous, depending on the perspective and affiliation of the person applying the label: the same group of people may be called terrorists by some and freedom fighters by others. In contrast, terrorist acts can be more easily identified according to two basic criteria. Violent acts are called terrorist if (a) they are not only used as direct means to achieve political aims, but also as instruments of publicity and intimidation; (b) they are directed at harming people other than the direct opponents in the political conflict. Both criteria underline that it is not the direct physical harm which is the primary objective of terrorist acts but their psychological effects in terms of attracting public attention and undermining the authority of the state in ensuring the safety of its citizens. Despite the worldwide notoriety achieved by individual terrorists, e.g. 'Carlos', terrorism is for the most part committed by groups, typically operating out of a position of relative weakness within their society. To explain when and why movements directed at social change resort to violence rather than accepted forms of political participation, several authors have transferred the frustration-aggression hypothesis from the individual to the group level. Terrorist violence is seen as the result of frustrations caused by social and political deprivation. In some cases, such as the IRA or the PLO, the perceived injustice leading to the emergence of terrorist movements is immediately traceable to historical developments. Other forms of terrorism, such as the acts of the ideologically motivated Red Army Faction in Germany, are attributed to the more elusive frustration caused by disappointment about not being able to make a significant impact on political decisions. However, given the widespread nature of social and political injustice affecting large numbers of people *without* turning them into terrorists, additional factors must be assumed to explain the conditions under which frustration is channelled into terrorist activities. Friedland offers an interactionist model, arguing that terrorism is a joint function of both situational and individual factors:

> The origin, in most instances, was a widespread social protest movement. Confrontations, often violent, with authorities and failure to elicit a popular response led to disillusion and deterioration of the movement. Remnants of the movement formed small, clandestine groups which maintained little external contact and a fierce ingroup loyalty and cohesion. These circumstances enhanced the status of violent individuals within the groups, elevated them to leadership positions and allowed them to establish terrorism as the groups' preferred modus operandi. (Friedland, 1988, p. 111)

The role of individual differences in support of aggressive strategies to resolve political conflicts was further explored by Feshbach (1994). He found that individual differences in dispositional aggressiveness failed to predict either support for nuclear armament or advocacy of military action. Instead, two more specific attitudes, nationalism and patriotism, were examined as potential candidates for predicting support for military options. While patriotism is defined in terms of pride in one's national identity, nationalism refers to feelings of national superiority and power over other nations. Feshbach (1994) argues that nationalism is more closely related to endorsement of military aggression than patriotism and reports a study which supports the functional distinction between the two types of attitudes. Subjects were exposed to either martial music (military marches) or patriotic music (the US National Anthem) and the effect of the music on nationalism and patriotism scores was examined. While martial music led to higher nationalism, but not patriotism, scores compared to a control group, patriotic music had the reverse effect. Feshbach (1994, pp. 289–90) concludes 'that it is possible to sustain and even reinforce patriotic attachments to one's nation while fostering internationally oriented attitudes that diminish the likelihood of war'.

Feelings of national superiority are also identified by Staub (1989) as precipitating factors of war, along with additional cultural preconditions conducive to the development of aggression towards other nations:

(a) the emergence of an 'ideology of antagonism', triggered by an initial ingroup–outgroup differentiation which then leads to the attribution of highly negative, often stereotype-based characteristics to the outgroup;

(b) an 'ideology of national security' in which the continuous assessment of and adaptation to the dangerousness of the opponent is replaced by the unquestioned aim to dominate the enemy at all costs; and

(c) the acceptance of a worldview which highlights the values fostered by war, such as companionship, loyalty, national pride, or the worthy cause. Toch refers to this aspect as the *myth of good violence*, which 'earns medals, commendations, and accolades' (Toch, 1993, p. 200).

The present analysis has focused on the psychological mechanisms involved in political violence. This focus should not disguise the fact that this form of aggressive behaviour is more strongly affected by nonpsychological factors than the other forms of aggression considered in this chapter. As Singer (1989) notes, *systemic conditions* (such as material resources, allegiance bonds) at the multinational level, *dyadic conditions* in the bilateral relationship between two nations (such as trade relationship, balance of military strength) and *national conditions* within a country (such as domestic instability) interact in a complex way, creating enormous problems in the search for regular patterns explaining the outbreak of wars.

Reducing aggression and violence

After reviewing the large-scale manifestation of aggression across almost all domains of social life, there can be no doubt about the pressing need to design strategies for the prevention and reduction of aggressive behaviour.

The development of such strategies is seriously impeded, however, by the fact that the causes and moderating variables leading to the manifestation of aggressive behaviour are still far from being fully understood. As long as we

---

General prerequisites
Awareness and involvement on the part of adults (parents, teachers)

Measures at the school level
Questionnaire survey
School conference day
Better supervision during recess
Parent–staff meetings

Measures at the class level
Class rules against bullying
Class meetings

Measures at the individual level
Serious talks with bullies and victims
Serious talks with parents of involved students
Teacher and parent use of imagination

Figure 13.4   *Interlocking measures for dealing with the problem of bullying in schools (adapted from Olweus, 1994, p. 123)*

do not have a clear understanding of why and when aggressive behaviour occurs and to what extent different forms of aggressive behaviour share the same underlying mechanisms, successful intervention strategies will have to be limited in scope, directed at specific types or contexts of aggressive behaviour. Alternatively, one can try to reduce the *manifestation* of aggressive behaviour, irrespective of its causal factors, by imposing sanctions and deterrents which suppress the performance of aggressive acts.

In reviewing the success of different measures for reducing and controlling aggression, we will first look at intervention *strategies directed at the individual* in the form of specific treatments or situational changes. In the second part of this section the focus will be on *strategies implemented at the societal level* to affect all members of the relevant target groups and bring down aggression and violence rates in the community as a whole.

In addition to the general intervention strategies which will be reviewed here, a variety of approaches have been developed to deal with particular kinds of aggressive behaviour, such as bullying (Olweus, 1994), ethnic hostility (Goldstein, 1994a) and gang violence (Goldstein, 1994b). While a discussion of these approaches is beyond the scope of the present chapter, they provide indications of how specific aggression-related problems in society may be addressed by a combination of individual intervention and social policy measures (Figure 13.4).

A fundamental obstacle in the way of effective strategies for dealing with aggression, according to Lore and Schultz (1993), is a public attitude which all too readily accepts aggression and violence as inherent features of human nature. These authors argue that this view ignores possibilities for controlling aggression suggested by research on both human and animal behaviour. Results from animal studies and behavioural observations of children are quoted to support the claim that the behavioural manifestation of aggression shows high intra-individual variability across situations and settings. This variability demonstrates, as they point out, that aggression is not an inevitable but an optional strategy for humans, which should lead researchers as well as political decision makers to be more concerned with the mechanisms by which the inhibitory forces against aggression can be strengthened.

Individual-centred interventions

Punishment is a possible control mechanism for aggressive behaviour which can be applied both at the individual level and at the societal level, in the form of legal sanctions. At the individual level, the idea is that punishment will reduce the frequency with which aggressive behaviour is shown by the individual in the future. The effectiveness of punishment as a control mechanism for aggression is called into question by most reviewers (e.g. Baron & Richardson, 1994; Berkowitz, 1993). Several limiting conditions have been identified which affect the impact of punishment as a deterrent to future aggression: anticipated punishment must be sufficiently adverse and have a high probability of being imposed to prevent aggressive behaviour; and actual punishment must follow immediately upon the transgression. Moreover, it only works if transgressors are not in a state of negative arousal strong enough to impede their assessment of the severity and likelihood of sanctions, if they perceive the punishment as contingent upon their behaviour and if attractive behavioural alternatives are available to them in the situation. Apart from the fact that the co-occurrence of these factors is relatively rare, critics have argued that punitive responses are in themselves instances of aggression. As such, they (a) convey the message that the use of aggression is an acceptable strategy of conflict resolution and (b) are likely to elicit negative affect in the target which, in turn, may instigate further aggressive acts. If it is to produce desirable consequences, punishment needs to be embedded in a more general approach to instrumental learning in which the primary aim is to reward desirable rather than penalizing undesirable behaviour (e.g. Patterson, Reid, Jones, & Conger, 1975).

Another strategy to be dismissed as largely inefficient or even counterproductive is the cathartic expression of hostile feelings to reduce the need for overt aggression. It is a widely accepted notion that bottling up one's aggressive feelings leads to problems of adjustment, carrying the risk of uncontrolled outbursts of aggression. According to the idea of catharsis endorsed by both Freud (1920) and Lorenz (1966), the ventilation of hostile feelings can lead to a discharge of aggressive impulses which temporarily reduces the likelihood of aggressive behaviour. A more general version of the catharsis hypothesis claims that any expression of aggressive feelings reduces the likelihood of subsequent aggression. However, empirical support for the effectiveness of catharsis in reducing aggression is equivocal, suggesting that the attributed positive effects are limited to highly specific contexts. Several studies indicate that the imaginary performance of aggressive behaviour, such as in pretend play or aggressive games, is more likely to enhance aggression than to reduce it. The same is true for the effects of watching violent actions in the media (cf. Berkowitz, 1993). Given the effects of cognitive priming in increasing aggression, which were discussed earlier in this chapter, it is not surprising that engaging in imaginary forms of aggression or watching others' violent behaviour may serve as an instigator of subsequent behavioural aggression. Overt expression of aggression in verbal or physical form has, indeed, been found to reduce negative affective arousal. Yet rather than acting against the subsequent performance of further aggression, the experience that negative feelings can be reduced through aggressive behaviour can promote rather than inhibit future aggression (Baron & Richardson, 1994).

In contrast to punishment and catharsis, approaches aimed at developing new skills, enabling the individual to engage in behavioural alternatives to aggression, have generally been more successful. One such approach is based on the proposition, reviewed above, that anger acts as a crucial mediator between a frustration and an aggressive response. Therefore, enabling the person to control his or her anger should prove to be effective in reducing hostile aggression. Anger management interventions have been developed as part of a clinical approach towards treating aggressive individuals. As Howells (1989) argues, anger management methods can only be expected to work with individuals who are aware of the fact that their aggressive behaviour results from a failure to control their aggressive impulses and who are motivated to change their inadequate handling of these impulses. The focus of this approach is on conveying to the aggressive individual 'an understandable model of anger and its relationship to triggering events, thoughts, and violent behaviour itself' (Howells, 1989, p. 166). Moreover, anger control can be improved by training individuals to consider the potential causes and mitigating circumstances for the other person's frustrating or negative behaviour. Here, evidence from several experimental studies shows that aggression can be reduced to the extent that the other's behaviour is interpreted as unavoidable or unintentional.

While anger management strategies require the full cooperation of the individual, a less obvious means of suppressing aggressive behaviour is to induce responses incompatible with the simultaneous performance of aggressive acts. *Empathy* with the target of an aggressive act may lead to a reduction in aggression, provided that the aggressor is not emotionally aroused to such an extent that he or she perceives the victim's suffering as a positive reinforcement. Similarly, inducing *humour* may block aggressive tendencies, unless the humorous material itself contains aggressive or hostile cues. Finally, *mild sexual arousal* seems to generate an affective state which is incompatible with the expression of aggressive impulses (Baron & Bell, 1977). However, each of these effects is restricted to the immediate context and will not result in decreased aggression over time and across situations.

In contrast, exposure to nonviolent role models is directed at the acquisition of new behavioural repertoires by which aggressive response patterns can be replaced in a more lasting way. Observing people behaving in a nonaggressive fashion has been found to decrease the performance of aggressive acts in the observers (Baron & Richardson, 1994). However, as Eron (1986) points out with respect to role models on the TV screen, the mere observation of non-aggressive models is less effective in changing aggressive response patterns than an integrated approach in which observation is combined with strategies for implementing the observed behaviour, such as role playing and performance feedback.

Societal-level strategies

Despite the fact that aggressive behaviour is ultimately to be changed at the level of the individual person, the social order in which people live can have a profound effect on the scale of aggression displayed by its members. For example, a systematic relationship has been identified between the availability of pornographic material and sexual violence rates (e.g. Scott & Schwalm, 1988). Moreover, any society is under the obligation to provide the best possible protection of its members against aggression and violence.

The prime mechanism at the societal level to control aggression and violence is the imposition of legal sanctions. Over and above the penalization of the individual offender once he or she has committed a criminal act of violence, the punishment of aggressive behaviour is designed to act as a deterrent to further violence. In his detailed review, Berkowitz (1993) concludes that there is little evidence to support the deterrent effect of legal sanctions. While some studies have found a short-term effect of more severe punishment (e.g. Sherman & Berk, 1984), overall support for the deterrence hypothesis is weak. In particular, no conclusive support was found for the claim that capital punishment is an effective means of restricting murder rates.

A related issue, raised in particular in connection with US homicide rates, refers to legal control of the availability of firearms to reduce the prevalence of violent assaults. Isolating the effects of legal firearm restrictions from the complex network of variables associated with the role of firearms in American society is an extremely difficult task. Accordingly, there is no consistent evidence supporting or rejecting the idea that gun control restrictions can bring down violence. While Berkowitz (1993) argues in favour of gun control legislation on the basis of the evidence he reviewed, Kleck and Patterson (1993) conclude from their own large-scale study that gun prevalence is not systematically related to violence rates and that gun control laws are largely ineffective in reducing violence rates.

An alternative way of imposing measures at the sociopolitical level to control violence is suggested by Goldstein (1994a). He presents a crime prevention approach based on creating a physical and social environment which restricts the opportunities for aggressive behaviour. Making it harder for the criminal to reach his or her target (through physical barriers or access control), controlling facilitators (e.g. banning the sale of alcohol at sports events), implementing formal or informal surveillance (e.g. neighbourhood watch schemes) and identifying property (e.g. through labels or electronic codes) are measures to reduce criminal opportunity. A crucial question, though, is whether these strategies can reduce the overall level of criminal behaviour or simply lead to a 'displacement' of criminal activities towards less protected targets. Given the limited evidence on the effectiveness of situational crime prevention, no conclusive answer can as yet be provided to this question.

The research reviewed in this section has illustrated once more how very difficult it is to come to terms with the problem of aggression between individuals and groups. While several firmly entrenched beliefs about effective control mechanisms, such as the role of cathartic release of aggressive feelings or the deterrent function of punishments and legal sanctions, need to be revised on the basis of this research, support for alternative courses of action is limited and far from conclusive. Progress towards reducing and preventing aggression is most likely to be achieved by focusing on specific types (e.g. sexual violence, bullying) and mediating processes (e.g. frustration, media consumption) of aggression. Given the diversity and complexity of aggressive behaviours, broad theoretical explanations need to be complemented by domain-specific predictor variables to account for the occurrence of particular forms of aggression. Developing a better understanding of the processes which lead individuals and groups to engage in aggressive, often lethal actions against each other and, on this basis, deriving guidelines for their prevention and control remains one of the greatest challenges for both basic and applied research in social psychology.

The present chapter has reviewed the main theoretical concepts and empirical findings of social psychological aggression research with a view to highlighting their contributions to the issues of (a) causation and (b) prevention of aggression and violence in society. Starting from a brief discussion of how to define and measure aggression and violence, the chapter offered a summary of the main theoretical approaches for explaining aggressive behaviour. This was followed by a look at attempts to identify determinants of aggression, distinguishing between determinants located at the level of the individual person (e.g. sex differences) and those located in the situation or social environment (e.g. media influences). Specific forms of aggression were examined in more detail, organized into the broad categories of interpersonal aggression and intergroup aggression. The final section considered strategies and proposals for reducing aggression and violence, ranging from individual-centred psychological intervention to global measures implemented at the sociopolitical level.

Further reading

Allison, J.A. & Wrightsman, L.S. (1993). *Rape. The misunderstood crime.* Newbury Park, CA: Sage. Provides a thorough, up-to-date discussion of the psychological research on rape, ranging from an analysis of different forms of sexual violence to the treatment of victims and offenders as well as the prevention of rape.

Archer, J. & Browne, K. (Eds) (1989). *Human aggression: Naturalistic approaches.* London: Routledge. Adopts a problem-oriented approach to the diverse manifestations of aggression and violence occurring in natural contexts, applying basic theoretical knowledge about aggression to the explanation and prevention of everyday aggression.

Baron, R.A. & Richardson, D.R. (1994). *Human aggression* (2nd ed.). New York: Plenum Press.

Berkowitz, L. (1993). *Aggression: Its causes, consequences, and control.* Philadelphia, PA: Temple University Press. Two authoritative accounts of the present state of psychological aggression research, covering theoretical and methodological issues as well as applied concerns.

Goldstein, A.P. (1994). *The ecology of aggression.* New York: Plenum Press. Examines the impact of ecological factors on aggression, following the distinction between physical and social ecology and placing special emphasis on ecological change and reduction of aggression.

14

Social Construction and Old Age: Normative Conceptions and Interpersonal Processes

Jutta Heckhausen and Frieder R. Lang

Contents

This chapter concerns the social construction of old age. Chronological age within the human life-span is conceived as a social marker, which structures the way people perceive each other, and which organizes the way people interact with each other, in a similar manner as other social markers such as gender, social class or ethnicity. Such social markers are a product of social construction in a given society. Across cultures, values and conceptions associated with old age may vary considerably, in that some cultures ascribe high status to individuals in old age (e.g. China), whereas others such as the Western industrial cultures tend to view old age in less favourable terms (Keith, 1985).

Like any other phase in the life span, old age is constructed in the social world the individual lives in. This social construction involves both the mental representations of old age as a unique and distinct phase of life, and relations with other members of the social community. The everyday interactions with other persons generate a developmental ecology in terms of the available social relationships and support, and thus constitutes a social reality of old age. In this sense, old age can be conceived of as a 'social construction of reality', a concept introduced by Berger and Luckmann's (1966) sociology of knowledge.

Social constructions of reality serve important functions in two ways. First, they provide constraints and give structure to behavioural options. For human individuals this is particularly important because of the extensive variability and ontogenetic potential of human behaviour. In order to optimize interactions with the external world, so that the individual successfully achieves intended outcomes by his or her own activity, behavioural resources have to be invested selectively (Baltes & Baltes, 1990; Heckhausen & Schulz, 1995). Social interactions and social norms help to provide a scaffold for behaviour selection. Social norms inform the individual which behaviours are adequate or appropriate, and realization of normative behaviours is regulated and evaluated in the social interactions of the individual.

Secondly, social constructions help the individual to compensate for the negative effects of losses and failure. This latter function is particularly prominent in old age, when losses become more frequent and severe (Baltes & Baltes, 1990). Failure and losses can be compensated either by investing more external resources into achieving a given goal or by disengaging from an unattainable goal and reinterpreting the failure in a self-protective way (Heckhausen & Schulz, 1993, 1995). Both aspects of compensation are facilitated by social interactions and constructions, in that other people may provide assistance to overcome a difficulty, and age-normative conceptions may help generate substitute goals and self-protective interpretations.

Social construction of development and ageing is understood here as a continuous process encompassing the entire life span, rather than pertaining only to old age as one specific phase of life. Therefore, social construction of ageing needs to be considered in the context of life-span developmental psychology and its key concepts, to be discussed briefly in the following section.

Developmental gains and losses as key concepts in life-span developmental psychology

Life-span developmental psychology conceptualizes ageing and old age as part of the human life span and its continuous dynamic between developmental gains and losses (Baltes, 1987). Developmental gains include increases in desirable attributes (e.g. motor abilities, wisdom) and decreases in undesirable attributes (e.g. dependency, agitation).

Analogously, developmental losses involve increases in undesirable attributes and decreases in desirable attributes. Developmental gains and losses occur at any time throughout the life span, from infancy to old age, and are closely interrelated: most developmental gains in a given domain of functioning imply the concurrent loss of alternative developmental advances in other areas. The potentials for developmental gains and losses, however, vary across the life span. At higher age levels, losses relative to gains become increasingly predominant, for example because the biological and mental resources decrease in old age (Baltes, 1987; Kliegl, Smith, & Baltes, 1990). Using an investment-consumption metaphor, Marsiske, Lang, Baltes and Baltes (1995)

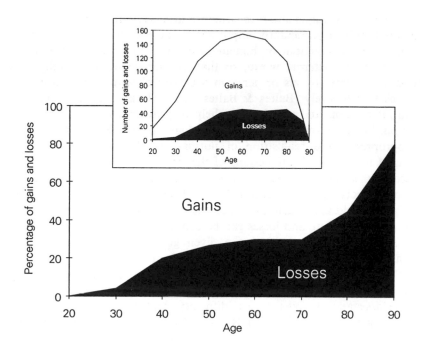

Figure 14.1   *Quantitative relation of gains and losses across the adult life-span (percentages and absolute numbers) (adapted from Heckhausen, Dixon, & Baltes, 1989)*

have argued that any investment of resources necessarily precludes investment of the same resources elsewhere, and, at the same time, developmental processes also produce 'consumption' costs, that is, invested resources are expended. Such dynamic between gains and losses in life-span development is based on biological ageing as well as on constraints on the social roles allocated to older individuals. Social constraints are seen to both scaffold and challenge regulation and management of resource investment, resource consumption, and resource protection in old age (see also Heckhausen, 1995).

Normative conceptions about old age communicate to the older person which behaviours are appropriate. Consequently, the increasingly unfavourable ratio between gains and losses at higher ages is also reflected in lay persons' conceptions about development and ageing as illustrated in Figure 14.1 (Heckhausen, Dixon, & Baltes, 1989).

The lifelong dynamic of developmental gains and losses is also reflected in the model of selective optimization with compensation. This model, developed by Baltes and Baltes (1980, 1990; Baltes, 1993) captures the fundamental adaptive strategies and mechanisms by which losses can be minimized while, simultaneously, gains are maximized. Selection, compensation and optimization are cornerstones of life-span models of successful development (Baltes & Baltes, 1990; Baltes & Carstensen, in press; Carstensen, Hanson, & Freund, 1995; Heckhausen & Schulz, 1993; Marsiske et al., 1995).

Selection refers to the choice of specific functional or behavioural domains or goals for growth or maintenance, such as in specialization in professional expertise. Moreover, selection includes the process of narrowing of developmental contexts throughout ontogeny (Marsiske et al., 1995), as in career tracks which preclude alternative occupational trajectories. *Compensation* refers to the acquisition of new internal or external means in the face of failure, loss or lack of resources (Marsiske et al., 1995). Compensatory strategies have to be used, in terms of other people's assistance, technical aids, and with regard to self-protection (Baltes, 1993). *Optimization* relates to mechanisms and strategies by which developmental potentials and functioning are enhanced or maintained (Marsiske et al., 1995). Even in old age, the individual can optimize functioning in a given domain by investing behavioural resources (e.g. time, effort, skills) in attaining or maintaining high standards of performance (Marsiske et al., 1995). The selective optimization with compensation model thus is seen as a set of interacting components that operate dynamically throughout the life span and across different functional and behavioural domains (Marsiske et al., 1995). The functional value of each component is determined by the specific contextual constraints of a given life phase. For example, for the domain of social behaviour and interpersonal functioning in old age, M. Baltes and Carstensen (in press) have applied the selective optimization with compensation model to integrate socioemotional selectivity theory (Carstensen, in press) with the model of learned dependency (M. Baltes, in press). This argument will be considered in greater detail later.

Heckhausen and Schulz (1993, 1995) have integrated the concepts of selection, compensation and optimization with their life-span theory of primary and secondary control (see also Schulz, 1986; Schulz, Heckhausen, & Locher, 1991). Primary control relates to those behaviours by which the environment is changed in accordance with one's own goals, whereas secondary control refers to those mechanisms that bring the self in line with the environment (see also Rothbaum, Weisz, & Snyder, 1982). When integrated with the concepts of selection and compensation, four types of strategy for selective and compensatory optimization of development across the life-span are identified: selective primary control refers to the focused investment of behavioural resources; compensatory primary control captures the employment of additional (e.g. unusual action means) and external means to achieve goals; selective secondary control to the volitional focusing of motivational resources on chosen goals; and compensatory secondary control addresses the strategies of internal regulation that serve to protect motivational resources from negative consequences of failures and losses. Heckhausen and Schulz (1993) conceive of optimization as a higher-order process for regulating the employment of the four types of control strategy illustrated in Table 14.1, so as to optimize primary control across the life span.

In the following section, the developmental dynamic of gains and losses in old age will be discussed in relation to two fundamental domains of the social construction in old age. First, social construction of old age will be discussed as it is generated by age-normative conceptions about development and ageing. Age-normative conceptions are discussed as social constraints of

Table 14.1   *Two-dimensional model of primary/secondary control and selection/compensation*

	Selection	Compensation
Primary control	*Selective primary control* Investment of internal resources: effort, time, abilities activity-inherent skills	*Compensatory primary control* Use of external resources: technical aids, other people's assistance, activity-external skills
Secondary control	*Selective secondary control* Metavolition: enhancement of goal commitment, remaining focused in order to avoid distractions	*Compensatory secondary control* Buffering negative effects of failure: goal change, strategic social comparison, or strategic causal attribution

Source: adapted from Heckhausen & Schulz (1993)

developmental regulation in old age. Secondly, we discuss the social construction in old age as it is determined by interpersonal processes in the old person's social network and personal relationships.

Social construction of old age as generated by normative conceptions about development

What is the function of age-normative conceptions about development? What role do they play in shaping individuals' lives? These questions are particularly relevant to the heated debate about whether the life course is increasingly institutionalized or deinstitutionalized (Held, 1986; Hogan, 1981; Marini, 1984; Mayer, 1986; Modell, Furstenberg, & Strong, 1978; Neugarten, 1979; Uhlenberg, 1974) by societal constraints. On the one hand, societal constraints to life-course timing and sequencing appear to have become more lenient, and the variability of individuals' life-course patterns has increased (Neugarten, 1979; Rindfuss, Swicegood, & Rosenfeld, 1987). On the other hand, life-course patterns that adhere to normative age structure and sequence still largely prevail even in highly industrialized Western societies with elaborate systems of labour division (Hogan, 1981; Marini, 1984; Modell et al., 1978; Uhlenberg, 1974). This paradox raised various questions: what is it that regulates life-course-relevant behaviour? What are the guiding influences on people's mental representations of desired and possible life-course trajectories? How do individuals arrive at goals to strive for in their effort to shape their own development?

An analogous question can be raised regarding the general regulation of individuals' behaviour according to rules of social conduct that are not enforced externally. Norbert Elias (1969) in his classic sociohistorical analysis of the process of civilization has answered this more general question by showing how the external enforcement of social rules has become transformed into internalized norms and rules of conduct subscribed to by all members of a given society. Elias has shown this process with regard to such behaviours as the expression of anger and aggression, but particularly with regard to everyday behaviours such as table manners (e.g. not wiping one's mouth with the table linen) or patterns of co-sleeping. Elias's analyses show how previously externally enforced norms become internalized, and thereby gain the status of naturalized and seemingly inevitable prescriptions for individual behaviour.

This line of thought converges with the argument made by cultural anthropologists that social conventions become transformed into institutionalized ways of thinking (Douglas, 1986). While social conventions are transparent and therefore malleable outcomes of negotiation between different interest groups in a given social community, institutionalized ways of thinking entail much less transparency and greater stability. They are more stable than mere social conventions, because their pragmatic base in group interests is less transparent and is viewed as grounded in nature. Institutional ways of thinking turn individual thought over to an 'automatic pilot', and society profits by a saving of energy from institutional coding and inertia (Douglas, 1986, p. 63). Similarly, from the perspective of the sociology of knowledge, Berger and Luckmann (1966) propose that reality is socially constructed. Social constructions of reality facilitate the stability of the social system and provide the individual with subjective certainty about a mutually habitualized, and thereby institutionalized, foundation of individual action.

A similar argument can be applied to the societal regulation of life-course patterns. Internalized conceptions about timing and sequencing of life-course transitions may gradually have replaced regulation externally enforced via objectified societal institutions (Heckhausen, 1990). An example maybe the age of marriage and first child-bearing, which in contemporary Western society is more individually determined than ever before, yet still normatively determined by the individual's self-regulation according to social norms. This way, processes of deinstitutionalization with regard to external institutions can go hand in hand with an institutionalization of the life course via internalized age norms and age-graded regulations. Age-normative conceptions about the life course that are shared by the individual members of a given society may have committing power as internalized, naturalized, and therefore hardly questionable ways of thinking about human life. Thus, age-normative conceptions about development have come to be a major constraint (Heckhausen, in press) to people's regulation of development throughout the life course. They provide structure and predictability to individuals' lives and are therefore most adaptive both for society and for individuals. On the societal level, age-graded predictability is conducive to the functioning of the labour market, family cycles and educational planning. On the individual level, age-normative conceptions provide signposts for individual aspirations, as well as markers for developmental deadlines after which futile goals need to be abandoned (Heckhausen, in press). Moreover, age-normative conceptions may function as social stereotypes and help to organize and render efficient social perception processes ('Tell me your age, and I tell you what you do'; Krueger, Heckhausen, & Hundertmark, in press).

Table 14.2   *Developmental tasks for early adulthood, middle age, and old age*

Early adulthood	Middle age	Late maturity
Selecting a mate	Assisting teenage children to become responsible and happy adults	Adjusting to decreasing physical strength and health
Learning to live with a marriage partner		Adjusting to retirement and reduced income
Starting a family	Achieving adult social and civic responsibility	
Rearing children		Adjusting to death of spouse
Managing a home	Reaching and maintaining satisfactory performance in one's occupational career	Establishing an explicit affiliation with one's age group
Getting started in an occupation	Developing adult leisure-time activities	
Taking on civic responsibility		Adopting and adapting social roles in a flexible way
Finding a congenial social group	Relating to one's spouse as a person	Establishing satisfactory physical living arrangements
	Accepting and adjusting to the physiological changes of middle age	
	Adjusting to ageing parents	

Source: adapted from Havighurst (1972)

To illustrate a scheme of age-normative prescriptions for important developmental tasks, Table 14.2 gives a list of developmental tasks for early adulthood, mid-life and old age, which has been compiled by Havighurst (1972).

Some sociologists have argued that people's age-normative conceptions about development are merely epiphenomenal, that is secondary reflections with no independent impact, to sociostructural systems of age-grading and their expression in statistical age norms (Marini, 1984; Mayer, 1987, in press). However, age-normative conceptions constitute social frames of reference (Festinger, 1954) and the dimension of consensus (Kelley, 1967) when it comes to attributing behaviour to causes: 'What is deviant needs to be explained.' Social frames of reference set the stage for personal aspirations: 'What other people can do, I can do too.' And in case of failure, this involves serious sanctions in terms of self-evaluation: 'If I cannot do what most people can, I must be particularly incompetent.' Thus, internalized age norms have much more far-reaching implications that merely being the reflections of statistical age norms in a given society. They set the social standards for individuals' developmental goals and therefore determine positive and negative effects on self-evaluation. Like any social norm they function as *ought rules* and failing to abide by them results in *social sanctions*.

The following sections discuss a number of phenomena related to and based on age-normative conceptions about development and ageing, that have important implications for people's behaviour towards their own and other people's ageing and development, their self-evaluation and subjective well-being.

Conceptions about age groups and the segmentation of the life course

When considering age-normative conceptions about development the most basic phenomenon is the segmentation of the life course into age periods or age groups. Various studies have addressed this topic and uncovered a consensual structure of five to six age groups (e.g. Fry, 1976; Shanan & Kedar, 1979–80). Shanan and Kedar (1979–80), for instance, asked subjects between the ages of 16 and 78 years to divide the life span (starting at age 11) into as many sections as they liked. Most subjects used six segments, comprising the following age categories: adolescence from 12 to 20 years, early adulthood from 20 to 30 years, adulthood from 30 to 50 years, middle adulthood from 50 to 60 years, advanced adulthood from 60 to 70 years, and old age at 65 years and above.

Further evidence supporting the consensual nature of age-related conceptions comes from studies on age estimates (Blau, 1956; Harris & Associates, 1975; Peters, 1971; Shanas, 1962; Tuckman & Lorge, 1953; Zola, 1962). Kogan (1975), for instance, presented photographs of women and men at different ages to young and old adults. There was substantial agreement in age estimates across subjects' age and gender. However, there was also a small but distinct tendency for older respondents to give higher age estimates than younger respondents. Moreover, for male targets both middle adulthood and old age begin later than for female targets (Kogan, 1979).

Research on the boundaries of certain age categories corroborate the conclusion that age-related conceptions about the segmentation of the life span involve substantial inter-individual consensus, but also show minor but significant distortions, which reflect the informant's own age status. In a study by Cameron (1969), for instance, young, middle-aged and old adults were requested to indicate age boundaries for the categories young, middle-aged, old and very old. Subjects of all age groups largely agreed on the following boundaries: young from 18 to 25 years, middle-aged from 40 to 50–55 years, old from 60 to 80 years, and very old over 80 years. However, the middle-aged adults delayed the end of mid-life from 50 to 55 years, and advanced the onset of old age from 60 to 65 years. By extending mid-life to a later age and putting off old age these middle-aged adults may have granted themselves a final delay of having to identify personally with the age category 'old'. An analogous distortion of the lower age boundary of old age has been identified by Drevenstedt (1976): this time older adults delayed old age until after 70.

The research reported provides strong support for the conclusion that age-normative conceptions are far from being 'cold cognitions'; instead they are charged with self-involvement (Heckhausen & Krueger, 1993). However, as social constructions of *reality* they cannot be arbitrary, but are constrained in their self-serving variability by their function to orient the individual within the social reality of the life course in a given society. Even conceptions about age groups that are at present distant from oneself are highly relevant to the individual, because these age groups will have been or will become the frame of social being for the self. In this way, conceptions about age groups differ from social stereotypes, which either include (ingroup) or exclude (outgroup) the individual. Accordingly, they reflect both social age norms and personal involvement, a characteristic which is most saliently expressed in stereotypes about old age, the topic we turn to next.

Stereotypes of ageing

An abundance of studies has demonstrated that negative stereotypes of ageing prevail in adults' perceptions about old age (see reviews in Green, 1981; Lutsky, 1980; McTavish, 1971), although recent findings from German representative surveys indicate that, at least in Germany, the image of ageing may have become more positive (Noelle-Neumann & Rothenberger, 1993). However, in the international literature findings of negative ageing stereotypes largely dominate the field. People above the age of 70 are generally considered to be the most unhappy of all age groups (e.g. Chiriboga, 1978; Tuckman & Lorge, 1952) and are evaluated less favourably than younger adults on various dimensions, including competence, independence, and mental and physical well-being (e.g. Golde & Kogan, 1959; Harris & Associates, 1975, 1981; Kogan, 1961; Kogan & Shelton, 1962; Palmore, 1977; and a critical review in Schonfield, 1982).

But even within the stereotypical images of ageing, not all aspects are negative. There are some select positive characteristics ascribed to old people in general (Braithwaite, 1986; Brubaker & Powers, 1976; Thorson, Whatley, & Hancock, 1974; Thomas & Yamamoto, 1975; Hummert, 1990, 1993). These include such attributes as wisdom, dignity, friendliness, patience, calmness and nurturance (Ahammer & Baltes, 1972; Heckhausen et al., 1989; Rothbaum, 1983). These positive images of old age have, of course, been highly emphasized as valuable counterparts to what many gerontologists referred to as the 'ageism' implied in negative stereotypes of ageing. However, we shall argue that negative stereotypic views of old age may not only deplete or threaten older persons' self-esteem. They may also serve important adaptive functions for the elderly, and therefore should not be discouraged, and in fact, prove to be highly resilient to political correctness.

A striking and recurrent feature of findings about ageing stereotypes was that a negative view of ageing only holds when 'old people in general' are the target of evaluation. As soon as the target is more specific, either in terms of a specifically described old person (Braithwaite, 1986; Braithwaite, Gibson, & Holman, 1985–86; Crockett, Press, & Osterkamp, 1979; Green, 1981; Lutsky, 1980; Weinberger & Millham, 1975) or the old subject him- or herself (Ahammer & Baltes, 1972; Brubaker & Powers, 1976; Borges & Dutton, 1976; Harris & Associates, 1975, 1981; Milligan, Powell, Harley, & Furchtgott, 1985; Mueller, Wonderlich, & Dugan, 1986; O'Gorman, 1980; Schulz & Fritz, 1988; Thomas, 1981) the image of ageing is much less negative, if not positive. Direct comparisons between ratings of specific old people and old people in general as targets indicated repeatedly that specific old people are viewed much more favourably than old people in general or the typical old person

(Bell & Stanfield, 1973; Braithwaite, 1986; Connor & Walsh, 1980; Connor, Walsh, Litzelman, & Alvarez, 1978; Harris & Associates, 1975, 1981). Under certain conditions older persons are regarded even more highly than young persons (Crockett et al., 1979; Sherman, Gold, & Sherman, 1978; Weinberger & Millham, 1975; see reviews in Green, 1981; Lutsky, 1980; McTavish, 1971).

These seemingly paradoxical findings can probably best be accounted for in the conceptual context of Weiner's (1985) attribution theory in achievement motivation (Banzinger & Drevenstedt, 1982; Blank, 1987; Green, 1984; Reno, 1979). According to this approach, the causal factor 'age' plays an inverse role in accounting for success and failure in young versus old adulthood. For old adults, age can, therefore, be construed as an inhibitory factor for success, and thereby render whatever is achieved a much more valuable outcome that attests to high underlying ability. For young adults, in contrast, age should facilitate success and therefore discredits whatever is achieved, and renders failures unrefutable testimonies of incompetence. In support of this reasoning, Banzinger and Drevenstedt (1982) found that age was more often used to explain the failure of an old target person, and the success of a young target person. Thus, any specific old person may be evaluated against the stereotypic expectation of low ability in old age. High or even moderate performances contradict the stereotypic expectations, and therefore may give rise to attributions of particularly high ability in the old person in question (Frieze, 1984; Green, 1981).

Converging evidence for the contrasting effect of specific old target persons against the general negative ageing stereotype was found in various studies (Crockett et al., 1979; Sherman et al., 1978; Weinberger & Millham, 1975). Weinberger and Millham (1975), for instance, report that the typical 75-year-old was described more negatively than the typical 25-year-old, but a 75-year-old specifically described in positive terms was evaluated more positively than a comparable 25-year-old target person. Sherman and colleagues (Sherman & Gold, 1978; Sherman et al., 1978) also found more positive evaluations of older as compared to younger target persons, who were specifically described in either positive or negative terms with regard to social interaction and achievement. Interestingly, they uncovered that older targets did receive particularly negative evaluations, if they were portrayed as socially inactive but active in achievement settings. Such a behaviour pattern may be so markedly discrepant from normative conceptions about old age that extreme and potentially pathological levels of personality disposition (e.g. ruthless careerist) were attributed to the target person. In sum, social stereotypes of ageing are largely negative, and seem to function as an unfavourable contrast to specific old persons, who appear as comparatively fortunate exceptions to an overwhelmingly negative image of ageing.

Social perception of being on-time versus off-time

Social norms about the age timing of behaviour were first studied in the 1960s by sociologists in the United States (Neugarten, Moore, & Lowe, 1965;

Neugarten & Petersen, 1957; Riley, Johnson, & Foner, 1972). It was found that people in a given society hold widely shared conceptions about the appropriate age timing of life-course transitions (e.g. getting married, peak of career) as well as specific behaviours (e.g. wearing a bikini, living in one's parents' house). Moreover and most importantly, these conceptions about normative age timing were applied to evaluate one's own status within the life course as being on-time or off-time (Neugarten et al., 1965; Sofer, 1970). These findings were replicated in the 1970s and 1980s in the US (Fallo-Mitchell & Ryff, 1982; Passuth & Maines, 1981; Zepelin, Sills, & Heath, 1986–87) and in Japan (Plath & Ikeda, 1975).

Age-normative conceptions about the timing of life-course transitions might also play an important role in the social perception of unfamiliar persons. Social stereotypes help to organize information about people in syndrome-like clusters. Knowledge about membership of a social category (e.g. related to age, gender, occupation) may be used to extrapolate information on various other dimensions, which are associated with the stereotype. This way, processes of social perception and interaction may be rendered more efficient. In the case of age-based stereotypes, a target person's age would give rise to a whole array of perceiver assumptions about his/her likely family status, number and age of children, and occupational position.

Krueger, Heckhausen and Hundertmark (1995) investigated the assumption that specific target persons are perceived, evaluated and interpreted in the normative framework of conceptions about age-appropriate timing of life-course events and transitions. Persons whose life-course status is incongruent with their chronological age provide a contrast to age-normative conceptions, a contrast which is perceived as atypical, surprising, and in need of explanation. The 'attribution-of-contrast' model (Heckhausen, 1990; Krueger et al., 1995) proposes that stereotype-incongruent persons elicit a search for causal attribution, which will typically result in the ascription of more extreme personality dispositions than in the case of stereotype-congruent persons (Krueger et al., 1995). Thus, for instance, an old person who is very active in strenuous athletic exercise would be perceived as particularly physically fit, tenacious and health-minded.

In sum, age-normative conceptions of being on-time versus off-time shape processes of social perception and evaluation. Based on the knowledge of chronological age, assumptions about age-congruent behaviour are made, and if violated give rise to polarized evaluations and causal attributions.

Normative conceptions about development in adulthood

Age-normative conceptions may pertain not only to life events and transitions, but also to psychological characteristics. In a research programme conducted at the Max Planck Institute for Human Development and Education, it was investigated whether lay persons hold consensual conceptions about age-related changes in psychological processes across the adult life span (Heckhausen, 1989, 1990; Heckhausen et al., 1989; Heckhausen & Baltes, 1991; Heckhausen

& Hosenfeld, 1988; Heckhausen & Krueger, 1993; Hundertmark & Heckhausen, 1994; Krueger & Heckhausen, 1993). The research paradigm used in a series of studies involved ratings of psychological attributes with regard to their perceived changeability over the adult life course, the expected ages of onset and closing of change, their desirability and perceived controllability. The findings revealed substantial consensus on the changeability of psychological characteristics, their timing and perceived controllability both within and across different subject age groups. Overall, the pattern of expected psychological change across the life span corresponded to a negative ageing stereotype, with decreasing potential for developmental gains and increasing risks of decline attributed to higher age levels. In accordance with this pattern, controllability of psychological change was perceived to be lower at higher ages. However, even for old age, some select developmental growth was expected. Within the overall consensus displayed by adults at various ages, the old adults exhibited more elaborate conceptions about developmental change, both in terms of the richness of dimensions perceived as changing, and with regard to the differentiation of timing-related expectations.

Given that age-normative conceptions are consensual and extend to expectations about psychological change, how do these relate to beliefs about developmental change for the self? Heckhausen and Krueger (1993) investigated this question by inquiring about psychological change both 'for most other people' and for 'yourself personally' throughout seven decades of the adult life span, ranging from 20 to 90 years of age. Again, ratings of psychological attributes with regard to change direction, strength, desirability, controllability and age timing were used to assess age-related conceptions of lay persons at different age levels. Figure 14.2 displays the findings for the three subject age groups, young (20 to 35 years), middle-aged (40 to 55 years), and old (over 60 years) adults. The trajectories are given separately for self- and other-related conceptions and for desirable and undesirable attributes.

The three panels of Figure 14.2 reveal an overall congruence of age trajectories expected for adult developmental change in the self and most other people. This indicates that age-normative conceptions may serve as guidelines for personal perceptions of developmental change. However, the middle-aged and especially the old adults also expressed characteristic differences pertaining to perceived change in old age. Selectively, with regard to old age, self-related conceptions were more favourable than other-related conceptions, in that more desirable attributes were expected to decline later and less for the self than for 'most other people', and undesirable attributes were expected to increase earlier and more for 'most other people' than for the self. It is quite noteworthy that this pattern of self-enhancement was particularly pronounced in the older adults. Apparently, old age represents a threat to self-esteem that is compensated by construing an even less fortunate image of the developmental course of other old people. Such social downgrading can be interpreted as a self-protective strategy of the 'resilient mind' (Baltes & Baltes, 1990; Staudinger, Marsiske, & Baltes, in press) and as such may function as compensatory secondary control of ageing-related losses (Heckhausen & Schulz, 1995).

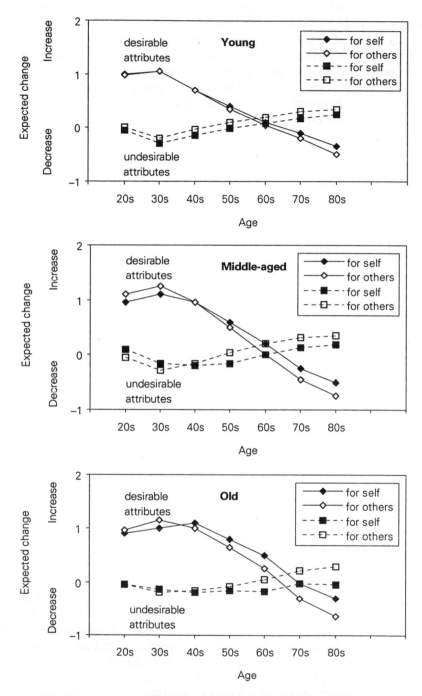

Figure 14.2 *Change in desirable and undesirable attributes expected for the self and most other people: separately for young, middle-aged and old adults (adapted from Heckhausen & Krueger, 1993)*

This interpretation also accords with other empirical findings on self–other differences in perceptions of ageing (Harris & Associates, 1975, 1981; O'Gorman, 1980). Cross-national survey research conducted in the United States has found substantially more favourable perceptions of own personal old age as compared to that of others on a variety of dimensions, such as loneliness, financial problems, and health status (Harris & Associates, 1975, 1981). O'Gorman undertook a secondary analysis of this survey data and uncovered a telling pattern underlying this self-enhancement effect. Those elderly who perceived personal problems in a given area of functioning (e.g. health) attributed more severe problems to their age peers than did those who did not perceive the respective domain as personally problematic. This finding leads us on to the final topic in this section about age-normative conceptions: the role of strategic social comparisons.

Social comparisons can be directed upwards towards comparison partners superior to oneself, downwards at inferior targets, or be lateral, when addressing similar others. Festinger's classic theory of social comparison comprised upward comparisons which serve to improve the self, and comparisons with similar others, which assist the individual in self-assessment (Festinger, 1954). Recent conceptual developments have extended the theory of social comparison to include downward comparisons, which serve to enhance the self-esteem of the individual (Wills, 1981; Wood, 1989). In the context of ageing-related change, each of these three kinds of social comparison may be essential to maintain optimal functioning and subjective well-being. Upward comparisons with those more advanced in developmental growth or less constrained by ageing-related losses can motivate the individual to strive for developmental growth and prevent developmental decline. Downward comparisons with those less advanced or more impaired, on the other hand, help to protect self-esteem and motivation in spite of inevitable losses associated with the ageing process and thus constitute attempts to compensate for negative effects by secondary control. Lateral comparisons, finally, guide the individual to identify age-appropriate challenges and in evaluating his or her own developmental status (Heckhausen, 1995; Heckhausen & Krueger, 1993).

As reported above, Heckhausen and Krueger (1993) have found evidence for select downward comparisons with regard to old age. Moreover, an investigation of developmental aspirations revealed that young adults identified with early mid-life, while middle-aged and old adults were oriented towards age groups younger than themselves (Heckhausen & Krueger, 1993; Heckhausen & Wrosch, 1995). Thus, at each age level adults selected a comparison age group with comparatively higher status, either more mature or being less aged. That is, old adults compare most frequently with comparison partners younger than themselves, and rarely with older individuals.

To summarize: age-normative conceptions about adult development involve substantial consensus within and across age groups in a given society. They provide a normative framework to evaluate one's own personal status in development. Moreover, they serve as a social reference for construing informative, favourable and challenging comparisons of oneself with others.

Social construction in old age as determined by interpersonal processes

In the remainder of this chapter we will focus on what Berger and Luckmann (1966) have called the 'fundamental experience of the other' that is, the experience of interacting and dealing with others in the construction of everyday life. As argued above, the experience of growing old is commonly shared with others who are themselves ageing or growing up. Thus, social construction in old age also implies the need to manage and adapt to changing interpersonal contexts. In the following, we argue that interpersonal processes constitute the relational context for social construction in old age. This relational context is defined by the structure of the personal network and by the social functions and provisions available to the old person. Interaction behaviours and personal relationships in old age – as argued above in the case of age-normative conceptions – follow specific life-course patterns and can therefore only be wholly understood from the perspective of life-span developmental psychology (Antonucci, 1985; Baltes & Silverberg, 1994; Skolnick, 1986). Such lifelong development of interpersonal processes determine the relational opportunity structures in old age and influence the successful mastery of developmental tasks which are specific to old age. We concentrate on three facets of interpersonal processes in late life.

First, the age-related changes in personal relationships and social networks in old age are discussed. What are the possible mechanisms that regulate the composition and functioning of social networks in late life? How can age-related change in interpersonal relationships be explained? For example, do old people seek and engage in interpersonal contact for other reasons and in other ways than they did when they were younger? Secondly, the differential structural and functional facets of friendship and family relationships in late life are described. For example, we ask how friendship relationships differ from family relationships in respect to what old people can gain or lose in such relationships. In a third part of this section the regulation and management of supportive transactions in old age is addressed. Specifically, we discuss the mechanisms that regulate supportive interactions and relationships in old age. To what extent can old people exert control over or optimize the outcomes of their social support networks?

Age-related changes in personal relationships and social networks

Most of the incisive experiences of late adulthood such as, for example, retirement and thus losing professional contacts (e.g. Block, 1984; Havighurst, Munnichs, Neugarten, & Thomae, 1970; Carp, 1972), the experience of one's children finally leaving the home (Lowenthal, Thurnher, Chiriboga et al., 1975; White & Edwards, 1990) or the personal loss of one's spouse, close relatives or long-term friends (Garrett, 1987; Stevens, 1988) are associated with changes in the structural and functional characteristics of the old individual's personal network and relationships. While such changes follow a more or less predictable pattern, other age-related changes in the structure and function of personal networks might be characterized by the old person's idiosyncratic and volitional efforts and interaction behaviours (e.g. Carstensen, 1993a; Lang, 1994). The issue of what social forces determine how old people organize and manage their personal relationships in order to adapt most adequately to age-related changes has been one of the major debates in social gerontology since the early 1960s (Lee, 1985; Osgood, 1989).

On the one side, disengagement theorists claimed that social withdrawal reflects an old individual's adaptive response to social forces such as age stereotypes and to personal losses (Cumming & Henry, 1961; Maddox, 1963). Old people disengage from social life as they become aware 'of the shortness of life and the scarcity of the time remaining [and that] available ego energy is lessened' (Cumming, Henry, & Damianopoulus, 1961). On the other side, from the perspective of activity theory (Havighurst, Neugarten, & Tobin, 1968; Lemon, Bengtson, & Peterson, 1972) it was argued that successful adaptation in late life requires old people to participate in social life and to be socially active. From a life-course perspective, Atchley (1977, 1993) claims that individuals in old age prefer those social interactions and relationships that allow for continuity of their lifelong role identities, experiences and competencies. Those old people who used to be socially active when they were middle-aged keep up their social roles, while those who never engaged in social activities will not change in late life. In contrast to this, Rosow (1974, 1982) proposed that successful adaptation to loss of social roles in old age can only be achieved when the ageing experience is shared with peers. Thus, socialization to old age requires old people to live in age-segregated communities where they can take over new social roles.

More recently, emphasis has been placed on the adaptive and motivational mechanisms in the social interaction behaviour of old people, according to which old people select and regulate their social relationships and their interaction partners primarily so that their emotional needs and preferences can be satisfied and optimized (Carstensen, 1993a; Carstensen et al., 1995; Lang & Carstensen, 1994; Lang, Staudinger, & Carstensen, 1995; Lang & Tesch-Römer, 1993; Marsiske et al., 1995). Age-related changes in social interaction behaviour and social networks are seen as reflecting a developmental process in which old people adapt to the changing demands and needs of late life. This perspective is paradigmatically reflected in the socioemotional selectivity theory that has been proposed by Laura Carstensen (1987, 1991, 1992, 1993a).

According to socioemotional selectivity theory, people throughout their life span are motivated to interact with other persons mainly for three reasons: because they want to acquire information or learn from other people; because they want to develop and maintain their self-definition in order to learn about themselves and find out who they are; and because they want to realize and experience meaningful and profound emotional exchanges with others. These three basic functions of social interaction (acquiring information, self-development and emotion regulation) operate in different constellations across the life span. While in earlier phases of life – childhood, youth, adolescence and early to middle adulthood – people prefer social partners from whom they can learn something about the world (i.e. information acquisition) and about themselves (i.e. self-development), in later phases of life, emotional regulation becomes the most salient motivation for individuals to interact with others.

Carstensen (1993a) argues that when individuals perceive close future endings, long-term future goals become less important, resulting in reduced interest in the informational or identity-related functions of social inter-actions. Consequently, emotional regulation becomes more important in old age because the reduced future perspective makes it seem more promising to seek and obtain short-term benefits and gratifications in the immediate relational context. Socioemotional selectivity theory brings together the different, above-mentioned perspectives on social ageing that are usually seen as diametrically opposed: activity theory and disengagement theory. Old people narrow down their social life and their social participation in order to intensify their engagement in a selected range of social functions and the close emotional relationships that seem to give the most meaning to their remaining lifetime.

Recently, Lang and Carstensen (1994) provided an empirical illustration of such social selectivity in late life, in reporting a cross-sectional age comparison with data from the Berlin Aging Study (BASE), a large multidisciplinary research project based on a representative sample of old and very old people aged 70 to 104 years (see Baltes, Mayer, Helmchen, & Steinhagen-Thiessen, 1993). Social networks in this study were measured using the circle diagram measure developed by Kahn and Antonucci (1980) that consists of three embedded concentric circles grouped around a small inner circle that contains the German word for 'I'. Respondents are asked to record in the inner, first circle those people to whom they feel *very close*, so close that they cannot imagine life without them. In the middle circle, respondents were asked to name those people they considered *close*, but not quite as close as those in the first circle, and in the outermost circle they reported the names of social partners who were *less close* to them but who were also important. Lang and Carstensen (1994) found evidence that the age-related differences in total number of social partners did indeed depend on the degree of emotional closeness to social partners (see Figure 14.3). While the number of network members described as very close did not differ between the older and younger subsamples, the number of less close social relationships was considerably fewer for very old than for old people. Thus, while there were differences in overall network size between people in their seventies, eighties, nineties and older, these differences mostly pertained to more peripheral social relation-ships.

Reduced social interactions and personal relationships in late life thus also seem to reflect the old individual's changed needs and motivations. Of course, this does not mean that the social worlds of elderly people reflect choice alone. In later adulthood, illness and deaths of social partners obviously reduce the availability of particular types of social relationships (e.g. with siblings, peer

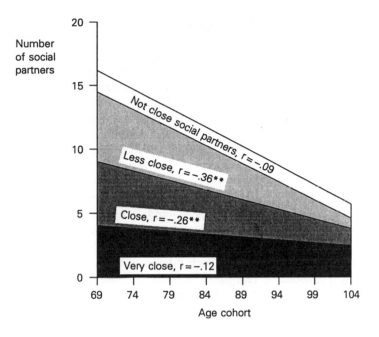

Figure 14.3 *Number of social partners and degree of emotional closeness as a function of age (adapted from Lang & Carstensen, 1994)*

friends) and interpersonal experiences. Personal losses such as losing a spouse, surviving one's own children or losing old friends are a rather common experience among those old people who survive into their late eighties or nineties (cf. Bury & Holme, 1991). Moreover, the structural composition of social networks in old age is also determined by the cumulative impact of decisions made throughout life concerning mate selection, career decisions and friendship networks that constitute social convoys over the life span (Antonucci, 1991; Kahn & Antonucci, 1980). In other words, the social worlds of the elderly not only reflect current preferences for social contact, but also effects that extend beyond individuals' control as well as choices and decisions that were made decades earlier.

Moreover, it is not the frequency of social interaction or the number of network partners but the quality, emotional meaningfulness and functional adequacy of enduring close ties that contribute to well-being in late life (Beckman, 1981; Ishii-Kuntz, 1990; Lang & Carstensen, 1994; Lee & Markides, 1990; Lowenthal & Haven, 1968; Rook, 1984). This also pertains to the well-established findings that the absence of close confidants and intimate relationships is associated with increased vulnerability and mortality in old age (e.g. Berkman & Syme, 1979; Blazer, 1982; Hammer, 1983; Orth-Gomer & Johnson, 1987; Steinbach, 1992; Sugisawa, Liang, & Liu, 1994). While such findings prove the adaptive function of personal relationships in late life, the differential contribution of specific role-related relationships in friendship and in family relationships remains to be discussed.

Finally, it is important to emphasize that the personal relationships and social networks of older people do not exclusively provide gratification and resources but also involve the unpleasant side of social interactions (e.g. Rook, 1984, 1989). Personal relationships are often a major source of daily stressors (Bolger & Kelleher, 1993). Most personal relationships go through times of conflict or periods of relational crisis that need to be mastered if the social partners are willing to maintain their relationship (Antonucci, 1985; Duck, 1986). Successfully managing the stable and varying, positive and negative aspects of family ties or friendships might be fundamental to high levels of social adaptivity throughout adulthood and late life (Lang, Featherman, & Nesselroade, 1995; Marsiske et al., 1995; Morgan, 1990).

Age-related changes in personal relationships are explained by old people's changed social motivations and needs, which results from limited future perspectives. Managing close emotional relationships in old age is also associated with some relational investment that precludes maintenance of less meaningful relationships. Finally, such interpersonal processes are moderated by the old individual's relational context as defined by the structural properties of friendship and family networks.

Structural and functional facets of friendship and family relationships

According to the concept of functional specificity of relations (Weiss, 1969; Litwak, 1985) different role relationships in an older individual's social network, such as, for example, with spouse, children, siblings, friends or neighbours, serve and fulfil specific tasks for the old person. Such task-specific functions of different role relationships are seen to be exclusive and so cannot be substituted for each other. This means, for example, that the tasks specific to a marital relationship can never be taken over by a child or a friend. In contrast to the notion of functional specificity of relations, the hierarchical-compensatory model (Cantor, 1979; Chatters, Taylor, & Jackson, 1986; Stoller & Earl, 1983) claims that friendship and family relationships are functionally equivalent and differ only in respect to their hierarchical structure; that is, spouses or children are closer to the old person than friends, and thus serve more functions in the network. When no spouse and children are available, other relatives or friends may take over their functions.

Empirical evidence for one of the two perspectives, functional specificity or hierarchical substitution, is still scarce. There is some evidence suggesting that friendship and family relationships differ both in respect to normative obligations and to the interpersonal processes that regulate them (Litwak, 1989; Simons, 1983; Verbrugge, 1978–79). For example, in contrast to family relationships that are constructed by genetic relatedness, kinship and legal ties, friendship is constructed by the voluntary and deliberately selected involvement of two or more partners with each other (Adams & Blieszner, 1994; Blau, 1973; Chappell, 1983; Ishii-Kuntz, 1990). Consequently, failure to abide by normative expectations in friendships (e.g. Roberto & Scott, 1986a, 1986b) may lead to the dissolution of the relationship. Moreover, longitudinal data suggests that while the relevance of family roles remains quite stable in old age, the significance of other social roles seems to decrease (Field & Minkler, 1993; Lehr & Minnemann, 1987).

In general, family relations prove to be reliable and stable ties in old and very old age, even if no special efforts are made to keep in touch or maintain these relationships (Carstensen, 1993b; Crohan & Antonucci, 1989; Field & Minkler, 1993). This seems to be equally valid for parent–child relationships in late life (Carstensen, 1992; Wagner & Settersten, 1993) and for sibling relationships (Cicirelli, 1989; Scott, 1990). Findings from the Berkeley older generation study revealed that family contacts even increased in old age (Field & Minkler, 1988, 1993). Moreover, the most often named source of instrumental and emotional social support in old age is the close family (Caplan, 1982; Depner & Ingersoll-Dayton, 1988; Sussman, 1985).

However, friendship relationships are associated with higher social satisfaction than relationships with family members who are not living in the same household (Chappell, 1983; Larson, Mannell, & Zuzanek, 1986). A possible explanation for this could be that friends are often discharged from tasks that are related to instrumental support exchange, and thus are less burdened than family members. Friends are often named as confidants of old people (Keith, Hill, Goudy, & Powers, 1984; Strain & Chappell, 1982) or are associated with pleasant interactions such as social companionship (Crohan & Antonucci, 1989; Rawlins, 1992). In this respect, friends might play a moderating role in older people's social networks by functioning as a counterbalance to the family (Johnson, 1983) and by providing opportunities for various social activities in the community (Peters & Kaiser, 1985). However, when it comes to supportive transactions between friends, satisfaction with the friendship is associated with the perceived equity of the exchange (Roberto, 1989; Roberto & Scott, 1986a; Rook, 1989). Nonreciprocal exchanges with friends seem to be even more detrimental than those with family members (Antonucci & Jackson, 1990). However, such findings might not pertain to close or best friends. Jones and Vaughan (1990) reported that older adults' satisfaction with their best friends was predicted by the absence of conflict and by the old individuals' communal orientation (cf. Clark, 1984) to the best friend rather than by characteristics of the social exchange. These findings nicely illustrate the basic argument made throughout this chapter emphasizing the idea that interpersonal processes do actually play a crucial role in determining the 'social construction of reality' in late life. The availability of specific social partners and types of relationships (i.e. 'best friend', 'just friend', spouse, child, etc.) constitutes the social context within which older people can select and evaluate the social attitudes and social behaviours that might contribute to an enhanced quality of life.

In sum, friendship and family relationships are associated with distinct social provisions and functions that cannot easily be substituted for each other. Thus, relational contexts determine to some extent the interpersonal processes that are adaptive in late life. Finally, there is also evidence that, in general, older people are satisfied with both their family relationships and their friendships (Field & Minkler, 1988; Herzog & Rodgers, 1981; Ryff, 1989).

Managing social support in late life

A fundamental challenge in late life is related to the experience of becoming increasingly dependent on other people's willingness and capacity to provide adequate social support. While the individual during middle adulthood typically was used to mastering daily routines and tasks easily and autonomously, in late life the same everyday activities may become strenuous and require additional effort. Old people find themselves confronted with the developmental task of accepting their dependence on others in some behavioural domains while simultaneously maintaining autonomy in some selected domains that are important to their self and well-being. It should be noted here that during all phases of the life course there is some developmental dynamic between autonomy and dependence, although these are different in content and function (for a seminal discussion of this topic see Baltes & Silverberg, 1994).

A basic function of personal relationships in old age is related to the receipt of social support and the possible effects of social support on well-being and mental health (Schwarzer & Leppin, 1991, see also Chapter 5 of the present book). In the literature, two models are predominantly discussed: (1) the direct-effect model, which claims that receiving social support generally leads to positive outcomes; and (2) the buffering-effect model, according to which social support is most adaptive when individuals face stressful situations or life events (Cassel, 1974; Cobb, 1979; Cohen & Wills, 1985; Thoits, 1985; Wills, 1991). It has been noted, however, that the two models are not exclusive and may not even be complementary (Pfaff, 1989). Another model of social support which also provides a framework for explaining links to subjective well-being is derived from exchange theory. According to this model, receipt of support will produce positive effects when the individual is able to reciprocate the support or subjectively believes that the support has been reciprocated at some point in the relationship (Sauer & Cauer, 1985). There is increasing empirical evidence for the supportive exchange model (e.g. Antonucci, 1990; Danigelis & Fengler, 1990).

Social exchange theory assumes that, analogous to patterns of economic exchange, individuals tend to maximize their benefits and minimize their costs in social interactions. Since social exchange resources can be material as well as immaterial it is important to note that this reflects a huge difference in economic exchanges. Costs and benefits of social exchange can be perceived differently by individuals. This gives rise to a certain amount of uncertainty about at which point a given exchange is perceived to be 'just' or 'equal'. The exchange of goods and services is also regulated by social norms. The most crucial is the norm of reciprocity. According to this universal norm, any individual who receives goods or services is supposed to reciprocate this action adequately (Gouldner, 1960). Whether a given exchange corresponds to this norm is governed by social- and culture-specific rules of exchange (Befu, 1980). These rules refer to a variety of attributes which characterize the social exchange process.

Such considerations are in line with suggestions that both characteristics of the person and of the environment and the transaction of personal and environmental resources should be considered (Lawton, 1989). Thus, the environmental context of social support exchanges need to be considered. The older person in need of help, for example, might not always be in a position to influence what kind of help or support is available. In some instances, social support might not be adequate or might even have detrimental aspects, particularly in the case of overprotection, or when too much support is offered, or when support is provided that is not needed. For example, when old people do not feel capable of reciprocating received support, this might lead to increased levels of stress. The adequacy of support received might also depend on the degree to which old people still feel 'in control' of such supportive transactions or the support relationship.

Exchange and resource theory approaches have also argued that the effect of social exchange on well-being depends on the nature of the interaction process as well as on the relation between the interaction partners (Adams, 1965; Homans, 1961; Walster, Berscheid, & Walster, 1973). Weinberger (1981), for example, in a field experiment found that older help-seekers were helped more often than younger help-seekers. Note that in this field experiment the help-giver did not expect to be reciprocated for their help. Characteristics of the help-receiver, such as old age or intensity of need, seem to facilitate giving help without expecting immediate response. This could be due to other social norms such as altruism or social responsibility. Older help-seekers are more likely to be helped because the norm of altruism is more salient in helping older people than in helping younger people. Hence, norms other than the norm of reciprocity could also influence the rules of exchange in old age.

Another facet of social behaviour towards support givers in late life is suggested by research on the learned dependency model in old age as proposed by Margret Baltes (1995). The learned dependency model claims that dependent behaviours not only imply losses but also entail gains. For example, empirical evidence in nursing homes revealed that staff members were most responsive to old residents who displayed dependent behaviours, whereas independent behaviours of old residents were mostly ignored. Thus, old residents who gave up their autonomy in one domain (e.g. self-care) actually succeeded in gaining some social attention from their social partners. Further research could demonstrate that residents' independent behaviours increased when social partners were trained to be more responsive to these (Baltes, Neumann, & Zank, 1994). Margret Baltes proposes that old people who live in nursing homes regulate and optimize the available resources in their environment by initiating such dependence-support and independence-ignore scripts (Baltes, 1995; Lang, Marsiske, Baltes, & Baltes, 1995). Bandura (1982) has proposed the concept 'proxy control' for such processes, when the individual assigns control in particular domains of functioning to other persons and thus exerts an indirect influence over the environment. Through use of proxy control in interpersonal contexts the old person may compensate for loss of direct control. Finally, life-span developmental psychology offers an additional explanation for the existence of specific interpersonal rules in old age. Kahn (1979; Kahn & Antonucci, 1980) proposed the convoy model of social support and the concept of the support bank as metaphors for lifelong and long-term exchange processes. According to the social convoy model, close relationships created during earlier phases of the life course have a strong influence on structural and functional properties of the social network in later life phases (Antonucci, 1990; Field, Minkler, Falk, & Leino, 1993; Kahn & Antonucci, 1980). Just like a convoy in traffic, a person is accompanied by a convoy of social ties throughout the life span. An individual's convoy changes, though, and has particular characteristics at different life phases. For example, the social convoy of an 82-year-old woman who married at the age of 25 and who gave birth to three children differs in many central features from that of an 81-year-old woman who never married and never had children. For example, both women might be good friends for more than 50 years, yet despite this long time of shared experiences, they might differ very much in respect to how central and important they are in the other friend's current personal network. While for the 82-year-old mother, her adult children might become an important source of support and satisfaction, the 81-year-old, childless woman might prefer to have contact with her best friends. It is a basic notion of the social convoy model that relationships are hierarchically organized and might change their hierarchical positions within a particular individual's social network across the life course (cf. Antonucci & Akiyama, in press; Carstensen & Lang, in press).

The concept of the support bank assumes that within an individual's convoy there is long-term reciprocal exchange; that is, any help one receives can be reciprocated later when there is an opportunity. Take, for example, the above-described 82-year-old mother. Most of her adult life, this mother might have spent bringing up and educating her three children and might now expect her children to feel as responsible for her as she did for them, when they were young. Another example might be her 81-year-old friend. It might be that more than 50 years ago this friend supported and helped the mother and her spouse very much, for example with getting a job and finding an apartment in the postwar years. So the 82-year-old mother might act as a support bank to her childless friend in times of increased need of support. As these examples illustrate, the concept of the support bank is not limited to old-age-specific exchange rules but broadens the perspective to a consideration of lifelong processes. It is an open question whether the support bank and particular exchange rules in old age are complementary or not and how they have to be combined (Morgan, Schuster, & Butler, 1991). It seems plausible, though, that both age-specific exchange rules and long-term support exchange influence the process of exchange in old age depending on the type of relationship with exchange partners and depending on what is exchanged.

In sum, managing social support and personal relationships in old age is seen as determined both by the old person's competence and social preferences as well as by the individual's social context. Thus, relational contexts also determine which interpersonal behaviours are adaptive for the old person in the process of regulating, selecting and constructing close emotional relationships and supportive exchanges.

Conclusion

In this chapter, two major domains of the social construction in old age have been described and discussed. First, age-normative conceptions about development in adulthood were seen as providing developmental constraints and challenges to the old person. They inform the individual about the age-graded structure of the life span, the developmental gains and losses to be expected during different phases of the life span, and provide normative social reference frames for assessing and evaluating one's own developmental status. In this way, age-normative conceptions guide active attempts to shape one's own development as well as attempts to compensate for inevitable ageing-related losses that are perceived as uncontrollable.

Secondly, we focused on the structural and functional facets of personal relationships and social networks in old age that constitute the relational opportunity structures for social construction in old age. Age-related changes in personal relationships and social support management are seen as the individual's adaptive responses to the changing developmental constraints and demands of old age. Old people narrow down their social networks and appear to focus their social behaviours on close friendship and family relationships that provide emotionally meaningful contacts (Carstensen, 1992; Lang & Carstensen, 1994). This change in social motivations and preferences reflects old people's conception of their limited remaining lifetime and changed social needs resulting from their increased vulnerability in late life. Managing personal relationships and social support thus requires that the old person gives up control over his or her life in some functional domains in order to free up resources for functioning in others.

Age-normative conceptions, besides the biological and societal sources of influence on the social construction in old age, determine the conceptions of others as well as the individual's behaviour, including interpersonal behaviours. Social stereotypes and conceptions about age groups function as guidelines for evaluating and influencing one's close personal relationships, and also serve as reference frames to generate self-protective interpretations. What is expected and how one behaves towards other people – friends, relatives or close family members – is strongly influenced by normative conceptions about age. Social interactions in old age inevitably confront the old person with the age-normative conceptions of social partners as well as with norms pertaining to social behaviours, best reflected in the processes of receiving and giving support. Normative conceptions regulate the social expectations and behaviours of interaction partners. Moreover, there is also evidence for age-specific rules regulating adaptive interpersonal processes and social motivations in old age (Antonucci, 1985; Carstensen, 1993a; Marsiske et al., 1995).

Social construction in old age is determined by age-normative conceptions that are also transmitted and carried on by the age-specific
interpersonal relationships of old people. Age-graded expectations about
developmental goals and losses at different stages of the life-span shape
the individual's attempts to influence his or her own development. Age-
related shifts in the dynamic of gains and losses also determine interpersonal processes in old age. In spite of considerable social and personal
losses, motivational and social-interactive processes enable the old
individual to maximize the socioemotional benefits of personal relationships.

In this respect, the model of selective optimization with compensation
(Baltes & Baltes, 1990; Marsiske et al., 1995) as well as the model of
primary and secondary control (Heckhausen & Schulz, 1995) can be
applied. Age-normative conceptions guide the selection of goals for
primary control and help generate secondary control in spite of ageing-
related losses. Moreover, age-normative conceptions assist social
perception with regard to the life-span timing of common life-course
transitions. Finally, selection, compensation and optimization are also
reflected in old people's social behaviours and social functioning.
Selection, compensation and optimization refer to those mechanisms
and processes that determine which social environments are preferred
and how social responses of interaction partners are solicited and relied
upon.

Further reading

Baltes, P.B. (1987). Theoretical propositions of life-span developmental psychology: On the
dynamics between growth and decline. *Developmental Psychology, 23*, 611–626. Good overview
of life-span developmental psychology.

Carstensen, L.L. (1991). Socioemotional selectivity theory: Social activity in life-span context.
Annual Review of Gerontology and Geriatrics, 11, 195–217. Describes the motivational and
emotional propositions of age-related changes in social interaction behaviours and social
activity in late life.

Hagestad, G. O. (1990). Social perspectives on the life course. In R. Binstock & L. George (Eds),
Handbook of aging and the social sciences (3rd ed. pp. 151–168). New York: Academic Press.
Comprehensive chapter on the social construction of the life course, including sociological
research on age norms.

Heckhausen, J. & Schulz, R. (1995). A life-span theory of control. *Psychological Review, 102*,
284–304. Conceptual and review article on life-span changes in primary and secondary control
behaviour.

Marsiske, M., Lang, F.R., Baltes, P.B., & Baltes, M.M. (1995). Selective optimization with
compensation: Life-span perspectives on successful human development. In R. Dixon & L.
Bäckman (Eds), *Psychological compensation: Managing losses and promoting gains* (pp. 35–79).
Hillsdale, NJ: Lawrence Erlbaum. Discusses successful social and cognitive development across
the life-span and reviews empirical research which illustrates selection, compensation and
optimization processes.

15

Culture and Migration

Günter Bierbrauer and Paul Pedersen

Contents

The increased volume of international migration is a major challenge to the world's social, political and economic systems. It is estimated that there are about 100 million immigrants, refugees, asylum-seekers and immigrant workers living outside their country of origin (Russel & Teitelbaum, 1992). It is expected that this number will rise sharply in the next millennium. Poverty, wars, political persecution and ecological disasters are among the main driving forces creating mass migration and these are increasing in frequency as well as intensity. Immigration has risen to the top of the international agenda because of the large numbers of migrants who moved from Third World countries towards industrial societies which are not only experiencing political insecurity and uncertainty but also facing new types of social and hitherto unknown ethnic tensions (Martin, 1992b).

Moghaddam, Taylor and Wright (1993) point out that historically there were differences of geography, institutionalized segregation and barriers to assimilation that limited migrations of people, and consequently, little attention was paid to cultural differences and similarities until fairly recently. 'This lack of interpersonal contact created little general interest in cultural differences. With groups either living isolated from one another or minority groups abandoning their divergent cultures, there was little interest in the study of cross-cultural contact. Today, however, cultural isolation is the exception rather than the rule' (p. 133).

The social psychological dynamics
of emigration and immigration

Krau (1991) points out the value of the sociopsychological approach to immigrant problems in discovering the 'hidden mechanisms of apparently illogical, contradictory and discriminatory behaviors on the one hand and maladaptive attitudes on the other' (p. xvii). The phenomenon of migration is complicated and multidimensional. First of all, each migration must be viewed in the context of historical and political events to be understood as a consequence of what has happened before and what is expected to happen in the future. Secondly, each migration is a social movement responding to the societal pressures to move from one place to another because of social, economic and political problems and opportunities. Thirdly, each migrant is motivated by personal considerations and psychologically perceived threats and opportunities so that individuals may migrate to the same place for different reasons.

The social and psychological dynamics of this process are extremely complex and not well understood. Comprehending the process of migration requires an analysis of how humans accommodate to environmental changes and how the environment is organized to induce such changes. Research on migration and cultural contact draws from subject matters covering the entire social sciences: sociology, anthropology, economics, history and other fields of study. A social psychological perspective can offer a conceptual and empirical base from which an analysis of both individual processes and environmental forces is possible. Foreshadowing one of the central arguments of this chapter is Smith and Bond's (1993) contention that migrants who place a higher value on their own traditions are better able to resist host culture pressures to conform. 'The net result in many immigrant societies is not the "melting pot" so many feared, but rather the subcultural mosaic so many sought' (p. 219).

Because of the complexity of the migration process we have to deal with five different levels of psychological analysis: (1) individual (e.g. cognition, affect, personality dispositions); (2) interpersonal (e.g. dyadic interactions); (3) intragroup (e.g. intragroup conflict); (4) intergroup (e.g. ingroup/outgroup conflicts); (5) cultural (e.g. cultural variation and immigration policy). An adequate understanding of migration requires a comprehensive view which simultaneously takes into account the five levels.

The present chapter will only deal with selected social psychological phenomena related to migration. It has to be acknowledged at the outset that there are many unclear and uncharted areas in the migration landscape. When projected against the myriad of social psychological dimensions of the migration experiences the topic appears to be unexplored and so diffuse as to be daunting. The difficulty of doing research focusing on the psychological aspects of migration has been recognized by others and the subject has not received the attention it deserves. For instance, a bibliographical search of articles published over a 19-year period (1974–93) in 21 primary psychological journals revealed that only slightly more than 1 per cent of more than 30,000 articles published during this period were in some way or other related to the issues of migration, refugees and relocation (Rogler, 1994). Despite its neglect by mainstream psychological research the process and dynamic of migration issues lend themselves almost naturally to the fundamental lessons of social psychology's Lewinian tradition which considers the complex relationships between objective circumstances and subjective interpretations.

According to Ross and Nisbett (1991), social psychology's most important and enduring contribution has been the theoretical and empirical demonstration of the profound influence of three forces on human behaviour: (1) the power of the social context producing or constraining behaviour; (2) the importance of people's subjective interpretation of the situation; and (3) the dynamic interplay of individual and social forces. The aim of this chapter is to show where in the process of migration it is desirable to design or apply interventions in the social context, in the individual perception or in the interaction of the two.

International migration is a major life episode, as it involves the transition of individuals and groups from one geographical location and culture to another and affects almost all spheres of life. The framework presented in Figure 15.1 is adopted from Rogler (1994) and draws attention to some of the key issues discussed in this chapter. The framework makes a distinction among the cultural level (e.g. immigration policies of the host societies), group level (e.g. immigrant category) and individual level (e.g. cultural orientation) and the resulting changes in socioeconomic status, social networks and acculturation patterns of the immigrants. The migration experience connects the different contexts of the sending and receiving societies as they influence immigrants' adaptation. The migration experience and the culture contact are mediated by personal variables like age, gender and education which exist prior to migration, and by category of immigrant group (e.g. migrant worker or refugee) as they affect the social psychological concomitants (e.g. socioeconomic status, social bonding and ethnic identity). Of course, this simplified framework does not include all possible patterns of independent influences that mediate the migration experience.

The remainder of the chapter is organized into three interrelated parts which describe the process of migration. The first part describes the immigration policies and histories of four main immigration countries; the second is organized around the issues that motivate people to migrate; and the third part deals with the dynamics of cultural contact.

Migration and national contexts

Most immigration countries identify immigration as the most important issue. They fear that if migration continues to the same extent as in the past, anti-immigrant parties and sentiments will gain influence in their countries. Although the membership states of the European Union have developed legal instruments to draw up uniform policies on the handling of asylum seekers, war refugees and immigrant workers, there are considerable differences in how immigration is dealt with.

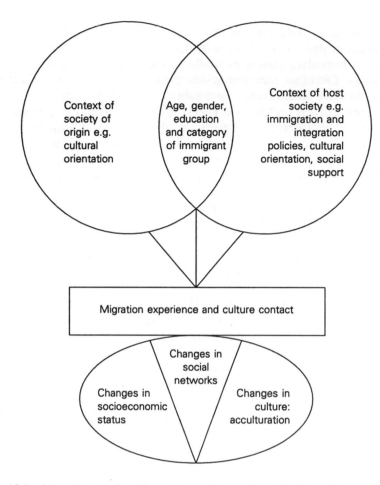

Figure 15.1   *International migration: contexts of the society of origin and host society, demographic characteristics and category of immigrant group, migration experience and culture contact (adapted from Rogler, 1994)*

Differences with regard to immigration history, political heritage and the degree to which there is a need to maintain their ageing population are some of the factors which may or may not play a role. What follows is a brief description of the immigration policies and histories of four main immigration countries: France, Germany, Great Britain and the USA. These four countries have been chosen because they show interesting and important differences. Although there are considerable differences in immigration policies due to their different traditions, the increasing number of illegal immigrants is a major issue in all four countries. Europe is likely to change its immigration and integration policies during the 1990s to include tightly regulated measures for asylum seekers and foreign workers and programmes to cut down on illegal immigration. Western Europe's open door policy dating from World War II is closing and countries are becoming less hospitable. The passing of new immigration laws and the changing climate of public opinion go hand in hand. In the United States changing public opinion sees immigration as a problem requiring drastic solutions. For example between 1965 and 1993 in the United States the percentage of persons believing that immigration should be decreased rose from 33 per cent to 61 per cent, whereas those who felt that it should remain the same decreased from 39 per cent to 27 per cent (Mydans, 1993).

Policies on integration will continue to vary widely – they range from the French assimilation model to the Swedish multicultural model – and the debate over immigration and integration is likely to continue. Thus, the receiving societies show a great deal of contextual variation. This has to be taken into account when we compare migration experiences such as the motivation to migrate, the role of social networks, and the social, economic and cultural transitions of migrants.

France

France experienced a demographic revolution in the nineteenth century by 'importing' huge waves of immigrants whereas most other European countries 'exported' them. This made it a country of immigration more than a century before other European nations. Large waves of immigrant workers from various European countries settled in France. It is estimated that one-third of the French population have at least one foreign-born grandparent. France today receives approximately 60,000 immigrants annually (Weil, 1991). Citizenship is conferred almost automatically on an immigrant's offspring born in the country. The French 'assimilation policy' is based on the Republican model which held that immigrants should behave like the French in public: celebration of ethnic differences should be confined to private life. The unwillingness of some new immigrants to obey the assimilation rules, such as Muslim schoolgirls wearing veils in public schools, is threatening to undermine the traditional ideology of the Republican heritage (Schnapper, 1995).

Germany

Unlike France, Germany did not experience large-scale immigration in the nineteenth century. However, from 1945 to 1990 more than 15 million refugees and displaced persons from the former East German regions, as well as ethnic Germans from Eastern Europe, came to West Germany. As reported by the United Nations (1994): 'Germany has been the country in the world with the largest number of immigrants in recent years. It had an annual average of almost 1.4 million for 1992 and 1993, compared with an annual average of 800,000 in the US' (p. 1). At the same time Germany is least prepared both politically and socially to become a country of immigrants. Large numbers of asylum seekers benefit from Germany's liberal asylum laws, which grant asylum to any individual who is politically persecuted. Between

1991 and 1993 the number of asylum seekers was 300–400,000 annually. Ethnic Germans whose forefathers had migrated to Russia are entitled to obtain German citizenship when they immigrate to Germany. Immigration of non-ethnic Germans started in about 1969 when guest workers, mostly from south European countries and Turkey, were attracted to Germany. Most of them settled, brought their families to Germany and stayed permanently.

There is no consensus on immigration and integration in Germany. Official government policy is that Germany is not a country of immigration, that foreigners should be persuaded to leave and those who want to stay should be 'integrated' into German society. Proponents of an active immigration policy demand immigration laws which specify numbers, quotas and dual citizenship as a key to integration (Heckmann, 1995). With regard to refugee movements, Germany is the country most affected by the collapse of the Soviet Union and Yugoslavia. Germany was not prepared for this development and recent acts of ethnic violence are signs of growing tensions within some segments of the German population. Nevertheless, right-wing parties who want foreigners out of Germany did fail in the recent elections.

Great Britain

Britain shares with the rest of Europe increasing pressure from illegal immigration and asylum seekers, as well as from new legal immigrants through family reunion. Britain's basic immigration law is the Aliens Registration Act of 1919. This law did not restrict the entry of British subjects from the colonies in Africa and Asia until 1971, and Irish nationals have had freedom of movement since 1922. Children of migrants born in Britain become British citizens, but political rights are not related to citizenship – a fact which furthers the process of integration. Today Great Britain accepts about 50,000 immigrants annually; the total of illegal aliens is estimated to be 100,000. In 1991 the number of asylum seekers reached 56,000. Only 3 per cent of these are granted asylum status; very few of those rejected are in fact removed from the United Kingdom.

Integration policy is based on targets that are similar to American quotas. Britain opposes EU-wide immigration policy because it fears that this would be too expensive (Coleman, 1995).

The United States

The United States has traditionally been a nation of immigration. US immigration policy went through several phases, first encouraging immigration and later restricting it by establishing preference systems to determine the number of people who have priority to enter and their qualifications. Immigration rose from 4.5 million in the 1970s to 7.3 million in the 1980s, up to an estimated 12 million for the 1990s (High, 1995). An estimated 2 million aliens enter the United States illegally each year. There is an ongoing debate between admissionists who want more immigrants and better conditions for them to ease the process of integration, and restrictionists who would like to see immigration reduced (Martin, 1995).

What motivates people to migrate

Often individuals base their decision to migrate on highly idiosyncratic factors such as prior contact, knowledge and influence. In general, however, migration is triggered by a host of complex objective situational conditions complemented by individual factors. In the following, migration is seen to occur as a consequence of three main structural factors which interact with specific group characteristics. Here the notions of 'demand', 'supply' and 'network' on the one hand and 'push' and 'pull' factors on the other may be useful. All factors can have positive as well as negative valences for the people involved. These combined conditions are as follows.

- *Demand*: Pull factors draw migrants into industrial countries. For instance, today's immigrant workforce was deliberately attracted by industrial countries in need of additional workers. During the 1950s and 1960s the United States imported almost 5 million Mexican workers, and 30 million people moved from southern Europe and north Africa to work in northern Europe (Martin, 1992a).
- *Supply*: Push factors motivate individuals to leave their country of residence: the prospect of employment and better living conditions attract migrants to leave their own countries. Despite high rates of unemployment in most EU countries, labour markets need cheap and unskilled workers. There are various job niches for immigrants to fill because many natives shun certain jobs. Job niches for immigrants can be found in various sectors, e.g. in agriculture, construction or tourism.
- *Networks*: 'Network factors' are the relatives and friends already in the receiving country who provide information, jobs and housing for prospective newcomers. Individuals and families bring relatives legally and illegally to the new society. Network factors often include the activities of middle men: labour brokers or contractors who promise, for a fee, to get immigrants into the country and to find them a job. Very often immigrants without language skills and knowledge of their rights are exploited.

Although demand (pull), supply (push) and network factors are the pressures which instigate migration it is not known how much weight should be assigned to each. To talk of general simple motives for migration would be misleading, as motives vary with structural and group factors. For instance, Morokvasic (1993) states that women seem to respond more readily to pull factors and consequently are more likely to be exploited than men. Furnham and Bochner (1986) criticize the fact that there is little empirical research on people's motives to migrate despite the voluminous literature on this topic. In addition, they remark that this literature is often simple minded and a-theoretical.

In order to understand the adaptation or acculturation of immigrants it is also important to study the native's perception of immigrant motives. For example, Furnham (Furnham & Bochner, 1986) asked native Britons for their attributions and explanations for why people immigrate to and emigrate from Britain. He found striking differences in their explanations for people leaving or coming to Britain. His respondents believed 'that the most important motives for both immigration and migration were personal advancement and better job opportunities' (p.45). The process of transition and adaptation to the host country is most likely to be affected by the different dynamic factors which cause people to migrate.

It is important to consider the positive and negative consequences of migration for the migrant, for the home country and for the host country.

First of all, almost every country and culture has stories of successful and unsuccessful migrants who moved voluntarily or involuntarily and achieved or failed to achieve success. It is astonishing that we are not yet able to explain the factors likely to result in success or failure of the individual migrant through empirical data (Pedersen, 1995; Furnham, 1988; Furnham & Bochner, 1986).

Secondly, each home country from which the migrant comes experiences both positive and negative consequences as a result of the migration. While the home country may lose population, migration may also decrease unemployment, provide new resources from money sent back home from abroad, establish professional networks in foreign countries and result in the delayed return of foreign trained experts.

Thirdly, each receiving country also experiences positive and negative consequences. Migrants to urban areas provide new and typically inexpensive labour for industrialization, as in the People's Republic of China today, and enrich the gene pool both biologically, and conceptually by introducing alternative perspectives. On the other hand, migrants place a burden, initially at least, on the welfare system. This led to Proposition 187 in California, for example, by which the government seeks to withdraw public aid and services from refugees and illegal immigrants. Proposition 187 was a 1994 ballot initiative to deny schooling, health care and other services to illegal immigrants. Florida, California, Arizona and Texas have also sued the US federal government, claiming that it has not reduced the flow of illegal immigrants but requires the state to spend its own budget to support them.

In order to understand why people migrate it may be useful to consider the following questions:

1. What promises lead migrants to break with their past and seek out an unknown future with all the risks and dangers it presents?
2. How do these migrants explain their own behaviour in their own words rather than in the words of outside experts?
3. What are the attributions and misattributions that the migrants make of themselves and others in their new surroundings?
4. What is the historical context leading up to the migration decision, in both the sending and receiving countries?

5. What stereotypes do the migrants assume about the host culture and what does the host culture assume about migrants?
6. What ideas and transfer of technology migrate along with the people and how do these ideas influence the future?
7. What does the migrant expect to happen as a result of the migration?
8. To what extent will each migrant continue to move internally from region to region or job to job?

Dynamics of cultural contact

The immigrants' first contacts usually occur under unfavourable conditions. They are often forced to accept low-paying jobs with low status that local inhabitants have rejected. They are forced to live in poor neighbourhoods and have difficulty moving out because they are not accepted elsewhere. The immigrant becomes trapped, with no way out. If relatives back home are depending on financial support from the immigrant then even returning home is impossible. Krau (1991) points out that this trapped condition may continue through the first and even the second generation of immigrants. The negative consequences of immigration for the host culture are typically exaggerated, which may in turn contribute to mutual hostility in a self-fulfilling prophecy. Resistance to integration is met by animosity from locals in a spiralling negativity that turns potential friends into enemies.

Categories of immigrant groups and stranger–host relationships

Not all migrants were voluntary travellers. To understand the dynamics of migration we have to consider structural factors in addition to the characteristics of specific categories of groups that migrate and come into contact with a host culture. Some of these groups enjoy special protection while others do not, some are welcomed by the host societies and others have to face prejudice and discrimination, some leave voluntarily while others have escaped from their home countries in order to survive. 'Immigrants' and 'refugees' are both first-generation newcomers by way of migration. The term 'ethnic group' is frequently used to refer to individuals who identify with a common heritage in the second or third generation after immigration (Berry, 1990). The process which results when two distinct cultural groups come in contact has been termed acculturation (Berry & Kim, 1988). In particular, we have to consider specific groups which have to leave or were expelled from their countries and therefore deserve special protection on humanitarian grounds. Refugees, according to the UN definition (1951), are people who have a well-founded fear of persecution because of race, religion, nationality, political opinion or membership of a particular group. A special subgroup are war and civil war refugees, who are granted temporary protection by most states.

Many people who flee are migrating from one part of their country to another. One of the most recent tragedies of massive internal displacement in Europe is occurring in the former Yugoslavia. The estimated number of refugees all over the world varies between 20 million and 500 million, depending on the definition of 'refugee' by the counting agency (Martin, 1992a). According to the Geneva Convention, asylum seekers deserve a special refugee status which entitles them to temporary or permanent protection by their host country. It is estimated that 2 million people who fear political, religious or ethnic persecution at home ask for asylum in Western countries (Martin, 1992a).

Most of these factors and conditions complement each other. Very often war refugees ask for asylum because this status seems to be more privileged. Many of those whose status as refugee or asylum seeker is not recognized become illegal immigrants. Other individuals who intended only a temporary stay as guest workers become permanent immigrants. On the other hand, there are legal immigrants from certain ethnic groups with an automatic right of entry. For example, Jews are entitled to Israeli citizenship and ethnic Germans in Eastern Europe are admitted as German citizens. The various categories of migrant are blurred as, for example, when student visitors or asylum seekers marry citizens or find employment and thus obtain legal immigrant status.

In addition to immigrants and refugees there are various groups who move for very different reasons and are met with very different reactions by their potential hosts. When members of one group come into contact with members of another group who are unknown and unfamiliar, they are interacting as strangers. Because strangers are not members of the ingroup and thus are not known as individuals, behaviour towards them is based on perceived group membership. In sociology there is a long history on the concept of the stranger going back to Georg Simmel's (1908) seminal essay, 'Der Fremde' (The Stranger).

According to Simmel, the stranger–host relationship is by its nature ambivalent, since the stranger may be experienced as near and far and because he comes today and goes tomorrow, or he may remain permanently. Based on Simmel's theorizing, a number of stranger–host typologies have been developed which examine the potential relationships between the two by taking into consideration, for instance, the stranger's motives in the host community and the host's reaction to the stranger. Gudykunst (1983) provided a useful taxonomy of the stranger–host relations which yields nine categories (Table 15.1).

What this typology attempts to illustrate is that migrants or refugees differ not only with respect to their cultural orientations or country of origin, but also according to their real or perceived motives and their real or perceived intentions to stay. It should be pointed out that various other dimensions could be considered. Because of different antecedent conditions under which stranger and host meet we can assume that each immigrant group has a unique transition history which is likely to affect the process of adaptation to the new environment.

Table 15.1 *A typology of stranger–host relations*

| Host's reaction to stranger | Stranger's interest in host community | | |
	Visit	Residence	Membership
Friendly (leaning to positive)	Guest	Newly arrived	Newcomer
Ambivalent (indifferent)	Sojourner	Simmel's stranger	Immigrant
Antagonistic (leaning to negative)	Intruder	Middle-man minority	Marginal persons
General area of research	Sociology of tourism	Intercultural adjustment	Acculturation/ Assimilation

Source: Gudykunst (1983)

Transition between cultures

International migration almost always involves a transition from one culture to another. When culturally disparate individuals and groups come into contact they will have an influence on each other's social structure, institutions, political processes and other social-cultural elements. Cross-cultural contacts almost always create misunderstanding, confusion and conflicts. In this section we shall focus on the issue of cultural contact, discuss the concept of culture and how it differs from ethnicity and review one major cultural dimension: individualism-collectivism, which is most important for our discussion of cultural transitions.

The cultural contact hypothesis

Extensive research has focused on the question: what type of contact between members of different groups can reduce intergroup prejudice and hostility? This line of research has been labelled 'studies of the contact hypothesis'. Amir (1969) in his research on the contact hypothesis discovered that groups experiencing conflict who meet together under favourable conditions are likely to work together in greater harmony. Groups who meet together under unfavourable conditions are likely to increase their disharmony still further. Finally, he discovered that most spontaneous contact between groups occurs under unfavourable conditions. Favourable conditions that reduce intergroup hostility include: (1) equal status contact between members of the two groups; (2) contact between representatives of the majority group and high-status minorities; (3) a positive social climate for contact; (4) intimate rather than casual contact; (5) pleasant and rewarding contact; and (6) functionally important outcomes. Unfavourable conditions that increase hostility include: (1) contact that produces competition between groups; (2) unpleasant or involuntary contact; (3) contact that lowers one or both groups' status and prestige; (4) contact leading to frustration and scapegoating; (5) contact where one or both sides' moral or ethical standards are violated. It is clear that migrants and refugees typically experience contact under unfavourable conditions.

What is culture?

Cultural patterns of thinking and acting are inherited from those who taught us the rules of life. Culturally learned assumptions control our life with or without our permission. As we learn about ourselves and others we learn how we are both similar and different in our assumptions. We come to believe that our way is the best of all possible ways and even when we find better ways it is difficult to change. Our perception of reality is culturally learned, using a 'self-reference criterion' to judge others according to our own perspective.

This inclusive definition of culture presumes that behaviours can best be understood in the cultural context where they occurred. Identifying more of our culture makes it possible to find common ground with others in shared positive expectation for trust, respect and success between persons who might otherwise consider their behaviours to be fundamentally different and potentially hostile. With increased movement to other places and roles individuals have the potential to become 'shape-shifters' (Lifton, 1993) adapting to new environments rather than 'fundamentalist' and unchanging in their perspective. Increased migration has potentially given each modern person multiple identities as a source of strength while discontinuous change is experienced as a permanent feature (Rosenau, 1992).

There is no single definition of culture. After reviewing more than a hundred different definitions, Kroeber and Kluckhohn (1952, p. 181) suggested one of the most comprehensive:

> Culture consists of patterns, explicit and implicit of and for behaviour acquired and transmitted by symbols, constituting the distinctive achievement of human groups, including their embodiment in artifacts; the essential core of culture consists of traditional (i.e. historically derived and selected) ideas and especially their attached values; culture systems may, on the one hand, be considered as products of action, on the other, as conditioning elements of future action.

Rohner (1984) made a distinction between the concepts of culture and of social system. He defines a social system as behaviours found within a culture, whereas culture is defined as the shared meanings which are given to events. According to Rohner, culture and social system are interwoven within the concept of society. Culture broadly defined includes all levels of analysis referred to in the introduction: demographic variables (e.g. age, sex, place of residence), status variables (e.g. social, educational, economic) and affiliations (formal and informal) as well as ethnographic variables such as nationality, ethnicity, language and religion (see Pedersen, 1991, p. 7). This broad definition of culture allows researchers to detect and explain within-group differences with regard to psychological dimensions among individuals in the same culture as well as differences between cultural groups.

Smith and Bond (1993) emphasize that locating individuals on a universally useful dimension that relates to behaviour (e.g. the belief that arbitration leads to reduction in animosity) proceeds in the same way for different cultural groups as well as for the same cultural group. The identification of constructs such as values, motives, expectations or beliefs which relate to behaviour is, according to Smith and Bond, the proper task for psychologists when they study culture. When culture is defined in terms of psychological constructs, it becomes amenable to measurement.

However, culture is more than a system of shared meaning for social orientation that is passed on through socialization. Culture also serves unique needs in human existence. As pointed out by Max Weber (1904/1956), culture gives meaning and importance to our lives in an otherwise meaningless universe. According to Solomon, Greenberg and Pyszczynski (1991), cultural beliefs represent an anxiety buffer that protects us from the awareness of our ultimate death. A threat to our cultural anxiety buffer leads to negative reactions by those who espouse different cultural beliefs. A much neglected area in this respect is the meaning of death and dying for migrants or families living in exile (Harrel-Bond & Wilson, 1990). Moreover, culture serves as a precious social resource, as the knowledge of relevant cultural skills entails obvious advantages in the process of adaptation to a new environment.

Each person belongs to many different cultures, although the salience of each culture is likely to change between places and times. Euro-American theories have often tried to capture culture in a fixed, monomodal and 'reliable' measure of consistency. Non-Western cultures have often been more tolerant of the elusive and dynamic qualities of cultural identity. Culture is complicated but it is not chaotic, and it presents itself through patterns or stories. We have been taught the cultural perspectives by which we interpret our own and others' behaviours. Behaviours result from expectations that in turn result from values which have been learned in a cultural context.

Cultural orientation and the conception of self

Today's international migration flows can be characterized by a movement of people from collectivistically oriented Third World countries to individualistically oriented Western countries of Europe and North America. In order to understand the process of transition and adaptation in the receiving society we must raise such questions as: in which way do people vary across cultures? How do cultures shape individuals' identity? What are the best strategies for adaptation to a new cultural context?

In this section the focus is on the first question: how do people vary across cultures? If we assume that a person's identity or self is shaped by his or her social environment (Markus & Kitayama, 1991), then we have to focus on how social relationships, values and norms vary across cultures. It will be argued that cultures differ systematically in the way individuals define themselves and their position in society. This has important consequences for their positive or negative experiences as migrants. For instance, when an actor perceives himself or herself as an individual whose identity and self is separate from the group or community, he or she is less likely to be concerned about social bonding and network factors. On the other hand, when an actor's identity or self is defined by close social relationships and obligations he or she is more likely to be concerned with or dependent on social network factors. Recently, a number of related conceptions of cultural variation have been suggested in the literature, e.g. tight vs. loose cultures (Pelto, 1968) and high vs. low context cultures (Hall, 1976). A somewhat related concept is individualism vs. collectivism. This dimension of cultural variation has received most attention from cross-cultural researchers (e.g. Kim, Triandis, Kagitcibasi, Choi, & Yoon, 1994; Triandis, 1989). According to Hofstede (1980), individualism refers to a society's cultural orientation in which the ties between individuals are loose, the emphasis is on 'I' consciousness and values such as autonomy, achievement orientation and self-sufficiency are important. Collectivism as its opposite stresses 'we' consciousness and values such as group solidarity, and the sharing of duties and obligations. Indeed it was Hofstede's ambitious research programme which isolated this dimension. In his now classic study *Culture's consequences* (1980) he analysed the responses of individuals in 40 countries with respect to their work-related values. When he factor-analysed his data he could classify the 40 countries along four dimensions, which he named 'individualism–collectivism', 'power distance', 'masculinity–femininity' and 'uncertainty avoidance'. According to Hofstede's analysis, the most individualistically oriented cultures are to be found in North America and Western Europe; the more collectivistically oriented countries in Asia, Africa and Latin America.

Since the majority of immigrants come from Third World countries in Africa and Asia, their cultural background is most likely to be collectivistic and their preferred destinations are likely to be the countries of Western Europe and North America. The culture contact and culture clash is likely to take place, so to speak, along the individualistic–collectivistic dimension.

Lalonde, Taylor and Moghaddam (1988) studied how individualistic or collectivistic orientation affects acculturation strategies of immigrant women in Canada. They found that the women in their sample who have a stronger desire to retain their ethnic identity were more likely to favour a collectivistic approach for getting ahead in Canadian society compared to those for whom heritage culture maintenance was less important.

The differences between individualistically oriented cultures and many collectivistically oriented cultures are also found with respect to important ideological and institutional differences. For instance, Western democratic societies place great emphasis on the rights, freedom and equality of the individual. In order to understand the different attitudes to law and legal institutions, Bierbrauer (1994) systematically analysed how individualistic and collectivistic orientations affect the perceived functions and components of law and the legal system by comparing asylum seekers in Germany with a presumed collectivistic orientation (Kurds and Lebanese) with individuals who have a presumed individualistic orientation. To independently assess the cultural orientation of the respondents they were asked to complete a scale measuring individualistic–collectivistic orientations (see Bierbrauer et al., 1994). The scale reflected attitudes mainly toward the family domain; for instance: 'Do people in your native country often feel lonely when not with their brothers, sisters, or close relatives?' As expected, German respondents showed a significantly lower degree of collectivistic orientation than the Kurds and Lebanese. In addition to measuring attitudes to the law and legal institutions, scenarios depicting forms of wrongdoing and conflict were employed to elicit respondents' conceptions of law and legal practices in their countries of origin. Thus, the construct of individualism–collectivism was used as an explanatory mechanism to examine variations in legal cultures. Among other things it was found that collectivistically oriented groups showed a higher preference to abide by the norms of tradition and religion and were less willing to let state law regulate family disputes than individualistically oriented respondents, who favoured formal procedures and guidelines. In the same vein, collectivistically oriented respondents preferred informal modes of dispute regulation to a greater extent and the use of persons from the ingroup as mediators. In addition, the collectivistically oriented participants responded with more shame following the violation of norms than individualistically oriented participants (Bierbrauer, 1992). These differences suggest that legal norms and legal institutions in Western societies may mean different things for different cultural groups. This should be taken seriously in multicultural societies, otherwise the legitimacy of the legal and political institutions of these societies is undermined.

Ethnicity and ethnic identity

The term 'ethnicity' is sometimes associated with the concept of culture as well as with 'race'. Often ethnicity is meant to embrace differences identified by colour, language, religion or some other attribute of common origin (Horowitz, 1985). Most members of an ethnic group identify themselves with others on the basis of imagined ancestry and they display some distinctive cultural patterns (Wilpert, 1989). Ethnic identity is established for most group members at birth and based on presumed shared sociocultural experiences. In social psychological analyses ethnic identity refers to the process of identity formation, whereas ethnicity is part of the structural relationship between groups (see Liebkind, 1989). Social psychological approaches to the study of ethnic identity focus on the processes by which individuals construe their relationship to certain persons or categories of persons within their own ethnic group and others (Weinreich, 1989). Clearly, ethnic identity is a dynamic phenomenon involving an interplay of individual, social and cultural levels of analysis. Cultural identity and ethnic identity are often used interchangeably. Wilpert (1989) distinguishes between the terms: cultural identity refers to shared values, group membership and common history, whereas ethnic identity means a form of ethnic consciousness. She points out that 'ethnicity is first and foremost a political question' (p. 8), because cultural and ethnic identity determine inclusion in or exclusion from the social structure. In other words, access to cultural resources, such as schooling, language learning and job opportunities, varies according to ethnic boundaries. Some commentators even believe that the twentieth-century notion of class struggle will be replaced by the notion of ethnic struggle in the twenty-first century as the major source of political and social conflict.

One final remark is necessary with regard to the term 'race', which is often used interchangeably with ethnicity, culture or nationality. Frequently in surveys or questionnaires respondents are required to indicate their race, ethnicity or national origin. We are particularly concerned with the loose and thoughtlessness way in which the term 'race' is used by researchers to explain differences between groups. Both in history (e.g. the use and abuse of the term 'race' by the Nazis) and today, the terms 'race' or 'racial' are used intentionally or unintentionally to discriminate against selected groups. The classification of people into 'races' has been criticized as arbitrary. Betancourt and Lopez (1993) argue that 'racial groups are more alike than they are different, even in physical and genetic characteristics' (p. 631). Even the use of the expression 'racial prejudice' by well-intentioned scientists to refer to xenophobic or ethnic prejudices can reinforce the notion in the public mind that 'races' do indeed exist and that the use of this concept has a scientific base. Therefore, we argue that the term 'race' or 'racial' should be relinquished as a scientific or science-based term and that observed differences between groups should be attributed to specific cultural or ethnic variables.

The process of acculturation

International migration almost always results in intercultural contact. Previously culturally isolated individuals or groups set up a new life in another country and culture. This transition forces them to engage in cultural and psychological adaptation in their new environment. How this process of acculturation proceeds is the focus of this section.

When immigrating to a new country there can be dramatic changes in language, culture, food, institutions and religion which challenge the immigrant and he or she is required to interpret, accept or reject these changes. The process where groups or individuals with different cultural backgrounds come into first-hand contact by influencing each other's culture has been termed acculturation. Berry (1990) distinguishes acculturation on the group level (ecological, cultural, social and institutional) from the individual level. At the individual level acculturation refers to psychological changes in behaviour and cognitions. According to Berry's ecological framework (Berry, 1994), the individual and the context are interactive. People have adapted in an ecological context in both their biological and their cultural identity. In this adaptation, the individual responds to ecological influences which may result from direct contact with others or be mediated by other influences in the new context. Adaptation results in a new identity for the migrating person, and this defines a new ecological framework.

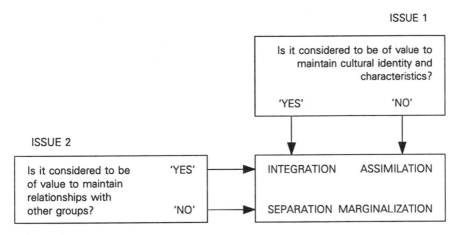

Figure 15.2 *Four varieties of acculturation defined in relation to two questions (Berry, 1990)*

Berry (1990) has developed a two-dimensional model of acculturation in pluralistic societies with four different options that result from separate questions which are answered either positively or negatively: (1) is it desirable to remain in one's heritage culture? and (2) is it desirable to maintain positive contact with other groups in the new society? When these two questions are posed simultaneously, a combination of four possible varieties of acculturation strategies results (Figure 15.2).

(1) The *assimilation* strategy implies that the individual rejects his or her original culture and seeks to become a member of the new culture. This strategy of developing a new cultural identity is captured by the idealized concept of the 'melting pot'; (2) *integration* represents an option in which the individual wants both to maintain the original culture and also to learn about the new culture; (3) *separation* implies that the individual wants to maintain his or her original culture and avoid the new culture; (4) *marginalization* implies that the individual rejects both the original and the new culture. Of course, acculturation is not a unidirectional process. The integration strategy, for example, can only be pursued in societies which have favourable policy conditions and where certain social psychological preconditions are established such as a widespread acceptance of cultural diversity and low levels of ethnocentrism and discrimination. When individuals or groups want to pursue closer contact with the dominant culture, but are rejected by the latter, segregation or exclusion results.

There are many studies which focus on the psychological correlates linked with the different strategies of acculturation (Berry, 1990; Berry & Kim, 1988; LaFromboise, Coleman, & Gerton, 1993). Those who feel marginalized or maintain a separation mode experience higher levels of conflict than those who seek integration and intermediate levels or those who want assimilation. For example, Prins, van Oudenhoven, and Bank (1994) studied the acculturation strategies of Turks and Moroccans in the Netherlands. They found that the majority of both groups are aiming at integration. In addition, those who integrate report higher levels of general well-being than assimilating individuals. Similarly, Third World immigrant youth in Norway (Sam & Berry, 1995) and immigrants to Germany (Schmitz, 1992) show that integration seems to be the most effective strategy in terms of health and well-being.

Individual factors existing prior to migration such as age, gender and education and group factors such as cultural orientation (see Figure 15.1) may have profound influences on the degree of adaptation. Each of these factors is likely to moderate or affect the acculturation process (see Berry & Kim, 1988). When acculturation begins early, the process is likely to be smoother than when relatively older persons move. There is substantial evidence that migrant women have poorer mental health than migrant men. Distance between cultural orientations may have an influence; the greater the cultural differences, the less positive is the adaptation. Higher education and knowledge of the new language and culture appear to be associated with positive adaptation: related to education is one's place in the social and economic world. Social changes mean disrupted communities and loss of social support. A common experience for migrants is a combination of status loss and limited status mobility. An immigrant's 'entry status' in the host society is frequently lower than his or her 'departure status' in the society of origin.

Multiculturalism

Berry and his colleagues (Berry, 1990; Berry, Poortinga, Segall, & Dasen, 1992) and others (Taylor, 1991) have developed a multicultural model which attempts to find an alternative to integration and assimilation while avoiding the negative consequences of separation and marginalization. This endeavour is of course only feasible where government policies promote and sustain such pluralism, as for instance in Canada. Multicultural or pluralistic societies differ, according to Berry (1990), from monocultural societies in two important ways: (1) they provide social and cultural networks for those who enter; and (2) they allow greater tolerance and acceptance of culturally diverse groups. Whether or not it is possible to maintain a truly multicultural society is questioned by some authors (Mallea, 1988).

Multiculturalism has become an emotionally loaded construct when it has been used to enforce the interests of ethnic groups on the larger society without regard for within-group variables such as age, gender, socioeconomic status, disability and other potentially salient variables. Wherever multiculturalism has been exclusively used to promote the self-interest of selected ethnic groups the term has become divisive. When a more inclusive definition has been used, recognizing the importance of within-group as well as between-group variables, multiculturalism has the potential to provide a level playing field where a multiplicity of groups can find common ground without giving up their cultural identity.

Friedman (1994) contends that with the increased awareness of ethnic identity and cultural affiliations both within each European country and across national boundaries there is a tendency for each group to perceive other groups as competing for limited resources.

Ethnocentrism and ethnic conflicts

When people from different cultures come into contact they face differences in language, habits, behaviours, dress, beliefs and more. In addition, several other factors come into play, e.g. conflicts over resources, social and legal status, and feelings of relative deprivation.

People tend to react to such differences 'ethnocentrically', that is, they use their own ethnic group or their own ingroup as the standard and judge others unfavourably. As summarized by Triandis (1990), research on ethnocentrism has shown that people tend to

- define their way of feeling, thinking and doing as natural and correct and what people in other cultures do as unnatural and incorrect;
- believe that their own ingroup norms, roles and values are absolutely correct;
- behave in ways that favour their ingroup;
- feel proud of their ingroup and act in a hostile way towards outgroup members.

Some level of ethnocentrism seems to be universal (LeVine & Campbell, 1972). Most members of a given cultural or ethnic group hold the habits and symbols of their group in higher regard than those of other groups. Since the norms and values in one culture are often very different from those in other cultures, behaviour that is taboo or inappropriate in one culture may be quite appropriate in another.

There can be ethnocentrism on the side of immigrants as well as on the side of the host culture. For instance, immigrants whose background is Islamic may view the secular lifestyle of individualistic countries as immoral. On the other hand, people in Western countries may view Islam as rigid and fundamentalistic. In this way, both the newcomers' own ethnocentrism and the ethnocentric attitudes of members of the host culture contribute to the difficulties in adjustment.

Ethnocentrism is predicated upon a sense of ingroup–outgroup differentiation and is related to positive ingroup attitudes coupled with negative outgroup attitudes. The study of factors influencing intergroup relations has been at the centre of social psychology. Much of this research is concerned with cognitive and affective processes between groups, such as stereotyping, prejudice, ethnocentrism, attitudes and attributions. Within social psychology several theories have been developed to understand the dynamic of intergroup conflicts. A classic example of intergroup conflict is Sherif's (1966) work known as the realistic group conflict approach. Within this framework intergroup conflict results from a negative interdependence of groups – that is, one group achieves its goals at the expense of the other group's goal attainment. While Sherif considered negative interdependence of groups to be the basic cause of negative intergroup behaviour, social identity theory, developed by Tajfel and Turner (1986), questions its necessity. Instead the mere perception of belonging to a group is sufficient by itself to produce positive ingroup attitudes and outgroup discrimination. According to this theory, intergroup discrimination occurs without real conflicts of interest or a history of antagonism. More recently, Brewer (1993) has proposed an optimal distinctiveness theory which posits that an individual's sense of self is shaped by a need to 'assimilate' to some group and also to 'differentiate' from other groups. Thus, social identification can be viewed as a compromise between assimilation and differentiation where the need for inclusion is satisfied within ingroups, while the need for distinctiveness is met through ingroup comparisons (see section on acculturation, p. 414ff.). For individuals in each culture there may be different points at which there is the right amount of differentiation and assimilation. For instance, collectivistically oriented individuals may feel most satisfied when the point is closer to assimilation, and individualistically oriented individuals when it is closer to differentiation.

The complex relationships between ethnocentrism and its potential for intergroup conflict are elaborated by Fisher (1990) and include the following levels:

- Real or false threat fosters ethnocentric reactions above and beyond simple intergroup differentiation; perceived threat causes ethnocentrism including ingroup solidarity and outgroup hostility.
- Ethnocentrism reduces trust and contributes to conflict escalation through ineffective communication and contention tactics.
- Ethnocentrism increases perceptual distortion and cognitive biases which can contribute to conflict escalation.
- Ethnocentrism decreases problem-solving competencies due to rigid and restrictive group norms with regard to the outgroup and thus promotes conflict escalation.

Further elaboration of these theories of intergroup behaviour is necessary to understand the complexity of situations in which several ethnic groups are living together. When ethnic groups interact, each having its own norms and values, differences in power, status and resources may hinder the often professed desirability of integration or multiculturalism. In particular, when one is interested in the determination of escalation or de-escalation of already existing or potential conflicts between ethnic groups, these theories need to be supplemented by social, structural, economical and political variables (Horowitz, 1985).

Counselling migrants and refugees

The individual migrant experiences 'culture shock' in adjusting to the new and unfamiliar context. Although culture shock used to be treated as a 'disease', it is now more frequently perceived as a painful but potentially positive educational experience. Immigration is even included in the *Diagnostic and statistical manual-III Revised* (American Psychiatric Association, 1980) as an example of a possible pervasive stressor contributing to pathology. More recent research describes it as a positive and growthful learning process, however painful, although it may be linked to pathology under certain conditions. Berry et al. (1992) prefer the term 'acculturative stress' to emphasize the developmental consequences of culture shock as one of the many forms of stress management. While there are ways to mediate the pain and discomfort of culture shock there are no accurate measures of the adjustment process.

A 'U-curve' pattern of adjustment describes the culture shock in five stages of detachment, disintegration, defensiveness, development and biculturation. This model has great heuristic value but mixed support in the research literature (Pedersen, 1995). Culture shock seems to be more of an intrapersonal phenomenon in response to interpersonal conflict or dissonance. The process is multidimensional and can result in learning crucial to the migrant's success. Kealey (1988) described culture shock as a necessary but not sufficient condition for long-term adaptation to a new culture.

There are two primary approaches to counselling migrants: (1) the communication approach presumes that problems are the result of bad communication. The methods and content of communication in different cultures are significantly different, requiring the provider to know several contrasting 'languages' of communication to match each unique cultural context; (2) the structural approach emphasizes the interlocking roles of migrants. The migrant's situation is constantly changing as the migrant structures and restructures the environment in response to each new crisis. The structural approach defines boundaries, creates alliances, identifies patterns and structures to mediate 'boundary disputes'. Migrants are likely to encounter xenophobia and poverty, conflicts between their old and new cultural values, confusion between their public and private identities, profound oppression by the host culture, language problems, and class differences in the new culture.

Oetting and Beauvais (1991) have developed a so-called orthogonal model of cultural identification to describe the complex interactive factors facing the migrant. Rather than polarize cultures, this model recognizes increased identification with one culture and does not require decreased identification with other cultures in a multiplicity of identities. The five most frequently used alternative models are less complex: (1) the 'dominant majority' model simply imposes a dominant culture on everyone; (2) the 'transitional model' presumes a movement towards the dominant culture as an appropriate adjustment; (3) the 'alienation model' seeks to avoid stress from anomie by assisting persons in transition to adjust; (4) multidimensional models presume transition on several dimensions at the same time with different degrees of change on each dimension; (5) bicultural models presume that one can adapt to one culture without losing contact with the earlier culture.

The orthogonal identification model suggests that adapting to any single culture is independent from adapting to many alternative cultures providing an unlimited combination of overlapping cultural identities. It presumes a higher level of complexity and a more comprehensive inclusion of cultural context. The orthogonal model offers several advantages over alternative

models: (1) cultural groups may exist in association without isolating themselves or competing with one another; (2) minority cultures need not be
eliminated or absorbed in order to coexist; (3) a permanent multicultural
society may be possible which is multifaceted and multidimensional without
becoming a melting pot; (4) conflicts of value and beliefs do not present
insurmountable barriers but may be combined in a realistic pluralism; (5)
cultural conflict may become a positive rather than a negative force from the
perspective of shared common-ground expectations; (6) members of minority
groups may be less inclined to militancy when their survival is not threatened;
(7) the interaction of minority and majority cultures may be less destructive
for all parties; (8) there are economic advantages of releasing resources
previously consumed by cultural conflict; and (9) there are already models of
orthogonal relationships in healthy bicultural and multicultural families or
social units where a family member may take on a specific identity at home
and a very different identity at work or in other settings.

Conclusion

Immigration and migration – both legal and illegal – are increasing both in
terms of absolute numbers of migrants and as a social issue in modern
society. Not only are people better able to move from one place to the other
through modern transportation facilities but the international migration of
ideas that prepares the way for migrants is also rapidly increasing. Until very
recently, the social sciences marginalized migration as a topic of concern and
attention but the increasing visibility of migrant issues in social science
publications demonstrates how the topic is no longer marginalized. Within
the social sciences the approach of social psychology offers unique advantages
by combining both the perspective of the group or society sending and
receiving migrants and the psychological perspective of the individual migrant
caught up in these movements. This chapter has focused on the social
psychology of three factors in migration issues: (1) social, historical and
political consequences of migration; (2) the motivation of migrants to move
from one place to another; and (3) the dynamics of cultural contact resulting
from migration.

There is no simple explanation for why people migrate. The decision to
migrate is based on complicated push and pull factors reviewed earlier in this
chapter. Not all migrants are voluntary and a surprising number of migrants
plan to or would like to return home as soon as possible. There is also a high
level of misattribution, both by the migrants about the host culture and by the
host culture about the migrants. This chapter has attempted to clarify the
complex motivations of migrants in the host culture context.

The dynamics of cultural contact are also complicated. Typically contacts
between migrants and the host culture occur under 'unfavourable' conditions
and are more likely to result in hostility than harmony. The victimization of
migrants was discussed, along with the data indicating that host cultures
typically benefit in the long term from immigrants. Our identity is culturally

learned, so migration is not just a change of location but involves learning a new identity along with the other problems of culture shock. The various modes of acculturation such as assimilation, integration, marginalization and separation were considered, along with the controversial issues of multiculturalism and ethnocentrism which accompany the migration phenomenon.

The historical, political and social consequences of migration are also important. Migrants are typically from Third World countries moving to Westernized-industrialized countries. This usually also means moving from a collectivistically oriented culture to a more individualistically oriented culture, with many problems in adapting to the new values. The function of ethnic communities has changed, with a rediscovery of ethnicity in European countries, for example as a rationale for exclusion and 'cleansing'. Counselling seeks to meet the social consequences of migration, offering a safety net for migrants through an orthogonal model approach that accommodates the client's multiple cultural identities in a pattern of relationships. The immigration policies and histories of France, Germany, Great Britain and the United States were briefly reviewed as examples of host cultures.

This chapter has reviewed the published literature on migration from a social psychological perspective to help the reader understand significant patterns in migration. The topic of migrants and migration is likely to become significantly more important in the near future.

The social psychological perspective of migration combines the perspective of the host culture society with that of the individual migrant. This chapter has discussed motivational issues, attributions and misattributions among the push and pull factors influencing migrants as well as the psychological dynamics of cultural contact. Ways to change the typically unfavourable conditions of contact toward a favourable and positive context have been suggested. The historical, political and social consequences of migration are becoming increasingly prominent and are likely to grow in importance with greater migration.

Further reading

Heckmann, F. & Bosswick, W. (Eds) (1995). *Migration policies: A comparative perspective.* Stuttgart: Enke. This volume examines the migration policies of major European countries and policies in classical immigration countries like the United States and Australia.

Kim, U., Triandis, H.C., Kagitcibasi, C., Choi, S.C., & Yoon, G. (Eds) (1994). *Individualism and collectivism. Theory, method, and applications.* Thousand Oaks, CA: Sage. An important collection of contemporary research on the topic of individualism and collectivism written by accomplished researchers who have made significant contributions to the ways in which individualism and collectivism might be understood both conceptually and methodologically.

Pedersen, P. (Ed.) (1987). *Handbook of cross-cultural counseling and therapy*. New York: Praeger. This is a comprehensive and well elaborated review of conceptual frameworks for counselling and therapy in cross-cultural problems written by prominent authors in the field.

Smith, P.B. & Bond, M.H. (1993). *Social psychology across cultures*. New York, London, Toronto: Harvester Wheatsheaf. The authors aim to remedy the neglect of cultural influences within social psychology by introducing a cross-cultural perspective to the field. Starting with the well-known classic studies in social psychology, they show how the validity of empirical findings can be extended to other cultures.

Triandis, H.C. (1994). *Culture and social behaviour*. New York: McGraw-Hill. Written by one of the foremost contributors to research and theory in the field of cross-cultural psychology. He shows why and how culture is indispensable to a fuller understanding of human nature.

References

Abelson, R.P., Kinder, D.R., Peters, M.D., & Fiske, S.T. (1982). Affective and semantic components in political person perception. *Journal of Personality and Social Psychology, 42*, 619–630.

Abraham, S.C.S., Sheeran, P., Spears, R., & Abrams, D. (1992). Health beliefs and the promotion of HIV-preventive intentions among teenagers: A Scottish perspective. *Health Psychology, 11*, 363–370.

Abrams, D. (1994). Political distinctiveness: An identity optimising approach. *European Journal of Social Psychology, 24*, 357–365.

Abrams, D. & Emler, N. (1991). Self-denial as a paradox of political and regional social identity: Findings from a study of 16- and 18-year-olds. *European Journal of Social Psychology, 22*, 279–295.

Abramson, L.Y., Seligman, M.E.P., & Teasdale, J. (1978). Learned helplessness in humans: Critique and reformulation. *Journal of Abnormal Psychology, 87*, 49–74.

Acre, R. (1995). Evidence evaluation in jury decision-making. In R. Bull & D. Carson (Eds), *Handbook of psychology in legal contexts*. Chichester: Wiley.

Acre, R., Sobral, J., & Farina, F. (1992). Verdicts of psychosocially biased juries. In F. Lösel, D. Bender, & T. Bliesener (Eds), *Psychology and law: International perspectives*. Berlin: de Gruyter.

Adams, J.S. (1965). Inequity in social exchange. In L. Berkowitz (Ed.), *Advances in experimental social psychology*, vol. 2 (pp. 267–299). New York: Academic Press.

Adams, R.G. & Blieszner, R. (1994). An integrative conceptual framework for friendship research. *Journal of Social and Personal Relationships, 11*, 163–184.

Adorno, T., Frenkel-Brunswick, E., Levinson, D., & Sanford, N. (1950). *The authoritarian personality*. New York: Harper & Row.

Ahammer, I.M. & Baltes, P.B. (1972). Objective versus perceived age differences in personality: How do adolescents, adults, and older people view themselves and each other? *Journal of Gerontology, 27*, 46–51.

Aitken, C.K., McMahon, T.A., Wearing, A.J., & Finlayson, B.L. (1994). Residential water use and reducing consumption. *Journal of Applied Social Psychology, 24*, 136–158.

Ajzen, I. (1985). From intentions to actions: a theory of planned behaviour. In J. Kuhl & J. Beckmann (Eds), *Action control: From cognition to behaviour* (pp. 11–39). Berlin: Springer-Verlag.

Ajzen, I. (1988). *Attitudes, personality and behavior*. Milton Keynes, UK: Open University Press.

Ajzen, I. (1991). The theory of planned behavior. *Organizational Behavior and Human Decision Processes, 50*, 179–211.

Ajzen, I. & Fishbein, M. (1977). Attitude–behavior relations: A theoretical analysis and review of empirical research. *Psychological Bulletin, 84*, 888–918.

Ajzen, I. & Fishbein, M. (1980). *Understanding attitudes and predicting social behavior*. Englewood Cliffs, NJ: Prentice-Hall.

Ajzen, I. & Madden, T.J. (1986). Prediction of goal-directed behavior: Attitudes, intentions and perceived behavioral control. *Journal of Experimental Social Psychology, 22*, 453–474.

Akehurst, L. & Köhnken, G. (1995). *Lay persons' and police officers' perception of deceptive behavior*. Unpublished manuscript, University of Portsmouth.

Akehurst, L., Köhnken, G., Vrij, A., & Bull, R. (in press). Lay persons' and police officers' beliefs regarding deceptive behaviour. *Applied Cognitive Psychology*.

Akiba, S., Kato, H., & Blot, W.J. (1986). Passive smoking and lung cancer among Japanese women. *Cancer Research, 46*, 4804–4807.

Albrecht, D., Bultena, G., Hoiberg, E., & Nowak, P. (1982). The New Environmental Paradigm scale: Measuring environmental concern. *Journal of Environmental Education, 13*, 38–43.

Aldag, R.J. & Riggs Fuller, S. (1993). Beyond fiasco: A reappraisal of the groupthink phenomenon and a new model of group decision processes. *Psychological Bulletin, 113*, 533–552.

424 References

Allport, G.W. (1935). Attitudes. In C. Murchison (Ed.), *Handbook of social psychology*, vol. 2 (pp. 798–844). Worcester, MA: Clark University Press.

Alonso-Quecuty, M.L. (1992). Deception detection and reality monitoring: A new answer to an old question? In F. Lösel, D. Bender, & T. Bliesener (Eds), *Psychology and law: International perspectives*. Berlin: de Gruyter.

Altemeyer, B. (1981). *Right-wing authoritarianism*. Winnipeg, Ontario, Canada: University of Manitoba Press.

Amabile, T.M. (1988). A model of creativity and innovation in organizations. In B.M. Staw & L.L. Cummings (Eds), *Research in organizational behavior*, Vol. 10 (pp. 123–167). Greenwich, CT: JAI Press.

American Cancer Society (1986). *Cancer, fact and figures*. New York: American Cancer Society.

American Psychiatric Association (1980). *Diagnostic and statistical manual III: Revised*. Washington, DC: American Psychiatric Association.

Amerio, P. (1991). Perspectives théoriques cognitives et sociales en psychologie politique. *Revue Internationale de Psychologie Sociale, 4*, 209–229.

Amir, Y. (1969). Contact hypothesis in ethnic relations. *Psychological Bulletin, 71*, 319–342.

Anderson, C.A. (1989). Temperature and aggression: ubiquitous effects of heat on occurrence of human violence. *Psychological Bulletin, 106*, 74–96.

Anderson, M.C. & Pichert, J.W. (1978). Recall of previously unrecalled information following a shift in perspective. *Journal of Verbal Learning and Verbal Behavior, 17*, 1–12.

Andison, F.S. (1977). TV violence and viewer aggression: A cumulation of study results 1956–76. *Public Opinion Quarterly, 41*, 314–331.

Andreoli, V. & Worchel, S. (1978). Effects of media, communicator, and message position on attitude change. *Public Opinion Quarterly, 42*, 59–70.

Antaki, C. (1981). *The psychology of ordinary explanations*. London: Academic Press.

Antonucci, T.C. (1985). Personal characteristics, social support, and social behavior. In R.H. Binstock & E. Shanas (Eds), *Handbook of aging and the social sciences* (2nd edn, pp. 94–128). New York: Van Nostrand Reinhold.

Antonucci, T.C. (1990). Social supports and social relationships. In R.H. Binstock & L.K. George (Eds), *Handbook of aging and the social sciences* (3rd edn, pp. 205–226). San Diego, CA: Academic Press.

Antonucci, T.C. (1991). Attachment, social support, and coping with negative life events in mature adulthood. In E.M. Cummings, A.L. Greene, & K.H. Karraker (Eds), *Life-span developmental psychology: Perspectives on stress and coping* (pp. 261–276). Hillsdale, NJ: Lawrence Erlbaum.

Antonucci, T.C. & Akiyama, H. (in press). Social support and the maintenance of competence. In S. Willis and K.W. Schaie (Eds), *Societal mechanisms for maintaining competence in old age*. New York: Springer.

Antonucci, T.C. & Jackson, J.S. (1990). The role of reciprocity in social support. In B.R. Sarason, I.G. Sarason, & G.R. Pierce (Eds), *Social support: An interactional view* (pp. 173–198). New York: Wiley.

Archer, D. & Akert, R.M. (1977). Words and everything else: Verbal and nonverbal cues in social interpretation. *Journal of Personality and Social Psychology, 35*, 443–449.

Archer, D., Iritani, B., Kimes, D.D., & Barrios, M. (1983). Faceism: Five studies of sex differences in facial prominence. *Journal of Personality and Social Psychology, 45*, 725–735.

Archer, J. (1989). From the laboratory to the community: Studying the natural history of human aggression. In J. Archer & K. Browne (Eds), *Human aggression: Naturalistic approaches* (pp. 25–41). London: Routledge.

Archer, J. & Browne, K. (1989). Concepts and approaches to the study of aggression. In J. Archer & K. Browne (Eds), *Human aggression: Naturalistic approaches* (pp. 3–24). London: Routledge.

Arcury, T.A., Johnson, T.P., & Scollay, S.J. (1986). Ecological worldview and environmental knowledge: The 'New Environment Paradigm'. *Journal of Environmental Education, 17*, 35–40.

Argote, L., Seabright, M.A., & Dyer, L. (1986). Individual versus group use of base-rate and individualizing information. *Organizational Behavior and Human Decision Processes, 38*, 65–75.

Argyle, M., Alkema, F., & Gilmour, R. (1971). The communication of friendly and hostile attitudes by verbal and non-verbal signals. *European Journal of Social Psychology, 1*, 385–402.

Argyle, M., Salter, V., Nicholson, H., Williams, M., & Burgess, P. (1970). The communication of inferior and superior attitudes by verbal and nonverbal signals. *British Journal of Social and Clinical Psychology, 9*, 222–231.

Arntzen, F. (1983). *Psychologie der Zeugenaussage*. Munich: C.H. Beck.

Aronson, E., Brewer, M., & Carlsmith, J.M. (1985). Experimentation in social psychology. In G.

Lindzey & E. Aronson (Eds), *Handbook of social psychology*, Vol. 1 (pp. 441–486). New York: Random House.

Aronson, E., Wilson, T.D., & Akert, R.M. (1994). *Social Psychology: The heart and the mind.* New York: HarperCollins.

Asch, S. (1951). Effects of group pressure on the modification and distortion of judgments. In H. Guetzkow (Ed.), *Groups, leadership, and men* (pp. 177–190). Pittsburgh, PA: Carnegie Press.

Asch, S.E. (1946). Forming impressions of personality. *Journal of Abnormal and Social Psychology, 41*, 258–290.

Aschermann, E., Mantwill, M., & Köhnken, G. (1991). An independent replication of the cognitive interview. *Applied Congitive Psychology, 5*, 489–495.

Atchley, R.C. (1977). *The social forces in late life.* Belmont, CA: Wadsworth.

Atchley, R.C. (1993). Continuity theory and the evolution of activity in later adulthood. In J.R. Kelly (Ed.), *Activity and aging* (pp. 5–16). Newbury Park, CA: Sage.

Autorengruppe Nationales Forschungsprogramm (1984). *Wirksamkeit der Gemeindeorientierten Präventionen Kardiovacularer Krankheiten* (Effectiveness of community-oriented prevention of cardiovascular diseases). Bern: Hans Huber.

Baddeley, A.D. & Hitch, G.J. (1977). Recency reexamined. In S. Dornic (Ed.), *Attention and performance*, Vol. 6 (pp. 647–667). Hillsdale, NJ: Lawrence Erlbaum.

Baddeley, A.D., Lewis, V., & Nimmo-Smith, J. (1978). When did you last . . .? In M.M. Gruneberg, P.E. Morris, & R.N. Sykes (Eds), *Practical aspects of memory* (pp. 77–83). London: Academic Press.

Baenninger, R. (Ed.) (1991). *Targets of violence and aggression.* Amsterdam: North-Holland.

Bales, R.F. (1968). Interaction process analysis. In D.L. Sills (Ed.), *International encyclopaedia of the social sciences*, Vol. 7. New York: Macmillan.

Ball-Rokeach, S.J., Rokeach, M., & Grube, J.W. (1984). *The great American values test.* New York: Free Press.

Baltes, M.M. (1995). Dependencies in old age: Gains and losses. *Current directions in Psychological Science, 4*, 14–19.

Baltes, M.M. & Carstensen, L.L. (in press). The process of successful ageing. *Ageing and Society.*

Baltes, M.M. & Silverberg, S.B. (1994). The dynamics between dependency and autonomy: Illustrations across the life-span. In D.L. Featherman, R.M. Lerner, & M. Perlmutter (Eds), *Life-span development and behavior*, Vol. 12 (pp. 41–90). Hillsdale, NJ: Lawrence Erlbaum.

Baltes, M.M., Neumann, E.-M., & Zank, S. (1994). Maintenance and rehabilitation of independence in old age: An intervention program for staff. *Psychology and Aging, 9*, 179–188.

Baltes, M.M., Wahl, H.-W., & Reichert, M. (1991). Successful aging in long-term care institutions. *Annual Review of Gerontology and Geriatrics, 11*, 311–337.

Baltes, P.B. (1987). Theoretical propositions of life-span developmental psychology: On the dynamics between growth and decline. *Developmental Psychology, 23*, 611–626.

Baltes, P.B. (1993). The aging mind: Potential and limits. *The Gerontologist, 33*, 580–594.

Baltes, P.B. & Baltes, M.M. (1980). Plasticity and variability in psychological aging: Methodological and theoretical issues. In G.E. Gurski (Ed.), *Determining the effects of aging on the central nervous system* (pp. 41–66). Berlin: Schering.

Baltes, P.B. & Baltes, M.M. (1990). Psychological perspectives on successful aging: The model of selective optimization with compensation. In P.B. Baltes & M.M. Baltes (Eds), *Successful aging. Perspectives from the behavioral sciences* (pp. 1–34). New York: Cambridge University Press.

Baltes, P.B., Mayer, K.U., Helmchen, H., & Steinhagen-Thiessen, E. (1993). The Berlin Aging Study (BASE): Overview and design. *Ageing and Society, 13*, 475–515.

Bandura, A. (1977). Self-efficacy: Toward a unifying theory of behavior change. *Psychological Review, 84*, 191–215.

Bandura, A. (1982). Self-efficacy mechanism in human agency. *American Psychologist, 37*, 122–147.

Bandura, A. (1983). Psychological mechanisms of aggression. In R.G. Geen & E.I. Donnerstein (Eds), *Aggression: Theoretical and empirical reviews*, Vol. 1 (pp. 1–40). New York: Academic Press.

Bandura, A. (1986). *Social foundations of thought and action: A cognitive social theory.* Englewood Cliffs, NJ: Prentice-Hall.

Bandura, A., Ross, D., & Ross, S.A. (1963). Imitation of film-mediated aggressive models. *Journal of Abnormal and Social Psychology, 66*, 3–11.

Banzinger, G. & Drevenstedt, J. (1982). Achievement attributions by young and old judges as a function of perceived age of stimulus person. *Journal of Gerontology, 37*, 468–474.

Barber, J.D. (1985). *Presidential character: Predicting performance in the White House.* Englewood Cliffs, NJ: Prentice-Hall.

Baron, J. (1992). The effect of normative beliefs on anticipated emotions. *Journal of Personality and Social Psychology, 63,* 320–330.

Baron, R.A. & Bell, P.A. (1977). Sexual arousal and aggression by males: Effects of type of erotic stimuli and prior aggression. *Journal of Personality and Social Psychology, 35,* 79–87.

Baron, R.A. & Byrne, D. (1991). *Social Psychology.* Boston: Allyn & Bacon.

Baron, R.A. & Richardson, D.R. (1994). *Human aggression* (2nd ed.). New York: Plenum Press.

Bar-Tal, D. (1990). Causes and consequences of delegitimization: Models of conflict and ethnocentrism. *Journal of Social Issues, 46,* 65–81.

Bartunek, J. M. (1993). The multiple cognition and conflicts associated with second order organizational change. In J. K. Murnighan (Ed.), *Social psychology in organizations: Advances in theory and research* (pp. 322–349). Englewood Cliffs, NJ: Prentice-Hall.

Bass, B.M. & Avolio, B.J. (1990). The implications of transactional and transformational leadership for individual, team, and organizational development. In W.A. Pasmore & R.W. Woodman (Eds), *Research in organizational change and development,* Vol. 4 (pp. 231–272). Greenwich, CT: JAI Press.

Baxter, J.S., Macrae, C.N., Manstead, A.S.R., Stradling, S.G., & Parker, D. (1990). Attributional biases and driver behaviour. *Social Behaviour, 5,* 185–192.

Baxter, J.S., Manstead, A.S.R., Stradling, S.G., Campbell, K.A., Reason, J.T., & Parker, D. (1990). Social facilitation and driver behaviour. *British Journal of Psychology, 81,* 351–360.

Beach, L.R. (1993). Image theory: Personal and organizational decisions. In G.A. Klein, J. Orasanu, R. Calderwood, & C.E. Zsambok (Eds), *Decision making in action: Models and methods* (pp. 148–157). Norwood, NJ: Ablex.

Beach, L.R. & Mitchell, T.R. (1987). Image theory: Principles, goals and plans. *Acta Psychologica, 66,* 201–220.

Beale, D.A. & Manstead, A.S.R. (1991). Predicting mothers' intentions to limit frequency of infants' sugar intake: Testing the theory of planned behaviour. *Journal of Applied Social Psychology, 21,* 409–431.

Becker, M.H. & Joseph, J.G. (1988). AIDS and behavioral change to reduce risk: a review. *American Journal of Public Health, 78,* 394–410.

Beckman, L.J. (1981). Effects of social interaction and children's relative inputs on older women's psychological well-being. *Journal of Personality and Social Psychology, 4,* 1075–1086.

Befu, H. (1980). Structural and motivational approaches to social exchange. In K.J. Gergen, M.S. Greenheim, & R.H. Willis (Eds), *Social exchange. Advances in theory and research* (pp. 197–214). New York: Plenum ·Press.

Beggan, J.K. (1991). Using what you own to get what you need: The role of possessions in satisfying control motivation. In F. W. Rudmin (Ed.), *To have possessions: A handbook of property and ownership* (pp. 129–146). Special issue of the *Journal of Social Behavior and Personality, 6.*

Beggan, J.K. (1992). On the social nature of nonsocial perception: The mere ownership effect. *Journal of Personality and Social Psychology, 62,* 229–237.

Beirness, D.J. & Simpson, H.M. (1988). Lifestyle correlates of risky driving and accident involvement among youth. *Alcohol, Drugs and Driving, 4,* 193–204.

Bekerian, D.A. & Dennett, J.L. (1993). The cognitive interview technique: Reviving the issues. *Applied Cognitive Psychology, 7,* 275–297.

Belk, R. (1978). Assessing the effects of visible consumption on impression formation. *Advances in Consumer Research, 5,* 39–47.

Belk, R. (1985). Materialism: Trait aspects of living in the material world. *Journal of Consumer Research, 12,* 265–280.

Belk, R. (1988). Possessions and the extended self. *Journal of Consumer Research, 15,* 139–168.

Belk, R., Mayer, R., & Driscoll, A. (1984). Developmental recognition of consumption symbolism. *Journal of Consumer Research, 9,* 4–17.

Bell, B.D. & Stanfield, G.C. (1973). Chronological age in relation to attitudinal judgments: An experimental analysis. *Journal of Gerontology, 28,* 491–496.

Bell, D.E. (1982). Regret in decision making under uncertainty. *Operations Research, 30,* 961–981.

Bem, D.J. (1972). Self-perception theory. In L. Berkowitz (Ed.), *Advances in Experimental Social Psychology,* Vol. 6 (pp. 1–62). New York: Academic Press.

Bentler, P.M. & Speckart, G. (1979). Models of attitude–behavior relations. *Psychological Review, 86,* 452–464.

Benton, D. (1992). Hormones and human aggression. In K. Bjorkqvist & P. Niemel (Eds), *Of mice and women: Aspects of female aggression* (pp. 37–48). San Diego, CA: Academic Press.

Berger, P. & Luckmann, T. (1966). *The social construction of reality*. New York: Doubleday.

Berkman, L.F. & Syme, S.L. (1979). Social networks, host resistance and mortality: A nine-year follow-up study of Alameda County residents. *American Journal of Epidemiology, 109*, 186–204.

Berkowitz, L. (1989a). Laboratory experiments in the study of aggression. In J. Archer & K. Browne (Eds), *Human aggression: Naturalistic approaches* (pp. 42–61). London: Routledge.

Berkowitz, L. (1989b). Frustration-aggression hypothesis: Examination and reformulation. *Psychological Bulletin, 106*, 59–73.

Berkowitz, L. (1993). *Aggression: Its causes, consequences, and control*. Philadelphia, PA: Temple University Press.

Berkowitz, L. & LePage, A. (1967). Weapons as aggression-eliciting stimuli. *Journal of Personality and Social Psychology, 7*, 202–207.

Bernardin, H.J. & Beatty, R.W. (1984). *Performance appraisal: Assessing human behavior at work*. Boston: Kent Publishing.

Berry, J.W. (1990). Psychology of acculturation. Understanding individuals moving between cultures. In R.W. Brislin (Ed.), *Applied cross-cultural psychology* (pp. 232–253). Newbury Park, CA: Sage.

Berry, J.W. (1994). Ecology of individualism and collectivism. In U. Kim, H.C. Triandis, C. Kagitcibasi, S.C. Choi, & G. Yoon (Eds), *Individualism and collectivism* (pp. 77–85). Thousand Oaks, CA: Sage.

Berry, J.W. & Kim, U. (1988). Acculturation and mental health. In P.R. Dasen, J.W. Berry, & M. Sartorius (Eds), *Health and cross-cultural psychology. Toward applications* (pp. 207–236). Newbury Park, CA: Sage.

Berry, J.W., Poortinga, Y.H., Segall, M.H., & Dasen, P.R. (1992). *Cross cultural psychology*. New York: Cambridge Press.

Berti, A. & Bombi, A. (1988). *The child's construction of economics*. Cambridge: Cambridge University Press.

Betancourt, H. & Lopez, S.R. (1993). The study of culture, ethnicity, and race in American psychology. *American Psychologist, 48*, 629–637.

Bierbrauer, G. (1992). Reactions to violation of normative standards: A cross-cultural analysis of shame and guilt. *International Journal of Psychology, 27*, 181–193.

Bierbrauer, G. (1994). Toward an understanding of legal culture: Variations in individualism and collectivism between Kurds, Lebanese, and Germans. *Law & Society Review, 28*, 243–264.

Bierbrauer, G. et al. (1994). Measurement of normative and evaluative aspects in individualistic and collectivistic orientations. The cultural orientation scale (COS). In U. Kim, H.C. Triandis, C. Kagitcibasi, S.C. Choi, & G. Yoon (Eds), *Individualism and collectivism: Theory, method, and application*. Thousand Oaks, CA: Sage.

Binet, A. (1905). La science de témoigne. *Année Psychologique, 1*, 128–138.

Bishop, G.F., Oldendick, R.W., & Tuchfarber, R.J. (1986). Opinions on fictitious issues: the pressure to answer survey questions. *Public Opinion Quarterly, 50*, 240–250.

Björkvist, K. & Niemelä, P. (Eds) (1992). *Of mice and women: Aspects of female aggression*. San Diego, CA: Academic Press.

Blair, E. & Burton, S. (1987). Cognitive processes used by survey respondents to answer behavioral frequency questions. *Journal of Consumer Research, 14*, 280–288.

Blank, T.O. (1987). Attributions as dynamic elements in a life-span social psychology. In R. Abeles (Ed.), *Life-span perspectives and social psychology* (pp. 61–84). Hillsdale, NJ: Lawrence Erlbaum.

Blaske, D.M., Borduin, C.M., Henggeler, S.W., & Mann, B.J. (1989). Individual, family, and peer characteristics of adolescent sex offenders and assaultive offenders. *Developmental Psychology, 25*, 846–855.

Blau, Z.S. (1956). Changes in status and age identification. *American Sociological Review, 21*, 198–203.

Blau, Z.S. (1973). *Old age in a changing society*. New York: Franklin Watts.

Blazer, D. (1982). Social support and mortality in an elderly community population. *American Journal of Epidemiology, 115*, 684–694.

Bless, H., Strack, F., & Schwarz, N. (1993). The informative functions of research procedures: Bias and the logic of conversation. *European Journal of Social Psychology, 23*, 149–165.

Bloch, P.H., Ridgway, N.M., & Nelson, J.E. (1991). Leisure and the shopping mall. *Advances in Consumer Research, 18*, 445–452.

Block, M.R. (1984). Retirement preparation needs of women. In H. Dennis (Ed.), *Retirement preparation. What retirement specialists need to know* (pp. 129–140). Lexington, MA: D.C. Heath.

Bloom, L. (1991). People and property: A psychoanalytic view. In F.W. Rudmin (Ed.), *To have possessions: A handbook of property and ownership* (pp. 427–444). Special issue of the *Journal of Social Behavior and Personality*, *6*.

Bocock, R. (1993). *Consumption*. London: Routledge.

Bodenhausen, G.V. & Wyer, R.S. (1987). Social cognition and social reality: Information acquisition and use in the laboratory and the real world. In H.J. Hippler, N. Schwarz, & S. Sudman (Eds), *Social information processing and survey methodology* (pp. 6–41). New York: Springer.

Bohner, G., Moskowitz, G., & Chaiken, S. (1995). The interplay of heuristic and systematic processing of social information. In *European Review of Social Psychology*, Vol. 6 (pp. 33–68). Chichester: Wiley.

Bolger, N. & Kelleher, S. (1993). Daily life in relationships. In S. Duck (Ed.), *Social context and relationships* (pp. 100–108). Newbury Park, CA: Sage.

Bolinger, D. (1973). Truth is a linguistic question. *Language*, *49*, 539–550.

Borges, M.A. & Dutton, L.J. (1976). Attitudes toward aging: Increasing optimism found with age. *The Gerontologist*, *16*, 220–224.

Boster, F.J. & Mongeau, P. (1984). Fear-arousing persuasive messages. In R.N. Bostrom (Ed.), *Communication yearbook*, Vol. 8 (pp. 330–375). Beverly Hills, CA: Sage.

Botha, M. (1990). Stability of aggression among adolescents over time: A South African study. *Aggressive Behavior*, *16*, 361–380.

Bothwell, R.K., Brigham, J.C., & Malpass, R.S. (1989). Cross-racial identification. *Personality and Social Psychology Bulletin*, *15*, 19–25.

Bowers, L., Smith, P.K., & Binney, V. (1994). Perceived family relationships of bullies, victims and bully/victims in middle childhood. *Journal of Social and Personal Relationships*, *11*, 215–232.

Bowling, B. (1993). Racial harassment and the process of victimization. Conceptual and methodological implications for the local crime survey. *British Journal of Criminology*, *33*, 231–250.

Bradac, J.J. (1990). Language attitudes and impression formation. In H. Giles & P. Robinson (Eds), *Handbook of language and social psychology* (pp. 387–412). New York: Wiley.

Bradburn, N.M. (1983). Response effects. In P.H. Rossi, J.D. Wright, & A.B. Anderson (Eds), *Handbook of survey research* (pp. 289–328). New York: Academic Press.

Bradburn, N.M. & Sudman, S. (1988). *Polls and surveys: Understanding what they tell us*. San Francisco: Jossey-Bass.

Bradburn, N.M., Huttenlocher, J., & Hedges, L. (1994). Telescoping and temporal memory. In N. Schwarz & S. Sudman (Eds), *Autobiographical memory and the validity of retrospective reports* (pp. 203–216). New York: Springer.

Bradburn, N.M., Rips, L.J., & Shevell, S.K. (1987). Answering autobiographical questions: The impact of memory and inference on surveys. *Science*, *236*, 157–161.

Braithwaite, V.A. (1986). Old age stereotypes: Reconciling contradictions. *Journal of Gerontology*, *41*, 353–360.

Braithwaite, V., Gibson, D., & Holman, J. (1985–86). Ageing stereotype: Are we oversimplifying the phenomenon? *International Journal of Aging and Human Development*, *22*, 315–325.

Brandon, R. & Davies, C. (1973). *Wrongful imprisonment*. London: Allen & Unwin.

Branwhite, T. (1994). Bullying and student distress: Beneath the tip of the iceberg. *Educational Psychology*, *14*, 59–71.

Breakwell, G.M. (1992). Predicting political party identification in new voters. In G.M. Breakwell (Ed.), *Social psychology of political and economic cognition*. London: Academic Press.

Brehm, J.W. (1966). *A theory of psychological reactance*. New York: Academic Press.

Brewer, M.B. (1993). Social identity, distinctiveness, and in-group homogeneity. *Social Cognition*, *11*, 150–164.

Brief, A.P. & Dukerich, J.M. (1991). Theory in organizational behavior: Can it be useful? In L.L. Cummings & B.M. Staw (Eds), *Research in organizational behavior*, Vol. 13 (pp. 327–352). Greenwich, CT: JAI Press.

Brigham, J.C. & Cairns, D.L. (1988). The effect of mugshot inspections on eyewitness identification accuracy. *Journal of Applied Social Psychology*, *18*, 1394–1410.

Brody, S. (1976). *The effectiveness of sentencing*. London: HMSO.

Brooks, H. (1976). *Waste management*. Paper presented at the international symposium on the management of wastes from the LWR Fuel Cycle, Denver, Colorado, 12 July.

Brown, C.L. & Geiselman, R.E. (1990). Eyewitness memory of mentally retarded: effect of the cognitive interview. *Journal of Police and Criminological Psychology*, *6*, 14–22.

Brown, J., Henderson, J., & Fielding, J. (1983). *Differing perspectives on nuclear related risks: An analysis of social psychological factors in the perception of nuclear power.* Paper presented at the meeting of the Operations Research Society, University of Warwick, England, September.

Brown, R. & Fish, D. (1983). The psychological causality implicit in language. *Cognition, 14,* 233–274.

Browne, K. (1989). The naturalistic context of family violence and child abuse. In J. Archer & K. Browne (Eds), *Human aggression: Naturalistic approaches* (pp. 182–216). London: Routledge.

Browne, K. (1994). Child sexual abuse. In J. Archer (Ed.), *Male violence* (pp. 210–230). London: Routledge.

Brubaker, T.H. & Powers, E.A. (1976). The stereotype of 'old': A review and alternative approach. *Journal of Gerontology, 31,* 441–447.

Bruner, J. & Goodman, C. (1947). Value and need as organizing principles in perception. *Journal of Abnormal and Social Psychology, 42,* 33–44.

Brunswik, E. (1956). *Perception and the representative design of psychological experiments.* Berkeley: University of California Press.

Bruun, K., Edwards, G., Lumio, M., Mäkelä, K., Pan, L., Popham, R.E., Room, R., Schmidt, W., Skog, O.-J., Sulkunen, P., & Österberg, E. (1975). *Alcohol control policies and public health perspective,* Vol. 25. Helsinki: Finnish Foundation for Alcohol Studies.

Bryant, J., Alexander, A., & Brown, D. (1983). Learning from educational television programs. In M.A.J. Howe (Ed.), *Learning from television: Psychological and educational research* (pp. 1–30). London: Academic Press.

Bugental, D.E. (1974). Interpretations of naturally occurring discrepancies between words and intonation: Modes of inconsistency resolution. *Journal of Personality and Social Psychology, 30,* 125–133.

Bugental, D.E., Kaswan, J.W., & Love, L.R. (1970). Perception of contradictory meanings conveyed by verbal and nonverbal channels. *Journal of Personality and Social Psychology, 16,* 647–655.

Bugental, D.E., Kaswan, J.W., Love, L.R., & Fox, M.N. (1970). Child vs. adult perception of evaluative messages in verbal, vocal, and visual channels. *Developmental Psychology, 2,* 367–375.

Bugental, D.E., Love, L.R., Kaswan, J.W., & April, C. (1971). Verbal–nonverbal conflict in parental messages to normal and disturbed children. *Journal of Abnormal Psychology, 77,* 6–10.

Bull, R. (1992). Obtaining evidence expertly: The reliability of interviews with child witnesses. *Expert Evidence, 1,* 5–12.

Bull, R. (1994a). Innovative techniques for the questioning of child witnesses especially those who are young and those with learning difficulty. In M. Zaragoza (Ed.), *Memory, suggestibility and eye-witness testimony in children and adults.* Newbury Park, CA: Sage.

Bull, R. (1994b). Good practice for video recorded interviews with child witnesses for use in criminal proceedings. In G. Davies, S. Lloyd-Bostock, M. McMurran, & C. Wilson (Eds), *Law and psychology.* Amsterdam: de Gruyter.

Bull, R. & Carson, D. (Eds) (1995). *Handbook of psychology in legal contexts.* Chichester: Wiley.

Buller, D.B. & Aune, R.K. (1987). Nonverbal cues to deception among intimates, friends, and strangers. *Journal of Nonverbal Behavior, 11,* 269–290.

Burgoon, J.K. & Buller, D.B. (1994). Interpersonal deception III: Effects of deceit on perceived communication and nonverbal behavior dynamics. *Journal of Nonverbal Behavior, 18,* 155–185.

Burgoyne, C.B. (1990). Money in marriage: How patterns of allocation both reflect and conceal power. *Sociological Review, 38,* 634–665.

Burgoyne, C.B. & Routh, D.A. (1991). Constraints on the use of money as a gift at Christmas: The role of status and intimacy. *Journal of Economic Psychology, 12,* 47–69.

Burns, K.L. & Beier, E.G. (1973). Significance of vocal and visual channels in the decoding of emotional meaning. *Journal of Communication, 23,* 118–130.

Bury, M. & Holme, A. (1991). *Life after ninety.* London: Routledge.

Bushman, B.J. & Cooper, H.M. (1990). Effects of alcohol on human aggression: An integrative research review. *Psychological Bulletin, 107,* 341–354.

Bushman, B.J. & Geen, R.G. (1990). Role of cognitive-emotional mediators and individual differences in the effects of media violence on aggression. *Journal of Personality and Social Psychology, 58,* 156–163.

Buss, A.H. (1961). *The psychology of aggression.* New York: Wiley.

Buss, A.H. & Perry, M. (1992). The aggression questionnaire. *Journal of Personality and Social Psychology, 63,* 452–459.

Butera, F. (1984). Designing work in automated systems: A review of case studies. In F. Butera & J.E. Thurman (Eds), *Automation and work design.* New York: Elsevier Science.

Cacioppo, J.T. & Petty, R.E. (1979). Effects of message repetition and position on cognitive response, recall and persuasion. *Journal of Personality and Social Psychology, 40,* 97–109.

Cacioppo, J.T. & Petty, R.E. (1985). Central and peripheral routes to persuasion: The role of message repetition. In L.F. Alwitt & A.A. Mitchell (Eds), *Psychological processes and advertising effects* (pp. 91—111). Hillsdale, NJ: Lawrence Erlbaum.

Calder, B.J. & Staw, B.M. (1975). Self-perception of intrinsic and extrinsic motivation. *Journal of Personality and Social Psychology, 31,* 599–605.

Cameron, P. (1969). Age parameters of young adult, middle-aged, old, and aged. *Journal of Gerontology, 24,* 201–202.

Campbell, A. (1981). *The sense of well-being in America.* New York: McGraw-Hill.

Campbell, A., Converse, P.E., Miller, W.E., & Stokes, D.E. (1960). *The American voter.* New York: Wiley.

Canter, D. (1994). *Criminal shadows.* London: HarperCollins.

Canter, D. (1995). Psychology of offender profiling. In R. Bull & D. Carson (Eds), *Handbook of psychology in legal contexts.* Chichester: Wiley.

Cantor, M.H. (1979). Neighbors and friends: An overlooked resource in the informal support system. *Research on Aging, 1,* 434–463.

Caplan, G. (1982). The family as a support system. In H.I. McCubbin, A.E. Cauble, & J.E. Patterson (Eds), *Family stress, coping, and social support* (pp. 200–220). Springfield, IL: Thomas.

Carlson, M., Marcus-Newhall, A., & Miller, N. (1989). Evidence for a general construct of aggression. *Personality and Social Psychology Bulletin, 15,* 377–389.

Carlson, M., Marcus-Newhall, A., & Miller, N. (1990). Effects of situational aggression cues: A quantitative review. *Journal of Personality and Social Psychology, 58,* 622–633.

Carp, F.M. (Ed.) (1972). *Retirement.* New York: Behavioral Publications.

Carstensen, L.L. (1987). Age-related changes in social activity. In L.L. Carstensen & B.A. Edelstein (Eds), *Handbook of clinical gerontology* (pp. 222–237). New York: Pergamon Press.

Carstensen, L.L. (1991). Socioemotional selectivity theory: Social activity in life-span context. *Annual Review of Gerontology and Geriatrics, 11,* 195–217.

Carstensen, L.L. (1992). Social and emotional patterns in adulthood: Support for socioemotional selectivity theory. *Psychology and Aging, 7,* 331–338.

Carstensen, L.L. (1993a). Motivation for social contact across the life span: A theory of socioemotional selectivity. In *Nebraska symposium on motivation* (pp. 209–254). Lincoln, NB: University of Nebraska Press.

Carstensen, L.L. (1993b). Perspective on research with older families: Contributions of older adults to families and to family theory. In P. Cowan, D. Field, D. Hansen, A. Skolnick, & G.E. Swanson (Eds), *Family, self, and society: Toward a new agenda for family research* (pp. 353–359). Hillsdale, NJ: Lawrence Erlbaum.

Carstensen, L.L. (1995). Evidence for a life-span theory of socioemotional selectivity. *Current Directions in Psychological Science, 5,* 151–156.

Carstensen, L.L. & Lang, F.R. (in press). Social relationships in context and as context: Comments on social support and the maintenance of competence in old age. In S. Willis and K.W. Schaie (Eds), *Societal mechanisms for maintaining competence in old age.* New York: Springer.

Carstensen, L.L., Hanson, K., & Freund, A.M. (1995). Selection and compensation in adulthood. In R.A. Dixon & L. Bäckman (Eds), *Psychological compensation: Managing losses and promoting gains.* Hillsdale, NJ: Lawrence Erlbaum.

Cartwright, D. & Zander, A. (1968). *Group dynamics.* New York: Harper & Row.

Casey, S.M. & Lund, A.K. (1987). Three field studies on driver speed adaptation. *Human Factors, 29,* 541–550.

Cassel, J. (1974). Psychosocial processes and 'stress': Theoretical formulation. *International Journal of Health Services, 4,* 471–482.

Castro, F.G., Newcomb, M.D., McCreary, C., & Baezconde-Garbanati, L. (1989). Cigarette smokers do more than just smoke cigarettes. *Health Psychology, 8,* 107–129.

Catania, J.A., Coates, T.J., Kegeles, S., Ekstrand, M., Guydish, J.R., & Bye, L.L. (1989). Implications of the AIDS risk-reduction model for the gay community: The importance of perceived sexual enjoyment and help-seeking behaviors. In V.M. Mays, G.W. Albee, & S.F. Schneider (Eds), *Primary prevention of AIDS.* Newbury Park, CA: Sage.

Catania, J.A., Coates, T.J., Stall, R., Bye, L., Kegeles, S.M., Capell, F., Henne, J., McKusick, L., Morin, S., Turner, H., & Pollack, I. (1991). Changes in condom use among homosexual men in San Francisco. *Health Psychology, 10,* 190–199.

Catania, J.A., Gibson, D.R., Chitwood, D.D., & Coates, T.J. (1990). Methodological problems in

AIDS behavioral research: Influences on measurement error and participation bias in studies of sexual behavior. *Psychological Bulletin, 108,* 339–362.

Catellani, P. (1990). I concetti di 'politica' e di 'uomo politico' nella percezione di militanti e non militanti. *Giornale Italiano di Psicologia, 17,* 625–650.

Catellani, P. (1995). *Political knowledge and the two faces of participation.* Manuscript submitted for publication.

Catellani, P., Balzarini, A., & Cardinali, R. (1995). *Local, national and European identity: Coexistence possibilities.* Manuscript submitted for publication.

Catellani, P., Pajardi, D., Galardi, A., & Semin, G. R. (1995). *Implicit attributions in question– answer exchanges: Analysing language in court.* Manuscript submitted for publication.

Catellani, P. & Quadrio, A. (1991). Ideal and real in the representation of politics. *Revue Internationale de Psychologie Sociale, 4,* 231–256.

Ceci, S.J. & Bruck, M. (1993). Suggestibility of the child witness: A historical review and synthesis. *Psychological Bulletin, 113,* 403–439.

Ceci, S.J., Crotteau, M.L., Smith, E., & Loftus, E.F. (in press). *Repeatedly thinking about non-events: Consciousness and cognition.*

Ceci, S.J., Leichtman, M.D., & Putnick, M.E. (Eds) (1992). *Cognitive and social factors in early deception.* Hillsdale, NJ: Lawrence Erlbaum.

Ceci, S.J., Leichtman, M., & White, T. (in press). Interviewing preschoolers: Remembrance of things planted. In D.C. Peters (Ed.), *The child witness: Cognitive, social and legal issues.* North Holland: Kluwer.

Ceci, S.J., Loftus, E.F., Leichtman, M.D., & Bruck, M. (1994). *The possible role of source misattributions in the creation of false beliefs among preschoolers.* Unpublished manuscript.

Ceci, S.J., Ross, D.F., & Toglia, M.P. (Eds) (1989). *Perspectives on children's testimony.* New York: Springer.

Ceci, S.J., Toglia, M.P., & Ross, D.F. (Eds) (1987). *Children's eyewitness memory.* New York: Springer.

Chaiken, S. & Eagly, A.H. (1976). Communication modality as a determinant of message persuasiveness and message comprehensibility. *Journal of Personality and Social Psychology, 34,* 605–614.

Chaiken, S., Liberman, A., & Eagly, A.H. (1989). Heuristic and systematic processing within and beyond the persuasion context. In J.S. Uleman & J.A. Bargh (Eds), *Unintended thoughts* (pp. 212–252). New York: Guilford.

Chance, J.E. & Goldstein, A.G. (1996). The other-race effect and eyewitness identification. In S.L. Sporer, R.M. Malpass, & G. Kölmken (Eds), *Psychological issues in eyewitness identification* (pp. 153–176). Hillsdale, NJ: Lawrence Erlbaum.

Chapanis, A., Parrish, R.N., Ochsman, R.B., & Weeks, G.D. (1977). Studies in interactive communication: II. The effects of four communication modes on the linguistic performance of teams during cooperative problem solving. *Human Factors, 19,* 101–126.

Chappell, N.L. (1983). Informal support networks among the elderly. *Research on Aging, 5,* 77–99.

Chatters, L.M., Taylor, R.J., & Jackson, J.S. (1986). Aged blacks' choices for an informal helper network. *Journal of Gerontology, 41,* 94–100.

Chen, K., Mathes, J.C., Jarboe, K., & Wolfe, J. (1979). Value oriented social decision analysis: Enhancing mutual understanding to resolve public policy issues. *IEEE Transactions on Systems, Man and Cybernetics, 9,* 567–580.

Chiriboga, D.A. (1978). Evaluated time: A life course perspective. *Journal of Gerontology, 22,* 388–393.

Cicirelli, V.G. (1989). Feelings of attachment to siblings and well-being in later life. *Psychology and Aging, 4,* 211–216.

Clark, C. (1969). Television and social controls: Some observation of the portrayal of ethnic minorities. *Television Quarterly, 8,* 18–22.

Clark, H.H. & Clark, E.V. (1977). *Psychology and language.* New York: Harcourt Brace Jovanovich.

Clark, H.H. & Haviland, S.E. (1977). Comprehension and the given-new contract. In R.O. Freedle (Ed.), *Discourse production and comprehension* (pp. 1–40). Norwood, NJ: Ablex.

Clark, H.H. & Schober, M.F. (1992). Asking questions and influencing answers. In J.M. Tanur (Ed.), *Questions about questions* (pp. 15–48). New York: Russell Sage.

Clark, M.S. (1984). A distinction between two types of relationships and its implications for development. In J.C. Masters & K. Yarkin-Levin (Eds), *Boundary areas in social and developmental psychology* (pp. 241–270). New York: Academic Press.

Clarke-Stewart, A., Thompson, W., & Lepore, S. (1989). *Manipulating children's interpretations through interrogation.* Paper presented at the biennial meeting of the Society for Research on Child Development, Kansas City.

Cline, M.E., Holmes, D.S., & Werner, J.C. (1977). Evaluations of the work of men and women as a function of the sex of the judge and type of work. *Journal of Applied Social Psychology, 7,* 89–93.

Cline, M.G. (1956). The influence of social context on the perception of faces. *Journal of Personality, 2,* 142–158.

Cline, M.G. (1964). Interpersonal perception. In B.A. Maher (Ed.), *Progress in experimental personality research,* Vol. 1 (pp. 221–284). New York: Academic Press.

Cobb, S. (1979). Social support and health through the life course. In M.W. Riley (Ed.), *Aging from birth to death* (pp. 93–106). Boulder, CO: Westview Press.

Cohen, S. & Wills, T.A. (1985). Stress, social support, and the buffering hypothesis. *Psychological Bulletin, 98,* 310–357.

Cohen, S., Evans, G.W., Stokols, D., & Krantz, D. (1986). *Behavior, health, and environmental stress.* New York: Plenum Press.

Coleman, D. (1995). Immigration policy in Great Britain. In F. Heckmann & W. Bosswick (Eds), *Migration policies: A comparative perspective* (pp. 113–136). Stuttgart: Enke.

Collins, A.M. & Loftus, E.F. (1975). A spreading activation theory of semantic processing. *Psychological Review, 82,* 407–428.

Collins, L.M., Graham, J.W., Hansen, W.B., & Johnson, C.A. (1985). Agreement between retrospective accounts of substance use and earlier reported substance use. *Applied Psychological Measurement, 9,* 301–309.

Combs, B. & Slovic, P. (1979). Causes of death: Biased newspaper coverage and biased judgments. *Journalism Quarterly, 56,* 837–843.

Connell, R.W. (1983). *Which way is up? Essays on sex, class and culture.* Sydney: Allen & Unwin.

Connor, C.L. & Walsh, R.P. (1980). Attitudes toward the older job applicant: Just as competent, but more likely to fail. *Journal of Gerontology, 35,* 920–927.

Connor, C.L., Walsh, R.P., Litzelman, D.K., & Alvarez, M.G. (1978). Evaluation of job applicants: The effects of age versus success. *Journal of Gerontology, 33,* 246–252.

Conway, M.A. (1990). *Autobiographical memory: An introduction.* Buckingham, UK: Open University Press.

Cook, S.W. & Berrenberg, J.L. (1981). Approaches to encouraging conservation behavior: A review and conceptual framework. *Journal of Social Issues, 37,* 73–103.

Cooper, A., Woo, D., & Dunkelberg, W. (1988). Entrepreneurs' perceived chances for success. *Journal of Business Venturing, 3,* 97–108.

Cope, J.G. & Grossnickle, W.E. (1986). An evaluation of three corporate strategies for safety belt use promotion. *Accident Analysis and Prevention, 18,* 243–251.

Corey, S.M. (1937). Professed attitudes and actual behavior. *Journal of Educational Psychology, 28,* 271–280.

Coutinho, R.A., van Griensven, G.J.P., & Moss, A. (1989). Effects of preventive efforts among homosexual men. *AIDS, 3,* 53–56.

Covello, V.T., von Winterfeldt, D., & Slovic, P. (1986). Risk communication: a review of the literature. *Risk Abstracts, 3,* 171–182.

Craik, F.I.M. & Lockhart, R.S. (1972). Levels of processing: A framework for memory research. *Journal of Verbal Learning and Verbal Behavior, 11,* 671–684.

Crant, J.M. & Bateman, T.S. (1993). Assignment of credit and blame for performance outcomes. *Academy of Management Journal, 36,* 7–27.

Crockett, W.H., Press, A.N., & Osterkamp, M. (1979). The effect of deviation from stereotyped expectations upon attitudes toward older persons. *Journal of Gerontology, 34,* 368.

Crohan, S.E. & Antonucci, T.C. (1989). Friends as a source of social support in old age. In R.G. Adams & R. Blieszner (Eds), *Older adult friendship* (pp. 129–146). Newbury Park, CA: Sage.

Cropanzano, R. (Ed.) (1993). *Justice in the workplace: Approaching fairness in human resource management.* Hillsdale, NJ: Lawrence Erlbaum.

Csikszentmihalyi, M. & Rochberg-Halton, E. (1981). *The meaning of things: Domestic symbols and the self.* Cambridge: Cambridge University Press.

Cumming, E. & Henry, W.E. (Eds) (1961). *Growing old: The process of disengagement.* New York: Basic Books.

Cumming, E., Henry, W.E., & Damianopoulus, E. (1961). A formal statement of disengagement theory. In E. Cumming & W.E. Henry (Eds), *Growing old: The process of disengagement* (pp. 210–218). New York: Basic Books.

Cunningham, S. (1985). The public and nuclear power. *American Psychological Association Monitor, 16,* 1.

Curran, J.W., Jaffe, H.W., Hardy, A.M., Morgan, W.M., Selik, R.M., & Dondero, P.J. (1988). Epidemiology of HIV infection and AIDS in the United States. *Science, 239*, 610–616.

Curran, J.W., Morgan, W.M., Hardy, A.M., Jaffe, H.W., Darrow, W.W., & Dowdle, W.R. (1985). The epidemiology of AIDS: Current status and future prospects. *Science, 229*, 1352–1357.

Curtis, K.A. (1992). Altering beliefs about the importance of strategy: An attributional intervention. *Journal of Applied Social Psychology, 22*, 953–972.

Cushman, P. (1990). Why the self is empty: Toward a historically situated psychology. *American Psychologist, 45*, 599–611.

Cutler, B.R. & Penrod, S.D. (1995a). Assessing the accuracy of eye-witness identification. In R. Bull & D. Carson (Eds), *Handbook of psychology in legal contexts*. Chichester: Wiley.

Cutler, B.R. & Penrod, S.D. (1995b). *The effectiveness of legal safeguards against erroneous conviction resulting from mistaken eyewitness identification*. New York: Cambridge University Press.

Cutler, B.R., Penrod, S.D., & Martens, T.K. (1987). Improving the reliability of eyewitness identifications: Putting context into context. *Journal of Applied Psychology, 72*, 629–637.

Daamen, D.D.L. & de Bie, S.E. (1992). Serial context effects in survey items. In N. Schwarz & S. Sudman (Eds), *Context effects in social and psychological research* (pp. 97–114). New York: Springer.

Damaska, M. (1973). Evidentiary barriers to conviction and two models of criminal procedure: A comparative study. *University of Pennsylvania Law Review*, 506.

Danigelis, N.L. & Fengler, A.P. (1990). Homesharing: How social exchange helps elders live at home. *Gerontologist, 30*, 162–170.

Davidson, A.R. & Jaccard, J. (1979). Variables that moderate the attitude–behavior relation: Results of a longitudinal survey. *Journal of Personality and Social Psychology, 37*, 1364–1376.

Davidson, L.M., Baum, A., & Collins, D.L. (1982). Stress and control-related problems at Three Mile Island. *Journal of Applied Social Psychology, 12*, 349–359.

Davies, G.M. (1996). Children's identification evidence. In S.L. Sporer, R.M. Malpass, & G. Köhnken (Eds), *Psychological issues in eyewitness identification* (pp. 233–258). Hillsdale, NJ: Lawrence Erlbaum.

Davis, J.H. (1989). Psychology and law: The last 15 years. *Journal of Applied Social Psychology, 19*, 199–230.

Dawes, R.M. (1988). *Rational choice in an uncertain world*. San Diego, CA: Harcourt Brace Jovanovich.

Dawes, R.M. (1994). AIDS, sterile needles, and ethnocentrism. In L. Heath, R. Scott-Tindale, J. Edwards, E.J. Posavac, F.B. Bryant, E. Henderson-King, Y. Suarez-Balcazar & J. Myers (Eds), *Applications of heuristics and biases to social issues* (pp. 31–44). New York: Plenum Press.

Dawes, R.M. & Smith, T.L. (1985). Attitude and opinion measurement. In G. Lindzey & E. Aronson (Eds), *Handbook of social psychology*, Vol. 1 (pp. 509–566). New York: Random House.

Deci, E.L. (1971). Effects of externally mediated rewards on intrinsic motivation. *Journal of Personality and Social Psychology, 18*, 105–115.

Deci, E.L. (1975). *Intrinsic motivation*. New York: Plenum Press.

Deci, E.L. & Ryan, R.M. (1980). The empirical exploration of intrinsic motivational processes. In L. Berkowitz (Ed.), *Advances in experimental social psychology*, Vol. 13 (pp. 39–80). New York: Academic Press.

Deci, E.L., Benware, C., & Landy, D.A. (1974). The attribution of motivation as a function of output and rewards. *Journal of Personality, 42*, 652–667.

De Dreu, C.W., Lualhati, J.C., & McCusker, C. (1994). Effects of gain–loss frames on satisfaction with self–other outcome differences. *European Journal of Social Psychology, 24*, 497–510.

DeFleur, M.L. & Westie, F.R. (1958). Verbal attitudes and overt acts: An experiment on the salience of attitudes. *American Sociological Review, 23*, 667–673.

DeMaio, T.J. (1984). Social desirability and survey measurement: A review. In C.F. Turner & E. Martin (Eds), *Surveying subjective phenomena*, Vol. 2 (pp. 257–281). New York: Russell Sage.

Dent, H.R. & Flin, R. (Eds) (1992). *Children as witnesses*. Chichester: Wiley.

Department of Transport (1989). *Road accidents Great Britain 1988: The casualty report*. London: HMSO.

Department of Transport (1994). *Road accidents Great Britain 1993: The casualty report*. London: HMSO.

DePaulo, B.M. & Pfeifer, R.L. (1986). On-the-job experience and skill at detecting deception. *Journal of Applied Social Psychology, 16*, 249–267.

DePaulo, B.M., Rosenthal, R., Eisenstat, R.A., Rogers, P.L., & Finkelstein, S. (1978). Decoding discrepant nonverbal cues. *Journal of Personality and Social Psychology, 36*, 313–323.

DePaulo, B.M., Stone, J.L., & Lassiter, G.D. (1985). Deceiving and detecting deceit. In B.R. Schenker (Ed.), *The self and social life*. New York: McGraw-Hill.

Depner, C.E. & Ingersoll-Dayton, B. (1988). Supportive relationships in later life. *Psychology and Aging, 3*(4), 348–357.

De Poot, C. & Semin, G.R. (1995) Pick your verbs with care when you formulate a question! *Journal of Language and Social Psychology, 14*, in press.

Detels, R., English, P., Visscher, B.R., Jacobson, L., Kingsley, L.A., Chmiel, J.S., Dudley, J.P., Eldred, L.J., & Ginzburg, H.M. (1989). Seroconversion, sexual activity and condom use among 2915 HIV seronegative men followed for up to three years. *Journal of Acquired Immune Deficiency Syndromes, 2*, 77–83.

Deutsch, M. & Hornstein, H.A. (1975). *Applying social psychology: Implications for research, practice, and training*. Hillsdale, NJ: Lawrence Erlbaum.

De Wit, J.B.F., de Vroome, E.M.M., Sandfort, T.G.M., van Griensven, G.J.P., Coutinho, R.A., & Tielman, R.A.P. (1992). Safe sex practices not reliably maintained by homosexual men. *American Journal of Public Health, 82*, 615–616.

De Wit, J.B.F., van den Hoek, J.A.R., Sandfort, T.G.M., & van Griensven, G.J.P. (1993). Increase in unprotected anogenital intercourse among homosexual men. *American Journal of Public Health, 2483*, 1451–1453.

DiCagno, D. & Hey, J.D. (1988). A direct test of the original version of regret theory. *Journal of Decision Making, 3*, 357–365.

Dickson, E. & Bowers, R. (1973). *The videotelephone: A new era in telecommunications*. Report to the National Science Foundation from Cornell University.

Diener, E. (1976). Effects of prior destructive behavior, anonymity, and group presence on deindividuation and aggression. *Journal of Personality and Social Psychology, 33*, 497–507.

Dietz, T. & Vine, E.L. (1982). Energy impacts of a municipal energy policy. *Energy, 7*, 755–758.

DiLalla, L.F. & Gottesman, I.I. (1991). Biological and genetic contributions to violence – Widom's untold tale. *Psychological Bulletin, 109*, 125–129.

Dillman, D.A. (1978). *Telephone and mail surveys: The total design method*. New York: Wiley.

Dittmann, A.T., Parloff, M.B., & Boomer, D.S. (1965). Facial and bodily expression: A study of receptivity of emotional cues. *Psychiatry, 28*, 239–244.

Dittmar, H. (1992a). *The social psychology of material possessions: To have is to be*. Hemel Hempstead, UK: Harvester Wheatsheaf; New York: St Martin's Press.

Dittmar, H. (1992b). Perceived material wealth and first impressions. *British Journal of Social Psychology, 31*, 379–391.

Dittmar, H. (1994). Material possessions as stereotypes: Material images of different socio-economic groups. *Journal of Economic Psychology, 15*, 561–585.

Dittmar, H. & Pepper, L. (1994). To have is to be: Materialism and person perception in British working-class and middle-class adolescents. *Journal of Economic Psychology, 15*, 233–251.

Dittmar, H., Beattie, J., & Friese, S. (1995). Gender identity and material symbols: Objects and decision considerations in impulse purchases. *Journal of Economic Psychology, 16*, 491–511.

Dohrenwend, B.P., Dohrenwend, B.S., Kasl, S.V., & Warheit, G.J. (1979). *Report of the Task Group on Behavioral Effects to the President's Commission on the accident at Three Mile Island*. Washington, DC: USA Government Printing Office.

Dollard, J., Doob, L.W., Miller, N.E., Mowrer, O.H., & Sears, R.R. (1939). *Frustration and aggression*. New Haven, CT: Yale University Press.

Domangue, B.B. (1978). Decoding effects of cognitive complexity, tolerance of ambiguity, and verbal-nonverbal inconsistency. *Journal of Personality, 46*, 519–535.

Donnerstein, M. & Donnerstein, E. (1978). Direct and vicarious censure in the control of interracial aggression. *Journal of Personality, 46*, 162–175.

Doob, A. & MacDonald, G.E. (1979). Television viewing and fear of victimization: Is the relationship causal? *Journal of Personality and Social Psychology, 37*, 170–179.

Doris, J. (Ed.) (1991). *The suggestibility of children's recollections: Implications for eyewitness testimony*. Washington, DC: American Psychological Association.

Douglas, M. (1986). *How institutions think*. Syracuse, NY: Syracuse University Press.

Dowrick, P.W. & Biggs, S.J. (Eds) (1983). *Using video: Psychological and social applications*. Chichester: Wiley.

Drevenstedt, J. (1976). Perceptions of onsets of young adulthood, middle age, and old age. *Journal of Gerontology, 31*, 53–57.

Drottz, B.M. & Sjöberg, L. (1990). Risk perception and worries after the Chernobyl accident. *Journal of Environmental Psychology, 10*, 135–150.

Dubrowsky, V.J., Kiesler, S., & Sethna, B.N. (1991). The equalization phenomenon: Status effects in computer-mediated and face-to-face decision making groups. *Human–Computer Interaction, 6*, 119–146.

Duck, S. (1986). *Human relationships*. London: Sage.

Dunand, M., Berkowitz, L., & Leyens, J.P. (1984). Audience effects when viewing aggressive movies. *British Journal of Social Psychology, 23*, 69–76.

Dunlap, R.E. & van Liere, K.D. (1978). The New Environmental Paradigm: A proposed measuring instrument and preliminary results. *Journal of Environmental Education, 9*, 10–19.

Dunlap, R.E. & van Liere, K.D. (1984). Commitment to the dominant social paradigm and concern for environmental quality. *Social Science Quarterly, 64*, 1013–1028.

Dunning, D., Griffin, D.W., Milojkovic, J.D., & Ross, L. (1990). The overconfidence effect in social prediction. *Journal of Personality and Social Psychology, 58*, 568–581.

Duval, S. & Wicklund, R.A. (1972). *A theory of objective self-awareness*. New York: Academic Press.

Eagly, A.H. (1987). *Sex differences in social behavior: A social role interpretation*. Hillsdale, NJ: Lawrence Erlbaum.

Eagly, A.H. & Chaiken, S. (1993). *The psychology of attitudes*. Fort Worth, TX: Harcourt Brace Jovanovich.

Eagly, A.H. & Steffen, F.J. (1986). Gender and aggressive behavior: A meta-analytic review of the social psychological literature. *Psychological Bulletin, 100*, 309–330.

Eastman, M. (1989). Studying old age abuse. In J. Archer & K. Browne (Eds), *Human aggression: Naturalistic approaches* (pp. 217–229). London: Routledge.

Eden, C., Jones, S., Sims, D., & Smithin, T. (1981). The intersubjectivity of issues and issues of intersubjectivity. *Journal of Management Studies, 18*, 37–47.

Edwards, D. & Potter, J. (1992). *Discursive psychology*. Newbury Park, CA: Sage.

Edwards, D. & Potter, J. (1993). Language and causation: A discursive action model of description and attribution. *Psychological Review, 100*, 23–41.

Edwards, W. (1954). The theory of decision making. *Psychological Bulletin, 51*, 380–417.

Efran, M.G. (1974). The effect of physical appearance on the judgement of guilt, interpersonal attraction and severity of recommended punishment on a simulated jury task. *Journal of Research in Personality, 85*, 395–461.

Egger, G., Fitzgerald, W., Frape, G., Monaem, A., Rubinstein, P., Tyler, C., & McKay, B. (1983). Result of a large scale media antismoking campaign in Australia: North cost 'Quit For Life' programme. *British Medical Journal, 286*, 1125–1128.

Egido, C. (1988). Videoconferencing as a technology to support group work: A review of its failure. *Journal of the Association for Computing Machinery, 9*, 13–24.

Einzig, P. (1966). *Primitive Money* (2nd ed.). Oxford: Pergamon Press.

Eiser, J.R. (1986). *Social psychology: Attitudes, cognition and social behaviour*. Cambridge: Cambridge University Press.

Eiser, J.R. & van der Pligt, J. (1979). Beliefs and values in the nuclear debate. *Journal of Applied Social Psychology, 9*, 524–536.

Eiser, J.R., van der Pligt, J., & Spears, R. (1995) *Nuclear neighbourhoods: Community responses to reactor siting*. Exeter, UK: Exeter University Press.

Ekman, P. & Friesen, W.V. (1978). *The facial action coding system*. Palo Alto, CA: Consulting Psychologists Press.

Ekman, P., Friesen, W.V., & Ellsworth, P. (1982). What are the relative contributions of facial behavior and contextual information to the judgement of emotion? In P. Ekman (Ed.), *Emotion in the human face* (2nd ed., pp. 111–127). New York: Cambridge University Press.

Ekman, P., Friesen, W.V., O'Sullivan, M., & Scherer, K.R. (1980). Relative importance of face, body, and speech in judgments of personality and affect. *Journal of Personality and Social Psychology, 38*, 270–277.

Ekstrand, M. & Coates, T. (1990). Maintenance of safer sexual behaviors and predictors of risky sex: The San Francisco Men's Health Study. *American Journal of Public Health, 180*, 973–977.

Elander, J., West, R., & French, D. (1993). Behavioral correlates of individual differences in road-traffic crash risk: An examination of methods and findings. *Psychological Bulletin, 113*, 279–294.

Elias, N. (1969). *Über den Prozess der Zivilisation: soziogenetische und psychogenetische Untersuchungen*. Bern: Francke Verlag.

Elliott, R. (1994). Addictive consumption: Function and fragmentation in postmodernity. *Journal of Consumer Policy, 17*, 159–179.

Ellis, T. (1988). Clean needles idea is a menace to society. *USA Today*, 10A (February 9).

Emler, N. & Dickinson, J. (1985). Children's representation of economic inequalities: The effects of social class. *British Journal of Developmental Psychology, 3*, 191–198.

Emler, N.S., Renwick, S., & Malone, B. (1983). The relationship between moral reasoning and political orientation. *Journal of Personality and Social Psychology, 45*, 1073–1080.

Erikson, R.S., Luttberg, N.R., & Tedin, K.T. (1988). *American public opinion* (3rd ed.). New York: Macmillan.

Eron, L.D. (1986). Interventions to mitigate the psychological effects of media violence on aggressive behavior. *Journal of Social Issues, 42*, 155–169.

Eron, L.D. (1994). Theories of aggression: From drives to cognitions. In L.R. Huesman (Ed.), *Aggressive behavior: Current perspectives* (pp. 3–11). New York: Plenum Press.

Esplin, P., Boychuk, T., & Raskin, D. (1988). *Application of statement validity analysis*. Paper presented at the NATO Advanced Study Institute on Credibility Assessment, Maratea, Italy.

Esterling, B., Antoni, M.N., Fletcher, M.A., Marguiles, S., & Schneiderman, N. (1994). Emotional disclosure through writing or speaking modulates Epstein-Barr virus antibody titers. *Journal of Consulting and Clinical Psychology, 62*, 130–140.

Etzioni, A. (1988). Normative-affective factors: Toward a new decision-making model. *Journal of Economic Psychology, 9*, 125–150.

Evans, G. (1993). Class, powerlessness and political polarization. *European Journal of Social Psychology, 23*, 495–511.

Evans, L. (1991). *Traffic safety and the driver*. New York: Van Nostrand Reinhold.

Eysenck, H.J. (1977). *Crime and personality* (2nd ed.). London: Routledge & Kegan Paul.

Eysenck, H.J. & Eysenck, S.B.G. (1978). Psychopathy, personality and genetics. In R.D. Hare & D. Schalling (Eds), *Psychopathic behaviour*. Chichester: Wiley.

Fagley, N.S. & Miller, P.M. (1990). The effects of framing on choice: Interactions with risk-taking propensity, cognitive style and sex. *Personality and Social Psychology Bulletin, 16*, 496–510.

Fallo-Mitchell, L. & Ryff, C. D. (1982). Preferred timing of female life events. *Research on Aging, 4*, 249–267.

Fanselow, M. (1975). How to bias an eyewitness: A review of research on expectancy applied to eyewitness identification testing. *Social Action and the Law, 2*, 3–4.

Farabollini, F. (Ed.) (1994). *Aggression, gender and sex*. Special issue of *Aggressive Behavior, 20*(3).

Farnham, B. (1990). Political cognition and decision-making. *Political Psychology, 11*, 83–107.

Farquhar, J.W., Maccoby, N., Wood, P.D., Alexander, J.K., Breitrose, H., Brown, B.W., Jr., Haskell, W.L., McAlister, A.L., Meyer, A.J., Nash, J.D., & Stern, M.P. (1977). Community education for cardiovascular health. *Lancet, 1*, 1192–1195.

Farrington, D.P. (1986). Stepping stones to adult criminal careers. In D. Olweus, J. Block, & M.R. Yarrow (Eds), *Development of anti-social and pro-social behaviour: Research, theories and issues*. New York: Academic Press.

Farrington, D.P. (1990). Age, period, cohort, and offending. In D.M. Gottfredson & R.V. Clarke (Eds), *Policy and theory in criminal justice: Contributions in honor of Leslie T. Wilkins*. Aldershot, UK: Gower.

Farrington, D.P. (1992). Psychological contributions to the explanation, prevention and treatment of offending. In F. Lösel, D. Bender, & T. Bliesener (Eds), *Psychology and law: International perspectives*.

Farrington, D.P. & West, D.J. (1990). The Cambridge study in delinquent development: A longterm follow-up of 411 London males. In H.J. Kerner & G. Kaiser (Eds), *Criminality: Personality, behavior, and life history*. Berlin: Springer Verlag.

Farrington, D.P., Biron, L., & LeBlanc, M. (1982). Personality and delinquency in London and Montreal. In J. Gunn & D.P. Farrington (Eds), *Abnormal offenders, delinquency and the criminal justice system*. Chichester: Wiley.

Farrington, D.P., Loeber, R., & van Kammen, W.B. (1990). Long-term criminal outcomes of hyperactivity-impulsivity-attention deficit and conduct problems in childhood. In L.N. Robins & M. Rutter (Eds), *Straight and devious pathways from childhood to adulthood*. Cambridge: Cambridge University Press.

Fazio, R.H. (1986). How do attitudes guide behavior? In R.M. Sorrentino & E.T. Higgins (Eds), *Handbook of motivation and cognition: Foundations of social behavior* (pp. 204–243). New York: Guilford.

Fazio, R.H. (1990). Multiple processes by which attitudes guide behavior: The MODE model as an integrative framework. In M.P. Zanna (Ed.), *Advances in experimental social psychology*, Vol. 23 (pp. 75–109). San Diego, CA: Academic Press.

Fazio, R.H. & Zanna, M.P. (1981). Direct experience and attitude–behavior consistency. In L.

Berkowitz (Ed.), *Advances in experimental social psychology*, Vol. 14 (pp. 161–202). San Diego, CA: Academic Press.

Fazio, R.H., Chen, J., McDonel, E.C., & Sherman, S.J. (1982). Attitude accessibility, attitude–behavior consistency, and the strength of the object–evaluation association. *Journal of Experimental Social Psychology, 18*, 339–357.

Feagin, J.R. (1972). Poverty: We still believe that God helps those who help themselves. *Psychology Today, 6*, 101–129.

Feldman, J.M. (1981). Beyond attribution theory: Cognitive processes in performance appraisal. *Journal of Applied Psychology, 66*, 127–148.

Feldman, J.M. & Lynch, J.G. (1988). Self-generated validity and other effects of measurement on belief, attitude, intention, and behavior. *Journal of Applied Psychology, 73*, 421–435.

Feldstein, R.S. & Rimé, B. (1991). *Fundamentals of nonverbal behavior.* Cambridge: Cambridge University Press.

Felson, R.B. & Tedeschi, J.T. (Eds) (1993). *Aggression and violence: Social interactionist perspectives.* Washington, DC: American Psychological Association.

Fenigstein, A. (1979). Does aggression cause a preference for viewing media violence? *Journal of Personality and Social Psychology, 37*, 2307–2317.

Feshbach, S. (1994). Nationalism, patriotism, and aggression. A clarification of functional differences. In L.R. Huesman (Ed.), *Aggressive behavior: Current perspectives* (pp. 275–291). New York: Plenum Press.

Festinger, L. (1954). A theory of social comparison processes. *Human Relations, 7*, 117–140.

Festinger, L. (1957). *A theory of cognitive dissonance.* Stanford, CA: Stanford University Press.

Festinger, L. (Ed.) (1964). *Conflict, decision and dissonance.* Stanford, CA: Stanford University Press.

Festinger, L. & Carlsmith, J.M. (1959). Cognitive consequences of forced compliance. *Journal of Abnormal and Social Psychology, 58*, 203–210.

Festinger, L. (1964). *Conflict, decision, and dissonance.* Stanford, CA: Stanford University Press.

Festinger, L. & Maccoby, N. (1964). On resistance to persuasive communications. *Journal of Abnormal and Social Psychology, 68*, 359–366.

Fhanér, G. & Hane, M. (1979). Seat belts: Opinion effects of law-induced use. *Journal of Applied Psychology, 64*, 205–212.

Fiedler, K. (1989). Suggestion and credibility: Lie detection based on content-related cues. In V. Gheorghiu, P. Netter, H.J. Eysenck, & R. Rosenthal (Eds), *Suggestibility, theory and research* (pp. 323–335). New York: Springer.

Fiedler, K. & Armbruster, T. (1994). Two halts may be more than one whole: Category-split effects on frequency illusions. *Journal of Personality and Social Psychology, 66*, 633–645.

Fiedler, K. & Semin, G.R. (1992). Attribution and language as a socio-cognitive environment. In G.R. Semin & K. Fiedler (Eds), *Language, interaction and social cognition* (pp. 79–101). London: Sage.

Fiedler, K. & Walka, I. (1993). Training lie detectors to use nonverbal cues instead of global heuristics. *Human Communication Research, 20*, 199–223.

Fiedler, K., Semin, G.R., & Finkenauer, C. (1993). The battle of words between gender groups: A language-based approach to intergroup processes. *Human Communication Research, 19*, 409–441.

Fiedler, F., Semin, G.R., & Koppetsch, C. (1991). Language use and attributional biases in close personal relationships. *Personality and Social Psychology Bulletin, 17*, 147–155.

Field, D. & Minkler, M. (1988). Continuity and change in social support between young-old and old-old or very-old age. *Journal of Gerontology: Psychological Sciences, 43*(4), P100–106.

Field, D. & Minkler, M. (1993). The importance of families in advanced old age: A family is 'forever'. In P. Cowan, D. Field, D. Hansen, A. Skolnick, & G.E. Swanson (Eds), *Family, self, and society: Toward a new agenda for family research* (pp. 331–351). Hillsdale, NJ: Lawrence Erlbaum.

Field, D., Minkler, M., Falk, R.F., & Leino, E.V. (1993). The influence of health on family contacts and family feelings in advanced old age: A longitudinal study. *Journal of Gerontology: Psychological Sciences, 48*, P18–P28.

Fielding, J.E. (1985). Smoking: Health effects and control. *New England Journal of Medicine, 313*, 555–561.

Fincham, F.D. (1985). Attribution processes in distressed and nondistressed couples: 2. Responsibility for marital problems. *Journal of Abnormal Psychology, 94*, 183–190.

Finkelhor, D. (1986). *A sourcebook on child sexual abuse.* Beverly Hills, CA: Sage.

Finn, P. & Bragg, B.W.E. (1986). Perception of the risk of an accident by young and older drivers. *Accident Analysis and Prevention, 18*, 289–298.

Fischhoff, B. (1983). Predicting frames. *Journal of Experimental Psychology: Learning, Memory and Cognition, 9*, 103–116.

Fischhoff, B. & Beyth, R. (1975). 'I knew it would happen': Remembered probabilities of once-future things. *Organizational Behavior and Human Performance, 13*, 1–16.

Fischhoff, B., Lichtenstein, S., Slovic, P., Derby, S.L., & Keeney, R.L. (1981). *Acceptable risk*. Cambridge: Cambridge University Press.

Fischhoff, B., Slovic, P., Lichtenstein, S., Read, S., & Combs, B. (1978). How safe is safe enough: A psychometric study of attitudes toward technological risks and benefits. *Policy Sciences, 8*, 127–152.

Fishbein, M. & Ajzen, I. (1975). *Belief, attitude, intention and behavior: An introduction to theory and research*. Reading, MA: Addison-Wesley.

Fishbein, M. & Ajzen, I. (1981). Attitudes and voting behavior: An application of the theory of reasoned action. In G.M. Stephenson & J.M. Davis (Eds), *Progress in applied social psychology*. Chichester: Wiley.

Fisher, J.D. & Fisher, W.A. (1992). Changing AIDS-risk behavior. *Psychological Bulletin, 111*, 455–474.

Fisher, R.J. (1990). *The social psychology of intergroup and international conflict resolution*. New York: Springer.

Fisher, R.P. & Geiselman, R.E. (1992). *Memory-enhancing techniques for investigative interviewing*. Springfield, IL: Charles C. Thomas.

Fisher, R.P. & McCauley, M.R. (in press). Improving eyewitness testimony with the cognitive interview. In M. Zaragoza, I. Graham, G. Hall, R. Hirschman, & Y. Ben-Porath (Eds), *Memory and testimony in the child witness*. London: Sage.

Fisher, R.P., Geiselman, R.E., & Amador, M. (1989). Field test of the cognitive interview: Enhancing the recollection of actual victims and witnesses of crime. *Journal of Applied Psychology, 74*, 722–727.

Fisher, R.P., Geiselman, R.E., Raymond, D.S., Jurkevich, L.M., & Warhaftig, M.L. (1987). Enhancing enhanced eyewitness memory: Refining the cognitive interview. *Journal of Police Science and Administration, 15*, 291–297.

Fisher, R.P., McCauley, M.R., & Geiselman, R.E. (1994). Improving eyewitness testimony with the cognitive interview. In D. Ross, J.D. Read, & M. Toglia (Eds), *Adult eyewitness testimony: Current trends and developments*. London: Cambridge University Press.

Fiske, J. & Hartley, J. (1978). *Reading television*. London: Methuen.

Fiske, S. & Pavelchak, M.A. (1986). Category-based vs. piecemeal-based affective responses: Developments in schema-triggered effects. In R.M. Sorrentino & E.T. Higgins (Eds), *Handbook of motivation and cognition*. New York: Guilford.

Fiske, S., Lau, R.R., & Smith, R.A. (1990). On the varieties and utilities of political expertise. *Social Cognition, 8*, 31–48.

Fiske, S.T. & Taylor, S.E. (1984). *Social cognition*. New York: Random House.

Flexser, A.J. & Tulving, E. (1978). Retrieval independence in recognition and recall. *Psychological Review, 85*, 152–172.

Flynn, C.B. (1979). *Three Mile Island Telephone Survey: A preliminary report*. Washington, DC: US Nuclear Regulatory Commission.

Flynn, C.B. (1981). Local public opinion. In T.H. Moss & D.L. Sills (Eds), The Three Mile Island nuclear accident: Lessons and implications. *Annuals of the New York Academy of Sciences*, Vol. 365 (pp. 146–158). New York: New York Academy of Sciences.

Foley, J.M. (1966). *The bilateral effect of film context*. Unpublished master's thesis, University of Iowa (cited in Isenhour, 1975).

Forgas, J.P. & Brown, L.B. (1977). Environmental and behavioral cues in the perception of social encounters: An exploratory study. *American Journal of Psychology, 90*, 635–644.

Forgas, J.P., Furnham, A., & Frey, D. (1988). Cross-national differences in attributions of wealth and economic success. *Journal of Social Psychology, 129*, 643–651.

Forgas, J.P., Morris, S.L., & Furnham, A. (1982). Lay explanations of wealth: Attributions for economic success. *Journal of Applied Social Psychology, 12*, 381–397.

Fosdick, J.A. & Tannenbaum, P.H. (1964). The encoder's intent and use of stylistic elements in photographs. *Journalism Quarterly, 41*, 175–182.

Fournier, S. & Richins, M. (1991). Some theoretical and popular notions concerning materialism. In F.W. Rudmin (Ed.), *To have possessions: A handbook of property and ownership* (pp. 403–414). Special issue of the *Journal of Social Behavior and Personality, 6*.

Fowler, F.J. (1991). Reducing interviewer-related error through interviewer training, supervision, and other means. In P. Biemer, R. Groves, N. Mathiowetz, & S. Sudman (Eds), *Measurement error in surveys* (pp. 259–278). Chichester: Wiley.

Frank, J. & Frank, B. (1957). *Not guilty*. London: Gollancz.

Freedman, J.L. (1986). Television violence and aggression: A rejoinder. *Psychological Bulletin, 100*, 372–378.

Freedman, J.L. (1988). Television violence and aggression: What the evidence shows. In S. Oskamp (Ed.), *Applied Social Psychology Annual*, Vol. 8 (pp. 144–162). Newbury Park, CA: Sage.

Frese, M. (1987). Human–computer interaction in the office. In C.L. Cooper & I.T. Robertson (Eds), *International Review of Industrial and Organizational Psychology*, Vol. 2 (pp. 117–165). Chichester: Wiley.

Freud, S. (1920). *Beyond the pleasure principle*. New York: Bantam Books.

Freudenburg, W.R. & Baxter, R.K. (1984). Nuclear reactions: Public attitudes and policies toward nuclear power. *Policy Studies Review, 5*, 96–110.

Frey, D. (1986). Recent research on selective exposure to information. In L. Berkowitz (Ed.), *Advances in Experimental Social Psychology*, Vol. 15 (pp. 41–80). Orlando, FL: Academic Press.

Frey, D. (1995). Information seeking among individuals and groups and possible consequences for decision-making in business and politics. In E. Witte & J. Davis (Eds), *Understanding group behavior, Vol. II: Small group processes and interpersonal relations*. Hillsdale, NJ: Lawrence Erlbaum.

Frey, D., Schulz-Hardt, S., Lüthgens, C., & Moscovici, S. (1995). *The heart of groupthink: Dissonance and consistency-construction in three-person decision-making groups*. Manuscript submitted for publication.

Frey, J.H. (1983). *Survey research by telephone*. Newbury Park, CA: Sage.

Frey, S. (1987). *Analyzing patterns of behavior in dyadic interaction*. Göttingen: Hogrefe.

Friedland, N. (1988). Political terrorism: A social psychological perspective. In W. Stroebe, A. Kruglanski, D. Bar-Tal, & M. Hewstone (Eds), *The social psychology of intergroup conflict* (pp. 103–114). New York: Springer.

Friedman, H.S. (1979). The interactive effects of facial expression of emotion and verbal messages on perceptions of affective meaning. *Journal of Experimental Social Psychology, 15*, 453–469.

Friedman, J. (1994). *Cultural identity and global process*. London: Sage.

Friedrich-Cofer, L. & Huston, A.C. (1986). Television violence and aggression: The debate continues. *Psychological Bulletin, 100*, 364–371.

Frieze, I.H. (1984). Causal attributions for the performances of the elderly: Comments from an attributional theorist. *Basic and Applied Social Psychology, 5*, 127–130.

Frijda, N.H. (1958). Facial expression and situational cues. *Journal of Abnormal and Social Psychology, 57*, 149–154.

Frijda, N.H. (1969). Recognition of emotion. In L. Berkowitz (Ed.), *Advances in experimental social psychology*, Vol. 4 (pp. 167–224). New York: Academic Press.

Fromm, E. (1978). *To have or to be?* Harmondsworth, UK: Penguin.

Frude, N. (1994). Marital violence: An interactional perspective. In J. Archer (Ed.), *Male violence* (pp. 153–169). London: Routledge.

Fry, C.L. (1976). The ages of adulthood: A question of numbers. *Journal of Gerontology, 31*, 170–177.

Fukuyama, F. (1995). *The social virtues and the creation of prosperity*. New York: Free Press.

Furby, L. (1978). Possessions: Towards a theory of their meaning and function throughout the life cycle. In P.B. Baltes (Ed.), *Life Span Development and Behavior*, Vol. 1 (pp. 297–336). New York: Academic Press.

Furnham, A. (1982). Why are the poor always with us? Explanations for poverty in Britain. *British Journal of Social Psychology, 21*, 311–322.

Furnham, A. (1983). Attributions for affluence. *Personality and Individual Differences, 4*, 31–40.

Furnham, A. (1984). Many sides of the coin: The psychology of money usage. *Personality and Individual Differences, 5*, 95–103.

Furnham, A. (1985). Why do people save? Attitudes to, and habits of saving money in Britain. *Journal of Applied Social Psychology, 15*, 354–373.

Furnham, A. (1986). Assertiveness through different media. *Journal of Language and Social Psychology, 5*, 1–11.

Furnham, A. (1988). The adjustment of sojourners. In Y.Y. Kim & W.B. Gudykunst (Eds), *Cross cultural adaptation: Current approaches. International and Intercultural Communication Annual Vol XI* (pp. 42–61). Newbury Park, CA: Sage.

Furnham, A. & Bochner, S. (1986). *Culture shock. Psychological reactions to unfamiliar environments*. London: Methuen.

Furnham, A. & Stacey, B. (1991). *Young people's understanding of society*. London: Routledge.

Furth, H. (1980). *The world of grown-ups.* Amsterdam: Elsevier.

Galbraith, J. (1982). Designing the innovating organization. *Organizational Dynamics, 10* (Summer), 5–25.

Garrett, J.E. (1987). Multiple losses in older adults. *Journal of Gerontological Nursing, 13,* 8–12.

Garrett, P. (1985). Effects of residential treatment of adjudicated delinquents: A meta-analysis. *Journal of Research in Crime and Delinquency, 22,* 287–308.

Geen, R.G. (1990). *Human aggression.* Milton Keynes, UK: Open University Press.

Geen, R.G. & O'Neal, E.C. (1969). Activation of cue-elicited aggression by general arousal. *Journal of Personality and Social Psychology, 11,* 289–292.

Geiselman, R.E. & Machlowitz, H. (1987). Hypnosis memory recall: Implications for forensic use. *American Journal of Forensic Psychology.*

Geiselman, R.E. & Padilla, J. (1988). Interviewing child witnesses with the cognitive interview. *Journal of Police Science and Administration, 16,* 236–242.

Geiselman, R.E., Fisher, R.P., Cohen, G., Holland, H.L., & Surtes, L. (1986). Eyewitness responses to leading and misleading questions under the cognitive interview. *Journal of Police Science and Administration, 14,* 31–39.

Geiselman, R.E., Fisher, R.P., Firstenberg, I., Hutton, L.A., Avetissian, I., & Prosk, A. (1984). Enhancement of eyewitness memory: An empirical evaluation of the cognitive interview. *Journal of Police Science and Administration, 12,* 74–80.

Geiselman, R.E., Fisher, R.P., MacKinnon, D.P., & Holland, H.L. (1985). Eyewitness memory enhancement in the police interview: Cognitive retrieval mnemonics versus hypnosis. *Journal of Applied Psychology, 70,* 401–412.

Geiselman, R.E., Fisher, R.P., MacKinnon, D.P., & Holland, H.L. (1986). Enhancement of eyewitness memory with the cognitive interview. *American Journal of Psychology, 99,* 385–401.

Geller, E.S., Kalsher, M.J., Rudd, J.R., & Lehman, G.R. (1989). Promoting safety belt use on a university campus: An integration of commitment and incentive strategies. *Journal of Applied Social Psychology, 19,* 3–19.

Gendreau, P. & Ross, R.R. (1979). Effective correctional treatment: Bibliotherapy for cynics. *Crime and Delinquency, 25,* 463–489.

George, R. (1991). *A field and experimental evaluation of three methods of interviewing witnesses and victims of crime.* Master's thesis, Polytechnic of East London.

Gerbner, G. & Gross, L. (1976). The scary world of TV's heavy viewer. *Psychology Today, 89*(4), 41–45.

Gerbner, G. & Signorelli, N. (1979). *Women and minorities in television drama 1969–1978.* Philadelphia, PA: Annenberg School of Communication.

Gerbner, G., Gross, L., Morgan, M., & Signorelli, N. (1986). Living with television: The dynamics of the cultivation process. In J. Bryant & D. Zillmann (Eds), *Perspectives on media effects* (pp. 17–40). Hillsdale, NJ: Lawrence Erlbaum.

Gerbner, G., Gross, L., Signorelli, N., & Morgan, M. (1980). The 'mainstreaming' of America: Violence profile no. 11. *Journal of Communication, 30,* 10–29.

Gerrard, M., Gibbons, F.X., Warner, T.D., & Smith, G.E. (1993). Perceived vulnerability to HIV-infection and AIDS preventive behavior: A critical review of the evidence. In J. Pryor & G. Reeder (Eds), *The social psychology of HIV infection* (pp. 59–84). Hillsdale, NJ: Lawrence Erlbaum.

Gigerenzer, G. (1991a). From tools to theories: A heuristic of discovery in cognitive psychology. *Psychological Review, 98,* 254–267.

Gigerenzer, G. (1991b). How to make cognitive illusions disappear: Beyond 'heuristics and biases'. In W. Stroebe & M. Hewstone (Eds), *European Review of Social Psychology,* Vol. 2 (pp. 83–115). Chichester: Wiley.

Gigerenzer, G. & Hoffrage, U. (1995). How to improve Bayesian reasoning without instruction: Frequency formats. *Psychological Review, 102,* 684–704.

Giles, H. (1973). Accent mobility: A model and some data. *Anthropological Linguistics, 15,* 87–105.

Giles, H., Mulac, A., Bradac, J.J., & Johnson, P. (1987). Speech accommodation theory: The first decade and beyond. In M.L. McLaughlin (Ed.), *Communication yearbook,* No. 10 (pp. 13–48). Beverly Hills, CA: Sage.

Gleicher, F. & Petty, R.E. (1992). Expectations of reassurance influence the nature of fear-stimulated attitude change. *Journal of Experimental Social Psychology, 28,* 86–100.

Global Programme on AIDS (1994). *The HIV/AIDS pandemic: 1994 overview.* Geneva: World Health Organization.

Godin, G. & Kok, G. (in press). The theory of planned behavior: A review of its applications to health-related behaviors. *American Journal of Health Promotion.*

Goffman, E. (1968). The inmate world. In C. Gordon & K.J. Gergen (Eds), *The Self in Social Interaction*, Vol. 1 (pp. 267–274). New York: Wiley.

Goffman, E. (1979). *Gender advertisements*. New York: Harper & Row.

Goldberg, H. & Lewis, R. (1978). *Money madness: The psychology of saving, spending, loving and hating money*. London: Springwood.

Goldberg, H.D. (1951). The role of 'cutting' in the perception of motion picture. *Journal of Applied Psychology*, *35*, 70–71.

Golde, P. & Kogan, N. (1959). A sentence completion procedure for assessing attitudes toward old people. *Journal of Gerontology*, *14*, 355–363.

Goldhaber, M.K., Houts, P.S., & Disabella, R. (1983). Moving after the crisis: A prospective study of Three Mile Island area population mobility. *Environment and Behavior*, *15*, 93–120.

Goldstein, A.P. (1994a). *The ecology of aggression*. New York: Plenum Press.

Goldstein, A.P. (1994b). Delinquent gangs. In L.R. Huesman (Ed.), *Aggressive behavior: Current perspectives* (pp. 255–273). New York: Plenum Press.

Goodenough, F.L. & Tinker, M.A. (1931). The relative potency of facial expression and verbal description of stimulus in the judgment of emotion. *Comparative Psychology*, *12*, 365–370.

Goodman, G.S. & Reed, D.S. (1986). Age differences in eyewitness testimony. *Law and Human Behavior*, *10*, 317–332.

Goodman, P.S., Ravlin, E., & Schminke, M. (1987). Understanding groups in organizations. In L.L. Cummings & B.M. Staw (Eds), *Research in organizational behavior*, Vol. 9 (pp. 121–173). Greenwich, CT: JAI Press.

Gorenstein, G.W. & Ellsworth, P. (1980). Effects of choosing an incorrect photograph on a later identification by an eyewitness. *Journal of Applied Psychology*, *65*, 616–622.

Gorn, G.J. & Goldberg, M.E. (1982). Behavioral evidence of the effects of televised food messages on children. *Journal of Consumer Research*, *9*, 200–205.

Gottfredson, M. & Hirschi, T. (1988). Science, public policy and the career paradigm. *Criminology*, *26*, 37–56.

Gottschalk, R., Davidson II, W.S., Gensheimer, L.K., & Mayer, J.P. (1987). Community-based interventions. In H.C. Quay (Ed.), *Handbook of juvenile delinquency*. New York: Wiley.

Gouldner, A.W. (1960). The norm of reciprocity: A preliminary statement. *American Sociological Review*, *25*(2), 161–178.

Grayson, G.B. (1991). Driver behaviour. In *Proceedings of Safety '91 Conference*. Crowthorne, UK: TRRL.

Grayson, G.B. & Maycock, G. (1988). From proneness to liability. In J.A. Rothengatter and R. de Bruin (Eds), *Road user behaviour: Theory and research* (pp. 234–242). Assen: Van Gorcum.

Green, S.K. (1981). Attitudes and perceptions about the elderly: Current and future perspectives. *International Journal of Aging and Human Development*, *13*, 99–119.

Green, S.K. (1984). Senility versus wisdom: The meaning of old age as a cause for behavior. *Basic and Applied Social Psychology*, *5*, 105–110.

Green, S.G. & Mitchell, T.R. (1979). Attributional processes of leaders in leader–member interactions. *Organizational Behavior and Human Performance*, *23*, 429–458.

Greenberg, D.F. (1977). The correctional effects of corrections: A survey of evaluations. In D.A. Greenberg (Ed.), *Corrections and punishment*. Newbury Park, CA: Sage.

Greenberg, J. (1990). Organizational justice: Yesterday, today, and tomorrow. *Journal of Management*, *16*, 399–432.

Greenwald, A.G. (1968). Cognitive learning, cognitive response to persuasion, and attitude change. In A.G. Greenwald, T.C. Brock, & T.M. Ostrom (Eds), *Psychological foundations of attitudes* (pp. 147–170). San Diego, CA: Academic Press.

Gresswell, D.M. & Hollin, C.R. (1994). Multiple murder. A review. *British Journal of Criminology*, *34*, 1–14.

Grice, H.P. (1975). Logic and conversation. In P. Cole & J.L. Morgan (Eds), *Syntax and semantics, Vol. 3: Speech acts* (pp. 41–58). New York: Academic Press.

Griffin, R.W. (1987). Toward an integrated theory of task design. In L.L. Cummings & B.M. Staw (Eds), *Research in organizational behavior*, Vol. 9 (pp. 79–120). Greenwich, CT: JAI Press.

Griffitt, W. & Jackson, T. (1973). Simulated jury decisions: The influence of jury defendant attitude similarity–dissimilarity. *Social Behavior and Personality*, *1*, 73–93.

Groeger, J.A. (1989). Conceptual bases of drivers' errors. *Irish Journal of Psychology*, *10*, 276–290.

Groeger, J.A. (1991). Acquiring and retaining driving skills. In M.J. Kuiken & J.A. Groeger (Eds), *Report on feedback requirements and performance differences of drivers*. (APU Report 2666). Cambridge, UK: MRC Applied Psychology Unit.

Grossbart, S., Carlson, L., & Walsh, A. (1991). Consumer socialization and frequency of shopping with children. *Journal of the Academy of Marketing Science, 19,* 155–163.

Groves, R.M. & Kahn, R.L. (1979). *Surveys by telephone: A national comparison with personal interviews.* New York: Academic Press.

Groves, R.M., Cialdini, R.B., & Couper, M.P. (1992). Understanding the decision to participate in a survey. *Public Opinion Quarterly, 56,* 475–495.

Gudjonsson, G. (1992). *The psychology of interrogations, confessions and testimony.* Chichester: Wiley.

Gudykunst, W.B. (1983). Toward a typology of stranger–host relationships. *International Journal of Intercultural Relations, 7,* 401–413.

Gulerce, A. (1991). Transitional objects: A reconsideration of the phenomenon. In F.W. Rudmin (Ed.), *To have possessions: A handbook of property and ownership* (pp. 187–208). Special issue of the *Journal of Social Behavior and Personality, 6.*

Gulian, E., Matthews, G., Glendon, A.I., Davies, D.R., & Debney, L.M. (1989). Dimensions of driver stress. *Ergonomics, 32,* 585–602.

Gunter, B. (1983). Do aggressive people prefer violent television? *Bulletin of the British Psychological Society, 36,* 166–168.

Gunter, B. & Furnham, A. (1992). *Consumer profiles: An introduction to psychographics.* London: Routledge.

Guzzo, R.A. (1988). Productivity research: Reviewing psychological and economic perspectives. In J.P. Campbell, R.J. Campbell & Associates (Eds), *Productivity in organizations: New perspectives from industrial and organizational psychology* (pp. 63–81). San Francisco: Jossey-Bass.

Haaland, G.A. & Vankatesan, M. (1968). Resistance to persuasive communications: An examination of the distraction hypotheses. *Journal of Personality and Social Psychology, 9,* 167–170.

Hacket, P.M.W. (1992). The understanding of environmental concern. *Journal of Social Behavior and Personality, 20,* 143–148.

Hackman, J.R. & Oldham, G.R. (1980). *Work redesign.* Reading, MA: Addison-Wesley.

Hall, E.T. (1976). *Beyond culture.* New York: Doubleday.

Hall, G.C.N. & Hirschman, R. (1991). Toward a theory of sexual aggression: A quadripartite model. *Journal of Consulting and Clinical Psychology, 59,* 662–669.

Hamill, R., Lodge, M., & Blake, F. (1985). The breadth, depth, and utility of class, partisan and ideological schemata. *American Journal of Political Science, 29,* 850–870.

Hamilton, D.L. & Gifford, R.K. (1976). Illusory correlation in interpersonal perception: A cognitive basis of stereotypic judgments. *Journal of Experimental Social Psychology, 12,* 392–407.

Hammer, M. (1983). 'Core' and 'extended' social networks in relation to health and illness. *Social Science and Medicine, 17,* 405–411.

Hammond, K.R., Stewart, T.R., Brehmer, B., & Steinmann, D.O. (1975). Social Judgment theory. In M. Kaplan & S. Schwartz (Eds), *Human judgments and decision processes.* New York: Academic Press.

Hans, V.P. & Vidmar, N. (1982). Jury selection. In N.L. Kerr & R.M. Bray (Eds), *The psychology of the courtroom.* London: Academic Press.

Hans, V.P. & Vidmar, N. (1986). *Judging the jury.* New York: Plenum Press.

Hanson, R.K. (1990). The psychological impact of sexual assault on women and children: A review. *Annals of Sex Research, 3,* 187–232.

Harkness, R.C. (1973). *Telecommunications substitutes for travel: a preliminary assessment of their potential for reducing urban transportation costs by altering office location patterns.* Unpublished PhD dissertation, University of Washington, Seattle.

Harper, R.G., Wiens, A.N., & Matarazzo, J.D. (1978). *Nonverbal communication: The state of the art.* New York: Plenum Press.

Harrel-Bond, B.E. & Wilson, K.B. (1990). Dealing with dying: Some anthropological reflections on the need for assistance by refugee relief programmes for bereavement and burial. *Journal of Refugee Studies, 3,* 228–243.

Harrington, D.M. & McBride, R.S. (1970). Traffic violations by type, age and sex and marital status. *Accident Analysis and Prevention, 2,* 67–79.

Harris, J.E. (1982). Self-directed weight control through eating and exercise. *Behavior Research and Therapy, 11,* 523–529.

Harris, L. & Associates (1975). *The myth and reality of aging in America.* Washington, DC: National Council on the Aging.

Harris, L. & Associates (1981). *Aging in the eighties: America in transition.* Washington, DC: National Council on the Aging.

Harris, P. & Middleton, W. (1994). The illusion of control and optimism about health: On being less at risk but no more in control than others. *British Journal of Social Psychology, 33,* 369–386.

Harris, R.J. (1989). *A cognitive psychology of mass communication.* Hillsdale, NJ: Lawrence Erlbaum.

Harrison, J.A., Mullen, P.D., & Green, L.W. (1992). A meta-analysis of studies of the Health Belief Model with adults. *Health Education Research, 7,* 107–116.

Hastie, R. (1986). Experimental evidence on group accuracy. In B. Grofman & G. Owen (Eds), *Information pooling and group decision-making: Proceedings of the second University of California, Irvine, Conference on Political Economy.* Greenwich, CT: JAI Press.

Haugtvedt, C.P. & Petty, R.E. (1992). Personality and persuasion: Need for cognition moderates the persistence and resistance of attitude changes. *Journal of Personality and Social Psychology, 63,* 308–319.

Havighurst, R. (1972). *Developmental tasks and education.* New York: David McKay.

Havighurst, R., Munnichs, J.M.A., Neugarten, B., & Thomae, H. (Eds) (1970). *Adjustment to retirement.* Assen: Van Gorcum.

Havighurst, R., Neugarten, B., & Tobin, S. (1968). Disengagement and patterns of aging. In B. Neugarten (Ed.), *Middle age and aging* (pp. 161–172). Chicago: University of Chicago Press.

Haward, L.R.C. (1988). Hypnosis in forensic practice. In M. Heap (Ed.), *Hypnosis: Current clinical, experimental and forensic practices* (pp. 357–368). London: Croom Helm.

Haward, L.R.C. (1990). *A dictionary of forensic psychology.* Chichester: Barry Rose.

Hearold, S. (1986). A synthesis of 1043 effects of television on social behavior. In G. Comstock (Ed.), *Public communication and behavior,* Vol. 1 (pp. 65–134). New York: Academic Press.

Heath, A.F., Jowell, R., & Curtice, J. (1985). *How Britain votes.* Oxford: Pergamon Press.

Heath, L., Bresolin, L.B., & Rinaldi, R.C. (1989). Effects of media violence on children: A review of the literature. *Archives of General Psychiatry, 46,* 376–379.

Heath, L., Scott Tindale, R., Edwards, J., Posavac, E.J., Bryant, F.B., Henderson-King, E., Suarez-Balcazar, Y., & Myers, J. (Eds) (1994). *Applications of heuristics and biases to social issues.* New York: Plenum Press.

Heaven, P.C.L. (1994). The perceived causal structure of poverty: A network analysis approach. *British Journal of Social Psychology, 33,* 259–271.

Heckhausen, J. (1989). Normatives Entwicklungswissen als Bezugsrahmen zur (Re)Konstruktion der eigenen Biographie [Normative conceptions about development as a frame of reference for (re)constructing one's own biography]. In P. Alheit & E. Hoerning (Eds), *Biographisches Wissen: Beiträge zu einer Theorie lebensgeschichtlicher Erfahrung* (pp. 202–282). Frankfurt: Campus.

Heckhausen, J. (1990). Erwerb und Funktion normativer Vorstellungen über den Lebenslauf: Ein entwicklungspsychologischer Beitrag zur sozio-psychischen Konstruktion von Biographien [Acquisition and function of normative conceptions about the life course: A developmental psychology approach to the socio-psychological construction of biographies]. *Kölner Zeitschrift für Soziologie und Sozialpsychologie, 31,* 351–373.

Heckhausen, J. (in press). *Developmental regulation in adulthood: Age-normative and socio-structural constraints as adaptive challenges.* New York: Cambridge University Press.

Heckhausen, J. & Baltes, P.B. (1991). Perceived controllability of expected psychological change across adulthood and old age. *Journal of Gerontology: Psychological Sciences, 46,* 165–173.

Heckhausen, J. & Hosenfeld, B. (1988). Lebensspannenentwicklung von normativen Vorstellungen über Lebensspannenentwicklung [Life-span development of normative conceptions about life-span development]. Paper presented at the 36th Kongress, Deutsche Gesellschaft fur Psychologie, Berlin, Germany.

Heckhausen, J. & Krueger, J. (1993). Developmental expectations for the self and most other people: Age grading in three functions of social comparison. *Developmental Psychology, 29,* 539–548.

Heckhausen, J. & Schulz, R. (1993). Optimisation by selection and compensation: Balancing primary and secondary control in life-span development. *International Journal of Behavioral Development, 16,* 287–303.

Heckhausen, J. & Schulz, R. (1995). A life-span theory of control. *Psychological Review, 102,* 284–304.

Heckhausen, J. & Wrosch, C. (1995). Social comparison as a strategy of developmental regulation in adulthood. Manuscript in preparation, Max Planck Institute for Human Development and Education, Berlin, Germany.

Heckhausen, J., Dixon, R.A., & Baltes, P.B. (1989). Gains and losses in development throughout adulthood as perceived by different adult age groups. *Developmental Psychology, 25,* 109–121.

Heckmann, F. (1995). Is there a migration policy in Germany? In F. Heckmann & W. Bosswick (Eds), *Migration policies: A comparative perspective* (pp. 157–179). Stuttgart: Enke.

Heider, F. (1958). *The psychology of interpersonal relations*. New York: Wiley.

Heilman, M.E. & Guzzo, R.A. (1978). The perceived cause of work success as a mediator of sex discrimination in organizations. *Organizational Behavior and Human Performance, 21*, 346–357.

Heilman, M.E., Simon, M.C., & Repper, D.P. (1987). Intentionally favoured, unintentionally harmed? Impact of sex-based preferential selection on self-perceptions and self-evaluations. *Journal of Applied Psychology, 72*, 62–68.

Held, T. (1986). Institutionalization and deinstitutionalization of the life course. *Human Development, 29*, 157–162.

Heller, R.F., Saltzstein, H.D., & Caspe, W.B. (1992). Heuristics in medical and non-medical decision-making. *Quarterly Journal of Environmental Psychology, 44a*, 211–235.

Heneman, R.L., Greenberger, D.B., & Anonyuo, C. (1989). Attributions and exchanges: The effects of interpersonal factors on the diagnosis of employee performance. *Academy of Management Journal, 32*, 466–476.

Herdan, G. (1964). *Quantitative linguistics*. London: Butterworths.

Herren, R. (1976). Das Vernehmungsprotokoll (the interview protocol). *Kriminalistik, 7*, 313–317.

Hershey, J.C. & Schoemaker, P.J.H. (1980). Prospect theory's reflection hypothesis: A critical examination. *Organizational Behavior and Human Performance, 25*, 395–418.

Herzog, R.A. & Rodgers, W.L. (1981). Age and satisfaction: Data from several large surveys. *Research on Aging, 3*, 142–165.

Hewstone, M. (1989). *Causal attribution: From cognitive processes to collective beliefs*. Oxford: Blackwell.

Higgins, E.T. (1989). Knowledge accessibility and activation: Subjectivity and suffering from unconscious sources. In J.S. Uleman & J.A. Bargh (Eds), *Unintended thought* (pp. 75–123). New York: Guilford Press.

High, G.B. (1995). Major issues of contemporary American immigration policy. In F. Heckmann & W. Bosswick (Eds), *Migration policies: A comparative perspective* (pp. 45–57). Stuttgart: Enke.

Hilton, D.J. (1990). Conversational processes and causal explanation. *Psychological Bulletin, 107*, 65–81.

Himmelweit, H.T., Humpreys, M., Jaeger, M., & Katz, M. (1985). *How voters decide*. New York: Academic Press.

Hinckley, J.J., Craig, H.K., & Anderson, L.A. (1990). Communication characteristic of provider–patient information exchanges. In H. Giles & P. Robinson (Eds), *Handbook of language and social psychology* (pp. 519–536). New York: Wiley.

Hinkle, S.W. & Brown, R.J. (1990). Intergroup comparisons and social identity: Some links and lacunae. In D. Abrams & M.A. Hogg (Eds), *Social identity theory: Constructive and critical advances*. Hemel Hempstead, UK: Harvester Wheatsheaf.

Hippler, H.J., Schwarz, N., & Sudman, S. (Eds) (1987). *Social information processing and survey methodology*. New York: Springer.

Hirsch, P.M. (1980). The 'scary world' of the non-viewer and other anomalies: A reanalysis of Gerbner *et al.*'s findings on the cultivation hypotheses. *Communication Research, 7*, 403–456.

Hirsch, P.M. (1981). On not learning from one's own mistakes. A reanalysis of Gerbner *et al.*'s findings on the cultivation hypotheses. *Communication Research, 8*, 3–37.

Höfer, E., Köhnken, G., Hanewinkel, R., & Bruhn, C. (1993). *Diagnostik und Attribution von Glaubwürdigkeit* [Assessment and attribution of credibility]. Final report for research grant Ko 882/4–1 of the Deutsche Forschungsgemeinschaft. Kiel, Germany: University of Kiel.

Hofstede, G. (1980). *Culture's consequences: International differences in work-related values*. Beverly Hills, CA: Sage.

Hogan, D. (1981). *Transitions and the life course*. New York: Academic Press.

Hogarth, R.M. (Ed.) (1990). *Insights in decision making: A tribute to Hillel J. Einhorn*. Chicago: Chicago University Press.

Hohenhemser, C. & Renn, O. (1988). Shifting public perceptions of nuclear risk: Chernobyl's other legacy. *Environment, 30*(3), 4–11, 40–45.

Hollin, C.R. (1989). *Psychology and crime*. London: Routledge.

Holmes, R.M. (1989). *Profiling violent crimes: An investigative tool*. Newbury Park, CA: Sage.

Homans, G.C. (1961). *Social behavior. Its elementary forms*. New York: Harcourt, Brace & World.

Hornick, J.P., McDonald, L., & Robertson, G.B. (1992). Elder abuse in Canada and the United States: Prevalence, legal, and service issues. In R.D. Peters, R.J. McMahon, & V.L. Quinsey (Eds), *Aggression and violence through the life-span* (pp. 301–335). Newbury Park, CA: Sage.

Horowitz, D.L. (1985). *Ethnic groups in conflict.* Berkeley: University of California Press.

Horowitz, S.W. (1991). Empirical support for statement validity analysis. *Behavioral Assessment,* *13,* 293–313.

Hospers, H.J. & Kok, G.J. (1995). Determinants of safe and risk-taking sexual behavior among gay men: A review. *AIDS Education and Prevention, 7,* 74–96.

Howells, K. (1989). Anger management methods in relation to the prevention of violent behaviour. In J. Archer & K. Browne (Eds), *Human aggression: Naturalistic approaches* (pp. 153–181). London: Routledge.

Hox, J.J., de Leeuw, E.D., & Kreft, I.G.G. (1991). The effect of interviewer and respondent characteristics on the quality of survey data: A multilevel model. In P. Biemer, R. Groves, N. Mathiowetz, & S. Sudman (Eds), *Measurement error in surveys* (pp. 393–418). Chichester: Wiley.

Hsieh, C.-C. & Pugh, M.D. (1993). Poverty, income inequality, and violent crime: A meta-analysis of recent aggregate data studies. *Criminal Justice Review, 18,* 182–202.

Huber, G.P. (1980). *Managerial decision making.* Glenview, IL: Scott, Foresman.

Huber, V.L., Neale, M.A., & Northcraft, G.B. (1987). Decision bias and personnel selection strategies. *Organizational Behavior and Human Decision Processes, 40,* 136–147.

Huesmann, L.R. (1986). Psychological processes promoting the relation between exposure to media violence and aggressive behavior by the viewer. *Journal of Social Issues, 42,* 125–139.

Huesmann, L.R. (Ed.) (1994). *Aggressive behavior: Current perspectives.* New York: Plenum Press.

Huesmann, L.R. & Eron, L.D. (1984). Cognitive processes and the persistence of aggressive behaviour. *Aggressive Behavior, 10,* 243–251.

Huesmann, L.R. & Eron, L.D. (Eds) (1986). *Television and the aggressive child: A cross-national comparison.* Hillsdale, NJ: Lawrence Erlbaum.

Huesmann, L.R. & Malamuth, N.M. (1986). Media violence and antisocial behavior. *Journal of Social Issues, 42,* 1–6.

Huesmann, L.R. & Miller, L.S. (1994). Long-term effects of the repeated exposure to media violence in childhood. In L.R. Huesmann (Ed.), *Aggressive behavior: Current perspectives* (pp. 153–186). New York: Plenum Press.

Hulley, S.B. & Hearst, N. (1989). The worldwide epidemiology and prevention of AIDS. In V.M. Mays, G.W. Albee, & S.F. Schneider (Eds), *Primary prevention of AIDS* (pp. 44–71). Newbury Park, CA: Sage.

Hummert, M.L. (1990). Multiple stereotypes of elderly and young adults: A comparison of structure and evaluation. *Psychology and Aging, 5,* 182–193.

Hummert, M.L. (1993). Age and typicality judgments of stereotypes of the elderly: Perceptions of elderly vs. young adults. *International Journal of Aging and Human Development, 37,* 217–226.

Hundertmark, J. & Heckhausen, J. (1994). Entwicklungsziele junger, mittelalter und alter Erwachsener. *Zeitschrift für Entwicklungspsychologie und Pädagogische Psychologie, 26,* 197–217.

Hyde, J.S. (1984). How large are gender differences in aggression? A developmental meta-analysis. *Developmental Psychology, 20,* 722–736.

Ilaria, G., Jacobs, J.L., Polsky, B., Koll, B., Baron, P., MacLow, C., Armstrong, D., & Schlegerl, P.N. (1992). Detection of HIV-1 DNA sequences in pre-ejaculatory fluid. *Lancet, 340,* 1469.

Ingham, R. (1991). *The young driver.* Paper presented at the meeting of Parliamentary Advisory Council for Transport Safety, London, October.

Isen, I.M. & Means, L. (1983). The influence of positive affect on decision making strategy. *Social Cognition, 2,* 18–31.

Isenhour, J.P. (1975). The effects of context and order in film editing. *AV Communication Review, 23,* 69–79.

Ishii-Kuntz, M. (1990). Social interaction and psychological well-being: Comparison across stages of adulthood. *International Journal of Aging and Human Development, 30*(1), 15–36.

Iyengar, S. & Ottati, V. (1994). Cognitive perspective in political psychology. In R.S. Wyer, Jr. & T.K. Srull (Eds), *Handbook of social cognition, vol. II, Applications.* Hillsdale, NJ: Lawrence Erlbaum.

Jabine, T.B., Straf, M.L., Tanur, J.M., & Tourangeau, R. (Eds) (1984). *Cognitive aspects of survey methodology: Building a bridge between disciplines.* Washington, DC: National Academy Press.

Jaccard, J. & Turrisi, R. (1987). Cognitive processes and individual differences in judgments relevant to drunk driving. *Journal of Personality and Social Psychology, 53,* 135–145.

Jaffé-Pearce, M. (1989). No mod cons. *Sunday Times Magazine,* 6 August, 8–10.

Janis, I.L. (1972). *Victims of groupthink.* Boston: Houghton-Mifflin.

Janis, I.L. (1982). *Groupthink: Psychological studies of policy decisions and fiascoes.* Boston: Houghton-Mifflin.

Janis, I.L. & Mann, L. (1977). *Decision making*. New York: Free Press.

Janz, N.K. & Becker, M.H. (1984). The health belief model: A decade later. *Health Education Quarterly, 11*, 1–47.

Jenkins, C.R. & Dillman, D.A. (in press). Towards a theory of self-administered questionnaire design. In L. Lyberg, P. Biemer, M. Collins, E. DeLeeuw, C. Dippo, & N. Schwarz (Eds), *Survey measurement and process quality*. Chichester: Wiley.

Jenkins, F. & Davies, G. (1985). Contamination of facial memory through exposure to misleading composite pictures. *Journal of Applied Psychology, 70*, 164–176.

Jepson, C. & Chaiken, S. (1990). Chronic issue-specific fear inhibits systematic processing of persuasive communications. *Journal of Social Behavior and Personality, 5*, 61–84.

Jessor, R. (1987). Risky driving and adolescent problem behaviour: An extension of problem-behavior theory. *Alcohol, Drugs and Driving, 3*, 1–11.

Jessor, R. & Jessor, S.L. (1977). *Problem behavior and psycho-social development: A longitudinal study of youth*. New York: Academic Press.

Jobe, J. & Loftus, E. (Eds) (1991). Cognitive aspects of survey methodology. Special issue of *Applied Cognitive Psychology, 5*.

Joffe, R. & Yuille, J. (1992). *Criteria-based content analysis: An experimental investigation*. Paper presented at the Meeting of the American Psychology-Law Society, San Diego.

Johnson, B.B. (1987). Public concerns and the public role in siting nuclear and chemical waste facilities. *Environmental Management, 11*, 571–586.

Johnson, C.L. (1983). Fairweather friends and rainy day kin: An anthropological analysis of old age friendship in the United States. *Urban Anthropology, 12*, 103–123.

Johnson, E.J. & Tversky, A. (1983). Affect, generalization, and the perception of risk. *Journal of Personality and Social Psychology, 45*, 20–31.

Johnson, M.D. (1984). Consumer choice strategies for comparing noncomparable alternatives. *Journal of Consumer Research, 11*, 741–753.

Johnson, M.K. & Foley, M.A. (1984). Differentiating fact from fantasy: The reliability of children's memory. *Journal of Social Issues, 40*, 33–50.

Johnson, M.K. & Raye, C.L. (1981). Reality monitoring. *Psychological Reviews, 88*, 67–85.

Johnson, R.D. & Downing, L.L. (1979). Deindividuation and valence of cues: Effects on prosocial and antisocial behavior. *Journal of Personality and Social Psychology, 37*, 1532–1538.

Jonah, B.A. (1986). Accident risk and risk-taking behavior among young drivers. *Accident Analysis and Prevention, 18*, 255–271.

Jonas, K. (1992). Modelling and suicide: A test of the Werther effect. *British Journal of Social Psychology, 31*, 295–306.

Jonas, K. (1993). Expectancy-value models of health behaviour: An analysis by conjoint measurement. *European Journal of Social Psychology, 23*, 167–183.

Jones, D.C. & Vaughan, K. (1990). Close friendships among senior adults. *Psychology and Aging, 5*, 451–457.

Jones, E.E. & Davis, K.E. (1965). From acts to dispositions: The attribution process in person perception. In I. Berkowitz (Ed.), *Advances in experimental social psychology*, Vol. 2 (pp. 219–266). San Diego, CA: Academic Press.

Jones, E.E. & Nisbett, R.E. (1972). The actor and the observer: Divergent perceptions of the causes of behavior. In E.E. Jones, D.E. Kanöuse, H.H. Kelley, R.E. Nisbett, S. Valius, & B. Weiner (Eds), *Attribution: Perceiving the causes of behavior* (pp. 79–94). Morristown, NJ: General Learning Press.

Joseph, J.G., Montgomery, S.B., Emmons, C.A., Kessler, R.C., Ostrow, D.G., Wortman, C.B., O'Brien, K., Eller, M. & Eshleman, S. (1987). Magnitude and determinants of behavioral risk reduction: Longitudinal analysis of a cohort at risk for AIDS. *Psychology and Health, 1*, 73–96.

Judd, C.M. & Krosnick, J.A. (1989). The structural bases of consistency among political attitudes: Effects of political expertise and attitude importance. In A.R. Pratkanis, S.J. Breckler, & A.G. Greenwald (Eds), *Attitude structure and function*. Hillsdale, NJ: Lawrence Erlbaum.

Junger. M. (1994). Accidents. In T. Hirschi and M.R. Gottfredson (Eds), *The generality of deviance* (pp. 81–113). New Brunswick, NJ: Transaction Publishers.

Kahn, R.L. (1979). Aging and social support. In M.W. Riley (Ed.), *Aging from birth to death* (pp. 77–91). Boulder, CO: American Association for the Advancement of Science.

Kahn, R.L. & Antonucci, T.C. (1980). Convoys over the life course. Attachment, roles and social support. In P.B. Baltes & O.G. Brim (Eds), *Life-span development and behavior* (pp. 254–283). New York: Academic Press.

Kahneman, D. & Tversky, A. (1973). On the psychology of prediction. *Psychological Review, 80*, 237–251.

Kahneman, D. & Tversky, A. (1979). Prospect theory: Analysis of decision under risk. *Econometrica, 47*, 263–291.

Kahneman, D. & Tversky, A. (1982). The simulation heuristic. In D. Kahneman, P. Slovic, & A. Tversky (Eds), *Judgment under uncertainty: Heuristics and biases* (pp. 201–210). New York: Cambridge University Press.

Kahneman, D. & Tversky, A. (1984). Choices, values, and frames. *American Psychologist, 39*, 341–350.

Kairys, D., Schulman, J., & Harring, S. (Eds) (1975). *The jury system: New methods for reducing prejudice.* Philadelphia: Philadelphia Resistance Book Shop.

Kalton, G. (1983). *Introduction to survey sampling.* Beverly Hills, CA: Sage.

Kalven, H., Jr., & Zeisel, H. (1966). *The American jury.* Boston: Little, Brown.

Kamptner, N.L. (1991). Personal possessions and their meanings: A life-span perspective. In F. Rudmin (Ed.), *To have possessions: A handbook of property and ownership* (pp. 209–228). Special issue of the *Journal of Social Behavior and Personality, 6*.

Kanfer, R. (1992). Motivation theory and industrial and organizational psychology. In M.D. Dunnette & L.M. Hough (Eds), *Handbook of Industrial and Organizational Psychology*, Vol. 2 (pp. 77–170). Chicago: Rand-McNally.

Kanter, R.M. (1988). When a thousand flowers bloom: Structural, collective, and social conditions for innovation in organizations. In B.M. Staw & L.L. Cummings (Eds), *Research in organizational behavior*, Vol. 10 (pp. 169–211). Greenwich, CT: JAI Press.

Kaplan, M.F. (Ed.) (1986). *The impact of social psychology on procedural justice.* Springfield, IL: Charles C. Thomas.

Kaplan, R.M. (1988). The value dimension in studies of health promotion. In S. Spacapan & S. Oskamp (Eds), *The social psychology of health.* Beverly Hills, CA: Sage.

Kasperson, R.E. (1985). *Rethinking the siting of hazardous waste facilities.* Paper presented at the conference on Transport, Storage, and Disposal of Hazardous Materials. IIASA, Vienna, Austria, July.

Kasperson, R.E., Derr, P., & Kates, R.W. (1983). Confronting equity in radioactive waste management: modest proposals for a socially just and acceptable program. In R.E. Kasperson & M. Berberian (Eds), *Equity issues in radioactive waste management* (pp. 331–368). Cambridge, MA: Oelgeschlager, Gunn & Hain.

Kasser, T. & Ryan, R.M. (1993). A dark side of the American dream: Correlates of financial success as a central life aspiration. *Journal of Personality and Social Psychology, 65*, 410–422.

Kates, R.W. & Braine, B. (1983). Locus, equity, and the West Valley nuclear wastes. In R.E. Kasperson & M. Berberian (Eds), *Equity issues in radioactive waste management* (pp. 301–331). Cambridge, MA: Oelgeschlager, Gunn & Hain.

Katz, D. & Kahn, R.L. (1978). *The social psychology of organizations* (2nd ed.). New York: Wiley.

Katzev, R., Blake, G., & Messer, B. (1993). Determinants of participation in multi-family recycling programs. *Journal of Applied Social Psychology, 23*, 374–385.

Kealey, D.J. (1988). *Explaining and predicting cross-cultural adjustment and effectiveness: A study of Canadian technical advisors overseas.* PhD thesis, Queens University, Kingston, Ontario, September.

Keeney, B.T. & Heide, K.M. (1994). Gender differences in serial murderers. *Journal of Interpersonal Violence, 9*, 383–398.

Keet, I.P.M., Albrecht-van Lent, N., Sandfort, T.G.M., Coutinho, R.A., & van Griensven, G.J.P. (1992). Orogenital sex and the transmission of HIV among homosexual men. *AIDS, 6*, 223–226.

Keith, J. (1985). Age in anthropological research. In R.H. Binstock & E. Shanas (Eds), *Handbook of aging and the social sciences* (pp. 231–263). New York: Van Nostrand.

Keith, P.M., Hill, K., Goudy, W.J., & Powers, E.A. (1984). Confidants and well-being: A note on male friendship in old age. *The Gerontologist, 24*, 318–320.

Kelley, H.H. (1967). Attribution theory in social psychology. In D. Levine (Ed.), *Nebraska symposium on motivation* (pp. 192–238). Lincoln: University of Nebraska Press.

Kelley, H.H. (1971). Attribution in social interaction. In E.E. Jones, D.E. Kanouse, H.H. Kelley, R.E. Nisbett, S. Valins, & B. Weiner (Eds), *Attribution: Perceiving the causes of behavior* (pp. 95–120). Morristown, NJ: General Learning Press.

Kelley, H.H. & Michela, J.L. (1980). Attribution theory and research. In M.R. Rosenzweig & L.W. Porter (Eds), *Annual review of psychology*, Vol. 31 (pp. 457–501). Palo Alto, CA: Annual Reviews, Inc.

Kelloway, E.K. & Barling, J. (1993). Members' participation in local union activities: Measurement, prediction, and replication. *Journal of Applied Psychology, 78*, 262–279.

Kelly, C. (1993). Group identification, intergroup perceptions and collective action. In W. Stroebe & M. Hewstone (Eds), *European review of social psychology*, Vol. 4. New York: Wiley.

Kelly, C. & Kelly, J. (1994). Who gets involved in collective action?: Social psychological determinants of individual participation in trade unions. *Human Relations, 47,* 63–88.

Kelly, J.A., St Lawrence, J.S., Brasfield, T.L., Lemke, A., Amidei, T., Roffman, R.E., Hood, H.V., Smith, J.E., Kilgore, H., & McNeill, C. (1990). Psychological factors that predict AIDS high-risk versus AIDS precautionary behavior. *Journal of Consulting and Clinical Psychology, 58,* 117–120.

Kelly, J.A., St Lawrence, J.S., Hood, H.V., & Brasfield, T.L. (1989). Behavioral intervention to reduce AIDS risk activities. *Journal of Consulting and Clinical Psychology, 57,* 60–67.

Kempton, W. (1990). Lay perspectives on global climate change (PU/CEES Report No. 251). Princeton University, Center for Energy and Environmental Studies.

Kempton, W., Darley, J.M., & Stern, P.C. (1992). Psychological research for the new energy problems. *American Psychologist, 47,* 1213–1223.

Kepplinger, H.M. (1987). *Darstellungseffekte: Experimentelle Untersuchungen zur Wirkung von Pressefotos und Fernsehfilmen.* Freiburg: Alber.

Kerr, N.L. & Bray, R.M. (Eds) (1982). *The psychology of the courtroom.* London: Academic Press.

Kerry Smith, V., Desvouges, W.H., & Payne, J.W. (1995). Do risk information programs promote mitigating behavior? *Journal of Risk and Uncertainty, 10,* 203–221.

Kiesler, C. (1971). *The psychology of commitment.* New York: Academic Press.

Kiesler, S. & Sproull, L. (1992). Group decision making and communication technology. *Organizational Behavior and Human Decision Processes, 52,* 96–123.

Kiesler, S., Siegel, J., & McGuire, T.W. (1984). Social psychological aspects of computer-mediated communication. *American Psychologist, 39,* 1123–1134.

Kilmann, R.H., Saxton, M.J., Serpa, R. & Associates (Eds) (1985). *Gaining control of the corporate culture.* San Francisco: Jossey-Bass.

Kim, U., Triandis, H.C., Kagitcibasi, C., Choi, S.C., & Yoon, G. (Eds) (1994). *Individualism and collectivism. Theory, method, and applications.* Thousand Oaks, CA: Sage.

Kinder, D.R. (1986). Presidential character revisited. In R.R. Lau & D.O. Sears (Eds), *Political cognition.* Hillsdale, NJ: Lawrence Erlbaum.

Kingsley, L.A., Kaslow, R., Rinaldo, C.R., Detre, K., Odaha, N., Van Raden, M., Detels, R., Polk, B.F., Chmiel, J., Kelsey, S.F., Ostrow, D., & Visscher, B. (1987). Risk factors for seroconversion to Human Immunodeficiency Virus among male homosexuals. *Lancet, 1,* 345–349.

Kintsch, W. & van Dijk, T.A. (1978). Toward a model of text comprehension and production. *Psychological Review, 85,* 363–394.

Kipnis, D., Castell, J., Gergen, M., & Mauch, D. (1976). Metamorphic effects of power. *Journal of Applied Psychology, 61,* 127–135.

Kirchler, E. (1995). *Wirtschaftspsychologie.* Goettingen: Hogrefe.

Klandermans, P.G. (1995). Principles of movement participation. Manuscript submitted for publication.

Kleck, G. & Patterson, E.B. (1993). The impact of gun control and gun ownership levels on violence rates. *Journal of Quantitative Criminology, 9,* 249–287.

Kleindorfer, P.R., Kunreuther, H.C., & Schoemaker, P.J.H. (1993). *Decision sciences: An integrative perspective.* New York: Cambridge University Press.

Kleinot, M.C. & Rogers, R.W. (1982). Identifying effective components of alcohol misuse prevention programs. *Journal of Studies on Alcohol, 43,* 802–811.

Kliegl, R., Smith, J., & Baltes, P.B. (1990). On the locus and process of magnification of age differences during mnemonic training. *Developmental Psychology, 26,* 894–904.

Kline, P. (1981). *Fact and Fantasy in Freudian Theory* (2nd ed.). London: Methuen.

Knowlton, W.A. & Mitchell, T.R. (1980). Effects of causal attributions on a supervisor's evaluation of subordinate performance. *Journal of Applied Psychology, 65,* 459–466.

Knudsen, H.R. & Mutzekari, L.H. (1983). The effects of verbal statements of context on facial expressions of emotion. *Journal of Nonverbal Behavior, 7,* 202–212.

Kogan, N. (1961). Attitudes toward old people: The development of a scale and an examination of correlates. *Journal of Abnormal Psychology, 62,* 44–54.

Kogan, N. (1975). Judgments of chronological age: Adult age and sex differences. *Developmental Psychology, 11,* 107.

Kogan, N. (1979). A study of age categorization. *Journal of Gerontology, 34,* 358–367.

Kogan, N. & Shelton, F.C. (1962). Images of 'old people' and 'people in general' in an older sample. *Journal of Genetic Psychology, 100,* 3–21.

Kohlberg, L. (1976). Moral stages and moralization: The cognitive developmental approach. In T. Lickona (Ed.), *Cognitive development and epistemology*. New York: Holt, Rinehart & Winston.

Köhnken, G. (1985). Speech and deception of eyewitnesses: An information processing approach. In F.L. Denmark (Ed.), *Sociallecological psychology and the psychology of women*. Amsterdam: North-Holland.

Köhnken, G. (1987). Training police officers to detect deception: Does it work? *Social Behaviour*, 2, 1–17.

Köhnken, G. (1990). *Glaubwürdigkeit*. Munich: Psychologie Verlags Union.

Köhnken, G. & Steller, M. (1988). Assessment of the credibility of child witness statements. In G.M. Davies & J. Drinkwater (Eds), *The child witness: Do the courts abuse children?* Division of Legal Criminological Psychology, Occ. Paper No. 13.

Köhnken, G. & Wegener, H. (1982). Zur Glaubwürdigkeit von Zeugenaussagen. Experimentelle Überprüfung ausgewählter Glaubwürdigkeitskriterien [Credibility of witness statements: experimental examination of selected reality criteria]. *Zeitschrift für experimentelle und angewandte Psychologie*, 29, 92–111.

Köhnken, G. & Wegener, H. (1985). Zum Stellenwert des Experiments in der Forensischen Aussagepsychologie [The role of experiments in eyewitness psychology]. *Zeitschrift für experimentelle und angewandte Psychologie*, 32, 104–119.

Köhnken, G., Malpass, R.S., & Wogalter, M.S. (1996). Forensic applications of lineup research. In S.L. Sporer, R.M. Malpass, & G. Köhnken (Eds), *Psychological issues in eyewitness identification*. Hillsdale, NJ: Lawrence Erlbaum.

Köhnken, G., Milne, R., Memon, A., & Bull, R. (1994). *Recall in cognitive interviews and standard interviews: A meta-analysis*. Paper presented at the conference of the American Psychology and Law Society, Santa Fe.

Köhnken, G., Schimossek, E., Aschermann, E., & Höfer, E. (1995). The cognitive interview and the assessment of the credibility of adults' statements. *Journal of Applied Psychology*, 80, 671–684.

Köhnken, G., Thürer, C., & Zoberbier, D. (1994). The cognitive interview: Are the interviewers' memories enhanced, too? *Applied Cognitive Psychology*, 8, 13–24.

Konecni, V.J. & Ebbesen, E.B. (Eds) (1982). *The criminal justice system: A social psychological analysis*. San Francisco: Freeman.

Koss, M.P. & Harvey, M.R. (1991). *The rape victim: Clinical and community interventions*. Newbury Park, CA: Sage.

Koss, M.P., Goodman, L.A., Browne, A., Fitzgerald, L.F., Keita, G.P., & Russo, N.F. (1994). *No safe haven: Male violence against women at home, at work, and in the community*. Washington, DC: American Psychological Association.

Krahé, B. (1988). Victim and observer characteristics as determinants of responsibility attributions to victims of rape. *Journal of Applied Social Psychology*, 18, 50–58.

Krahé, B. (1991). Social psychological issues in the study of rape. In W. Stroebe & M. Hewstone (Eds), *European Review of Social Psychology*, Vol. 2 (pp. 279–309). Chichester: Wiley.

Kramer, R.M. (1991). Intergroup relations and organizational dilemmas: The role of categorization processes. In L.L. Cummings & B.M. Staw (Eds), *Research in organizational behavior*, Vol. 13 (pp. 191–227). Greenwich, CT: JAI Press.

Krampen, G. (1991). Political participation in an action-theory model of personality: Theory and empirical evidence. *Political Psychology*, 12, 1–25.

Krau, E. (1991). *The contradictory immigrant problem: A sociopsychological analysis*. New York: Peter Lang.

Kraus, S.J. (1995). Attitudes and the prediction of behavior: A meta-analysis of the empirical literature. *Personality and Social Psychology Bulletin*, 21, 58–75.

Krauss, R.M. (1980). Impression formation, impression management and nonverbal behaviors. In E.T. Higgins, E.P. Herman, & M. Zanna (Eds), *The Ontario Symposium: Vol. I. Social cognition* (pp. 323–341). Hillsdale, NJ: Lawrence Erlbaum.

Kraut, R.E. & Poe, D. (1980). On the line: The deception judgements of customs inspectors and laymen. *Journal of Personality and Social Psychology*, 36, 380–391.

Krebs, D.L. & Miller, D.T. (1985). Altruism and aggression. In G. Lindzey & E. Aronson (Eds), *Handbook of social psychology*, Vol. 2 (pp. 1–71). New York: Random House.

Kristaponis, B. (1981). The myth of no-frame in the video session. *TV in Psychiatry*, 14(2), 1–5.

Kroeber, A.L. & Kluckhohn, F. (1952). Culture: A critical review of concepts and definitions. In *Peabody Museum Papers, Vol. 47, No. 1*. Cambridge, MA: Harvard University.

Krueger, J. & Heckhausen, J. (1993). Personality development across the adult life span: Subjective conceptions versus cross-sectional contrasts. *Journal of Gerontology: Psychological Sciences*, 48, 100–108.

Krueger, J., Heckhausen, J., & Hundertmark, J. (1995). Perceiving middle-aged adults: Effects of stereotype-congruent and incongruent information. *Journal of Gerontology: Psychological Sciences, 508*, 82–93.

Krüger, H. & Schmidt, F. (1989). Leichtrauchen ist kein Ausweg. *Die Medizinische Welt, 40,* 1091–1094.

Kuiper, J. (1958). *The relationship between context and the meaning of a single shot in a motion picture sequence.* University of Iowa, Department of Speech and Dramatic Art (cited in Isenhour, 1975).

LaFromboise, T., Coleman, H.L.K., & Gerton, J. (1993). Psychological impact of biculturalism: Evidence and theory. *Psychological Bulletin, 114,* 395–412.

Lalonde, R.M., Taylor, D.M., & Moghaddam, F.M. (1988). Social integration strategies of Haitian and Indian immigrant women in Montreal. In J. W. Berry & R.C. Annis (Eds), *Ethnic Psychology: Research and practice with immigrants, refugees, native peoples, ethnic groups and sojourners* (pp. 114–124). Amsterdam: Swets & Zeitlinger.

Lamb, M.E., Sternberg, K.J., & Esplin, P.W. (in press). Factors influencing the reliability and validity of statements made by young victims of sexual maltreatment. *Journal of Applied Developmental Psychology.*

Landry, K.L. & Brigham, J.C. (1992). The effect of training in criteria-based content analysis on the ability to detect deception in adults. *Law and Human Behavior, 16,* 663–676.

Lane, D.A. (1989). Bullying in school: The need for an integrated approach. *School Psychology International, 10,* 211–215.

Lang, F.R. (1994). *Die Gestaltung informeller Hilfebeziehungen im hohen Alter – Die Rolle von Elternschaft und Kinderlosigkeit* [Social support management in late life – The role of parenthood and childlessness]. Berlin: Max-Planck-Institut für Bildungsforschung, Studien und Berichte, Band 59.

Lang, F.R. & Carstensen, L.L. (1994). Close emotional relationships in late life: Further support for proactive aging in the social domain. *Psychology and Aging, 9,* 315–324.

Lang, F.R. & Tesch-Römer, C. (1993). Erfolgreiches Altern und soziale Beziehungen: Selektion und Kompensation im sozialen Kontaktverhalten [Successful aging and social relationships: Selection and compensation in social contact behavior]. *Zeitschrift für Gerontologie, 26,* 321–329.

Lang, F.R., Featherman, D.L., & Nesselroade, J.R. (1995). *Managing short-term variability in personal relationships: Evidence from the MacArthur Successful Aging Studies.* Unpublished paper, Free University, Berlin.

Lang, F.R., Marsiske, M.M., Baltes, P.B., & Baltes, M.M. (1995). *Selective optimization with compensation: Different facets of control?* Paper presented at the 13th biennial meeting of the International Society for the Study of Behavioral Development, Amsterdam, 28 June–2 July.

Lang, F.R., Staudinger, U.M., & Carstensen, L.L. (1995). *Socioemotional selectivity in late life: How personality and social context does (and does not) make a difference.* Unpublished paper, Free University Berlin, Berlin.

Langer, E.J. (1975). The illusion of control. *Journal of Personality and Social Psychology, 32,* 311–328.

Langley, T., O'Neal, E.C., Craig, K.M., & Yost, E.A. (1992). Aggression-consistent, -inconsistent, and -irrelevant priming effects on selective exposure to media violence. *Aggressive Behavior, 18,* 349–356.

LaPiere, R.T. (1934). Attitudes versus actions. *Social Forces, 13,* 230–237.

Larson, R., Mannell, R., & Zuzanek, J. (1986). Daily well-being of older adults with friends and family. *Psychology and Aging, 1,* 117–126.

Larwood, L. & Whittaker, W. (1977). Managerial myopia: Self-serving biases in organizational planning. *Journal of Applied Psychology, 62,* 194–198.

Lasswell, H. (1927). *Propaganda technique in the world war.* New York: Knopf.

Lasswell, H.D. (1948). *Power and personality.* New York: Norton.

Lau, R.R. & Sears, D.O. (Eds) (1986). *Political cognition.* Hillsdale, NJ: Lawrence Erlbaum.

Lawton, M.P. (1989). Behavior-relevant ecological factors. In K.W. Schaie & C. Schooler (Eds), *Social structure and aging: Psychological processes* (pp. 57–78). Hillsdale, NJ: Lawrence Erlbaum.

Lawton, R., Parker, D., Stradling, S.G., & Manstead, A.S.R. (1994). *Predicting road traffic accidents: The role of social deviance and violations.* Unpublished manuscript, University of Manchester.

Lazarsfeld, P., Berelson, B., & Gaudet, H. (1944). *The people's choice.* New York: Meredith.

Lea, S.E.G., Tarpy, R.M., & Webley, P. (1987). *The individual in the economy.* Cambridge: Cambridge University Press.

Lea, S.E.G., Webley, P., & Levine, R. M. (1993). The economic psychology of consumer debt. *Journal of Economic Psychology, 14*, 85–119.

Leahy, R.L. (1983). The development of the conception of economic inequality. *Developmental Psychology, 19*, 111–125.

Leahy, R.L. (1990). The development of concepts of economic and social inequality. *New Directions for Child Psychology, 46*, 107–120.

LeBon, G. (1896). *The crowd: A study of the popular mind.* London: T. Fisher Unwin.

Lee, D.J. & Markides, K.S. (1990). Activity and mortality among aged persons over an eight-year period. *The Journals of Gerontology: Social Sciences, 45*, S39–S42.

Lee, G.R. (1985).Theoretical perspectives on social networks. In W. Sauer & R.T. Coward (Eds), *Social support networks and the care of the elderly: Theory, research, and practice* (pp. 21–37). New York: Springer.

Lefkowitz, M.M., Eron, L.D., Walder, L.O., & Huesmann, L.R. (1977). *Growing up to be violent.* New York: Pergamon Press.

Lehr, U. & Minnemann, E. (1987). Veränderung von Quantität und Qualität sozialer Kontakte vom 7. bis 9. Lebensjahrzehnt [Changes of quantity and quality of social contact from the 7th to the 9th decade of life]. In U. Lehr & H. Thomae (Eds), *Formen seelischen Alterns* (pp. 80–91). Stuttgart: Enke.

Leichtman, M.D. & Ceci, S.J. (in press). The effects of repeated questions and stereotypes on preschoolers' reports. *Developmental Psychology.*

Leiser, D., Roland-Lévy, C., & Sevón, G. (Eds) (1990). *Economic socialization.* Special issue of the *Journal of Economic Psychology, 11.*

Lemon, B.W., Bengtson, V.L., & Peterson, I.A. (1972). An exploration of the activity theory of aging: Activity types and life satisfaction among inmovers to a retirement community. *Journal of Gerontology, 27*, 511–523.

Lepore, S.J. & Sesco, B. (1994). Distorting children's reports and interpretations of events through suggestion. *Journal of Applied Psychology, 79*, 108–120.

Lepper, M.R. & Greene, D. (Eds) (1978). *The hidden costs of reward.* Hillsdale, NJ: Lawrence Erlbaum.

Lepper, M.R., Greene, D., & Nisbett, R.E. (1973). Undermining children's intrinsic interest with extrinsic reward: A test of the 'overjustification' hypothesis. *Journal of Personality and Social Psychology, 28*, 129–137.

Lester, J. (1991). *Individual differences in accident liability: A review of the literature.* (Transport and Road Research Laboratory Research Report 306) Crowthorne, UK: TRRL.

Leventhal, H. (1970). Findings and theory in the study of fear communication. In L. Berkowitz (Ed.), *Advances in experimental social psychology*, Vol. 5 (pp. 120–186). New York: Academic Press.

Levin, I.P., Johnson, R.D., & Davis, M.J. (1987). The effect of information frame on risky decisions. *Journal of Economic Psychology, 8*, 43–54.

Levin, I.P., Snyder, M.A., & Chapman, D.P. (1988). The interaction of experimental and situational factors and gender in a simulated risky decision-making task. *Journal of Psychology, 122*, 173–181.

Levine, J.M. & Moreland, R.L. (1990). Progress in small group research. In M.R. Rosenzweig & L.W. Porter (Eds), *Annual review of psychology*, Vol. 41 (pp. 585–634). Palo Alto, CA: Annual Reviews, Inc.

LeVine, R. & Campbell, D. (1972). *Ethnocentrism.* New York: Wiley.

Lewis, A. (1981). Attributions and politics. *Personality and Individual Differences, 2*, 1–4.

Lewis, A., Webley, P., & Furnham, A. (1994). *The new economic mind: The social psychology of economic behaviour.* Hemel Hempstead, UK: Harvester Wheatsheaf.

Lewit, E.M. & Coate, D. (1982). The potential for using excise taxes to reduce smoking. *Journal of Health Economics, 1*, 121–145.

Leyens, J.P., Herman, G., & Dunand, M. (1982). The influence of an audience upon the reactions to filmed violence. *European Journal of Social Psychology, 12*, 131–142.

Liebkind, K. (1989). Conceptual approaches to ethnic identity. In K. Liebkind (Ed.), *New identities in Europe* (pp. 25–40). Aldershot: Gower.

Lifton, R.J. (1993). *The protean self.* New York: Basic Books.

Lindell, M.K. & Earle, T.C. (1983). How close is close enough: Public perceptions of the risk of industrial facilities. *Risk Analysis, 3*, 245–253.

Lindsay, D.S. (1994). Memory source monitoring and eyewitness testimony. In D.F. Ross, D. Read, & M.P. Toglia (Eds), *Adult eyewitness testimony.* Cambridge: Cambridge University Press.

Lindsay, D.S., Gonzales, V., & Eso, K. (1994). Aware and unaware uses of postevent suggestions.

In M. Zaragoza (Ed.), *Memory, suggestibility, and eyewitness testimony in children and adults.* Beverly Hills, CA: Sage.

Lindsay, D.S., Johnson, M.K., & Kwon, P. (1991). Developmental changes in memory source monitoring. *Journal of Experimental Child Psychology, 52,* 297–318.

Lindsay, R.C.L. & Wells, G.L. (1980). What price justice? Exploring the relationship of lineup fairness to identification accuracy. *Law and Human Behavior, 4,* 303–313.

Lindsay, R.C.L., Wallbridge, H., & Drennan, D. (1987). Do the clothes make the man? An exploration of the effect of lineup attire on eyewitness identification accuracy. *Journal of Applied Psychology, 76,* 463–477.

Linn, L.S., Spiegel, J.S., Mathews, W.C., Leake, B., Lien, R., & Brooks, S. (1989). Recent sexual behaviors among homosexual men seeking primary medical care. *Archives of Internal Medicine, 149,* 2685–2690.

Linstone, H.A. & Turoff, M. (1975). *The Delphi method: Techniques and applications.* Reading, MA: Addison-Wesley.

Linton, M. (1975). Memory for real-world events. In D.A. Norman & D.E. Rumelhart (Eds), *Explorations in cognition* (pp. 376–404). San Francisco: Freeman.

Linton, M. (1982). Transformations of memory in everyday life. In U. Neisser (Ed.), *Memory observed: Remembering in natural contexts* (pp. 77–91). San Francisco: Freeman.

Linz, D. & Malamuth, N. (1993). *Pornography.* Newbury Park, CA: Sage.

Linz, D., Wilson, B.J., & Donnerstein, E. (1992). Sexual violence in the mass media: Legal solutions, warnings, and mitigation through education. *Journal of Social Issues, 48,* 145–171.

Lipmann, O. (1906). Die Wirkung von Suggestivfragen. *Zeitschrift für pädagogische Psychologie, 8,* 89–96.

Lipsey, M.W. (1992). The effect of treatment on juvenile delinquents: Results from metaanalysis. In F. Lösel, D. Bender, & T. Bliesener (Eds), *Psychology and law: International perspectives.* Berlin: de Gruyter.

Lipton, D., Martinson, R., & Wilks, J. (1975). *The effectiveness of correctional treatment: A survey of treatment evaluation studies.* New York: Praeger.

Liska, A.E. (1984). A critical examination of the causal structure of the Fishbein–Ajzen attitude–behavior model. *Social Psychology Quarterly, 47,* 61–74.

Litwak, E. (1985). *Helping the elderly.* New York: Guilford Press.

Litwak, E. (1989). Forms of friendships among older people in an industrial society. In R.G. Adams & R. Blieszner (Eds), *Older adult friendship* (pp. 65–88). Newbury Park, CA: Sage.

Litwak, E., Messeri, P., & Silverstein, M. (1991). *Choice of optimal social support among the elderly: A meta-analysis of competing theoretical perspectives.* Paper presented at the annual meeting of the American Sociological Association, Cincinnati, OH, August.

Livingstone, S.M. & Lunt, P.K. (1992). Predicting personal debt and debt repayment: Psychological, social and economic determinants. *Journal of Economic Psychology, 13,* 111–134.

Locke, E.A. & Schweiger, D.M. (1979). Participation in decision-making: One more look. In B.M. Staw (Ed.), *Research in organizational behavior,* Vol. 1 (pp. 265–340). Greenwich, CT: JAI Press.

Lodge, M. & Hamill, R. (1986). A partisan schema for political information processing. *American Political Science Review, 80,* 505–519.

Loeber, R. & Stouthamer-Loeber, M. (1986) Family factors as correlates and predictors of juvenile conduct problems and delinquency. In M. Tonry & N. Morris (Eds), *Crime and justice,* Vol. 7. Chicago: University of Chicago Press.

Loftus, E. (1975). Leading questions and the eyewitness report. *Cognitive Psychology, 7,* 560–672.

Loftus, E. (1979). *Eyewitness testimony.* Cambridge, MA: Harvard University Press.

Loftus, E. & Fathi, D.C. (1985). Retrieving multiple autobiographical memories. *Social Cognition, 3,* 280–295.

Loftus, E.F. & Marburger, W. (1983). Since the eruption of Mt St Helens, has anyone beaten you up? *Memory and Cognition, 11,* 114–120.

Lonsway, K.A. & Fitzgerald, L.F. (1994). Rape myths. *Psychology of Women Quarterly, 18,* 133–164.

Loomes, G. & Sugden, R. (1982). Regret theory: an alternative theory of rational choice under uncertainty. *Economic Journal, 92,* 805–825.

Loomes, G. & Sugden, R. (1986). Disappointment and dynamic consistency in choice under uncertainty. *Review of Economic Studies, 53,* 271–282.

Lord, R.G. & Foti, R.J. (1986). Schema theories, information processing, and organizational behavior. In H.P. Sims, Jr, D.A. Gioia, & Associates (Eds), *The thinking organization: Dynamics of organizational social cognition* (pp. 20–48). San Francisco: Jossey-Bass.

Lord, R.G. & Kernan, M.C. (1987). Scripts as determinants of purposeful behavior in organizations. *Academy of Management Review, 12,* 265–277.

Lore, R.K. & Schultz, L.A. (1993). Control of human aggression. A comparative perspective. *American Psychologist, 48,* 16–25.

Lorenz, K. (1966). *On aggression.* New York: Harcourt, Brace & World.

Lorenz, K. (1974). *Civilized man's eight deadly sins.* New York: Harcourt Brace Jovanovich.

Lösel, F. (1992). Psychology and the law: Overtures, crescendos, and reprises. In F. Lösel, D. Bender, & T. Bliesener (Eds), *Psychology and law: International perspectives.* Berlin: de Gruyter.

Lösel, F. (1995). The efficacy of correctional treatment: A review and synthesis of metaevaluations. In J. McGuire (Ed.), *What works: Reducing reoffending guidelines from research and practice.* Chichester: Wiley.

Lösel, F. & Köferl, P. (1989). Evaluation research on correctional treatment in West Germany: A meta-analysis. In H. Wegener, F. Lösel, & J. Haisch (Eds), *Criminal behavior and the justice system: Psychological perspectives.* New York: Springer.

Lösel, F., Bender, D., & Bliesener, T. (Eds) (1992). *Psychology and law: International perspectives.* Berlin: de Gruyter.

Lowenthal, M.F. & Haven, C. (1968). Interaction and adaptation: Intimacy as a critical variable. *American Sociological Review, 33,* 20–30.

Lowenthal, M.F., Thurnher, M., Chiriboga, D. et al. (1975). *Four stages of life.* San Francisco: Jossey-Bass.

Lubin, J.H., Blot, W.J., Berrrino, F., Flamant, R., Gillis, C.R., Kunze, M., Schmähl, D., & Visco, G. (1984). Modifying risk of developing lung cancer by changing habits of cigarette smoking. *British Medical Journal, 288,* 1953–1956.

Ludwig, T.D. & Geller, E.S. (1991). Improving the driving practices of pizza deliverers: Response generalisation and moderating effects of driving history. *Journal of Applied Behavior Analysis, 24,* 31–44.

Lunt, P.K. & Livingstone, S.M. (1992). *Mass consumption and personal identity.* Buckingham, UK: Open University Press.

Lurigo, A.J., Carroll, J.S., & Stalans, L.J. (1994). Understanding judges' sentencing decisions: Attributions of responsibility and story construction. In L. Heath, R. Scott Tindale, J. Edwards, E.J. Posavac, F.B. Bryant, E. Henderson-King, Y. Suarez-Balcazar, & J. Myers (Eds), *Applications of heuristics and biases to social issues* (pp. 91–115). New York: Plenum Press.

Lutsky, N.S. (1980). Attitudes toward old age and elderly persons. In C. Eisdorfer (Ed.), *Annual review of gerontology and geriatrics,* Vol. 1 (S. 287–336). New York:

Luus, C.A.E. & Wells, G.L. (1991). Eyewitness identification and the selection of distractors for lineups. *Law and Human Behavior, 14,* 43–57.

Lykken, D.T. (1979). The detection of deception. *Psychological Bulletin, 86,* 47–53.

Lynn, R. (1991). *The secret of the miracle economy: Different national attitudes to competitiveness and money.* London: SAU.

Maass, A. & Arcuri, L. (1992). The role of language in the persistence of stereotypes. In G.R. Semin & K. Fiedler (Eds), *Language, interaction and social cognition* (pp. 129–143). London: Sage.

Maass, A., Arcuri, L., Salvi, D., & Semin, G.R. (1989). Language use in intergroup contexts. *Journal of Personality and Social Psychology, 57,* 981–993.

Maass, A., Corvino, P., & Arcuri, L. (1995). Linguistic intergroup bias and the mass media. *Revue de Psychologie Sociale.*

Maass, A., Milesi, A., Zabbini, S., & Stahlberg, D. (1995). Linguistic intergroup bias: Differential expectancies or in-group protection. *Journal of Personality and Social Psychology, 68,* 116–126.

MacDonald, T.K., Zanna, M.P., & Fong, G.T. (1995). Decision-making in altered states: The effects of alcohol on attitudes toward drinking and driving. *Journal of Personality and Social Psychology, 68,* 973–985.

MacLean, D. (1983). A moral requirement for energy policies. In D. Maclean & P.G. Brown (Eds), *Energy and the future* (pp. 180–196). Totowa, NJ: Rowman & Littlefield.

Macrae, C.N., Milne, A.B., & Griffith, R.J. (1993). Counterfactual thinking and the perception of criminal behaviour. *British Journal of Psychology, 84,* 221–226.

Madden, T.J., Ellen, P.S., & Ajzen, I. (1992). A comparison of the theory of planned behavior and the theory of reasoned action. *Personality and Social Psychology Bulletin, 18,* 3–9.

Maddox, G.L. (1963). Activity and morale: A longitudinal study of selected elderly subjects. *Social Forces, 42,* 195–204.

Maddux, J.E. & Rogers, R.W. (1983). Protection motivation and self-efficacy: A revised theory of fear appeals and attitude change. *Journal of Experimental Social Psychology, 19*, 469–479.

Maguire, M. (1980). The impact of burglary upon victims. *British Journal of Criminology, 20*, 262–275.

Majchrzak, A. (1988). *The human side of factory automation.* San Francisco: Jossey-Bass.

Maletzke, G. (1978). *Psychologie der Massenkommunikation.* Hamburg: Hans Bredow Institut.

Mallea, J. (1988). Canadian dualism and pluralism: Tensions, contradictions and emerging resolutions. In J.W. Berry & R.C. Annis (Eds), *Ethnic psychology: Research and practice with immigrants, refugees, native peoples, ethnic groups and sojourners* (pp. 13–37). Amsterdam: Swets Zeitlinger.

Malpass, R.S. & Devine, P.G. (1983). Measuring the fairness of eyewitness identification lineups. In S.M.A. Lloyd-Bostock & R.B. Clifford (Eds), *Evaluating witness evidence.* Chichester: Wiley.

Malpass, R.S. & Devine, P.G. (1984). Research on suggestion in lineups and photospreads. In G.L. Wells & E.F. Loftus (Eds), *Eyewitness testimony: Psychological perspectives.* New York: Cambridge University Press.

Mandell, L.M. & Shaw, D.L. (1973). Judging people in the news unconsciously: Effects of camera angle and bodily activity. *Journal of Broadcasting, 17*, 353–362.

Manstead, A.S.R. & Parker, D. (1995). Evaluating and extending the theory of planned behaviour. In W. Stroebe and M. Hewstone (Eds), *European review of social psychology*, Vol. 6 (pp. 69–95). Chichester: Wiley.

Manstead, A.S.R., Parker, D., Stradling, S.G., Reason, J.T., & Baxter, J.S. (1992). Perceived consensus in estimates of driving errors and driving violations. *Journal of Applied Social Psychology, 22*, 509–530.

Manstead, A.S.R., Proffitt, C., & Smart, J.L. (1983). Predicting and understanding mothers' infant–feeding intentions and behavior: Testing the theory of reasoned action. *Journal of Personality and Social Psychology, 44*, 657–671.

Mantwill, M., Köhnken, G., & Aschermann, E. (1995). Effects of the cognitive interview on the recall of familiar and unfamiliar events. *Journal of Applied Psychology, 80*, 68–78.

Marbe, K. (1913). *Grundzüge der forensischen Psychologie* [Elements of forensic psychology]. Munich: Beck.

Marin, B.V., Holmes, D.L., Guth, M., & Kovac, P. (1979). The potential of children as eyewitnesses. *Law and Human Behavior, 3*, 295–305.

Marini, M.M. (1984). Age and sequencing norms in the transition to adulthood. *Social Forces, 63*, 229–244.

Marks, G. & Miller, N. (1987). Ten years of research on the false-consensus effect: An empirical and theoretical review. *Psychological Bulletin, 102*, 72–90.

Markus, G.B. (1986). Stability and change in political attitudes: Observed, recalled, and explained. *Political Behavior, 8*, 21–44.

Markus, H.R. & Kitayama, S. (1991). Culture and the self: Implications for cognition, emotion, and motivation. *Psychological Review, 98*, 224–253.

Marsiske, M., Lang, F.R., Baltes, P.B., & Baltes, M.M. (1995). Selective optimization with compensation: Life-span perspectives on successful human development. In R. Dixon & L. Bäckman (Eds), *Psychological compensation: Managing losses and promoting gains* (pp. 35–79). Hillsdale, NJ: Lawrence Erlbaum.

Marteau, T.M. (1989). Framing of information: Its influence upon decisions of doctors and patients. *British Journal of Social Psychology, 28*, 89–94.

Martin, B. & Mason, S. (1987). Current trends in leisure. *Leisure Studies, 6*, 93–97.

Martin, J.L. (1987). The impact of AIDS on gay male sexual behavior patterns in New York City. *American Journal of Public Health, 77*, 578–581.

Martin, P.L. (1992a). International migration: A new challenge. *International Economic Insights*, March/April, 2–6.

Martin, P.L. (1992b). The migration issue. *Migration World, 5*, 11–15.

Martin, P.L. (1995). The United States: Benign neglect toward immigration. In F. Heckmann & W. Bosswick (Eds), *Migration policies: A comparative perspective* (pp. 21–44). Stuttgart: Enke.

Martinson, R. (1974). What works? Questions and answers about prison reform. *Public Interest, 10*, 22–54.

Mathieu, J.E. & Zajac, D.M. (1990). A review and meta-analysis of the antecedents, correlates, and consequences of organizational commitment. *Psychological Bulletin, 108*, 171–194.

Mathiowetz, N.A. (1986). *Episodic recall and estimation: Applicability of cognitive theories to survey data.* Paper presented at the Social Science Research Council seminar on retrospective data, New York, June.

Matthews, M.L. & Moran, A.R. (1986). Age differences in male drivers' perception of accident risk: The role of perceived driving ability. *Accident Analysis and Prevention, 18*, 299–313.

Mayer, K.U. (1986). Structural constraints on the life course. *Human Development, 29*, 163–170.

Mayer, K.U. (1987). Lebenslaufforschung [Life course research]. In W. Voges (Ed.), *Methoden der Biographie- und Lebenslaufforschung.* Opladen: Leske & Buderich.

Mayer, K.-U. (in press). Lebensverläufe und gesellschaftlicher Wandel – eine Theoriekritik und eine Analyse zum Zusammenhang von Bildungs- und Geburtenentwicklung. In J. Behrens & W. Voges (Eds), *Statuspassagen und Institutionalisierung.* Frankfurt am Main.

McArthur, L.Z. & Eisen, S.V. (1976). Television and sex-role stereotyping. *Journal of Applied Social Psychology, 6*, 329–351.

McCain, T.A., Chilberg, J., & Wakshlag, J. (1977). The effect of camera angle on source credibility and attraction. *Journal of Broadcasting, 22*, 35–46.

McCauley, M.R. & Fisher, R.P. (1995). Facilitating children's recall with the revised cognitive interview. *Journal of Applied Psychology, 80*, 510–516.

McCombs, M.E. & Shaw, D.L. (1972). The agenda setting function of mass media. *Public Opinion Quarterly, 36*, 176–187.

McCracken, G. (1990). *Culture and consumption.* Indianapolis: Indiana University Press.

McCusker, J., Zapka, J.G., Stoddard, A.M., & Mayer, K. (1989). Responses to the AIDS epidemic among homosexually active men: factors associated with preventive behavior. *Patient Education and Counseling, 13*, 15–30.

McDermott, R. (1992). Prospect theory and Soviet policy towards Syria, 1966–1967. *Political Psychology, 13*, 237–263.

McEwan, J. (1995). Adversarial and inquisitorial proceedings. In R. Bull & D. Carson (Eds), *Handbook of psychology in legal contexts.* Chichester: Wiley.

McGinnis, J.M., Shopland, D., & Brown, C. (1987). Tobacco and health: Trends in smoking and smokeless tobacco consumption in the United States. *Annual Review of Public Health, 8*, 441–467.

McGraw, K.D. (1978). The detrimental effect of reward on performance: A literature review and a prediction model. In M.R. Lepper & D. Greene (Eds), *The hidden costs of reward* (pp. 33–60). Hillsdale, NJ: Lawrence Erlbaum.

McGraw, K., Pinney, N., & Neumann, D. (1991). Memory for political actors: Contrasting the use of semantic and evaluative organizational strategies. *Political Behavior, 13*, 165–189.

McGregor, D.M. (1960), *The human side of enterprise.* New York: McGraw-Hill.

McGuire, W.J. (1985). The nature of attitude and attitude change. In G. Lindzey & E. Aronson (Eds), *Handbook of social psychology* (pp. 233–246). New York: Random House.

McGuire, W.J. (1986). The myth of massive media impact: Savagings and salvagings. In G. Comstock (Ed.), *Public communication and behavior,* Vol. 1 (pp. 173–258). New York: Academic Press.

McGuire, W.J. (1993). The poly-psy relationship: Three phases of a long affair. In W.J. McGuire & S. Iyengar (Eds), *Explorations in political psychology.* Durham, NC: Duke University Press.

McKenna, F.P. (1992). Paper to Behavioural Research in Road Safety III seminar, University of Kent at Canterbury, 22–23 September.

McKenna, F.P. (1993). It won't happen to me: Unrealistic optimism or illusion of control? *British Journal of Psychology, 84*, 39–50.

McKenna, F.P. & Lewis, C. (1991). Illusory judgments of driving skill and safety. In G.B. Grayson & J.F. Lester (Eds), *Behavioural research in road safety* (pp. 124–131). (Proceedings of a seminar at Nottingham University, September 1990.) Crowthorne, UK: Transport Research Laboratory.

McKinlay, J.B. & McKinlay, S.M. (1981). Medical measures and the decline of mortality. In P. Conrad & R. Kern (Eds), *The sociology of health and illness* (pp. 12–30). New York: St Martin's Press.

McKusick, L., Coates, T.J., Morin, S.F., Pollack, L., & Hoff, C. (1990). Longitudinal predictors of reductions in unprotected anal intercourse among gay men in San Francisco: The AIDS Behavioral Research Project. *American Journal of Public Health, 80*, 978–983.

McLuhan, H.M. (1964). *Understanding media: The extensions of men.* New York: McGraw-Hill.

McNeal, J.U. (1987). *Children as consumers: Insights and implications.* Lexington, MA: Lexington Books.

McNeil, B.J., Pauker, S.G., & Tversky, A. (1988). On the framing of medical decisions. In D. Bell, H. Raiffa, & A. Tversky (Eds), *Decision making. Descriptive, normative, and prescriptive interactions* (pp. 562–568). Cambridge: Cambridge University Press.

McPhail, C. (1994). The dark side of purpose: Individual and collective violence in riots. *Sociological Quarterly, 35*, 1–32.

McTavish, D.G. (1971). Perceptions of old people: A review of research methodologies and findings. *Gerontologist, 11*, 90–101.

Mehrabian, A. (1971). Non-verbal betrayal of feeling. *Journal of Experimental Research in Personality, 5*, 64–73.

Mehrabian, A. (1972). *Nonverbal communication*. Chicago: Aldine-Atherton.

Memon, A. & Köhnken, G. (1992). Helping witnesses to remember more: The cognitive interview. *Expert Evidence, 1*, 39–48.

Memon, A., Holley, A., Milne, R., Köhnken, G., & Bull, R. (1994). Towards understanding the effects of interviewer training in evaluating the cognitive interview. *Applied Cognitive Psychology, 8*, 641–659.

Messick, D.M. & Brewer, M.B. (1983). Solving social dilemmas: A review. In L. Wheeler & P. Shaver (Eds), *Review of Personality and Social Psychology*, Vol. 4 (pp. 11–44). Beverly Hills, CA: Sage.

Meyer, J.P. & Allen, N.J. (1991). A three-component conceptualization of organizational commitment. *Human Resource Management Review, 1*(1), 61–89.

Meyerowitz, B.E. & Chaiken, S. (1987). The effects of message framing on breast self-examination attitudes, intentions, and behavior. *Journal of Personality and Social Psychology, 52*, 500–510.

Meyrowitz, J. (1985). *No sense of place*. New York: Cambridge University Press.

Michela, J.L., Peplau, L.A., & Weeks, D.G. (1982). Perceived dimensions of attributions for loneliness. *Journal of Personality and Social Psychology, 43*, 929–936.

Mick, D.G. & Demoss, M. (1990). Self-gifts: Phenomenological insights from four contexts. *Journal of Consumer Research, 17*, 322–332.

Milavsky, J.R., Kessler, R., Sipp, H., & Rubens, W.S. (1982). Television and aggression: Results of a panel study. In D. Pearl, L. Bouthilet, & J. Lazar (Eds), *Television and behavior: Ten years of scientific progress and implications for the 80s*, Vol. 2. Washington, DC: Government Printing Office.

Milbrath, L. (1984). *Environmentalists: Vanguard for a new society*. Albany, NY: State University of New York Press.

Milbrath, L. (1986). Environmental beliefs and values. In M. Hermann (Ed.), *Political psychology* (pp. 97–138). San Francisco: Jossey-Bass.

Milgram, S. (1963). Behavioral study of obedience. *Journal of Abnormal and Social Psychology, 67*, 371–378.

Miller, N.E. (1941). The frustration-aggression hypothesis. *Psychological Review, 48*, 337–342.

Miller, P.M. & Fagley, N.S. (1991). The effects of framing, problem variations, and providing rationale on choice. *Personality and Social Psychology Bulletin, 17*, 517–522.

Miller, T.Q., Heath, L., Molcan, J.R., & Dugoni, B.L. (1991). Imitative violence in the real world: A reanalysis of homicide rates following championship prize fights. *Aggressive Behavior, 17*, 121–134.

Milligan, W.L., Powell, D.A., Harley, C., & Furchtgott, E. (1985). Physical health correlates of attitudes toward aging in the elderly. *Experimental Aging Research, 11*, 75–80.

Mintzberg, H. (1973). *The nature of managerial work*. New York: Harper & Row.

Mitchell, J. & Dodder, R.A. (1983). Types of neutralization and types of delinquency. *Journal of Youth and Adolescence, 12*, 307–318.

Mitchell, T.R. & Wood, R.E. (1980). Supervisor's responses to subordinate poor performance: A test of an attributional model. *Organizational Behavior and Human Performance, 25*, 123–138.

Mitchell, T.R., Green, S.G., & Wood, R.E. (1981). An attributional model of leadership and the poor performing subordinate: Development and validation. In L.L. Cummings & B.M. Staw (Eds), *Research in organizational behavior*, Vol. 3 (pp. 197–234). Greenwich, CT: JAI Press.

Modell, J., Furstenberg, F.F., & Strong, D. (1978). The timing of marriage in the transition to adulthood: Continuity and change, 1860–1975. *American Journal of Sociology, 84*, 120–150.

Modigliani, F. & Brumberg, R. (1954). Utility analysis and the consumption function: An interpretation of the data. In K.K. Kurihara (Ed.), *Post-Keynesian Economics*. New Brunswick, NJ: Rutgers University Press.

Moghaddam, F.M., Taylor, D.M., & Wright, S.C. (1993). *Social psychology in cross-cultural perspective*. New York: W.H. Freeman.

Montgomery, H. (1993). The search for a dominance structure in decision making: Examining the evidence. In G.A. Klein, J. Orasanu, R. Calderwood, & C.E. Zsambok (Eds), *Decision making in action: Models and methods* (pp. 182–187). Norwood, NJ: Ablex.

Morgan, D.L. (1990). Combining the strengths of social networks, social support, and personal relationships. In S. Duck & R.C. Silver (Eds), *Personal relationships and social support* (pp. 190–215). Newbury Park, CA: Sage.

Morgan, D.L., Schuster, T.L., & Butler, E.W. (1991). Role reversals in the exchange of social support. *Journal of Gerontology: Social Sciences, 46*, S278–287.

Morokvasic, M. (1993). 'In and out' of the labour market: Immigrant and minority women in Europe. *New Community, 19*, 459–483.

Morris (1989). The admissibility of evidence derived from hypnosis and polygraphy. In D.C. Raskin (Ed.), *Psychological methods in criminal investigation and evidence* (pp. 333–376). New York: Springer.

Morton, A.Q. & Farringdon, M.G. (1992). Identifying utterance. *Expert Evidence, 1*, 84–92.

Moscovici, S. (1976). *Social influence and social change.* London: Academic Press.

Moscovici, S. (1988). Notes towards a description of social representations. *European Journal of Social Psychology, 18*, 211–250.

Moston, S. (1987). The suggestibility of children in interview studies. *Child Language, 7*, 67–78.

Mourant, R.R. & Rockwell, T.H. (1972). Strategies of visual search by novice and experienced drivers. *Human Factors, 14*, 325–335.

Mowen, J.C. & Mowen, M.M. (1991). Time and outcome valuation: Implications for marketing decision making. *Journal of Marketing, 55*, 54–62.

Mueller, J.H., Wonderlich, S., & Dugan, K. (1986). Self-referent processing of age-specific material. *Psychology and Aging, 1*, 293–299.

Mulilis, J.-P. & Lippa, R. (1990). Behavioral change in earthquake preparedness due to negative threat appeals: A test of protection motivation theory. *Journal of Applied Social Psychology, 20*, 619–638.

Mullen, B. & Hu, L. (1988). Social projection as a function of cognitive mechanisms: Two meta-analytic integrations. *British Journal of Social Psychology, 27*, 333–356.

Mullen, B., Atkins, J.L., Champion, D.S., Edwards, C., Hardy, D., Story, J.E., & Vanderklok, M. (1985). The false consensus effect: A meta-analysis of 115 hypothesis tests. *Journal of Experimental Social Psychology, 21*, 262–283.

Mummendey, A. & Otten, S. (1993). Aggression: Interaction between individuals and social groups. In R.B. Felson & J.T. Tedeschi (Eds), *Aggression and violence: Social interactionist perspectives* (pp. 145–167). Washington, DC: American Psychological Association.

Munn, N.L. (1940). The effect of knowledge of the situation upon judgment of emotion from facial expression. *Journal of Abnormal and Social Psychology, 35*, 324–338.

Münsterberg, H. (1908). *On the witness stand: Essays on psychology and crime.* New York: Clark, Boardman, Doubleday.

Murnighan, J.K. (Ed.) (1993). *Social psychology in organizations: Advances in theory and research.* Englewood Cliffs, NJ: Prentice-Hall.

Murphy, P., Williams, J., & Dunning, E. (1990). *Football on trial: Spectator violence and development in the football world.* London: Routledge.

Murray, E.J., Lamnin, A.D., & Carver, C.S. (1989). Emotional expressions in written essays and psychotherapy. *Journal of Social and Clinical Psychology, 8*, 414–429.

Mydans, S. (1993). Poll finds tide of immigration brings hostility. *New York Times*, 27 June, 1, 16.

Narby, D.J., Cutler, B.L., & Penrod, S.D. (1996). The effects of witness, target, and situational factors on eyewitness identifications. In S.L. Sporer, R.M. Malpass, & G. Köhnken (Eds), *Psychological issues in eyewitness identification* (pp. 23–52). Hillsdale, NJ: Lawrence Erlbaum.

Nau, P.A., van Houten, R., Rolider, A., & Jonah, B.A. (1993). The failure of feedback on alcohol impairment to reduce impaired driving. *Journal of Applied Behavior Analysis, 26*, 361–367.

Nealey, S.M., Melber, B.D., & Rankin, W.L. (1983). *Public opinion and nuclear energy.* Lexington, MA: Lexington Books.

Neisser, U. (1986). Nested structure in autobiographical memory. In D.C. Rubin (Ed.), *Autobiographical memory* (pp. 71–88). Cambridge: Cambridge University Press.

Neugarten, B.L. (1979). Time, age, and the life cycle. *American Journal of Psychiatry, 136*, 887–894.

Neugarten, B.L. & Peterson, W.A. (1957). *A study of the American age-grade system.* Paper presented at the fourth congress of the International Association of Gerontology.

Neugarten, B.L., Moore, J.W., & Lowe, J.C. (1965). Age norms, age constraints, and adult socialization. *American Journal of Sociology, 70*, 710–717.

Neuman, W.R. (1991). *The future of the mass audience.* Cambridge: Cambridge University Press.

Newhouse, N. (1990). Implications of attitude and behavior research for environmental conservation. *Journal of Environmental Education, 21*, 20–26.

Ng, S.H. (1990). Language and control. In H. Giles & P. Robinson (Eds), *Handbook of language and social psychology* (pp. 271–285). New York: Wiley.

Nilson, L.B. (1981). Reconsidering ideological lines. *Sociological Quarterly, 22*, 531–548.

Nisbett, R.E. (1993). Violence and US regional culture. *American Psychologist, 48*, 441–449.

Nisbett, R. & Ross, L. (1980). *Human inference: Strategies and shortcomings of social judgment.* Englewood Cliffs, NJ: Prentice-Hall.

Noble, T. (1981). *Structure and change in modern Britain.* London: Batsford Academic.

Noelle-Neumann, E. & Rothenberger, W. (1993). Erfahrung und Einstellungen zum Alter [Experience and attitudes toward aging]. In H.-U. Klose (Ed.), *Bevölkerungsentwicklung und dynamische Wirtschaft* (pp. 199–212). Opladen.

Noordzij, P. (1990). *Individual differences and accident liability: A review of the German literature* (Transport and Road Research Laboratory Contractor's Report 195). Crowthorne, UK: TRRL.

Novotny, T.E., Romano, R.A., Davis, R.M., & Mills, S.L. (1992). The public health practice of tobacco control: Lessons learned and directions for the States in the 1990s. *Annual Review of Public Health, 13,* 287–318.

O'Brien, T.M. (1987). The interracial nature of violent crimes: A reexamination. *American Journal of Sociology, 92,* 817–835.

OECD (Organization for Economic Co-operation and Development) Road Research Group Report (1970). *Driver behaviour.* Paris: OECD.

Oetting, E.R. & Beauvais, F. (1991). Orthogonal cultural identification theory: The cultural identification of minority adolescents. *International Journal of Addictions, 25,* 655–685.

O'Gorman, H.J. (1980). False consciousness of kind: Pluralistic ignorance among the aged. *Research on Aging, 2,* 105–128.

O'Guinn, T. & Faber, R. (1989). Compulsive buying. *Journal of Consumer Research, 16,* 147–157.

Olweus, D. (1991). Bully/victim problems among schoolchildren: Basic facts and effects of a school based intervention program. In D. Pepler & K. Rubin (Eds), *The development and treatment of childhood aggression* (pp. 411–448). Hillsdale, NJ: Lawrence Erlbaum.

Olweus, D. (1994). Bullying at school. Long-term outcomes for the victims and an effective school-based intervention program. In L.R. Huesmann (Ed.), *Aggressive behavior: Current perspectives* (pp. 97–130). New York: Plenum Press.

Orlikowski, W. J. (1992). The duality of technology: Rethinking the concept of technology in organizations. *Organization Science, 3,* 398–427.

Orne, M.T. (1979). The use and misuse of hypnosis in court. *International Journal of Clinical and Experimental Hypnosis, 27,* 311–341.

Orth-Gomer, K. & Johnson, J.V. (1987). Social network interaction and mortality. A six year follow-up study of a random sample of the Swedish population. *Journal of Chronic Diseases, 40,* 949–957.

Osborn, J.E. (1989). A risk assessment of the AIDS epidemic. In V.M. Mays, G.W. Albee, & S.F. Schneider (Eds), *Primary prevention of AIDS* (pp. 23–38). Newbury Park, CA: Sage.

Osgood, N.J. (1989). Theory and research in social gerontology. In N.J. Osgood & A.H. Sontz (Eds), *The science and practice of gerontology. A multidisciplinary guide* (pp. 55–87). New York: Greenwood Press.

Oskamp, S. (1965). Overconfidence in case study judgments. *Journal of Consulting Psychology, 29,* 261–265.

Oskamp, S. (1984). *Applied social psychology.* Englewood Cliffs, NJ: Prentice-Hall.

Oskamp, S. (1986). Applied social psychology to the year 2000 and beyond. *Contemporary Social Psychology, 12,* 14–20.

Oskamp, S., Harrington, M.J., Edwards, T.C., Sherwood, D.L., Okuda, S.M., & Swanson, D. (1991). Factors influencing household recycling behavior. *Environment and Behavior, 23,* 494–519.

Ostrom, T.M. & Upshaw, H.S. (1968). Psychological perspective and attitude change. In A.C. Greenwald, T.C. Brock, & T.M. Ostrom (Eds), *Psychological foundations of attitudes.* New York: Academic Press.

Ottati, V.C. & Wyer, R.S., Jr. (1993). Affect and political judgement. In W.J. McGuire & S. Iyengar (Eds), *Explorations in political psychology.* Durham, NC: Duke University Press.

Ottati, V.C., Fishbein, M., & Middlestadt, S. (1988). Determinants of voters' beliefs about the candidates' stands on the issues: The role of evaluative bias heuristics and the candidates' expressed message. *Journal of Personality and Social Psychology, 55,* 517–529.

Otten, W. & van der Pligt, J. (1992). Risk and behavior: The mediating role of risk appraisal. *Acta Psychologica, 80,* 325–346.

Otway, H.J. & Fishbein, M. (1976). *The determinants of attitude formation: An application to nuclear power* (Research Memorandum RM76–80). Laxenburg, Austria: International Institute for Applied Systems Analysis.

Otway, H.J., Haastrup, P., Connell, W., Gianitsopoulos, G., & Paruccini, M. (1987). *An analysis of the print media in Europe following the Chernobyl accident.* Report of the Joint Research Center of the Commission of the European Community. Ispra, Italy, April.

Palmer, T. (1975). Martinson revisited. *Journal of Research in Crime and Delinquency, 12,* 133–152.

Palmore, E. (1977). Facts on aging: A short quiz. *Gerontologist, 17,* 315–320.

Pan, H.S., Neidig, P.H., & O'Leary, K.D. (1994). Male–female and aggressor–victim differences in the factor structure of the modified Conflict Tactics Scale. *Journal of Interpersonal Violence, 9,* 366–382.

Pandy, J., Sinha, Y., Prakash, A., & Tripathi, R.C. (1982). Right–left political ideologies and attribution of the causes of poverty. *European Journal of Social Psychology, 12,* 327–331.

Parducci, A. (1983). Category ratings and the relational character of judgment. In H.G. Geissler, H.F.J.M. Bulfart, E.L.H. Leeuwenberg, & V. Sarris (Eds), *Modern issues in perception* (pp. 262–282). Berlin: VEB Deutscher Verlag der Wissenschaften.

Park, W.W. (1990). A review of research on groupthink. *Journal of Behavioral Decision Making, 3,* 229–245.

Parker, D., Manstead, A.S.R., & Stradling, S.G. (1995). Extending the theory of planned behaviour: The role of personal norm. *British Journal of Social Psychology, 34,* 127–137.

Parker, D., Manstead, A.S.R., & Stradling, S.G. (1996). Modifying beliefs and attitudes to exceeding the speed limit: An intervention based on the theory of planned behavior. *Journal of Applied Social Psychology, 26,* 1–19.

Parker, D., Manstead, A.S.R., Stradling, S.G., & Lawton, R. (1995). *Attitudes to driving violations: The role of affective and instrumental beliefs.* Unpublished manuscript, University of Manchester.

Parker, D., Manstead, A.S.R., Stradling, S.G., Reason, J.T., & Baxter, J.S. (1992a). Intentions to commit driving violations: An application of the theory of planned behaviour. *Journal of Applied Psychology, 77,* 94–101.

Parker, D., Manstead, A.S.R., Stradling, S.G., Reason, J.T., & Baxter, J.S. (1992b). Determinants of intention to commit driving violations. *Accident Analysis and Prevention, 24,* 117–131.

Parker, D., Reason, J.T., Manstead, A.S.R., & Stradling, S.G. (1995). Driving errors, driving violations and accident involvement. *Ergonomics, 38,* 1036–1048.

Parrot, A. & Bechhofer, L. (Eds) (1991). *Acquaintance rape: The hidden crime.* New York: Wiley.

Pasmore, William A. (1988). *Designing effective organizations: The sociotechnical systems perspective.* New York: Wiley.

Passuth, P.M. & Maines, D.R. (1981). *Transformations in age norms and age constraints: Evidence bearing on the age-irrelevancy hypothesis.* Hamburg: World Congress on Gerontology.

Patterson, G.R., Reid, J.B., Jones, R.R., & Conger, R.E. (1975). *A social learning approach to family intervention, Vol. 1: Families with aggressive children.* Eugene, OR: Castalia.

Payne, J.W., Bettman, J.R., & Johnson, E.J. (1992). Behavioral decision research: A constructive processing perspective. *Annual Review of Psychology, 43,* 87–132.

Payne, J.W., Bettman, J.R., & Johnson, E.J. (1993). *The adaptive decision maker.* Cambridge: Cambridge University Press.

Payne, S.L. (1951). *The art of asking questions.* Princeton, NJ: Princeton University Press.

Pedersen, P. (1991). Multiculturalism as a generic approach to counseling. *Journal of Counseling & Development, 70,* 6–12.

Pedersen, P. (1995). *The five stages of culture shock.* Westport, CT: Greenwood Press.

Pelto, O. (1968). The difference between 'tight' and 'loose' societies. *Transaction,* April, 37–40.

Pence, E.C., Pendleton, W.C., Dobbins, G.H., & Sgro, J.A. (1982). Effects of causal explanations and sex variables on recommendations for corrective action following employee failure. *Organizational Behavior and Human Performance, 29,* 227–240.

Pennebaker, J. (1989). Confessions, inhibition and disease. In L. Berkowitz (Ed.), *Advances in experimental social psychology,* Vol. 22 (pp. 211–244). New York: Academic Press.

Pennebaker, J., Kiecolt-Glaser, J.K., & Glaser, R. (1988). Disclosure of traumas and immune function: Health implications for psychotherapy. *Journal of Consulting and Clinical Psychology, 56,* 239–245.

Pennington, N. & Hastie, R. (1981). Juror decision making models: The generalization gap. *Psychological Bulletin, 89,* 246–287.

Pennington, N. & Hastie, R. (1986). Evidence evaluation in complex decision making. *Journal of Personality and Social Psychology, 51,* 242–258.

Pennington, N. & Hastie, R. (1990). Practical implications of psychological research on juror and jury decision making. *Personality and Social Psychology Bulletin, 16,* 90–105.

Pepper, S.C. (1981). Problems in the quantification of frequency expressions. In D.W. Fiske (Ed.),

Problems with language imprecision (New Directions for Methodology of Social and Behavioral Science, Vol. 9). San Francisco: Jossey-Bass.

Peters, G.R. (1971). Self-conceptions of the aged, age identification, and aging. *Gerontologist, 11,* 69–73.

Peters, G.R. & Kaiser, M.A. (1985). The role of friends and neighbors in providing social support. In W.J. Sauer & R.T. Coward (Eds), *Social support networks and the care of the elderly* (pp. 123–158). New York: Springer.

Peters, J.F. (1989). Youth clothes-shopping behaviour: An analysis of gender. *Adolescence, 24,* 575–588.

Peters, R.-D., McMahon, R.-J., & Quinsey, V.-L. (Eds) (1992). *Aggression and violence throughout the life span.* Newbury Park, CA: Sage.

Pettit, F., Fegan, M., & Howie, P. (1990). *Interviewer effects on children's testimony.* Paper presented at the International Congress on Child Abuse and Neglect, Hamburg, September.

Petty, R.E. & Cacioppo, J.T. (1986a). *Communication and persuasion: Central and peripheral routes to attitude change.* New York: Springer.

Petty, R.E. & Cacioppo, J.T. (1986b). The elaboration likelihood model of persuasion. In L. Berkowitz (Ed.), *Advances in experimental social psychology,* Vol. 19 (pp. 123–205). San Diego, CA: Academic Press.

Petty, R.E., Cacioppo, J.T., & Goldman, R. (1981). Personal involvement as a determinant of argument-based persuasion. *Journal of Personality and Social Psychology, 41,* 847–855.

Petty, R.E., Ostrom, T.M., & Brock, T.C. (Eds) (1981). *Cognitive responses in persuasion.* Hillsdale, NJ: Lawrence Erlbaum.

Petty, R.E., Priester, J.R., & Wegener, D.T. (1994). Cognitive processes in attitude change. In R.S. Wyer, Jr. & T.K. Srull (Eds), *Handbook of social cognition,* Vol. 2 (pp. 69–142). Hillsdale, NJ: Lawrence Erlbaum.

Petty, R.E., Wells, G.L., & Brock, T.C. (1976). Distraction can enhance or reduce yielding to propaganda: Thought disruption versus effort justification. *Journal of Personality and Social Psychology, 34,* 874–884.

Pfaff, H. (1989). *Streßbewältigung und soziale Unterstützung* [Coping with stress and social support]. Weinheim: Deutscher Studien Verlag.

Phillips, D.P. (1979). Suicide, motor vehicle fatalities, and the mass media: Evidence toward a theory of suggestion. *American Journal of Sociology, 84,* 1150–1174.

Phillips, D.P. (1982). The impact of fictional television stories on US adult fatalities: New evidence on the effect of mass media on violence. *American Journal of Sociology, 87,* 1340–1359.

Phillips, D.P. (1983). The impact of mass media violence in US homicides. *American Sociological Review, 48,* 560–568.

Phillips, D.P. (1986). The found experiment: A new technique for assessing the impact of mass media violence on real-world aggressive behavior. In G. Comstock (Ed.), *Public communication and behavior,* Vol. 1 (pp. 259–308). New York: Academic Press.

Pinder, C.C. (1984). *Work motivation: Theory, issues, and applications.* Glenview, IL: Scott, Foresman.

Plath, D.W. & Ikeda, K. (1975). After coming of age: Adult awareness of age norms. In T.R. Williams (Ed.), *Socialization and communication in primary groups* (pp. 107–123). The Hague: Mouton.

Plous, C. (1993). *The psychology of judgment and decision making.* New York: McGraw-Hill.

Poole, D.A. & White, L.T. (1991). Effects of question repetition and retention interval on the eyewitness testimony of children and adults. *Developmental Psychology, 27,* 975–986.

Pooling Project Research Group (1978). *Relationship of blood pressure, serum cholesterol, smoking habit, relative weight and ECG-abnormality to incidence of major coronary events: Final report of the Pooling Project* (American Heart Association Monographs No. 60). Dallas, TX: American Heart Association.

Porac, J.F., Ferris, G.R., & Fedor, D.B. (1983). Causal attributions, affect, and expectations of a day's performance. *Academy of Management Journal, 26,* 285–296.

Porter, S. & Yuille, J.C. (1995). Credibility assessment of criminal suspects through statement analysis. *Psychology, Crime & Law, 1,* 319–331.

Postman, N. (1985). *Amusing ourselves to death. Public discourse in the age of show business.* New York: Viking.

Pratkanis, A.R. & Greenwald, A.G. (1989). A sociocognitive model of attitude structure and function. In L. Berkowitz (Ed.), *Advances in experimental social psychology,* Vol. 22 (pp. 245–285). New York: Academic Press.

Prentice, D. (1987). Psychological correspondence of possessions, attitudes, and values. *Journal of Personality and Social Psychology, 53,* 993–1003.

Prentky, R. & Burgess, A.W. (1992). Rehabilitation of child molesters: A cost-benefit analysis. In A.W. Burgess (Ed.), *Child trauma I: Issues and research*. New York: Garland.

Prince, M. (1993a). Self-concept, money beliefs and values. *Journal of Economic Psychology, 14*, 161–174.

Prince, M. (1993b). Women, men and money styles. *Journal of Economic Psychology, 14*, 175–182.

Prince-Embury, S. (1992). Psychological symptoms as related to cognitive appraisals and demographic differences among information seekers in the aftermath of technological disaster at Three Mile Island. *Journal of Applied Social Psychology, 22*, 38–54.

Prins, K.S., van Oudenhoven, J.P., & Bank, B.P. (1994). *Adaptation strategies in the Netherlands. Consequences for Turks and Moroccans*. Paper presented at the Second International Congress on Prejudice, Discrimination and Conflict, Jerusalem.

Puska, P., Nissinen, A., Tuomilehto, J., Salonen, J.T., Koskela, K., McAlister, A., Kottke, T.E., Maccoby, N., & Farquhar, J.W. (1985). The community-based strategy to prevent coronary heart disease: Conclusions from ten years of the North Karelia Project. *Annual Review of Public Health, 6*, 147–194.

Quattrone, G.A. & Tversky, A. (1984). Causal versus diagnostic contingencies: On self-deception and the voter's illusion. *Journal of Personality and Social Psychology, 46*, 237–248.

Quattrone, G.A. & Tversky, A. (1988). Contrasting rational and psychological analyses of political choice. *American Political Science Review, 82*, 719–736.

Quiggin, J. & Horowitz, J. (1995). Time and risk. *Journal of Risk and Uncertainty, 10*, 37–55.

Quimby, A. & Downing, C. (1991). *Road users' attitudes to some road safety and transportation issues* (Transport and Road Research Laboratory Contractor's Report 277). Crowthorne, UK: TRRL.

Raine, A. & Venables, P.H. (1981). Classical conditioning and socialisation – a biosocial interaction. *Personality and Individual Differences, 2*, 273–283.

Raskin, D.C. (1989). Polygraph techniques for the detection of deception. In D.C. Raskin (Ed.), *Psychological methods in criminal investigation and evidence*. New York: Springer.

Raskin, D.C. and Esplin, P.W. (1991). Statement Validity Assessment: Interview procedures and content analysis of children's statements of sexual abuse. *Behavioral Assessment, 13*, 265–291.

Rattner, A. (1988). Convicted but innocent: Wrongful conviction and the criminal justice system. *Law and Human Behavior, 12*, 283–293.

Rawlins, W.K. (1992). *Friendship matters. Communication, dialectics, and the life course*. New York: de Gruyter

Razran, G. (1950). Ethnic dislikes and stereotypes: A laboratory study *Journal of Abnormal and Social Psychology, 45*, 7–27.

Reason, J.T., Manstead, A.S.R., Stradling, S.G., Baxter, J.S., & Campbell, K. (1990). Errors and violations on the road: A real distinction? *Ergonomics, 33*, 1315–1332.

Reicher, S.D. (1984). The St Paul's riot: An explanation of the limits of crowd action in terms of a social identity model. *European Journal of Social Psychology, 14*, 1–21.

Reid, J.E. & Inbau, F.E. (1977). *Truth and deception: The polygraph ('lie-detector') technique*. Baltimore, MD: Williams & Wilkins.

Reiser, B.J., Black, J.B., & Abelson, R.P. (1985). Knowledge structure in the organization and retrieval of autobiographical memories. *Cognitive Psychology, 17*, 89–137.

Reiser, M. (1980). *Handbook of investigative hypnosis*. Los Angeles: Lehi.

Renn, O. (1990). Public responses after Chernobyl: Effects on attitudes and public policies. *Journal of Environmental Psychology, 10*, 151–168.

Reno, R. (1979). Attribution for success and failure as a function of perceived age. *Journal of Gerontology, 34*, 709–715.

Richard, R., van der Pligt, J., & de Vries, N. (1995a). Anticipated affect and behavioural choice. *British Journal of Social Psychology, 34*, 9–21.

Richard, R., van der Pligt, J., & de Vries, N. (1995b). Anticipated affective reactions and prevention of AIDS. *British Journal of Social Psychology, 34*, 23–30.

Richard, R., van der Pligt, J., & de Vries, N.K. (1996). Anticipated regret and time perspective: Changing sexual risk-taking behavior. *Journal of Behavioral Decision Making* (in press).

Richins, M. (1994a). Special possessions and the expression of material values. *Journal of Consumer Research, 21*, 522–533.

Richins, M. (1994b). Valuing things: The public and private meanings of possessions. *Journal of Consumer Research, 21*, 504–521.

Richins, M. & Dawson, S. (1992). Materialism as a consumer value: Measure development and validation. *Journal of Consumer Research, 19*, 303–316.

Riley, M.W., Johnson, M.E., & Foner, A. (Eds) (1972). *Aging and society: A sociology of age stratification*, Vol. 3. New York.

Rindfuss, R.R., Swicegood, C.G., & Rosenfeld, R.A. (1987). Disorder in the life course: How common and does it matter? *American Sociological Review, 52*, 785–801.

Rippetoe, P.A. & Rogers, R.W. (1987). Effects of components of protection-motivation theory on adaptive and maladaptive coping with a health threat. *Journal of Personality and Social Psychology, 52*, 596–604.

Rivers, I. & Smith, P.K. (1994). Types of bullying behavior and their correlates. *Aggressive Behavior, 20*, 359–368.

Roberto, K.A. (1989). Exchange and equity in friendships. In R.G. Adams & R. Blieszner (Eds), *Older adult friendship: Structure and process* (pp. 147–165). London: Sage.

Roberto, K.A. & Scott, J.P. (1986a). Equity considerations in the friendships of older adults. *Journal of Gerontology, 41*, 241–247.

Roberto, K.A. & Scott, J.P. (1986b). Friendships of older men and women: Exchange patterns and satisfaction. *Psychology and Aging, 1*, 103–109.

Roberts, D.F. & Bachen, C.M. (1981). Mass communication effects. *Annual Review of Psychology, 32*, 307–356.

Robins, L.N. (1979). Sturdy childhood predictors of adult outcomes: Replications from longitudinal studies. In J.E. Barrett, R.M. Rose, & G.L. Klerman (Eds), *Stress and mental disorder*. New York: Raven Press.

Rogers, R.W. (1975). A protection motivation theory of fear appeals and attitude change. *Journal of Psychology, 91*, 93–114.

Rogers, R.W. (1983). Cognitive and physiological processes in fear appeals and attitude change: A revised theory of protection motivation. In J.T. Cacioppo & R.E. Petty (Eds), *Social psychophysiology: A source book* (pp. 153–176). New York: Guilford Press.

Rogers, R.W. & Mewborn, C.R. (1976). Fear appeals and attitude change: Effects of noxiousness, probability of occurrence, and the efficacy of coping responses. *Journal of Personality and Social Psychology, 58*, 499–511.

Rogler, L. (1994). International migrations. A framework for directing research. *American Psychologist, 49*, 701–708.

Rohner, R. (1984). Toward a conception of culture for cross-cultural psychology. *Journal of Cross-Cultural Psychology, 15*, 111–138.

Rokeach, M. (1973). *The nature of human values*. New York: The Free Press.

Rokeach, M. & Ball-Rokeach, S.J. (1988). *Stability and change in American values priorities, 1968–1981*. Paper presented at the meeting of the American Association of Public Opinion Research. Toronto.

Rolls, G.W.P., Hall, R.D., Ingham, R., & McDonald, M. (1991). *Accident risk and behavioural patterns of younger drivers*. Basingstoke, UK: AA Foundation for Road Safety Research.

Ronis, D.L., Yates, J.F. & Kirscht, J.P. (1989). Attitudes, decisions, and habits as determinants of repeated behavior. In A.R. Pratkanis, S.J. Breckler, & A.G. Greenwald (Eds), *Attitude structure and function* (pp. 213–239). Hillsdale, NJ: Lawrence Erlbaum.

Rook, K.S. (1984). The negative side of social interaction: Impact on psychological well-being. *Journal of Personality and Social Psychology, 46*, 1097–1108.

Rook, K.S. (1989). Strains in older adults' friendship. In R. G. Adams & R. Blieszner (Eds), *Older adult friendship* (pp. 166–194). Newbury Park, CA: Sage.

Rosa, E.A. & Freudenburg, W.R. (1993). The historical development of public reactions to nuclear power: Implications for nuclear waste policy. In R.E. Dunlap, M.E. Kraft, & E.A. Rosa (Eds), *Public reactions to nuclear waste: Citizens' views of repository siting* (pp. 33–63). Durham, NC and London: Duke University Press.

Rosch, E. (1978). Principles of categorization. In E. Rosch & B.B. Lloyd (Eds), *Cognition and Categorization*. Hillsdale, NJ: Lawrence Erlbaum.

Rosenau, P.M. (1992). *Post-modernism and the social sciences*. Princeton, NJ: Princeton University Press.

Rosenberg, M.J. & Hovland, C.I. (1960). Cognitive, affective, and behavioral components of attitudes. In C.I. Hovland & M.J. Rosenberg (Eds), *Attitude organization and change: An analysis of consistency among attitude components* (pp. 1–14). New Haven, CT: Yale University Press.

Rosenstock, I. (1974). The health belief model and preventive health behavior. *Health Education Monographs, 2*, 354–386.

Rosenthal, R. (1986). Media violence, antisocial behavior, and the social consequences of small effects. *Journal of Social Issues, 42*, 141–154.

Rosenthal, R., Hall, J.A., DiMatteo, M.R., Rogers, P.L., & Archer, D. (1979). *Sensitivity to nonverbal communication.* Baltimore, MD: Johns Hopkins University Press.

Rosenzweig, S. (1981). The current status of the Rosenzweig Picture-Frustration Study as a measure of aggression in personality. In P.F. Brain & D. Benton (Eds), *Multidisciplinary approaches to aggression research* (pp. 113–126). Amsterdam: Elsevier.

Rosow, I. (1974). *Socialization to old age.* Berkeley, CA: University of California Press.

Rosow, I. (1982). Intergenerational perspectives on aging. In G. Lesnoff-Caravaglia (Ed.), *Aging and the human condition* (pp. 40–53). New York: Human Sciences Press.

Ross, D., Read, J.D., & Toglia, M. (Eds) (1994). *Adult eyewitness testimony: Current trends and developments.* London: Cambridge University Press.

Ross, L. (1977). The intuitive psychologist and his shortcomings. In L. Berkowitz (Ed.), *Advances in experimental social psychology*, Vol. 10 (pp. 174–221). New York: Academic Press.

Ross, L. & Nisbett, R. E. (1991). *The person and the situation.* New York: McGraw-Hill.

Ross, L., Greene, D., & House, P. (1977). The 'false consensus' effect: An egocentric bias in social perception and attribution processes. *Journal of Experimental Social Psychology, 13,* 279–301.

Ross, M. (1989). The relation of implicit theories to the construction of personal histories. *Psychological Review, 96,* 341–357.

Ross, M. & Sicoly, F. (1979). Egocentric biases in availability and attribution. *Journal of Personality and Social Psychology, 37,* 322–336.

Rossi, P.H., Wright, J.D., & Anderson, A.B. (Eds) (1983). *Handbook of survey research.* New York: Academic Press.

Roter, D.L. (1984). Patient question asking in physician–patient interaction. *Health Psychology, 3,* 395–409.

Rothbaum, F. (1983). Aging and age stereotypes. *Social Cognition, 2,* 171–184.

Rothbaum, F., Weisz, J., & Snyder, S. (1982). Changing the world and changing the self: A two process model of perceived control. *Journal of Personality and Social Psychology, 42,* 5–37.

Rothengatter, J.A., de Bruin, R.A., & Rooijers, A.J. (1989). The effects of publicity campaigns and police surveillance on the attitude-behaviour relationship in different groups of road users. In N. Muhlrad (Ed.), *Proceedings of the second workshop on recent developments in road safety research.* Arcueil, France: INRETS.

Rousseau, D.M. & Parks, J.M. (1993). The contracts of individuals and organizations. In L.L. Cummings & B.M. Staw (Eds), *Research in organizational behavior*, Vol. 14 (pp. 1–43). Greenwich, CT: JAI Press.

Rowlingson, K. & Kempson, E. (1994). *Paying with plastic: A study of credit card debt.* London: Policy Studies Institute.

Rule, B.G. & Ferguson, T.J. (1986). The effects of media violence on attitudes, emotions, and cognitions. *Journal of Social Issues, 42,* 29–50.

Rumelhart, D.E. (1977). Understanding and summarizing brief stories. In D. LaBerge & S.J. Samuels (Eds), *Basic processes in reading: Perception and comprehension.* Hillsdale, NJ: Lawrence Erlbaum.

Russel, S.S. & Teitelbaum, M. (1992). *International migration and international trade.* Washington, DC: World Bank.

Russell, D.H. (1990). *Rape in marriage.* Bloomington, IN: Indiana University Press.

Rutherford, G.W., Lifson, A.R., Hessol, N.A.H., Darrow, W.W., O'Malley, P.M., Buchbinder, S.P., Barrenhart, J.L., Bodecker, T.W., Cannon, L., & Doll, L.S. (1990). Course of HIV-1 infection in a cohort of homosexual and bisexual men: An 11 year follow up study. *British Medical Journal, 301,* 1183–1188.

Ryff, C.D. (1989). Beyond Ponce de Leon and life satisfaction: New directions in quest of successful aging. *International Journal of Behavioral Development, 12,* 35–55.

Rzewnicki, R. & Forgays, D. (1987). Recidivism and self-cure of smoking and obesity: An attempt to replicate. *American Psychologist, 42,* 97–100.

Sabey, B.E. & Taylor, H. (1980). *The known risks we run: The highway* (Transport and Road Research Laboratory Supplementary Report 567). Crowthorne, UK: TRRL.

Salancik, G.R. & Porac, J.F. (1986). Distilled ideologies: Values derived from causal reasoning in complex environments. In H.P. Sims, Jr., D.A. Gioia & Associates (Eds), *The thinking organization: Dynamics of organizational social cognition* (pp. 75–101). San Francisco: Jossey-Bass.

Sam, D.L. & Berry, J.W. (1995). Acculturative stress among young immigrants in Norway. *Scandinavian Journal of Psychology, 35,* 10–24.

Sampson, E.E. (1993). *Celebrating the other: A dialogic account of human nature.* Hemel Hempstead, UK: Harvester Wheatsheaf.

Sarbin, T.R. (1979). The myth of the criminal type. In T.R. Sarbin (Ed.), *Challenges to the criminal justice system: The perspectives of community psychology*. New York: Human Science.

Sauer, W.J. & Cauer, R.T. (1985). The role of social support networks in the care of the elderly. In W. Sauer & R.T. Coward (Eds), *Social support networks and the care of the elderly: Theory, research, and practice* (pp. 3–20). New York: Springer.

Saunders, P. (1990). *A nation of home owners*. London: Unwin.

Saywitz, K.J., Geiselman, R.E., & Bornstein, G.K. (1992). Effects of cognitive interviewing and practice on children's recall performance. *Journal of Applied Psychology*, 77, 744–756.

Schachter, S. (1982). Recidivism and self-cure of smoking and obesity. *American Psychologist*, 37, 436–444.

Schank, R.C. & Abelson, R.P. (1977). *Scripts, plans, goals, and understanding*. Hillsdale, NJ: Lawrence Erlbaum.

Schein, E.H. (1992). *Organizational culture and leadership* (2nd ed.). San Francisco: Jossey-Bass.

Scherer, K.R. & Ekman, P. (Eds) (1982). *Handbook of methods in nonverbal behavior research*. Cambridge: Cambridge University Press.

Scherer, K.R., Scherer, U., Hall, J.A., & Rosenthal, R. (1977). Differential attribution of personality based on multichannel presentation of verbal and nonverbal cues. *Psychological Research*, 39, 221–247.

Schifter, D. & Ajzen, I. (1985). Intention, perceived control, and weight loss: An application of the theory of planned behavior. *Journal of Personality and Social Psychology*, 49, 843–851.

Schlosser, S., Black, D., Repertinger, S., & Freet, D. (1994). Compulsive buying: Demography, phenomenology, and comorbidity in 46 subjects. *General Hospital Psychiatry*, 16, 205–212.

Schmid, J. & Fiedler, K. (1996). *Language and implicit attributions in the Nuremberg Trials: Analyzing prosecutors' and defense attorneys' closing speeches. Human Communication Research*, 22(3), 371–398.

Schmitz, P. (1992). Acculturation styles and health. In S. Iwawaki, Y. Kashima, & K. Leung (Eds), *Innovations in cross-cultural psychology* (pp. 360–370). Amsterdam: Swets & Zeitlinger.

Schnapper, D. (1995). The significance of French immigration and integration policy. In F. Heckmann & W. Bosswick (Eds), *Migration policies: A comparative perspective* (pp. 99–111). Stuttgart: Enke.

Schonfield, D. (1982). Who is stereotyping whom and why? *Gerontologist*, 22, 267–272.

Schulz, R. (1986). Successful aging: Balancing primary and secondary control. *Adult Development and Aging News*, 13, 2–4.

Schulz, R. & Fritz, S. (1988). Origins of stereotypes of the elderly: An experimental study of the self–other discrepancy. *Experimental Aging Research*, 13, 189–195.

Schulz, R., Heckhausen, J., & Locher, J.L. (1991). Adult development, control, and adaptive functioning. *Journal of Social Issues*, 47, 177–196.

Schuman, H. & Kalton, G. (1985). Survey methods. In G. Lindzey & E. Aronson (Eds), *Handbook of social psychology*, Vol. 1 (pp. 635–697). New York: Random House.

Schuman, H. & Presser, S. (1981). *Questions and answers in attitude surveys*. New York: Academic Press.

Schunk, D.H. & Carbonari, J.P. (1984). Self-efficacy models. In J.D. Matarazzo, S.M. Weiss, J.A. Herd, N.E. Miller, & S.M. Weiss (Eds), *Behavioral health: A handbook of health enhancement and disease prevention*. New York: Wiley.

Schwartz, J.L. (1987). *Smoking cessation methods: The United States and Canada, 1978–1985* (Division of Cancer Prevention and Control, National Cancer Institute, US Department of Health and Human Services, Public Health Service. HIH Publication 87–2940). Washington, DC: US Government Printing Office.

Schwartz, S. (1994). Heuristics and biases in medical decision making. In L. Heath, R. Scott, J. Edwards, E.J. Posavac, F.B. Bryant, E. Henderson-King, Y. Suarez-Balcazar, & J. Myers (Eds), *Applications of heuristics and biases to social issues* (pp. 45–72). New York: Plenum Press.

Schwarz, N. (1990). Assessing frequency reports of mundane behaviors: Contributions of cognitive psychology to questionnaire construction. In C. Hendrick & M.S. Clark (Eds), *Research methods in personality and social psychology* (Review of Personality and Social Psychology, Vol. 11, pp. 98–119). Beverly Hills, CA: Sage.

Schwarz, N. (1994). Judgment in a social context: Biases, shortcomings, and the logic of conversation. In M. Zanna (Ed.), *Advances in experimental social psychology*, Vol. 26 (pp. 123–162). San Diego, CA: Academic Press.

Schwarz, N. (1995). Social cognition: Information accessibility and use in social judgment. In D. N. Osherson & E. E. Smith (Eds), *Thinking. An invitation to cognitive science*, Vol. 3 (2nd ed.) (pp. 345–376). Cambridge, MA: MIT Press.

Schwarz, N. & Bless, H. (1992). Constructing reality and its alternatives: Assimilation and contrast effects in social judgment. In L.L. Martin & A. Tesser (Eds), *The construction of social judgments* (pp. 217–245). Hillsdale, NJ: Lawrence Erlbaum.

Schwarz, N. & Bless, H. (in press). Mental construal processes and the emergence of context effects in attitude measurement. *Bulletin de Methodologie Sociologique.*

Schwarz, N. & Hippler, H.J. (1991). Response alternatives: The impact of their choice and ordering. In P. Biemer, R. Groves, N. Mathiowetz, & S. Sudman (Eds), *Measurement error in surveys* (pp. 41–56). Chichester: Wiley.

Schwarz, N. & Kurz, E. (1989). What's in a picture? The impact of face-ism on trait attributions. *European Journal of Social Psychology, 19,* 311–316.

Schwarz, N. & Strack, F. (1991). Context effects in attitude surveys: Applying cognitive theory to social research. In W. Stroebe & M. Hewstone (Eds), *European review of social psychology,* Vol. 2 (pp. 31–50). Chichester: Wiley.

Schwarz, N. & Sudman, S. (Eds) (1992). *Context effects in social and psychological research.* New York: Springer.

Schwarz, N. & Sudman, S. (1994). *Autobiographical memory and the validity of retrospective reports.* New York: Springer.

Schwarz, N. & Sudman, S. (1996). *Answering questions: Methodology for determining cognitive and communicative processes in survey research.* San Francisco: Jossey-Bass.

Schwarz, N., Hippler, H.J., Deutsch, B., & Strack, F. (1985). Response categories: Effects on behavioral reports and comparative judgments. *Public Opinion Quarterly, 49,* 388–395.

Schwarz, N., Knäuper, B., Hippler, H.J., Noelle-Neumann, E., & Clark, F. (1991). Rating scales: Numeric values may change the meaning of scale labels. *Public Opinion Quarterly, 55,* 570–582.

Schwarz, N., Strack, F., Hippler, H.J., & Bishop, G. (1991). The impact of administration mode on response effects in survey measurement. *Applied Cognitive Psychology, 5,* 193–212.

Schwarz, N., Strack, F., & Mai, H.P. (1991). Assimilation and contrast effects in part–whole question sequences: A conversational logic analysis. *Public Opinion Quarterly, 55,* 3–23.

Schwarz, N., Strack, F., Müller, G., & Chassein, B. (1988). The range of response alternatives may determine the meaning of the question: Further evidence on informative functions of response alternatives. *Social Cognition, 6,* 107–117.

Schwarzer, R. & Leppin, A. (1991). Social support and health: A theoretical and empirical overview. *Social and Personal Relationships, 8,* 99–127.

Scott, J.E. & Schwalm, L. (1988). Rape rates and the circulation rates of adult magazines. *Journal of Sex Research, 24,* 241–250.

Scott, J.P. (1990). Sibling interaction in later life. In T.H. Brubaker (Ed.), *Family relationships in later life* (2nd ed., pp. 86–99). Beverly Hills, CA: Sage.

Sealy, A.P. (1989). Decision processes in the jury room. In H. Wegener, F. Lösel, & J. Haisch (Eds), *Criminal behavior and the justice system: Psychological perspectives.* New York: Springer.

Sechrest, L.B., White, S.O., & Brown, E.D. (1979). *The rehabilitation of criminal offenders: Problems and prospects.* Washington, DC: National Academy of Sciences.

Self, C.A. & Rogers, R.W. (1990). Coping with threats to health: Effects of persuasive appeals on depressed, normal, and antisocial personalities. *Journal of Behavioral Medicine, 13,* 343–357.

Semin, G.R. (1990). Social constructivist approaches to personality. In G. Semin & K.J. Gergen (Eds), *Everyday understanding: Social and scientific implications* (pp. 151–175). London: Sage.

Semin, G.R. (1995). Interfacing language and social cognition. *Journal of Language and Social Psychology, 14,* 182–194.

Semin, G.R. & de Poot, C. (1995). *You might regret it if you don't notice how a question is worded!* Manuscript submitted for publication.

Semin, G.R. & Fiedler, K. (1988). The cognitive functions of linguistic categories in describing persons: Social cognition and language. *Journal of Personality and Social Psychology, 54,* 558–568.

Semin, G.R. & Fiedler, K. (1991). The linguistic category model, its bases, applications, and range. In W. Stroebe & M. Hewstone (Eds), *European review of social psychology,* Vol. 2 (pp. 1–30). Chichester: Wiley.

Semin, G.R. & Marsman, G. (1994). On the information mediated by interpersonal verbs: Event precipitation, dispositional inference and implicit causality. *Journal of Personality and Social Psychology, 67,* 836–849.

Semin, G.R., Rubini, M., & Fiedler, K. (1995). The answer is in the question: The effect of verb causality upon locus of explanation. *Personality and Social Psychology Bulletin, 21,* 834–841.

Seydel, E., Taal, E., & Wiegman, O. (1990). Risk-appraisal, outcome and self-efficacy

expectancies: Cognitive factors in preventive behavior related to cancer. *Psychology and Health,*
  4, 99–109.

Shanan, J. & Kedar, H.S. (1979–80). Phenomenological structuring of the adult life span as a
  function of age and sex. *International Journal of Aging and Human Development, 10,* 343–357.

Shanas, E. (1962). *The health of older people: A social survey.* Cambridge.

Shapiro, P. & Penrod, S.D. (1986). A meta-analysis of facial identification studies. *Psychological
  Bulletin, 100,* 139–156.

Sheffield, C.J. (1993). The invisible intruder: Women's experiences of obscene phone calls. In P.B.
  Bart & E.G. Moran (Eds), *Violence against women: The bloody footprints* (pp. 73–83).
  Newbury Park, CA: Sage.

Shefrin, H.M. & Thaler, R. (1988). The behavioral life-cycle hypothesis. *Economic Inquiry, 26,*
  609–643.

Shepherd, J.W. & Ellis, H.D. (1996). Face recall – methods and problems. In S.L. Sporer, R.M.
  Malpass, & G. Köhnken (Eds), *Psychological issues in eyewitness identification* (pp. 87–115).
  Hillsdale, NJ: Lawrence Erlbaum.

Sheppard, B.H., Hartwick, J., & Warshaw, P.R. (1988). The theory of reasoned action: A meta-
  analysis of past research with recommendations for modifications and future research. *Journal
  of Consumer Research, 15,* 325–343.

Sherif, M. (1936). *The psychology of social norms.* New York: Harper & Row.

Sherif, M. (1966). *Group conflict and cooperation: Their social psychology.* London: Routledge &
  Kegan Paul.

Sherman, L.W. & Berk, R.A. (1984). The specific deterrent effects of arrest for domestic assault.
  American Sociological Review, 49, 261–272.

Sherman, N.C. & Gold, J.A. (1978). Perceptions of ideal and typical middle and old age.
  International Journal of Aging and Human Development, 9, 67–73.

Sherman, N.C., Gold, J.A., & Sherman, M.F. (1978). Attribution theory and evaluations of older
  men among college students, their parents, and grandparents. *Personality and Social
  Psychology Bulletin, 4,* 440–442.

Shetzer, L., Stackman, R.W., & Moore, L.F. (1991). Business-environment attitudes and the New
  Environmental Paradigm. *Journal of Environmental Education, 22,* 14–21.

Shiloh, S. (1994). Heuristics and biases in health decision making: Their expression in genetic
  counseling. In L. Heath, R. Scott Tindale, J. Edwards, E.J. Posavac, F.B. Bryant, E.
  Henderson-King, Y. Suarez-Balcazar, & J. Myers (Eds), *Applications of heuristics and biases to
  social issues* (pp. 13–30). New York: Plenum Press.

Siegel, K., Mesagno, F.P., Chen, J.-Y., & Christ, G. (1989). Factors distinguishing homosexual
  males practising risky and safer sex. *Social Science and Medicine, 28,* 561–569.

Simmel, G. (1908). *Soziologie,* Chapter 9: 'Exkurs über den Fremden' (pp. 685–691). English
  translation: K.H. Wolff (Ed.) (1950), *The sociology of Georg Simmel.* New York: Free Press.

Simon, H.A. (1957). *Models of man: Social and rational.* New York: Wiley.

Simons, R.L. (1983). Specificity and substitution in the social networks of the elderly. *International
  Journal of Aging and Human Development, 18,* 121–139.

Simonson, I. (1989). Choice based on reasons: The case of attraction and compromise effects.
  Journal of Consumer Research, 16, 158–174.

Simonson, I. (1992). The influence of anticipating regret and responsibility on purchase decisions.
  Journal of Consumer Research, 19, 105–118.

Singelis, T. M. (1994). The measurement of independent and interdependent self-construals.
  Personality and Social Psychology Bulletin, 20, 580–591.

Singer, J.D. (1989). The political origins of international war: A multifactorial review. In J.
  Groebel & R.A. Hinde (Eds), *Aggression and war: Their biological and social bases* (pp. 202–
  220). Cambridge: Cambridge University Press.

Singer, J.L. & Singer, D.J. (1981). *Television, imagination, and aggression: A study of preschoolers.*
  Hillsdale, NJ: Lawrence Erlbaum.

Sivak, M. (1983). Society's aggression level as a predictor of traffic fatality rate. *Journal of Safety
  Research, 14,* 93–99.

Skolnick, A. (1986). Early attachment and personal relationships across the life course. In P.B.
  Baltes, D.L. Featherman, & R.M. Lerner (Eds), *Life-span development and behavior,* Vol. 7
  (pp. 173–206). Hillsdale, NJ: Lawrence Erlbaum.

Slovic, P. (1987). Perception of risk. *Science, 236,* 280–285.

Slovic, P., Fischhoff, B., & Lichtenstein, S. (1979). Rating the risk. *Environment, 21,* 14–39.

Slovic, P., Lichtenstein, S., & Fischhoff, B. (1979). Images of disaster: Perception and acceptance
  of risk for nuclear power. In G. Goodman & W. Rowe (Eds), *Energy risk management.*
  London: Academic Press.

Slovic, P., Lichtenstein, S., & Fischhoff, B., (1988). Decision making. In R.D. Atkinson, R.J. Herrnstein, G. Lindzey, & R.D. Luce (Eds), *Stevens' handbook of experimental psychology, Vol. 2: Learning and cognition* (pp. 673–738). New York: Wiley.

Smetana, J.G. & Adler, N. (1980). Fishbein's value x expectancy model: An examination of some assumptions. *Personality and Social Psychology Bulletin, 6*, 89–96.

Smith, J.E., Pleban, R.J., & Shaffer, D. (1982). Effects of interrogator bias and a police trait questionnaire on the accuracy of eyewitness identification. *Journal of Social Psychology, 116*, 19–26.

Smith, M. (1983). Hypnotic memory enhancement of witnesses: Does it work? *Psychological Bulletin, 94*, 387–407.

Smith, P.B. & Bond, M. H. (1993). *Social psychology across cultures.* New York, London, Toronto: Harvester Wheatsheaf.

Smith, T.W. (1979). Happiness. *Social Psychology Quarterly, 42*, 18–30.

Smith, T.W. (1992). Thoughts on the nature of context effects. In N. Schwarz & S. Sudman (Eds), *Context effects in social and psychological research.* New York: Springer.

Smith, W.E. (1974). The effects of social and monetary rewards on intrinsic motivation. Unpublished doctoral dissertation, Cornell University.

Snelders, H.M., Hussein, G., Lea, S.E.G., & Webley, P. (1992). The polymorphous concept of money. *Journal of Economic Psychology, 13*, 71–92.

Snyder, M. (1974). The self-monitoring of expressive behavior. *Journal of Personality and Social Psychology, 30*, 526–537.

Snyder, M. (1984). When belief creates reality. In L. Berkowitz (Ed.), *Advances in experimental social psychology*, Vol. 18. New York: Academic Press.

Social Trends (1994). Volume 24, Government Statistical Office Publication. London: HMSO.

Sofer, C. (1970). *Men in mid-career.* New York: Cambridge University Press.

Solomon, M. (1985). *The psychology of fashion.* Lexington, MA: Lexington Books.

Solomon, S., Greenberg, J., & Pyszczynski, T. (1991). A terror management theory of social behavior: The psychological functions of self-esteem and cultural world views. In M.P. Hanna (Ed.), *Advances in experimental social psychology, 24*, 93–159.

Sparks, G.G. & Fellner, C.L. (1986). Faces in the news: Gender comparisons of magazine photographs. *Journal of Communication, 36*, 76–79.

Spears, R. & Manstead, A.S.R. (1990). Consensus estimation in social context. In W. Stroebe & M. Hewstone (Eds), *European review of social psychology*, Vol. 1 (pp. 81–109). Chichester: Wiley.

Spencer, J. & Flin, R. (1993). *The evidence of children.* London: Blackstone Press.

Sperber, D. & Wilson, D. (1986). *Relevance: Communication and cognition.* Cambridge, MA: Harvard University Press.

Spignesi, A. & Shor, R.E. (1981). The judgment of emotion from facial expressions, contexts, and their combination. *Journal of General Psychology, 104*, 41–58.

Sporer, S.L. (1982). A brief history of the psychology of testimony. Current *Psychological Reviews, 2*, 323–340.

Sporer, S.L. (1995). *Training people to discriminate true from invented stories by their content.* Unpublished manuscript, University of Aberdeen.

Sporer, S.L. (1996). Psychological aspects of person descriptions. In S.L. Sporer, R.M. Malpass, & G. Köhnken (Eds), *Psychological issues in eyewitness identification: New evidence and practical guidelines.* Hillsdale, NJ: Lawrence Erlbaum.

Sporer, S.L., Malpass, R.M., & Köhnken, G. (Eds) (1996). *Psychological issues in eyewitness identification.* Hillsdale, NJ: Lawrence Erlbaum.

Sporer, S.L., Penrod, S.D., Read, J.D., & Cutler, B.L. (in press). Choosing, confidence, and accuracy: A meta-analysis of the confidence–accuracy relation in eyewitness identification studies. *Psychological Bulletin.*

Srivastva, S., & Associates (Eds) (1986). *Executive power.* San Francisco: Jossey-Bass.

Stacey, B.G. (1982). Economic socialization in the pre-adult years. *British Journal of Social Psychology, 21*, 159–173.

Stall, R., Ekstrand, M., Pollack, L., McKusick, L., & Coates, T.J. (1990). Relapse from safer sex: the next challenge for AIDS prevention efforts. *Journal of Acquired Immune Deficiency Syndromes, 3*, 1181–1187.

Starr, C. (1969). Social benefits versus technological risk. *Science, 165*, 1232–1238.

Staub, E. (1989). *The roots of evil: The origins of genocide and other group violence.* New York: Cambridge University Press.

Staudinger, U.M., Marsiske, M., & Baltes, P.B. (in press). Resilience and reserve capacity in later adulthood: Potentials and limits of development across the life span. In D. Cicchetti & D. Cohen (Eds), *Manual of developmental psychopathology*. New York: Wiley.

Steblay, N.M. (1992). A meta-analytic review of the weapon focus effect. *Law and Human Behavior, 16*, 413–424.

Steeh, C. (1981). Trends in nonresponse rates. *Public Opinion Quarterly, 45*, 40–57.

Steele, C.M. & Josephs, R.A. (1990). Alcohol myopia: Its prized and dangerous effects. *American Psychologist, 45*, 921–933.

Steger, M.A.E., Pierce, J., Steel, B.S., & Lovrich, N.P. (1989). Political culture, postmaterial values, and the New Environmental Paradigm: A comparative analysis of Canada and the United States. *Political Behavior, 11*, 233–254.

Steinbach, U. (1992). Social networks, institutionalization, and mortality among elderly people in the United States. *Journals of Gerontology: Social Sciences, 47*, S183–S190.

Steiner, I.D. (1986). Paradigms and groups. In L. Berkowitz (Ed.), *Advances in experimental social psychology*, Vol. 19 (pp. 251–289). New York: Academic Press.

Steller, M. & Boÿchuk, T. (1992). Children as witnesses in sexual abuse cases: Investigative interview and assessment techniques. In H. Dent & R. Flin (Eds), *Children as witnesses*. Chichester: Wiley.

Steller, M. & Köhnken, G. (1989). Statement analysis: Credibility assessment of children's testimonies in sexual abuse cases. In D.C. Raskin (Ed.), *Psychological methods in criminal investigation and evidence*. New York: Springer.

Steller, M., Wellershaus, P., & Wolf, T. (1992). Realkennzeichen in Kinderaussagen: empirische Grundlagen der Kriterienorientierten Aussageanalyse [Reality criteria in child witness statements: Empirical foundations of the criteria-based content analysis]. *Zeitschrift für Experimentelle und Angewandte Psychologie, 39*, 151–170.

Stephenson, G.M. (1992). *The psychology of criminal justice*. Oxford: Blackwell.

Stern, P.C. (1992). Psychological dimensions of global environmental change. *Annual Review of Psychology, 43*, 269–302.

Stern, P.C. & Oskamp, S. (1987). Managing scarce environmental resources. In I. Altman & D. Stokols (Eds), *Handbook of environmental psychology* (pp. 1044–1088). New York: Wiley.

Stern, W. (1903). *Beiträge zur Psychologie der Aussage*, 1. Heft. Leipzig: Barth.

Stevens, N.L. (1988). Aanpassing aan het verlies van de partner bij oudere weduwen: Een typologie [Adaptation to loss of the partner among older widows: A typology]. *Tijdschrift vorr Gerontologie en Geriatrie, 19*, 169–175.

Stiles, W.B. (1979). Discourse analysis and the doctor–patient relationship. *International Journal of Psychiatry in Medicine, 9*, 263–274.

Stoll, F.C., Hoecker, D.G., Krueger, G.P., & Chapanis, A. (1976). The effects of four communication modes on the structure of language used during cooperative problem solving. *Journal of Psychology, 94*, 13–26.

Stoller, E.P. & Earl, L.E. (1983). Help with activities of everyday life: Sources of support for the noninstitutionalized elderly. *Gerontologist, 23*, 64–70.

Stone, G.P. (1954). City shoppers and urban identification: Observations of the social psychology of city life. *American Journal of Sociology, 60*, 36–45.

Stone, J., Aronson, E., Crain, A.L., Winslow, M.P., & Fried, C.B. (1994). Inducing hypocrisy as a means of encouraging young adults to use condoms. *Personality and Social Psychology Bulletin, 20*, 116–128.

Storie, V.J. (1977). *Male and female car drivers: Differences observed in accidents* (Department of Transport TRRL Supplementary Report SR761). Crowthorne, UK: Transport Research Laboratory.

Storms, M.D. (1972). Videotape and the attribution process: Reversing actors' and observers' points of view. *Journal of Personality and Social Psychology, 27*, 165–175.

Strack, F. (1992). Order effects in survey research: Activative and informative functions of preceding questions. In N. Schwarz & S. Sudman (Eds), *Context effects in social and psychological research* (pp. 23–34). New York: Springer.

Strack, F. (1994). *Zur Psychologie der standardisierten Befragung*. Heidelberg: Springer Verlag.

Strack, F. & Martin, L. (1987). Thinking, judging, and communicating: A process account of context effects in attitude surveys. In H.J. Hippler, N. Schwarz, & S. Sudman (Eds), *Social information processing and survey methodology* (pp. 123–148). New York: Springer.

Strack, F. & Schwarz, N. (1992). Implicit cooperation: The case of standardized questioning. In G. Semin & F. Fiedler (Eds), *Social cognition and language* (pp. 173–193). Beverly Hills, CA: Sage.

Strack, F., Argyle, M., & Schwarz, N. (Eds) (1991). *Subjective well-being. An interdisciplinary perspective*. Oxford: Pergamon Press.

Strack, F., Martin, L.L., & Schwarz, N. (1988). Priming and communication: The social determinants of information use in judgments of life-satisfaction. *European Journal of Social Psychology, 18*, 429–442.

Strack, F., Schwarz, N., Chassein, B., Kern, D., & Wagner, D. (1990). The salience of comparison standards and the activation of social norms: Consequences for judgments of happiness and their communication. *British Journal of Social Psychology, 29*, 303–314.

Strack, F., Schwarz, N., & Wänke, M. (1991). Semantic and pragmatic aspects of context effects in social and psychological research. *Social Cognition, 9*, 111–125.

Strain, L.A. & Chappell, N.L. (1982). Confidants. Do they make a difference in quality of life? *Research on Aging, 4*, 479–502.

Straus, M.A. & Gelles, R.J. (1990). *Physical violence in American families: Risk factors and adaptations to violence in 8,145 families*. Brunswick, NJ: Transaction Publishers.

Strickland, L.H. (1958). Surveillance and trust. *Journal of Personality, 26*, 206–215.

Strickland, L.H., Guild, P.D., Barefoot, J.C., & Paterson, S.A. (1978). Teleconferencing and leadership emergence. *Human Relations, 31*, 583–596.

Stroebe, W. & Stroebe, M.S. (1995). *Social psychology and health*. Buckingham, UK: Open University Press.

Strube, G. (1987). Answering survey questions: The role of memory. In H.J. Hippler, N. Schwarz, & S. Sudman (Eds), *Social information processing and survey methodology* (pp. 86–101). New York: Springer.

Sudman, S. (1976). *Applied sampling*. New York: Academic Press.

Sudman, S. & Bradburn, N.M. (1983). *Asking questions*. San Francisco: Jossey-Bass.

Sudman, S., Bradburn, N., & Schwarz, N. (1996). *Thinking about answers: The application of cognitive processes to survey methodology*. San Francisco: Jossey-Bass.

Sugisawa, H., Liang, J., & Liu, X. (1994). Social networks, social support, and mortality among older people in Japan. *Journals of Gerontology: Social Sciences, 49*, S3–S13.

Sussman, M.B. (1985). The family life of old people. In R.H. Binstock & E. Shanas (Eds), *Handbook of aging and the social sciences* (2nd ed., pp. 415–449). New York: Van Nostrand Reinhold.

Sutton, S.R. (1982). Fear-arousing communications: A critical examination of theory and research. In J.R. Eiser (Ed.), *Social psychology and behavioral medicine* (pp. 303–337). Chichester: Wiley.

Svenson, O. (1981). Are we all less risky and more skillful than our fellow drivers? *Acta Psychologica, 47*, 43–148.

Svenson, O. (1993). Differentiation and consolidation theory of human decision making: A frame of reference for the study of pre- and post-decision processes. In O. Huber, J. Mumpower, J. van der Pligt, & P. Koele (Eds), *Current themes in psychological decision research* (pp. 143–168). Amsterdam: North Holland.

Szucko, J.J. & Kleinmuntz, B. (1981). Statistical versus clinical lies. *American Psychologist, 36*, 488–496.

Tajfel, H. (1981). *Human groups and social categories*. London: Academic Press.

Tajfel, H. & Turner, J.C. (1979). An integrative theory of intergroup conflict. In S. Worchel & W.G. Austin (Eds), *The social psychology of intergroup relations* (pp. 33–47). Monterey, CA: Brooks/Cole.

Tajfel, H. & Turner, J. (1986). The social identity theory of intergroup behavior. In S. Worchel & W. Austin (Eds), *Psychology of intergroup relations* (pp. 7–24). Chicago: Nelson-Hall.

Tang, T. (1992). The meaning of money revisited. *Journal of Organizational Behaviour, 13*, 197–202.

Tannenbaum, P.H. & Fosdick, J.A. (1960). The effect of lighting angle on the judgment of photographed subjects. *AV Communication Review, 8*, 253–262.

Tanur, J.M. (Ed.) (1992). *Questions about questions*. New York: Russell Sage.

Taylor, D.M. (1991). The social psychology of social and cultural diversity: Issues of assimilation and multiculturalism. In A.G. Reynolds (Ed.), *Bilingualism, multiculturalism, and second language learning* (pp. 1–19). Hillsdale, NJ: Lawrence Erlbaum.

Taylor, S.E. (1982). The availability bias in social perception and interaction. In D. Kahneman, R. Slovic, & A. Tversky (Eds), *Judgment under uncertainty: Heuristics and biases* (pp. 190–201). New York: Cambridge University Press.

Taylor, S.E. & Brown, J.D. (1988). Illusion and wellbeing: A social psychological perspective on mental health. *Psychological Bulletin, 103*, 193–210.

Taylor, S.E. & Crocker, J. (1980). Schematic bases of social information processing. In E.T. Higgins, C.P. Herman, & M.P. Zanna (Eds), *Social cognition: The Ontario symposium*, Vol. 1 (pp. 89–134). Hillsdale, NJ: Lawrence Erlbaum.

Tedeschi, J.T. & Norman, N. (1985). Social power, self-presentation, and the self. In B.R. Schlenker (Ed.), *The self and social life*. New York: McGraw-Hill.

Tetlock, P.E. (1983). Accountability and complexity of thought. *Journal of Personality and Social Psychology, 45*, 74–83.

Tetlock, P.E. (1986). A value pluralism model of ideological reasoning. *Journal of Personality and Social Psychology, 50*, 819–827.

Tetlock, P.E. (1993). Cognitive structural analysis of political rhetoric: Methodological and theoretical issues. In W.J. McGuire & S. Iyengar (Eds), *Explorations in political psychology*. Durham, NC: Duke University Press.

Tetlock, P.E. & Boettger, R. (1989). Cognitive style and political ideology in the Soviet Union. *Political Psychology, 10*, 209–231.

Tetlock, P.E. & Kim, J.I. (1987). Accountability and judgment processes in a personality prediction task. *Journal of Personality and Social Psychology, 52*, 700–709.

Tetlock, P.E. & Levi, A. (1982). On the inconclusiveness of the cognition-motivation debate. *Journal of Experimental Social Psychology, 18*, 68–88.

Tetlock, P.E., Peterson, R.S., McGuire, C., Chang, S., & Feld, P. (1992). Assessing political group dynamics: A test of the groupthink model. *Journal of Personality and Social Psychology, 63*, 403–425.

Thibaut, J. & Walker, L. (1975). *Procedural justice: A psychological analysis*. New York: Spectrum.

Thoits, P.A. (1985). Social support and psychological well-being: Theoretical possibilities. In I.G. Sarason & B.R. Sarason (Eds), *Social support: Theory, research and application* (pp. 51–72). Dordrecht: Nijhoff.

Thomas, E.C. & Yamamato, K. (1975). Attitudes toward age: An exploration in school-age children. *International Journal of Aging and Human Development, 6*, 117–129.

Thomas, W.C. (1981). The expectation gap and the stereotype of the stereotype: Images of old people. *Gerontologist, 21*, 402–407.

Thompson, C.P. (1982). Memory for unique personal events: The roommate study. *Memory & Cognition, 10*, 324–332.

Thompson, S.C. & Kelley, H.H. (1981). Judgments of responsibility for activities in close relationships. *Journal of Personality and Social Psychology, 41*, 469–477.

Thornhill, R. & Thornhill, N.W. (1991). Coercive sexuality of men: Is there psychological adaptation to rape? In E. Grauerholz & M.A. Koralewski (Eds), *Sexual coercion* (pp. 91–107). Lexington, MA: Lexington Books.

Thorson, J.A., Whatley, J.L., & Hancock, K.A. (1974). Attitudes toward the aged as a function of age and education. *Gerontologist, 14*, 316–318.

Thyer, B.A. & Geller, E.S. (1987). The 'Buckle Up' dashboard sticker: An effective environmental intervention for safety belt promotion. *Environment and Behavior, 19*, 484–494.

Tichenor, P.J., Donohue, G.A., & Olien, C.N. (1970). Mass media flow and differential growth in knowledge. *Public Opinion Quarterly, 34*, 159–170.

Tichy, N.M. (1983). *Managing strategic change*. New York: Wiley.

Tiemens, R.K. (1970). Some relationships of camera angle to communicator credibility. *Journal of Broadcasting, 14*, 483–490.

Timmermans, D.R.M. (1991). *Decision aids for bounded rationalists*. PhD dissertation, University of Groningen, the Netherlands.

Tindale, R.S. (1989). Group versus individual information processing: The effects of outcome feedback on decision making. *Organizational Behavior and Human Decision Processes, 44*, 454–473.

Tobey, A. & Goodman, G. (1992). Children's eyewitness memory: Effects of participation and forensic content. *Child Abuse and Neglect, 16*, 779.

Toch, H. (1993). Good violence and bad violence: Self-presentations of aggressors through accounts and war stories. In R.B. Felson & J.T. Tedeschi (Eds), *Aggression and violence: Social interactionist perspectives* (pp. 193–206). Washington, DC: American Psychological Association.

Todd, A.D. & Fisher, S. (1988). *Gender and discourse: The power of talk*. Norwood, NJ: Ablex.

Tourangeau, R. (1984). Cognitive science and survey methods: A cognitive perspective. In T. Jabine, M. Straf, J. Tanur, & R. Tourangeau (Eds), *Cognitive aspects of survey methodology: Building a bridge between disciplines* (pp. 73–100). Washington, DC: National Academy Press.

Tourangeau, R. & Rasinski, K.A. (1988). Cognitive processes underlying context effects in attitude measurement. *Psychological Bulletin, 103*, 299–314.

Townsend, P. (1979). *Poverty in the United Kingdom.* London: Allen Lane.

Traugott, M.W. (1987). The importance of persistence in respondent selection for preelection surveys. *Public Opinion Quarterly, 51*, 48–57.

Triandis, H.C. (1989). The self and social behavior in differing cultural contexts. *Psychological Review, 96*, 506–520.

Triandis, H.C. (1990). Theoretical concepts that are applicable to the analysis of ethnocentrism. In R.W. Brislin (Ed.), *Applied cross-cultural psychology* (pp. 34–55). Newbury Park, CA: Sage.

Trice, H.M. & Beyer, J.M. (1993). *The cultures of work organizations.* Englewood Cliffs, NJ: Prentice-Hall.

Truffaut, F. (1975). *Mr. Hitchcock, wie haben Sie das gemacht?* Munich: Heyne (Original: *Le cinema selon Hitchcock.* Paris: R. Laffont, 1966).

Tuckman, J. & Lorge, I. (1952). The best years of life: A study in ranking. *Journal of Gerontology, 8.*

Tuckman, J. & Lorge, I. (1953). When does old begin and a worker becomes old? *Journal of Gerontology, 8.*

Tulving, E. (1974). Cue-dependent forgetting. *American Scientist, 62*, 74–82.

Tulving, E. & Thomson, D.M. (1973). Encoding specificity and retrieval processes in episodic memory. *Psychological Review, 80*, 353–370.

Turhan, M. (1960). Über die Bedeutung des Gesichtsausdrucks. *Psychologische Beiträge, 5*, 440–495.

Turner, C.E. & Martin, E. (1984). *Surveying subjective phenomena,* Vol. 1. New York: Russell Sage.

Turner, J.C., Hogg, M.A., Oakes, P.J., Reicher, S.J., & Wetherell, M.S. (1987). *Rediscovering the social group.* Oxford: Blackwell.

Turner, M.E. & Pratkanis, A.R. (1994). Affirmative action as help: A review of recipient reactions to preferential selection and affirmative action. *Basic and Applied Social Psychology, 15*, 43–69.

Turner, R.E., Edgley, C., & Olmstead, G. (1975). Information control in conversation: Honesty is not always the best policy. *Kansas Journal of Sociology, 11*, 69–89.

Turrisi, R. & Jaccard, J. (1991). Judgment processes relevant to drunk driving. *Journal of Applied Social Psychology, 21*, 89–118.

Tversky, A. & Kahneman, D. (1973). Availability: A heuristic for judging frequency and probability. *Cognitive Psychology, 5*, 207–232.

Tversky, A. & Kahneman, D. (1974). Judgment under uncertainty. Heuristics and biases. *Science, 185*, 1124–1131.

Tversky, A. & Kahneman, D. (1981). The framing of decisions and the psychology of choice. *Science, 211*, 453–548.

Tversky, A. & Kahneman, D. (1992). Advances in prospect theory: Cumulative representation of uncertainty. *Journal of Risk and Uncertainty, 5*, 297–323.

Tybout, A.M. & Artz, N. (1994). Consumer psychology. *Annual Review of Psychology, 45*, 131–169.

Tyler, T.F. & Cook, F.L. (1984). The mass media and judgments of risk: Distinguishing impact on personal and societal level judgments. *Journal of Personality and Social Psychology, 47*, 693–708.

Ugwuegbu, D.C.E. (1979). Racial and evidential factors in juror attribution of legal responsibility. *Journal of Experimental Social Psychology, 15*, 133–146.

Uhlenberg, P. (1974). Cohort variations in family life cycle experiences of US females. *Journal of Marriage and the Family, 36*, 284–292.

Undeutsch, U. (1967). Beurteilung der Glaubhaftigkeit von Aussagen [Evaluation of statement credibility]. In U. Undeutsch (Ed.), *Handbuch der Psychologie, Vol. 11: Forensische Psychologie.* Göttingen: Hogrefe.

Undeutsch, U. (1984). Courtroom evaluation of eyewitness testimony. *International Review of Applied Psychology, 33*, 51–67.

Undeutsch, U. (1992). Highlights of the history of forensic psychology in Germany. In F. Lösel, D. Bender, & T. Bliesener (Eds), *Psychology and law: International perspectives.* Berlin: de Gruyter.

United Nations (1951). United Nation Convention Relating to the Status of Refugees. Conference of Plenipotentiaries, Article 1, Paragraph A Clause (2), July.

United Nations (1994). *International Migration Bulletin, 4*(1).

Unruh, D. (1983). Death and personal history: Strategies of identity preservation. *Social Problems, 30*, 340–351.

Ury, W.L., Brett, J.M., & Goldberg, S.B. (1988). *Getting disputes resolved: Designing systems to cut the costs of conflict.* San Francisco: Jossey-Bass.

US Department of Health and Human Services (1982). *The health consequences of smoking. Cancer: A report of the Surgeon-General.* Rockville, MD: Office on Smoking and Health.

US Department of Health and Human Services (1985). *Fact book fiscal year 1985.* Bethesda, MD: National Heart, Lung and Blood Institute.

US Department of Health and Human Services (1986). *The health consequences of involuntary smoking: A report of the Surgeon-General.* Office on Smoking and Health. DHHS Publication no. (CDC) 87–8398. Washington, DC: Government Printing Office.

US Surgeon-General (1984). *The health consequences of smoking: Chronic obstructive lung disease.* Washington, DC: US Government Printing Office.

Valdiserri, R.O., Lyter, D., Leviton, L.C., Callahan, C.M., Kingsley, L.A., & Rinaldo, C.R. (1988). Variables influencing condom use in a cohort of gay and bisexual men. *American Journal of Public Health, 78,* 801–805.

Valdiserri, R.O., Lyter, D.W., Leviton, L.C., Callahan, C.M., Kingsley, L.A., & Rinaldo, C.R. (1989). AIDS prevention in homosexual and bisexual men: Results of a randomized trial evaluating two risk reduction interventions. *AIDS, 3,* 21–26.

Vallacher, R.R., Wegner, D.M., & Frederick, J. (1987). The presentation of self through action identification. *Social Cognition, 5,* 301–322.

Van den Putte, B. (1993). *On the theory of reasoned action.* Doctoral dissertation, University of Amsterdam, the Netherlands.

Van der Pligt, J. (1992). *Nuclear energy and the public.* Oxford: Blackwell.

Van der Pligt, J. & Eiser, J.R. (1984). Dimensional salience, judgment and attitudes. In J.R. Eiser (Ed.), *Attitudinal judgment.* New York: Springer.

Van der Pligt, J. & Richard, R. (1994). Changing adolescents' sexual behaviour: perceived risk, self efficacy and anticipated regret. *Patient Education and Counseling, 23,* 187–196.

Van der Pligt, J. & van Schie, E.C.M. (1990). Frames of reference, judgment and preference. In W. Stroebe & M. Hewstone (Eds), *European Review of Social Psychology,* Vol. 1 (pp. 61–80). Chichester: Wiley.

Van der Pligt, J., Eiser, J.R., & Spears, R. (1987). Comparative judgment and preference: The influence of the number of response alternatives. *British Journal of Social Psychology, 26,* 269–280.

Van der Pligt, J., Otten, W., Richard, R., & van der Velde, F. (1993). Perceived risk of AIDS: Unrealistic optimism and self-protective action. In J. Pryor and G. Reeder (Eds), *The social psychology of HIV-infection* (pp. 39–58). Hillsdale, NJ: Lawrence Erlbaum.

Van der Pligt, J., van der Linden, J. & Ester, P. (1982). Attitudes to nuclear energy: Beliefs, values and false consensus. *Journal of Environmental Psychology, 2,* 221–231.

Van der Velde, F.W., van der Pligt, J., & Hooykaas, C. (1994). Perceiving AIDS-related risks: Accuracy as a function of differences in actual risk. *Health Psychology, 23,* 25–33.

Van der Zouwen, J., Dijkstra, W., & Smit, J. H. (1991). Studying respondent-interviewer interaction: The relationship between interviewing style, interviewer behavior, and response behavior. In P. Biemer, R. Groves, N. Mathiowetz, & S. Sudman (Eds), *Measurement error in surveys* (pp. 419–438). Chichester: Wiley.

van de Vliert, E. & Mastenbroek, W.F.G. (in press). Negotiation. In H. Thierry, P.J.D. Drenth, & C.J. Wolff (Eds), *A new handbook of work and organisational psychology.* Hove, UK: Lawrence Erlbaum.

Van Griensven, G.J.P., Samuel, M.C., & Winkelstein, W. (1993). The success and failure of condom use by homosexual men in San Francisco. *Journal of Acquired Immune Deficiency Syndromes, 6,* 430–431.

Van Houten, R. & Nau, P.A. (1983). Feedback interventions and driving speed: A parametric and comparative analysis. *Journal of Applied Behaviour Analysis, 16,* 253–281.

Van Koppen, P.J. (1995). Judges' decision making. In R. Bull & D. Carson (Eds), *Handbook of psychology in legal contexts.* Chichester: Wiley.

Van Maanen, J. (1978). People processing: Strategies of organizational socialization. *Organizational Dynamics, 7* (1), 18–36.

Van Schie, E.C.M. & van der Pligt, J. (1994). Getting an anchor on availability in causal judgment. *Organizational Behavior and Human Decision Making Processes, 57,* 140–154.

Van Schie, E.C.M. & van der Pligt, J. (1995). Influencing risk-preference in decision-making: The effects of framing and salience. *Organizational Behavior and Human Decision Processes, 63,* 264–275.

Verbrugge, L.M. (1978–79). Multiplexity in adult friendship. *Social Forces, 57,* 1286–1309.

Verplanken, B., Aarts, H., van Knippenberg, A., & van Knippenberg, C. (1994). Attitude versus general habit: Antecedents of travel mode choice. *Journal of Applied Social Psychology, 24,* 285–300.

Vinacke, W.E. (1949). The judgment of facial expressions by three national-racial groups in Hawaii: I. Caucasian faces. *Journal of Personality, 17,* 407–429.

Vining, J. & Ebreo, A. (1992). Predicting recycling behavior from global and specific environmental attitudes and changes in recycling opportunities. *Journal of Applied Social Psychology, 22,* 1580–1607.

Vlek, C. & Keren, G. (1992). Behavioral decision theory and environmental risk management: Assessment and resolution of four 'survival' dilemmas. *Acta Psychologica, 80,* 249–278.

Vogel, R. & Rothengatter, J.A. (1984). *Motieven van snelheidsgedrag op autosnelwegen: Een attitude onderzoek* [Motives for speeding behaviour on motorways: An attitudinal study]. Report VK 84–09. Traffic Research Centre, University of Groningen, the Netherlands.

Vogels, T. & Danz, M.J. (1990). De intentie tot veilig seksueel gedrag. In T. Vogels & R. van der Vliet (Eds), *Jeugd en seks.* Den Haag: SDU.

Vollrath, D.A. & Davis, J.H. (1980). Jury size and decision rule. In R.J. Simon (Ed.), *The jury: Its role in American society.* Lexington, MA: Lexington Books.

Vollrath, D.A., Sheppard, B.H., Hinsz, V.B., & Davis, J.H. (1989). Memory performance by decision-making groups and individuals. *Organizational Behavior and Human Decision Making Processes, 43,* 289–300.

Von Neumann, J. & Morgenstern, O. (1944). *Theory of games and economic behavior.* New York: Wiley.

Von Winterfeldt, D. & Edwards, W. (1986). *Decision analysis and behavioral research.* Cambridge: Cambridge University Press.

Vrij, A. (1991). *Misverstanden tussen politie en allochtonen: sociaal-psychologische aspecten van verdacht zijn.* Amsterdam: VU Uitgeverij.

Vrij, A. (1994). The impact of information and setting on detection of deception by police detectives. *Journal of Nonverbal Behavior, 18,* 117–136.

Vrij, A. & Semin, G.R. (in press). Lie experts' beliefs about nonverbal indicators of deception. *Journal of Nonverbal Behavior.*

Vrij, A. & Winkel, F.W. (1992). Crosscultural police–citizen interactions: The influence of race, beliefs and nonverbal communication on impression formation. *Journal of Applied Social Psychology, 22,* 1546–1559.

Vrij, A. & Winkel, F.W. (1993). Perceptual distortions in crosscultural interrogations: The impact of skin color, accent, speech style and spoken fluency on impression formation. *Journal of Cross-Cultural Psychology.*

Vrij, A. & Winkel, F.W. (1994). Objective and subjective indicators of deception. In N.K. Clark & G.M. Stephenson (Eds), *Children, evidence and procedure. Issues in Criminological and Legal Psychology,* Vol. 20.

Wagenaar, W.A. (1986). My memory: A study of autobiographical memory over six years. *Cognitive Psychology, 18,* 225–252.

Wagenaar, W.A. (1988). People and places in my memory: A study on cue specificity and retrieval from autobiographical memory. In M.M. Gruneberg, P.E. Morris, & R.N. Sykes (Eds), *Practical aspects of memory: Current research and issues,* Vol. 1 (pp. 228–232). Chichester: Wiley.

Wagner, J.A. (1994). Participation's effect on performance and satisfaction: A reconsideration of research evidence. *Academy of Management Review, 19,* 312–330.

Wagner, M. & Settersten, R. S. (1993). *Generational structures and intergenerational ties of the old and very old in Berlin: Possibilities and realities.* Paper presented at the XVth congress of the International Association of Gerontology, Budapest.

Wagstaff, G.F. (1984). The enhancement of witness testimony by 'hypnosis': A review and methodological critique of the experimental literature. *British Journal of Experimental and Clinical Hypnosis, 22,* 3–12.

Wall, T.D. & Davids, K. (1992). Shopfloor work organization and advanced manufacturing technology. In C.L. Cooper & I.T. Robertson (Eds), *International review of industrial and organizational psychology,* Vol. 7 (pp. 363–398). Chichester: Wiley.

Wall, T.D., Corbett, J.M., Martin, R., Clegg, C.W., & Jackson, P.R. (1990). Advanced manufacturing technology, work design, and performance: A change study. *Journal of Applied Psychology, 75,* 691–697.

Wallbott, H.G. (1986). Person und Kontext: Zur relativen Bedeutung von mimischem Verhalten und Situationsinformationen im Erkennen von Emotionen. *Archiv für Psychologie, 138,* 211–231.

Wallbott, H.G. (1988). Faces in context: The relative importance of facial expression and context information in determining emotion attributions. In K.R. Scherer (Ed.), *Facets of emotion* (pp. 139–160). Hillsdale, NJ: Lawrence Erlbaum.

Wallbott, H.G. (1989). Die 'euphorisierende' Wirkung von Musik-Videos – eine Untersuchung zur Rezeption von 'bebilderter' Musik. *Zeitschrift für Experimentelle und Angewandte Psychologie, 36,* 138–161.

Wallbott, H.G. (1990). *Mimik im Kontext: Die Bedeutung verschiedener Informationskomponenten für das Erkennen von Emotionen.* Göttingen: Hogrefe.

Wallbott, H.G. (1991). The robustness of communication of emotion via facial expression: Emotion recognition from photographs with deteriorated pictorial quality. *European Journal of Social Psychology, 21,* 89–98.

Wallbott, H.G. (1992a). Effects of distortion of spatial and temporal resolution of stimuli on emotion attributions. *Journal of Nonverbal Behavior, 16,* 5–20.

Wallbott, H.G. (1992b). Sex, violence, and rock n' roll: Die Rezeption von Musikvideos unterschiedlichen Inhalts. *Medienpsychologie, 4,* 3–14.

Wallbott, H.G. (1994). 'Ein Ausländer war der Täter': Beeinflußt ethnische Charakterisierung in Zeitungsmeldungen Schuld- und Strafzuschreibungen?' *Medienpsychologie, 2,* 90–102.

Wallbott, H.G. (1995). Kommunikation von Emotionen: zur Bedeutung der Sprechstimme. *Wege zum Menschen, 47,* 201–214.

Wallbott, H.G. & Schleyer, C. (1990). Von sympathischen fremden Frauen und unsympathischen fremden Männern: Elizitierung von Stereotypen durch Eigennamen. *Zeitschrift für Sozialpsychologie, 21,* 113–117.

Wallendorf, M. & Arnould, E. J. (1988). My favourite things: A cross-cultural inquiry into object attachment, possessiveness, and social linkage. *Journal of Consumer Research, 14,* 531–547.

Walsh, D.C. & Gordon, N.P. (1986). Legal approaches to smoking deterrence. In L. Breslow, J.E. Fielding, & L.B. Lave (Eds), *Annual review of public health,* Vol. 7 (pp. 127–149). Palo Alto, CA: Annual Review Inc.

Walstedt, J.J., Geis, F.L., & Brown, V. (1980). Influence of television commercials on women's self-confidence and independent judgment. *Journal of Personality and Social Psychology, 38,* 203–210.

Walster, E., Berscheid, E., & Walster, G.W. (1973). New directions in equity research. *Journal of Personality and Social Psychology, 6,* 435–441.

Ward, S. (1980). Consumer socialization. In H.H. Kassarjian & T.S. Robertson (Eds), *Perspectives on Consumer Behavior* (pp. 380–396). Robertson, IL: Scott Foresman.

Wärneryd, K.-E. (1989). On the psychology of saving: An essay on economic behavior. *Journal of Economic Psychology, 10,* 515–541.

Wasserman, I.M. (1984). Imitation and suicide: A reexamination of the Werther effect. *American Sociological Review, 49,* 427–436.

Watson, D. (1982). The actor and the observer: How are their perceptions of causality divergent? *Psychological Bulletin, 92,* 682–700.

Watson, S.G. (1972). Judgment of emotion from facial and contextual cue combinations. *Journal of Personality and Social Psychology, 24,* 334–342.

Weary, G., Stanley, M.A., & Harvey, J.H. (1989). *Attribution.* New York: Springer.

Weber, M. (1904/1956). Die 'Objektivität' sozialwissenschaftlicher Erkenntnis. In J. Winckelmann (Ed.), *Soziologie. Weltgeschichtliche Analysen. Politik,* Vol. 229 (pp. 186–262). Stuttgart: Kröner Verlag.

Webley, P. & Lea, S.E.G. (1993). The partial unacceptability of money as repayment for neighbourly help. *Human Relations, 46,* 65–76.

Webley, P., Lea, S.E.G., & Portalska, R. (1983). The unacceptability of money as a gift. *Journal of Economic Psychology, 4,* 233–238.

Weeks, G.D. & Chapanis, A. (1976). Cooperative versus conflictive problem solving in three telecommunication modes. *Perceptual and Motor Skills, 42,* 879–917.

Wegener, H., Lösel, F., & Haisch, J. (1989). *Criminal behavior and the justice system: Psychological perspectives.* New York: Springer.

Wegner, D.M., Wenzlaff, R., Kerker, R.M., & Beattie, A.E. (1981). Incrimination through innuendo: Can media questions become public answers? *Journal of Personality and Social Psychology, 40,* 822–832.

Weick, K.E. (1993). Sensemaking in organizations: Small structures with large consequences. In J.K. Murnighan (Ed.), *Social psychology in organizations: Advances in theory and research* (pp. 10–37). Englewood Cliffs, NJ: Prentice-Hall.

Weigel, R.H. & Newman, L.S. (1976). Increasing attitude–behavior correspondence by broadening the scope of the behavioral measure. *Journal of Personality and Social Psychology, 33,* 793–802.

Weil, P. (1991). Immigration and the rise of racism in France: The contradictions in Mitterand's policies. *French Politics & Society, 9,* 82–100.

Weinberger, A. (1981). Responses to old people who ask. *Research on Aging, 3,* 345–368.

Weinberger, L.E. & Millham, J. (1975). A multi-dimensional multiple method analysis of attitudes toward the elderly. *Journal of Gerontology, 30,* 343–348.

Weiner, B. (1979). A theory of motivation for some classroom experiences. *Journal of Educational Psychology, 71,* 3–25.

Weiner, B. (1982). The emotional consequences of causal attributions. In M.S. Clark & S.T. Fiske (Eds), *Affect and cognition: The Seventeenth Annual Carnegie Symposium on Cognition.* Hillsdale, NJ: Lawrence Erlbaum.

Weiner, B. (1985). An attributional theory of achievement motivation and emotion. *Psychological Review, 92,* 548–573.

Weiner, B., Frieze, I., Kukla, A., Reed, L., Rest, S., & Rosenbaum, R.M. (1971). Perceiving the causes of success and failure. In E.E. Jones, D.E. Kanouse, H.H. Kelley, R.E. Nisbett, S. Valins, & B. Weiner (Eds), *Attribution: Perceiving the causes of behavior* (pp. 95–120). Morristown, NJ: General Learning Press.

Weinreich, P. (1989). Variations in ethnic identity: Identity structure analysis. In K. Liebkind (Ed.), *New identities in Europe* (pp. 41–75). Aldershot, UK: Gower.

Weinstein, N.H. (Ed.) (1988). *Taking care: Understanding and encouraging self-protective behavior.* Cambridge: Cambridge University Press.

Weisberg, H.F., Krosnick, J.A., & Bowen, B.D. (1989). *An introduction to survey research and data analysis* (2nd ed.). Glenview, IL: Scott, Foresman.

Weiss, R.S. (1969). The fund of sociability. *Trans-Action, 9,* 36–43.

Wells, G.L. (1978). Applied eyewitness research: System variables and estimator variables. *Journal of Personality and Social Psychology, 36,* 1546–1557.

Wells, G.L. (1986). Eyewitness identification: The importance of lineup models. *Psychological Bulletin, 99,* 320–329.

Wells, G.L. (1993). What do we know about eyewitness identification? *American Psychologist, 48,* 553–571.

Wells, G.L. & Gavanski, I. (1989). Mental simulation of causality. *Journal of Personality and Social Psychology, 56,* 161–169.

Wells, G.L. & Luus, C.A.E. (1990). Police lineups as experiments: Social methodology as a framework for properly conducted lineups. *Personality and Social Psychology Bulletin, 16,* 106–117.

Wells, G.L. & Turtle, J.W. (1986). Eyewitness identification: The importance of lineup models. *Psychological Bulletin, 99,* 320–329.

Wernimont, P. & Fitzpatrick, S. (1972). The meaning of money. *Journal of Applied Psychology, 56,* 218–261.

Wertheimer, M. (1906). Experimentelle Untersuchungen zur Tatbestandsdiagnostik. *Archiv für die gesamte Psychologie, 6,* 59–131.

West, D.J. & Farrington, D.P. (1973). *Who becomes delinquent?* London: Heinemann.

West, M.A. (1990). The social psychology of innovation in groups. In M.A. West & J.L. Farr (Eds), *Innovation and creativity at work* (pp. 309–333). Chichester: Wiley.

West, R., Elander, J., & French, D. (1993). Mild social deviance, Type-A behavior pattern and decision making style as predictors of self-reported driving style and traffic accident risk. *British Journal of Psychology, 84,* 207–219.

West, R., French, D., Kemp, R., & Elander, J. (1993). Direct observation of driving, self reports of driver behaviour and accident involvement. *Ergonomics, 36,* 557–567.

White, L. & Edwards, J.N. (1990). Emptying the nest and parental well-being: An analysis of national panel data. *American Sociological Review, 55,* 235–242.

Whitehead, J.T. & Lab, S.P. (1989). A meta-analysis of juvenile correctional treatment. *Journal of Research in Crime and Delinquency, 26,* 276–295.

Whitten, W.B. & Leonard, J.M. (1981). Directed search through autobiographical memory. *Memory and Cognition, 9,* 566–579.

Wicker, A.W. (1969). Attitudes versus actions: The relationship of verbal and overt behavioral responses to attitude objects. *Journal of Social Issues, 25,* 41–78.

Wicker, A.W. (1971). An examination of the 'other-variables' explanation of attitude–behavior inconsistency. *Journal of Personality and Social Psychology, 19,* 18–30.

Wicklund, R.A. (1975). Objective self-awareness. In L. Berkowitz (Ed.), *Advances in experimental social psychology,* Vol. 4 (pp. 233–275). New York: Academic Press.

Wicklund. R. & Gollwitzer, P. (1982). *Symbolic self-completion.* Hillsdale, NJ: Lawrence Erlbaum.

Widom, C.S. (1989). Does violence beget violence? A critical examination of the literature. *Psychological Bulletin, 106,* 3–28.

Wiener, R.L. & Pritchard, C.C. (1994). Negligence law and mental mutations: A social inference model of apportioning fault. In L. Heath, R. Scott Tindale, J. Edwards, E.J. Posavac, F.B. Bryant, E. Henderson-King, Y. Suarez-Balcazar, & J. Myers (Eds), *Applications of heuristics and biases to social issues* (pp. 117–136). New York: Plenum Press.

Williams, M.D. & Hollan, J.D. (1981). The process of retrieval from very long term memory. *Cognitive Science, 5,* 87–119.

Wills, T.A. (1981). Downward comparison principles in social psychology. *Psychological Bulletin, 90,* 245–271.

Wills, T.A. (1991). Social support and interpersonal relationships. In M.S. Clark (Ed.), *Prosocial behavior.* Newbury Park, CA: Sage.

Wilpert, C. (1989). Ethnic and cultural identity: Ethnicity and the second generation in the context of European migration. In K. Liebkind (Ed.), *New identities in Europe* (pp. 6–24). Aldershot, UK: Gower.

Wilson, D.K., Kaplan, R.M., & Schneiderman, L.J. (1987). Framing of decisions and selections of alternatives in health care. *Social Behaviour, 2,* 51–59.

Wilson, J.Q. & Herrnstein, R.J. (1985). *Crime and human nature.* New York: Simon & Schuster.

Wilson, M. & Daly, M. (1985). Competitiveness, risk taking and violence: The young male syndrome. *Ethology and Sociobiology, 6,* 59–73.

Wilson, T.D. & Hodges, S.D. (1992). Attitudes as temporary constructions. In L.L. Martin & A. Tesser (Eds), *The construction of social judgments* (pp. 37–65). Hillsdale, NJ: Lawrence Erlbaum.

Wilson, T.D. & Linville, P.W. (1982). Improving the academic performance of college freshmen: Attribution therapy revisited. *Journal of Personality and Social Psychology, 42,* 367–376.

Wimer, S. & Kelley, H.H. (1982). An investigation of the dimensions of causal attribution. *Journal of Personality and Social Psychology, 43,* 1142–1162.

Winkelstein, W., Lyman, D.M., Padian, N., Grant, R., Samuel, M., Wiley, J.A., Anderson, R.E., Lang, W., Riggs, J., & Levy, J.A. (1987a). Sexual practices and risk of infection by the Human Immunodeficiency Virus. *Journal of the American Medical Association, 257,* 321–325.

Winkelstein, W., Samuel, M., Padian, N.S., Wiley, J.A., Lang, W., Anderson, R.E., & Levy, J.A. (1987b). The San Francisco Men's Health Study III: Reduction in Human Immunodeficiency Virus transmission among homosexual/bisexual men, 1982–1986. *American Journal of Public Health, 77,* 685–689.

Winterhoff-Spurk, P. (1989). *Fernsehen und Weltwissen.* Opladen: Westdeutscher Verlag.

Withey, S.B. (1954). Reliability of recall of income. *Public Opinion Quarterly, 18,* 31–34.

Wittenbraker, J., Gibbs, B.L., & Kahle, L.R. (1983). Seat belt attitudes, habits and behaviours: An adaptive amendment to the Fishbein model. *Journal of Applied Social Psychology, 13,* 406–421.

Wolfgang, M.E. (1958). *Patterns of criminal homicide.* Philadelphia, PA: University of Pennsylvania Press.

Wood, J.V. (1989). Theory and research concerning social comparison of personal attributes. *Psychological Bulletin, 106,* 231–248.

Wood, R. & Bandura, A. (1989). Social cognitive theory of organizational management. *Academy of Management Review, 14,* 361–383.

Wood, W., Wong, F.Y., & Chachere, J.G. (1991). Effects of media violence on viewers' aggression in unconstrained social interaction. *Psychological Bulletin, 109,* 371–383.

Wurtele, S.K. & Maddux, J.E. (1987). Relative contributions of protection motivation theory components in predicting exercise intentions and behavior. *Health Psychology, 6,* 453–466.

Wynne, B. (1989). Sheepfarming after Chernobyl. *Environment, 31*(2), 11–39.

Yamauchi, K. & Templer, D. (1982). The development of a money attitude scale. *Journal of Personality Assessment, 46,* 522–528.

Yates, J.F. (Ed.) (1992). *Risk-taking behavior.* Chichester: Wiley.

Yuille, J. (1988). The systematic assessment of children's testimony. *Canadian Psychologist, 29,* 247–262.

Yuille, J.C. & McEwan, N.H. (1985). Use of hypnosis as an aid to eyewitness memory. *Journal of Applied Psychology, 70,* 389–400.

Yule, G.U. (1944). *The statistical study of literary vocabulary.* Cambridge, MA: Cambridge University Press.

Zani, B. & Kirchler, E. (1991). When violence overshadows the spirit of sporting competition: Italian football fans and their clubs. *Journal of Community and Applied Social Psychology, 1,* 5–21.

Zepelin, H., Sills, R.A., & Heath, M.W. (1986–87). Is age becoming irrelevant? An exploratory study of perceived age norms. *International Journal of Aging and Human Development, 24,* 241–256.

Zillmann, D. (1978). Attribution and misattribution of excitatory reactions. In J.H. Harvey, W.J. Ickes, & R.F. Kidd (Eds), *New directions in attribution research*, Vol. 2 (pp. 335–368). Hillsdale, NJ: Lawrence Erlbaum.

Zillmann, D. (1979). *Hostility and aggression*. Hillsdale, NJ: Lawrence Erlbaum.

Zillmann, D., Harris, C.R., & Schweitzer, K. (1993). Effects of perspective and angle manipulations in portrait photographs on the attribution of traits to depicted persons. *Medienpsychologie, 5*, 106–123.

Zimbardo, P. (1969). The human choice: Individuation, reason, and order versus deindividuation, impulse, and chaos. In W.J. Arnold & D. Levine (Eds), *Nebraska Symposium on Motivation*, Vol. 17 (pp. 273–307). Lincoln, NB: University of Nebraska Press.

Zola, I. (1962). Findings about age among older people. *Journal of Gerontology, 17*, 65–68.

Zuckerman, M. (1986). On the meaning and implications of facial prominence. *Journal of Nonverbal Behavior, 10*, 215–229.

Zuckerman, M. & Driver, R.E. (1985). Telling lies: Verbal and nonverbal correlates of deception. In A.W. Siegman & S. Feldstein (Eds), *Multichannel integrations of nonverbal behaviour*. Hillsdale, NJ: Lawrence Erlbaum.

Zuckerman, M., DePaulo, B.M., & Rosenthal, R. (1981). Verbal and nonverbal communication of deception. In L. Berkowitz (Ed.), *Advances in experimental social psychology*, Vol. 14 (pp. 1–59). New York: Academic Press.

Zuckerman, M., Koestner, R., & Alton, A.O. (1984). Learning to detect deception. *Journal of Personality and Social Psychology, 46*, 519–528.

Zuckerman, M., Koestner, R., & Colella, M.J. (1985). Learning to detect deception from three communication channels. *Journal of Nonverbal Behavior, 9*, 188–194.

Zuckerman, M., Koestner, R., & Driver, R.E. (1981). Beliefs about cues associated with deception. *Journal of Nonverbal Behavior, 6*, 105–114.

Zuckerman, M., Lipets, M.S., Hall, J.A., & Rosenthal, R. (1975). Encoding and decoding nonverbal cues of emotion. *Journal of Personality and Social Psychology, 32*, 1068–1076.

Name Index

Subject Index